Principles
of
International Business Transactions, Trade and Economic Relations

By

Ralph H. Folsom
Professor of Law
University of San Diego

Michael Wallace Gordon
John H. and Mary Lou Dasburg Professor of Law
University of Florida

John A. Spanogle, Jr.
William Wallace Kirkpatrick Professor of Law
The George Washington University

CONCISE HORNBOOK SERIES®

THOMSON

™

WEST

Mat #40264771

© 2005 Thomson/West
    610 Opperman Drive
    P.O. Box 64526
    St. Paul, MN 55164–0526
    1–800–328–9352

Printed in the United States of America

ISBN 0–314–15415–9

TEXT IS PRINTED ON 10% POST CONSUMER RECYCLED PAPER

Preface

The authors have collaborated for decades on *International Business Transactions: A Problem-Oriented Coursebook* (new editions annually). Many students studying with this popular coursebook, and others interested in an introduction to the field, have enjoyed our easy-to-read *International Business Transactions* Nutshell (Seventh Edition, 2004) and its companion, *International Trade and Economic Relations* Nutshell (Third Edition, 2004). Students and professionals seeking a comprehensive, footnoted treatise worthy of a law firm or law school library should consider our hardback *International Business Transactions* Hornbook (Second Edition, 2001).

Principles of International Business Transactions, Trade and Economic Relations is part of the West Group's Concise Hornbook series. *Principles* is intended to provide more depth and citations than Nutshells permit, and can be used with any international business, trade or economic law coursebook. Our coverage moves sequentially from international sales and letters of credit to regulation of international trade to transfers of technology to foreign investment to dispute settlement. Thus one advantage for students of this Concise Hornbook, depending on the scope of your course, is that you need not purchase both Nutshells.

RALPH H. FOLSOM
MICHAEL W. GORDON
JOHN A. SPANOGLE

June 2005

*

iii

Summary of Contents

Table of Contents

*

PRINCIPLES
OF
INTERNATIONAL BUSINESS TRANSACTIONS, TRADE AND ECONOMIC RELATIONS

*

Chapter 1

INTERNATIONAL SALES LAW

Table of Sections

Most students who have taken the first-year Contracts course believe that Uniform Commercial Code (UCC) Article 2 is the United States law that governs all contracts for the sale of goods, both domestic and international. However, there is a U.S. federal law which governs contracts for the international sale of goods, and which pre-empts state laws like the UCC. This federal law on sales of goods was created by the ratification by the United Nations Convention on Contracts for the International Sale of Goods (1980). The parties to a contract can "opt out" of that convention, but it must be the starting point for any analysis of international sales law.

§ 1.1   Introduction to CISG

The United Nations Convention on Contracts for the International Sale of Goods (1980)[1] (hereafter CISG) governs the sale of goods between parties in the United States and parties in over sixty other countries, unless the parties to the sale contract have expressly "opted out" of the Convention. CISG entered into force on January 1, 1988, thirteen months after the United States had ratified the Convention and deposited its instruments of ratification with the United Nations. As a self-executing treaty, no separate implementing legislation is needed. As federal law, it pre-empts Article 2 of the UCC where it is applicable. CISG is available to be used by private parties in ordinary commercial litigation before both federal and state courts in the United States.

At the time of ratification, the United States declared one reservation, a reservation under Article 95 that the United States is not bound by Article 1(1)(b). The effect of this reservation is that the courts of the United States are bound under international law to use CISG only when the places of business of both parties to the sale contract are each in different States, and both of those different States are Contracting States to CISG. Thus, CISG governs all contracts for the international sale of goods (unless the parties "opt out" under Article 6) between parties whose principle places of business are in the United States and other Contracting States.

As of July 1, 2004, there were sixty-two Contracting States to CISG representing two thirds of the world's trade in goods. In addition to the United States, they included: Argentina, Australia, Austria, Belarus, Belgium, Bosnia and Herzegovina, Bulgaria, Burundi, Canada, Chile, China, Columbia, Croatia, Cuba, Czech Republic, Denmark, Ecuador, Egypt, Estonia, Finland, France, Georgia, Germany, Greece, Guinea, Honduras, Hungary, Iceland, Iraq, Israel, Italy, Kyrgystan, Latvia, Lesotho, Lithuania, Luxembourg, Mauritania, Mexico, Moldova, Mongolia, the Netherlands, New Zealand, Norway, Peru, Poland, Romania, the Russian Federation,

---

§ 1.1

1. United Nations Convention for the International Sale of Goods, Apr. 11, 1980, U.N. Doc. A/CONF. 97/18, Annex I (1980), 19 I.L.M. 671 (entered into force Jan. 1, 1988).

Saint Vincent and Grenadines, Singapore, Slovakia, Slovenia, Spain, Sweden, Switzerland, Syria, Uganda, Ukraine, Uruguay, Uzebekistan, Yugoslavia and Zambia.

Other states are expected to ratify or adopt CISG in the near future. This will increase the impact and effectiveness of CISG in unifying international sales law. A current and complete list of Contracting States to this Convention can be obtained on the internet at www.uncitral.org.

CISG was drafted by the United Nations Commission on International Trade Law (UNCITRAL), and adopted and opened for signature and ratification by a U.N.-sponsored diplomatic conference held at Vienna in 1980. The mandate of UNCITRAL is the unification and harmonization of international trade law. The purpose of such unification is to reduce legal obstacles to international trade, and to promote the orderly development of new legal concepts to assist further growth in international trade.

In addition to CISG, UNCITRAL has adopted the UNCITRAL Model Law on International Commercial Arbitration (1985),[2] which has been enacted in 28 nations and four states in the United States; the UNICITRAL Model Law on Electronic Commerce (1996),[3] which has influenced more than twenty enactment laws to date, including uniform acts in Canada and the U.S., and EU directives; and a Legal Guide on Drawing Up International Contracts for Construction of Industrial Works,[4] which has been widely used in LDC development projects, even before its final adoption by UNCITRAL, because of its perceived balance, fairness and attention to detail. UNCITRAL is continuing its tradition of promoting unification in "unconventional" areas of commercial law, such as government procurement law.

UNCITRAL is not the only international organization currently making proposals for the unification and harmonization of international law. The International Institute for the Unification of Private Law (UNIDROIT) held a diplomatic conference in Toronto in 1988 to adopt the Convention on International Lease Financing,[5] which has eight Contracting States and entered into force in 1995,

---

2. Model Law on International Commercial Arbitration, in Report of the United Nations Commission on International Trade Law, 18th Sess., U.N. Doc. A/40/17 Annex (1985); Y.B. Int'l Trade L.Com'n 393, U.N. Doc. A/CN.9/Ser.A/1985.

3. Model Law on Electronic Commerce, in Report of the United Nations Commission on International Trade Law, 39th Sess., U.N. Doc. A/51/17 Annex (1996); 4.8 Int'l Trade L. Com'n 237, Vol. XXVII, U.N. Doc. A/CN.9/5ER.A/1996.

4. Legal Guide on Drawing Up International Contracts for Construction of Industrial Works, U.N. Commission on International Trade Law, U.N. Doc. A/CN.9/SER.B/2.

5. UNIDROIT Convention International Financial Leasing, May 28, 1988, 27 I.L.M. 931. The United States has signed this convention.

and the Convention on International Factoring,[6] which has six Contracting States and entered into force in 1995. These two conventions, together with CISG, may form an alternative source of law in international transactions for issues now analyzed under UCC Articles 2 and 9. The OAS has also been active in this field on a hemisphere-wide basis.

In addition, UNIDROIT has prepared and issued in 1994 the Principles of International Commercial Contracts.[7] The Principles are applicable to all contracts, not just sales of goods, and their provisions are set forth in more general terms. If CISG is the international analogue to UCC Article 2 in the United States law, then the Principles are the international analogue to the Restatement of Contracts in U.S. law. They are not intended to be adopted as a convention or enacted as a uniform model law. Instead, they are expected to be used by international commercial arbitrators, and even by judges where local law is ambiguous. Some of the specific concepts are discussed later in this chapter. The substantive rules of the Principles are often different from those of CISG, because the Principles were not drafted by official delegations of governments, and the individual drafters could adopt what they considered to be "best practices" in commerce.

§ 1.2   The Sphere of Application of CISG

The first six articles of CISG define its sphere of application. Under CISG Article 1 the Convention is applicable only to contracts for the sale of goods which are international and which have a minimum amount of contact with a contracting State. Article 1 requires that a sale of goods contract be both "international" and also bear a stated relation to a Contracting State before the contract can be governed by the Convention. In determining whether "a contract is for the international sale of goods," the convention does not define "contract" on "sale" or "goods", but Article 1 does define in some detail the amount of "internationality" required, and the necessary amount of contact with a Contracting State or States.

Under Article 1, a contract is sufficiently international to be governed by the convention if the seller's and the buyer's "places of business are in different States."[1] There is no requirement that the goods be shipped between different states, nor that the offer and

---

6. UNIDROIT Convention on International Factoring, May 28, 1988, 27 I.L.M. 943. The United States has signed this convention.

7. See Perillo, UNIDROIT Principles of International Commercial Contracts:

The Black Letter Text and a Review, 63 Fordham L.Rev. 281 (1994).

§ 1.2

1. CISG art. 1(1).

acceptance occur in different nations.[2] Neither the location of the goods themselves, nor the location of negotiations between the parties, is necessarily dispositive. Instead, the "place of business" of each party must be located, and must be in a different State. In a contract involving two Austrian citizens one of whom had his place of business in Italy, the court held that CISG applied, and not Austrian law.[3]

The application of the Convention depends upon both parties being aware that the transaction is international, and that the places of business are in different nations. Thus, if the foreign place of business of one of the parties is not disclosed to the other party by a local agent, the Convention cannot govern the transaction.[4]

What is "a place of business"? Although the term in the English language version may be ambiguous, the term in the French (tablissemant) and Spanish (establecimiento) language versions refer to a permanent place of business.[5] CISG does not define what a "place of business" is, although the drafting history of the Convention suggests that a permanent establishment is required and that neither a warehouse nor the office of a seller's agent qualifies as a "place of business." This interpretation has been adopted by the courts. A seller's "liaison office" in buyer's nation was held by the Paris Court of Appeal not to be a "place of business," because it was not an autonomous legal entity, so that orders through that office were subject to CISG.[6] Even the presence of a liaison office combined with a lengthy stay by one party's representatives in the nation of the other party to enter into and complete contract negotiations did not create a "place of business" in that country by the first party, as long as the first party's foreign place of business was disclosed.[7] There is an arbitral discussion to the contrary,[8] but the decision may be better analyzed as one involving multiple offices under CISG Art. 10, with the foreign office being more closely connected to the transaction.

This "place of business" criterion will cause difficulty whenever one or both parties have more than one place of business. However, CISG does provide some help in such situations by specifying which "place of business" is to be considered. If a party has multiple places of business, one of which is in the same State as the other party's place of business, the issue of "internationality"

---

2. Cf., Uniform Law on the Formation of Contracts for Goods (ULF).

3. UNILEX Case D. 1998–17.2.

4. CISG, art. 1(2).

5. Official Records of the 1980 Conference 73, Analysis of Comments and Proposals: (Comment by ICC); Honnold,

Documentary History of the Uniform Law for International Sales 394 (189).

6. UNILEX Case D–1995–1, CLOUT 155.

7. UNILEX Case D. 1994–31.

8. ARB. ICC (Paris) 7531/1993 (1994).

becomes more complicated. Which place of business is used to determine the applicability of the Convention? CISG Article 10(a) directs that use of the place of business having "the closest relation to the contract *and* its place of business."[9] Thus, the determinative "place of business" in the Convention analysis is different from those which use the place of incorporation,[10] or the "seat." Instead, it depends upon the relationship of the transaction to a particular office. It is further limited to the transaction-office relationship according to the facts which appear from (1) the contract form, (2) the dealings between the parties, or (3) information disclosed by the parties before the contract if formed.[11]

Where one office is more closely associated with the formation of the contract and a second office is more closely associated with a party's performance of its contractual obligations, there is an unresolved issue concerning which of those offices is the relevant "place of business." The only assistance furnished by Article 10(a) in such situations is to limit the usable facts in making a choice between multiple offices to those circumstances known to "the parties" before a binding contract is formed. However, this process limitation should permit well-advised parties to resolve possible ambiguities by stating in the contract which office of each party they believe to have "the closest relationship to the contract." Since the literal limitation in the Convention is to circumstances known to "the parties," each party should ensure that the other party is aware of its status.

What minimum amount of contact with Contracting States is required? There are two methods available to meet this requirement, but in the some States the second method is precluded by a permissible reservation under CISG Article 95. One method of meeting the requirement, which is universally available, is that each party has its relevant "place of business" in a different Contracting State.[12] This method does not depend upon the vagaries of conflicts of law doctrines, and provides certainty to the parties in designing the transaction and to courts in analyzing and deciding issues from such transactions.

The Convention does not govern all contracts for the international sale of goods, but only those contracts which have a substantial relation to one or more Contracting States—that is, States which ratified, accepted, approved or acceded to the Convention so as to become parties to the Convention. CISG Article 1 makes the Convention applicable to sales contracts where the places of busi-

---

9. CISG, art. 10 (a) (emphasis added).

10. Barcelona Traction [1970] I.C.J. Rep. 3.

11. CISG art. 1(2).

12. CISG art. (1) (a).

ness of the parties are in different States, and either (a) both states are Contracting States,[13] or (b) only one State is a Contracting State and private international law choice-of-law rules lead to the application of the law of a Contracting State.[14] Thus, CISG will govern a contract of sale between parties, where each party has its place of business in a different Contracting State. For a United States buyer or seller, that means that CISG will govern any transactions, in the absence of any contrary choice of law clause, where the other party to the transaction has its place of business in France, China, Italy or any of the other Contracting States.[15]

The other method of meeting the requirement of sufficient contact with a Contracting State, is to have one of the parties have its place of business in a Contracting State, and for that State's laws to govern the contract under the normative rules of "private international law" choice of law doctrines.[16] Thus, a contract between a seller in Germany (a Contracting State) and a buyer in the United Kingdom (not a Contracting State) would be governed by CISG if the applicable choice of law doctrines made the law of the seller's place of business the governing law.[17]

This second method of meeting the requirement of sufficient contact with a Contracting State is not normally available, however, to a buyer or a seller which has its principal place of business in the United States. When it ratified CISG, the United States declared a reservation that its courts would not be bound by Article 1(1)(b).[18] The United States' version of the Convention is that it is not applicable when a contract is between parties having places of business in different States and only one State is a Contracting State, even though choice-of-law rules lead to the application of the law of the Contracting State. Thus, a contract of sale between a United States party and another party in N, a non-Contracting State, will not be governed by CISG, even though United States law is applicable under usual choice-of-law rules. If United States law applies, but CISG does not, what law does govern the contract? Instead of CISG, United States law for domestic sales transactions would govern, which means the Uniform Commercial Code (UCC) is applicable in forty-nine states (all but Louisiana).[19]

13. *Id.*

14. CISG art. (1)(b).

15. See the list of Contract States at www.uncitral.org/en-index.htm.

16. CISG art. 1 (1)(b).

17. See, the Convention the Law Applicable to Contractual Obligations (EC) (Rome, 1998), Art. 4.

18. This reservation is permitted under CISG art. 95.

19. Although the reservation formally states that U.S. courts are "not bound" by CISG, they are not expressly prohibited from using CISG either. How should a court make that choice? The State Department explanation for the U.S. reservation under Article 95 is premised on the concept that use of the UCC is preferable to use of CISG. U.S. State Department, Legal Analysis of the United Nations Convention on Contract

This reservation was included in the Convention by UNCI-TRAL to prevent the possibility that the formation of the contract by would be governed by the law of one state and the performance of the contract would be governed by the law of a different state.[20] However, the motivation for the United States declaration is probably a belief that the UCC is superior as a sales law to CISG. Therefore CISG was considered helpful to United States interests only where it provided a clear resolution of the choice-of-law issues.[21] It was believed that, if a court first had to resolve such choice-of-law issues and determined that United States law applied, it might as well apply the "best" United States law—the UCC. Thus, a sales contract between a United States party and another party in N, a non-Contracting State, will not be governed by CISG.

This analysis of the non-application of CISG to a contract between a party whose place of business is in the United States and a party whose place of business is in a non-contracting state should be consistent, whether the action is brought in the courts of the United States or in the courts of France, which has no reservation concerning CISG Article 1(1)(b). For the purposes of interpreting CISG Article 1(1)(a), the United States is a Contracting State in all jurisdictions. But, for the purposes of interpreting CISG Article 1(1)(b) the United States is not to be regarded as a Contracting State.

§ 1.3   Choice of Law Clauses

Under CISG the parties may expressly determine not to be governed by ("opt out of") the Convention.[1] Thus, even if CISG is applicable under its Article 1, the parties may choose a different law to govern the contract. If such a decision is made, care must be used in drafting the statement of exclusion. The parties can attempt to exclude the Convention either by expressly choosing a different law or by stating that CISG is not applicable. However, only if parties have done both will their intent be clear enough that they can be certain that it will be followed by courts.

For example, in the United States, a simple statement that a contract "shall be governed by New York law" is ambiguous, because a court could hold that the New York law concerning international sales is CISG, through federal pre-emption doctrines. Thus, if the parties decide to exclude the Convention, it should be expressly excluded by language which states that it does not apply

---

for the Internal Sale of Goods (1980), Appendix B.

20. J. Honnold, Uniform Law for International Sales under the 1980 United Nations Convention (3d ed. 1999), at § 47.

21. See note 19, supra.

§ 1.3

1. CISG art. 6.

and also states what law shall govern the contract. ("This contract shall not be governed by the United Nations Convention on Contracts for the International Sale of Goods, 1980, but shall be governed by the New York Uniform Commercial Code for domestic sales of goods and other New York laws.") It is necessary to designate the law of a particular jurisdiction, in addition to CISG, in any choice of law clause because CISG, like any other single statute, will not furnish a complete legal regime.

Opting out of CISG in other legal regimes of Contracting States requires equal clarity. A simple statement that a contract "shall be governed by the law of France" is not so ambiguous, because CISG was incorporated into the laws of France when the Convention was adopted.[2] If the parties choose "the law of France," under French law the contract is one for an international sale, and the French law governing international sales is CISG.[3] In order to "opt out" of CISG would require at least: "This contract shall be governed by the laws of France applicable to domestic contracts of sale, and shall not be governed by the United Nations Convention on Contracts for the International Sale of Goods, 1980." Clauses with less clarity may fail. For example, references in a contract to the law of domestic contracts (the German Civil Code) were held to be not sufficient to indicate that the parties intended to derogate from CISG and apply the law for domestic contracts.[4]

Partial derogation from CISG provisions is also permitted.[5] Thus, specific clauses in contracts establishing different rules for transmission errors[6] and time for notification[7] have been held to derogate from CISG Articles 27 and 39, respectively.

If the parties can "opt out" of CISG, can they also "opt in"? Under CISG Article 1(1)(b), the parties may also use the rules of "private international law" including choice of law clauses, to "opt in" to the Convention.[8] The choice of law clause used to accomplish this result can be relatively simple ("this contract shall be governed by the laws of France") for the reasons explained above.[9] However, because at least one court has misperceived such language,[10] it is probably better to provide additional clarity here, also: "This contract shall be governed by the laws of France, including the United Nations Convention on Contracts for the International Sale of Goods, 1980."

2. UNILEX Case D. 1994–32. At least one Italian court misperceived the issue and applied Italian domestic law in such circumstances. UNILEX Case D. 1993–3.

3. See, e.g., Cases D. 1993–1, 1994–30.

4. UNILEX Case D. 1995–12.

5. CISG art. 6.

6. UNILEX Case D. 1991–6.

7. UNILEX Case D. 1994–18.

8. See text at § 1.4, note 16, supra.

9. See text and authorities at notes 2–4, supra.

10. See UNLIEX Case D. 1993–3.

There are many attorneys who will seek to "opt out" of CISG for all contracts under all conditions, simply because they do not understand it as well as they understand the UCC. However, such action may be a disservice to the clients' interests. There may be many circumstances when a seller of goods in an international transaction will be placed in a much more awkward position by the UCC and its "perfect tender" and "rejection" rules than it will be under the rules of CISG. In such transaction, automatic rejection of CISG should be resisted, unless the attorney is willing to write comparable seller-friendly rules into the contract as express terms of the contract. At least one author has stated that negotiating an international sales contract, or automatically opting out of CISG, without understanding how it affects the client's interests, constitutes malpractice.[11]

§ 1.4   Transactions Excluded from the Convention

CISG Articles 2 and 3 exclude a series of types of transactions from the Convention's application. Sales to consumers were excluded in order for CISG not to conflict with special national legislation (usually "mandatory law") to protect consumers.[1] The criteria for such consumer transactions is whether the goods are "bought for personal family or household use," which will be familiar to U.S. attorneys, since it is derived from language used in the UCC[2] and the federal Truth in Lending Act (TILA).[3] The issues which arise under that language will also be familiar to U.S. attorneys. One ambiguity is whether the goods must be so used by the immediate buyer in the transaction. Or, can it be eventually used by that buyer's sub-buyer or other remote buyer? U.S. interpretation has uniformly held the former, that the buyer must intend to so use the goods. Other issues relate to whether buyer's intended use must be known to seller at the time of the conclusion of the contract, whether seller has a duty to inquire about intended use, and effect actual changes in use. An Austrian court, in a contract for the sale of Lamborghini automobile, stated that application of the exclusion

---

11.   Brand, Professional Responsibility in a Transnational Practice, 17 J. Law & Com. 301, 335–36 (1998).

See also Gordon, Some thoughts on the Receptiveness of Contract Rules in the CISG and the UNIDROIT Principles as Reflected in One State's (Florida) Experience of (1) Law School Faculty, (2) Members of the Bar with an International Practice and (3) Judges, 46 Am. J. Comp. L. 361 (1998). In it only 30% of practitioners who were members of the international law section indicated a "reasonable" knowledge of CISG, and only 2% claimed a "strong" knowledge

of it. Although 40% of the judges handled international contracts cases, most were unfamiliar with CISG, and some believed that "CISG must be a federal law which is applicable in federal courts, not in state courts." Most faculty did not include CISG in their contracts or sales courses.

§ 1.4

1.   CISG Art. 2(a).

2.   UCC § 9–109.

3.   15 USC § 1663 (h), TILA § 103 (h).

language depended upon the proposed use of the car as understood by the parties, and not on the actual use, and ruled that CISG did not govern the sale.[4]

The exclusion of consumer goods contains an exception which allows CISG to apply if seller "neither knew or ought to have known" of buyer's use for personal purposes.[5] Thus, if buyer's purchase is in fact for "personal, family, or household use," seller would seem to have the burden of proving that it neither knew of that use, nor should have realized such intended use from the transaction facts. This may explain the results in some cases. In the Lamborghini sale, the Austrian court observed that seller had not presented evidence that it neither knew nor ought to have known of buyer's personal use.[6] However, a contract for the sale of a generator and spare parts for "a sailing yacht cruising the Carribean Sea" was held to be governed by CISG by a German court.[7]

Sales of ships, vessels, hovercraft and aircraft are also expressly excluded.[8] This exclusion seems to be derived from the prior conventions ULIS and ULF,[9] which excluded sales of such goods because they were often treated as "immovables" (real property) under civil law national legislation, because such goods were precisely identifiable by serial number and subject to registration. The ULIS and ULF exclusions were intended to apply only to those ships, etc., which were subject to such registration. This limitation does not appear in the text of CISG, however. Thus, there is an issue of whether either the registration or the size of the ship, etc., is relevant to this exclusion. Since most individual "rowboat" sales are sales to consumers, they would already be excluded under CISG art. 2(a). However, it is unclear whether CISG covers commercial sales of large numbers of such "rowboats" by a manufacturer to a dealer. The one issue settled by the caselaw is that sales of parts of aircraft are covered by CISG, even though those parts themselves may be precisely identifiable by serial number and may be subject to registration.[10] Implicitly, this decision indicates that the necessity of registration may be irrelevant to an interpretation of the exclusion under CISG art. 2(e).

Growing crops and timber have traditionally been considered part of the realty until severance (harvesting). If the crops or timber were sold in a present sale while growing, the harvest had

---

4. UNILEX Case D. 1997–4.3; CLOUT Case 190

5. CISG Art. 2(a).

6. UNILEX Case D. 1997–4.3, CLOUT Case 190.

7. UNILEX Case D. 1995–27.1.

8. CISG Art. 2(e).

9. ULIS Art. 5(1)(b), ULF Art. 1(6)(b).

10. United Technologies Int'l Pratt & Whitney Com'l Engine Bus. v. Malev Hungarian Airlines, UNILEX Case D. 1992–40. The decision is translated and published in full text in 13J. Law and Com 31 (1993).

not yet occurred and the sale was of realty. Even in a contract to sell crops or timber in the future, the sale was of realty if the severance was to be done by buyer. Only if seller contracted to sever as well as to sell could the contract be construed as the sale of "future" goods. At the turn of the century, sales statutes began to incorporate the doctrine of "constructive severance." If the growing corps were to be severed as part of the contract of sale, they were "constructively severed" from the realty by the conclusion of the contract, and were therefore converted into personality. In this manner the sale of growing corps could become a sale of chattels. Other legal regimes constructed similar legal fictions to allow such sales to be considered sales of personality. It is not clear whether these local doctrines are to be incorporated into CISG.

Sales of some intangible rights or claims—investment securities (stocks, shares), negotiable instruments, money and electricity—are expressly excluded from CISG, even though they may have a tangible "token."[11] Although CISG does not define the word "goods," these two provisions attempt to limit the concept to tangible items. A Swiss court has held that a contract for the purchase of corporate shares is not covered by CISG,[12] and an arbitral tribunal determined that a contract for the transfer of a quota relating to goods was not governed by CISG.[13]

Contracts for the transfer of information (an intangible) which is contained in a tangible (e.g., a computer disc) creates special difficulties in interpreting the term "goods" under CISG. While it is presumed that contracts concerning intellectual property rights (patent, copyright and trademark) are not for the sale of goods, but are licences, the intellectual property may be contained in a disc or a computer or a camera, each of which is a "good." In a non-electronic transaction, a German court held that a contract for market research was not a contract for the sale of "goods," even though the market research was to be contained in a written report to be furnished to the buyer.[14] The court emphasized that the concept of goods required that the tangible thing delivered be the principal object of the contract.

In contracts for the sale of things electronic, the sale of computer hardware, such as computer components, has been held to be governed by CISG.[15] Should that line of analysis be extended to cover the software that is included in the sale of "loaded" computer, or the sale of a car or a camera with "embedded" software? The purchase of software downloaded over the internet

---

11. CISG Art. 2(d) and (f).

12. UNILEX Case D. 1998–17.1.

13. UNILEX Case D. 1993–27.

14. UNILEX Case D. 1994–21, CLOUT Case 122.

15. UNILEX Case D. 1993–23, CLOUT Case 281.

would at least seem not to involve a sale of "goods." In the United States, the National Conference of Commissioners on Uniform State Laws (NCCUSL) has wrestled extensively with these questions, and seems to provide different answers depending upon the composition of the drafting committees.[16] The one CISG decision on the issue, by a German court, held a sale of software to be governed CISG.[17] The court identified the computer program as "standard software," this implying that it was not specially designed for the buyer, and perhaps that it was a mass-marketed, pre-packaged product. Both considerations could influence a court to consider the software product to be goods. More importantly, however, the court does not indicate that the sale was subject to any written contract of sale or license for use.

An analogy from the non-electronic world may be helpful in analyzing software sales. A contract calling for the submission of a manuscript for a book is not a contract for the sale of goods, even thought the manuscript will be on paper or a disc.[18] It is basically a contract for the author's services. However, a contract for the sale of a commercial lot of printed books (or only one book) is for the sale of tangible items—the books, and not the printer's services. There is no such clear bright line in software sales, since many software sales involve some adaptation to the user's precise situation. Nevertheless, a criterion which is based on the difference between "off the shelf" software and individually designed software may be helpful even when the software sold exhibits some characteristics of each, because one characteristic or the other may predominate.

§ 1.5 Types of Sales Transactions Excluded from the Convention

Although there are many issues concerning the definition of "goods,"[1] there are also many "transactions in goods" which may or may not be "sales." Neither the term "goods" nor the term "transactions" is defined in the Convention.

Auction sales are excluded from CISG. Like consumer contracts, this is another type of contract which is often subject to specialized national legislation. However, a court in the Netherlands has ruled that CISG did govern a sale in which Dutch seller directed a German "buyer," which was itself an auctioneer, to sell a

---

16. Compare the drafts of UCITA (Uniform Computer Information Act) with each of the two proposed drafts of UCC Article 2. For further discussion of this subject, see Chapter 8, infra.

17. UNILEX Case D. 1995–3.1, CLOUT Case 131.

18. See case cited at note 14, supra.

§ 1.5

1. CISG art. 2(b).

painting "by auction."[2] The decision draws a distinction between a sale "by auction" and "an order to sell by auction." The analysis of this case turns upon the fact that the auctioneer, the party plaintiff, was the "buyer" in the transaction in litigation, and the court characterized the auction as a second contract which was not the subject of the litigation. Thus, although the sale by the auctioneer to the subsidiary buyer was "by auction," that sale was not involved in the litigation. The transfer by the seller to the auctioneer was not "by auction," but the court found that it was subject to the rules governing "sales" of goods.

Execution sales and sales order by governmental authority are also excluded from CISG.[3] Such sales are often subject to special rules of court and legislature rules. The scope of this exclusion is not well-defined. It may include, for example, sales of goods which were warehoused, or collateral which is seized by the warehouse or a creditor "under authority of law," and which are then sold at public or private sale under the provision of that same law.[4]

"Services" contracts are also expressly excluded from CISG.[5] However, there are many contracts which involve both obligations to provide goods and also obligations to provide related services. In such transactions, when is CISG the governing law? The stated criterion is that CISG does not apply when the "preponderant part of the obligations of the party who furnishes the goods consists of … labor or other services."[6] The authorities seem to be in agreement that a "preponderant part" requires that more than 50% of the purchase price be attributed to labor or other services. Thus, the sale of a water tank did not become a "services contract" just because the contract required both provision and installation of the goods.[7] Further, if a CISG is applicable to a mixed service and sale contract it will govern both sales and services aspect of that contract, unless the contract is severable under national domestic law.[8]

Distribution agreements in their usual form are not covered by CISG,[9] although the Convention will govern the separate contracts under those distribution agreements which are actual orders for goods.[10] Thus, distribution agreements, like franchising and marketing contracts, are regarded as "service contracts and not con-

---

2. UNILEX Case D. 1997–12.1.

3. CISG art. 2(c).

4. See, e.g., UCC §§ 2–710, 9–504.

5. CISG art. 3(2).

6. Id.

7. UNILEX Case D. 1996–15.1, CLOUT Case 196.

8. P. Schlechtriem, Uniform Sales Law 32 (1986).

9. UNILEX Cases D. 1996–3.3, CLOUT Case 126.

10. UNILEX Case D. 1996–9, CLOUT Case 169; UNILEX Cases D. 1997–11, 12.

tracts for sale of goods."[11] The same analysis applies to joint venture agreements.[12] As one U.S. court stated, a distribution contract would be within CISG only if it contained definite terms of the delivery of specific goods.[13] That case involved a contract for sale of identified goods, but no breach of the contract was claimed concerning those identified goods. The breach was claimed only for goods ordered later, and not identified in the distribution agreement.

Another excluded type of contract is the traditional "maquiladora" transaction, in which a United States party ships parts of a product to a party in Mexico (or other low-wage country) for the non-U.S. party to assemble the parts and ship the assembled product back to the United States. Is this transaction a pair of cross-border sales of goods, and thus governed by CISG, or a contract for the services of the non-U.S. party, which is not governed by CISG? CISG Article 3(b) excludes contracts where the preponderant part of the obligations of one party are labor or other services. However, there is a second CISG provision which is expressly applicable when the party who "orders the goods" also supplies some of the materials for producing those goods.

This provision first states that contracts for sales of future goods ("goods to be manufactured of produced" after the conclusion of the contract) are governed by CISG.[14] It then makes an exception, however, for those transactions in which the purported buyer ("the party who orders the goods") will provide "a substantial part of the materials necessary" for the completed goods. Note that the deliberate use of "a substantial part" in CISG Article 3(1) is in contrast with the use of "the preponderant part" in CISG Article 3(2), and indicates that the purported buyer need not provide as much as 50% of the necessary materials in order for this exclusion to become applicable. An Austrian court has ruled that a transaction was excluded from CISG in which an Austrian firm provided that raw materials to a Yugoslav company to process into brushes and brooms.[15] There was no discussion of any materials being furnished by the Yugoslav company.[16]

Barter transactions provide an issue of applicability which is outside CISG articles 2 and 3. Is a barter transaction, in which

11. UNILEX Case D. 1997–2, CLOUT Case 192.

12. UNILEX Case D. 1998–24.

13. Helen Kaminski PTY Ltd. v. Marketing Australia Products Inc. (S.D.N.Y. 1997), UNILEX Case D. 1997–14.

14. UNILEX Case D. 1991–9, CLOUT Case 2.

15. UNILEX Case D. 1994–27, CLOUT Case 105.

16. An interpretation which seems more problematic, at least on the reported facts, is UNILEX Case D. 1993–7, in which a French Court excluded CISG from application because the purported buyer provided "specification and design" to the seller, but not materials.

goods are exchanged for other goods, a "sale"? Professor Honnold argues that such transactions are "sales" because CISG Article 53 refers to buyer's obligation to "pay the price for the goods" without requiring that he "price" be a monetary obligation.[17] However, the word "pay" is usually related to tender of money and not to a tender of goods, so Article 53 may not settle this point.[18]

Where a countertrade transaction is structured to use three interrelated contracts—one for the sale of the primary goods, a second for the exchange sale of the countertrade goods, and a protocol to define the relationship between other two[19]—there often is a price specified for each of the goods involved, the two sale contracts in such transactions would be governed by CISG. However, many such sales contracts, especially those for the sale of the exchange goods, are not sufficiently specific in identifying the quantities and types of goods to be purchased under the counter- trade agreement. Thus, although the purported contract would be governed by CISG, the Convention might well determine that no valid contract was formed.[20]

§ 1.6   Issues Excluded from the Convention

The Convention expressly includes two sets of issues which arise under a sale contract, and expressly excludes three sets of issues from its coverage—thereby remanding those latter issues of the substantive law of the legal regime indicated by choice of law doctrines (private international law rules). The issues covered by the Convention are the formation of the contract and the rights and obligations of the parties to the contract.[1] The excluded issues are the "validity" of the contract,[2] property (or title) issues,[3] and liability for death or personal injury.[4]

The language in the preamble to CISG art. 4 concerning "formation" refers to Part II of the Convention[5] and the language concerning "rights and obligations" of the parties refers to Part III of the Convention.[6] Included within the concept of "obligations" is the concept of remedies for beach.[7]

---

17. J. Honnold, Uniform Law for International Sales § 56.1 (3d ed. 1999).

18. See also, P. Schlechtriem, Commentary on the U.N. Convention on Contracts for the International Sale of Goods, at 22 (1998).

19. McVey, Countertrade: Commercial Practices, Legal Issues and Policy Dilemmas, 16 Law & Pol'y Int'l Bus. 1 (1984).

20. For further discussion of this issue, see § 1.9, infra.

§ 1.6

1. CISG art. 4 (preamble).

2. CISG art. 4(a).

3. CISG art. 4(b).

4. CISG art. 5.

5. CISG art. 14–24.

6. CISG arts. 25–88.

7. Part III of the Convention, Chapter II covers obligations of the seller, and Section III of that chapter comprises the remedies for seller's breach of its

In the language of the preamble to CISG Article 4, only the obligations of the buyer and the seller are expressly mentioned, which has lead to some debate over whether CISG would also govern the rights and obligations of persons who were not immediate parties to the sale contract.[8] Such persons would include manufacturers of the product or its parts which had sold their product to seller or to persons in the chain of distribution who were prior to the seller, and sub-buyers of the goods who purchased from the buyer.

The archetypical example is the manufacturer of a car or electric blanket who attaches a standard form "warranty in a box" to the goods, while the retailer (seller) sells the goods "as is."[9] If the courts read the "buyer-seller" language of CISG Article 4 literally, CISG provides no basis for a claim against the manufacturer, as it is not a seller in this contract. Note, however, that since CISG does not cover this aspect of the contract, local domestic law should be consulted and may provide a cause of action. To the extent that the courts are willing to recognize that the manufacturer has been involved in the sale contract through its "warranty in a box," even though not a formal party, then CISG may be used to provide the cause of action.

To date, the cases have held that such lawsuits are not covered by CISG.[10] Although a French appellate court considered that a "warranty in a box" ("document of guarantee") was a sale contract and gave a right of action against the manufacturer, the Cour de Cassation reversed.[11] It held that the document of guarantee did not create a sale contract, and that CISG Article 4 limited the application of CISG to the buyer-seller relationship.

CISG Article 4 has also been used to exclude many non-sale issues, especially agency issues, from analysis under CISG. Such issues include the liability of a purported "agent" who represented a non-existing principal,[12] whether a person paid by a buyer was an agent of the seller or not,[13] and whether a right to payment could be assigned.[14] Non-agency issues excluded have included estoppel,[15]

---

obligations. Likewise, in Part III of the Convention, Chapter III covers obligations of the buyers, and Section III of that chapter comprises the remedies for buyer's breach of its obligations.

8. Honnold, § 1.5 note 17, supra, at 63.

9. See Reitz, "Manufacturers' Warranties of Consumer Goods," 75 Wash. U.L. Rev. 357 (1997).

10. UNILEX Case D. 1994–16 (Manufacturer not a party to the sales contract).

11. UNILEX Case D. 1999–1.

12. UNILEX Case D. 1990–6, CLOUT Case 5.

13. UNILEX Case D. 1997–8.2.

14. UNILEX Case D. 1994–3, CLOUT Case 80.

15. UNILEX Case D. 1994–24.

promissory estoppel,[16] unjust enrichment claims,[17] the validity of forum selection clauses[18] and the assignments of burdens of proof.[19]

CISG Article 4(a) excludes issues of "validity" from the coverage of the Convention but does not define "validity." There are concepts which are clearly within this concept (capacity illegality, fraud and duress), and other issues which present much closer cases. Thus, the domestic law rules which invalidate sale of contraband items would not be affected by CISG, and the local courts would continue to apply such local rules to international sales transactions. Would duress include only "gun at the head" type duress, or also economic duress? CISG provides no guidance other than to indicate that these issues are determined outside the Convention. Thus, a court should consult the local domestic law on the subject, or other law made applicable under the transaction.

The impact of other local, domestic regulatory statutes, such as unfair competition laws, would also be preserved under CISG art. 4(a). Thus, German domestic unfair competition laws were held to be outside CISG and applicable to an asserted franchising agreement. However, the German law involved did not invalidate the individual sales contracts under the flawed franchising agreement, as those individual sales contracts were considered to be valid.[20]

The impact of general doctrines concerning mistake, hardship and unfairness presents a more difficult analytical problem. The courts have reached different conclusions concerning whether "mistake" doctrines are outside CISG, so that domestic law my be consulted. In one Swiss case, a buyer sought excuse from an agreement under Swiss domestic mistake doctrines, because the buyer had not read the contract it signed.[21] The court held that claims of mistake created "validity" issues, so that Swiss domestic law could be consulted. However, a German court has held that it was precluded from considering the German domestic law of mistake, since CISG exhaustively covered the subject-matter area.[22]

There has been a fair amount of litigation concerning general terms of the contracting parties, statutes regulating the use of "general terms", and CISG, especially Article 4(a). Most of the court decisions on this issue have held that questions of the validity of general conditions must be determined by local law and not by CISG principles.[23] A clause disclaiming seller liability for conformity of the goods was subject to German domestic law on such clauses and ruled invalid.[24] Contractual "penalty" clauses have been both

---

16. UNILEX Case D. 1997–8.

17. UNILEX Case D. 1997–15.1.

18. UNILEX Case D. 1993–24.

19. UNILEX Case D. 1993–1, CLOUT Case 103.

20. UNILEX Case D. 1997–13.

21. UNILEX Cases D. 1995–23. Accord, UNILEX Case D. 1997–6.

22. UNILEX Case D. 1993–16.

23. UNILEX Case D. 1994–12, D. 1995–1, D. 19972.1; CLOUT Case 232.

24. UNILEX Cases D. 1996–5.5.

upheld[25] and invalidated,[26] but in all cases the court ruled that the analysis of such clauses involved concepts outside of CISG, so domestic law must be consulted. However, in one case, a Hungarian court struck down a liquidated damages clause using CISG Article 4(a), and allowed a greater recovery under the Convention provisions.[27]

One issue under United States law is whether the restrictions in the UCC on disclaimers of warranty create a "validity" issue or not. The UCC provision requires that a disclaimer of the warranty of merchantability use the term "merchantability" and be conspicuous.[28] Is this an issue of "validity" under United States law? A second issue concerns the UCC restrictions on seller's clauses which limit the buyer's remedies to repair or replacement, and thereby exclude the remedies of avoidance of the contract (rejection of the goods) or an action for damages, especially consequential damages.[29] A third issue concerns penalty clauses which provide for a significantly larger payment to the aggrieved party than any actual damages which reasonably could be expected. The relevant UCC provision makes such clauses "void as a penalty."[30]

To date, there are no judicial decisions on any of these issues in the United States arena. The academic analyses of the first two issues take widely different approaches. Professor Murray has argued that "validity" issues can only arise if the entire contract is voided by the domestic law, not just a single clause within the contract.[31] Thus, CISG would allow a court to go outside CISG and consult domestic law only for sales of heroin or sales of stolen goods—and then only if the actual thief was the seller.[32] Thus, neither the UCC rules on disclaimers of warranty or limitations on remedy could never be considered to be rules of validity.

Professor Hartnell argues that CISG Article 4(a) is designed to protect domestic law rules designed to protect the fairness of a particular clause or of the bargain as a whole.[33] Since the UCC provisions restricting clauses that disclaim warranties or limit remedies are designed to protect fairness, they would qualify as rules of "validity" under CISG and the United States domestic rules would apply to international sales contracts governed by CISG.

25. UNILEX Case D. 1995–22.

26. UNILEX Case D. 1992–2, 1997–2.1.

27. UNILEX Case D. 1992–2.

28. UCC § 2–316(2).

29. UCC § 2–719 (2).

30. UCC § 2–718(1), last sentence.

31. J.E. Murray, Contracts, § 155B (1990).

32. Transfers of the thief could have "voidable title" UCC § 2–403.

33. Hartnell, Rousing the Sleeping Dog: The Validity Exception to the Convention on Contracts for the International Sale of Goods, 18 Yale Int'l L.1 (1993).

Professor Honnold argues that whether such rules are rules of validity depends in part, on the factual situation in which they are used.[34] He would turn first to the provisions of CISG Article 8 on the proper construction of the contract, and believes that proper construction could obviate the need to consult domestic rules on validity. However, he also suggests that where the same operative facts are covered by both a CISG provision and a domestic law rule, the CISG rule should prevail.

Despite all this sophisticated analysis, the CISG cases from other jurisdictions, especially those concerning general terms in contracts, suggest a far lower standard. Those decisions indicate that, if certain conduct or a certain clause is prohibited under the domestic law applicable to the contract, the courts will look outside the Convention and apply the prohibitive rules to the contract as rules of validity.[35] Thus, the standard adopted abroad resembles the standard proposed by Professor Hartnell.[36]

The long debate about the status of the UCC warranty disclaimer and remedy limitation provisions should be contrasted with the wide acceptance of the status of the limitation on penalty clauses.[37] There seems to be general agreement that common law courts will hold such clauses to be invalid, even in contracts otherwise subject to CISG. That wide acceptance may be due to the fact that the UCC makes such clauses "void," rather than merely prohibited or unconscionable. It may also be due to the fact that the rule arises out of the common law cases and pre-dates the UCC.[38] Or, it may be due to the foundations of their rule on public policies against non-compensatory remedies and potential *in terrorem* use of contract language.[39]

Another set of issues excluded from CISG coverage concerns property rights to the goods, including title to the goods and the rights and obligations of third parties to the contract.[40] The primary issue raised in litigation over this provision has been the effect of "retention of title" clauses, in which seller attempts to retain title in the goods after they are delivered to the buyer until the buyer pays for the goods. The legal status of such clauses is a property issue and is therefore outside the scope of CISG.[41] Thus, any determination of the effect of such clauses depends upon applicable

---

34. J. Honnold, § 1.2, note 20, supra, at §§ 65, 67. See also, Winship, Commentary on Professor Kastely's Rhetorical Analysis, 8 Nw. J. Int'l L. & Bus. 623 (1988).

35. See text and authorities at notes 23–27, supra.

36. Supra, note 33.

37. UCC § 2–718(1), last sentence.

38. A. Farnsworth, Contracts 935–37 (3d ed. 1990).

39. See, Lloyd, Penalties and Forfeitures, 29 Harv. L. Rev. 117 (1915).

40. CISG art. 4 (b).

41. UNILEX Case D. 1992–4.

domestic law, even though CISG applies to the analysis of the remainder of the contract.[42]

§ 1.7   General Provisions of CISG

Articles 7–13 contain its "general principles." These provisions deal with interpretation of the Convention and filling gaps in its provisions,[1] interpretation of international sales contracts,[2] a few definitions,[3] and a replacement for the Statute of Frauds.[4] Article 7 is designed to assist in interpretation of the Convention itself, while Articles 8 and 9 are designed to assist in interpretation of the contract terms. Article 8 concentrates on statements and conduct by the parties themselves as indications of contract terms, while Article 9 concentrates on sources external to the parties, such as trade usage. The provisions of Article 10 concerning multiple business offices have already been discussed in relation to their impact on Article 1.[5]

At first glance, CISG Article 7(1) appears to be a set of "pious platitudes," without any particular analytical content. However, it is intended to provide several inhibitions to the local courts of a State which will decide disputes under the Convention from applying their local law, rather than the Convention, to these international disputes. Thus, in interpreting the concepts stated in the Convention, such as "reasonable time," regard for the "international character" of the Convention is imposed upon courts in an attempt to lead them to use international practice rather than domestic practice or precedent. This preference for international practice is stressed further by the directive "to promote uniformity of its application." The latter is intended to establish foreign decisions under CISG as more persuasive than local decisions on domestic sales law.[6] Even the doctrine of "good faith," well-known in most local law, is muted. Although the UCC imposes an obligation of good faith on each of the parties to a sale,[7] CISG Article 7(1) only refers to good faith in relation to interpretation of the Convention, not of the contract, by courts.

Article 7(2) continues this approach in regard to supplementary principles of law, or "gap-fillers." Unlike the corresponding provision in the UCC, these supplementary principles are not to be

---

42.   UNILEX Case D. 1995–15.1.1.

§ 1.7

1.   CISG art. 7.

2.   CISG arts. 8 and 9.

3.   CISG arts. 10 and 13.

4.   CISG arts. 11 and 12.

5.   See text and authorities supra § 1.2, notes 10–13.

6.   Compare the effect of UCC § 1–102 (2)(c) in persuading the courts of the different individual states of the United States to regard decisions under the UCC of courts in other states as persuasive (not binding) precedent. The hope is for the same effect under CISG art. 7(1).

7.   UCC § 1–203.

gathered from United States domestic law, but either from "general principles" found within the Convention or international law or, if none can be found, from principles found in the law applicable under normal choice-of-law rules. The danger to uniform application is that local courts will discover many "gaps," no usable "general principles" derivable from the Convention, choose their own law as applicable, and easily fall back on their own familiar supplementary principles of law.

Article 8 attempts to establish rules for interpreting the contract itself, and its terms. It establishes a three-tier hierarchy: (1) Where the parties have a common understanding or intent concerning the meaning of a provision, that common understanding is to be used in any interpretation. (2) Where the understandings or intent of the parties diverge, and one party "knew or could not have been unaware" of the other party's intent, the latter party's interpretation prevails.[8] And (3), where the parties were unaware of the divergence, their statements and conduct are each to be subjected to a "reasonable person" standard.[9] The Convention does not attempt to resolve the interpretation problems created if each party's understanding of the other's statements is possible under this "reasonable person" scrutiny.[10] In evaluating party conduct and statements, a court can look to the negotiating history of the contract and to the actual administration of terms of the contract by the parties.[11] (Termed "course of performance" under the UCC).[12]

Article 8(1) has been interpreted to require courts to consider subjective intent while interpreting both the statements and the conduct of the parties.[13] Article 8(3) also can direct a court to a very different approach to contract interpretation than is usual in other U.S. contract cases. Its requirement that a court give consideration to all relevant circumstances is a clear direction to consider parol evidence even when there is a subsequent written agreement. It has also been suggested that both provisions can be used to promote the actual intent of the parties in the battle of the forms transaction, to avoid the "last shot" doctrine.[14]

Article 9(1) allows the parties to include "any usage" to which they have agreed. The drafting history indicates that this paragraph refers only to express agreements to include usage, although the express agreement need not be written. Further, "any" usage

---

8. CISG art. 8(1).

9. CISG art. 8(2).

10. See discussion of "mistake" doctrines in § 1.6. supra.

11. CISG art. 8(3).

12. UCC § 2–208.

13. *MCC–Marble Ceramic Center, Inc. v. Ceramica Nuova d'Agostino, S.p.A.*, 144 F.3d 1384 (11th Cir.1998), *cert. denied* 526 U.S. 1087, 119 S.Ct. 1496, 143 L.Ed.2d 650 (1999).

14. See discussion at § 1.11, notes 16–21 infra.

may be so incorporated, including local ones, not just international usage. If so incorporated, usage is considered to be part of the express contract items, but is not the governing law of the contract. However, since Article 6 allows the express terms of the contract to vary the provisions of the Convention, agreed usages will prevail over CISG provisions where CISG is the governing law. The one exception to the last statement is Article 12, which is applicable only if one of the parties has its place of business in a Contracting State which has declared a reservation under Article 96. Under that reservation, which is considered to be "mandatory law" and may not be derogated by the contract terms, contracts must be evidenced by a writing if so required by the local law of the Contracting State.

Article 9(2) concerns the incorporation of usages by implication. Both less developed countries (LDCs) and nonmarket economies (NMEs) sought to limit the application of implied usages. Thus, if the parties do not expressly agree to incorporate a usage, it is available in interpreting the contract only if "the parties knew or ought to have known" of it, it must be a usage in international (not merely local) trade, it must be widely known to others in this international trade, and it must be "regularly observed" in that trade. This seems to set a very high standard for any party assuming the burden of proof, although the principle issue in litigation is likely to concern the delineation of the specific "trade" involved.

Article 11 provides that a contract for the international sale of goods is enforceable, even though it is not written, and may be proven by any means. Thus, there is no equivalent in the Convention of the common law Statute of Frauds. However, Articles 12 and 96 allow a Contracting State to declare a reservation that the local law of that Contracting State shall govern the form requirements of the sale contract "where any party has his place of business in that State." Such a reservation may be declared at any time, but it is applicable only to the extent that the domestic law of the State making the reservation "requires contracts of sale" to be in writing. The United States has not made this declaration, so its Statute of Frauds provisions in the UCC are not applicable to contracts under the Convention.[15] However, the local law of parties from other States may be applicable if they have the required local legislation. The former Soviet Union was the strongest proponent of the Article 96 reservation, and the Russian Federation, Belarus and the Ukraine made this declaration when they adopted the Convention.

15. UCC § 2–201.

If the Article 96 reservation has been declared, the parties may not under CISG Article 6 agree otherwise.[16] This gives the local law the effect of "mandatory law" under the Convention. However, it should be noted that a telex or a telegram can be used under Article 13 to satisfy the "writing" requirement.[17] Further, a telex or a telegram qualify as a "writing" regardless of the formal requirements of the local law. Articles 12 and 96 only make unenforceable those contracts which are "other than in writing" (a Convention term), and Article 13 then defines "writing," as used in CISG, to include a telex or telegram.

§ 1.8   Contract Formation in General

The contract formation provisions (Articles 14–24) form a separate "part" of CISG–Part II. A Contracting State may declare a reservation at the time of ratification that it will not be bound by Part II, even though it is bound by the rest of CISG.[1] This is an historical appendix to the Convention, arising out of the separation between ULF and ULIS.[2] The Article 92 reservation has been declared by the Scandinavian nations,[3] which have also made a declaration under Article 94 that CISG will not apply to contracts between parties which have their places of business in Scandinavian states.

Although every first-year American law student studies about "offer, acceptance and consideration," those three elements of contract formation are not present in other legal systems. Civil law emphasizes the agreement process, and does not include a "consideration" requirement.[4] An examination of most commercial transactions will show that there is no real issue concerning consideration in most of them. An examination of most "consideration" cases will show that few of them are commercial contracts—rather, they are aunts attempting to induce nephews not to smoke.[5] Thus, it should not be surprising to learn that CISG has no requirement of "consideration" in its contract formation provisions.

As was discussed in the previous section, the writing requirements of the Statute of Frauds are also not applicable, unless one of the parties has a place of business in a Contracting State which has

---

16. CISG art. 12.

17. CISG art. 13.

§ 1.8

1. CISG art. 92.

2. Uniform Law on the International Sale of Goods (ULIS) and Uniform Law on the Formation of Contracts for Goods (ULF).

3. Denmark, Finland, Norway and Sweden.

4. See generally, Nicholas, "Introduction to the French Law of Contract," in Contract Law Today: Anglo–French Comparisons (. Harris & D. Tallon, eds. 1989).

5. Hamer v. Sidway, 124 N.Y. 538, 27 N.E. 256 (1891).

declared a reservation under Article 96.[6] However, the parties to an informal contract may agree to require any formalities they desire, including requiring that a contract may be validly concluded only with a written, signed final agreement. Such a term, if agreed by both parties is an enforceable derogation from CISG Article 23.

Part II of CISG focuses on "offer"[7] and "acceptance."[8] In Convention terminology, a contract "is concluded" (becomes binding) "when an acceptance of an offer becomes effective."[9] There is no need for consideration, and no formal requirements.

However, it is also clear that agreements can be reached without clearly identifiable elements of offer and acceptance, and that such offers fall within the scope of CISG rules.[10] Such agreements may be formed by the conduct of the parties, which recognize the existence of an agreement, and would establish that a contract had indeed been concluded without a formal offer or acceptance.[11]

§ 1.9   The Offer

Under CISG, the concept of an "offer" has three requirements.[1] First, it must be "a proposal for concluding a contract," which is a standard provision. Second, it must indicate "an intention to be bound in case of acceptance," which will distinguish an offer from a general sales catalogue or advertisement or a purchase inquiry.[2] Article 14 (2) elaborates on this concept by making proposals addressed to the general public to be presumptively not offers "unless the contrary is clearly indicated." Third, an offer must be "sufficiently definite." This provision is directed toward only three contract terms: the description of the goods, their quantity and their price. Other terms can be left open, but not those three. The criteria for judging definiteness are somewhat ambiguous. The offer is definite enough if the goods are "indicated," which does not seem to require that they be described with any particularity. Similarly, an offer is definite if it "expressly or impliedly fixes or makes provision for determining the quantity and the price."

However, the caselaw seems to be more restrictive. Where "during the course of negotiations" the parties agreed on the quantity of the test-tubes but did not agree on the quality of the

---

6. See § 1.7, above.
7. CISG arts. 14–17.
8. CISG arts. 18–22.
9. CISG art. 23.
10. P. Schlechtriem, Commentary on the U.N. Convention on Contracts for the International Sale of Goods 102 (2d., 1998)

11. CISG art. 9 (1); CLOUT Case 52 (Hungary, 1992).

§ 1.9

1. CISG art. 14.
2. CISG art. 14 (1).

test-tubes, the court concluded that the buyer and the seller had not created an agreement through the exchange of messages.[3] Therefore, there was no contract, and the seller had no right to recover the price of the test-tubes. The abstract does not state whether the parties agreed upon the price. If they had done so, the court could have found that the price was evidence that there had been agreement as to the quality of the test tubes.

This CISG provision seems more restrictive than the comparable UCC provision on open, or flexible, price contracts, and it was intended to be more restrictive, because many civil law states do not recognize such open-price contracts. Article 55 might seem to be helpful, but its provisions are available only where a contract has already been "validly concluded," which assumes either a valid offer or the creation of a contract without an identifiable offer and acceptance.[4] The Convention language is flexible enough, however, to authorize most forms of flexible pricing. Thus, the contract does "make provision for determining the price" where the price is to follow an index specified in the contract, has an escalator clause, or is to be set by a third party. Arguably, the latter would include "lowest price to others" clauses. The principal problem not resolved under the foregoing analysis may be only the order for a replacement part in which no price is stated. It is here that Article 55 is certainly useful. The offeror may have "implicitly" agreed to pay seller's current price for such goods, and Article 55 fixes the price as that generally charged at the time the contract is "concluded."

Open quantity contracts, such as those for requirements, output and exclusive dealings, may cause less difficulty. In each such contract, there arguably is a "provision for determining the quantity" through facts which will exists after the parties become bound, even if the precise number cannot be fixed in advance. Thus, an order for an approximate quantity of natural gas met the requirements of Article 14, because it complied with usage regularly applied in the natural gas trade.[5] Similarly, an order for "a certain quantity" of furs, followed by receipt and resale of specific furs, satisfied the definiteness requirements.[6] However, in view of the requirements of CISG Article 14, it is usually preferable to include either estimated quantity amounts or minimum quantity amounts, to assure that there is a fixed or determinable quantity provision.

Assortment is a final problem concerning "definiteness."[7] However, a clause which permits either the buyer or the seller to specify a changing assortment during the period of the contract would

3. CLOUT Case 135 (Germany, 1995)

4. See notes 10 and 11 to § 1.13, *supra.*

5. UNILEX Case D. 1996–3.1.

6. UNILEX Case D. 1994–29.

7. Compare UCC § 2–311.

seem to make a provision for determining both quantity and type of goods. The major hurdle in such cases is the requirement that the offer "indicate the goods" and be "sufficiently definite." But Article 14 (1) does not require that the offer "specify" the goods, and so clauses which allow later selection of assortment are presumably authorized, if the parties take care in describing the type of goods from which the assortment will be selected.

§ 1.10   Firm Offers

CISG Article 14 provides the prerequisites of an offer, but the three following articles concern the withdrawal, revocation and termination of an offer.[1] Many of these provisions resemble the civil law in substance, scope and style, more than comparable common law models. "Withdrawal" of an offer is permissible only before the offer is received by the offeree.[2] After such receipt, the only recourse of the offeror is to attempt to "revoke" the offer.

Under CISG, any attempt to revoke an offer must be received by the offeree before the offeree has dispatched an acceptance.[3] However, not all offers are revocable.

One of the consequences of the abandonment by CISG of the "consideration" requirement is that the traditional common law analysis of the revocability of an unaccepted offer has no foundation without the consideration doctrine. The traditional common law doctrine made an offer revocable at will until accepted, unless there was an agreement supported by consideration to keep it open (such as an option).[4] In German law, an offer is binding and irrevocable, unless the offeror states that it is revocable.[5] These two approaches are opposites, and the compromise adopted by CISG uses neither of these approaches.

Under the second paragraph of Article 16, an offer originating under the Convention is revocable unless "it indicates" that it is not revocable. In adopting this position, the Convention rejects both the common rule that an offer is always revocable and the German civil law rule that an offer is not revocable unless it is expressly stated to be revocable. This basic concept is similar to that used in creating a "firm offer" under the UCC,[6] but no "signed writing" is required. There are two ways in which an offer can become irrevo-

§ 1.10

1. CISG arts 15–17

2. CISG art 15 (2)

3. CISG art. 16(1).

4. Dickenson v. Dodds, L.R.2 Ch. Div. 463 (1876).

5. Eorsi, "Article 16," in Commentary on the International Sales Law: The 1980 Vienna Convention 155 (C. Bianca & M. Bonell, eds., 1987).

French law permits revocation, but requires indemnification of the offeree for revocation. However, this approach was not discussed at the Vienna Conference. Id.

6. UCC § 2–205.

cable under Article 16: (1) through the offeror's statements and (2) through reasonable reliance by the offeree. The first of these approaches incorporates civil law norms, while the second applies common law norms.

An offeror can indicate that an offer is irrevocable "by stating a fixed time for acceptance or otherwise." The first reference seems relatively clear, and would include a statement that an offer will be held open for a specified period and no longer. But, what is included in "or otherwise"? For example, does it include a statement that an offer will *lapse* after a specified period? That does not necessarily waive the offeror's right to withdraw the offer earlier, but the delegates at the Diplomatic Conference could not agree on how their language applied in that hypothetical case.[7] The criteria for irrevocability of an offer after reasonable reliance by an offeror under Article 16(2)(b) seem to follow United States caselaw and the Second Restatement of Contracts, Section 87.

Despite the seeming ambiguity of these concepts and the Convention language, no cases been reported which arise under Article 16(2). Courts which are presented with these issues may consult the principles of CISG Article 8 on the interpretation of the statement of parties. Under 8(1), the issue would be whether the offeree knew or could not have been unaware that the offeror intended the offer to be revocable. If both offeror and offeree are from common law states, there may be such an intention, although it is not conclusive since both parties' understandings arise from a common law background in which offers are revocable in the absence of consideration, or a signed writing. If both parties are from civil law backgrounds the opposite construction of intention may be possible. It could be argued that Article 8 is irrelevant to this determination, since the language of CISG Article 16(2)(a) asks what the offer indicates, not what the person making the offer intended to indicate. However, it is unlikely that the drafters of CISG intended to set aside the general interpretive rules of Art. 8 in interpreting any of the substantive provisions, including the provisions of Article 16.

§ 1.11 Acceptance

CISG defines "acceptance" as either a statement or "other conduct" by an offeree "indicating assent to an offer."[1] Silence is not necessarily acceptance, although the negotiations and other

---

7. Eorsi supra note 4. "The common law delegations maintained that even if the offer states a fixed time for acceptance, this, in itself, does not necessarily mean that the offer is irrevocable. After all, revocability was stated in the offer. Thus, the common law delegations were inclined to read the civil law language in the common law way." Id.

§ 1.11

1. CISG Art. 18(1).

prior conduct of the parties may establish an implicit understanding that lengthy silence followed by affirmative conduct is acceptance. But in *Filanto*, the first CISG case decided by a United States court, the court used the prior relations of the parties, including exchanges of draft contracts, to find that a lengthy failure to object by one party to a proposed final draft of the other party, followed by the beginning of performance by the proposing party, was an acceptance which created an express "agreement in writing" for purposes of the Federal Arbitration Act.[2]

The Filantro decision has been criticized many times.[3] In part, the decision seems to state that there can be a contract to arbitrate which is separate from the sales contract and is separately formed. The concept that the dispute resolution clause can create valid obligations, when no sales contract was ever formed to support it, seems contrary to CISG Art. 8(1). The antecedents of such an analysis are all in arbitration cases and not in sales cases. However, the federal law governing formation of an arbitration contract may be different from the state law governing formation of the underlying sales contracts. The decision's determination that the silence of one party is acceptance relies on past conduct, without indicating which actions were referenced. *Filanto* and a recent German decision both represent judicial hostility to the possible return under CISG to the "last shot" doctrine in the "battle of the forms" transaction, discussed below.

Article 18(2) determines when an "indication of acceptance" is effective for "concluding" the contract. Thus, along with Articles 16(1) and 22, it forms the Convention's analog to "the mailbox rule"—except that the CISG rules are different. At common law, "the mailbox rule" passed the risk of loss or delay in the transmission of an acceptance to the offeror, once the offeree has dispatched the acceptance.[4] It also chose that point in time to terminate the offeror's power to revoke an offer and to terminate the offeree's power to withdraw the acceptance. Under CISG however, an acceptance is not effective until it "reaches" (is delivered to) the offeror.[5] Thus, risk of loss or delay in transmission is on the offeree, who must now inquire if the acceptance is not acknowledged. On the

2. Filanto, S.p.A. v. Chilewich Int'l Corp., 789 F.Supp. 1229 (S.D.N.Y.1992). Ironically, the opinion is principally an analysis of the "federal law of contracts" that has grown up around the 1958 New York Convention on the Recognition and Enforcement of Arbitral Awards and the federal legislation implementing that treaty. 9 U.S.C. §§ 201–209.

3. See, e.g., Winship, The U.N. Convention and the Emerging Caselaw,

Emptio–Venditio Internationes 227–237 (1997); Van Alstine, Consensus, Dissensus and Contractual Obligation Through the Prism of Uniform International Sales Law, 37 Van. Int'l L. 1 (1996); Nakata, Filanto SPA v. Chilewich Int'l Corp., 7 Transnat.Law.141 (1994).

4. See Adams v. Lindsell, 1 B. & Ald. 631, 106 Eng. Rep. 250 (K.B.1818).

5. CISG art 18(2).

other hand, the offeror's power to revoke under CISG is terminated upon dispatch of the acceptance[6]—which is the common law rule. However, the offeree's power to withdraw the acceptance terminates only when the acceptance reaches the offeror. Thus, an acceptance sent by a slow transmission method allows the offeree to speculate for a day or two while the offeror is bound. A telex will release the offeree from the acceptance.

Even though Article 18(1) states that acceptance by conduct alone is possible, the remaining paragraphs of Article 18 seem to imply that in the usual case the offeree must notify the offeror that acceptance by conduct is forthcoming. Article 18(3) indicates that acceptance by conduct without notice is possible only when that procedure is allowed by the offer, by usage or by the parties' prior course of performance. If so allowed by the offer, the acceptance by conduct, such as shipping the goods without notice, is effective upon dispatch of the goods, rather than upon their delivery to the offeror. However, notification of the acceptance may reach the offeror indirectly through third parties, such as banks or carrier.

The traditional analysis of the CISG approach to the "battle of the forms" is quite different than that of the UCC, and closer to the common law "mirror-image" analysis.[7] Under CISG, if the buyer's purchase order form and seller's order acknowledgment form differ as to any material term, there is no offer and acceptance.[8] Instead, there is an offer, followed by a rejection of that offer and a counter offer (usually the seller's order acknowledgment form). The rejection of the original offer terminates the original offer under CISG.[9] Thus, (theoretically) the parties cannot "conclude" a contract by exchanging conflicting forms; and if one party reneges on its obligations, before performance, it probably is not bound to perform.

Under an express exception to the "mirror-image" rule, a non-mirror image response can be an acceptance if it contains additional or different terms which do not materially alter the terms of the offer.[10] However, "materially alter" is defined in the last paragraph of Article 19, and would include any term which relates to the quality of the goods or the extent of one party's liability to the other.[11] Most order acknowledgment forms contain an additional or different term which does materially alter the terms of most purchase orders. Thus, the express exception will not be applicable in the majority of "battle of the forms" cases.

---

6. CISG art. 16 (1).

7. Poel v. Brunswick—Balke—Collender, 216 N.Y. 310, 110 N.E. 619 (1915).

8. CISG art. 19(1).

9. CISG art. 17.

10. CISG art. 19(2).

11. CISG art. 19(3).

However, the vast majority of transactions involving exchanges of such forms are performed by the parties, despite the lack of a contract formed by the exchange of forms. Once the goods have been shipped, accepted and paid for, there has been a transaction; and a contract underlying that transaction has been formed by the parties—what are its terms? To put the same question in a different way, is the seller's shipment of the goods "conduct" by the seller which accepts the terms in the buyer's purchase order? Or, is the buyer's acceptance and payment for the goods "conduct" which accepts the terms in the seller's acknowledgment form? The common law analysis would make the terms of the form last sent to another party controlling,[12] since that last form (usually seller's) would be a counter offer and a rejection and termination of all prior unaccepted offers. If the Convention is the governing law, and if no contract has been formed by the exchange of forms, when seller ships the goods, they are shipped under the terms of the only non-terminated offer, which often is the seller's order acknowledgment form.[13] When buyer accepts the goods, it may be argued that buyer also accept seller's terms as contained in the order acknowledgment form. Thus, buyer would be bound by the terms as set forth in seller's order acknowledgment form.[14]

If the buyer accepts the seller's terms by accepting the goods, no contract would be formed until the goods have been shipped by the seller and have been accepted by the buyer, so that the contract would be formed by the conduct of the parties. It may be worth noting that both the United States and civil law regimes have developed more sophisticated methods of dealing with the "battle of the forms" than the "mirror-image" rule followed by the "last shot" principle, but they each use different mechanisms, and the Convention drafters were unable to agree on any of them.[15] Despite the seeming clarity of CISG Articles 18 and 19, there is great resistance against going back to 19th century contract principles. A

---

12. See Poel, supra note 7.

13. CISG art. 17.

14. CISG art. 18(1). So held in UNI-LEX Case D. 1996-10.1.

15. Compare UCC § 2-207.

Under the UCC, one can argue for several different analytical approaches. However, the traditional analysis is that an agreement was formed by the writings of the parties under 2-207(1), and the terms in the offeree's response (often the seller's acknowledgment form) drop out under UCC § 2-207(2). This is a "first shot" rule which rewards the initiator of the transaction (the first offer-ror) by giving it the terms of that offer.

Under the proposed Amendments to Article 2 of the UCC, amended UCC § 2-207 would create a "Knock-out" risk to replace the "first shot" rule of original UCC § 2-207.

For the analysis under French law, see Vergne, the "Battle of the Forms" under the 1980 United Nations Convention Contract for the International Sale of Goods, 33 Am J. Comp. L. 233, 250-51 (1985).

For an analysis under German law, see H. Silberberg, The German Standard Contracts Act 18-19 (1979). The German statute results in the use of a "knock out" rule for the battle of the forms.

German decision held that a variation in an acceptance was nonmaterial which limited the buyer's ability to notify the seller of product defects to a 30–day period.[16] Professor Honnold would use the gap-filling provisions of CISG when the parties are not in actual agreement on the terms that lead to a dispute, adopting a "knock-out" doctrine in principal.[17] In *Filanto*, discussed above,[18] the court used prior conduct of the parties to find the existence of a contract where exchange of forms was followed by one party's silence. All of these authorities seem to agree that the mirror-image and last-shot doctrines should not be resurrected, and that there are more sophisticated analytical tools to resolve the battle of forms under CISG.

Professor Van Alstine argues that the problem with the traditional analysis relying on CISG art. 18(1) is the assumption that the buyer's act of accepting the goods indicates assent to the counter-offer.[19] It is far more likely that the buyer acted without knowledge of the terms of the seller's form. He would argue that the buyer's act should be interpreted in accordance with CISG art. 8(1) or (2). In some cases this analysis will lead to the determination that there is a contract. In other cases, however, the result is indeterminate under the Convention because the buyer did not intend to accept the seller's terms. In these latter cases, the failure to provide an answer may be designated as a gap to be filled in accordance with CISG Article 7(2). If so, it may be argued that the Convention has a general principle that the parties must act in good faith, which means in this context that contract terms are those that the parties agree upon, together with the gap-filling provisions of the Convention. Alternatively, if the general principle of good faith is deemed unsatisfactory, the answer may be filled by recourse to the national law designated by of conflict of laws rule.

One recent German decision may have adopted Professor Honnold's approach to this issue, not only finding a contract in the "battle of the forms" situation, but using a "knock out" rule to determine the terms of the contract.[20] The parties exchanged standard forms, but the abstract does not state which form was the "last" sent. The court held that seller's choice of law clause had not become part of the contract. Instead, because their intention to be bound was shown by their performance of the contract, the court reasoned that the parties intended implicitly to derogate from CISG

---

16. UNILEX Case D. 1991–7. See also Bundesgerichtshof VIII ZR304/00, Jan. 9, 2002, effectively applying a "Knock-out rule" to the battle of the forms situation.

17. J. Honnold, supra § 1.2, note 20, at § 170.4.

18. Supra, note 2.

19. Van Alstine, supra note 3. Compare this reasoning to the analytical pattern used in MCC–Marble, supra § 1.9, note 13.

20. UNILEX Case D. 1995–26.

Article 19(1) and to permit a non-mirror image positive response to be an "acceptance." The court then ruled that the terms of the contract consisted of the agreed terms, plus "any standard terms which were common in substance," and the conflicting standard terms were excluded.[21]

It is always possible to attempt to "win" the battle of the forms, through derogation of Articles 7 and 8, by inserting a clause in the acknowledgment form that states: "Our obligations are conditional upon your assent to all our terms." However, if everyone uses such clauses in their forms, then no contract is ever formed by the writings, and we return to the "last shot" doctrine, with fax machines working overtime.

In summary and in comparison to the UCC, CISG reduces the flexibility of the parties by prohibiting some open price terms; CISG expands the "firm offer" concept and applies it to more offers; and in the battle of the forms, CISG may delay the formation of a contract through the "mirror image" rule, and may use the "last shot" principle to make to offeree's (usually seller's) terms control the transaction. However, on the last points, both the courts and the authors who have written on the subject have suggested ways of avoiding this traditional analysis.

§ 1.12 Seller's Obligations—Delivery

The seller is obligated to deliver the goods and any related documents and to transfer "the property in the goods" to the buyer.[1] In addition, the seller is obligated to deliver goods which conform to the contract as to quantity, quality and title.

Some of these obligations are governed by domestic law, and not the Convention, because the Convention "is not concerned with" the effect of the contract on "the property in the goods sold."[2] Domestic law, therefore, determines whether "the property" passes from seller to buyer at the "conclusion" (formation) of the contract, upon delivery, or at some other time;[3] whether a certificate of title is required; and whether seller may retain title as security for the purchase price or other debts.[4]

"Delivery" under CISG is a limited concept, relating to transfer of possession or control of the goods. The CISG draftsmen did

---

21. Note that this result is comparable to the result under local domestic law, The German Standard Contracts Act. See authority cited at note 15, supra.

§ 1.12

1. CISG Art. 30.

2. CISG Art. 4(b).

3. For such domestic law in the United States, see UCC §§ 2–401 to 2–403.

4. In the United States, any retention of title of security under UCC Article 2 is subject to the secured transactions provisions of UCC Article 9.

not attempt to consolidate all the incidents of sale—physical delivery, passing of risk of loss, passing of title, liability for the price, and ability to obtain specific performance, etc.—into a single concept or make them turn on a single event, as has been done in many sales statutes.[5] Instead, they followed the format of the UCC in providing separate provisions for each of these concepts.[6]

As to the place of delivery, CISG recognizes four distinct types of delivery terms: (1) delivery contracts in which the seller must deliver to the place specified in the contract; (2) shipment contracts, in which the contract "involves carriage of the goods," but does not require delivery to any particular place; (3) sales of goods at a known location which are not expected to be transported; and (4) sales of goods whose location is not known or specified, and which are not expected to be transported.[7]

In "destination" or delivery contracts, the seller may be obligated to deliver the goods to the buyer's place, or to a sub-buyer's place, or to any location specified. However, it should be noted that CISG has no provisions directly describing seller's duties in such contracts, for they are expressly excluded from Article 31, and all interpretation is left to contract terms only. The goods must be conforming when delivered,[8] not merely when shipped, unless performance is excused by force majeure.[9]

In a shipment contract, the seller is not obligated to accomplish delivery of goods to their destination, or to any particular place, but it is clear that transportation of the goods by an independent third party carrier is involved. The usual reference such a contract is through commercial terms like "FOB" or "CIF."[10] Since the goods are to be "handed over" to the carrier and not to the buyer, transactions involving carriage by the buyer seem to be excluded from this provision.

The shipment contract may require seller to take more than one action to accomplish its obligation of "delivery." First, the seller must transfer ("hand over") the goods to a carrier—the first carrier.[11] There is no duty under CISG for seller to arrange for the carriage of the goods, such as the one imposed by the UCC.[12] Commercial terms may impose such a duty,[13] but the Convention does not. Second, depending upon the sale contract terms, seller must either "effect insurance" coverage of the goods during transit

---

5. See, e.g., the Sale of Goods Act 1893 (U.K.)

6. CISG arts. 31, 69, 57 and 46, respectively. The comparable UCC provisions are UCC §§ 2–509, 2–509, 2–511, and 2–716.

7. CISG art. 31.

8. CISG arts. 36, 69.

9. CISG art. 79.

10. See discussion of "commercial terms" in Chapter 2, infra.

11. CISG art. 31(a).

12. See UCC § 2–504 (a).

13. See generally, Chapter 2, infra.

or, at buyer's request, provide the buyer all available information necessary to effect insurance.[14] Third, if the goods are not "clearly identified to the contract" by the shipping documents or by their own markings, seller must notify buyer of the consignment specifying the goods.[15] Finally, the contract may require seller to arrange for the transportation of the goods, in which case seller must contract for "appropriate" carriage under "usual terms."[16]

Where carriage of the goods is not "involved," the buyer may or may not be told where the goods are or will be. Absent a contrary provision in the contract, in such a transaction, if buyer is told the location of the goods she is expected to pick them up at that location; otherwise at the seller's place of business. The seller's obligation under CISG is to put the goods "at buyer's disposal" at the appropriate place.[17] The Convention is not clear as to whether this requires notification to buyer, but it would require notification to any third party bailees to allow the buyer to take possession.

Where the delivery of the goods is to be accomplished by tender or delivery of documents, CISG merely requires that the seller conform to the terms of the contract.[18] The second and third sentences of Article 34 establish the principle that a seller who delivers defective documents early may cure the defects until the date due under the contract, if possible, and buyer must take the cured documents, even though the original tender and cure has caused damage to buyer.

The time requirements for seller's performance, as stated in CISG, all relate to the contract terms: the goods or documents must be delivered on or before a stated or determinable date set in the contract, within a stated or determinable span of time specified in the contract, or, if no date or span of time is set, within a "reasonable time."[19] "Reasonable time" is not defined, and will depend on trade usage, but at least it precludes demands for immediate delivery.

The Convention has no provisions concerning seller's duties in regard of export and import licenses and taxes, but leaves the determination of these incidents of delivery to the contract terms, or usage. Where these issues are not covered by the contract terms or usage, the concepts are to be interpreted according to the general principles of CISG.

§ 1.13   Seller's Obligations—Quality of the Goods

Under CISG, the seller's obligation is to deliver goods of the quantity, quality, description and packaging required by the con-

---

14. CISG art. 32(3).

15. CISG art. 32(1).

16. CISG art. 32(2).

17. CISG art. 31(b), (c).

18. CISG art. 34.

19. CISG art. 33.

tract.[1] In determining whether the quality of the goods conforms to the contract, the Convention eschews such separate and independent doctrines as "warranty" and "strict product liability" from the common law analysis, as well as "fault" or "negligence" from civil law. Instead, CISG focuses on the simpler concept that the seller is obligated to deliver the goods as described in the contract, and then elaborates on the connotations of that contractual description. This approach, however, produces results which are comparable to the "warranty" structure of the UCC, but without the divisions between express and implied warranties.[2] This is a pattern of analysis which has long been urged by Professor John Honnold for the UCC itself.[3]

The basic requirements are that the goods conform to the contract description,[4] that the goods be fit for ordinary use and properly packaged,[5] that they be fit for any particular use made known to the seller,[6] and that they conform to any goods which seller has held out as a sample or model.[7] Each of these obligations, however, arises out of the contract, so that the parties may "agree otherwise" and limit seller's obligations concerning quality.[8]

In *Rotorex*, the court held that failure of the goods to comply with affirmative contractual performance standards (contractual specifications regarding cooling capacity and power consumption) constituted a breach.[9] Any trade usage recognized by CISG would also be applicable to the contractual description.[10]

There are no conditions on the imposition on seller of the obligation of fitness for ordinary use. All the contracts governed by CISG will be commercial contracts,[11] so that there is no need for the UCC limitation to a "merchant" seller.[12] One issue not expressly resolved is whether the "ordinary use" is defined by seller's location or by buyer's location, if "ordinary use" in each is different. One United States court has cited, with seeming approval, the

---

§ 1.13

1. CISG art. 35.

2. Compare CISG art. 35 to UCC §§ 2–314 and 2–315. The UCC creates a series of "warranties" from seller to buyer. Some warranties are "express" under UCC § 2–313, others are "implied" under UCC §§ 2–314 and 2–315. The primary reason for the differentiation under UCC concepts is that "implied" warranties can be "disclaimed" under UCC § 2–316(2), while "express" warranties cannot.

3. See, e.g., J. Honnold, Law of Sales and Sales Financing, 28–32 (4th ed. 1976).

4. CISG art. 35(1). Compare UCC § 2–313.

5. CISG art. 35(2)(a) and (d). Compare UCC § 2–314.

6. CISG art. 35(2)(b). Compare UCC § 2–315.

7. CISG art. 35(2)(c). Compare UCC § 2–313(1)(c).

8. CISG art. 6. Compare UCC § 2–316 (disclaimers of warranty).

9. Delchi Carrier SpA v. Rotorex Corp., 71 F.3d 1024 (2d Cir.1995).

10. CISG art. 9(2).

11. CISG art. 1(1).

12. See UCC § 2–314(1).

analysis of a German court that the seller is generally not obligated to supply goods that conform to public laws and regulations enforced at buyer's place of business, but with three recognized exceptions.[13] The exceptions enumerated were: (1) if the public laws and regulations of the buyer's state are identical to those enforced in the seller's state; (2) if the buyer informed the seller about those regulations; *or* (3) if, due to special circumstances, seller knew or should have known about the regulations in the buyer's state. The concept of "special circumstances" includes the seller having a branch office in the buyer's state.

The obligation of fitness for a particular purpose arises only if (1) the buyer makes the particular purpose known to the seller (expressly or impliedly) at or before the "conclusion of the contract," (2) the buyer also relies on seller's skill and judgment, and (3) such reliance is reasonable.[14] There is no express requirement that the buyer inform the seller of the buyer's reliance, but only that the buyer inform the seller of the particular purpose. More importantly, there is no requirement that the buyer inform the seller of any of the difficulties which the buyer may know are involved in designating or designing goods to accomplish this particular use. However, it is likely that courts can avoid any abuse of these gaps in the statute by the "reasonable reliance" criterion. In the text of the Convention, the assignment of burdens of proof on such issues is not clear. Most courts have usually placed this burden on the buyer,[15] although one court placed it on the seller,[16] or have allocated it according to the domestic law of the forum.[17]

Seller is relieved of any of the obligations under Article 35(2) against defects in quality whenever buyer is aware or "could not have been unaware" of a defect at the time the contract is "concluded." However, knowledge gained at the time of delivery or inspection of the goods will not affect seller's obligation.[18] The "could not have been unaware" language is the subject of much dispute among common law and civil law authorities. Most common law authorities consider it to be "subjective" and relate to buyer's actual state of mind, rather than to impose "constructive knowledge" on the buyer for items he should have learned. In practice, the usual dispute seems to arise out of the sale of used goods or "seconds," where the courts refuse to allow claims for defects

13. Medical Marketing Int'l, Inc. v. Internazionale Medico Scientifica, S.R.L., 1999 WL 311945 (E.D.La.1999), cert. den., 526 U.S. 1087, 119 S.Ct. 1496, 143 L.Ed.2d 650 (1999). The court held that the decision of an arbitral tribunal was not in manifest disregard of the German Supreme Court decision. See UNILEX Case. D. 1995-9.

14. CISG art. 35(2)(b).

15. UNILEX Cases D. 1993-22; D 1994-20.1.

16. UNILEX Case D. 1996-10.5.

17. UNILEX Cases D. 1993-1; D. 1998-1.1.

18. CISG art. 35(3).

which were not notified to the buyer, but which seem to be predictable for such goods.[19] A court will refuse to relieve the seller of its obligation of non-conformity, even though the buyer "could not have been unaware" of the non-conformity, when the seller was aware of non-conformity and did not inform the buyer of it.[20]

Under CISG Article 35, a seller is generally not obligated to supply goods that conform to the public laws and regulations in the buyer's state. However, there are at least three exceptions to this general rule. First, if those laws and regulations are identical to those in the seller's state, the goods must conform to them. Second, if the buyer informs the seller about the laws and regulations in its state, the goods must conform to them. And, third, if the seller knew or should have known of the laws and regulations in the buyer's state due to special circumstances, such as having a branch office in buyer's state, then the goods must conform to them.[21]

Under CISG the conformity of the goods to all the contract, and to these standards, is to be tested "at the time when the risk [of loss] passes to the buyer."[22] The time at which the risk of loss passes will be explored in depth later.[23] How long do these obligations continue? Although the less developed countries sought a statutory provision requiring "a reasonable time" for the duration of such obligations, such a provision was not included. Instead, CISG defers to the contract, and speaks of long term obligations of quality which arise from a "guarantee ... for a period of time."[24] However, it is clear that any nonconformity concerning the quality of the goods which exists at the time the risk of loss passes is actionable, even if discovered later. Thus, the buyer is still able to recover for any nonconformity which becomes apparent long after delivery, but the buyer may have to prove that the defect was present at delivery and was not caused by buyer's use, maintenance or protection of the goods.[25]

If the goods are defective, seller may have a disclosure obligation. Under Article 40 there is an obligation to notify buyer of any nonconformity not only if known to seller, but also if "he could not have been unaware." If seller does know of a defect and does not notify, then seller may not be able to rely on buyer's failure to inspect the goods quickly or to notify seller of any discovered

---

19. UNILEX Case D. 1997–20.

20. UNILEX Case D. 1996–5.5. Compare CISG art. 40.

21. See Medical Marketing Int'l, Inc. v. Internazionale Medico Scientifica, S.R.L., 1999 WL 311945 (E.D.La.1999).

22. CISG art. 36(1).

23. See § 1.22, infra.

24. CISG art. 36(2).

25. See UNILEX Case D. 1996–5.2.1, in which the goods, delivered under an FOB contract, were non-conforming when they reached their destination. The Commission held that the goods were not canned or packaged properly, so the non-conformity related back to a time before delivery.

defects. Thus, even though the buyer may lose its right to rely on a nonconformity because the buyer did not inspect the goods "within as short a time as is practicable,"[26] or did not notify the seller of any defects, specifying the nature of the defects, within a reasonable time after it discovered or "ought to have discovered" them,[27] the buyer's right to rely on the nonconformity revives if the seller, in turn, knew of the nonconformity and did not notify the buyer of it.

Can seller exclude these obligations concerning the quality of the goods by terms in the contract—and, if so, how? CISG Article 6 states that the parties may, by agreement, derogate from any provision of the Convention, and Article 35(2) supports that ability to limit obligations concerning the quality of the goods. However, it is also clear that the standard United States formulation in domestic contracts—disclaiming implied warranties[28]—will be inapposite, since the CISG obligations are neither "warranties" nor "implied." New verbal formulations should be found, which deal directly with the description of the goods and their expected use.

If a contract is framed in the usual language, which is appropriate for contracts subject to the UCC,[29] but the contract is actually governed by CISG, a court would have two possible analytical approaches. One would arise from the concept that the term "warranties" has little meaning in the CISG context, and the drafters deliberately avoided using it, because the term has many different meanings in different legal regimes. Thus, use of such language by a seller should not be allowed to destroy the legislatively imposed duties of quality. The other approach would allow a court to inquire of the parties whether they understood the concepts of "warranty," "express" and "implied"—i.e., whether they were familiar with the United States domestic legal approach in this area. If so, CISG Article 8(1) would allow the court to interpret the language according to the parties intentions.[30]

The major unresolved issue is the extent to which local law regulating disclaimers will impact on the international contracts governed by CISG. Such local law covers a spectrum from prohibitions on disclaimers in printed standard terms[31] to the "how to do it

---

26. CISG art. 38.

27. CISG art. 39.

28. The so-called "standard manufacturers warranty," usually reads as follows:

Seller warrants this product to be free from defects in material and workmanship for [amount of time]. Seller makes No other EXPRESS WARRANTY and NO IMPLIED WARRANTIES. Seller's obligation is limited to repair or replace-

ment of defective parts without charge to Buyer.

29. See UCC § 2–316(2), (3).

30. The *MCC–Marble* case, supra § 1.9, note 13, would allow U.S. courts to examine the background of the transaction to determine the parties' intentions.

31. The German Standard Contracts Act, translated and published in H. Sil-

manual" set out in UCC § 2–316. It is likely that the former raises a question of "validity," and therefore governs contracts arising under CISG; but there is a three-way argument as to whether the UCC provisions raise issues of "validity," and therefore whether they govern CISG contracts. The distinction drawn seems to depend upon whether the local public policy prohibits conduct completely, or allows it but only within certain conditions.[32] Whether the United States courts will accept such a distinction is conjectural at this point. However, they should, at the least, draw a distinction between those UCC provisions which require language to be "conspicuous" and those provisions which require a particular linguistic formula, such as use of the word "merchantability."

§ 1.14   Seller's Obligations—Property Issues

Even though CISG Art. 4(b) states that the Convention is not concerned with property or title to the goods sold, CISG does impose obligations on sellers that the goods be sold free of any claims concerning title to the goods or claims on infringement of intellectual property rights.[1] Seller's obligation concerning title to the goods under CISG is to deliver the goods not only free from any encumbrances on their title, but also free from any claim of a third party.[2] The issue concerning who actually has valid title to particular goods is outside the scope of the Convention under Article 4(b), and would be left to local law. But the scope of seller's obligation to deliver what it has promised is within the scope of the Convention.

A second issue is whether seller is required to convey only a valid title to the goods, or is also required to convey title that will not be contested–a warranty of "quiet possession." The common law required that seller provide a warranty of "quiet possession."[3] The legal issue is whether the Convention language should be interpreted to require that seller convey title that is free from all claims, or only title that is free from valid claims. The language in the English version is not clear and, the debates and legislative history suggest conflicting interpretations, but the language in the French and Spanish versions suggest that the goods are to be free

berberg. The German Standard Contracts Act, 27–29 (1979).

32. See Hartnell, "Rousing the Sleeping Dog: The Validity Exception to the CISG," 18 Yale Int'l L. 1 (1993); S. Honnold, supra § 1.2, note 20, at § 236; Longobardi, "Disclaimers of Implied Warranties: The 1980 United Nations Convention on Contracts for the International Sale of Goods", 53 Fordham L. Rev. 863 (1985).

§ 1.14

1.   CISG arts. 41, 42.

2.   CISG art. 41.

3.   See UCC § 2–312, and especially Comment 1.

from all claims.[4] There are no CISG cases yet which analyze the issue.[5]

Although the obligation is very broad, it probably is not breached by claims which are frivolous on their face or by state restrictions on use of the goods. The parties may derogate from the terms of these provisions of CISG by agreement, but buyer's knowledge that the goods are subject to a bailee's lien does not necessarily imply such an agreement. Instead, buyer may expect seller to discharge the lien before tender of delivery.

In addition to good title, seller is obligated to deliver the goods free from patent, trademark and copyright claims assertable under the law of the buyer's "place of business" or the place where both parties expect the goods to be used or resold.[6] This obligation is, however, subject to multiple qualifications. First, seller's obligations arise only with respect to claims of which "seller knew or could not have been unaware."[7] Second, seller has no obligation with respect to intellectual property rights or claims of which buyer had knowledge when the contract was formed.[8] Third, seller is not liable for claims which arise out of its use of technical drawings, designs or other specifications furnished by buyer, if seller's action is in "compliance with" buyer's specifications.[9] It is clear that this provision applies when seller is following specifications required by the contract, but its application is not clear when seller is merely following "suggestions" of buyer as to how best to meet more general contract provisions. Fourth, seller is excused from these obligations if buyer does not give notice of breach[10]—unless seller knew of the claim, which knowledge may be required in order to create liability initially.[11]

With all these qualifications on the seller's obligation, does the mere assertion of an intellectual property infringement claim create a violation of seller's title obligations? In order to have a violation, the buyer must show that "seller knew or could not have been unaware" the third party claims. One survey of the legislative history concludes that it does not require the seller to research the trademark and copyright registries of the buyer's country, but only requires seller to use due care.[12] That interpretation would preclude

4. See Honnold supra § 1.2, note 20, at § 266, and especially authorities cited in his note 4.

5. The one case to date citing CISG art. 41 dealt with seller's ability to place geographic limits on buyer's resale of the goods. See UNILEX Case D. 1996–3.1.

6. CISG art. 42.

7. CISG art. 42(1).

8. CISG art. 42(2)(a).

9. CISG art. 42(2)(b).

10. CISG art. 43(1).

11. CISG art. 43(2). Compare UCC § 2–312(3).

12. Shinn, "Liabilities Under Article 42 of the U.N. Convention on the International Sale of Goods", 2 Minn. J. Global Trade 115 (1993).

The only CISG decision to date, involves a situation in which the third party claimant had already obtained an infringement judgment against the buyer. See UNILEX Case D. 1996–6.0.1.

a warranty of quiet enjoyment, because buyer has no absolute claim, but only a knowledge or negligence-based claim.

It can also be argued that mistake of law will excuse seller, or at least that the seller has performed its obligations concerning intellectual property rights if it has relied on trustworthy information from a lawyer that there are no such rights which might be infringed by use or resale of the goods, because seller could not then "know" of the possible claims of infringement.

The UCC approach to these problems is to allow buyer, when sued by a third party claimant, to "vouch in" the seller, so as to allow the seller to defend itself directly.[13] However, there is no "vouching in" provision in CISG. Thus, buyers who are confronted with third party claims are left to local procedural devices for protection, such as collateral estoppel.

§ 1.15 Buyer's Obligations

Buyer has two primary obligations in a sale contract under CISG: to pay the price, and to take delivery of the goods.[1] The former duty is the more important of the two. In addition, there are several derivative preliminary duties called "enabling steps."[2]

Unless the sale contract expressly grants credit to buyer, the sale is a cash sale, and payment and delivery are concurrent conditions. Further, payment is due when seller places the goods, or their documents of title, "at buyer's disposal according to the contract."[3] If the sales contract involves carriage of the goods, seller may ship the goods under negotiable documents of title and demand payment against those documents,[4] even though no particular method of payment was actually agreed upon by the parties. In such circumstances, buyer still has a right of inspection before payment. If, however, buyer has expressly agreed to "pay against documents" (such as through the use of CFR or CIF term), the buyer has agreed to pay upon tender of the documents, regardless of whether the goods have yet arrived, and without inspection of the goods.[5]

If the buyer is to pay against "handing over" of the documents, or handing over the goods, the place of "handing over" is the place of payment. Otherwise, the place of seller's business is the place of payment, unless the contract provides otherwise.[6] Such a provision requires the buyer to "export" the funds to seller, which is a

---

13. See UCC § 2–607(5)

§ 1.15

1. CISG art. 53.

2. J. Honnold, supra § 1.2, note 20, at § 323.

3. CISG art. 58.

4. CISG art. 58(2).

5. CISG art. 58(3).

6. CISG art. 57.

critical issue when buyer is from a country with a "soft" currency, or with other restrictions on the international transfer of funds. In addition the buyer has an obligation to cooperate and take all necessary steps to enable payment to be made, including whatever formalities may be imposed by the buyer's country to obtain administrative authorization to make a payment abroad.[7] Failure to take such steps may create a breach by the buyer even before payment is due.

The cases, however, have not been so doctrinaire. Where the offer indicated a range of prices for goods with a range of quality, the court held that the offer was sufficiently definite, since it was possible to price each item according to its quality.[8] Where the parties agreed to a sale without stating a price, but essentially "agreed to agree" later on the price for each shipment, the purported offer neither contained a price term nor made a provision for determining the price.[9] However, in two cases where the seller and buyer agreed to a sale with no price term, then the goods were shipped and accepted by buyer, the courts found that a binding contract existed.[10] In each case, seller had included an invoice stating a price with the goods, and buyer had not contested that price at the time of receipt.

The buyer's second obligation, to take delivery, also poses duties of cooperation. The buyer must not only take over the goods, but also do everything that could reasonably be expected in order to enable the seller to make delivery.[11] This includes a duty to make the expected preparations to permit seller to make delivery and may include such acts as providing for containers, transportation, unloading and import licenses.[12]

§ 1.16   Buyer's Inspection and Notice of Defects

The buyer has a right to inspect the goods before taking delivery and the duty to notify the seller of any non-conformities.[1] Where the contract involves the carriage of goods, the buyer may defer the inspection until the goods have arrived at their destina-

---

7. CISG art. 54.

8. UNILEX Case D. 1994–29.

9. UNILEX Case D. 1995–7.2.

10. UNILEX Cases D. 1995–15 and D. 10.1.

11. CISG art. 60.

12. *Id.*

§ 1.16

1. CISG art. 38(1). Compare UCC § 2–513, which gives the buyer a right to inspect the goods before it must ei-

ther accept or pay for them. Even when shipment of the goods is involved, buyer may inspect after arrival at their destination before acceptance or payment, unless otherwise agreed. UCC § 2–513(1). However, buyer is not permitted to inspect before payment where the contract provides for payment against documents, UCC § 2–513(3).

tion.[2] Timeliness of inspection is important, and several decisions hold that the buyer is not permitted to pass the goods on to sub-purchasers and await their complaints, but has an affirmative duty to inspect the goods immediately when they arrive.[3]

The buyer may also have a natural incentive to inspect at the place of delivery (e.g., shipment) because the goods must be con-forming at the time the risk passes, which will be at the place or port of shipment in the usual FCA, FOB or CIF contract.[4] There are numerous specialized inspection companies that will, for a fee, inspect goods for a distant buyer.

The buyer must notify the seller within a reasonable after the buyer discovers any nonconformity.[5] The notice must specify the nature of the lack of conformity. If it fails to duly notify the seller without a reasonable excuse, the buyer may not rely on the lack of conformity in any remedy proceeding. If there is a reasonable excuse, the buyer may still reduce the price of the goods in accordance with the special formula of Art. 50.[6] This latter provi-sion was included in the CISG as a result of pressure from develop-ing countries who complained that it was often difficult for them to inspect and notify promptly.

There has been more litigation over the effectiveness of such notices than over any other single issue, but the results are usually not surprising.[7] For example, where buyer notified seller that the goods (shoes) had "poor workmanship and improper fitting," the court held that the notice was defective in that it was not specific enough.[8]

The contract may include such terms as a provision on how many days the buyer will have to inspect, where the inspection will take place, how many days the buyer will have to notify the seller of the defects, how and where the notice is to be sent, and a statement as to when specification of a defect is sufficient.

§ 1.17   Cure

If the seller delivers non-forming goods, it will often wish to cure any defects in the goods delivered. It is for that reason that

---

2. CISG art 38(2).

3. See, e.g., UNILEX Case D. 1995–10.1. A delay of twenty days to inspect frozen bacon is unreasonably long. Buy-er did not inspect but waited for its customs to do so.

4. See, generally, Chapter 2, infra.

5. CISG art. 39. Compare UCC § 2–607, which requires the buyer which has accepted nonconforming goods to notify seller "of breach" within a reasonable

time of discovery, or its "barred from any remedy" under the UCC—unless the contract terms provide otherwise, UCC § 2–607(3)(a).

6. CISG art. 44.

7. Consult the "Cases listed by Is-sue" section of UNILEX under Article 39.

8. CLOUT Case 3.

the Convention requires early notice by the buyer to the seller of any defects in the goods or their tender of delivery. The primary issues arise from defects in quantity or quality of the goods or the timeliness of the delivery. The Convention has different rules for cure which depend upon whether the defects were discovered before or after the contract date for delivery.

Where a non-conforming tender is made before the contract date for delivery, the seller has the right to remedy any lack of conformity, "provided that the exercise of this right does not cause the buyer unreasonable inconvenience or unreasonable expense."[1] The cure may be repair, replacement or making up a shortage in quantity. If seller cures the non-conformity, it is still liable to the buyer for any damages caused by the defects.[2]

CISG Article 37 speaks of the seller having a "right" to cure the non-conformity of a tender before the date for delivery. Thus, the buyer is obligated to permit the seller to cure.[3] If the buyer prohibits the seller from attempting cure, that is a breach of buyer's obligations, so the buyer will be responsible for any damages which arise from not permitting the cure.[4] That article expressly contemplates repair or replacement as recognized forms of cure. Whether other forms of redress, such as offering of a money allowance,[5] can be used is not clear.[6] Given the objectives of Article 37, the list of specific forms of remedy should not be read as exclusive and the buyer should be obligated to accept a tendered cure as long as it does not cause the buyer unreasonable inconvenience or unreasonable expense.

Even after the date for delivery has passed, the seller may remedy the non-conformity but its right to do so is subject to more conditions. In addition to not causing the buyer unreasonable inconvenience or unreasonable expense, the seller must cure without unreasonable delay.[7] Unlike the specific references in CISG Article 37 to various ways a non-conformity tender might be remedied, CISG Article 48 says only that the seller may remedy any failure. Given that the basic objectives of Article 48 are the same as

---

§ 1.17

1. CISG art. 37. Compare UCC § 2–508(1), which allows a seller who had tendered delivery before the contract delivery date to cure any non-conforming tender, if there is notice and cure be accomplished before the contract delivery date.

2. *Id.*

3. CISG art. 61(1).

4. See CISG art. 74.

5. Compare CISG art. 50.

6. Compare UCC § 2–508(2).

7. CISG art. 48. Compare UCC § 2–508(2) which gives to the seller a more limited right to cure even after the contract delivery date. It is available only if the seller had "reasonable grounds to believe" that the non-conforming tender "would be acceptable" to buyer, even though defective. If so, seller must notify buyer of the intention to cure, and then may "substitute a conforming tender" within a reasonable time of the contract date.

that of Article 37, the seller should not be limited in the form of cure as long as the conditions (e.g., no unreasonable delay, expense or inconvenience) are satisfied.

If asked whether it will accept cure, the buyer apparently has the option to say "No" under CISG.[8] If the buyer does so and the seller proceeds nevertheless to make a conforming tender, the buyer would not be obligated to accept the tender. One arbitral award has stated that the seller's right to cure after the delivery date is dependent on the consent of the buyer.[9] If the buyer does agree to the seller's offer of cure, it may not seek a remedy which as inconsistent with seller's offered performance, such as avoidance of the contract.

If the buyer wishes to avoid the contract after seller has made an offer to cure the non-conformities, that is still possible under the opening clause of CISG Article 48(1). However, to be authorized to avoid the contract, the buyer must comply with all of the requirements of CISG Article 49.[10] It is not clear whether an attempt by the seller to cure, where the performance remains non-conforming is a satisfactory performance under CISG.

§ 1.18   Risk of Loss

Most international sales will involve transportation of the goods, even though no such transportation is necessary for CISG to apply.[1] The basic rule, under CISG and domestic law, is that the buyer bears the risk of loss to the goods during their transportation by a carrier, unless the contract provides otherwise.[2] The contract will often contain a term which expressly allocates the risk of loss, such as "FOB" or "CIF," and such terms supersede the CISG provision.[3] If there is no such delivery term, under CISG the risk in a shipment contract passes to the buyer when the seller completes its delivery obligations under CISG Article 31, which is when the goods are "handed over" by the seller to the first carrier.[4] They need not be on board the means of transportation, or even pass a ship's rail—any receipt by a carrier will do. Further, they need not be "handed over" to an ocean-going or international carrier—possession by the local trucker who will haul them to the port is

---

8. CISG art 48 (2).

9. UNILEX Case D. 1994–31.

10. See further discussion with respect to the remedy of avoidance at § 1.22.

§ 1.18

1. See discussion of CISG art. 1 at § 1.2, supra.

2. CISG art. 67(1), UCC § 2–509(1).

3. See discussion of risk of loss, generally, throughout Chapter 2 on Incoterms. However, use of commercial terms is a derogation from CISG art. 67, even when there is no reference to Incoterms. See, e.g., UNILEX Case D. 1995–28.1.1.

4. The risk of loss passes to the buyer when the seller has completed its delivery obligations under CISG art 31(a).

sufficient. However, if the seller uses its own vehicle to transport the goods, seller bears the risk of loss until the goods are handed over to an independent carrier, or to the buyer.

Where the contract requires that the seller deliver the goods to buyer's location, or that seller provide part of the transportation and then "hand the goods over to a carrier at a particular place," seller bears the risk of loss to that location or particular place.[5] Thus, in a contract between a Buffalo, N.Y., seller and Beijing, China, buyer: (1) in a shipment contract (FCA Buffalo), the risk would pass to buyer when the goods were delivered to the first carrier in Buffalo;[6] (2) in a destination contract (DDU Beijing), the seller would bear the risk during transit, and risk would not pass to buyer until the goods were delivered in Beijing; and (3) in a transshipment contract (FAS New York City), the seller would bear risk from Buffalo to "along side" a ship in New York harbor, and buyer would bear the risk thereafter.

If the goods are not to be transported by a carrier (e.g., when the buyer or an agent are close to the seller and will pick up the goods), the risk passes to buyer when the buyer picks them up or, if the buyer is late in doing so, when the goods are "at his disposal" and the delay in picking them up causes a breach of contract.[7] The goods cannot, however, be "at his disposal" until they have first been identified to the contract.

In most situations, title and risk are treated separately. Thus, manipulation of title through the use of title retention clauses or documents of title, such as negotiable bills of lading, is irrelevant and has no effect on the point of transfer of risk of loss. However, if the goods are already in transit when sold, the risk passes when the contract is "concluded."[8] This rule reflects a use of "title" concepts in risk allocation, even though it may be practically impossible to determine whether damage to goods in a ship's cargo hold occurred before or after a sale contract was signed.

Just as title and risk are treated separately, so also breach and risk are treated separately. If seller is in breach of contract when the goods are shipped, these basic risk of loss rules are not changed, which is contrary to the position of the UCC.[9] Thus, a breach by seller, whether it is a "fundamental beach" under CISG Article 25 or not, is irrelevant to determine risk allocation or the point when the risk of loss passes to the buyer. However, if the seller does commit a fundamental breach of contract in shipment contract,

---

5. CISG art. 67(1), second sentence.

6. See § 2.7, infra. Even if the contract had a C & F term, the risk of loss would pass upon delivery to the carrier at the port of shipment, Buffalo. See UNILEX Case D. 1995–28.1.1.

7. CISG art. 69.

8. CISG art. 68.

9. UCC § 2–510.

further damage to the goods during transit will not deprive buyer of its right to avoid the contract under CISG.[10] Likewise, a non-fundamental breach in a shipment contract, plus damage in transit, will not create a right for buyer to avoid the contract.

§ 1.19 Excused Performance

Under CISG, performance of an obligation of a party is excused when that party's failure to perform the obligation was due to an "impediment" which was beyond that party's control, and which the party "could not reasonably be expected to have taken [it] into account" when the contract was made.[1] In addition, the party seeking excuse must prove that it could neither avoid nor overcome the "impediment." The excuse is available only so long as the impediment continues,[2] and the party seeking excuse must notify the other party to the contract both of the "impediment" and of its effect on performance.[3]

Even if the party seeking excuse proves all these elements, it is protected only from damage claims.[4] It is not protected from other remedial actions by the other party, such as avoidance of the contract or restitution of benefits received from the other party or derived from goods received.

This brief summary of the provisions of Article 79 should demonstrate that great weight is placed on the concept of "impediment." In part, that word was chosen because it was believed to be not an operative word used to define excused performance in any current legal regime.[5] Thus, it is not connected to the operation of any domestic legal system; it creates a blank slate for development of CISG concepts,[6] although the of the word "impediment" does create nuances from which analytical conclusions may be drawn. The drafters of the CISG provisions deliberately rejected a proposal to use the word "circumstances," rather than "impediment."[7] "Impediment" was thought to reflect a requirement of an outside force which arose to prevent performances, rather than a change in the general economic climate. Thus, recessions or increases in inflation rates were not expected to qualify as impediments, al-

---

10. CISG art. 49

§ 1.19

1. CISG art. 79(1).

2. CISG art. 79(3).

3. CISG art. 79(4).

4. CISG art. 79(5).

5. See J. Honnold, supra § 1.5, note 17 at §§ 425–432.

6. For example, CISG art. 79 is deliberately different from UCC § 2–615, which would be the analogous UCC provision. The CISG provision can be used by both buyer and seller, while the UCC provision is expressly limited to use by sellers only. Further, the CISG provision can be used to excuse "any" obligation, while the UCC provision is limited to late delivery. It was the limitations (or sometimes expansions) in domestic laws that the drafters sought to avoid by using a new word which started with no precedential interpretation baggage.

7. Honnold, supra note 5, at § 427.

though even Professor Honnold accepts that extreme cases of economic dislocation may qualify as an "impediment."[8] The language in Article 79 does not, however, resolve the issue of whether it can excuse only a complete failure to perform (deliver or pay for goods), or whether it can also be used to excuse defective performance (late delivery or delivery of non-conforming goods). Professor Honnold argues for the former interpretation, although that argument seems to ignore the literal language of the provision which allows excuse of "any" obligation. The debates in the Working Group indicate that it was intended to excuse only the obligation to deliver or pay, and not to include obligation to deliver conforming goods.[9]

While the CISG provisions may seem open-ended and subject to widely varying interpretation, the cases involving CISG Article 79 are clear. With one possible exception,[10] the decisions have all ruled against the party seeking excuse. Thus, a buyer is not excused from payment because the funds were stolen from "a foreign bank" through allegedly criminal conduct.[11] Transferring the funds to seller is part of buyer's obligations,[12] and at buyer's risk.

Most of the cases involve defaults by seller's suppliers. The CISG provisions establish a high standard for obtaining excuse because a third party, such as seller's supplier, has defaulted. The party to the sales contract (seller) is excused by a default of a third party (supplier) only if both the seller and the supplier can show that they failed due to an impediment which was beyond their control, not expected, and unavoidable and not overcomable.[13] Thus, the seller must be able to prove that some "impediment" prevented the supplier from performing. Financial difficulties of the supplier do not meet that standard, and seller assumes the risk of supplier's ability to continue to perform.[14] If the supplier furnished non-conforming goods to the buyer, there is no excuse unless the problems causing the non-conformity were beyond the supplier's ability to control, as well as the seller's.[15] Where the goods are not delivered at all, seller faces a double difficulty. First, it must prove that the problems causing the non-delivery were beyond the supplier's ability to control.[16] In addition, the seller must prove that it was not possible for it (the seller) to obtain conforming substitute

---

8. *Id.*, at § 432.2.

9. B. Nicholas, Chapter 5, in International Sales (Galston & Smit, eds. 1984).

10. See UNILEX Case D. 1995–15.2. However, that case seems to turn more on an interpretation of German agency law than on CISG art. 79.

11. UNILEX Case D. 1998–5.2.

12. CISG art. 57(1)(a).

13. CISG art. 79(2).

14. UNILEX Case D. 1996–3.4.

15. UNILEX Case D. 1999–3.

16. UNILEX Case D. 1995–34; UNILEX Case 1995–10.0.1, CLOUT Case 140.

goods from another source.[17] To date no seller has overcome this double burden.

It is relatively clear that there is no excuse for performance under CISG Article 79 for cases involving "hardship" or economic difficulty. Thus, relief has been denied where the price of goods increased by 30%.[18]

§ 1.20   Remedies in General

The organization of CISG treats buyer's remedies for seller's breach in a separate chapter of the convention from the seller's remedies for buyer's breach.[1] Thus, the buyer has four potential types of remedies under CISG: "avoidance" of the contract,[2] price adjustment,[3] specific performance,[4] and an action for damages.[5] The first two of these remedies may be undertaken without judicial intervention, the latter two involve proceedings in court or before an arbitral tribunal.

If the buyer breaches, the seller has five potential types of remedies: suspension of performance,[6] "avoidance" of the contract,[7] reclamation of the goods (including protection of them if they have been delivered),[8] an action for the price,[9] and an action for damages.[10] The first of these remedies may be undertaken without judicial intervention, the third may or may not involve judicial assistance, and the last two involve proceedings in court or before an arbitral tribunal.

The informal remedies which do not require judicial intervention are preferred by merchants because of their low cost; and merchants who have traded with each other in the past, and hope to do so in the future, are much more likely to use these remedies than to go to court. Thus, to your authors, the more important differentiation is between informal (non-judicial) remedies and remedies which require formal proceedings in court or an arbitral tribunal; and we have organized the following discussion of CISG remedies around that principle.

---

17. UNILEX Case D. 1997–4.4.

18. CLOUT Case No. 54 (1994); see also CLOUT Case No. 102.

§ 1.20

1. Buyer's remedies are in CISG Part III, Chapter II, arts. 45–52. Seller's remedies are in CISG Part III, Chapter III, arts. 61–65. The measurement of damages for both parties, however, is aggregated in still another chapter: CISG Part III, Chapter V, arts. 74–77.

2. CISG art. 49.

3. CISG art. 50.

4. CISG art. 46, which in the United States is also subject to art. 28.

5. CISG art. 45(1)(b), referring to arts. 74–77.

6. CISG art. 71.

7. CISG art. 64.

8. CISG arts. 85–88.

9. CISG art. 62, which in the United States may or may not be subject to art. 28.

10. CISG art. 61(1), referring to arts. 74–77.

§ 1.21   Suspending Performance

Under CISG, a party who has yet to perform may suspend its performance if "it becomes apparent" that the other party "will not" render the required counterperformance.[1] Thus, a seller who has not yet shipped the goods may suspend that performance if it learns that the buyer is insolvent or that there is a "serious deficiency . . . in his creditworthiness."[2] The seller may also suspend its performance if the buyer fails to perform necessary, agreed upon preliminary steps, such as a failure to open a letter of credit[3] or to provide specifications for the goods.[4]

The provision is neutral between buyers and sellers. Thus, a buyer who has agreed to pay, or to prepay, for the goods may suspend that performance if it learns that there is a "serious deficiency" in seller's ability to perform,[5] or that necessary preparations for performance have not been made.[6] Seller's preparations for performance which are necessary include making shipping insurance arrangements[7] or obtaining the proper documents.[8]

Despite the facial neutrality of the provision between sellers and buyers, the cases all involve suspensions of performance by sellers, usually because they have not been paid for prior deliveries. There seems to be a split in the reasoning in the decisions to date. The Austrian Supreme Court has held that a seller may not suspend performance merely because the buyer has failed to pay for prior installments of goods shipped under a contract.[9] It stated that the seller was entitled to suspend its performance only if it could establish that the buyer was unable to pay (financial difficulty or insolvency), and that proof of the buyer's unwillingness to pay was insufficient.

The two other decisions on this issue seem to disagree. In one, a Belgian court held that a seven month delay in buyer's payment for an initial installment of goods allowed a seller to suspend performance in delivering the second installment.[10] The court reasoned that the seller could have a reasonable suspicion that the buyer would not pay for the second installment, but there is no indication that the buyer was in any financial difficulties or had

---

§ 1.21

1. CISG art. 71. Compare UCC § 2–702 which permits a seller to suspend performance, but relates this power to the buyer's insolvency.

2. CISG art. 71(1)(a).

3. CISG arts. 71(1)(b), 54. See UNILEX Case D. 1995–28.2 (failure to secure bank guarantee allows suspension of performance).

4. *Id.*, CISG art. 65.

5. CISG art. 71(1)(a).

6. CISG art. 71(1)(b).

7. CISG art 32(2), (3).

8. CISG art. 34.

9. UNILEX Case D. 1998–5.1, CLOUT Case 238.

10. UNILEX Case D. 1995–7.0.

any inability to pay. Thus, the unwillingness of the buyer to pay for prior deliveries was sufficient.

The second case involves a standard scenario. The seller delivers defective, but repairable goods. The buyer refuses to pay until the goods are repaired. The seller refuses to repair until paid. A sole arbitrator ruled that the seller was entitled to suspend its repair performance until it was paid.[11] Again, there was no discussion of the buyer's inability to pay.

This division of authority arises from the Austrian court's focus on CISG Article 71(1)(a), which requires inability to pay, and the other decisions focus on the preamble to Article 71(1) ("apparent that the other party *will not* perform"). Certainly the conditions stated in subparagraphs (a) and (b) to Article 71(1) are an exclusive list. Thus, the analysis of the other two decisions would depend upon ruling that it was apparent that buyer would not pay in the future as a result of buyer's "conduct ... in performing the contract." (failure to pay for prior installments) under Article 71(1)(b).

A party who suspends performance must notify the other party of that suspension.[12] Failure to notify triggers the other party's rights to a remedy in accordance with the remedies provisions of CISG.[13] None of these remedies authorizes the other party to treat the suspension as ineffective because no notice has been given. However, the non-notified party may have an immediate cause of action for damages.[14]

The CISG permits a seller to suspend performance, if possible, after shipment of the goods but before delivery of them—stoppage in transit.[15] The CISG provision, however, only deals with rights and duties between the parties to the contract. There is a second question concerning whether a carrier will comply with the seller's direction to stop delivery. CISG does not require the carrier to do so, and the carrier's obligations are left to other law.[16] If the seller has possession of a negotiable bill of lading to its order, then the carrier is obligated under the contract of carriage to deliver the footwear to the seller. The CISG provision does not state any criteria for determining whether the stoppage is authorized, so the buyer has no ground under the sales contract to object to seller's stoppage or to challenge it.

However, if the buyer is the holder of the negotiable bill of lading, then the carrier is obligated to deliver the buyer.[17] If the

---

11. UNILEX Case D. 1995–29.

12. CISG art. 71(3).

13. For the buyer, see CISG art. 45(1). For the seller, see CISG art. 61(1).

14. UNILEX Case D. 1991–1.

15. CISG art. 71(2).

16. CISG art. 71(2), last sentence.

17. See discussion in Chapter 3, infra.

carrier does so, then CISG provides no relief for the seller. If the carrier has not delivered the goods to the buyer, the seller may seek to obtain the bill of lading from the buyer and to enjoin the buyer from presenting the bill to the carrier. These remedies are not expressly provided for by the CISG, but the first sentence of CISG Article 71(2) expressly states that the seller is entitled to stop delivery even the buyer "holds a document which entitles [it] to obtain [the goods]." The remedies discussed merely give effect to this right.

The reasoning of the previous paragraph also applies to a transaction in which the buyer is the consignee of a non-negotiable bill of lading.

After the carrier has delivered the goods to the buyer, then it is no longer possible to stop delivery under CISG.[18] All that seller would have is an in personam claim against for the purchase price.[19] The CISG is silent on whether the seller might have an in rem right to recover the goods.[20]

§ 1.22 "Avoidance" of a Contract—Refusal to Accept Nonconforming Performance

Either a seller or a buyer can "avoid" a contract, under certain conditions, due to nonperformance or defective performance by the other party.[1] "Avoidance of the contract," in CISG terminology, is the equivalent of "cancellation of the contract" at common law and under the UCC.[2] Also note that "avoidance of the contract" under CISG is a different concept than "avoidance" under the UCC.[3]

For buyers, "avoidance of the contract" is a method of refusing to accept or keep defective goods or to pay for them. Thus, it is comparable to the rights of buyers under the UCC to "reject" the goods actually delivered before "acceptance,"[4] or to "revoke the acceptance" of goods previously accepted.[5] However, CISG does not adopt the distinctions between "rejecting of the goods" acceptance and "revocation of acceptance" contained in the UCC.[6] Further, CISG does not employ the concept of "acceptance" of the goods; so the buyer's taking delivery of the goods is not a crucial factual step in the analysis of buyer's position under the CISG.

---

18. CISG art. 71(2).

19. CISG arts. 61(1)(a), 62.

20. CISG art. 4(b).

§ 1.22

1. CISG arts. 49(1), 64(1).

2. UCC § 2–106(4). In both, the ending of the contract is for breach; and an

action for damages survives the end of the contract.

3. See, UCC § 2–613.

4. UCC §§ 2–601, 2–612.

5. UCC §§ 2–606, 2–608.

6. UCC §§ 2–601, 2–602, 2–608, 2–612.

Instead, the fundamental concept under CISG is to limit use of this remedy to situations which involve "fundamental breach" by seller, regardless of when the breach occurs.[7] What constitutes a "fundamental breach"? The Convention definition requires "such detriment to the other party as to substantially deprive him of what he is entitled to expect."[8] The drafting history of CISG indicates that "fundamental breach" seems to impose a stricter standard on buyer than the "substantial impairment" test of the UCC.[9] However, there is no indication that the drafters contemplated the old English "fundamental breach" test, which required that the breach "go to the root" of the contract, but which was repudiated by the House of Lords in 1980.[10]

The seller must be substantially deprived of what it could reasonably expect. The reference to expectation is a reference to the quantity and quality of the goods, not to their market price. The focus is on the contract and what the seller is entitled to expect. This is an objective test, comparing the claimed defect in the goods to the reasonable expectation after buyer. The second clause of the CISG Article 25 requires a consideration of whether the substantial detriment was foreseeable. The motivation of the seller, such as an economic desire to get out of the contract is not legally relevant to the interpretation of CISG Article 25. However, it can also be argued that interpreting "fundamental breach" to promote the observance of good faith allows a court to consult the motivations for a breach. The current Common Law concept allowing parties to perform or pay damages is not accepted by civil law jurists. They seek to promote the performance of promises as an independent goal.

The two United States court decisions have not created an overwhelmingly high standard to meet the "fundamental breach" test. Nor have they required "perfect tender" or allowed non-functional defects to be considered as fundamental breaches. In one case, compressors for air conditioning units were delivered which did not have either the cooling capacity or the power consumption contained in the contract specifications. The court held that cooling capacity was an important factor in determining the value of air conditioner compressors, so that the buyer did not in fact receive the goods it was entitled to expect.[11] In the other case, mammography units were seized for non-compliance with U.S. administrative regulations. When the court decided that the seller in this case was

---

7. CISG art. 49(1)(a).

8. CISG art. 25.

9. UCC §§ 2–608, 2–612.

10. Photo Production Ltd. v. Securicor Transport Ltd., [1980] 1 All Eng. Rep. 556.

11. Delchi Carrier SpA v. Rotorex Corp., 71 F.3d 1024 (2d Cir.1995)

obligated to furnish goods that conformed to the buyer's laws,[12] it also held that a breach of that obligation was a fundamental breach.[13]

Foreign cases have adopted the same approach. Where the buyer stated that "it was unable to work with" the substandard steel wire delivered by the buyer, the court held that since seller was unable to use the goods the defect was a fundamental breach.[14] However, where the buyer alleged only that the material used in the goods was different from the contract specifications, but did not allege that the goods could not be used or resold, the breach was not considered fundamental.[15] When a seller contracted to deliver in "July, August, September" and the buyer expected monthly installment deliveries, it was not a fundamental breach to deliver the goods on September 26.[16] Such tender of delivery was within the agreed delivery period, so any delay was not a fundamental defect.

Where there was an exclusive dealership arrangement between seller and buyer, the fact that an agent of the seller sold to another retailer in the buyer's exclusive territory was held not to be a fundamental breach.[17] The court reasoned that because the seller had no knowledge of the agent's conduct, and that knowledge could not be imputed to the seller. On the other hand, where a seller stated that the resale location of the goods was critically important, and the buyer stated an intention to resell in South America, resale elsewhere was a fundamental breach.[18] At the conclusion of the contract, the buyer knew that it was important to the seller that the buyer not resell the goods in areas where other distributors sold those goods. The buyer breached the contract term with respect to the clothing delivered in the first installment. That breach could be treated as a fundamental breach, because the seller was substantially deprived of what it was entitled to expect under the contract,[19] and the buyer could foresee that the detriment would be substantial for the seller.[20]

Where as installment contract is involved, there are separate criteria for the avoidance with respect to an individual installment[21] and with respect to the whole contract.[22] For example, in the last case in the previous paragraph, although the resale of the first installment outside South America was a fundamental breach with

---

12. See discussion in text at § 1.13, supra.

13. Medical Marketing Int'l, Inc. v. Internazionale Medico Scientifica, S.R.L., 1999 WL 311945 (E.D.La.1999).

14. CLOUT Case 235 (Ger. 1997).

15. UNILEX Case 1994–2.

16. CLOUT Case 7 (Ger. 1990).

17. CLOUT Case 6 (Ger. 1991).

18. UNILEX Case 1995–7, CLOUT Case 154.

19. CISG art. 25, first clause.

20. CISG art. 25, second clause.

21. CISG art. 73(1).

22. CISG art. 73(2).

respect to the first installment, it might not be a fundamental breach for the whole contract. To permit avoidance with respect to the whole contract, the seller would have to give "good grounds to conclude" that a fundamental breach will reoccur with respect to future installments. In that case, the buyer had stated unequivocally that "its resale actions are of no concern to" the seller.[23] That statement gave the seller good grounds to conclude that the buyer would continue to breach the contract with regard to future installments as it had with respect to the first installment. If the buyer continued to breach the contract as it did, the seller would be deprived of what it is entitled to expect with respect to those installments and the buyer should have been able to foresee this.[24]

Given the uncertainties of the "fundamental breach" test, it will be very difficult for buyer, or buyer's attorney, to know how to react to any particular breach—and whether "avoidance" (cancellation) of the contract is permissible or not. Incorrect analysis could put buyer in the position of making a fundamental breach through its response. CISG Articles 47 and 49(1)(b) attempt to cure these uncertainties by offering buyer a method of formulating a supposedly strict standard for performance. If the seller fails to deliver the goods on the agreed delivery date, the buyer may notify the seller that performance is due by a stated new date (after the contract date for performance), and the seller's failure to perform by the new date permits the buyer to declare the contract avoided. However, the provision in CISG Article 49(1)(b) is available only for nondelivery by seller, not for delivery of nonconforming goods, and avoidance seems to be available only if seller does not deliver during the additional period allowed by the notice. Thus, it is not clear whether seller's delivery of nonconforming goods during the additional period permits avoidance or not. In other words, must the quality of a late delivery by seller meet a strict standard of "nonconformity," or only the standard of the "fundamental breach" test? There are other interesting issues of interpretation of this provision. How long an additional period must buyer give seller? Article 47 requires that it be "of reasonable length," but unless there is a custom on this issue, the buyer has no certainty that the period it gives in the Article 49(1)(b) notice is long enough, especially if long distances are involved.

The cases mostly involve buyers who quickly complain about the goods, hoping that the seller will cure the defect, and officially declare avoidance months later. They usually are not permitted to avoid the contract—the courts holding that their original complaints about the goods do not amount to a formal declaration of

---

23. UNILEX Case D. 1995–7, **24.** CISG arts. 72(2), 25.
CLOUT Case 154.

avoidance, and that their later declarations come too late.[25] However, in one case where the seller did unsuccessfully attempt to repair the defects, the period for sending a notice of avoidance seems to have been extended—for five weeks—even after the end of the unsuccessful repairs.[26]

As to the time period to be set by this notification to perform or else, the principle case involved "items related to printing machinery." The seller delivered only three out of nine promised items. The buyer then fixed an additional period of 11 days which was "too short to organize carriage by sea." But when seller still failed to deliver, the court held that the buyer could avoid the contract.[27] Thus, there is precedent for allowing the buyer's time desires to override the seller's time requirements for ordinary transport measures. The holding may be influenced by the fact that the buyer sent its declaration of avoidance seven weeks after delivery of the non-conforming goods. This delay was approved by the court because seller had offered only a partial delivery of the conforming goods in the interim.

The right to declare the contract avoided for the fundamental breach is lost if the buyer does not make the declaration within a reasonable time after he knew or ought to have known of the breach.[28] The purpose of this notice is to give the seller an opportunity to cure the defects.[29]

Even if buyer seeks to "avoid the contract" after a "fundamental breach" by the seller, the seller has a right to "cure" any defect in its performance before avoidance is declared.[30] If seller's nonconforming tender is early, seller may cure by making a conforming tender up to the delivery date in the contract, whether the nonconformity would create a fundamental breach or not. However, seller's right to cure after the delivery date may be more problematic. Does the right to cure survive buyer's actual declaration of "avoidance of the contract"? Conceptually, it is difficult to sustain a finding of fundamental beach where seller has made a timely offer of cure. If seller's tender or offer of cure is made after the delivery date in the contract, seller still has a right to cure through late performance, but only if it can be done "without unreasonable

---

25. See, e.g., UNILEX Case D. 1994–7, UNILEX Case 1994–10.

26. UNILEX Case D. 1995–1.2. Compare that fact pattern to on in which the buyer declared the contract avoided four weeks after discovering the defect, and was held to be too late UNILEX Case D. 1995–15.1.

27. UNILEX Case D. 1995–16, translated by P. Winship in J. Spanogle and

P. Winship, International Sales Law at 257 (2000).

28. CISG art. 49 (2)(b)(i). UNILEX Case D, 1992–10.

29. See discussion of "cure" at § 1.17, supra.

30. CISG art. 48(1).

delay," inconvenience or uncertainty of reimbursement expenses.[31] The cases have announced two different analytical approaches, one case held that the buyer could avoid the contract, despite the seller's offer to cure, because the seller's right to cure after the delivery date was dependent upon the buyer's consent.[32]

In the second case, the court found that the seller's breach was not fundamental, and that the seller had offered to furnish substitute conforming goods, but this offer was not accepted. The court ruled that determining the competing rights of the buyer to avoid the contract and the seller to cure defects in performance depended upon whether the defect was a fundamental breach of contract or not.[33] The buyer's right to avoid the contract could prevail over the seller's right to cure if there was a fundamental breach of contract. But, in this case, where the breach was not fundamental, the language of CISG Article 48 lead the court to decide that the seller's right to cure prevailed over the buyer's right to avoid the contract.

Must performance offered as cure meet a strict "nonconformity" test, or is it still subject to the "fundamental breach" test? CISG has no provisions on this issue. It is possible to argue that, if the seller delivers any attempt at cure, the buyer is not entitled to avoid under Art. 49(1)(b), but may only recover any damages it has suffered. On the other hand, it seems strange to argue that the delivery a second round of defective goods constitutes "delivery of the goods" under Art. 49(1)(b). Perhaps the seller, having breached once, should be considered to be on probation and must "get it right" during that probationary period.

The cases demonstrate that, for the buyer to be able to avoid the contract, it must inspect the goods in "as short a [time] as is practicable"[34]; notify seller of the nonconformity "within a reasonable time"[35]; and permit seller to attempt to cure any nonconformity, if the cure does not cause "unreasonable delay" or "inconvenience,"[36] To avoid the contract, the buyer must not only comply with the requirements of CISG Article 48(1), but also those of CISG Article 49. Otherwise it is entitled only to seek the remedy of damages[37] or price reduction.[38] The thrust of the combination of all of these CISG provisions on avoidance is to require cooperation

---

31. Id.

32. UNILEX Case D.1994–31. The analysis seems to emphasize the conditions stated in CISG art. 48(2) and (3).

33. UNILEX Case D. 1997–4.

34. CISG art. 38. See further discussion at § 1.16, supra.

35. CISG arts. 39, 48, see further discussion at § 1.16, supra.

36. CISG art. 48. See further discussion at § 1.17, supra.

37. CISG arts. 74–77. See further discussion at §§ 1.28–1.30, infra.

38. CISG art. 50. See further discussion at § 1.23, infra.

between the parties in resolving disputes over timeliness of delivery and quality of goods.

If the buyer properly avoids the contract and returns the goods, the buyer can still get its money back, even if it has already paid for the goods, under the restitutionary provisions of Article 81. However, the buyer must also return the goods "substantially in the condition which he receives them",[39] unless excused under CISG article 82(2). In the interim, the buyer must take reasonable steps to preserve them.[40] The seller must account for the goods if it is unable to return them "substantially in the condition in which it received them"[41] The buyer has right to deposit the goods in a public warehouse at the expense of the seller.[42] The buyer has a right to sell the goods under specified circumstances.[43]

Note that the seller of goods may be in a significantly better position under CISG than under the UCC, if the buyer claims a relatively minor fault in the goods. Although seller has a right to cure any defects under either statute, this right under the UCC has either time limitations or expectation requirements not stated in CISG.[44] Rejection merely because of a tender which is not "perfect" seems to be available under the UCC,[45] but is definitely not available under CISG.[46] Thus, the seller is less likely to find the goods rejected for an asserted minor non-conformity, and stranded an ocean or continent away, without any effective legal remedy.

§ 1.23   Non–Judicial Price Adjustment

In addition to refusing to accept goods which do not conform to the contract through "avoidance" (cancellation) of the contract,[1] the aggrieved buyer has another informal remedy which appears to give it the power of self-help. Under CISG, the buyer who receives nonconforming goods "may reduce the price" it pays to seller.[2] This remedy is available whether the buyer has already paid or not. If the buyer has paid, the remedy is likely to require an action in court, rather than self help.

The Convention provision spells out a mathematical formula for calculating the permissible amount of the price reduction. The reduction requires a comparison of the value that the goods actually delivered at the time of that delivery to the value that conforming goods would have had at the time of that actual delivery. That

---

39.   CISG arts. 81(2), 82(1).

40.   CISG art. 86(1).

41.   CISG art. 84(2).

42.   CISG art. 87.

43.   CISG art. 88.

44.   Compare UCC § 2–508 with CISG art. 37.

45.   UCC § 2–601. Cf. UCC §§ 2–608, 2–612.

46.   CISG art. 49(1).

§ 1.23

1.   See discussion at § 1.22, supra.

2.   CISG art. 50.

ratio is to be applied to the contract price to determine the price to be paid under CISG Article 50. If the price of the goods has not changed between the time of contracting and, the delivery date, that formula gives the same result as would a damages calculation under the UCC. However, if the price of the goods has changed during the period, then the resulting calculations clash with normative results under common law doctrine, whether they are used to calculate expectation (benefit of the bargain), reliance or restitution interests.[3]

This type of self-help provision is familiar at civil law, as a method of compensating a aggrieved buyer when the seller is not "at fault," when there is no civil law cause of action for damages.[4] There is also a UCC provision which allows an aggrieved buyer to exercise self help in reducing the price of non-conforming goods, but it appears to be not widely used under the UCC.[5] Unlike the UCC provisions, there is no requirement of prior notice to the seller by the buyer before exercising this option. Proposals at the Diplomatic Conference to require a "declaration of price reduction" by the buyer were not accepted.[6]

There is little guidance in the provision on how to determine the value of the actual goods delivered at the time of delivery, or as to what evidence of value should be sent to the seller. The provision, therefore, seems better suited to deliveries which are defective as to quantity, rather than as to quality. One United States decision has indicated that, if the buyer resells the defective goods, the resale price is evidence of their value at the time of delivery; and that the seller is entitled to discover the resale prices.[7] Several foreign courts have dispensed with the formula stated in the provision and, where the buyer had the defective goods repaired, have given the buyer the costs of repair under CISG article 50.[8]

If the provision may be used for defects in quality, may it also be used in cases where the defect arises from claims under patent or other intellectual property regimes? A buyer attempting to use this self-help remedy must allow seller to attempt to cure, if seller so requests. On the other hand, a seller who is excused from performance by an Article 79 "impediment"[9] will still be vulnerable

---

3. Flechter, More U.S. Decisions on the U.N. Sales Convention: Scope, Parol Evidence, "Validity," and Reduction of Price Under Article 50, 14 J. Law & Com. 153 (1995).

4. On the civil law foundation of Article 50, see Bergsten and Miller, The Remedy of Reduction of Price, 27 Am. J. Comp. L. 255 (1979).

5. UCC § 2–717.

6. See Bergsten and Miller, supra note 4. Cf. UNILEX Case D. 1994–7.

7. Interag Co. Ltd. v. Stafford Phase Corp., 1990 WL 71478 (S.D.N.Y.1990).

8. UNILEX Cases D. 1992–10, D. 1995–29.

9. See discussion at § 1.18, supra.

to a price reduction under Article 50, even though the buyer could not bring an action for damages.[10]

§ 1.24 Reclamation of the Goods

If an unpaid seller is unable (for any reason) to obtain the price, it may seek to obtain the return of its goods from the defaulting buyer, after delivery, by "avoiding" the contract and seeking to reclaim them. Such reclamation is difficult at common law,[1] but the Convention may allow such reclamation. CISG Article 64 gives the seller the power to declare the contract "avoided" and does not distinguish between pre-and post-delivery situations. Article 81 requires "restitution ... of whatever the first party has supplied" after avoidance. This analysis, however, is available only so long as third parties (buyer's creditors and trustees in bankruptcy) are not involved, for CISG does not affect title to the goods and third party rights,[2] and does not require a court to order "specific performance" which it would not order under its own law.[3]

A buyer who is in possession of goods after a contract has been avoided must take "reasonable" steps to preserve them.[4] Such steps may include depositing the goods in a warehouse at seller's expense.[5] If the seller has no agent in buyer's location, a buyer who avoids a contract or refuses to take delivery of goods which have been "placed at his disposal at their destination" must take possession of them "on behalf of the seller" if this can be done without payment of the price (i.e., without paying a negotiable bill of lading) and without "unreasonable inconvenience" or expense.[6] After such a taking of possession on behalf of the seller, the buyer must again take "reasonable" steps to preserve them.[7] If the goods are perishable, the buyer in possession may have to try to sell them and remit any proceeds to the seller, less the buyer's expenses of preserving and selling them.[8] CISG does not, however, contain any provisions which require a buyer in possession who has rejected the seller's tender to follow seller's instructions, such as to resell on seller's behalf, whether seemingly reasonable or not.

§ 1.25 Judicial Remedies

The more formal remedies available to an aggrieved party through court or arbitral tribunal proceedings are the buyer's

---

10. This aspect conforms to the civil law derivation of the price reduction concept, to make the remedy available when the seller is not at "fault."

§ 1.24

1. See, e.g., UCC §§ 2–507 and 2–702, and their comments.

2. CISG art. 4.

3. CISG art. 28. See discussion at § 1.26, infra.

4. CISG art. 85.

5. CISG art. 87.

6. CISG art. 86(2).

7. CISG art. 86(2), last sentence.

8. CISG art. 88.

action for specific performance, the seller's action for the price, and an action by either the buyer or the seller for damages.

This scheme is roughly comparable to the remedies available to an aggrieved buyer under the UCC. The difficulty facing the drafters of the Convention is illustrated by two facts: First, specific performance is the preferred remedy at civil law, while the action for damages is preferred at common law. Second, at civil law, a finding of "fault" is usually required for imposition of any recovery of damages, while the common law aggrieved party need show only "nonconformity." CISG had to bridge both gaps.

§ 1.26 Seller's Action for Specific Performance

CISG gives to the buyer who has not received the agreed performance from the seller a specifically enforceable right to "require performance" by the seller.[1] This reflects the basic civil law theory that legal compulsion of performance is the best relief to an aggrieved buyer, and that seller's actual performance is preferable to substitutional relief (such as a monetary award).[2] The reference to seller's "obligations" is not limited, and so can include court compulsion to provide goods of the agreed description quantity, quality and title (including intellectual property rights), as well as adhering to the agreed time, place & manner of delivery.

The provision permits the buyer to seek specific performance, but *does not require* it to do so. The buyer may still elect between seeking a performance remedy or a substitutional (i.e., damages) remedy. There are two limitations on the buyers' right to compel performance, One is that the buyer must not have previously sought an "inconsistent" remedy. For example, the buyer must not have previously "avoided", or sought to avoid, the contract. Since avoidance would terminate the contract, there would be no contract to enforce (specifically) after avoidance. The second limitation is that the court would order such performance under its own law in a similar case not governed by the Convention.[3] Thus, the buyer usually should not bring its action for specific performance in a common law court.

The CISG provision gives buyer the right to seek specific performance, rather than damages, but does not require it to do so. Thus, any preference for this remedy must arise from buyer's perspective, not from the court's. Even in civil law jurisdictions, buyers will often prefer to recover damages and purchase substitute

---

§ 1.26

1. CISG art. 46(1).

2. See Beardsy, Compelling Contract Performance in France, 1 Hastings Int'l and Comp. L. Rev. 93 (1977). For the contrasting common law approach, see Farnsworth, Damages and Specific Relief, 27 Am.J.Comp.L. 247 (1979).

3. CISG art. 28.

goods, because of the expense and delays inherent in litigation.[4] Even if a court should prefer specific performance, buyer can terminate this option by declaring the contract "avoided," which is an inconsistent remedy.

The CISG Article 28 limitation that the court "is not bound" to order specific performance unless it would do so in a case outside this Convention is applicable to all courts, both civil law and common law. However, it has a negligible effect on civil law courts because they are authorized to order seller's performance in many more cases.[5] Thus, if specific performance is sought in a civil law court, it will usually apply CISG Article 46 and order the seller to perform its obligations.

However, that would not be the analytical approach of a common law court. Under CISG Aricle 28, a United States court would not be required by CISG Article 46 to issue an order compelling the delivery if it would not do so in a similar domestic case. Although the UCC is designed to encourage courts to order specific performance, the case law does not demonstrate widespread interest in compelling performance.[6] If the goods are "unique" and they exist, then it is more likely the court will order specific performance. If, however, substitute goods are readily available in the market, it is less likely that the court would order specific performance. A United States court would be likely to issue a specific performance order if a requirements or a performance contact was involved.[7]

There are special provisions for specific performance orders which order seller to deliver substitute goods or to repair goods already delivered. Where the goods have been delivered, but are not conforming to the contract, the buyer may require specific performance in the form of delivery of conforming substitute goods only if the nonconformity amounts to a "fundamental breach,"[8] and the buyer has given the seller proper notice.[9] Likewise, buyer may require seller to repair the goods only if that is reasonable, "having regard to all the circumstances."[10] The principal difference between replacement and repair is that a buyer need not show that the nonconformities constitute a fundamental breach when requesting repair.

---

4. There is significant evidence that substitutional relief is often sought in civil law commercial disputes. See, e.g., Ziegel, The Remedial Provisions of the Vienna Sales Convention: Common Law Perspectives, Ch. 9 in International Sales (N. Galston and H. Smit, eds. 1984).

5. Tallon, Remedies, French Report in Contract Law Today: Anglo–French

Comparison, 263–88 (D. Harris and D. Tallon, eds. 1989).

6. UCC § 2–716(1).

7. UCC § 2–716, comment 2.

8. See discussion at § 1.25, notes 7–24.

9. CISG art. 46(2).

10. CISG art. 46(3).

§ 1.27   Buyer's Action for the Contract Price

There is also a CISG provision which permits a court to issue a specific performance order against a buyer, requiring the buyer to perform its obligations.[1] The preferred remedy for an aggrieved seller, if buyer should breach, is a cause of action for the price, which is seller's functional equivalent of an action for specific performance. A cause of action for damages, but not the price, is distinctly secondary. In addition, seller may wish to reclaim the goods if they are delivered or obtain some protection for them if they are refused.

As to the seller's recovery of the price, CISG Article 62 gives the seller a right to require buyer to pay the price unless the seller has resorted to an "inconsistent remedy."[2] Of course, there are implicit conditions on this right, first, that seller has itself performed to the extent required by the terms of the contract[3] and, second, that payment of the price is due.[4]

However, in common law jurisdictions, there is an issue of whether the seller's action for the price under CISG Article 62 an action for "specific performance," which is subject to the limitations of CISG Article 28. In other words, may a court order the buyer to pay the contract price of the goods, rather than mere damages, only if "the court would do so under its own law in respect of similar contracts of sale not governed by" CISG?[5] If it is an action for specific performance, then an aggrieved seller in the United States court would have to meet the requirements of the UCC[6] as well as the CISG,[7] before a United States court would order buyer to pay the price rather than damages. Under CISG Article 28, the issue is whether a judgment for the price requires the entry of a "judgment for specific performance." If not, then CISG Article 28 would seem to be inapplicable; and seller need meet only the requisites of CISG Article 62. The problem with this analysis is that the Convention and the UCC have different concepts of "specific performance."

From the UCC perspective the only provision which specifically mentions an action for "specific performance" is UCC § 2–716, which is expressly limited to a cause of action by seller. The buyer is given no comparable general cause of action to compel performance of buyer's obligations, except for a limited right to seek

---

§ **1.27**

1. CISG art. 62.

2. "Avoidance" of the contract would be such an inconsistent remedy. See discussion at § 1.29, supra.

3. CISG art. 30.

4. CISG art. 58.

5. CISG art. 28.

6. UCC § 2–709.

7. CISG art. 62.

payment of the price—a monetary award.[8] Thus, from the UCC perspective the action for the price under UCC § 2–709 is merely another action for a monetary judgment, not one to compel conduct.

From the CISG perspective there is no separate action for the price as a monetary judgment, only CISG Article 62, which allows a court to compel three different types of conduct—payment of the price, taking delivery, or performance of other obligations. Payment of the price is within a list of specific performances which a court is authorized to compel.

On the issue of the applicability of Article 28, Professors Honnold and Farnsworth publicly disagree.[9] The question would seem to be open at this time, because no common law courts have ruled on the issues presented by CISG Article 28. The only ruling involving a U.S. party in an action for the price was by a Mexican arbitral tribunal which did not need to discuss the Article 28 issue.[10]

Some of the buyer's obligations are not monetary, such as preparing to take delivery of the goods or opening a letter of credit. CISG authorizes a court to compel such conduct by the buyer,[11] if the court would do so in a non-convention case.[12] However, each of these may require the discretionary actions of third parties who may not be subject to the jurisdiction of the court.

§ 1.28 Damages

CISG Articles 74–78 provide the aggrieved buyer with an action for damages for any breach of a party's obligations, and damages can be available when the contract has been "avoided" (cancelled) and also even when seller has successfully cured defects in its performance.[1] There is no requirement that buyer prove that seller was "at fault" as a prerequisite to damage recovery. Nor is there a requirement that buyer prove what caused the defect, only that the goods were defective. Both direct and consequential damages are recoverable; and expectancy, reliance and restitutionary

---

8. UCC § 2–709. There are other non-monetary obligations of the buyer, such as duties of cooperation (UCC § 2–311), preparing to receive the goods, and opening a letter of credit. See text at not 12 infra.

The committee to revise UCC Article has considered revising UCC § 2–719 to permit buyer's to seek "specific performance."

9. Farnsworth, supra § 1.26, note 2; Honnold, supra § 1.2, note 20, at § 348.

10. UNILEX Case D. 1993–13.

11. CISG art. 62.

12. CISG art. 28. It is problematic whether a United States court could enter such an order. UCC § 2–716 is expressly limited to actions by sellers. The UCC approach instead is to make the buyer's conduct a condition precedent to seller's responsive conduct, and to award the seller damages if the buyer fails to perform.

§ 1.28

1. CISG arts. 45(2), 61(2), and 75. See also, CISG arts. 47(2), 48(1), 63(2).

interests are all protected.[2] Under *Delchi Carrier v. Rotorex*,[3] a buyer who planned to resell the goods and properly rejects them does recover the profits from any lot sales, measured by the price less variable costs only—and the variable costs do not include fixed overhead costs. Consequential damages are limited in the familiar manner that losses may not be recovered, which were neither actually foreseen nor should have been foreseen.[4] However, this may not be the same as the common law *Hadley v. Baxendale* test,[5] because recovery is available if the loss suffered is foreseeable as a "possible consequence of the breach of contract".[6] The aggrieved buyer must take "reasonable measures" to mitigate its damages.[7] Incidental damages relating to interest are covered separately.[8]

§ 1.29 Buyer's Damages

Where similar goods may be purchased in the market, the most usual measures of the aggrieved buyer's damages are either (1) the difference between the price of "cover" (substitute goods actually purchased) and the contract price, or (2) the difference between the market price for the goods and the contract price. The Convention provides for the recovery of each of these measures of damages,[1] but if buyer does purchase cover only the first measure is available.[2] The Convention gives no guidance on how to determine whether any particular purchase by buyer is a purchase of cover, or is ordinary inventory build-up. Where the market price differential is used, the market price is to be measured at the time of "avoidance" (cancellation),[3] unless buyer has "taken over" the goods, before cancelling, in which case, the market price is measured at the time of "taking over."[4]

The CISG measures of buyer's damages are remarkably similar to those in the UCC.[5] In the one CISG damage measurement case decided by United States courts, the court ruled that UCC caselaw

2. Flechtner, Remedies under the New International Sales Convention: The Perspective from Article 2 of the U.C.C., 8 J. Law & Com. 53 (1988).

3. 71 F.3d 1024 (2d Cir.1995).

4. CISG art. 74.

5. 9 Ex. 341, 156 Eng. Rep. 145 (1854).

6. CISG art. 74, last sentence.

7. CISG art. 77.

8. CISG art. 78.

§ 1.29

1. The difference between "cover" and the contract price is provided in CISG Article 75. Compare UCC § 2–712.

The difference between market price and the contract price is provided in CISG Article 76(1). Compare UCC § 2–713.

2. CISG art. 76(1): "if he has not made a purchase or resale under Article 75."

3. CISG art. 76(1), first sentence.

4. CISG art. 76(1), second sentence.

5. Flechtner, supra § 1.28, note 2.

could not be used to interpret CISG provisions unless the language of the UCC provision tracks that of the CISG provision.[6] The court also held that the broad, general language of CISG Article 74[7] was the primary criterion for damage measurement, and that all the subsequent provisions[8] were subsidiary to it. Finally, the court also ruled that, where there are gaps in the CISG provisions on measuring damages, that those gaps may be filled in by domestic law—the UCC.

The case involved a buyer which had lost sales due to seller's delivery of nonconforming goods, and which sought loss of profits for the sales lost until substitute, conforming goods had been found. The court found that the standard contract price—market price differential would not fully compensate the buyer for the "loss, including lost profits, suffered by" the buyer,[9] and chose Article 74 as its guide to damage measurement, not Articles 75 or 76. The lost profit damages were, however, recoverable only to the extent that they were reasonably foreseeable by the parties.[10] In measuring buyer's lost profits, the court found that CISG had no specific provision on the treatment of fixed and variable costs in determining buyer's lost profits. It therefore adopted the domestic law rule in which only the variable costs saved by the buyer are to be deducted from the lost sales revenues.

The courts also allowed the buyer to recover, as additional consequential and incidental damages:

(1) costs of buyer's attempts to cure, including reinspection and testing;

(2) costs of expedited delivery of substitute conforming goods from another seller;

(3) costs of storing the non-conforming goods;[11]

(4) shipping and customs costs for the non-conforming goods;

(5) cost of materials and tools usable only with the non-conforming goods; and

(6) labor costs related to the production line shutdown.[12]

§ 1.30 Seller's Damages

CISG Articles 74–78 provide the unpaid seller (as well as an aggrieved buyer) with an action for damages and the general

6. Delchi Carrier SpA v. Rotorex Corp., 71 F.3d 1024 (2d Cir. 1995).

7. "Damages ... consist of a sum equal to the loss ... suffered by the other party as a consequence of the breach." CISG art. 74.

8. CISG arts. 75–77.

9. CISG art. 74.

10. Delchi Carrier, S.p.A. v. Rotorex Corp., 1994 WL 495787 (N.D.N.Y.1994), *aff'd in part, rev'd in part* 71 F.3d 1024 (2d Cir.1995).

11. *Id.*

12. Rotorex, supra note 6.

principles are the same as the discussion of buyer's remedies for seller's breach.[1] The most usual measures of an unpaid seller's damages are either (1) the difference between the contract price and the resale price if the goods were actually resold or (2) the difference between the contract price and market price for the goods at the time of avoidance of the contract. The Convention provides for recovery of each of these measures of damages,[2] but if seller resells the goods only the first measure is available.[3] The major practical problem concerning unpaid sellers is that the "lost volume" seller is not adequately protected by the above two measures of damages.[4] However, the CISG provisions which establish these measures state that they are not exclusive, and the basic principles of Article 74 specifically include recovery of lost profits.[5] Since the *Rotorex* case has established the primacy of Article 74 over the subsequent provisions, a court should be able to protect the lost volume seller. The *Rotorex* court awarded "lost profits" damages to a buyer, which should be persuasive precedent for making a comparable award to a "lost volume" seller.

The CISG measures of seller's damages are remarkably similar to those in the UCC.[6] The principal difference is that the CISG provisions on the difference between the contract price and the resale price contain no provisions covering notice of the resale of the goods, nor do they regulate the resale.[7]

§ 1.30

1. See § 1.29, supra.

2. The difference between the contract price and the resale piece is provided in CISG Article 75. Compare UCC § 2–706.

The difference between the contract price and the market price is provided for in CISG Article 76(1) Compare UCC § 2–708(1).

3. CISG art. 76(1): "if he has not made a purchase or resale under Article 75."

4. Compare UCC § 2–708(2).

5. *Rotorex*, supra § 1.29, note 6.

6. Flechtner, supra § 1.28, note 2.

7. Compare UCC § 2–706(2)–(6).

Chapter 2

COMMERCIAL TERMS

Table of Sections

§ 2.1 Introduction

Chapter 1 illustrated how different rules are applicable to domestic and international sales of goods—respectively the Uniform Commercial Code (UCC) and the Convention on Contracts for the International Sales of Goods (CISG).[1] There are also differences between domestic and international commercial terms that provide rules for the delivery term in a contract for the sale of goods.

The UCC has its own definitions of such terms as "F.O.B." and "C.I.F."[2] The CISG does not have such definitions, and the CISG rules on delivery terms are very sparse.[3] Instead of incorporating detailed rules on the meaning of individual commercial delivery terms for the international sale, the drafters of the CISG could rely upon a written formulation of industry understanding of the meaning of such terms.[4] That written formulation is contained in Incoterms, published by the International Chamber of Commerce.[5] At

---

§ 2.1

1. *United Nations Convention on Contracts for the International Sale of Goods*, I.N. GAOR, U.N. DOC A/CONF.97/18 (1980), *reprinted in* 19 I.L.M. 671 (1980) [hereinafter CISG].

2. U.C.C. §§ 2–319 to–324.

3. CISG, *supra* note 1, art. 31. See discussion at § 1.12, supra.

4. *See* John Honnold, Uniform Law for Internation Sales Under the 1980 United Nations Convention ¶¶ 208, 211 (3d ed. 1999).

5. International Chamber of Commerce Incoterms 2000 (I.C.C. Publ. No. 560, 2000 Ed.) [Hereinafter Incoterms 2000].

least one author has concluded that Incoterms would qualify as an international "usage" under the CISG, and therefore would be available to fill in gaps in CISG provisions.[6]

Incoterms is an acronym for "International Commercial Terms" and was first published in 1936. It has been updated periodically since that time. Incoterms underwent major revisions in 1953 and 1990, and it was republished with new terms in 1967, 1976, and 1980.[7] The current version of Incoterms was published in 2000, and is known as Incoterms 2000.[8] It is substantially similar to the 1990 revision of Incoterms. These revisions of Incoterms have made the Incoterms definitions of commercial terms substantially different from the UCC definitions of similar terms.

§ 2.2 The Purpose of Commercial Terms

Where the goods are to be carried from one location to another as part of the sale transaction, the parties will often adopt a commercial term to state the delivery obligation of the seller. Such terms include F.O.B. (Free on Board), F.A.S. (Free Alongside) and C.I.F. (Cost, Insurance and Freight). These terms are defined in the UCC,[1] but the UCC definitions are seldom used intentionally in international trade. In fact, the UCC definitions are becoming obsolescent in domestic trade also, because the abbreviations used are now associated primarily with water-borne traffic, and the statutory terms do not include the new terminology associated with air freight, containerization, or multi-modal transportation practices. Thus, in this proposed amendments to UCC Article 2, adopted by the Uniform Commissioners, these statutory amendments are deleted. However, to date, no state has enacted those proposed amendments.

In International commerce the dominant source of definitions for commercial delivery terms is "Incoterms," published by the International Chamber of Commerce (I.C.C.) and last revised by them in 2000.[2] Incoterms provides rules for determining the obligations of both seller and buyer when different commercial terms (like F.O.B. or C.I.F.) are used. They state what acts seller must do to deliver, what acts buyer must do to accommodate delivery, what costs each party must bear, and at what point in the delivery process the risk of loss passes from the seller to buyer. Each of

---

6. Jan Ramberg, *Incoterms 1980, in* The Transnational Law of International Commercial Transactions 137 151 (Norbert Horn & Clive M. Schmitthoff eds., 1982); *see also* Texful Textile Ltd. v. Cotton Express Textile, Inc., 891 F.Supp. 1381 (C.D.Cal.1995).

7. *See* Peter Winship, *Introduction* in Basic Instruments in International Eco-

nomic Law, at 707 (Stephen Zamora & Ronald Brand eds., 1990).

8. Incoterms 2000, *supra* note 5.

§ 2.2

1. *See*, e.g., U.C.C. §§ 2–319, 2–320.

2. *See* Incoterms 2000, § 2.1, note 5, *infra.*

these obligations may be different for different commercial terms. Thus, the obligations, costs, and risks of seller and buyer are different under F.O.B. than they are under C.I.F.

There are other sources of such definitions, in addition to the UCC and Incoterms, such as the American Revised Foreign Trade Definitions (1941).[3] It has been widely used in Pacific Ocean trade, but may be replaced by the more recently revised Incoterms.

§ 2.3   Incoterms as a Trade Usage

Since the I.C.C. is a non-governmental entity, Incoterms is neither a national legislation nor an international treaty. Thus, it cannot be "the governing law" of any contract. Instead, it is a written form of custom and usage in the trade, which can be, and often is, expressly incorporated by a party of the parties to an international contract for the sale of goods. Alternatively, if it is not expressly incorporated in the contract, Incoterms could be made an implicit term of the contract as part of international custom. Courts in France and Germany have done so, and both treatises and the UNCITRAL Secretariat describe Incoterms as a widely-observed usage for commercial terms.[1] This description should allow Incoterms to qualify under CISG Article 9(2) as a "usage ... which in international trade is widely known to, and regularly observed by, parties to" international sales contracts, even if the usage is not global.[2]

Although the UCC has definitions for some commercial terms (e.g., F.O.B., F.A.S., C.I.F.), these definitions are expressly subject to "agreement otherwise."[3] Thus, an express reference to Incoterms will supercede the UCC provisions, and United States courts have so held.[4] Such incorporation by express reference is often made in American international sales contracts, especially in Atlantic Ocean trade. If there is no express term, and the UCC is the governing law rather than CISG, Incoterms can still be applicable as a "usage of trade" under the UCC.[5] The UCC criteria for such a usage is "a practice. . . . having such regularity of observance ... as to justify an expectation that it will be observed with respect to the transaction in question."[6] A usage need not be "universal" nor

---

3. Revised American Foreign Trade Definitions, *excerpted in* Andreas F. Lowenfeld, International Private Trade ds–151–158 (1977).

§ 2.3

1. *See* Winship, *§ 2.1,* note 7, *supra* at 707–10.

2. CISG, art. 9(2), at 674.

3. U.C.C. §§ 2–319(1)(2), 2–320(2).

4. Phillips Puerto Rico Core, Inc. v. Tradax Petroleum Ltd., 782 F.2d 314 (2d Cir.1985).

5. U.C.C. § 1–205(2).

6. U.C.C. § 1–205, cmt. 5; *see* Ramberg, *§ 2.1,* note 6, *supra.*

"ancient," just "currently observed by the great majority of decent dealers."[7]

§ 2.4   Categories of Commercial Terms

Incoterms gives the parties a menu of thirteen different commercial terms to describe the delivery obligations of the seller and the reciprocal obligations of the buyer to accommodate delivery. They include:

1) EXW (Ex Works)

2) FCA (Free Carrier)

3) FAS (Free Alongside Ship)

4) FOB (Free On Board)

5) CFR (Cost and Freight)

6) CIF (Cost, Insurance and Freight)

7) CPT (Carriage Paid To)

8) CIP (Carriage and Insurance Paid To)

9) DAF (Delivered at Frontier)

10) DES (Delivered Ex Ship)

11) DEQ (Delivered Ex Quay)

12) DDU (Delivered Duty Unpaid)

13) DDP (Delivered Duty Paid)

There are several types of divisions which one may make of these thirteen different terms. One is a division between the one term which does not assume that a carrier will be involved (EXW), and all the twelve other terms. A second division is between those six terms which require the involvement of water-borne transportation (FAS, FOB, CFR, CIF, DES and DEQ) and those six other terms which are applicable to any mode of transportation, including multi-modal transportation (FCA, CPT, CIP, DAF, DDU, and DDP). The UCC has none of the latter six terms, although the types of transactions they are designed for arise routinely, and can be handled under the UCC designations "F.O.B. place of shipment,"[1] "C. & F.", "C.I.F.,"[2] and "F.O.B. named place of destination."[3]

The twelve terms requiring transportation can also be divided into "shipment contract" terms (FCA, FAS, FOB, CFR, CIF, CPT, and CIP) and "destination contract" terms (DAF, DES, DEQ, DDU,

---

7. U.C.C. § 1–205, cmt. 5.

§ **2.4**

1. U.C.C. § 2–319(1)(a).

2. U.C.C. § 2–320(1)(2).

3. U.C.C. § 2–319(1)(b).

and DDP.). The UCC and CISG both use this terminology.[4] The underlying concept is that, in shipment contracts seller puts the goods in the hands of a carrier and arranges for their transportation, but transportation is at buyer's risk and expense.[5] On the other hand, in destination contracts seller is responsible to put the goods in the hands of the carrier, arrange their transportation, and bear the cost and risk of transportation.[6] Unfortunately, many aspects of transportation usages have changed since 1952, and the UCC concepts do not always fit the practices now described in Incoterms.

The I.C.C. suggests that these thirteen commercial terms be divided into four principal categories, one for each of the different first letters of the constituent terms, E,F,C and D. The "E" term (EXW) is where the goods are made available to buyer, but use of a carrier is not expressly required. All other terms require the use of a carrier. The "F" terms (FCA, FAS, FOB) require seller only to assume the risks and costs to deliver the goods to a carrier, and to a carrier nominated by the buyer. The "C" terms require seller to assume the risks and costs to deliver the goods to a carrier, arrange and pay for the "main transportation" (and sometimes insurance), but without assuming additional risks due to post-shipment events. Thus, under "C" terms, seller bears risks until one point in the transportation (delivery to a carrier), but pays costs to a different point in the transportation (the agreed destination). The "D" terms (DAF, DES, DEQ, DDU and DDP) require the seller to deliver the goods to a carrier, arrange for their transportation, and assume the risks and costs until the arrival of the goods at an agreed country of destination.

§ 2.5　Revisions of Incoterms

Incoterms are periodically revised, lately about once every ten years. The last revision was in 2000 and is set forth in I.C.C. Publication 560. It has few changes from its immediately previous edition. The primary changes concern loading and unloading obligations under FCA, customs clearance and duty obligations under FAS DEQ, and numerous wording changes to clarify various obligations.

The last significant revisions were in 1990 and are set forth in I.C.C. Publication No. 460.[1] In that 1990 revision, the I.C.C. included references to electronic messages and to new types of transport

---

4. CISG, art. 31; U.C.C. §§ 2–504, 2–509.

5. U.C.C. § 2–504.

6. *See*, e.g., U.C.C. § 2–319(1)(b) ("F.O.B. place of destination" contracts).

§ 2.5

1. International Chamber of Commerce, Incoterms 1990 (I.C.C. Publ. No. 460, 1990 Ed.) [Hereinafter Incoterms 1990].

documents, such as air waybills, railway and road consignment notes, and "multimodal transport documents." The I.C.C. explained that these changes were needed because of "the increasing use of electronic data interchange (EDI)" and "changed transportation techniques," including "containers, multimodal transport and roll on-roll off traffic."[2]

§ 2.6 The Format of Incoterms

The Incoterms 2000 obligations are arranged in a mirror-image format that sets forth the obligations of sellers and buyers in adjacent columns. Each column has numbered paragraphs, and each numbered paragraph refers to the comparable obligation of each party. The obligations covered include licenses and other formalities, contracts of carriage and insurance, physical delivery, risk of loss, division of costs, notices, transportation documents or equivalent electronic messages, and inspections.

Thus, the first set of paragraphs in the statement of rules for the interpretation of any Incoterm is a statement of the basic obligations of seller and buyer—to deliver the goods and a commercial invoice (or its electronic equivalent), and to pay the contract price. The second set of paragraphs allocates the responsibilities of the parties to procure export and import licenses and to carry out customs formalities. The third set of paragraphs allocates the responsibilities of the parties to arrange and pay for carriage and insurance during transportation of the goods. The fourth set of paragraphs specifies both the extent of seller's delivery obligation and buyer's obligation to take delivery. The fifth set of paragraphs specifies when the risk loss is transferred from the seller to the buyer.

The sixth set of paragraphs allocates the costs of transportation between the parties, including not only the freight and insurance costs already allocated in the third paragraph, but also loading costs and the administrative costs of customs clearance, even when no import duties are charged. The seventh set of paragraphs determines what notice each party must give to the others, when to give notice, and what each notice should say. The eight set of paragraphs specifies the type of transport document or other proof of delivery which seller must provide to buyer. The ninth set of paragraphs allocates who must pay the costs of packaging the goods, marking the packages, "checking operations" (measuring, weighing, counting), and any pre-shipment inspection. It does not, however, state when and whether buyer has a right to post-

---

2. Incoterms 1990, *supra note*, at 6. *See also* Jan Ramberg, Guide to Incoterms 1990 (I.C.C. Publ. No. 461/90, 1991 & No. 505, 1996) for further expla- nation and elaboration on the use and meaning of the 1990 revision of Incoterms.

shipment inspection before paying for the goods. Finally, the tenth set of paragraphs sets forth miscellaneous obligations, such as duties of assistance and cooperation.

§ 2.7   The Free Carrier (FCA) Term

Under the Incoterms Free Carrier (FCA) commercial term,[1] the seller is obligated to deliver the goods into the custody of a carrier, usually the first carrier in a multi-modal transportation scheme. The Incoterms definition of "carrier" includes freight forwarders. Seller has no obligation to pay for transportation costs or insurance. Usually the carrier will be named by, and arranged by, the buyer. However, seller "may" arrange transportation at buyer's expense if requested by the buyer, or if it is "commercial practice" for a seller to do so. But, even under such circumstances, seller may refuse to make such arrangements as long as it so notifies buyer. Even of seller does arrange transportation, it has no obligation to arrange for insurance coverage during transportation, and need only notify buyer "that the goods *have been* delivered into the custody of the carrier."[2] The risk of loss transfers to buyer upon delivery to the carrier, but buyer may not receive notice until after that time. The seller must provide a commercial invoice or its equivalent electronic message, any necessary export license, and usually a transport document that will allow buyer to take delivery- or an equivalent electronic data interchange message.

§ 2.8   The Free on Board (FOB) Term

Under the Incoterms Free on Board (FOB) commercial term,[1] the seller is obligated to deliver the goods on board a ship arranged for and named by the buyer at a named port of shipment. Thus, this term is also appropriate only for water-borne transportation, and seller must bear the costs and risks of inland transportation to the named port of shipment, and also of loading the goods on the ship (until "they have passed the ship's rail").[2] Seller has no obligation to arrange transportation or insurance, but does have a duty to notify buyer "that the goods *have been delivered* on board" the ship.[3] The risks of loss will transfer to the buyer also at the time the goods have "passed the ship's rail."[4] The seller must provide a commercial invoice, or its equivalent electronic message,

---

§ 2.7

1. Incoterms 2000, § 2.1, note 5, *supra,* at 33–39.

2. *Id.,* at 36 (emphasis added).

§ 2.8

1. Incoterms 2000, § 2.1, note 5, *supra,* at 49–55

2. *Id.,* at 50, ¶ A5

3. *Id.,* at 51 (emphasis added).

4. *Id.,* at 51.

any necessary export license, and usually a transport document that will allow buyer to take delivery—or an equivalent electronic data interchange message.[5] The seller must also provide an export license, and clear the goods for export from the place of delivery.[6] The seller must therefor pay any costs of customs formalities and export taxes.

In addition, the seller must provide all customary packaging and working, and pay for checking operations. The latter include measuring, weighing, counting, and checking of the goods considered necessary to accomplish delivery. However, buyer must pay the cost of any pre-shipment inspection not required by the country of export.

§ 2.9   The Cost, Insurance and Freight (CIF) Term

Under the Incoterms Cost, Insurance and Freight (CIF) commercial term,[1] the seller is obligated to arrange for both transportation and insurance to a named destination port and then to deliver the goods on board the ship arranged for by the seller. Thus, the term is appropriate only for water-borne transportation. Seller must arrange the transportation, and pay the freight costs to the *destination port*, but has completed its delivery obligations when the goods are "on board the vessel at the port of shipment." The seller must pay the freight and unloading costs of the carrier at the destination port under the CIF term, but the buyer must pay all other costs, including unloading costs not collected by the carrier. However, demurrage charges for the cost of docking the ship longer than agreed are to be borne by the party causing the delay.[2]

Significant litigation has arisen when the CIF contract specifies the arrival date at the port of destination. The U.S. courts have held that, since the 1980 Incoterms C & F was a shipment contract, the seller's obligations were fulfilled when the carrier took delivery of the goods. Thus, the buyer could not specify an arrival or delivery date after the sale contract has been formed.[3] If a CIF contract specifies an arrival or delivery date rather than a shipment date, the British decisions are split. One case held that, under an Incoterms CIF contract which specified a delivery date, the buyer

---

5. For a more detailed analysis of the F.O.B. and FOB terms, see A. Frecom, *Practical Considerations in Drafting F.O.B. Terms in International Sales,* 3 Int'l Tax & Bus. Law 346 (1986).

6. Incoterms 2000, § 2.1, note 5, *supra,* at 51.

§ 2.9

1. Incoterms 2000, § 2.1, note 5, *supra,* at 66–71.

2. *In re* Commonwealth Oil Refining Co., 734 F.2d 1079 (5th Cir.1984).

3. Phillips Puerto Rico Core, Inc. v. Tradax Petroleum Ltd., 782 F.2d 314 (2d Cir.1985).

could calculate an "appropriate latest delivery date," and that the seller is then entitled to calculate a "late date for loading" the goods on board the carrier. As long as the seller met that loading date, it was not liable for the carrier's subsequent late delivery to the port of destination, since seller's duties were completed upon a timely loading of the goods and notification to the buyer.[4] However, another court has held that a delivery date term is not inconsistent with Incoterms CIF. The court rejected an interpretation of CIF that requires the seller only to deliver to carrier and thereafter the risk of delay is on the buyer.[5]

The seller must arrange and pay for insurance during transportation to the *port of destination*, but the risk of loss transfers to the buyer at the time the goods "pass the ship's rail" at the *port of shipment*. The buyer bears the risk of damages that occur to the goods during transit, even though the seller has a duty to procure insurance against such risks.[6] Seller must notify buyer "that the goods have been delivered on board" the ship to enable buyer to receive the goods.[7] Seller must provide a commercial invoice, or its equivalent electronic message, any necessary export license, and "the usual transport documents" for the destination port.

The transportation document "must ... enable the buyer to sell the goods in transit by the transfer of the document to a subsequent buyer ... or by notification to the carrier," unless otherwise agreed.[8] The traditional manner of enabling buyer to do this, in either the "payment against documents" transaction or the letter of credit transaction, is for seller to obtain a negotiable bill of lading from the carrier and to tender that negotiable document to buyer through a series of banks. The banks allow buyer to obtain possession of the document (and control of the goods) only after buyer pays for goods. Thus, buyer "pays against documents," while the goods are at sea, and pays for them before any post-shipment inspection of the goods is possible. The ICC's Introduction to the 1990 Incoterms recognized that the use of nonnegotiable documents is inappropriate in a "payment against documents" situation and thus would not "enable the buyer to sell the goods in transit by surrendering the paper document" to the sub-buyer.[9]

---

4. P&O Oil Trading Ltd. v. Scanoil AB, [1985] 1 Lloyd's Rep. 389 (Q.B. 1984).

5. CEP Interagra SA v. Select Energy Trading, GmbH (Q.B. 1990), LEXIS, UK Library, Engcas File.

6. Establissements El Hadj Ousmanou Chetima risk of loss issues under Incoterms, see Daniel E. Murray, *Risk of Loss of Goods in Transit: A Comparison of the 1990 Incoterms with Terms from Other Voices,* 23 U. Miami Inter–Am. L. Rev. 93 (1991).

7. Incoterms 2000, § 2.1 note 5, *supra,* at 68.

8. Incoterms 2000, § 2.1, note 5, *supra,* at 70.

9. *Id.,* at 15.

*

Chapter 3

BILLS OF LADING

Table of Sections

§ 3.1 Introduction to Bills of Lading

A bill of lading is a document that is issued by a carrier to a shipper upon receipt of goods from the shipper. Bills of lading make it possible to have a cash international sales transaction without requiring a letter of credit by using a negotiable bill of lading and a series of collecting banks to require the buyer's payment of the price in full prior to obtaining physical possession of the negotiable bill of lading, and therefore prior to access to the goods.

A bill of lading is (1) the shipper's contract with the carrier which sets forth the terms of that contract expressly or incorporates a carrier's terms and tariffs by reference,(2) a contract of bailment as a receipt from the carrier to the shipper, and (3) a document of title.

At common law and under the U.S. Federal Bills of Lading Act,[1] there are two different types of bills of lading: a "straight," or non-negotiable, bill of lading, and an "order," or negotiable, bill of lading. These are also known in the trade as "white" and "yellow" for the different colors of paper on which they are often printed. They are specifically described below in §§ 3.3 and 3.4.

Shippers and carriers often refer to an "on board" bill of lading. An "on board" or "loaded" bill of lading is issued once the goods have been loaded on board the vessel. A "clean" bill of lading is one that has no clause or notation on the face of the bill indicating visible or possible defects in the packaging or condition of the goods. Therefore, simple comments regarding amount, weight or other descriptions as provided by the shipper will not "foul" the bill of lading, provided that they do not incorporate other documents indicating defects in the cargo.

In addition, the parties can negotiate either a "through" bill of lading, or a "multimodal" or "combined transport" bill of lading, when the carrier agrees to transport and deliver the goods to their final destination using connecting carriers such as railroads, trucks, and air carriers so that the bill of lading governs all of the links of transportation.

Finally, this area of law, like many others, is entering into the electronic age. Electronic substitutes for non-negotiable bills of lading have been in use for about two decades and have proved to be successful. However, electronic substitutes for negotiable bills of lading have been less successful and are still in the developmental stage. (See Electronic Bills of Lading below.)

§ 3.2   Non-negotiable or Straight Bills of Lading

A non-negotiable, or "straight," bill of lading is a receipt for the goods, and serves as a contract with the carrier stating the terms and conditions of carriage. A straight bill of lading is issued to a named person, the consignee.[1] Under the U.S. Federal Bills of Lading Act, a straight bill of lading must have the language "non-negotiable" or "not negotiable" on the bill of lading itself.[2]

Possession of the actual straight bill of lading does not confer rights over the goods or against the carrier to a person in possession of the paper who is not the consignee. In fact, the consignee does not need to be in possession of the bill of lading or produce the

---

§ 3.1

1. 49 U.S.C. §§ 80101–80116.

§ 3.2

1. A straight bill of lading under the Pomerene Act, the predecessor to the Federal Bills of Lading Act, was defined as "a bill in which it is stated that the goods are consigned or destined to a specified person."

2. 49 U.S.C. § 80103(b)(2).

document in order to obtain the goods from the carrier.[3] The carrier fulfills its duty under the straight bill of lading by delivering and transferring title to the goods to the consignee.[4] The shipper can even change its mind at any time prior to the delivery of the goods and stop delivery or reroute delivery to another party by instructing the carrier in writing. Straight bills of lading are commonly used between related parties or merchants with ongoing business as it is the simplest method of conducting business. Straight bills of lading are often used in container transport and on short sea routes.[5]

Straight bills of lading are not negotiable documents and are not documents of title. Further, indorsements on straight bills of lading are irrelevant in making the bill negotiable or to giving rights to the indorsee.[6]

Straight bills of lading are also called "air waybills," "sea waybills" and "freight receipts," depending upon the intended method of main transportation for the goods. In fact, the sea waybill is the European equivalent to the U.S. straight bill of lading, and is referred to by Incoterms (in addition to the air waybill).[7]

§ 3.3　Negotiable or Order Bills of Lading

An "order," or negotiable, bill of lading serves as (1) a contract with the carrier, (2) a receipt for the goods, and (3) a document of title for the goods. A negotiable bill of lading is issued to a named person "or order." This allows the named person (the consignee) to indorse the bill of lading to "order" delivery of the goods to others.

If possession of the bill of lading is transferred to a third party, and the bill of lading is indorsed to that third party by the payee or a "holder" (either specially or in blank), then the third party becomes a "holder" of the bill of lading. Therefore, possession of the actual negotiable bill of lading, properly indorsed, confers rights

---

3. For a discussion of the cases stating that the physical document need not be presented, see Chan, A Plea for Certainty: Legal and Practical Problems in the Presentation of Non-negotiable Bills of Lading, 29 Hong Kong L.J. 44, 52 (1999).

4. 49 U.S.C. § 80110(b)(2). See Poly-Gram Group Distrib., Inc. v. Transus, Inc., 990 F.Supp. 1454, 1459 (N.D.Ga. 1997) (holding that delivery to a street address specified as consignee's place of business on a straight bill of lading and obtaining signature of general contractor working at that address satisfied de-

livery requirements imposed by the bill of lading).

5. See Chan, supra note 3, at 45.

6. See Kasden et al. v. New York, New Haven & Hartford R.R. Co., 104 Conn. 479, 133 A. 573, 574 (1926) (stating that a straight bill issued by the carrier to the shipper and indorsed as "nonnegotiable" was not made negotiable by the shipper's subsequent indorsement on the bill of lading to deliver the goods to a third party or order). See also, 49 U.S.C. § 80108.

7. International Chamber of Commerce, Incoterms 2000, Pub. N. 560a.

over the goods and against the carrier to the person in possession of the document, the "holder." But a "proper" indorsement can be made only by a payee or a holder. A forgery of the payee's or holder's signature is not effective as an indorsement.[1]

The original consignee may indorse the negotiable bill of lading either "in blank" by a bare signature (e.g., "Ralph Folsom") or by a "special indorsement," which specifies the name of the intended holder (e.g., "Deliver the goods to Michael Gordon, or order, Ralph Folsom").[2]

Under a blank indorsement, any person in possession becomes a holder, and is entitled to demand delivery from the carrier. Under a special indorsement, only the named indorsee can become a holder, and only that person can demand delivery from the carrier or indorse the bill of lading to another party so as to make it a holder. Thus, the special indorsement better protects the interest of the parties from thieves and forgers than a blank indorsement.

A carrier under a negotiable bill of lading is required to obtain the original bill of lading prior to releasing the goods. If the carrier does not obtain the original bill of lading, it will be held liable to the shipper for misdelivery and conversion.[3] The negotiable bill of lading is used in the "payment against documents" transaction described below, and is required for CIF and CFR (C & F) contracts,[4] as well as the letter of credit transaction.[5]

Some commercial nations only recognize straight bills of lading and not negotiable bills of lading, but most commentators believe the United States' system of recognizing both types of bills of lading is preferable.

§ 3.4 Overview of the Payment Against Documents Transaction

How does the "payment against documents" transaction work? When the buyer and the seller are forming their contract for the sale of the goods, the seller will insist that the buyer "pay against the documents," rather than after delivery and inspection of the

§ 3.3

1. See Adel Precision Products Corp. v. Grand Trunk Western R. Co., 332 Mich. 519, 51 N.W.2d 922 (1952).

2. 49 U.S.C. § 80104(a).

3. See Velco Enters., Ltd. v. S.S. Zim Kingston, Zim Israel Navigation Co., et al., 858 F.Supp. 36, 38 (S.D.N.Y.1994) (holding that when a carrier releases goods without requiring the person receiving the goods to produce the original bill of lading, the carrier is liable for conversion of the goods and misdelivery under the Federal Bills of Lading Act because a carrier has delivered the goods to one who is not lawfully entitled to possession of them.)

4. 3 J. White & R.S. Summers, Uniform Commercial Code § 29–4(a) (4th ed. 1995).

5. Id. at § 29–1(a).

goods themselves. Such a payment term must be bargained for and expressed in the sales contract since it will normally not be implied.

The seller will then pack the goods and prepare a commercial invoice. If the commercial term requires it (e.g., under a "CIF" or a "Cost, Insurance and Freight" term) [See Chapter 2 on Commercial Terms] seller will also procure an insurance certificate (another form of contract) covering the goods during transit. The seller then delivers the goods to the carrier, which issues a bill of lading and designates to whom the goods should be delivered. In the case of a negotiable bill of lading, it will require the carrier to deliver the goods only "to seller or order" i.e., only to the seller or a person the seller may designate by an appropriate endorsement.

As stated above, a bill of lading serves as both a carrier contract and as a receipt for the cargo being sent. Under the terms of the bill of lading contract, in return for payment of the freight charge, the carrier promises to deliver the goods to either (1) the named "consignee" in a straight or non-negotiable bill of lading, or (2) the person in possession or the "holder" of a properly endorsed order or negotiable bill of lading. The issuance by the carrier of a bill of lading serves to assure the parties that (1) the goods have been delivered to the carrier, and (2) that they are destined for the buyer either as consignee under a straight bill of lading or as the holder of a negotiable bill of lading.

§ 3.5   The Necessity of a Negotiable Bill of Lading

The negotiable bill of lading should be used in the payment against documents sale. Because the negotiable bill of lading acts as a document of title, the buyer is able to obtain delivery of goods *only if* the buyer has physical possession of a properly endorsed bill of lading. The buyer can only have physical possession of a properly endorsed bill of lading by paying in full the balance owed on the goods for the shipment.

Since a negotiable bill of lading controls the right to obtain the goods from the carrier, the collecting banks can control the carrier's delivery of the goods to the buyer by simply retaining possession of the order bill of lading. In other words, when a bank undertakes to collect funds from the buyer for the seller, it receives the bill of lading from the seller that has been issued by the carrier. The bank's control over the negotiable bill of lading as a document of title confers control over the goods. The buyer cannot obtain possession of the goods from a carrier without physical possession of the negotiable bill of lading, so after the banks have received that piece of paper from the seller, they can obtain payment (or assurances that the buyer will pay them) before the buyer receives the physical possession of the negotiable bill of lading and therefore the ability to obtain the goods from the carrier.

If a straight bill of lading is used in the payment against documents transaction, the buyer would be able to obtain delivery of the goods as the consignee even if no payment was made, and thus the seller would lose a valuable protection.

§ 3.6 Payment

Once the seller has obtained a negotiable bill of lading to his own order, how does he obtain payment? First, he attaches a "draft" to it, together with an invoice and any other documents required by the sales contract. Then the seller uses the banking system as a collection agent. The "draft" (sometimes also called a "bill of exchange") will usually be a "sight draft," which is payable "on demand" when presented to buyer. The draft is drawn for the amount due under the sales contract, and it is payable to the seller's order.

At the bank, the seller endorses both the draft and the negotiable bill of lading to the seller's bank, and will also transfer the other documents required by the sales contract. If no letter of credit is involved in the transaction, the bank will usually take these documents only "for collection," although it is also possible for the bank to "discount" or buy the documents outright and become the owner.

To understand the collection transaction by the banking system, consult the flow chart on the next page. The seller's bank is required to send the draft and its accompanying documents for presentment to the buyer by the buyer's bank. The seller's bank deals with "for collection" items individually, without assuming that they will be honored, and therefore without giving the seller a provisional credit in the seller's account until the buyer pays the draft.

See flow chart below showing payment against document transaction.

The draft, with its attached documents, will pass through "customary banking channels" to the buyer's bank (the "presenting bank"), which will notify the buyer of the arrival of the documents. The buyer's bank will demand that the buyer "honor" the draft, at which time the buyer can pay the amount of a demand draft, or "accept" or promise to pay a time draft later. The buyer may require the bank to "exhibit" the draft and documents to it to allow the buyer to determine whether they conform to the contract. If the buyer receives mere notice that the documents have arrived, the buyer has three banking days after the notice is sent to decide whether to "honor" the draft. However, if the draft and documents are exhibited directly to the buyer, the buyer must decide whether or not to honor the draft by the close of business on that same day, unless there are extenuating circumstances.

The buyer must "pay against the documents" and not the goods themselves, which is why it is preferable to specify the terms of the documents in the original contract for the sale of goods. Once the buyer has paid or made arrangements to pay the buyer's bank, it will obtain possession of the negotiable bill of lading and only then will it be entitled to obtain the goods from the carrier. The buyer never sees the goods, only the documents B so it inspects the documents rigorously to determine that they comply exactly with the requirements of the sale contract. Substantial performance by the seller in the tender of documents is not acceptable.

An international sale of goods involving payment against documents is diagramed on this page.

§ 3.7   Risks of the Parties

Both parties face certain risks in this type of transaction that will affect both sides regardless of whether the buyer or seller is ultimately responsible for bearing the risks. For example, the goods could be lost or stolen. In such a situation, the value of the goods, the amount of time required to secure additional or replacement goods, and the demand for the goods on the buyer are factors that may be taken into account.

Some of these problems are recognized and dealt with in the standard handling of the "payment against documents" transaction. For example, insuring the goods against loss or theft is standard practice in the CIF transaction. Other problems, such as payment before inspection, make buyers feel unprotected, and they have searched for devices within the transaction that can afford them more protection. Such a device, in common use in modern transactions, is the Inspection Certificate.

Other risks relate directly to potential liabilities regarding bills of lading and are discussed under E. Inherent Risks and Liabilities Regarding Bills of Lading.

§ 3.8   Seller's Risks

What can go wrong from the seller's point of view? The seller will be paid before the documents or the goods are released to the buyer. If the buyer pays the buyer's bank, the proceeds are remitted immediately and automatically to the seller's bank account in the seller's nation. Therefore, the seller will not lose control of the goods without being paid for them.

However, the seller has shipped the goods to a foreign buyer prior to receiving any payment, and with no guarantee of payment from anyone other than the buyer. The buyer may refuse to pay the sight draft with documents attached when it arrives. This would give the seller a cause of action, but often the seller would have to go to a court in the buyer's jurisdiction for relief, which means bringing a suit abroad with its extra expense, delay and uncertainty. In addition, the seller could feel that it will be the target of discrimination in the courts of the buyer's nation.

The seller would still have control of the goods because after dishonor of the draft, the bill of lading will be returned to the seller. However, the goods would either be in transit or would have reached their foreign destination B one at which the seller is likely to have no agents and no particular prospects for resale. If the seller wanted to bring the goods back to its base of operations (and normal sales territory), it would have to pay a second transportation charge, and this may be substantial in relation to the value of the goods. Thus, the dishonor of the draft by the buyer can create economic circumstances where the seller's only rational option is a distress sale in the buyer's nation. This risk to the seller is inherent in the payment against documents transaction, unless the seller requires that the buyer also procure the issuance of a letter of credit. (See Chapter 6 for a complete description and discussion of the letter of credit transaction.)

§ 3.9   Buyer's Risks

What can go wrong from the buyer's point of view? In exchange for its payment of the purchase price of the goods, the buyer has a document from the carrier entitling it to delivery of the goods, an insurance certificate protecting the buyer against casualty loss, and perhaps an inspection certificate warranting that the goods conform to the sale contract. Therefore, the buyer should receive what it bargained for B delivery of conforming goods or insurance proceeds sufficient to cover any loss.

However, without the ability to inspect the actual goods before payment, the buyer cannot be absolutely assured that they conform to the contract. The buyer is forced to rely on information provided in the bill of lading, such as a description of the goods, quantity of boxes or weight of the cargo prior to payment for the goods. There could be misstatements or errors on the bill of lading so that the description conforms to the sales contract, but upon delivery, the buyer could find that the goods shipped are non-conforming. This non-conformity could range from the seller shipping scrap paper, to the seller shipping the correct goods in the wrong size or color. Similarly, the buyer could find that the labeling on the packaging is incorrect (which can cause problems with customs agents in both countries).

The buyer faces other risks—that the goods could have been stored or handled inappropriately by the carrier such that they are damaged in transit, or the bill of lading has been obtained by fraud or forgery. Some of these risks are inherent to any transaction using a bill of lading, and will be considered in the materials below.

§ 3.10   International Conventions

Regulation of the terms of a bill of lading, or the relationship between a carrier and its customers, is the subject of three international conventions and three United States federal statutes. The three international conventions (the Hague Rules,[1] the Hague–Visby Rules,[2] and the Hamburg Rules[3]) all encompass contracts of carriage and bills of lading, but have differing approaches and are progressively more customer-oriented.[4]

The Hague Rules were adopted in 1924, and set forth rules governing shipowner liability to shippers for cargo loss and damage. The Hague Rules provide 17 defenses against carrier and shipowner liability, preclude contractual exculpatory clauses in bills of lading, and limit liability to a minimum of $500 per package or customary freight unit.[5] The Visby Amendment was adopted in 1968 and

---

§ 3.10

1. Convention for the Unification of Certain Rules of Law Relating to Bills of Lading, Aug. 25, 1924, 51 Stat. 233, T.S. No. 931, 120 L.N.T.S. 155, reprinted in 3 T.J. Schoenbaum, Admiralty and Maritime Law 747 (2d ed. 1994) (hereinafter the Hague Rules) (enacted as 46 U.S.C. App. §§ 1300–1315 (1988).

2. See Protocol to Amend the International Convention for the Unification of Certain Rules of Law Relating to Bills of Lading, Brussels, Feb. 23, 1968, 2 U.N. Register of Texts ch. 2, at 180 (entered into force June 23, 1977), reprinted in 3 Schoenbaum, supra note 1, .5, at 753 (hereinafter the Visby Amendments) (together with the Hague Rules, the Hague–Visby Rules). The Hague–Visby Rules have been ratified by many countries, including Belgium, Denmark, Ecuador, Egypt, Finland, France, Germany, Italy, the Netherlands, Norway, Poland, Singapore, South Africa, Spain, the United Kingdom, and other signatory countries that represent a large percentage of the U.S. trade. 6 Benedicts Admiralty 1–30 (7th ed. 1996).

3. United Nations Convention on the Carriage of Goods by Sea, Hamburg,

Mar. 31, 1978, U.N. Doc A/Conf.89/13, 17 I.L.M. 608 (1978) (hereinafter the Hamburg Rules). Entered into force on Nov. 1, 1992, U.N. Doc. A/RES/48/34. As of Jan. 1, 2005, there are twenty-nine Contracting States to the Hamburg Rules. See UNCITRAL Status of Conventions and Model Laws at http://www.uncitral.org/en-index.htm.

4. For discussions on the development and changes of these international conventions, see Samuel Robert Mandelbaum, Creating Uniform Worldwide Liability Standards for Sea Carriage of Goods Under the Hague, COGSA, Visby and Hamburg Conventions, 23 Transp. L.J. 471, 477 (1996); see also Yancey, Admiralty Law Institute: Symposium on American and International Maritime Law: Comparative Aspects of Current Importance: The Carriage of Goods: Hague, COGSA, Visby and Hamburg, 57 Tul. L. Rev. 1238 (1983).

5. See Mandelbaum, supra note 4, at 477.

amended the Hague Rules; thus, they are referred to as the Hague–Visby Rules. The Visby Amendment addressed certain issues that had arisen under the Hague Rules, such as the broadness of the carrier defenses and the inadequacy of the $500 per package provision in light of multimodal transportation and containerized packaging. The Hague–Visby Rules define the term "package" to include containerized cargo, increase the per package liability to $663 (or $2 per kilogram, whichever is higher), and restrict a carrier's limitations of liability for damage caused by its own intentional or reckless actions.[6] The Hamburg Rules of 1978 is a major departure from the Hague and Hague–Visby Rules by substantially decreasing carrier and shipowner defenses and increasing potential liability. It eliminates many defenses leaving three from the 17 defenses provided in the previous conventions, increases liability per package to approximately $1,169 per package or customary shipping unit and provides the shipper an opportunity to recover based on the weight of the cargo instead, and includes liability for on deck cargo and shipments without a bill of lading for the first time (these items are specifically excluded by the prior conventions).[7] The Hamburg Rules have not been widely adopted, and a number of the adopting states are developing and/or landlocked states.

Some nations have chosen one set of rules to apply as mandatory law;[8] others such as Hague–Visby signatories apply different rules depending on the country of origin or whether the shipment is inbound or outbound, since the rules are not applicable of their own force for inbound shipments to a signatory country.[9]

The United States has enacted the Hague Rules into its domestic law as the Carriage of Goods by Sea Act (COGSA), but also has non-conforming pre-COGSA legislation (the Harter Act) in force. English law is based on the Hague/Visby Rules.

§ 3.11 Overview of United States Law

U.C.C. Article 7 would appear to regulate the relationship governing the transfer of the bill of lading, but in fact, except for intrastate transactions, the U.C.C. is preempted by federal law.[1]

---

6. See Edelman, Proposed Changes for Cargo Liability, 208 N.Y.L.J. 3 (1992).

7. See Mandelbaum, supra note 4, at 482–484. For an in-depth review of the Hamburg Rules, see Robert Force, A Comparison of the Hague, Hague–Visby, and Hamburg Rules: Much Ado About (?), 70 Tul. L. Rev. 2051 (1996).

8. For country-by-country information regarding the adoption of the

Hague, Hague–Visby or Hamburg conventions and the effective date, see www.admiraltylaw.com/cargo_regimes.htm.

9. Visby Amendment, supra note 2, Article 5.

§ 3.11

1. See National Union Fire Ins. Co. v. Allite, Inc., 430 Mass. 828, 724 N.E.2d 677, 679 (2000) (holding that the Feder-

The Federal Bills of Lading Act[2] (formerly called the Pomerene Act), governs the transfer and transferability of all bills of lading originating in the United States and generated to cover both international and interstate shipments;[3] but UCC, Article 7 covers the transfer of intrastate, inbound international, and international shipments that do not reach the United States.[4] The form and content of bills of lading are also governed by the Harter Act,[5] and the Carriage of Goods by Sea Act.[6] There is a Revised UCC Article 7 which as of Jan. 1, 2005, has been enacted in six states, and can be expected to obtain more enactments in the future. With this multiplicity of statutes governing the terms of the bill of lading and its use, conflicting concepts from overlapping statutes can be expected.

§ 3.12 The Harter Act

The Harter Act, codified under the shipping title of the United States Code (46 U.S.C. §§ 190–96), governs liability for cargo between the vessel owner or carrier and the shipper in the domestic trade. The Harter Act was a restatement of the common law as of 1893 that applied to the duties and liabilities of a vessel to its cargo.[1]

The Harter Act prohibits and nullifies language in a bill of lading that limits a carrier's liability for "negligence, fault, or failure in proper loading, stowage, custody, care, or proper delivery of any and all lawful merchandise or property committed to its or their charge."[2] Basically, the Harter Act limits the carrier's ability to contract away its liability for exercising due diligence in preparing the vessel (and all aspects related thereto) for the carriage of the goods, and in exercising due care in its handling of the goods while in the carrier's possession.

§ 3.13 Carriage of Goods by Sea Act (COGSA)

COGSA, codified under the shipping title of the United States Code (46 U.S.C. App. §§ 1300–15), is derived from the Hague Rules.[1] At the time it was enacted in 1936, there was no interna-

---

al Bills of Lading Act preempts Article 7 of the UCC, which applies only in cases of intrastate transportation of goods).

2. 49 U.S.C. §§ 80101–80116.

3. See 49 U.S.C. § 80102.

4. Thypin Steel Co. v. Certain Bills of Lading, in Rem, 1996 WL 223896 (S.D. N.Y. 1996); T.C. Ziraat Bankasi v. Standard Chartered Bank, 84 N.Y.2d 480, 619 N.Y.S.2d 690, 644 N.E.2d 272 (1994).

5. 46 U.S.C. §§ 190–196.

6. 46 U.S.C. App. §§ 1300–1315.

§ 3.12

1. See The Delaware, 161 U.S. 459, 471–72, 16 S.Ct. 516, 40 L.Ed. 771 (1896).

2. 46 U.S.C. § 190.

§ 3.13

1. For a description of the Hague Rules, see supra § 3.10.

tional uniformity regarding cargo liability derived from bills of lading. For example, in the U.S., carriers could not limit their liability and were treated as insurers of the cargo, while in the U.K., carriers were permitted under the principle of freedom of contract to exonerate themselves from liability. COGSA was enacted to establish uniform ocean bills of lading to govern the liability for cargo between the vessel owner or carrier and the shipper in international trade.[2]

COGSA applies to every bill of lading or document of title that evidences a contract for the carriage of goods by sea to or from a U.S. port, but does not automatically apply to solely domestic bills of lading.[3] COGSA sets forth the responsibilities and liabilities of the carrier and the ship, including seaworthiness of the vessel (which includes the proper manning, maintenance, equipment, supplies, and preparation of the vessel so that it is fit for the cargo),[4] and proper care and loading of cargo.[5] Unlike the Harter Act, COGSA does not require due diligence as a condition precedent to the use of a statutory defense, except for liability under the seaworthiness requirement.[6] In addition, COGSA states that a carrier will be held liable for damaged cargo resulting from an unreasonable deviation from the terms of the contract of carriage, for example, discharging the cargo and reloading it on another vessel, stowage in contravention to specific terms of contract of carriage, or a change in route to take on cargo resulting in delay of delivery.[7] Furthermore, COGSA provides a carrier with 17 defenses for "uncontrollable causes of loss," including defective navigation or management of the ship, fire, dangers of the sea, acts of God, seizure, acts or omissions of the shipper or owner of the goods, certain labor problems, inherent defects in the goods, insufficiency of packing or marks.[8]

One of the most well-known provisions of COGSA is the $500 per package limitation of liability for loss or damage to cargo,[9] which may be increased if the shipper declares a higher valuation or maximum amount of liability in the bill of lading.[10] Regardless of

---

2. See Robert C. Herd & Co., Inc. v. Krawill Mach. Corp., 359 U.S. 297, 301, 79 S.Ct. 766, 3 L.Ed.2d 820 (1959). International counterparts include the British Carriage of Goods by Sea Act of 1924 and the Barbados Carriage of Goods by Sea Act of 1926.

3. 46 U.S.C. App. §§ 1300 and 1312.

4. 46 U.S.C. App. § 1303(1).

5. 46 U.S.C. App. § 1303(2).

6. 46 U.S.C. App. § 1304(1).

7. See 46 U.S.C. App. § 1304(4). Note that deviations are often not covered by a ship's P & I insurance.

8. 46 U.S.C. App. § 1304(2).

9. 46 U.S.C. App. § 1304(5) ("Neither the carrier nor the ship shall in any event be or become liable for any loss or damage to or in connection with the transportation of goods in an amount exceeding $500 per package ... ")

10. See Atlantic Mut. Ins. Co. v. Poseidon Schiffahrt, 206 F.Supp. 15, 19 (N.D.Ill.1962), aff'd, 313 F.2d 872 (7th

the valuation or maximum amount of liability, a carrier or ship will not be held liable for more than the damage actually sustained.[11] An additional protection or limitation of liability under COGSA is that claims must be filed within a year following delivery of the subject goods.[12]

COGSA contains provisions that overlap with the Harter Act. COGSA will prevail for any loss or damage arising from an act, negligence or default in navigation or management of a vessel used for carriage of goods by sea.[13] When damage to goods occurs on land, the Harter Act will prevail and prohibit any disclaimers against liability.[14] The Harter Act by its terms still governs prior to loading and after discharge of cargo until delivery under the bill of lading is made.[15]

§ 3.14   Federal Bills of Lading Act

The Federal Bills of Lading Act (hereinafter the FBLA) (formerly called the Pomerene Act), codified under the transportation title of the United States Code (49 U.S.C.A. §§ 80101–80116), governs the transfer and transferability of all bills of lading generated to cover both international and interstate shipments. Congress enacted the FBLA in 1916, and recodified the FBLA in 1994. It did not intend to change the substance of the Act, but it did reword and consolidate the prior provisions and change all the section numbers.

The FBLA governs all interstate and outbound international shipments that use a bill of lading issued by a common carrier. By its terms, the statute governs the bill of lading if the goods are shipped from the United States to another country. The FBLA defines the different types of bills of lading (negotiable and non-negotiable),[1] and sets forth the rules that apply to a negotiable bill

Cir.1963), *cert. denied*, 375 U.S. 819, 84 S.Ct. 56, 11 L.Ed.2d 53 (1963). This concept is embodied in the doctrine of "fair opportunity" to declare a higher value. Note that neither the carrier nor the ship will be liable for an increased liability if the shipper has knowingly and fraudulently misstated the value of the goods on the bill of lading. Furthermore, the carrier may be subject to higher liability if damage is due to "unreasonable deviation" as described in this § 3.13.

11. 46 U.S.C. App. § 1304(5).

12. 46 U.S.C. App. § 1303(6).

13. 46 U.S.C. App. § 1301(e) defining carriage of goods by sea.

14. Compare 46 U.S.C. App. § 1304(2)(a) with 46 U.S.C. § 190. See Baker Oil Tools, Inc. v. Delta S.S. Lines,

Inc., 562 F.2d 938, 940–41 (5th Cir.1977) (refusing to apply COGSA to liability caused by land transportation), *reh'g denied*, 571 F.2d 978 (5th Cir.1978), *reh'g denied*, 577 F.2d 1134 (5th Cir.1978).

15. 46 U.S.C. App. § 1311 (stating that COGSA does not supercede the Harter Act or other federal statutes insofar as they relate to duties, responsibilities and liabilities of the ship or carrier prior to the time when the goods are loaded or after the time the goods are discharged from the ship.) See Allied Chem. Int'l Corp. v. Companhia de Navegacao Lloyd Brasileiro, 775 F.2d 476, 482 (2d Cir.1985), *cert. denied*, 475 U.S. 1099, 106 S.Ct. 1502, 89 L.Ed.2d 903 (1986).

§ 3.14

1. 49 U.S.C. § 80103.

of lading[2] and non-negotiable bill of lading,[3] outlining the rights and duties attached to each type.

There are several notable provisions in the FBLA regarding potential liability for bills of lading: (1) a carrier's liability for misdelivery and conversion, (2) a carrier's liability for nonreceipt, misdescription and improper loading, and (3) the warranty liability of a person negotiating or transferring a bill of lading for value. The FBLA sets forth the requirements for a carrier to fulfill its duty to deliver goods, thus describing what is required to prove liability for a claim for conversion or misdelivery by the carrier, and some of the carrier's defenses to such a claim.[4] For example, the carrier must deliver the goods to a person entitled to possession (consignee in of a non-negotiable bill of lading or holder of a negotiable bill of lading),[5] and must obtain and cancel a negotiable bill of lading at the time of delivery.[6]

A carrier is liable for nonreceipt and misdescription if it either indicates its receipt of cargo on a bill of lading where no cargo was received, or if the goods do not correspond with the carrier's description of them on the bill of lading.[7] The FBLA does provide certain exceptions for a carrier's nonreceipt, misdescription and improper loading liability, such as when the goods are loaded by the shipper, the bill of lading indicates that the goods were "shippers weight, load and count" or the "contents are unknown," and in the case of nonreceipt or misdescription, the carrier does not have information contrary to that included on the bill.[8] This defense is not available for an indication of the weight of bulk freight on a bill of lading if a shipper provides facilities for the carrier to determine the weight and requests that the carrier provide such information in the bill of lading, or for the kind and quantity of bulk freight when the goods are loaded by a carrier.[9]

As further described below, the FBLA provides for automatic representations and warranties by a person negotiating or transferring a bill of lading for value, including that the bill is genuine, the transferor has title to the goods and the right to transfer the bill, and the transferor is not aware of any fact affecting the validity of the bill.[10] These representations and warranties often arise in the context of a forged signature or a forged bill of lading.

The word "carrier" is not defined in the FBLA, so it is not clear whether documents issued by freight forwarders are covered

---

2. 49 U.S.C. §§ 80104 and 80105 (regarding indorsement, delivery and possession of the bill of lading, and title to the goods).

3. 49 U.S.C. § 80106.

4. 49 U.S.C. §§ 80110 and 80111.

5. 49 U.S.C. § 80111(a).

6. 49 U.S.C. § 80111(c).

7. 49 U.S.C. § 80113.

8. 49 U.S.C. § 80113(b) and (c).

9. 49 U.S.C. § 80113(d).

10. 49 U.S.C. § 80107(a).

by the FBLA. Further, the term "bill of lading" is not defined, so it is not clear whether air waybills or inland waterway documents are included.

§ 3.15   Inherent Risks and Liabilities Regarding Bills of Lading

There are certain problems that are uniquely related to any transaction using a bill of lading, and will be considered in the materials below:

(1) The loss of the bill of lading, followed by the forgery of a necessary indorsement and the carrier's misdelivery (delivery of the goods to the wrong person under a bill of lading).

(2) The misdescription of the goods by the shipper in the bill of lading followed by the carrier's delivery of goods which do not conform to the description in the bill of lading.

(3) The forgery of a complete bill of lading by the shipper without the carrier's knowledge.

§ 3.16   Misdelivery

Under a non-negotiable bill of lading, the carrier obligates itself to deliver the goods at the destination point to the consignee named in the bill of lading.[1] In short, the carrier is liable to the consignee of a straight bill of lading for misdelivery if it delivers the goods to anyone but the consignee or a person to whom the consignee delegates to receive them.[2] Thus, straight bills of lading are not appropriate for a "payment against documents" transaction, and the case reports are full of litigation where an attorney tried a short-cut using a straight bill of lading as the "easy" way to do this transaction, and sacrificed the client's interests.

Under a negotiable bill of lading, the carrier obligates itself to deliver the goods to the "holder" of the bill of lading at the destination point.[3] Thus, possession of the negotiable bill of lading becomes crucial and confers title over the goods. The carrier must see the actual bill of lading both to determine who has possession and to determine to whom the indorsements run.

In certain situations where the actual bill of lading is not available, the carrier will not be liable for delivery to a person

---

§ 3.16

1. 49 U.S.C. § 80110.

2. See Richardson v. Railway Express Agency, Inc., 258 Or. 170, 482 P.2d 176, 178–79 (1971) (holding carrier liable under a straight bill of lading where shipper instructed carrier to hold the goods for pickup and instead the carrier delivered the goods to an address listed as shipper's street address on the bill of lading and did not obtain evidence that the person signing for the goods was entitled to possession).

3. 46 U.S.C. § 80110.

entitled to possession of the goods pursuant to the FBLA.[4] For example, the New York Supreme Court held that a carrier was not liable for delivery without requiring the surrender of the bill of lading where the buyer was the true owner of the goods under the buyer's f.o.b. contract (in which the shipper passes title to the goods to the buyer upon delivery to the carrier).[5] More recently, a New Jersey District Court held that Honduran customs authorities were "persons entitled to possession" of jute bags since the bill of lading was not available for presentment to the customs authorities; therefore, the carrier was not liable for the bags being stolen while in the possession of the customs authorities.[6]

Notwithstanding the above situation, the carrier is liable to the holder of a negotiable bill of lading for misdelivery if it delivers the goods to anyone but the holder.[7] As stated above, the negotiable bill of lading is a document of title because possession of it, properly indorsed, controls title to the document, title to the goods, and the direct obligation of the carrier to hold the goods and deliver them to the holder of the document. For this reason, the negotiable bill of lading is appropriate for a "payment against documents" transaction. The collecting banks can use their possession of such bills of lading to control title to both the goods and the document until they have collected the purchase price from the buyer.

The carrier has an obligation to take possession of the bill of lading and cancel it. Under § 80111(c) of the FBLA, "if a common carrier delivers goods for which a negotiable bill of lading has been issued without taking and canceling the bill, the carrier is liable for damages for failure to deliver the goods to a person purchasing the bill for value in good faith whether the purchase was before or after delivery and even when delivery was made to the person entitled to the goods."[8] The statute does provide certain exceptions to this provision.[9]

The holder of the bill of lading has absolute title to the goods in almost all cases. If the seller is not the owner of the goods, for example if the goods have been stolen at gunpoint from the "true owner," then no holder of the bill of lading will have title because the seller's claim of title is void. However, if the original owner

---

4. 46 U.S.C. § 80110(b)(1).

5. Miller v. New York Cent. R.R. Co., 205 App.Div. 663, 200 N.Y.S. 287 (1923).

6. Ace Bag & Burlap Co., Inc. v. Sea–Land Serv., Inc., 40 F.Supp.2d 233, 239–40 (D.N.J.1999).

7. 46 U.S.C. § 80111; see also 46 U.S.C. § 80114(b) (stating that delivery of goods pursuant to a court order "does not relieve a common carrier from liability to a person to whom the negotiable

bill has been or is negotiated for value without notice of the court proceeding or of the delivery of the goods"). Note that under 46 U.S.C. § 80114(a) the court order requiring delivery of goods may require the posting of a surety bond prior to delivery.

8. 49 U.S.C. § 80111(c).

9. 49 U.S.C. § 80111(d).

voluntarily parted with the goods but was defrauded by the seller (for example, a cash sale in which the check bounces later), then the seller obtains voidable title[10] and can pass good title to a holder of the document who purchases it in good faith for value without notice.[11] The rights of such a good faith holder for value are also superior to any seller's lien or right to stop delivery of the goods in transit.

Under the FBLA, as under the UCC, any forgery of a necessary indorsement is not effective to create or transfer rights, regardless of whether the forgery is perfect. Further, any unauthorized signature by an agent is treated as a forgery, as long as it was made without actual, implied or apparent authority. The protection is illustrated in the situation where a thief steals a negotiable bill of lading from the holder who was in possession of the document under a special indorsement. As such, the holder's indorsement is necessary to transfer rights to the document or goods to any other party. Without that indorsement, the thief is not a holder and still has no rights. If the thief transfers the document to another party, that party also is not a holder and cannot obtain rights under the document without the holder's signature. The carrier is still obligated to deliver the goods only to the holder, the victim of the theft.[12] Thus, if a collecting bank or another party takes the document under a special indorsement, it is protected from loss from theft of the paper and forgery, and even from unauthorized transfer by an agent.

If the carrier does deliver to the forger, or to someone who received the document from the forger without the holder's indorsement, the carrier is liable for misdelivery.[13] The forger is also liable, if he can be found. The person who received the goods and other transferees have all made warranties hat they had "a right to transfer the bill and title to the goods," when they had no such rights or title.[14]

In the case of a person who purchases or otherwise gives value for a valid bill of lading without notice that the bill of lading was obtained by breach of duty, fraud, accident, mistake, duress, loss, theft or conversion, the validity of the bill of lading will be upheld to the detriment of the original or rightful owner.[15] The rightful owner will have the same remedies for misdelivery as described herein.

The concept is that each person who takes the bill of lading should "know his indorser." If the goods are misdelivered, the

10. U.C.C. § 7–502, 7–503. See also, UCC § 2–403.

11. 49 U.S.C. § 80105.

12. 49 U.S.C. § 80111(b).

13. 49 U.S.C. § 80111.

14. 49 U.S.C. § 80107.

15. 49 U.S.C. 80104(b).

party most easily found is the one who received the goods, and that party is liable. That party then has a warranty action against its transferor B and it is the person involved that is most likely to be able to find that transferor. The transferor, in turn, has a warranty action against its transferor B and so on back up the chain of transfers. This is not very efficient, however the purpose is to push liability back up the chain of transfers to the person who took from the forger, or even to the forger himself. In the meantime, the holder collects from the misdelivering carrier, which collects from its insuror.

Even collecting banks that transfer the document for value can be subject to this warranty liability. If the buyer pays, and those funds are transmitted to the forger, then the collecting banks have received value. However, such banks have some potential escape valves. One is to disclaim such warranty liability when indorsing the negotiable bill of lading. The statutory warranties do not arise if "a contrary intention appears."[16] Thus, a specific indorsement "XYZ Bank. Prior indorsements not guaranteed," or a general indorsement that the bank will not be responsible for quantity, quality, condition or delivery of the goods described in the bill would clearly disclaim liability for such a warranty.[17] A second avenue is to claim that the bank is only holding the document "as security for a debt," for the statute exempts such holders from warranty liability.[18] The difficulty with this avenue is that a collecting bank does not pay the seller until after it receives payment, so it never becomes a creditor, secured or otherwise. Any bank found to have warranty liability can pass this liability back to the transferor, as long as it can identify that transferor.

If the UCC is applicable, such as under an "inbound" international shipment, in which the bill of lading was issued abroad and is subject to U.S. law, the collecting bank will not make any warranties as to forgeries of indorsements, or of the bill itself. Although some transferors do make such warranties under the UCC, "mere intermediaries," such as collecting banks do not, by statutory rule.[19]

---

16. 49 U.S.C. 80107(a). The statute reads "unless a contrary intention appears," and then describes the general warranties and liabilities assigned to a person negotiating or transferring a bill of lading.

17. See e.g, American State Bank v. Mueller Grain Co., 15 F.2d 899, 904 (7th Cir.1926), rev'd on other grounds, 275 U.S. 493, 48 S.Ct. 34, 72 L.Ed. 390 (1927); Johnston v. Western Md. Ry. Co., 151 Md. 422, 135 A. 185 (1926).

18. 49 U.S.C. 80107(b) ("A person holding a bill of lading as security for a debt and in good faith demanding or receiving payment of the debt from another person does not warrant by the demand or receipt (1) the genuineness of the bill; or (2) the quantity or quality of the goods described in the bill.")

19. UCC §§ 2–507, 2–508. These provisions are not changed in Revised UCC Article 7.

§ 3.17   Misdescription

The carrier in a shipment transaction has no privity with the contract between the buyer and the seller for the sale of goods, and therefore has no obligation to deliver goods that conform to the sale contract. However, the goods are described in the bill of lading, which constitutes part of the carriage contract. Thus, the carrier does have an obligation to deliver goods that conform to the description in the bill of lading. Under the FBLA, a carrier is liable for any failure to deliver goods that correspond to the description in the bill of lading, either as to quantity or as to quality.[1] This obligation is owed to the owner of the goods under a non-negotiable bill of lading and to the holder of a negotiable bill of lading. Therefore, if a bill of lading describes goods, and the described goods differ from the delivered goods, the carrier may be held liable to the shipper.[2]

The problem with this obligation is that the carrier usually does not know what it is carrying, since the goods are often in containers. Thus, the carrier knows that it received a container that was labeled "100 IBM word-processing computers." It will not, and is not expected to, open the container to check whether it contains computers, or to count how many items are in the container. Even if the carrier opened the container, it would not be expected to check whether each computer is in working order. Even if it did so check, it is not likely to have the expertise to determine whether each computer can perform the necessary routines to be a word processor. Thus, the carrier is not expected to warrant the description and capability of packaged goods given to it to transport.

To solve this problem, carriers are allowed, under the FBLA and COGSA, to effectively disclaim their obligations to deliver goods that conform to the description.[3] Appropriate disclaimer language is set forth in the statute and includes: "contents or condition of contents of packages unknown," "said to contain," and "shipper's weight, load and count." Other language conveying the same meaning can be used; the statutory linguistic formulas are not required.

According to these statutory provision, all of these disclaimers are effective only if the seller loads the goods.[4] This restriction seems appropriate for disclaimers of the "shipper's weight, load and

§ 3.17

1. 49 U.S.C.A. § 80113.

2. See Industria Nacional Del Papel, CA. v. M/V "Albert F", 730 F.2d 622, 624 (11th Cir.1984) (holding the vessel liable for non-delivery when goods received did not conform to the goods de-

scribed in the bill of lading), *cert. denied,* 469 U.S. 1037, 105 S.Ct. 515, 83 L.Ed.2d 404 (1984).

3. 49 U.S.C.A. § 80113(b); 46 U.S.C. App. § 1303(3)(c).

4. 49 U.S.C.A. 80113(b)(1).

count" variety, but seems inappropriate for disclaimers of the "said to contain" or "contents or condition of contents of packages unknown" variety. There are cases in which the carrier is held liable for misdescription despite stating "shipper's weight, load and count" in a bill of lading if the carrier issues a bill of lading and the shipper has in fact never loaded anything on board the carrier's cars.[5]

The disclaimers are not effective if the carrier knows that the goods do not conform.[6] The protection is available only to the uninformed carrier. However, when goods are loaded by a carrier, the carrier is obligated to count the number of packages and is expected to note the condition of the packages.[7] The carrier is also obligated to "determine the kind and quantity" (but not the quality) of any bulk freight that it loads.[8] For bulk freight, even where it is loaded by the seller, the carrier must still determine the kind and quantity of the freight if the seller so requests and provides adequate facilities for the carrier to weigh the freight.[9] In situations where the carrier must count packages or weigh the goods, disclaimers (such as "shipper's weight, load and count" or others indicating that the shipper described or loaded the goods) will not be effective.[10]

The disclaimers are also not effective if the carrier has reasonable grounds for suspecting that the goods do not conform, or has no reasonable means of checking for marks, number, quantity or weight.[11] In such situations, the carrier is expected to omit such information from the bill of lading. A carrier that instead uses disclaimer language such as "shipper's load and count" and "said to contain," will face potential liability.[12]

Thus, what is established is a system in which the carrier is responsible for checking some quantity terms, the number of car-

---

5. See, e.g., Chicago and N. W. Ry. Co v. Stephens Nat. Bank, 75 F.2d 398, 400 (8th Cir.1935). See also, Portland Fish Co. v. States S.S. Co., 510 F.2d 628, 630–31 (9th Cir.1974) (stating that since the cargo was loaded by the carrier, the carrier should not have issued a bill of lading with a weight description if it had no reasonable means to check the weight of the cargo and therefore held that the carrier was estopped from denying that they had received anything other than what was listed on the bill of lading, despite a "shipper's load and count" clause).

6. 49 U.S.C. § 80113(b)(3).

7. 49 U.S.C. § 80113(d)(2); see Elgie & Co. v. S.S. "S. A. Nederburg", 599 F.2d 1177, 1180–81 (2d Cir.1979) (stat-

ing that carrier loading packaged goods is obligated to count packages and indicate that number in the bill of lading), *cert. denied*, 444 U.S. 1072, 100 S.Ct. 1016, 62 L.Ed.2d 753 (1980).

8. 49 U.S.C. § 80113(d)(2).

9. 49 U.S.C. § 80113(d)(1).

10. 49 U.S.C. § 80113(d)(2).

11. 46 U.S.C. ann. § 1303(3)(c), stating that "no carrier, master or agent of the carrier, shall be bound to state or show in the bill of lading any marks, number, quantity or weight which he has reasonable ground for suspecting not accurately to represent the goods actually received, or which he has had no reasonable means of checking."

12. See supra note 5.

tons and the weight of a shipment. These are items that the carrier is likely to check in any event, to be certain that some cartons are not inadvertently left behind, and to determine the appropriate freight charge. However, the carrier is not required to check most quality terms, such as what goods are in a container and whether they are in operating condition.[13] The carrier can truthfully say that it has received 100 cartons "said to contain" IBM word processing computers, without opening the cartons; but it does need to count the number of cartons.

The intersection of these rules arise when the carrier accepts a sealed container supposed to contain 2000 tin ingots weighing 35 tons, and issues a bill of lading for a container "said to contain 2000 tin ingots." If the container is empty or weighs less than a ton and the carrier does not weigh it, the carrier's disclaimer is not likely to protect it.[14] The disclaimer will, however, protect the carrier if the shipper actually loaded the sealed container itself.[15]

§ 3.18　Forged Bills of Lading

If the carrier issues a bill of lading for which there are no goods, the carrier will likely be held liable to the holder of a negotiable bill of lading. However, suppose the carrier never issued any bill of lading. Instead, a person unrelated to the carrier created a false bill of lading or forged a bill of lading, without authority from the carrier. The buyer who purchases such a forged bill of lading has paid funds to a forger, probably through a series of banks, and finds that the carrier has no goods to deliver. There is no misdelivery or misdescription claim against the carrier, for there never were any goods delivered to the carrier for it to redeliver or to describe. If the carrier did not issue the bill of lading and its "signature" is a forgery or is unauthorized, that signature is not "effective," and carrier will not be liable on the bill, absent some sort of actionable negligence.

The forger is liable for the fraud, if he can be found. Unlike the forged indorsement situation, there is no one who has received any goods, for there never were any goods to deliver. However, like the

---

13. See e.g., Mannell v. Luckenbach S.S. Co., 26 F.2d 908 (W.D.Wash.1928) (stating that the purchaser was not entitled to recover from a carrier for misdescription of the damaged goods where the bill of lading correctly described the kind and quantity of articles, without any description of the condition of the goods).

14. Berisford Metals Corp. v. S/S Salvador, 779 F.2d 841, 847–48 (2d Cir. 1985), *cert. denied*, 476 U.S. 1188, 106 S.Ct. 2928, 91 L.Ed.2d 556 (1986).

15. See Dei Dogi Calzature S.P.A. v. Summa Trading Corp., 733 F.Supp. 773, 775–76 (S.D.N.Y.1990) (stating that carrier is not liable to shipper for losses resulting from receipt of container filled with water instead of leather items where bill of lading description of contents was prefaced by "said to contain" and the bulk freight was loaded by the shipper).

forged indorsement situation, each party that transferred the bill of lading for value makes warranties to later parties, and the first warranty is that "the bill is genuine."[1] If the bill of lading itself is forged, that warranty is breached. Thus, all parties who transferred the bill and received payment funds can be liable to breach of warranty actions against them by later parties. The concept is that the last person to purchase the bill will "know its indorser," and be able to recover against its transferor. That transferor can, in turn, recover against its transferor, and so on up the chain of transfers, until the loss falls either on the forger or upon the person who dealt with and took the bill from the forger.

Collecting banks that have transferred the document for value can be subject to this warranty liability, but have the same potential escape options discussed under forged indorsements: a disclaimer of warranty through making "a contrary intention appear," and a claim that the bank is holding the document only "as security for a debt." Both of these approaches have analytical difficulties, as discussed above, but they may indicate a blanket intention to disclaim the statutory warranties implicitly. Any bank that is found to have warranty liability can pass this liability back to its transferor, as long as it can identify and find that transferor.

If UCC Article 7 is applicable, it does exempt banks which are "mere intermediaries" (collecting banks) from any warranties of genuineness of the documents.[2]

§ 3.19 Electronic Bills of Lading

The FBLA does not define "bills of lading" and does not require that a bill of lading be written on a piece of paper or signed by anyone. Thus, use of electronic bills of lading would seem to be a technical possibility. However, all of the primary rules of the federal law are filled with an implicit assumption that the bill of lading is a paper document. In fact, international maritime business law has been called a "law of document."[1] The references to indorsements in blank or to a specified person, transfer by delivery, and "person in possession" (holder) make sense only in a paper document transaction.

In the arena of electronic bills of lading, the largest challenge has been in making an electronic bill of lading negotiable so that it

---

§ 3.18

1. 49 U.S.C. § 80107(a)(1).

2. UCC §§ 7–507, 7–508. These provisions are not changed under Revised UCC Article 7.

§ 3.19

1. See Dube, Canadian Perspectives on the Impact of the CMI Rules for Electronic Bills of Lading on the Liability of the Carrier Towards the Endorsee, 26 Transp. L. J. 107, 110 (Fall 1998).

remains authentic and confidential.[2] Telecommunications technology can provide electronic messages that perform the main functions of the bill of lading as a receipt, transport contract and document of title. Thus, several types of bills of lading equivalents are currently in use, but most of them are used only as receipts for the goods and are generated by the carrier.

There have been several programs to create electronic carrier-issued international receipts for goods. Atlantic Container Lines used dedicated lines between terminals at its offices in different ports to send messages between those offices. It generated a Data Freight Receipt that was given to the consignee or notify party. Such a receipt was not negotiable and gave buyers and banks little protection from further sale or rerouting of the goods by shipper in transit. The Cargo Key Receipt was similar, but also an advance over the prior approach, because it included a "no disposal" term in the shipper-carrier contract. Thus, this electronic message protected buyer from further sale or rerouting by seller in transit. It still could not be used to finance the transfer, however, because the electronic receipt, even if it named a bank as consignee, was not formally a negotiable document of title. The receipt was believed to give the bank only the right to prevent delivery to the buyer, not a positive right to take control of the goods for itself.

The Chase Manhattan Bank and the International Association of Independent Tanker Owners (Intertanko), created the SEADOCS Registry, which was intended to create a negotiable electronic bill of lading for oil shipments. The Registry acted as custodian for an actual paper negotiable bill of lading issued by a carrier, and maintained a registry of transfers of that bill from the original shipper to the ultimate "holder." The transfers were made by a series of electronic messages, each of which could be authenticated by "test keys," or identification numbers, generated by SEADOCS. SEADOCS would then, as agent, endorse the paper bill of lading in its custody. At the end, SEADOCS would electronically deliver a paper copy of the negotiable bill of lading to the last endorsee to enable it to obtain the goods from the carrier. While SEADOCS was a legal success, showing that such a program was technically feasible, it was not a commercial success and lasted less than a year when Chase discontinued its efforts.[3]

The Comite Maritime International has adopted Rules for Electronic Bills of Lading (hereinafter the CMI Rules).[4] Under the

---

2. See Dube, supra note 1, at 110.

3. See Chandler, Maritime Electronic Commerce for the Twenty–First Century, 22 Mar. Law. 463, 469 (1998).

4. Comite Maritime International Rules for Electronic Bills of Lading (1990), reprinted in Kelly, Comment: The CMI Charts a Course on the Sea of Electronic Data Interchange: Rules for

CMI Rules, any carrier can issue an electronic bill of lading as long as it will act as a clearinghouse for subsequent transfers. Each carrier has its own registry (usually per ship) and is not dependant upon the technology or software of any other party or a central registry.[5] Upon receiving goods, the carrier sends an electronic message to the shipper describing the goods, the contract terms, the location and date that the goods were received, and a "private key" which can be used to transfer shipper's rights to a third party. Under the CMI Rules, the shipper now has the "right of control and transfer" over the goods, and is called a "holder." Under Rules 4 and 7, an electronic message from a shipper, which includes the private key, can be used to transfer the shipper's rights to a third party. The third party becomes a new holder when it sends a confirmation to the carrier that it intends to accept the transfer of ownership rights from the shipper. The carrier then cancels the shipper's private key and issues a different private key to the new holder. Upon arrival, the carrier will deliver the goods to the then-current holder or consignee designated by the holder.

To take advantage of the CMI Rules, the original parties to the transaction must agree that the CMI Rules will govern the "communications" aspects of the transaction B the rules are voluntary and do not automatically have the force of law.[6] The CMI Rules are not intended to govern the substantive laws of bills of lading provisions, only the electronic transfers of the electronic bill of lading. All parties also agree that electronic messages satisfy any national law requirements that a bill of lading be in writing. This is an attempt to create an "electronic" writing that is a negotiable document of title by contract and estoppel. Some commentators have observed that this is an attempt by private parties to create a negotiable document, a power usually reserved to legislatures. In addition, there is some concern that the CMI Rules do not address certain issues, such as what constitutes receipt of an offer or acceptance, or what happens when there is a system failure.[7]

The Commission of the European Committees has sponsored the BOLERO electronic bill of lading initiative, which is based on the CMI Rules, and supported by a consortium of carriers, shippers, banks, insurers and telecommunication companies. However, under the BOLERO system, neither a bank nor a carrier is the repository of the sensitive information of who has bought and sold the cargo covered by the electronic bills of lading. Instead BOLERO establishes a third party who is independent of the shipper, the carrier,

---

Electronic Bills of Lading, 16 Mar. Law. 349 (1992).

5. See Dube, supra note 1, at 109.

6. See Chandler, supra note 3, at 475.

7. See Livermore and Euarjai, Electronic Bills of Lading: A Progress Report, 28 J. Mar. L. & Com. 55, 57 (1997).

the ultimate buyer and all intermediate parties as the operator of the central registry. The central registry and user-carriers, shippers, freight forwarders, and banks communicate through computer workstations that also permit communications between the parties themselves. The central registry maintains the shipping details in "consignment records," and access to such records is limited to those possessing authority through strong security controls and digital signatures. The digital signatures authenticate the message sender and prevent modification of transactions. The BOLERO project has not been broadly accepted in the industry and has faced much difficulty it has changed management and continues to struggle to maintain funding.[8]

American bankers have been skeptical of the device created by the CMI Rules. The registries maintained by each carrier do not have the same level of security associated with SWIFT procedures (Society for Worldwide Interbank Financial Telecommunication). [See "Electronic Letters of Credit" in Chapter 6.] In addition to fraudulent transactions, there is a risk of misdirected messages. Thus, a bank could find itself relying on "non-existent rights based upon fraudulent information in a receipt message transmitted to it by someone pretending to be the carrier." The banks are concerned as to whether carriers will accept liability in their new role as electronic registrars for losses due to such fraudulent practices.[9] The banks are also concerned that the full terms and conditions of the contract of carriage are not available to the subsequent "holders." Thus, use of the CMI Rules does not yet seem to be widely adopted, and bills of lading are still primarily paper-based in both the "payment against documents" and letter of credit transactions.

8. Bills of Lading for Europe (BOLERO). See Laryea, Paperless Shipping Documents: An Australian Perspective, 25 Mar. Law 255 (2000); Chandler, supra note 1, at 486–87; Livermore and Euarjai, Electronic Bills of Lading and Functional Equivalence, at http://eljiwarwick.ac.uk./jilt/ecomm/82liv/livermore.htm.

9. See Winship, in Current Developments Concerning the Forms of Lading (A.N. Yiannaopolis ed. 1995).

*

Chapter 4

SALES AGENT AND DISTRIBUTORSHIP AGREEMENTS

Table of Sections

---

§ 4.1   Need for a Written Agreement

Most products sold to purchasers in foreign lands involve the use of some person or entity in the foreign nation as the sales representative or distributor.[1] A small company may retain a representative in the foreign nation who handles many different, but usually compatible, products. A large company will have its own foreign agent or distributor.[2] It should be obvious that the commercial relationship between a U.S. producer and its foreign agent or distributor *must* be reduced to a written agreement. Because two different nations' laws may be involved, and probably two different cultures, the agreement should be sufficiently detailed to deal with the legal consequences reflecting such differences.[3]

§ 4.1

1. Certainly a company in one nation may accept orders placed from abroad. Such sales require no foreign, local representation. The retention of a foreign agent or distributor often follows periodic but increasing sales placed directly to the home office from abroad.

2. While the direct sale from an order placed from abroad may be the pre-lude to the use of an agent or distributor, the successful use of an agent or distributor may in turn lead subsequently to manufacturing the products in the foreign nation. Subsequent chapters deal with licensing such production, and direct foreign investment.

3. Eberhard H. Rohm & Robert Koch, Choice of Law in International

105

§ 4.2   Problems Most Prevalent Upon Termination

A U.S. producer/seller may have its own complete distribution network in each foreign country in which it does business. Much more likely is that the U.S. company will use some local person or entity for the distribution of its goods. Local distributors are used by U.S. companies just beginning to sell goods abroad, as well as by large multinationals with long experience abroad, but which do not have their own distribution networks. As in the case of any commercial contract, there are many possible areas for disagreement. But the most difficult issues involving distribution agreements arise upon termination, especially when the foreign agent or distributor is terminated against its will. Termination issues are often difficult when both parties are in the United States. But they are exacerbated when the seller is in one nation, such as the United States, and the distributor is in another nation, particularly a developing nation.[1] The foreign distributor, often an individual or comparatively small corporation, may believe that it has been treated unfairly by the quite likely much larger foreign seller. This is especially true when the local distributor has worked to develop clients and goodwill for the foreign company. The consequence of complaints by local agents and distributors that they have been mistreated, especially terminated unfairly, by large foreign corporations, has been the enactment of host-nation regulation of many forms of distribution agreements.[2] These laws may be very favorable to the local agent or distributor, but one may look in vain for provisions in these foreign laws which offer the foreign producer or supplier compensation when the local distributor has performed unsatisfactorily.

Distribution Contracts: Obstacle or Opportunity, 11 N.Y. Int'l L. Rev. 1 (1998).

§ 4.2

1. It is not only developing nations which attempt to regulate the distribution of goods. Agency law in general affects such distribution and may be quite different and quite complex in other countries. See for example the law of Mexico, as discussed by Ignacio Gomez Palacio in Symposium, Establishing an Agency or Distributorship in Mexico, 4 U.S.-Mexico L. J. 72 (1996); or the law of Italy, as discussed in G. LaVilla & M. Caetella, The Italian Law of Agency and Distributorship Agreements (1977); or the law of Germany, as discussed in F. Staubach, The German Law of Agency and Distributorship (1977); or the law of

France, as discussed in J. Guyenot, The French Law of Agency and Distributorship Agreements (1976).

2. For example, the "Statement of Motives" of the Puerto Rican law applicable to distribution agreements states:

The Commonwealth of Puerto Rico cannot remain indifferent to the growing number of cases in which domestic and foreign enterprises, without just cause, eliminate their dealers, concessionaries [sic], or agents, as soon as these have created a favorable market and without taking into account their legitimate interests.

Quoted in Fornaris v. Ridge Tool Co., 423 F.2d 563, 565 (1st Cir.1970), *reversed* 400 U.S. 41, 91 S.Ct. 156, 27 L.Ed.2d 174 (1970).

§ 4.3 Effect of Changing Export Laws in the United States

A company dealing abroad through a foreign agent or distributor must be aware also of U.S. laws that may affect the distribution of goods abroad. The United States has exerted with some frequency extraterritorial authority by way of laws that affect U.S. businesses doing business abroad. These rules have usually been motivated by political goals (e.g., the removal of a dictator from office), and have no direct relation to either the U.S. seller or the foreign buyer. The political goals may be strongly rejected by the foreign agent's or distributor's government. These rules may have significant impact. The U.S. party may be prohibited from exporting to the foreign nation, which leaves the foreign agent or distributor without products to sell, and therefor in jeopardy of serious financial losses. The U.S. exporter may be in breach of a distribution agreement if it is unable to fulfill orders. The agreement should have an excuse for nonperformance clause which covers such an event. Which U.S. laws may have such an effect are not easily identified. Foreign policy has caused various U.S. presidents to use export controls as a response to foreign political actions, such as in 1982 when the United States limited the transfer of goods to Europe that were destined for use in the construction of a gas pipeline from the then-USSR.

§ 4.4 Choice of Form

The two forms most frequently used to distribute products abroad are (1) an independent foreign agent, or (2) an independent foreign distributor. Usually the choice is made by the U.S. exporter. But in doing business abroad, especially in developing nations, the choice of the form of distribution may not be the prerogative of the U.S. company. The choice may be mandated by local law. Furthermore, there may be quite different choices.

§ 4.5 Independent Foreign Agent

An independent foreign agent, who may be called a "sales representative" or "commission agent", is a person in the foreign nation who does not take title to the goods and who usually is paid in some combination of salary and commissions. This person does not bear the risk that the buyer might not pay. That risk remains with the U.S. supplier. The foreign agent usually does not have the power to bind the U.S. supplier,[1] but may be considered to have

---

§ 4.5

1. The word "agent" in foreign sales use may mean more than or less than the legal meaning of the word in U.S. law. United States agency law usually involves a consensual relationship where the agent has certain power to bind the principal. But that power may be limited

implied power to do so, and certainly may be given express authority to do so.[2] The independent agent obtains orders for sales abroad
and sends those orders to the U.S. seller. Thus, there usually is no
need for the agent to store goods in its nation.

The use of an independent foreign agent tends to create more
legal problems for the company selling abroad than would the use
of an independent foreign distributor. The agent, who may be called
a distributor without regard to the legal distinction between the
two, thus receives the greater focus of this chapter. Agency law may
differ substantially in a foreign nation, especially nations with civil
law tradition systems.[3] Furthermore, the laws of some nations blur
the distinction between the two forms of distribution, and thus use
of one form may not achieve the protection sought.

One important factor to understand is that the law of the
agent's nation may regulate the nature of the agency relationship
substantially more than is the practice in the United States. Civil
law commercial codes may provide extensive detail regarding the
agency relationship. Additionally, these rules may be mandatory
and not subject to alteration by contract. Foreign law may outline
different forms of agency with quite carefully delineated powers.
The powers may or may not be in conflict with what the U.S. party
might wish to arrange by contract. It is essential to understand the
forms of agency which exist, and their respective roles, in any
nation where the use of an agent is contemplated.

§ 4.6   Independent Foreign Distributor

An independent foreign distributor, in contrast to the usual
kind of agent, buys the company's products and resells them
through the foreign distributor's network.[1] The foreign distributor,
in taking title to the goods, consequently assumes such risk as not
being able to resell them. The distributor is the one whom the
purchaser must pay, and therefore the distributor is at risk for
nonpayment. Because the distributor is essentially buying the goods
for resale, it must find storage for the goods prior to final sale and
distribution.

---

or removed altogether. It is important to
realize that the general meaning of
"agent" may differ from country-to-
country, which emphasizes the need for
contractual clarity in defining the relationship.

2. Agents are frequently used for
sales to foreign governments, where contracts are often for very substantial
amounts.

3. The civil law tends not to recognize the responsibility of a principal for
acts of an undisclosed agent.

§ 4.6

1. The distributor, in contrast to an
agent, thus has to make a financial commitment, and consequently is usually a
larger and more formal entity than a
foreign direct agent.

Unlike the uncertainty existing in the case of the independent agent, the independent distributor does not have power to bind the supplier. That is because the distributor buys the goods for resale, rather than entering into contracts on behalf of the principal as in the case of an agent. Of course the distributor might additionally have power to act as an agent for goods it does not obtain as a distributor. In such case, the issue of the power to bind the principal is present.

If an independent foreign distributor is chosen, the language in the distribution agreement should be as clear as possible in noting the principal-principal as opposed to principal-agent relationship. Language used when establishing an independent contractor relationship may be useful in establishing an independent distributor relationship.

§ 4.7   Laws Protecting Agents and Distributors

Countries often have special laws which govern the distribution agreement between their nationals *as agents* and foreign businesses.[1] This is in addition to the domestic agency laws that apply to any agency relationship.[2] There are far fewer countries that have laws governing agreements between foreign business and local independent *distributors*.[3] However, the distinction between the two is sometimes blurred, but nevertheless remains an important distinction. For example, antitrust laws in some nations are enforced against distributorships but not against agencies. This may affect assigning a distributor exclusive selling rights.[4] Of course, when the agency form is that of an *employee* agent rather than an *independent* agent, the agency may clearly be exclusive. Some developing nations do not even recognize the distinction between their nationals as agents and their nationals as distributors, and govern both in one law.[5] But to be fair, what the U.S. supplier calls its foreign distributor is less important than being able to determine and formalize the characteristics of the relationship. If the characteristics suggest an agency, the host nation is likely to

§ 4.7

1. Some nations mandate the use of local agents for the distribution of foreign goods. This tends to be the rule in developing nations, and includes much of the middle-East.

2. Appointment of an agent, particularly with power to bind the principal, may constitute doing business and subject the foreign business to jurisdiction and taxation.

3. An example is Belgium, one of the very few nations in the European Union to have legislation regulating distributorship agreements.

4. Chile allows an exclusive agency but not an exclusive distributorship.

5. This is true of many Latin American nations, but not of Brazil. Developing nations in other areas of the world, i.e., Africa and Asia, are more inclined to follow the general rule of regulating agents but not distributors.

consider the person as an agent. The same is true for distributors.[6]

Where foreign laws applicable to distribution agreements have been enacted, they are likely to be designed to (1) benefit local agents/distributors, especially in the area of termination; (2) restrict (or prohibit) the use of agents/distributors, essentially to protect the public from unfair agents/distributors; or (3) apply domestic *labor* law to the distribution agreement, in addition to any special laws applicable to the distribution agreement. How these laws influence the distribution agreement is discussed below in the separate sections covering various distribution agreement provisions.

Civil law tradition nations tend to be more likely to restrict freedom to contract than common law tradition nations. Laws regulating agency and distributorship agreements in civil law countries may be separate and specific, or may be found in the civil or commercial codes.[7] Developing nations are most likely to have special laws affecting the agency/distributorship relationships.

Even where host nation law mandates use of local agents or distributors, it may be possible to use a local business entity as the agent even though the agency is majority owned by the U.S. company. But many host nations which mandate the use of local distributors additionally require at least majority host-nation ownership of artificial entities (i.e., local corporations).[8]

§ 4.8   Aspects of Control

The sale of goods abroad to an independent distributor usually means the seller relinquishes control over such aspects as where the product may be resold and the price.[1] Loss of control over

6. Carolita L. Oliveros, International Distribution Issues: Contract Materials, ALI–ABA 19th Annual Advanced Course, March 18–20, 2004, SJ075 ALI–ABA 777 (an extensive coverage of some 44 nations); Michael Dean, International Distribution Overview of Relevant Distribution Laws: Europe, SJ075 ALA–ABA 245 (2004); E. Charles Routh, Agency, Representation and Distribution Agreements in Asia, SJ078 ALI–ABA 397 (2004); Dennis Campbell & Louis Lafili, Distributorships, Agency and Franchising in an International Arena: Europe, The United States, Japan and Latin America (1990).

7. Distribution of products within the European Union involves national laws and EU law. Common or civil law tradition-based national laws, depending on the EU member state involved, are likely to govern the nature of the rela-

tionship, such as the powers of persons designated as agents. European Union law is likely to govern such aspects of distribution as territorial restrictions and price maintenance.

8. Many nonmarket economies mandated local sales through a government state trading organization (STO) or foreign trade organization (FTO), a requirement which has substantially been abandoned along with many other trade restrictions. But remnants of state involvement persist in some nations in transition from nonmarket to market economies, and there remain a number of nations still firmly committed to nonmarket policies.

§ 4.8

1. The U.S. export-control laws govern reexport and may place a burden on the U.S. exporter to assure that the

establishing the price may be enough to cause the seller to adopt an independent *agency* form of distribution, which may but does not assure ability to set the resale price.[2] Because title remains in the U.S. seller until the goods are sold in the foreign country by the agent, the seller should be able to set the price.[3] The agent only has authority to find a buyer, but not set the terms of the sale. That remains the function of the seller.

A further element of control is the ability to appoint sub-agents or sub-distributors without the approval of the principal. An agent normally has no such authority, but an independent distributor will be able to hire and fire at will, unless there is some agreement regarding whom the distributor uses to deal with the foreign company's products.

If the agent is actually *employed* by the U.S. company, there is no question about the issue of control.[4] But when an agent is an employee, the employer becomes subject to labor laws of the host nation. That may create such problem as being unable to terminate the employee at will, at least without making a substantial severance payment.[5] It is not only developing nations' laws which grant greater rights to employees. The industrialized nations of Europe treat labor in a very different way than does the United States.[6] The U.S. company therefore may prefer to use an independent agent who is carefully kept independent of the company, and linked to the company as an agent by contract rather than by employment. Control will be contractually designated, but host-nation laws are likely to affect the contract. Some foreign nations do not distinguish carefully between an agent who is an employee and an agent who is not.[7] Where the distinction is made, and statutory protection is not given to the independent agent, the choice of an agent who is not an employee will usually be the preference of the U.S. company.

---

goods are not reexported to certain destinations. See infra Chapter 16.

2. In many developing nations the government establishes price controls.

3. That may be a wholesale price and the U.S. seller may not be able to further control the retail price.

4. An employee-agent may be on commissions alone or a salary plus commissions. The independent agent is more likely to be solely on commissions.

5. Many developing nations have special agency/distributor laws because their labor laws do not apply to these relationships. Agents and distributors are thought to be able to bargain better than employees, but when that has proven not to be the case, it has been "remedied" by either enacting a special agent/distributor law, or by applying the labor laws to the agency/distributorship relationships.

6. See Clyde W. Summers, Worker Participation in the U.S. and West Germany: A Comparative Study from an American Perspective, 28 Am.J.Comp.L. 367 (1980).

7. Italy grants to self-employed agents nearly all the rights granted to employee agents. See A.H. Puelinck & H.A. Tielemans, The Termination of Agency and Distributorship Agreements: A Comparative Survey, 3 Nw.J.Int'l L. & Bus. 452, 456 (1981).

The fact that some laws may not acknowledge the distinction between an employee-agent and an independent agent does not mean that all laws will overlook that distinction. For example, the tax laws will generally accept the distinction, and thus income from sales by an employee-agent is income to the corporation, but not necessarily so in the case of an independent agent. Furthermore, a foreign nation may exert extraterritorial jurisdiction over the U.S. company which *employs* an agent in the foreign nation, but decline to do so when the U.S. company uses an *independent* agent in the foreign nation.

Choice of an independent distributor rather than an employee-agent may create antitrust problems. The distributorship agreement becomes an agreement between two different and independent entities, and provisions such as an exclusive distributorship arrangement may conflict with local laws. The European Union imposes rules on exclusive distributorships which differ from those in the United States. Prohibitions on selling outside an exclusive territory, such as one of the EU nations, will not be recognized, although one may be able to mandate that the distributor *solicit* business exclusively in the applicable territory. European Union rules also address and prohibit resale price maintenance and minimum prices.

Antitrust concerns similar to those involving exclusive distributorship arrangements may exist where the foreign independent distributor is prohibited from selling competing goods. This may create a problem with U.S. law in that it may foreclose other U.S. companies from entering the foreign market. It may conflict with host nation antitrust principles as well.

Use of an employee-agent may avoid these issues, because there is only a single entity involved and the control over the employee is obviously greater than over an independent agent. When there is any question regarding restraints on competition, the antitrust laws of both the United States and the foreign host nation must be consulted. The most developed antitrust law outside the United States is in the European Union. While many of the EU antitrust concepts parallel those in the United States, there are many significant differences, mandating an understanding of both.

The ability to control the agent by means of the distribution agreement may depend upon whether the agent is in a country with a common law tradition or a country with a civil law tradition. Common law tradition nations tend to allow greater freedom to contractually create the full terms of the agreement, including termination provisions. Civil law tradition nations, contrastingly, more often include statutory restraints on freedom to contract, especially with regard to the right to terminate and rights created upon termination. Whether the nation has a common law or civil law tradition system, laws are dynamic and the attitude toward distribution agreements may change. Laws governing the transfer of technology and intellectual property have very substantially changed in the past two decades in developing nations, several of which realized that restrictive laws diminished the amount and quality of technology offered. Knowing foreign law usually means associating with local counsel. No one distributing products in many countries can be an expert in all the host-nation laws—the use of local counsel is critical.

§ 4.9　Areas to Consider

There are many areas of control which should be considered, not only those mentioned above dealing with setting prices and hiring sub-agents. Where control exists, the agent/distributor may be limited in many actions. That may include the ability to incur expenses on behalf of the principal, or to carry competing lines of products. Such actions as making corrupt payments to foreign officials may be closely monitored where control exists. There is an obvious benefit to having control. But with control may come responsibility for actions of the agent appearing to a third party to be within the agent's authority. Such responsibility may be avoided by using a distributor who is fully independent of the company. But where the host foreign nation does not recognize this independence, the worst of both worlds may exist. The company may have no control over the agent/distributor, but may be held responsible for much of the conduct of the agent/distributor.

*

Chapter 5

COUNTERTRADE AGREEMENTS

Table of Sections

§ 5.1   Countertrade in the Post World War II Years

Countertrade is barter in modern clothes. It developed rapidly as a form of doing business with the USSR and Eastern European nations in the 1970s and 1980s, before major economic and political reforms tended to diminish its emphasis as a means of doing business.[1] Although some nations announced that as part of their reforms from nonmarket to market economies they would discontinue the use of countertrade, some of the same reasons that previously existed which encouraged the use of countertrade, i.e., shortage of hard currency, have persisted and have caused these nations to continue its use. Increased countertrade has been part of the dynamic growth in world trade since World War II, and part of the changing conditions in trading patterns.[2]

The use of countertrade has not depended on the size of the transaction. It has been used for some very large natural resource

---

§ 5.1

1. The Council for Mutual Economic Aid (CMEA or COMECON), the socialist bloc's modest attempt at economic integration, had requirements that member-nation sellers had to obtain contracts to sell their goods before they could import Western goods.

2. It has been estimated as accounting for 8B10 percent of world trade. Group of Thirty (G30) Report (Mar. 1986). A United States International Trade Commission report in 1985 suggested that 5.6 percent of U.S. exports involved countertrade.

ventures in the former Soviet Union, and for many relatively small transactions in Eastern European nations. The success that countertrade achieved in nonmarket economy nations caused it to spread; it has been used increasingly in transactions with developing nations.[3] Countertrade is not limited to nonmarket or developing nation trade, however. One form of countertrade, offsets (discussed below), is being used for many military equipment and large civilian aircraft sales to developed nations. It is thus no longer considered the "dark" side of international trade, but a legitimate form of doing business.

The above comments illustrate classifying the use of countertrade by the characteristics of a nation's economy, such as nonmarket economy nations, developing nations and developed or industrialized nations. The classification might also be based upon a product or service, such as aircraft. Countertrade has often been the only form of sales available where the goods or services were not of sufficiently high priority to gain import permission and consequent access to scarce hard currency. The exporter of sophisticated computer hardware usually has had little trouble in demanding traditional forms of documentary sales, cash in the form of some hard currency in return for the needed goods. But where the goods or services are of less priority for a nation's perceived development needs,[4] or where the goods or services are available from many sources, countertrade may be the only way to successfully market them.

§ 5.2 Why Engage in Countertrade?

Before one characterizes countertrade as any form of rightful heir to free trade, it must be acknowledged as a form of trade which is often an involuntary transaction. It consumes more time than a cash transaction. It gives the U.S. exporter products it may not want and cannot easily sell, sometimes because of poor quality. In view of such unattractive characteristics of countertrade, why do U.S. and other industrialized nations' companies engage in countertrade? In a great many cases not because they want to, but because it is the only way to trade or invest in the particular product or service. Additionally, it may be the way to gain a foothold in a market, to be positioned favorably for the time when countertrade is not mandatory and exchangeable currency is available.

3. It was largely the product of the debt crisis in the early 1980s, certainly as much so as the product of witnessing the success of countertrade by nonmarket economies.

4. This is especially true where there is a development plan which outlines what the nation's needs are for the next 5–10 years. If the products planned for export to such a country are not on the "list", they will be unlikely to be approved as a transaction involving scarce hard currency.

The U.S. company would almost always prefer to be paid in dollars or another hard currency. Those currencies are freely convertible. The reason for countertrade is often that the foreign party (or that party's nation) is short of convertible currency. It is easier to understand the complexities of countertrade when it is accepted that it is usually not the preferred method of trade, but does have some justifications that lead parties to agree to one form of countertrade or another.

One might use countertrade to avoid or evade taxation, but that is not a common characteristic of a professional, commercial transaction. It is rather more common between individuals who know each other, such as a person who has a hobby making concrete garden statuary and trades a fountain to a local restaurant for a dozen "free" dinners. Or the plumber who does some work on a lawyer's house in exchange for a will.[1] Tax avoidance was probably not an issue, but a consequence of not even thinking it might be necessary to include the value of each item received as income. These simple transactions constitute countertrade, but in its most simple formCbarter.

Countertrade as a form of international trade may be used to penetrate new markets which have been closed due to traditional trading relationships or patterns. Some persons have viewed countertrade as a necessary way of prying open formerly closed markets.[2] Purchasers often build good relations with suppliers and tend to avoid even listening about other available substitutes. It is commonplace in Japan especially, and often misunderstood in the United States as creating intentional trade barriers. Coerced or voluntary countertrade may be an effective way to create new markets for new products.[3]

Countertrade is not only intended to keep scarce hard currency within the nation that demands countertrade, but to create jobs as well. It thus is not only practiced by third world and nonmarket economies, but by many industrialized nations.[4] Selling military

§ 5.2

1. This is obviously more likely in a small town where people frequently "exchange" their work products, than in a large city. One may reasonably doubt that a large New York City law firm engages in such barter of its services.

2. Stanislaw J. Soltysinski, "Statement: In Defense of Countertrade," 5 J. Com. Bus. & Capital Market L. 341 (1983).

3. It is estimated that countertrade grew from about two percent of world trade in 1976 to something between five percent and 25 percent by the mid-

1980s. Philip Rowberg, Jr., Countertrade as a Quid Pro Quo for Host Government Approval of a Joint Venture, in David N. Goldsweig (ed.), Joint Venturing Abroad: A Case Study (ABA 1985). The movement towards market economies in Eastern Europe and former USSR countries has reduced countertrade because some of those nations consider countertrade a characteristic identified with the socialist, nonmarket form of economy they have rejected.

4. Australia, Belgium and Canada, for example. See Cedric Guyot, Countertrade Contracts in International Business, 20 Int'l Lawyer 921, 943 (1986).

equipment, or large aircraft, is very likely to involve some counter-trade as part of the sales agreement. This is a voluntary form of countertrade, part of the negotiating process to obtain a sale, and viewed as a legitimate part of fair trade, or trading on an "even playing field." Selling commercial aircraft from the United States to Japan is likely to involve manufacturing some of the aircraft parts in Japan. If the U.S. company does not agree to such countertrade, Airbus in Europe is likely to win the contract by agreeing to this form of countertrade.

The motivation and even government mandate or private inter-est decision to engage in countertrade will vary from country-to-country. Some Eastern European nations made countertrade man-datory, before 1988, but the trend is away from such restrictive use. Some nations use countertrade to attempt to maintain a general balance of trade in all industries, and others try to maintain a balance in each industrial sector (e.g., vehicles) or even each sepa-rate industry (e.g., trucks). Because countertrade tends to increase when a nation has a serious shortage of hard currency, the rules of the countertrade game are constantly changing. Participants enter and exit usually not according to any philosophical commitment to or rejection of countertrade, but because sales are best or only achieved by playing the countertrade game.

Because various forms of countertrade are often given different names, some definitions should be useful. They are not always carefully separated in use, but they help to illustrate how many variations of centuries-old "barter" modern commerce has been able to create.

§ 5.3 Barter

"Countertrade" has many faces. It is often nothing more than simple "barter," two parties exchanging goods, usually of similar value. Any difference in the values is normally paid in cash, but barter is often thought of as a transaction without cash, partly because the parties lack any currencies. It is actually the one form of countertrade that is usually accomplished without any cash involvement. As young people we probably all at one time engaged in barter, trading "things" with friends, perhaps stamps, or base-ball cards, or dolls, or marbles or Pokemon cards. We never thought of involving any money in the exchange. The reason for the exchange may well have been that we did not have any money, and thus added to our collections by disposing of items less desired or duplicated. That sounds remarkably like a modern countertrade transaction by a nation short of hard currency or lacking credit.

Barter may be on a much larger scale than exchanging marbles or one rifle for fifteen buffalo hides. Many commercial transactions, particularly with Eastern European countries in the 1970s and 1980s, were basically barter transactions. But countertrade has never been exclusively a characteristic of nonmarket nations. New Zealand has exchanged lamb for Iranian oil. A U.S. liquor company exported bourbon in exchange for bananas. The list of such examples is very long.

Barter agreements are not always simple, cash-less, single-document arrangements. They sometimes involve two separate documentary sales, often with letters of credit, and a linking or protocol agreement which includes provisions that make the transaction an exchange or barter transaction. But this tends to be more descriptive of a more complex form of barter, most likely *counterpurchase*.

§ 5.4 Counterpurchase

Counterpurchase occurs usually after one party, for example a company in the United States, finds a market for its goods in another, for example Poland. The U.S. company agrees to purchase Polish products of the same value as the U.S. company's proposed exports. The Polish goods are usually unrelated to the U.S. goods. It sounds like barter described above. But barter usually has two parties interested in each other's goods. In much counterpurchase, where it may be fairly called an involuntary transaction, one party would prefer to sell its goods for cash, but is forced into a countertrade agreement because of the currency shortage of the other nation. A company, whether Boeing or Airbus, selling commercial aircraft to Poland, would prefer to be paid in dollars or francs or pounds or deutschmarks. The company really does not want glassware, or canned hams, or coal. But if it wishes to sell the aircraft, it may have to accept the Polish products and arrange for their sale in the United States or some third nation.[1]

The counterpurchase agreement will provide for the date by which the seller must purchase the agreed amount of countertrade goods. Some nations require all agreements to be 100 percent counterpurchase, that is the seller must purchase as much as it sells. Such an arrangement means there will effectively be no net exchange of currency. But the nation demanding countertrade may even attempt to negotiate 150 percent countertrade, requiring that the foreign party essentially sell, on behalf of the nation demanding countertrade, some of its products and return hard currency for the

§ 5.4

1. Because it involves imports of the Polish products into the United States

or a third nation, tariffs and non-tariff barriers may have to be confronted.

50 percent excess. For example, a U.S. company sells a lathe valued at $10,000 to a Chilean company, and must take $15,000 in value in Chilean goods. But the U.S. company does not keep the $15,000 received for selling those goods, it must turn over to the Chilean company $5,000. The U.S. company has become little more than a sales agent for Chilean goods, at least with respect to the $5,000 worth of goods.

There is always concern that if the U.S. exporter purchases the foreign countertrade goods *before* selling its own goods, the foreign nation will use the hard currency obtained from such sale for some purpose other than to obtain the U.S. exporter's products. In such case it is wise for the U.S. company to demand the establishment of an escrow account in a third nation and have all the hard currency resulting from the U.S. purchase deposited in that account, to be used by the foreign nation only to buy specified products from the U.S. exporter.

Counterpurchase accounts for a considerable percentage of countertrade, perhaps as much as 50–60 percent. There are many potential problems, both with regard to locating products for countertrade in the foreign nation, establishing their value, drafting the agreement, and selling the products in the United States or a third nation. The countertrade or protocol agreement must be carefully drafted, although it is likely that some control of its terms will be maintained by the foreign nation, which may have laws or regulations governing such issues as the required percentage of counterpurchase, time limits for meeting such purchase commitment, and penalties for failure to meet the time limit.

One issue frequently involved in either common barter or the more sophisticated counterpurchase is setting a value for the goods. Returning to trading items as a child, if you were trying to trade an 1898 postage stamp, you might have said it was "worth" three 1904 stamps. But your friend may have disagreed, saying the 1904 stamps were rarer and at best the trade should be one for one. The same problem may occur in modern countertrade. In establishing the price you wish to receive for your lathe sold to the Chilean party, you may inflate the price above what would be the cash price so as to cover the "extra" costs attributable to countertrade. One of these costs is the uncertainty of the value of the products received from Chile. You may be asked to and accept Chilean wine as the countertrade products. But at what price will the wine sell in the United States—$6 or $12 a bottle? The Chilean company may argue the latter, but unless there is an established market for such wine in the United States, the price agreed per bottle is somewhat of a "rolling of the dice". One can understand why companies forced into countertrade may increase substantially the price of their goods in order to cover some very unknown costs of countertrade.[2]

§ 5.5   Compensation or Buyback

Compensation or buyback involves a relationship linking the seller's product and the countertrade goods.[1] The seller's "product" is sometimes equipment, or technology, or even an entire manufacturing plant. In return the seller receives products produced by the foreign purchaser with the equipment or technology, or in the manufacturing plant constructed by the seller. Obviously, it may take a long period of time to pay for the value of a plant by way of accepting products produced in that plant, and the agreement will be for a considerable duration. One of the most notable examples of buyback involved the Occidental Petroleum Company's sale to the USSR of an ammonia plant, paid for by taking part of the ammonia production once the plant was operating.

There is usually less concern about the disposition of *compensation* goods in contrast to *counterpurchase* goods. Counterpurchase may involve very different goods than what the U.S. company sold, i.e., airplanes for canned hams, or liquor for bananas. In compensation agreements, the goods are often products with which the seller is familiar, and possibly even sells in the regular course of its business. Thus, a U.S. automobile manufacturer might establish a plant in China, and take in exchange a percentage or fixed number of the production, which it in turn markets along with the production of its own U.S. plants.[2] An obvious concern in such case is to assure that the Chinese products meet quality standards of the U.S. company's other plants. Returning countertrade products is costly and has proven all too frequent in many countertrade arrangements with nonmarket and developing nations. At least in a compensation agreement, the seller may have some say over quality in the production of the goods. In a counterpurchase agreement, contrastingly, it will be necessary to carefully examine any prospective products to assure that they will be marketable in the United States or a third nation.

Compensation agreements are often for very large dollar amounts. A chemical plant may be constructed in return for many

2. Waide Warner, Jr., William Megevick, Emily Altman, Credit Agreements and Collateral Arrangements in International Infrastructure Projects, PLI 2000 Project Financing, PLI No. A0–003F, Mar. (2000)

§ 5.5

1. See Leo G.B. Welt, Unconventional Forms of Financing: Buyback/Compensation/Barter, 22 N.Y.U. J. Int'l L. & Pol. 461 (1990); Jerzy Rajski, Some Legal Aspects of International Compensation Trade, 35 Int'l & Comp.L.Q. 128 (1986).

2. The experience of producing the "Jeep" in the People's Republic of China is related in Jim Mann, Beijing Jeep (1989).

years of a percentage of the production. An automobile manufacturing plant may also require many automobiles over many years to pay for the cost of the plant. Counterpurchase agreements may be for large amounts, such as the sale of airplanes, but they are usually much smaller-value contracts than compensation agreements.

§ 5.6   Offsets

Sometimes used interchangeably to describe either counterpurchase or compensation forms of countertrade, an *offset* arrangement is technically quite different. It is frequently used in the aerospace industry, especially in the defense industry where there may be military alliances such as NATO. But it is also important for civilian aircraft sales. Offsets constitute an agreement by the foreign seller (e.g., Boeing or Airbus)to include as part of the sale in the foreign nation (e.g., China) the use of parts or services from local suppliers. It is really a local content requirement and is becoming increasingly more common.[1] The local supplier could be owned by the U.S. party (a foreign subsidiary), and might be established for that very purpose. Often a joint venture is established to provide the local production. The net result is that some of the production takes place in the foreign nation which is purchasing the item, expectantly at less cost to the nation's possibly limited supply of hard currency, and with an increase in local jobs.

The U.S. government has been sufficiently concerned that offset agreements have a damaging impact on the U.S. economy that Congress in 1984 amended the Defense Production Act to require annual reporting by the President on the impact of offsets on "defense preparedness, industrial competitiveness, employment, and trade."[2] The general view of the U.S. government is not favorable toward countertrade, yet it realizes that countertrade is often required for U.S. firms to be competitive. Curiously, it (actually the Department of Defense) has promoted the use of offsets for many defense-related items.

Offsets have been used and encouraged by such nations as Belgium and Canada for 20 years. Most firms in Western Europe, as well as Canada, Australia and New Zealand, use offsets for large military contracts. For example, Boeing in the United States agreed

---

§ 5.6

1. It might also involve regular counterpurchase, buying unrelated products and selling them in the home nation or a third nation.

2. 50 U.S.C.A. app. § 2099 (1986). Subsequent amendments have extended the reporting requirements. The reporting process and results of the report prepared in 1985 are discussed in Judith K. Cole, Evaluating Offset Agreements: Achieving a Balance of Advantages, 19 Law & Pol'y Int'l Bus. 765, 781 (1987).

with the United Kingdom to use a 130 percent offset in sales of military aircraft.[3]

The Feingold Amendment to the Foreign Relations Authorization Act in 1995 amended the Arms Export Control Act to require the President to certify to Congress whether an offset agreement involving certain high-value weapon sales abroad constitutes a government-to-government or a direct commercial sale.[4] U.S. contractors may not give incentive payments to U.S. persons to persuade them to buy goods or services from a foreign country which has an offset agreement with the contractor. The amendment arose from concern that Northrop offered more than $1 million to a customer of Harnischfeger Industries to encourage the customer to buy machinery from a Finnish company to help meet Northrup's offset obligations in a $3 billion sale of jet fighters to Finland. A Memorandum of Understanding (MOU) between Finland and the United States only discouraged offsets, it did not prohibit them.

Offsets are prohibited in the NAFTA agreement, but there is a major exception for defense procurement.[5]

§ 5.7 Switch Trading

Switch trading is less a form of countertrade than a procedure for clearing accounts among a number of transactions, or even among a number of nations. If a U.S. seller of airplanes to Brazil is unable to find sufficient Brazilian products to meet the counterpurchase percentage requirement in the contract, it may learn that Brazil is selling certain goods to Canada and has a surplus of Canadian dollars which the Brazilian government is willing to apply to the agreement. These Canadian dollars are called "clearing dollars." But Brazil may wish to retain all the Canadian-transaction hard currency for other uses, because it lacks scarce hard currencies of any denomination.

If the clearing transaction is with a nation with soft currency, it may be easier to work the switch. For example, if the Brazilian goods are sold in Argentina rather than Canada, Brazil may welcome the U.S. seller taking Argentine currency, since it is not acceptable in many international transactions (and may be available to the seller at a discounted price). The U.S. seller may be

---

3. Economist 89 (Dec. 20, 1986).

4. Current reporting requirements are in the Defense Production Act Amendments of 1992. Contractor reporting where involved in offset agreements exceeding $5 million for the sale of weapons systems or defense related items to foreign purchasers. 15 C.F.R. Part 701—"Reporting of Offsets Agree-

ments in Sales of Weapons Systems or Defense Related Items to Foreign Countries or Foreign Firms." See 59 FR 61796 (2 Dec. 1994).

5. See Richard J. Russin, Offsets in International Military Procurement, 24 Pub. Cont. L.J. 65 (1994).

willing to take the Argentine currency if it is buying products from Argentina, or commencing an investment there and needs some local currency.[1]

Companies usually turn to professional help for switch trading. There are a number of multinational companies which act as countertrade facilitators using computer technology. Usually based in developed nations, e.g., London or Vienna, these facilitators bear the risk, buying the product from the seller, paying for it with vouchers (which are exchangeable for products or services from the firm's clients), or sometimes cash plus vouchers. The services obtained might even be travel (accommodations) and advertising.[2] The persons who arrange these clearing transactions are called "switch traders". They obviously add an additional cost to the transaction. Indeed, countertrade has several "hidden" costs which may arise to take away or diminish an expected profit. One of those costs is the higher cost of negotiating a countertrade agreement than a simple single documentary sale. Such costs will be added to the selling price.

§ 5.8   Bilateral Clearing Accounts

Occasionally two nations will agree to purchase goods from each other in a determined amount. They are "clearing units" or an artificial use of a set currency, usually the dollar. The trade is designed to remain in balance. If it becomes out of balance the clearing units may be sold, often at a discount and often using a switch trader.

§ 5.9   Investment Commitment

In this form the seller agrees to invest a certain amount of money in the foreign country. The amount to be invested may be a percentage of the sales of the seller's products, or a fixed amount to be taken out of the proceeds of such sales in a fixed amount/percentage over a period of time. In some cases, companies invest the proceeds of their sales not because of any investment commitment, but because there is a shortage of hard currency in the foreign nation and the seller is essentially locked into leaving the proceeds of the sale of the goods in the country. An investment is often the most appropriate use of such funds.

§ 5.7

1. The Argentine adoption of the dollar as a dual currency will increase the acceptability of the Argentine peso in international transactions, including switch trading.

2. See G. Cassidy, Financing Strategies—Barter's Rebirth, East–West Commersant, Dec. 1, 1995.

§ 5.10   Future of Countertrade

Countertrade began to intensify in use a decade or two after World War II, mainly as the hard currency-short Eastern European nations increased trade with Western nations that were reluctant to buy the former nations' products. But countertrade quite rapidly spread to many other parts of the world, especially developing nations that were also short of hard currency. Latin American countertrade increased substantially in the early 1980s. Once free of Soviet domination, most of the Eastern European nations stated that they would reduce countertrade as part of their market economy oriented reforms, but that has proven to depend on these nations' ability to successfully market their products abroad.

Some countertrade may distort free or nearly free markets, partly because it is bilateral rather than multilateral trade.[1] Imports under a countertrade agreement may disadvantageously affect the market, and may cause unemployment and depressed prices. Because it is often difficult to identify a true price for the countertrade goods, it is hard to identify and measure dumping. Whatever distortions in free trade are attributed to countertrade, it is a method of international trading that sophisticated trading enterprises must learn and add to more common forms. The expertise in countertrade transactions has lagged behind the number of transactions. Experience and a long-term approach to countertrade are necessary ingredients to success. Some companies have suggested that it takes at least three years to show results from an in-house countertrade entity, and a General Electric spokesperson noted that GE had "nurtured" its trading capability over a 20 year period.[2] Countertrade is thus usually considered to be a service center in the same way as market research or finance, rather than a separate profit center.[3] However it is considered, company willingness to use countertrade may result in rewards for the additional effort.

Countertrade is here to stay. To be successful in countertrade arrangements, a company must learn how to accomplish some very complex negotiating, which cannot but help it in other trading as new, esoteric forms arise. Additionally, a company that has been willing to accept countertrade to gain entry to a market may be in a

§ 5.10

1. William D. Zeller, Countertrade, The GATT, and the Theory of the Second Best, 11 Hastings Int'l & Comp. L. Rev. 247 (1988).

2. Int'l Trade Rpt. 489 (Oct. 17, 1984). But in 1986 GE Trading announced that it was halting its countertrade program. Losses on large transactions caused several major countertraders to make similar announcements. But others, including Mitsui and Mitsubishi, were making announcements to increase countertrade.

3. The company may bill product divisions for the countertrade services when a sale is made.

very advantageous position when the nation becomes better off in accumulating hard currency required for direct cash purchases.[4]

4.   UNCITRAL Legal Guide on International Countertrade Transactions, U.N. Doc. A/CN.9/Ser.B/31 (1993).

Chapter 6

DOCUMENTARY LETTERS OF CREDIT

Table of Sections

§ 6.1   Introduction—The Transactional Problem

Unlike most domestic sales transactions, in a sale of goods across national borders the exporter-seller and importer-buyer may not have previously dealt with one another; or each may know nothing about the other, or the other's national legal system. The seller does not know: (1) whether the buyer is creditworthy or trustworthy; (2) whether information received on these subjects from the buyer's associates and bankers is reliable; (3) whether exchange controls will hinder movement of the payment funds (especially if payment is in "hard currency" from a "soft currency" country); (4) how great the exchange risk is if payment in buyer's currency is permitted; and (5) what delays may be involved in receiving unencumbered funds from buyer.

On the other hand, the buyer does not know: (1) whether the seller can be trusted to ship the goods if buyer prepays; (2) whether the goods shipped will be of the quantity and quality contracted for; (3) whether the goods will be shipped by an appropriate carrier and properly insured; (4) whether the goods may be damaged in transit;

(5) whether the seller will furnish to the buyer sufficient ownership documentation covering the goods to allow the buyer to claim them from the customs officials; (6) whether the seller will provide the documentation necessary to satisfy export control regulations and import customs and valuation regulations (e.g., country of origin certificates, health and other inspection certificates); and (7) what delays may be involved in receiving unencumbered possession and use of the goods in the buyer-importer's location.

Where the parties are strangers, these risks are significant, possibly overwhelming. Since they operate at a distance from each other, seller and buyer cannot concurrently exchange the goods for the payment funds *without the help of third parties*. The documentary sale, involving the use of a letter of credit, illustrates how these potentially large risks can be distributed to third parties who have special knowledge, can properly evaluate each risk assumed, and thereby can reduce the transaction risks to insignificance.

§ 6.2   The Documentary Sale Transaction

The third party intermediaries enlisted are banks (at least one in buyer's nation and usually a second one in seller's nation) and at least one carrier. Thus, the parties involved are: (1) a buyer, who is also presumably a "customer" of (2) a Buyer's Bank, (3) a seller, (4) a bank with an office in seller's nation (hereafter "Seller's Bank"), and (5) at least one carrier. Among them, these parties are able to take a large risk which is not subject to any firm evaluation, and divide it into several small, calculable risks, each of which is easily borne by one party. Thus, the documentary sale is an example that not all risk allocation is a "zero sum game," but may in fact create a "win-win" situation.

These parties will be related by a series of contracts—but not all of the parties to the transaction will be parties to each contract. The contracts include (A) the sale of goods contract between the buyer and the seller; (B) the bill of lading, a receipt and contract issued by the carrier; and (C) the letter of credit, a promise by Buyer's Bank (and, if confirmed, also by Seller's Bank) to pay seller under certain conditions concerning proof that seller has shipped the goods.

(A) The contract underlying the entire series of transactions is the contract for the sale of goods from buyer to seller. The buyer and the seller are parties to this contract, but the banks and the carrier are not parties. The seller is responsible to deliver the contracted quantity and quality of goods, and buyer is responsible for taking the goods and paying the stated price. (For conditions and further elaborations on this point, see the discussion of the

Convention on Contracts for the International Sale of Goods in Chapter 1.)

(B) In documentary sales, buyers and sellers are usually distant from each other, and the goods must be moved. Thus, an international carrier of the goods is usually employed, and either the seller or the buyer will make a contract with the carrier to transport the goods. (For our illustration, seller will make that contract). The seller (or, in the language of a contract of carriage, "shipper") makes a contract with carrier that the goods will be transported to the buyer's ("consignee's") location.

This second contract in our transaction will be expressed in the "bill of lading" issued by the carrier. Under the terms of the bill of lading contract, in return for payment of the freight charge, carrier promises to deliver the goods to either (1) the named "consignee" in a "straight" (or non-negotiable) bill of lading, or (2) the person in possession ("holder") of an "order" (or negotiable) bill of lading.[1] The order (negotiable) bill of lading should be used in the documentary sale (letter of credit transaction), so that the buyer is able to obtain delivery of goods *only if* buyer has physical possession of the bill of lading.[2] Such a bill of lading controls access to and delivery of the goods, so that the bill of lading is also a "document of title."

(C) Before the seller ("shipper") delivers the goods to the carrier, the seller wants assurance that payment will be forthcoming. A promise from the buyer may not be sufficient. Even a promise from a bank in the buyer's nation may not be sufficient, because the seller does not know them or know about them. Instead, the seller wants a promise from a bank known to it, and preferably in the seller's location.

What the seller wants is the third contract in our transaction— a confirmed, irrevocable letter of credit. A letter of credit is a contract—an undertaking (promise) by a bank (usually the Buyer's Bank) that it will pay to seller (or, "will honor drafts drawn on this bank by seller for") the amount of the contract price. The bank's promise is conditioned upon seller's presenting evidence that the goods have been shipped via carrier to arrive in buyer's port, along with any other documents required by the contract for the sale of goods. What would furnish such evidence? The bill of lading between the seller and the carrier, the second contract in our transaction, furnishes the evidence that the seller has shipped the goods.

Further, if it is a negotiable bill of lading, it also controls the right to obtain the goods from carrier. Thus, a negotiable bill of lading delivered by the seller to the Seller's Bank will assure the

---

§ 6.2

1. See § 3.3, supra.

2. See § 3.3, notes 2–4, supra.

Bank that: (1) the goods have been delivered to carrier, (2) they are destined for the buyer and not some third party, and (3) Bank can control the carrier's delivery of the goods to the buyer by simply retaining possession of the order bill of lading. In other words, when a bank pays seller, it receives from seller a "document of title" issued by carrier which gives the bank control of the carrier's delivery of the goods. The buyer cannot obtain possession of the goods from a carrier without physical possession of the bill of lading, so after the banks have paid the seller for that piece of paper, they can obtain payment (or assurances that the buyer will pay them) before the buyer receives the ability to obtain the goods from the carrier.

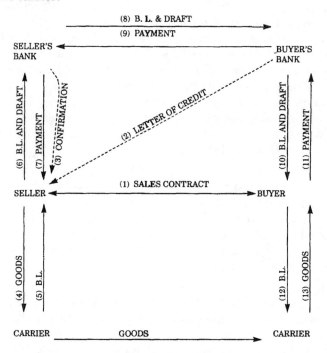

How does the international documentary sales transaction work? An international documentary sale is diagramed above. When the buyer and the seller are forming their contract for the sale of the goods, the seller will insist that the contract have both a "Price" term and a "Payment" term. For maximum protection, the seller will seek payment to be by "Confirmed, Irrevocable Letter of Credit," and should specify what documents are required with great detail. The reason for putting this payment term in the sales contract is that, since the buyer is expected to establish a letter of credit and "to pay against the documents," rather than after delivery and inspection of the goods themselves, that payment term must be bargained for and expressed in the sales contract. It will not normally be implied.[3]

What documents will be required? Usually, they include:

(1) a transport document, usually a negotiable bill of lading (showing transportation company's receipt of the goods to be shipped and the obligation to deliver them only to the holder of the document).[4]

(2) a commercial invoice (which sets out the terms of purchase such as grade and number of goods, price, etc.)

(3) an insurance document, such has a policy of marine insurance (if goods are to go by sea)[5]

(4) a certificate of inspection (issued by a commercial inspecting firm and confirming that the required number and type of goods are being shipped)[6]

(5) certificate of origin (relevant to the rules of origin used by customs personnel in importer's country for determining tariff assessments).[7]

Other documents may be required by the contract between the parties,[8] but it may not require the beneficiary to perform non-documentary conditions.[9]

If buyer agrees to a letter of credit payment term, buyer (or, in the language of the letter of credit, the "applicant"[10] or the "customer"[11] or an "account party") will contract with Buyer's Bank ("issuer" or "issuing bank") to issue a letter of credit ("credit") to seller ("beneficiary"). The letter of credit is a direct promise by the issuing bank that it will pay the contract price to the seller ("beneficiary"), on the condition that the seller presents to it the documents specified in the letter of credit (and also specified

---

3. See § 1.15, supra.

4. *See* ICC, Uniform Customs and Practices for Documentary Credits, art. 23 (ICC Publ. 500, 1993) (hereafter, the UCP).

In addition to the negotiable bill of lading, the UCP also permits the use of non-negotiable sea waybills (UCP art. 24), charts party bills of lading (UCP art. 25), multi modal transport documents (UCP art. 26), air transport documents (UCP art. 27), road, rail or inland waterway transport documents (UCP art. 28), courier and post receipts (UCP art. 29), and transport documents issued by freight forwarder.

5. *See* UCP arts. 34, 35.

6. *See* UCP arts. 20, 21. Inspection certificates may be issued either by an independent inspection company contracted for by either the buyer or the seller, or by a governmental entity.

7. *See* UCP arts. 20, 21.

8. *E.g.,* an export license or a health inspection certificate may be required to show that the goods are cleared for export.

9. UCP art. 13(c). The provision in Revised UCC § 5–108(g) is significantly more limited.

10. Uniform Customs Practices art. 2; Revised UCC § 5–102(a)(2).

11. UCC (1962) § 5–103(1)(g).

The UCP uses both terms in UCP art. 2, and uses "the Applicant" thereafter.

previously in the sales contract). The Buyer's Bank will be aware of the buyer's creditworthiness, and there will be a contract between the buyer and the Buyer's Bank (the "credit application agreement") which makes appropriate arrangements to obtain the funds from the buyer (through either immediate payment or future repayment of a loan). These arrangements will be made before the letter of credit is issued, for the Buyer's Bank is bound to the letter of credit terms after issuance if it is irrevocable.

If the seller requires an obligation of a bank in the seller's jurisdiction, the letter of credit must be confirmed by a Seller's Bank ("confirming bank").[12] The Buyer's Bank will forward its letter of credit to the seller through another bank, the Seller's Bank, which is usually a correspondent bank to the Buyer's Bank. By merely indicating "We confirm this credit," the Seller's Bank makes a direct promise to the seller that it will pay the contract price to the seller, if the seller presents the required documents to it. Confirmation of a letter of credit must be bargained for and specified in the sales contract.

If no confirmation of the credit is required by the sales contract, Buyer's Bank can forward the letter of credit through a "notifying bank" or an "advising bank"[13] which is near the seller. These banks act as the agents of the issuing bank and have only a duty to communicate the terms of the credit accurately. They are not obligated to the seller, but will take the documents and forward them to the Buyer's Bank for collection purposes only.

There are many other categories of banks which may be involved in the letters of credit transaction. Any bank which is authorized to pay against the documents is a "nominated bank",[14] whether it also undertakes an obligation to pay or not. "Nominated banks" are usually located in the same jurisdiction but may be located elsewhere. Thus, a "confirming bank" is a nominated bank which also undertakes to pay the credit. A bank which is a nominated bank and has given value for the documents is a "negotiating bank."[15] A "collecting bank" is one which acts as an agent of the beneficiary to take the documents for collection only, and to forward them to the issuer or confirmer.

Once the letter of credit is issued and confirmed, the seller will pack the goods and prepare a commercial invoice, and procure an insurance certificate (another form of contract) covering the goods during transit. If an inspection certificate is required, the goods will be made available to the inspector designated in the sales contract,

---

12. UCP art. 9; Revised UCC § 5–10 2(a)(4).

13. UCP art. 7; Revised UCC § 5–102(a)(1).

14. UCP art. 10(b)(i), (c)(i) Revised UCC § 5–102 (a)(11).

15. UCP art. 10(b)(ii).

and the inspecting firm will issue a certificate (another contract) stating that the goods conform to the description in the sales contract. The seller will also prepare the necessary documents for the customs officials in its nation (e.g., export license) and in the buyer's nation (certificate of origin). The seller then sends the goods to the carrier, which issues a negotiable bill of lading as a combination receipt and contract. This bill of lading will commonly be a negotiable document and require carrier to deliver the goods only "to seller or order"—i.e., only to seller, to such other persons as seller may designate by an appropriate endorsement.[16]

The Seller now has the complete set of documents needed, and takes these documents to the Seller's Bank, which (as a confirming bank) is obligated to pay the seller the contract price upon presentation of the documents. To obtain payment, the seller attaches a "draft"[17] to the documents; and in the letter of credit the banks have promised to honor such a draft. The draft (sometimes also called a "bill of exchange)" resembles a check written by the seller and drawn on the Seller's Bank or on the Buyer's Bank for the amount of the contract price.[18] A draft can be payable on demand ("at sight") in a cash sale, or payable at a later time (e.g. "30 days after sight") in a credit sale. If a "demand draft" is used, the bank will pay the amount immediately, usually by crediting the seller's account either in the Seller's Bank or in some other bank designated by the seller.

If the sales contract has been a sale on credit, the draft will be a "time draft" (e.g. "pay 30 days after sight") and is different from a check in that respect.[19] In that case, the issuer or confirming bank need not pay upon presentment of the draft and documents, but it must "accept"[20] the time draft when it is presented. This "acceptance" creates a promise, an obligation on the part of the issuer or confirming bank, a promise or undertaking that it will pay at the later time stated in the draft.[21] This promise through "acceptance of the draft" is directly enforceable against the party accepting by the "holder"[22] of the draft, and against a "holder in due course,"[23] deprives the acceptor of most of its potential defenses against payment.[24] Thus, if the confirming bank accepts a time draft and the buyer later becomes insolvent, the confirming bank which has accepted the draft must still pay the time draft when it matures. With the bank obligated on the time draft, the seller can immedi-

---

16. *See* discussion in Chapter 3, supra.

17. Revised UCC § 3–104(e).

18. Revised UCC § 3–104(f).

19. Revised UCC § 3–104(f).

20. Revised UCC § 3–401(a).

21. *Id.*

22. UCC § 1–201 (20); Revised UCC § 3–301

23. Revised UCC § 3–302.

24. Revised UCC §§ 3–305(b), 3–306.

ately raise funds by selling the paper on the strength of the bank's credit.

In return for the bank's payment, the seller will endorse both the draft and the negotiable bill of lading to the Seller's Bank and transfer the other documents to it. The Seller's Bank, in turn, will endorse and will forward the draft, with the required documents attached to the Buyer's Bank. It thus, presents the draft (with the accompanying documents) to the Buyer's Bank for payment.[25] The Buyer's Bank is obligated under the letter of credit to "honor" (accept) the draft and to reimburse the Seller's Bank if the documents attached to the draft are conforming. Since there is already a correspondent relationship between the two banks, the Buyer's Bank will credit the Seller's Bank's account with the amount of the draft. The Buyer's Bank then advises the buyer that the documents have arrived and that payment is due. Since the buyer and the Buyer's Bank usually have an established relationship, the usual course of events will be for the bank to be authorized to charge the amount of the draft to the buyer's bank account, and to forward the documents to the buyer. If the buyer has arranged for credit from the Buyer's Bank, the credit will be advanced when the draft and documents arrive. If there was not an established relationship between the buyer and its bank, the buyer would be required to pay (or to arrange sufficient credit for) the draft before the documents were released to it. As the draft and documents are forwarded from the seller to the Seller's Bank to the Buyer's Bank to the buyer, each of these parties will endorse the bill of lading to the next party.

The buyer, like the banks, must pay "against the documents" and not the goods themselves, which is why it is necessary to specify the terms of the documents in the original contract for the sale of goods, and then repeat those specifications precisely in the letter of credit. Once the buyer had paid, or arranged to pay, the Buyer's Bank, it will obtain possession of the bill of lading and only then will it be entitled to obtain the goods from carrier.

After it has obtained possession and endorsement of the bill of lading, the buyer uses the negotiable bill of lading to obtain the goods from the Carrier. Note that the buyer has effectively paid for the goods while they were at sea, long before their arrival. In fact, the buyer was bound to pay for the goods as soon as the draft and required documents were presented to the Seller's Bank. If the goods failed to arrive the buyer must look to its Insurance Certificate for protection and reimbursement.[26] When the goods arrive, carrier may not release them to the buyer unless it is in possession

---

25. Revised UCC § 3–501.

26. See discussion of CIF in Chapter 2, supra.

of the negotiable bill of lading, properly endorsed *to* the buyer.[27] Further, the terms of the bill of lading will prohibit the buyer from even inspecting the goods unless it has obtained physical possession of the bill of lading. Thus, until the banks are satisfied that they will be paid by the buyer, they can control the goods by controlling the bill of lading.

§ 6.3   Risk Allocation in the Letter of Credit Transaction—In General

Note the limited risks to each party. If the seller ships conforming goods, it has independent promises of payment from both the buyer and two banks. The banks' promises are enforceable despite assertions of non-conformity of the goods, so long as the documents conform. Seller's Bank never sees the goods, only the documents—so the bank inspects the documents rigorously to determine that they comply exactly with the requirements of the letter of credit, for the documents are its only protection. Substantial performance by seller is not acceptable.[1]

Thus, as a practical matter, the seller is at risk only if the Seller's Bank fails (and also the Buyer's Bank and the buyer), a risk it can probably evaluate. If the Seller's Bank unjustifiably refuses to perform its obligation, the seller has a cause of action in a local court against a "deep pockets defendant."

Even though the Seller's Bank is obligated to pay the seller on the documents, it is entitled to reimbursement from the Buyer's Bank and from the buyer, and practically is at risk only if the Buyer's Bank (and the buyer) fails or refuses to perform its obligations. Thus, a Seller's Bank has the credit risk concerning solvency of the Buyer's Bank, which it can evaluate better than either the buyer or the seller, and concerning breach of contract, which, since it has multiple level relationships with Buyer's Bank, it is in a better position to induce compliance than the other parties. Thus, when the seller ships and procures conforming documents, there is a risk of nonpayment only if both Buyer's Bank and Seller's Bank fail.

The Buyer's Bank is at risk only if the buyer fails or refuses to perform. If the buyer cannot pay (becomes insolvent) or will not (wrongfully rejects the goods), the Buyer's Bank must still pay the seller against conforming documents. The Buyer's Bank has protec-

---

27. See discussion in Chapter 3, supra.

§ 6.3

1. UCP art. 13(a). For further discussion of this issue, see text at § 6.6, notes 7–17, infra.

tion from the bill of lading, including possible resale of the goods, but it is also in a particularly good position to investigate and to evaluate the risk of the buyer's insolvency, and to either obtain funds from the buyer when issuing the letter of credit or sue the buyer for breach of contract if there is a wrongful refusal to pay. Further, the Buyer's Bank had an opportunity to evaluate all of these risks before issuing the letter of credit, and it could adjust its price (fee or interest rate) to compensate for any increased risk.

On the other hand, for its payment of the price, the buyer has a document from the carrier entitling it to delivery of the goods, an insurance certificate protecting the buyer against casualty loss and perhaps an inspection certificate warranting that the goods conform to the sale contract. In other words, the buyer should receive what it bargained for—delivery of conforming goods or insurance proceeds sufficient to cover any loss.

One large risk has been reduced to several smaller ones, and each smaller risk placed on a party which can fairly evaluate it. The lack of substantial risk in the vast bulk of these transactions can be seen by looking at the usual bank charges for this service.

§ 6.4   The Governing Rules

The law relating to letters of credit developed before World War I principally in England, and thereafter by courts in the United States.[1] In the United States, the governing law is usually the applicable state's version of Article 5 of the Uniform Commercial Code. However, most of UCC Article 5 is not mandatory law, and therefore most Article 5 provisions defer to the contract terms of the parties as expressed in the contract.[2]

UCC Article 5 had recently been revised. The Revised Article 5 was adopted by the Uniform Commissioners and the American Law Institute in 1995, and has been enacted by 47 state legislatures, including, after a long delay, the state of New York.[3] In this chapter there will be references to both versions of the UCC, which will distinguish between the original UCC Article 5[4] (hereafter the 1962 version) and the Revised UCC Article 5.[5]

The International Chamber of Commerce (I.C.C.) has developed and published the Uniform Customs and Practices for Documentary Credits (the UCP), which is incorporated by reference in

---

§ 6.4

1. See J. Dolan, The Law of Letters of Credit (rev. ed. 1999) at §§ 3.01–3.04.

2. For a list of the few provisions in Revised UCC Article 5 which are not open to variant by agreement of the parties, see Rev. UCC § 5–103(c).

3. See   http://www.nccusl.org/ uniformact_factsheets/uniformacts-fs-ucca5.htm.

4. E.g., UCC § 5–102 (1962).

5. E.g., Rev. UCC § 5–102.

most international letters of credit. The UCP constitutes a rather detailed manual of operations for banks, but they are a restatement of "custom" in the industry, and they do not purport to be law. They are incorporated as an express statement of contract terms and banking trade usage, and the UCP contract terms furnish the rules which usually determine the actions of the parties.

The I.C.C. published the original version of the UCP in 1933, and has published a revision of the UCP about every ten years. The most recent version of the UCP is the 1993 Revision (I.C.C. Publ. No. 500).[6] The rules set forth in the 1993 version are relatively similar to those of prior versions, but there are some differences.

According to the UCP, it is binding if "incorporated into the text of the Credit."[7] Thus, the UCP is applicable to any letter of credit which expressly incorporates the UCP into its terms. However, the UCP is silent as to implicit incorporation of its terms, such as by custom and usage. The language in the 1993 version of the UCP was amended supposedly to require express incorporation,[8] but it used neither the word "expressly," nor the word "only."

There is no need for a "choice of law" conflict between the UCC and the UCP. One is legislation, the other represents the agreed terms of the parties. Since most of the provisions in UCC Article 5 are not mandatory law,[9] the UCP provisions would prevail over the "gap-filler" provisions of UCC Article 5. The Revised UCC Article 5 provides that the UCP, if expressly chosen by the parties, prevails over all the non-mandatory UCC provisions.[10]

The primary difference between the UCC provisions and the UCP is that the UCC has provisions on fraud and on enjoining payment against documents where fraud or forgery exist,[11] and the UCP has none. Otherwise, their scope, coverage and substance are quite similar.[12] The absence of provisions on fraud and enjoining payment should be expected, however, in the drafting of a set of contract terms to be consented to by the parties. Thus, the UCP provisions will have more impact on the analysis of non-fraud issues, and the UCC Article 5 provisions will be used to resolve issues related to allegations of fraud. Therefore, this chapter will describe the UCP rules for all non-fraud issues, and the fraud

---

6. I.C.C. Uniform Customs and Practices for Documentary Credits (hereafter the UCP) (I.C.C. Publ. No. 500, 1993).

7. UCP art. 1.

8. Dolan, supra note 1, Unofficial Comment to UCP art. 1. However, UCC § 1–205(2) allows inclusion of a proven trade usage. As to whether UCC Article 5 allows consultation of custom, see Dolan, supra note 1, at § 4.07.

9. See note 2, supra.

10. Revised UCC § 5–116(c).

11. Revised UCC § 5–109; UCC § 5–114 (1962).

12. See, e.g., Gustavus, Letter of Credit Compliance under Revised UCC Article 5 and UCP 500, 114 Banking L.J. 55 (1997); Comment, Letters of Credit: A Comparison of Article 5 of the UCP, 41 Loy. L. Rev. 735 (1996).

issues will be covered in the next chapter[13] on standby letters of credit. Even though there is one significant documentary credit case that involves fraud issues, most of the fraud cases involve standby letters of credit, and are analyzed under the UCC. Thus, the UCC provisions on fraud will be described in the next chapter.

§ 6.5 Applicable Law

One provision which is noticeably absent from the UCP is a term which selects the law applicable to the transaction in the absence of an express choice of law by the parties. The UCC both allows the parties to select the law of any jurisdiction as the law applicable to the letter of credit,[1] and also provides "gap-filler" provisions if the parties do not make such a choice.[2] If no choice is made, "the liability" of each party is governed by the law of the jurisdiction where it is "located."[3] Presumably, the rights of each party are not governed by the law where it is located, but are co-extensive with the liabilities of each of the other parties. However, the Revised UCC provisions concern only the liabilities of each of the issuer, the nominated person and the advisor, and does not include the applicant. Apparently, the choice of law for the applicant is left to the contract between the applicant and the issuer, or to general conflict doctrines.

The UCP establishes four categories of banks in the letter of credit transaction: an issuing bank an advising bank, a confirming bank, and a nominated bank, and they are located in different jurisdictions. An issuing bank is usually located in the buyer's jurisdiction and promises to honor drafts on itself, if the documents stated in the letter of credit (conforming documents) are presented to it.[4] An advising bank is usually located in the seller's jurisdiction and advises the beneficiary (usually the seller) of the documentary credit, but makes no promise to pay against documents.[5] It is obligated to take "reasonable care" to check the authenticity of the credit before advising, but is not otherwise obligated. A confirming bank is also usually located in seller's jurisdiction and receives the

---

13. See § 7.10, infra.

§ 6.5

1. Revised UCC § 5–116(a). The general choice of law provisions in UCC Article 1 allow choice of the law of any state or nation if the "transaction bears a reasonable relation to" that state or nation. UCC § 1–105(1).

2. Revised UCC § 5–116(b). The general choice of law provisions in UCC Article 1 provide that the court in a state which has enacted the UCC shall use its own law (its own state's version of the UCC) if the transaction bears an

"appropriate relation" to the forum state. UCC § 1–105(1), last sentence.

3. Revised UCC § 5–116(b). A person is "located" at the address stated on the person's undertaking, from which the undertaking was issued.

4. UCP art. 9(a). The UCC equivalent is the "issuer," Rev. UCC § 5–102(a)(9).

5. UCP art. 7. The UCC equivalent is the "advisor," Rev. UCC§ 5–102(a)(1).

credit from the issuing bank and adds its own promise to honor drafts presented to it if accompanied by conforming documents.[6] A nominated bank is often located in Seller's jurisdiction, but may be in a third jurisdiction, and is designated by the issuing bank to pay or negotiate the drafts which accompany the required documents.[7] It may, or may not, be a confirming bank, but a confirming bank is a nominated bank. Outside the United States, the courts will not use the UCC provisions, but will use their own choice of law doctrines. They will uphold a choice of law clause stated in the letter of credit contract,[8] but a choice of law clause stated in the underlying sale contract is not necessarily applicable to the letter of credit contract. If there is no choice of law clause, the traditional doctrine is that the applicable law is the law of the place of performance of the contract, or, in the letter of credit context, the place of payment of the credit against presentation of the documents. Thus, where a straight credit is issued (only the issuer may pay), the law of the issuer's location is applicable.[9] Where there is a confirmed letter of credit, the law of the confirming bank is applicable, because that is the jurisdiction where payment of the beneficiary is made against presentation of the documents.[10]

The traditional doctrine applies the same law to all segments of the credit transaction. The Revised Article 5 doctrine will change this approach, however, and apply different rules to the obligations of the issuer and of the confirmer. This, in turn, could lead to the use of different standards for determining strict compliance, or different rules for transmission errors or effectiveness of communication. The law which governed the liability of the nominated bank in a "freely negotiated credit"[11] could not be determined until after the seller had presented the credit to that bank for honor.

§ 6.6   Basic Legal Principles

There are two basic principles of the letter of credit rules promulgated by the UCP (and also of UCC Article 5). One is that the banks' obligations under the letter of credit are independent of

---

6. UCP art. 9(b). The UCC equivalent is the "confirmer," Rev. UCC § 5–102(a)(4).

7. UCP art. 10(b)(i), (c). The UCC equivalent is the "nominated person," Rev. UCC § 5–102(a)(ii).

Under the UCP, if the letter of credit does not state expressly that honor is available only with the issuing band, either the credit must designate a specific bank that is authorized to honor it or it becomes "freely negotiable credit" and any bank is authorized to honor it.

8. Bonny v. Society of Lloyd's, 3 F.3d 156 (7th Cir.1993), *cert. denied,* 510 U.S. 1113, 114 S.Ct. 1057, 127 L.Ed.2d 378 (1994).

9. Sinotani Pacific Pte Ltd. v. Agricultural Bank of China, 1999–4 Singapore L. R. 34 (C.A. 1999).

10. Power Curber Int'l Ltd. v. National Bank of Kuwait, [1981] 3 All Eng. Rep. 607 (CA), noted (1981) J. Bus. Law 384; Offshore Int'l SA v. Banco Cent. SA, [1976] 2 Lloyd's Rep. 402 (QB).

11. See note 7.

the buyer's and seller's obligations under the contract for the sale of goods—the Independence Principle.[1] The promises of an issuing bank or a confirming bank are not subject to claims or defense by the applicant (Buyer) that the beneficiary (Seller) has not performed its obligations under the sales contract.[2] The issuing and conforming banks have made their own undertakings to the beneficiary that the banks will perform if the beneficiary (Seller) performs its obligations under the letter of credit contract, regardless of whether those obligations fulfill the sales contract obligations or not. Although the bank's obligations may not be subject to contract claims and defenses, they may still be subject to claims by the applicant (Buyer) relating to fraud by the beneficiary (Seller),[3] as will be discussed below.[4] As has been discussed previously,[5] the UCP has no provisions concerning fraud, and therefore such issues must be analyzed under UCC Article 5, where U.S. law is applicable.

The second principle is that banks deal only with documents, and not with the goods or any issues concerning performance of the sale contract.[6] However, since the banks pay the beneficiary (Seller) against the documents, and never see the goods, banks insist on "perfect tender" and "strict compliance" with all documentary conditions.[7] The primary document for describing the goods in a documentary sale transaction is the commercial invoice. The description in the commercial invoice must be specific and must "correspond with the description in the credit;" descriptions in all other documents can be general and need only be "consistent" with the description in the credit.[8] Thus, where a credit called for "100% acrylic yarn" and the invoice merely stated "imported acrylic yarn," the credit was not satisfied, even though the packing list stated "100% acrylic yarn."[9] The archetypical case of the strict

---

§ 6.6

1. UCP art. 3; Newport Indus. NA v. Berliner Handels Und Frankfurter Bank, 923 F.Supp. 31 (S.D.N.Y.1996).

2. UCP art. 3(a); Banca Del Sempione v. Provident Bank, 160 F.3d 992 (4th Cir.1998).

3. Rev. UCC § 5–109, UCC (1962) § 5–114.

4. See § 7.10, infra.

5. See supra § 6.4, at note 15.

6. UCP art. 4.

7. UCP art. 13(a). Buckley, The 1993 Revision of the UCP, 28 Geo. Wash. J. Int'l and Econ. 256 (1994), raises the issue of whether the language added in the 1993 revisions referring to "international standard banking practice" loosens the "strict compliance" doctrine, and concludes that it does not, because of the reference to "as reflected in these Articles."

A "substantial performance standard under several First Circuit cases appears to be no longer viable. Flagship Cruises, Ltd. v. New England Merchants Nat. Bank, 569 F.2d 699 (1st Cir.1978); Banco Espanol de Credito v. State Street Bank and Trust, 385 F.2d 230 (1st Cir. 1967), cert. denied, 390 U.S. 1013, 88 S.Ct. 1263, 20 L.Ed.2d 163 (1968). See Rev. UCC § 5–108 and Comment.

8. UCP art. 37(c).

9. Courtaulds North America, Inc. v. North Carolina Nat. Bank, 528 F.2d 802 (4th Cir.1975).

compliance doctrine was an English court's determination that "machine shelled groundnut kernels" was not the same description as "Coromandel groundnuts," even though it was agreed that the same goods were described by either label. Bankers could not be expected to know that, or to find it out.[10]

Many of the cases which litigate issues concerning the strict conformity of documents seem to revolve around discrepancies in transportation terms. Express conditions in the credit that loading, presentment or other acts must be performed by a certain time will be strictly enforced.[11] So also, a discrepancy in the location of shipment or delivery will fail to comply with the terms of a credit.[12] A credit calling for "Full Set Clean on board ocean bills of lading" is not satisfied by a tender of "truckers bills of lading," even though evidence was presented that the bills of lading were in customary Mexican form and that Mexican truckers did not specify on the bill of lading that the goods were "on board."[13] Nor is the "Full Set Clean on Board Bills of Lading" requirement satisfied by air waybills, even though air delivery may be preferable.[14] Discrepancies which seem not to warrant rejection include technically invalid clauses in bills of lading which limit the carrier's liability.[15] There is authority that questions concerning strict compliance are issues of law, and not issues of fact for a jury.[16]

Recent cases often involve typographical errors. When the letter of credit mistakenly identified the beneficiary as Sung Jin Electronics, while the documents were correctly addressed to Sung Jun Electronics, the banks were allowed to refuse payment.[17] But this decision has been criticized by practicing lawyers as being "too

10. J.H. Rayner & Co. Ltd. v. Hambros Bank Ltd. [1943] 1 K.B. 37 (Court of Appeal).

11. Voest–Alpine Int'l Corp. v. Chase Manhattan Bank, NA, 545 F.Supp. 301 (S.D.N.Y.1982), *aff'd in part, rev'd in part* 707 F.2d 680 (2d Cir. 1983).

12. Bank of Nova Scotia v. Angelica–Whitewear Ltd., 36 Dom. L.R. 4th 161 (Can. 1987); Bucci Imports, Ltd. v. Chase Bank Int'l, 132 A.D.2d 641, 518 N.Y.S.2d 15 (1987).

In a pre-UCC case, the seller-shipper did not prepay the freight charges on a CIF contract, but instead credited the freight charges against the amount of the invoice price, and then submitted the resulting documents to the issuing bank. The issuing bank rejected the documents, and refused to pay the draft accompanying the documents, as non-conforming. It argued that the documents did not strictly comply with CIF terms. However, in Dixon, Irmaos & Cia, Ltda v. Chase Nat. Bank, 144 F.2d 759 (2d Cir.1944), the court held that the documents were conforming because of "ancient usage" which permitted shippers to take such action.

13. Marine Midland Grace Trust Co. of N.Y. v. Banco Del Pais, S.A., 261 F.Supp. 884 (S.D.N.Y.1966).

14. Board of Trade v. Swiss Credit Bank, 597 F.2d 146 (9th Cir.1979).

15. British IMEX Indus., Ltd. v. Midland Bank, Ltd., [1958] 1 All Eng. Rep. 264.

16. Siderius, Inc. v. Wallace Co., 583 S.W.2d 852 (Tex.Civ.App.1979).

17. Hanil Bank v. Pt. Bank Negara Indonesia (Persero), 41 U.C.C. Rep. Serv.2d 618 (S.D.N.Y.2000).

narrow."[18] A line of American cases which seemed to permit payment upon substantial performance by the beneficiary, has now been rejected by the Revised Article 5.[19]

Recent UCP cases have involved substitutes for original documents. In *Western Int'l Forest Products v. Shinhan Bank*,[20] the letter of credit required the presentation of an original of an inspection certificate along with other documents. The designated inspector executed an inspection certificate and faxed it to the seller. The seller stamped the faxed copy "original" and sent it to the freight forwarder. When the documents were presented to the issuer, it refused payment, and the court upheld its action. Only the inspector could authenticate a copy. In another case, the letter of credit required the presentation of the original letter of credit and a promissory note. The beneficiary presented copies of both, an indemnity, and an affidavit that the originals were lost. The bank refused payment, and the court upheld that action.[21]

Not all discrepancies are permit the banks to refuse payment, however. In *Automation Source Corp. v. Korea Exchange Bank*,[22] the issuing bank detected two discrepancies. First, the shipping documents listed two "notifying parties," while the letter of credit required that the shipping documents instruct the consignee to notify the applicant. Second, two of the packages in the shipping documents listed identical contents, but had different weights. The court noted that the second notify party had been added at the request of the applicant and rejected any claim that listing an extra notify party created an ambiguity; but the court remanded the case for a factual determination as to whether any banking custom existed on duties to deliver documents to such parties. The court held that, since the letter of credit did not refer to the weight of the shipment, any discrepancy in weights would relate to the sales contract; and, under the "independence principle" be irrelevant to the issuer's obligation under its letter of credit contract.

§ 6.7 Wrongful Dishonor of a Credit

If the issuing bank or the confirming bank dishonors the credit, and refuse to pay when the documents are presented, the dishonor may be rightful or wrongful. If there truly are discrepancies between the specifications in the credit and the documents

---

18. See Barnes and Byrne, Survey: Letters of Credit: The 2000 Cases, 56 Bus.Law.1805, 1808 (2001).

19. See Revised UCC § 5–108(a) and Comment 1.

20. 860 F.Supp. 151 (S.D.N.Y.1994).

21. Brul v. MidAmerican Bank and Trust Co., 820 F.Supp. 1311, 22 U.C.C.

Rep.Serv. 2d 1125 (D.Kan.1993). UCC (1962) § 5–113 permitted issuers to take indemnities, but did not require them to do so. Rev. UCC Article 5 has no such provisions.

22. 249 A.D.2d 1, 670 N.Y.S.2d 847, 37 U.C.C. Rep.Serv.2d 372 (App.Div. 1998).

actually presented (and they are not waived),[1] the banks are entitled to dishonor, although they must follow the notice procedures specified in the UCP to protect themselves.[2] If the procedures are correctly followed, there is no liability of anyone on the credit, and no successful litigation on the credit[3] should ensue. For example, in *Western International Forest Products*, supra,[4] the issuer properly dishonored under the "strict compliance" principle, the beneficiary (seller) sued the issuing bank—and lost. Most of the cases involving rightful dishonor involve litigation over the timeliness and effectiveness of the notice of dishonor to prior parties.

If the issuer dishonors a presentation of documents which do comply strictly to the letter of credit, that is a wrongful dishonor. It is also a breach of one or more contracts. First, it is a breach of the letter of credit contract, for which the beneficiary will have a cause of action. Second, it may be a breach of the credit application agreement between the applicant and the issuer for which the applicant may have a cause of action. The former is governed by statute the letter is not. The UCP has no provisions on the subject.

The Revised Article 5 gives the beneficiary of a letter of credit whose presentation was wrongfully dishonored a cause of action against the issuer.[5] In addition it establishes the amount of damages which the aggrieved beneficiary may claim as "the amount of money that is the subject of the dishonor."[6] This amount does not necessarily equate to the actual damages suffered by the beneficiary. The beneficiary has no obligation to mitigate damages, but if it does actually avoid part of the loss, the recovery is reduced by the amount of the loss avoided. In addition, the aggrieved beneficiary can recover incidental damages and interest, but not consequential damages.

If the issuer wrongfully dishonors a presentation, the applicant may also be damaged. The most common harm is damage to the applicant's reputation in the trade, and an unwillingness of suppliers to accept subsequent letters of credit from the applicant. Prior to the revisions of UCC Article 5, it was usually held that the applicant was not actually a party to the letter of credit, so that it could not bring an action on the letter of credit itself for wrongful

---

§ 6.7

1. UCP art. 14 (c). See further discussion at § 6.10, notes 8–11, infra.

2. See generally UCP art. 14. For further discussion see § 6.10, infra.

3. There may well, however, be successful litigation between the buyer and the seller for breach of the sale of goods contract. See UCC article 2.

4. Supra, § 6.6, note 17.

5. Rev. UCC § 5–111 (a). The provision in the original version was UCC § 5–115(1)(1962).

6. *Id.* Under the 1962 version, however, the damages measurement provision produced a recovery closer to actual damages.

dishonor of the credit.[7] Instead, the applicant's right to sue the issuer for wrongful dishonor would arise out of the credit application agreement, and would be analyzed under ordinary contract law. It would also depend upon the terms of the credit application agreement, which might or might not include a clause disclaiming liability of the issues for wrongful dishonor.[8]

That analytical approach may be pre-empted under the revisions to UCC Article 5. Under Revised UCC Article 5, the applicant is given a statutory cause of action against the issuer for wrongful dishonor of the credit.[9] This cause of action would arise out of the statute, not the agreement, and would be analyzed according to the statutory terms, not the terms of the agreement. The most important statutory term regulating this cause of action is that the applicant can never recover consequential damages, even if foreseeable.[10] Thus, applicant's recovery for the most common form of harm—damage to reputation—would seem to be foreclosed in the statutory action. However, the contract cause of action under the credit application agreement may survive the enactment of the statutory cause of action, because the Official Comments state that "this section does not bar recovery ... for breach ... of common law duties outside of this article."[11]

The Comments do pose one circumstance in which the statutory action by the applicant is expected to be successful. Where the applicant has back-to-back credits, the wrongful dishonor of the documents under the first credit prevents the applicant from properly performing its obligations as beneficiary under the second credit. The Official Comments indicate that recovery of damages to the applicant from the issuer of the first credit should be expected in such a situation.[12]

§ 6.8   Wrongful Honor of the Credit

The issuing or confirming bank may honor the credit, paying the beneficiary or accepting a time draft when the documents are presented and this honor may be rightful or wrongful. If there are no discrepancies between the specifications in the credit (or they are waived)[1] and the documents actually presented, the banks are obligated to honor the presentation, and are entitled to reimbursement from the applicant. After the letter of credit is honored, the beneficiary has received payment or the acceptance of its time

---

7. Interchemicals Co. v. Bank of Credit, 222 A.D.2d 273, 635 N.Y.S.2d 194 (App.Div.1995).

8. *Id.* In *Interchemicals*, the application agreement did include such a waiver.

9. Rev. UCC § 5–111 (b).

10. *Id.*

11. Rev. UCC § 5–111, Comment 4.

12. Rev. UCC § 5–111, Comment 2.

§ 6.8

1. See discussion in § 6.9, infra.

draft,[2] so its claims should be satisfied and no litigation on the credit should ensue.

After a letter of credit has been honored, the issuer will seek reimbursement from the applicant under the credit application agreement. Alternatively, if that is not available, the issuer can seek reimbursement under banking custom or applicable law.[3] If the documents are conforming, so that the banks rightfully honored the beneficiary's presentation, the applicant has no defense to the issuer's reimbursement claim. The issuer has performed its contractual obligation to the applicant and is entitled to counterperformance. If the issuer granted credit to the applicant, the issuer has consciously taken the risk that the applicant would be unable to pay, and should have made provision for that possibility through taking collateral, obtaining a third party's guarantee, or seeking pre-payment.

On the other hand, if the documents have discrepancies and the issuer honors the beneficiary's presentation, that is a wrongful honor. The issuer may still seek reimbursement from the applicant, arguing that it has a right to such reimbursement even if it paid against documents that did not strictly comply with the letter of credit. The issuing bank may even debit the applicant's account with the bank, and compel the applicant to litigate to seek an order to re-credit that account.[4] There is a split of opinion as to whether the issuer is entitled to be reimbursed for a wrongful honor.[5]

The division of opinion arises from the difference between the letter of credit contract and the credit application agreement. The former is governed by statute, the latter is not. the standards for breach of each type of contract may be different.[6] Before either the UCC or the UCP, the law was relatively clear. A wrongful honor was a bar to recovery from the applicant by the issuer.[7]

The UCP has no provisions directly addressing the subject, although two UCP Articles can be used to formulate the various conflicting arguments. One argument is that, although the beneficiary is held to a "strict compliance" standard under the letter of credit,[8] the issuing bank is held to a lesser standard, because its

---

2. See discussion in § 6.2, supra.

3. See, e.g., Rev. UCC § 5–108(i).

4. Oei v. Citibank N.A., 957 F.Supp. 492 (S.D.N.Y 1997).

5. See Dolan, supra § 6.4, note 1 at § 9.03.

6. Id.

7. Anglo–South Am. Trust Co. v. Uhe, 261 N.Y. 150, 184 N.E. 741 (1933); Equitable Trust Co. v. Dawson Partners, Ltd., 27 Lloyd's Rep. 49 (H.L. 1927), H.

Harfield, Bank Credits and Acceptances, 105–108 (5th ed. 1974). Cf., Bank of New York and Trust Co. v. Atterbury Bros., 226 App.Div. 117, 234 N.Y.S. 442 (1929) (proper person paid under variant of specified name); Bank of Montreal v. Recknagel, 109 N.Y. 482, 17 N.E. 217 (1888) (non-material variation excused).

8. See discussion supra, § 6.6 at notes 7–19.

liability arises under the credit application agreement, not the letter of credit. This argument finds some support in UCP Article 13(a), which fixes a standard of examination for banks that only requires them to use "reasonable care, to ascertain whether or not [the documents] appear, on their face, to be in compliance ... "[9] They argue that "reasonable care" and "appearance" language, when applied to ordinary contracts, connotes only a substantial performance standard.

The contrary position draws support from the construction of UCP Article 14, which equates the examinations of nominated banks, confirming banks and issuers, and then applies the same standards to each.[10] There seems to be agreement that nominated banks and confirming banks must meet a strict compliance standard, and that, for those banks, the "reasonable care" and "appearance" language applies to the examination process, not to the standard of compliance.[11]

The Revised UCC Article 5 also has no provisions directly addressing the issue. The applicant is not given (or denied) a cause of action for wrongful honor.[12] The obligation of the issuer, that it "shall dishonor a presentation that does not appear [on its face strictly] to comply"[13] is made clear, but the UCC standard is ambiguous. The UCC ambiguity has many of the same dimensions as the similar ambiguity in the UCP, but the "appearance" must be one of strict compliance. These statutory duties can probably be modified by "agreement otherwise," so interpretation of the credit application agreement may be more important than interpretation of either the UCC or the UCP. Such agreements may include issuer disclaimers of liability for wrongful honor as well as wrongful dishonor.[14]

The cases are split, with a majority favoring no reimbursement from the applicant to the issuer after the issuer has wrongfully honored the presentation,[15] but in many of these cases the pronouncement is dictum.[16] The latter group of cases more often turns

9.   UCP art. 13(a).

10.   UCP art. 14(a).

11.   Bank of Cochin Ltd. v. Manufacturers Hanover Trust Co., 612 F.Supp. 1533 (S.D.N.Y.1985), aff'd 808 F.2d 209 (2d Cir.1986).

12.   Note that Rev. UCC § 5–111(b) applies only to cases of wrongful dishonor.

13.   Rev. UCC § 5–108(a), (e).

14.   See Interchemicals, § 6.7, note 7, supra.

15.   Oei v. Citibank, N.A., 957 F.Supp. 492 (S.D.N.Y.1997); Pioneer

Bank and Trust Co. v. Seiko Sporting Goods USA Co., 184 Ill.App.3d 783, 132 Ill.Dec. 886, 540 N.E.2d 808 (1989); Gulf So. Bank and Trust Co. v. Holden, 562 So.2d 1132 (La.App.1990). Contra: Transamerica Delaval Inc. v. Citibank, 545 F.Supp. 200 (S.D.N.Y.1982); and case cited in notes 17, 18, infra.

16.   Bank of Nova Scotia v. Agelica–Whitewear Ltd., 36 Dom. Rep. 4th 161 (Can.1987); Computer Place Services Pte Ltd. v. Malayan Bank Bhd, 1996–3 Singapore L.R.287 (High Ct. 1996); Philadelphia Gear Corp. v. Central Bank, 717 F.2d 230 (5th Cir.1983); Interna-

on the effectiveness, or lack thereof, of notices and other process requirements between the parties. The cases which apply a standard of less than strict compliance for the issuer to obtain reimbursement after wrongful honor involve a failure of the issuer to certify documents before forwarding them to the applicant[17] and a change of status by an employee designated to sign for a corporation—but the correct party did sign.[18]

If the issuer debits the applicant's account, the applicant may sue the issuer to have the account recredited.[19] If the applicant cannot, or does not wish to, sue the issuer, it probably does not have a cause of action against the confirming bank. The applicant is not a party to the letter of credit, has no contractual relationship with the confirming bank, and therefore lacks the necessary privity of contract to sue.[20]

If the issuer has wrongfully honored the beneficiary's presentation, and cannot obtain reimbursement from the applicant, it may seek to recover from the beneficiary. It may seek to recover directly from the beneficiary on a breach of warranty, or indirectly as an assignee or subrogee of the applicant's rights. The UCC provides that the beneficiary gives a warranty to the issuer that there is no fraud or forgery of the documents, but that warranty is not so broad as to cover all discrepancies in the documents, or even simple breach of contract.[21] The beneficiary also gives a warranty to the applicant but it is different in substance. The beneficiary warrants to the applicant that the documents do not violate the sales agreement.[22] The difference between these warranties is to promote finality to the letter of credit transaction, so that litigation between parties to the letter of credit transaction does not continue over obligations on the sales transaction, after the letter of credit is paid.[23] Except in New York, and other states with the same non-uniform amendment, incorporation of the UCP by the parties should not limit the availability of the UCC warranties.[24]

tional Leather Distributors, Inc. v. Chase Manhattan Bank, N.A., 464 F.Supp. 1197 (S.D.N.Y.1979), *aff'd* 607 F.2d 996 (2d Cir.1979).

17. Morgan Guaranty Trust Co. v. Vend Technologies, Inc., 100 A.D.2d 782, 474 N.Y.S.2d 67 (1984).

18. First National Bank v. Carmouche, 504 So.2d 1153 (La.Ct.App.), *rev'd on other gnds.* 515 So.2d 785 (La. 1987).

19. Oei, supra note 16.

20. Dulien Steel Products, Inc. v. Bankers Trust Co., 298 F.2d 836 (2d

Cir.1962); United States v. Foster Wheeler Corp., 639 F.Supp. 1266 (S.D.N.Y.1986).

21. Rev. UCC § 5–110(a)(1). See Mennen v. J.P. Morgan and Co., 91 N.Y.2d 13, 666 N.Y.S.2d 975, 689 N.E.2d 869 (1997).

22. Rev. UCC § 5–110(a)(2).

23. Rev. UCC § 5–110; Comment 2.

24. Chase Manhattan Bank v. Am–Tak Furniture Importers, Inc., 269 A.D.2d 882, 706 N.Y.S.2d 297 (App.Div. 2000).

§ 6.9   Examination   of   the   Documents   for Discrepancies

Discrepancies in tendered documents are an everyday occurrence. The Preface to the 1993 version of the UCP states that some surveys find that fifty percent of documents presented are rejected for discrepancies.[1] There is also expert testimony in one case stating that discrepancies are discovered in nearly one half of all documentary transactions.[2] Other commentary and cases indicate between one half and two thirds of all such presentations contain at least one discrepancy.[3] That rate of error should not be surprising if one understands that the presentation may consist of 967 pages of documents.[4] However, it is clear that the "strict compliance" standard itself causes problems.

Under the UCP, "banks must examine all documents . . . with reasonable care, to ascertain whether or not they appear, on their face, to be in compliance . . ." and "Compliance . . . shall be determined by international standard banking practice as reflected in these Articles."[5] According to the draftsmen, the reference to "international banking practice" was added to the 1993 version of the UCP in order to prevent "sharp, dishonest or negligent" use of strict compliance standards, and therefore to add some flexibility to the previous standards. But, since the "international . . . practice" must be "as reflected in these Article," it is difficult to be certain whether any change is intended at all, since no other UCP provision deals with the issue.[6] Further, there may be no "international standard banking practices," since practices in London are different from those in developing countries. Thus, the prior "strict compliance" standard, with all its rejections of documents, is likely to continue.

When documents are tendered to an issuing or a confirming bank (or a nominated bank acting for them), it has two duties. One is to examine the documents to determine whether they conform to the terms of the letter of credit.[7] The second is to act upon any discrepancies found.[8]

The examination must be, not only thorough, but also quick. If the bank does discover discrepancies, it may reject the documents without consulting its customer, the applicant (Buyer). However, in

§ 6.9

1. UCP, Preface

2. Banker's Trust Co. v. State Bank of India, [1991] 1 Lloyd's Rep. 587, affirmed [1991] 2 Lloyd's Rep. 443 (C.A.).

3. Buckley, The 1993 Revision of the UCP, 28 Geo. Wash. J. Int'l Law and Econ. 256 (1994).

4. Banker's Trust Co., supra note 2.

5. UCP art. 13(a).

6. Buckley, supra note 3.

7. UCP art. 13(a).

8. See § 6.10, infra.

many situations, the discrepancies may be trivial or typographical, and the applicant-buyer may want the payment made, and the goods delivered, despite the discrepancy. Thus, the UCP allows, but does not require, the bank to consult the applicant, its customer, for a waiver of the discrepancies it has discovered.[9] That provision does not permit the bank to seek help from the applicant to find further discrepancies.[10] About 90% of the time that they are consulted by the issuing bank, applicants will in fact waive the discrepancies discovered by the bank.[11] Thus, the system continues to work despite possible rejection of the documents in half the cases, because the non-bank parties (Buyer and Seller) want the transaction to be completed despite the technical difficulties imposed by the banking system.

The UCP gives the bank a "reasonable time, not to exceed seven banking days ... to determine whether to take up or refuse the documents."[12] This does not mean that all banks have seven days to examine the documents. Instead, banks have a "reasonable time" with an outside fixed time limit. As will be discussed in the next section,[13] the length of a reasonable time will vary with the amount and complexity of the documents, whether the defects are curable within the life of the credit, whether consultation with the applicant is required to seek a waivers of discrepancies, and whether any discrepancies are found.

However, if the bank discovers no discrepancies, so that there is no need for consultation with the applicant, the reasonable time for examination may be very short. For example, in one reported case, the employees of the issuing bank were able to examine 967 pages of documents twice in the period of two and a half days.[14] If the bank decides to accept the documents, it must honor the accompanying draft, and remit any proceeds to the beneficiary.[15]

§ 6.10 Notification of Discrepancies

On the other hand, if the bank discovers discrepancies, it must act to notify the person presenting the documents. It is under these circumstances that the "reasonable time" and the "seven banking days" limits may generate time pressures. This is due to the number of different actions which usually must be squeezed into the relevant time period. First, the bank must examine the document for discrepancies, as was discussed in the preceding section.

---

9. UCP art. 14(a).

10. So held in Banker's Trust Co., supra note 2, and E & H Partners v. Broadway Nat. Bank, 39 F.Supp.2d 275 (S.D.N.Y.1998).

11. Buckley, supra note 3.

12. UCP art. 13(b).

13. See discussion § 6.10, notes 11–12 infra.

14. Banker's Trust Co., supra note 2.

15. UCP art. 14(a).

Second, if discrepancies are found, the bank is authorized by the UCP to "approach the Applicant for a waiver of the discrepancy."[1] Third, if discrepancies are found, the bank must prepare a notification of dishonor which specifies all, not merely some, of the discrepancies relied upon to dishonor the presentation.[2]

The seven-day deadline should not become a "reasonable time" in all transactions, especially in simple transactions where all the documents can be examined in an hour or two. If seven banking days did become the norm, a beneficiary would not know for three weeks whether the funds were firm or not in transactions involving a non-confirmed letter of credit with a local nominated bank. Current practice is much quicker than that.

The cases make it clear that "seven banking days" is not a safe harbor provision. The bank has only a "reasonable time," and that may be significantly less than seven days.[3] Delays of over seven banking days are almost always too long,[4] although there are cases in which longer delays have been permitted under special circumstances.[5] Several cases have held that the reasonableness of any delay is an issue of fact for the jury or other trier of fact,[6] but this has been criticized.[7]

If the bank discovers discrepancies, as it will in half of the presentations,[8] it is authorized to contact the applicant, describe the discrepancies, and ask the applicant whether it chooses to waive the discrepancies or not.[9] Although the UCP does not require banks to do this, it may be expected by the applicant, the bank's customer, and therefore be commercially necessary, even if it is not legally necessary. It has been estimated that such waivers are granted in 90% of the transactions in which they are sought.[10] However, the bank must seek a waiver from the applicant based on the bank's

---

§ 6.10

1. UCP art 14(d)(i).

2. UCP art. 14(e).

3. Datapoint Corp. v. M and I Bank, 665 F.Supp. 722 (W.D.Wis.1987) But see Bombay Industries, Inc. v. Bank of New York, 27 U.C.C. Rep.Serv.2d 987 (Sup. Ct. 1995), *rev'd* 233 A.D.2d 146, 649 N.Y.S.2d 784 (App.Div.1996).

4. Bank of Cochin, Ltd. v. Manufacturers Hanover Trust Co., 808 F.2d 209 (2d Cir.1986); Kuntal, S.A. v. Bank of New York, 703 F.Supp. 312 (S.D.N.Y. 1989); Hamilton Bank, N.A. v. Kookmin Bank, 44 F.Supp.2d 653, 38 UCC Rep. Serv.2d 930 (S.D.N.Y.1999), *aff'd in part, vac'd in part* 345 F.3d 82 (2d Cir. 2001).

5. Alaska Textile Co., Inc. v. Chase Manhattan Bank, N.A. 982 F.2d 813 (2d Cir.1992).

6. Hellenic Republic v. Standard Chartered Bank, 244 A.D.2d 240, 664 N.Y.S.2d 434, 36 U.C.C. Rep.Serv.2d 502 (App.Div.1997); Rhode Island Hospital Trust Nat. Bank v. Eastern General Contractors, Inc., 674 A.2d 1227 (R.I. 1996) (Standby letters of credit).

7. Barnes and Byrne, Survey: Letters of Credit: 1998 Cases, 54 Bus. Law. 1885 (1999).

8. See authorities cited at § 6.9, notes 1–3, supra.

9. UCP art. 14(c).

10. See Buckley, § 6.9, note 3, supra.

examination of the documents, not assistance from the applicant in discovering discrepancies.[11]

Thus, the "seven banking days" deadline includes not only time to examine the documents presented, but also time to consult the bank's customer (Buyer) about waiving the discrepancies *and* notifying the party from whom the documents were received. It is the latter two requirements which can create difficulties. It is easier to deduce a "reasonable time" for clerks to examine documents than it is to determine such a time period for consulting with the customer, the applicant, and obtaining a response. The issuing bank may also wish to delay notification of prior parties about any discrepancies, because it must be very careful in making that notification.

If the bank discovers discrepancies, and the applicant does not waive the discrepancies, then the issuer should dishonor the presentation of the draft and documents.[12] If it does determine to dishonor the presentation, then it must act to notify the person who presented the documents both of the fact of dishonor and the reasons for dishonor. In its notice of dishonor, simply stating that the documents are defective ("discrepant docs") is not sufficient, the notice must also specify what the discrepancies are.[13] If it fails to notify, on a timely basis,[14] specifying the defects, it "shall be *precluded* from claiming that the documents are not in compliance with the terms and conditions of the Credit."[15] Most of the reported cases involve some dispute over whether the dishonoring bank has properly fulfilled its notification obligations or whether it is "precluded" to defend its dishonor on this basis.

In addition to specifying what the discrepancies are, the UCP also requires any bank which rejects a presentation of documents to "state all discrepancies" that it will rely upon in its notice to the person who presented the documents.[16] Failure to state all the discrepancies "precludes" the bank from claiming non-compliance due to any unstated discrepancies,[17] without the necessity of proving waiver or estoppel. Thus, banks which reject documents have only one chance to identify all the discrepancies on which they can ever rely. The rationale for this rule is to inform the beneficiary (Seller) of all the discrepancies at once, so that it can determine

---

11. See Banker's Trust Co., § 6.9, note 2, supra.

12. UCP art. 14(b) states that the bank "may" refuse to take-up the documents. However, if it does take them up, it may not be entitled to reimbursement. See § 6.8, supra, on Wrongful Honor.

13. See., e.g., Creaciones Con Idea, S.A. v. MashreqBank PSC, 51 F.Supp.2d 423, 38 UCC Rep.Serv.2d 946 (S.D.N.Y. 1999); Hamilton Bank, supra note 4.

14. See discussion at notes 11–12, supra.

15. UCP art. 14(e). (emphasis added).

16. UCP art. 14(d). See authorities cited at note 14, supra.

17. UCP art. 14(e).

whether they all can be cured and whether such cure is cost-effective. But the rule can also lead the issuing bank to delay notification for additional re-examinations to ensure that all defects are discovered.

In addition to provisions specifying time limits and specification of discrepancies of the notification of dishonor, the UCP also has provisions specifying the manner in which the notice must be communicated. The notice must be sent "by telecommunication" if possible;[18] use of a courier will not be proper.[19] However, a telephone call is subject to misinterpretation, or at least different interpretations, and is likely to produce litigation.[20]

The bank may not be required to follow this procedure if the credit has expired.[21] However, the simple fact that the beneficiary sent documents which were clearly discrepant, or that the beneficiary knew that they were discrepant, will not excuse the issuing bank from strict compliance with the notice requirements.[22] The price of not strictly following the UCP is "preclusion" from being able to raise the discrepancies at all in defense of the dishonor.

§ 6.11 The Documents in the Letter of Credit Transaction

Under the UCP, banks deal only in documents.[1] The parties may provide conditions upon the credit, as long as compliance with those conditions can be satisfied through documentary evidence. Thus, letters of credit must state precisely the documents, and the terms of the documents, against which payment is to be made.[2] It is the responsibility of the issuing bank and its customer, the applicant (Buyer), to ensure that satisfaction of each condition can be evidenced by documents. Otherwise, the condition need not be satisfied. The UCP provides that if a letter of credit contains any condition which is not satisfied by a document to be presented to evidence compliance with it, the bank can ignore that condition as though it were not written.[3]

The most important of the documents required by a letter of credit is the transportation document. Under prior versions of the UCP, this had referred to ocean bills of lading, evidencing an assumption that the goods would be carried by sea. However, there are new developments in the transport industry and new technolog-

---

18. UCP art. 14(d)(1).

19. Hamilton Bank, supra note 4.

20. Bombay Industries, Inc. v. Bank of New York, 32 U.C.C. Rep. Serv. 2d 1155 (N.Y.Sup.Ct.1997).

21. Todi Exports v. Amrav Sportswear, 1997 WL 61063 (S.D.N.Y.1997).

22. Hamilton Bank, supra note 4, Bombay Indus., supra note 21.

§ 6.11

1. UCP art. 4.

2. UCP art. 5(b).

3. UCP art. 13(c).

ical applications. Thus, the 1993 revision of the UCP provides separate articles for negotiable ocean bills of lading,[4] non-negotiable sea waybills,[5] charter party bills of lading,[6] multi-modal transport documents,[7] air transport documents,[8] road, rail or inland waterway transport documents,[9] and courier and post receipts.[10]

Under the UCP, an ocean bill of lading must name the port of loading, the port of discharge, the carrier and specify the parties which will be acceptable signatories.[11] Banks have no duty, however, to check the signature or initials accompanying an "on board" notation, absent a special arrangement with the bank.[12] The bill of lading may indicate an "intended vessel." In such cases, any "on board" notation must specify the vessel on which the goods have been loaded.[13] The medieval custom of issuing "a set" of bills of lading, and hoping one of them would arrive and be honored, is now disapproved; and the UCP seeks to have only a single original bill of lading issued as the norm.[14]

In multimodal transportation arrangements, the bill of lading is likely to be issued by a freight forwarder and not by a carrier. Thus, it does not name a carrier and it does not contain a receipt by the bailee (who is the carrier), which is the norm for documents of title.[15] However, if the letter of credit authorizes its use, such a transportation document may be used, if the freight forwarder issues it as either a multi-modal transport operator or an agent for a carrier.[16] Otherwise, such "house bills" of freight forwarders are not acceptable transport documents for letters of credit under the UCP.

If the original documents are lost or destroyed, a bank may accept copies of the documents as originals, if the copies have been signed.[17] Allowable signatures includes handwriting, facsimiles, perforated signatures, stamps, symbols, and other mechanical and electronic methods.[18] In the past, many civil law countries (e.g., Germany) have not accepted facsimile signatures and have ruled that *any* non-handwritten signature is invalid, but these rules are changing with the advent of e-commerce.[19]

---

4. UCP art. 23.

5. UCP art. 24.

6. UCP art. 25.

7. UCP art. 26.

8. UCP art. 27.

9. UCP art. 28.

10. UCP art. 29.

11. UCP art. 23. Compare the discussion in Chapter 3, supra.

12. UCP art. 23(a)(i).

13. UCP art. 23 (a)(ii).

14. UCp art. 23(a)(iv).

15. UCP art. 25(b).

16. UCP art. 26(a).

17. UCP art. 30.

18. UCP art. 20(b).

19. The provisions of the German Civil Code are now supplemented by the German Digital Signature Law. That law will be further amended to comply with the EU Electronic Signature Directive. For further discussion, see § 8.11, infra.

§ 6.12   Electronic Letters of Credit

Electronic communication has taken over some aspects of letters of credit practice, but not others. They dominate the issuance process in bank-to-bank communications, and are sometimes used by applicants to stimulate the issuance process. However, at this time they have not been able to create an entirely paperless transaction pattern for many reasons. First, the beneficiary still wants a piece of paper committing the banks to pay upon specified conditions. Second, electronic bills of lading still are not accepted in most trades as transferable documents of title for the reasons discussed in Chapter 3, supra. Thus, in the collection of the letter of credit, physical documents will be forwarded, while funds settlement may be electronic.

About three quarters of letter of credit communication between banks, for other banks' issuance, advice, confirmation or negotiation of letters of credit is paperless; and the communication is electronic. While bank-to-bank communication is electronic, bank-to-beneficiary (Seller) communication is still paper-based. Letter of credit issuers can now communicate directly with beneficiaries' computers, however, and use of this practice should be expected to increase. The UCP rules are now written in terms of "teletransmissions," rather than paper-based terminology, which facilitates the use of electronic practices.

Most bank-to-bank communication concerning letters of credit are routed through the dedicated lines of SWIFT (the Society for Worldwide Interstate Financial Telecommunications). SWIFT is a Belgian not-for-profit organization owned by banks as a cooperative venture for the transmission of financial transaction messages. A bank issuing a letter of credit communicates that message to the nearest SWIFT access point. The message is then routed on a dedicated data transmission line through SWIFT processors to the receiving bank. The bank which receives a SWIFT electronic letter of credit message does not have to send a reply stating that it accepts the request to advise or the authorization to negotiate or pay the letter of credit. It needs only to perform by advising, negotiating or paying, and it is entitled to reimbursement by the issuing bank. However, the SWIFT messages only transmit the letter of credit and their authorizations and requests. SWIFT messages do not effect the settlements of letters of credit or other transfers of funds between issuing banks and other banks. SWIFT is not a clearing house for bank settlements. Participating banks must use other arrangements (such as clearing houses) to settle their accounts and accomplish a transfer of funds.

It is now possible for an applicant (Buyer, in the documentary credit transaction) to draft a proposed electronic letter of credit.

The electronic proposed credit can then be transmitted to the issuing bank for it to issue over the SWIFT system. On the other end of the electronic communications, the beneficiary (Seller, in the documentary sale), who must be induced to part with value on the basis of the bank's promises, wants a "hard copy", a written letter of credit in the traditional form. The receiving bank therefore will convert the SWIFT electronic message into such a written, paper credit. However, the SWIFT message has been designed for bank-to-bank use, and not necessarily for use by beneficiaries, which creates some problems. First, it does not bear a signature in the traditional sense, even though it has been thoroughly authenticated within the computer-based transmission mechanisms. Thus, the beneficiary is entitled to doubt whether the sending bank is bound to the beneficiary to perform by the written credit derived from the SWIFT electronic message.

The issue is usually framed as: "Is the SWIFT message to be considered to be *the* operative credit instrument as far as the beneficiary is concerned?" The issue is of importance to beneficiaries not only in the original issuance of the credit, but also in the myriad of amendments to the credit which may follow. Under SWIFT rules, SWIFT users treat the electronic message as a binding obligation, and treat the authentication as the functional equivalent of a signature. However, the beneficiary is not a SWIFT user, and banking practice has been that a beneficiary can rely on an electronic message only after it has been issued in a paper-based format, properly signed or otherwise authenticated. The Revised UCC states that a letter of credit "may be issued in any form," including an electronic format,[1] but that provision does not necessarily answer the question as to whether the unsigned, paper-based transcription of a SWIFT message, generated by the recipient of that message, is the operative credit instrument and binds the issuing bank.

Under the UCP, whether an electronic message is the operative credit instrument or not depends upon the terminology in the message itself. The UCP provides that, if the electronic message states "full details to follow," or states that a mail confirmation will be the operative credit instrument, then the electronic message is not that instrument, and the subsequent message is.[2] However, another provision of the UCP states that other authenticated electronic messages to advise or amend credits *are* the operative credit instrument.[3] In the latter transactions, mail confirmations should not be sent, and are to have no effect if sent.

---

§ 6.12

1. Rev. UCC § 5–104.

2. UCP art. 11(a)(ii).

3. UCP art. 11(a)(i).

However, there is some doubt as to whether SWIFT-generated transcriptions are subject to the UCP. SWIFT internal rules provide that credits issued through its system are subject to the UCP, but the transcription into a hard copy may bear no reference to the UCP. The UCP states that the UCP provisions govern "where they are incorporated into the text of the credit."[4] That language is deemed, in some parts of the world, to require an express reference to the UCP in the message to the beneficiary.

The attempts to create an electronic bill of lading have been discussed earlier in Chapter 3. If successful, an electronic bill of lading could help facilitate the electronic letter of credit transaction. However, to date, while electronic bills of lading have been used successfully to replace the straight (non-negotiable) bill of lading, its use to replace the negotiable bill of lading has been met with skepticism. American bankers have been skeptical of their rights to any actual goods under electronic bills of lading issued under CMI (Comite Maritime International) Rules of BOLERO.

---

4. UCP art. 1.

Chapter 7

STANDBY LETTERS OF CREDIT

Table of Section

§ 7.1   Introduction

Just like traditional letters of credit, standby letters of credit, are mechanisms for allocating risks among parties in commercial transactions. By placing in the hands of a neutral third party the responsibility for making payment when certain conditions are met, one party to a transaction is able to avoid the risk of nonpayment or nonperformance.

Third world governments often require a financial assurance (by way of a financial guarantee) that foreign firms which undertake to supply goods or to perform a construction project will do so competently and in accordance with the terms of the contract covering the sale or project. Performance bonds can serve as an adequate assurance, but the United States banks are barred from issuing insurance contracts, including performance bonds. They have, however, developed an alternative—the *"standby" letter of credit*, which is a second type of letter of credit transaction. It involves a letter of credit which is issued by the seller's bank and runs in favor of the buyer—truly a backwards arrangement—and payable against a writing which certifies that the seller has not performed its promises. Such a standby letter of credit is not for the purpose of ensuring payment to the seller for the goods shipped. Instead, this standby letter of credit is used as a guarantee, or a performance bond, or as insurance of the seller's performance. Under prior federal law, banks were not allowed to issue guarantees or performance bonds or insurance policies.[1] However, the use of standby letters of credit could accomplish the same results, and was not prohibited by bank regulatory agencies. The result was the creation of a new commercial device, which is now commercially accepted for its own value, and which has supplanted the performance bond in many fields of endeavor.

The standby letter of credit has become an indispensable tool for financing international commercial transactions, with a two fold increase in use since 1970. Standby Letters of credit now exceed Commercial Letters of Credit by a five to one ratio.[2]

§ 7.2   Transaction Pattern of the Standby Letter of Credit

Below is an example of a standby letter of credit issued by seller's bank from *Dynamics Corp. of America v. Citizens & Southern Nat. Bank,* 356 F.Supp. 991 (N.D.Ga.1973).

" .. TO: THE PRESIDENT OF INDIA

INDIA

BY ORDER OF: ELECTRONICS SYSTEMS

DIVISION OF DYNAMICS CORPORATION OF AMERICA

For account

of same

GENTLEMEN:

§ 7.1

1. 12 U.S.C.A § 24 (Seventh).

2. Based on the Call Reports for the Second Quarter of 1999, the top 300 U.S. banks reported outstanding standby obligations of U.S. $29 billion in commercial LCs. The more recently available figures place the amount of standbys outstanding by non-U.S. banks to U.S. beneficiaries at $450 billion. Assuming conservatively that the amount of standbys by non-U.S. beneficiaries is $100 billion, that would place the amount of standbys outstanding at $765 billion. See Byrne, *Overview of Letter of Credit Law and Practice in 1999,* Documentary Credit World.

WE HEREBY ESTABLISH OUR IRREVOCABLE CREDIT IN
YOUR FAVOR, FOR THE ACCOUNT INDICATED ABOVE, FOR
A SUM OR SUMS NOT EXCEEDING IN ALL FOUR HUNDRED
TEN THOUSAND FOUR HUNDRED SEVENTY TWO AND
60/100 US DOLLARS (US $410,472.60)—AVAILABLE BY YOUR
DRAFT(S) AT sight,

DRAWN ON: us

Which must be accompanied by:

1. Your signed certification as follows: "The President of
India being one of the parties to the Agreement dated March 14,
1971 signed and exchanged between the President of India and the
Dynamics Corporation of America for the license to manufacture,
purchase and supply of radio equipment as per Schedule I thereof
for the total contract value of $1,368,242.00, does hereby certify in
the exercise of reasonable discretion and in good faith that the
Dynamics Corporation of America has failed to carry out certain
obligations of theirs under the said Order/Agreement. . . . "

In it, the seller (account party) has contracted to have the
seller's bank (issuing bank) issue an irrevocable letter of credit in
favor of the third world government (beneficiary) that payment will
be made upon presentation of a document which is only a simple
statement by the beneficiary that the account party has failed to
carry out its obligations under a contract (called a "suicide credit").
Some require no document, but provide for payment to be made
upon the beneficiary's demand.

This transaction is almost a mirror image of the letter of credit
in the documentary sale. In the standby credit, the account party is
the seller or contractor (more analogous to the seller than to the
buyer), the beneficiary is the purchaser (not the seller), and the
documents do not control goods and have no independent value of
their own. Often the required documentation is a mere certification
by the beneficiary that the contractor has failed to perform under
the contract, or perhaps, has failed to return an advance payment.

§ 7.3 Differences with Commercial Letter of Credit

The function of a standby letter of credit differs substantially
from that of the traditional letter of credit, even though both are
governed by the same substantive rules of law and practice. The
fundamental difference between a standby and a commercial letter
of credit is that the obligation for the commercial letter of credit
arises out of documents showing that the beneficiary has performed. In contrast, the obligation of a standby letter of credit
arises from documents showing that the principal has failed to
perform.

The standby letter of credit is primarily a risk-shifting device, with the advantage of providing the beneficiary with swift and easy access to funds in case of a default by the customer, much as if the customer had left a cash deposit with the beneficiary. The standby letter of credit is often preferable to a cash deposit, however, because it does not require the customer to part with any funds until after payment is demanded on the standby letter of credit.

Under the standby letter of credit the beneficiary may draw only after the customer defaults on the underlying contract. The traditional letter of credit usually requires a third party to generate some of the documents that the beneficiary must present to the issuer (usually a bill of lading); under the standby letter of credit, the beneficiary usually generates all of the necessary documents himself (usually a simple statement that the customer is in default).

Due to their contingent nature, standby letters of credit are riskier to a bank than ordinary letters of credit. The bank does not and cannot "look behind" the allegation of its customer's non-performance or delay payment in order to investigate the validity of the allegation. The bank cannot assert any defenses (except fraud) which the customer may have against the beneficiary. Standby letters of credit typically are unfounded (that is, they are not supported by funds on deposit with the bank), because banks do not anticipate having to pay out on them; the customer simply guarantees that the bank will be reimbursed if it is forced to pay out on the letter.

Under suicide credits payable upon unilateral demands, the account party's exposure may be enormous and the legal protections against arbitrary demands are limited to the fraud exception. Thus, standby credits tend, by their nature, to rely more heavily on the good faith of the parties than the commercial credit. This reliance on good faith exist because under a commercial credit it is more difficult for the beneficiary to make a fraudulent call on the credit as it has to present documents generally prepared by third parties, such as shipping companies and freight forwarders, in support of a call under the credit.

§ 7.4   Sources of Law and Rules/Governing Rules

Standby letters of credit are governed by the Uniform Customs and Practices for Documentary Credits (UCP)[1], and are governed by the same rules as those applicable to documentary credits "to the extent they may be applicable."[2]

§ 7.4

1. Uniform Customs and Practices for Documentary Credits (UCP500) (International Chamber of Commerce, Pub. No.500 (1993).

2. UCP Art. 1.

Standby letters of credit share two basic principles of commercial letters of credit. One is that the banks' obligations under the letter of credit are *independent* of the buyer's and seller's obligations under the contract for the sale of goods.[3] The "independence principle" posits that the contract for sale of goods between buyer and seller is conceptually and actually independent from the letter of credit contract. Historically, the independence principle has been recognized for the predictability and certainty that it offered to sellers, who were often reluctant to send goods abroad without payment.

The second is that banks deal only with documents, and not with performance of the underlying sales contract.[4] If the documents presented conform precisely to the terms of the letter of credit, the Confirming Bank and the Issuing Bank are obligated to pay the beneficiary or to honor its draft. The beneficiary is not subject to defenses arising out of the underlying sales transaction, so the conformity of the goods is, with exceptions noted below, irrelevant to the bank's decision. The decision is to be based upon the documents alone. Further, the documents need not conform to the underlying sales contract either, so long as they comply with the letter of credit.[5] However, the bank's promises may still be subject to claims by the applicant (Buyer) of fraud by the beneficiary (Seller). The UCP has no provisions concerning fraud, and therefore such issues must be analyzed under U.C.C. Article 5[6], where U.S. law is applicable.

Some legal commentators question whether the traditional "independence principle" of letter of credit rules is being or should be applied to standby credits, in light of the facts that such letters do not assure an exporter about payment for goods to be shipped, but serve principally a non-payment function to assure an importer (beneficiary) about payment if an exporter (the account party) does not deliver on its contract (to supply goods, services or raw materials). However, the text of both the UCP and Revised Article 5 make it clear that the drafters intended to cover standby letters of credit, and to apply the "independence principle" to such bank obligations.

Both U.C.C. Article 5 and the UCP have recently been revised. The Revised Article 5 was adopted by the Uniform Commissioners and the American Law Institute in 1995, and by the end of 2000, 47 U.S. and the District of Columbia had adopted the revision.[7] The

---

3. UCP Article 3.

4. UCP Article 4.

5. UCP Article 3(a).

6. Article 5 of the Uniform Commercial Code (U.C.C. §§ 5–101–117 (1999)).

7. See table of adoptions available in: *http://www.nccusl.org/uniformact_factsheets/uniformacts-fs-ucca5.htm*.

most recent version of the UCP is the 1993 Revision.[8] The rules set forth in each are relatively similar, but there are some differences. The UCP provisions will have more impact on the analysis of non-fraud issues, and the U.C.C. Article 5 provisions will be used to resolve issues related to allegations of fraud.

§ 7.5   Revised UCC Article 5

U.C.C. Article 5 has considerable significance in the field of letters of credit. Until the formulation of the United Nations Convention on Independent Guarantees and Standby Letters of Credit[1], it was the only modern attempt at a statute regulating letters of credit. Although a model code, it was adopted by every U.S. state. Moreover, it has provided a context for the development of U.S. letter of credit law which, because of the economic and political position of the U.S., has been influential beyond its borders. While the original version of U.C.C. Article 5, released in 1952, was largely declaratory of general principles of letter of credit law, it captured the fraud exception in a manner that has been highly influential. During the last decade the model code was completely revised. The process occurred simultaneously with the formulation of the U.N. Convention and the revision of the UCP and was influenced considerably by these efforts.

Revised Article 5 "clearly and forcefully states the independence of the letter of credit obligations from the underlying transaction that was unexpressed in, but was a fundamental predicate for, the original Article 5."[2] Certainty of payment, independent of other claims, setoffs or other causes of action, is a core element of the commercial utility of letters of credit.

The revision authorizes the use of electronic technology[3]; expressly permits deferred payment letters of credit.[4]

UCC Section 116–5(c) expressly recognizes that if the UCP is incorporated by reference into the letter of credit, the agreement varies the provisions of Article 5 with which it may conflict except for the non-variable provisions of Article 5.

§ 7.6   Uniform Customs and Practices for Documentary Credits (UCP)

The UCP is a set of industry rules that banks and trade finance institutions submit to voluntarily through express provision in the terms of a commercial letter of credit.

---

8. I.C.C. Publ. No. 500.

§ 7.5

1. UN Convention on Independent Guarantees and Standby Letters of Credit, available in *www.uncitral.org*.

2. Prefatory Note, Art. 5 (UCC §§ 5–103(d) and 5–108(f)).

3. UCC § 102(a)(14) and 5–104.

4. (UCC § 102 (a)8).

The International Chamber of Commerce (I.C.C.) has developed and published the Uniform Customs and Practices for Documentary Credits (UCP), which is incorporated by reference in most international letters of credit. The UCP constitutes a rather detailed manual of operations for banks, but they are a restatement of "custom" in the industry, and they do not purport to be law.

The UCP apply only if the operating banks, particularly the issuing bank, make the credit subject to the UCP. The general provisions of the UCP stipulate that the Customs govern all credits that do not expressly provide for the contrary. If the parties expressly incorporate the UCP, they become terms of the engagement and will apply. If the parties expressly reject the Uniform Customs, under the terms of Article 1 they do not apply. If the credit is silent, to the extent that a party proves that the UCP "fill in points that the parties have not considered and in fact agreed upon."

The UCP have, since 1983, included standby letters of credit within their scope. Article 1 of the UCP brings out more sharply than its predecessor the need for textual incorporation: "The Uniform Customs and Practice for Documentary Credits ... shall apply to all Documentary Credits (including to the extent to which they may be applicable, Standby letter(s) of credit) where they are incorporated into the text of the credit. They are binding on all the parties thereto, unless otherwise expressly stipulated in the credit." However, UCP 500 is essentially a set of rules for commercial letters of credit.

The beneficiary of the standby credit is not a performing party of the underlying transaction, but the party entitled to receive performance, and his entitlement to make a demand for payment arises not because of his own performance, but because of the other party's failure to perform. The result of this fundamental distinction is that most of the provisions of the UCP are simply not applicable to standby credits.

Despite persistent talk of the impending revision of UCP500, the I.C.C. Banking Commission agreed that any revision be postponed several years in order to permit necessary studies as to the need and extent of any revisions and to assess the impact of ISP98.[1]

§ 7.6

1. Statement of the Revision of UCP (ICC Commission on Banking Technique & Practice, Nov. 1999 DCW 8.

§ 7.7   New International Rules for Standby Letters of Credit

Even though both the UCP and Revised U.C.C. Article 5 expressly include standby letters of credit within their coverage, it is clear that they were designed to cover the documentary letter of credit transaction and not the standby transaction. Thus, they impose many unnecessary document-related conditions on the use of standbys. In response to these difficulties, the United Nations Commission on International Trade Law (UNCITRAL) has developed the United Nations Convention on Independent Guarantees and Stand-by Letters of Credit (1995) which entered into force on January 1, 2000. For the same reason, the International Chamber of Commerce (I.C.C.) has developed the Rules on International Standby Practices (ISP 98)[1], which became effective on January 1, 1999. The Convention currently has five Contracting States (Ecuador, El Salvador, Kuwait, Panama and Tunisia). The ISP 98 was designed to replace the UCP and be its equivalent to international practice regarding standby letters of credit.

§ 7.8   United Nations Convention on Independent Guarantees and Stand-by Letters of Credit (1995)

The United Nations Commission on International Trade Law (UNCITRAL) prepared the United Nations Convention on Independent Guarantees and Stand-by Letters of Credit (CIGSLC). The UN Convention was adopted and opened for signature by the General Assembly by its resolution 50/48 of December 11, 1995,[1] and entered into force on January 1, 2000.[2] The Convention is designed to facilitate the use of independent guarantees and standby letters of credit. The CIGSLC uses the term "undertaking" to refer to both type of instruments.

The Convention gives legislative support to the autonomy of the parties to apply agreed rules of practice such as the UCP and the Uniform Rules for Demand Guarantees (URDG).[3] It supplements their operation by dealing with issues beyond the scope of such rules. It does so in particular regarding the question of

---

§ 7.7

1. International Standby Practices 1998 (ISP 98) (I.C.C. Pub. No 590).

§ 7.8

1. Explanatory Note by UNCITRAL secretariat of the United Nations Convention on Independent Guarantees and Standby Letters of Credit, available in *www.uncitral.org*).

2. The Convention has been signed by four states (including the US) and ratified by five (but not the US), Ecuador, El Salvador, Kuwait, Panama and Tunisia. See UNCITRAL Status of Conventions and Model Laws, at http://www.uncitral.org/en-index.htm.

3. Uniform Rules for Demand Guarantees (URDG) (I.C.C., Pub. No 458, (1992)).

fraudulent or abusive demands for payment and judicial remedies in such instances.

The focus of the Convention is on the relationship between the issuer and the beneficiary. The relationship between the issuer and the account party largely falls outside its scope.

Full freedom is given to the parties to exclude completely the coverage of the Convention,[4] with the result that another law becomes applicable. Since the Convention, if it is applicable, is to a large extent suppletive rather than mandatory, wide breath is given to exclude or alter the rules of the Convention in any given case.

Letters of credit other than standby letters of credit are not covered by the Convention. However, the Convention does recognize a right of parties to international letters of credit to "opt into" the Convention.[5]

The Convention applies to an "international" undertaking if the place of business of the issuer is in a state that has adopted the Convention or if the rules of private international law lead to the application of the laws of such a state, unless the undertaking excludes the application of the CIGSLC.[6] The Convention also applies if it expressly states that it applies to an international letter of credit.[7] An undertaking is international if any of two of the issuer, the applicant, the confirmer or the beneficiary are located in different states.[8]

The Convention defines as "independence,"[9] an undertaking which is not dependent upon the existence or validity of the underlying transaction, or upon any other undertaking. An independent undertaking must not be subject to any terms or conditions not appearing in the undertaking. To be independent from the underlying transactions, the undertakings covered by the Convention must possess a "documentary" character. The effect of this rule is that an undertaking which is subject to "non-documentary" conditions is outside the scope of the Convention.

The Convention contains a general rule that interpretation of the Convention should be with a view to its international character and the need to promote uniformity in its application.[10] In addition, interpretation is to have regard for the observance of good faith in international practice.

The Convention provides rules on several aspects of the form and content of undertakings. The rights and obligations of the

---

4. CIGSCL Article 1.

5. CIGSCL Article 1(2).

6. CIGSLC Art. 1(1).

7. CIGSLC Art. 1(2).

8. CIGSLC Art. 4(1).

9. CIGSCL Article 3.

10. CIGSLC Article 5. Compare to CISG art. 7(1), discussed in § 1.6, supra.

issuer and the beneficiary are determined by the terms and conditions of the undertaking.[11] Express reference is made in the Convention to rules of practice, general conditions or usages (e.g. UCP, URDG) to which the undertaking may be expressly made subject.

The United Nations Convention complements the UCP and reinforces its use. The United Nations Convention differs from the UCP in that it is public law, not private law. Unlike the UCP, it also provides for injunctive relief to thwart fraudulent demands.

Now that the Convention has entered into force, letters of credit can be issued subject to its provisions. Indeed, even in countries where the Convention has not been adopted, standby letters of credit may be issued subject to it if so permitted by the choice of law rules of the issuer's state. Since many such rules emphasize party autonomy, such a result may be possible in a number of different countries.

§ 7.9 The Rules on International Standby Practices (ISP 98)

The International Institute of Banking Law and Practice has drafted the International Standby Practices (ISP 98) and the I.C.C. ultimately agreed to publish them to become effective in 1999. ISP 98 endeavors to set forth uniform rules and regulations governing standby letters of credit that would be widely accepted, as well as to streamline and standardize customs and practices. It also addresses issues unique to standby letters of credit, and clarifies the application of rules to standby letters of credit.

There are basic similarities with the UCP because standby and commercial practices are fundamentally the same. However, ISP 98 differs from the UCP in style and approach. The ISP 98 contains 89 rules in contrast to the UCP's 49 and cover many areas with regard to which the UCP is silent. The most significant differences between the UCP and the ISP 98 exist in the issuer's and the beneficiary's respective rights and obligations.

Like the UCP and the URDG, the ISP will apply to any independent undertaking issued subject to it. The choice of which set of rules to select is, therefore, left to the parties. The ISP is designed to be compatible with the UN Convention and also with local law, whether statutory or judicial, and to embody standby letter of credit practice under that law.

ISP 98 clarifies terminology used in letters of credit, and restates basic principles of letter of credit law in order to obviate

11. CIGSLC Article 13(1).

the need for placing these principles in each standby letter of credit.[1]

ISP 98 applies to both domestic and international standby credits expressly stated to be subject to it (notwithstanding that "international" is used in the title of ISP 98).[2] It is intended to apply to any standby Letter of Credit that is issued subject to ISP 98. Parties need to incorporate ISP 98 by reference before it becomes applicable as the "governing law" of the standby letter of credit.

ISP 98, like the UCC and the UCP, contains only a few provisions concerning the contract between the issuer and the account party. These concern the issuer's right to be paid certain charges for issuing the credit, to reimbursement and limitations on its liability to the applicant.

Neither the UCP nor ISP 98 prescribe rules concerning when the issuer may or should refuse an otherwise complying presentation because the beneficiary's draw is fraudulent. The UCP does not mention the exception. The ISP 98 states expressly that it does not provide "defenses to honor based on fraud, abuse or similar matters."[3] Some have raised a question as to whether this difference between the UCP and ISP 98 leaves open the possibility of banks becoming defendants in securities fraud litigation by having aggressive plaintiffs' counsel alleging the bank permitted a drawing because of a reckless state of mind.

ISP 98 rule 3.06 is the first existing rule actually permitting electronic presentation of documents under a standby LC. It enables members of S.W.I.F.T. to make electronic presentation in situations where the only required document is a demand whether or not the credit expressly permits it. In addition, ISP 98 proposes basic definitions should the standby permit or require presentation of documents by electronic means. While electronic presentation is relatively easy for standbys, it is much more difficult for commercial letters of credit that require presentation of documents of title.

ISP 98 applies to the obligation of the applicant to reimburse the issuer of a standby letter of credit, and even create indemnification obligations on the part of the applicant against certain cost of the issuer.[4] The UCP does not specifically address these obligations.

Under ISP 98, certain provisions of a standby letter of credit may be waived unilaterally by the issuer, without effect on the applicant's reimbursement obligations to the issuer.[5]

§ 7.9

1. ISP 98, Rules 1.06, 1.07, 1.10.
2. ISP 98, Rule 1.01(b).
3. ISP 98, Rule 1.01(b).
4. ISP 98, Rule 8.03.
5. ISP 98, Rule 3.11.

The ISP establishes a three-day safe harbor for examination of documents, within which notice of dishonor is deemed to be reasonable.[6] It continues the seven-day rule of the UCP, beyond which notice of dishonor is deemed to be unreasonable. The statement of discrepancies need not be detailed.[7]

The ISP also sets out standards for documentary compliance.[8] Regarding the extent to which the documents presented under a standby must match the wording of the letter of credit, Rule 4.01 states the general principle that demands must comply on their face with the terms and conditions of the standby. Rule 4.09 contains specific rules for applying this principle. The UCP does not provide such detail in determining when a presentation is in compliance.

§ 7.10   The "Fraud Defense"

Where the documents are forged or fraudulent, or there is a fraud in the transaction, however, a different analysis is applied. The "independence principle" promotes the utility of the letter of credit transaction, by offering certainty of payment to the beneficiary who complies with a credit's requirements. But where there is fraud or forgery, rather than a "mere" breach of the underlying sales contract, a counter principle comes into play. "There is as much public interest in discouraging fraud as in encouraging the use of letters of credit."[1] Where the seller's fraud has been called to the bank's attention before the drafts and documents have been presented for payment, the principle of the "independence of the bank's obligation under the letter of credit" should not be extended to protect the unscrupulous seller.[2]

Thus, there are two competing principles, and the courts have created compromise which limit the impact of the independence principle when there are forged or fraudulent documents, or fraud in the transaction. Vexing problems are raised by claims of fraud and, more particularly, of "fraud in the transaction", but the doctrine that there is a "fraud exception" to the "independence principle" seems to be generally recognized. However, there is still a significant debate about how broad and extensive the fraud exception should be.

6. ISP 98, Rule 5.01.

7. ISP 98, Official Comments to Rule 5.02.

8. ISP 98, Rule 4.09.

§ 7.10

1. *Dynamics Corp. of America v. Citizens & Southern Nat. Bank,* 356 F.Supp. 991 (N.D.Ga.1973).

2. *Sztejn v. J. Henry Schroder Banking Corp.,* 177 Misc. 719, 31 N.Y.S.2d 631 (1941).

This "fraud exception" is available where the credit is expressly subject to the UCP, even though the UCP has no specific provisions on the subject. Since the UCP is silent, the courts have generally held that the UCC provisions govern as a "gap filling provision." The principle underlying this approach is that the courts will not allow their process to be used by a dishonest person to carry out a fraud.

While the concept of enjoining payment due to fraud has not been widely used in the documentary letter of credit transaction, there has been at least one significant case involving documentary credits. In *Mid–America Tire, Inc. v. PTZ Trading Ltd.*,[3] the Supreme Court of Ohio held that (1) the UCP did not displace the UCC's provisions on fraud; (2) the fraud provisions of the UCC applied to both fraud in the letter of credit transaction and fraud in the underlying sales transaction; (3) that the necessary "material fraud"[4] required that the fraud "vitiate the transaction," making the letter of credit a "vehicle for fraud," and depriving the applicant of the benefits of the underlying contract; and (4) the fraudulent acts of agents of the beneficiary must be considered by the courts.

On the other hand, injunctions against payment due to fraud have been widely sought in the standby letter of credit transaction. Some limiting concepts in the documentary letter of credit transaction, such as "strict compliance" of the documents, become somewhat meaningless when the "document" becomes a mere allegation by one party that the other party failed to perform properly under the contract. When the limitations which give structure to the transaction become meaningless, the transaction can become a breeding ground for fraud.

Under Revised UCC 5–109, there is a series of limitations on the availability of the fraud exception for use by the beneficiary. The first limitation is that "the issuer shall honor presentation, if honor is demanded by a nominated person who has given value in good faith without notice of material injury or fraud." Thus, confirming banks who have paid against the documents in good faith and without notice of any defense to, or defect in, the documents are entitled to reimbursement, despite fraud on the beneficiary. So also is an advising bank which has been authorized to pay against the documents, rather than merely to accept the documents for collection. Under the UCC, if the documents are presented by such a confirming bank, or authorized advising bank, and the documents appear on their face to comply with the credit, the issuing bank *must* pay the confirming bank, even though the

---

3. 95 Ohio St.3d 367, 768 N.E.2d 619 (2002).   **4.** Revised UCC § 5–109(b).

documents are forged or fraudulent or there is fraud in the transaction.

A second limitation is that, if the documents are presented by anyone else (beneficiary, advising bank authorized to take for collection only, confirming bank which took with notice of defects or defenses, etc.), the issuing bank *may* still pay, even though it has been notified that the documents are forged or fraudulent, or that there is fraud in the transaction, as long as it acts in good faith. In the latter case, the issuing bank may also refuse to pay, but that is not very likely. Reasons for the issuing bank not refusing to pay range from its reluctance to be known as an unreliable source of funds in letter of credit transactions to its inability to evaluate the available evidence of fraud, especially on an *ex parte* basis. Banks are paid to handle documents, not to become judge and jury.

The account party is, however, given the power to obtain a court order against payment, so long as it can prove forgery, fraud or fraud in the transaction. Thus under the UCC, if the account party obtains a court injunction against payment form a court having proper jurisdiction, the issuing bank is permitted to dishonor the presentment. But the Revised UCC Article 5 leaves only a very narrow avenue for the account party to seek and obtain judicial intervention through injunctive relief in the letter of credit transaction. To beneficiaries, the concept creates great uncertainty about prompt payment, because they know nothing about the judicial system and fear the worst. To account parties, the concept has created a theoretical argument, but there have been very few reported cases in which they were successful.

The Revised Article 5 limits itself in several ways:

First, the fraud must be "material," but material is not defined. The Comments to Revised 5–109 cite some prior decisions favorably, but its meaning will be decided on a case by case basis.

Second, the account party must present sufficient evidence of fraud or forgery, not merely allegations of it.

Third, all the procedural requirements for injunctive or other relief must be met.

Fourth, the relief can be denied if third parties are not "adequately protected," and no relief will be granted if a confirming or advising bank has paid funds to the beneficiary. However, this concept has been expanded in the Comments to include protection against incidental damages, such as legal fees, by *bonds* or otherwise. All of these are limitations which have been found in the prior cases and which would be expected in an action for injunctive relief.

The principal new limitation is one stated in Revised 5–109. A forgery or a fraud in the document may permit an injunction of payment if perpetrated by anyone, but a fraud in the underlying transaction is cognizable only if it is "committed by the beneficiary," and not by some third party, such a carrier. The difference between the two concepts is illustrated by the approach of English and Canadian courts to the fraud exception.

The English and Canadian courts have each recognized the "fraud exception," based upon the persuasive precedent of the American cases. However, each of them, in addition to the requirements of the pre-Revision UCC, place great stress on the *scienter* requirements of common law fraud and require the account party to establish that the beneficiary itself made, or was responsible for, the misrepresentation that was the foundation for the fraud claim. A misrepresentation made by any other party to the transaction would not permit an injunction against payment of the beneficiary. Thus, the House of Lords, while recognizing, the basic fraud concept, refused to extend it to protect the buyer when the fraud was committed by a third party (a loading broker) without seller's knowledge.[5] Under the English–Canadian formulation: (1) Where the credit requires loading by May 15 and the bill of lading shows loading on the 16th, the bank must dishonor. (2) Where the credit requires loading on May 15, and bank knows that the beneficiary has altered a document in a non-apparent manner, the bank must dishonor. (3) But, where the credit requires loading by May 15, and bank knows that a freight forwarder has altered a document in a non-apparent manner, the bank must *honor* the credit.

Under Revised 5–109, American courts would reach such a result if the misrepresentation was considered a fraud in the underlying transaction. However, such a misrepresentation is more likely to be considered arising out of the document itself. If so, the identity of the perpetrator would be irrelevant. Revised 5–109 does not attempt to define fraud, which is a product of case law and varies widely from state to state.

The traditional difference between fraud doctrines and breach of contract concepts was that the former consider the state of mind of the seller, while breach of contract concerns only whether the goods lived up to a particular objective standard set by their description. Fraud concepts have expanded enormously since 1952, and conduct which not have been actionable during the first half of the 20th Century is now routinely within current case law concepts. The modern fraud doctrines often do not require any evil intent, but only that seller know that a particular fact is not true—or, that

5. *United City Merchants (Investments) Ltd. v. Royal Bank of Canada* *(The American Accord),* [1983] 1 A.C. 168 (H.L.1982)

he does not know whether a particular fact is true or not when he
states it—or, that he believes that a fact is true when is not, and a
court decides that he should have made a more thorough investigation before speaking.

As an outgrowth of the 1979 change of government in Iran,
increased attention was given to the potential that a standby
letter's beneficiary could require payment for what was characterized as "bad faith" or "arbitrary" reasons, or at least for reasons
not related to the contractor's intentional failure to perform on the
contract (e.g., perhaps because of conditions surrounding a civil
insurrection).

Many courts have declined to enjoin payment because of insufficient evidence of fraud. Other courts have been willing to issue a
"notice of injunction" requiring issuers to give some prior notice
(usually three to ten days) to the account party before transferring
money to the beneficiary of a standby credit after demand for
payment, while a few courts have granted preliminary injunctions
of indefinite duration.

Although the customer may sometimes have payment enjoined
when fraud is present, he is obligated to reimburse the bank if the
bank has made a payment in good faith, even upon a fraudulent
demand.

The fraud in the transaction exception created in *Stejn* has
been codified in section 5–114 of the UCC, and has been accepted
by courts in England. In cases involving traditional letters of credit,
the courts have given the fraud in the transaction exception a
narrow reading, confining its application to cases of egregious fraud
on the part of the beneficiary. This narrow reading apparently is
justified on the ground that a broader rule would defeat the
certainty of letter of credit transactions and undermine of the basic
purposes of the letter of credit—assuring prompt payment to the
beneficiary.

§ 7.11   Fraudulent or Abusive Demands for Payment Under the United Nations Convention on Independent Guarantees and Stand-by Letters of Credit

A main purpose of the UN Convention on Independent Guarantees and Stand-by Letters of Credit is to establish greater uniformity internationally in the manner in which issuers and courts
respond to allegations of fraud or abuse in demands for payment
under standby letters of credit.

Article 19 of the Convention indicates the situations in which a
court may interfere with a complying drawing under an indepen-

dent undertaking. As is apparent from the drafting history of the provision, it is intended to provide a rigorous standard by which the availability of relief is to be determined.

The Convention provides a general definition of the types of situations in which an exception to the obligation to pay against a facially compliant demand would be justified.[1] The definition encompasses fact patters covered in different legal systems by notions such as "fraud" or "abuse of right." The definition refers to situations in which is manifest and clear that any document is not genuine or has been falsified, that no payment is due on the basis asserted in the demand or that the demand has no conceivable basis. Additionally, the Convention provides examples of cases in which a demand would be deemed to have no conceivable basis.[2]

The Convention seeks to strike a balance between different interests and considerations at play. By allowing discretion to the issuer acting in good faith, the Convention takes into account the concern of issuers over preserving the commercial reliability of undertakings as promises that are independent from underlying transactions.

At the same time, the Convention affirms that the applicant, in the situations referred to, is entitled to provisional court measures to block payment.[3] This recognizes that it is proper role of courts, and not of issuers, to investigate the facts of underlying transactions.

Apart from entitling an applicant or an instructing party to provisional court measures blocking payment or freezing proceeds of an undertaking in the types of cases referred to above, the Convention establishes a standard of proof to be met in order to obtain such provisional measures on the basis of immediately available strong evidence of a high probability that the fraudulent or abusive circumstances are present. Reference is also made to consideration of whether the applicant would be likely to suffer serious harm in the absence of the provisional measures and to the possibility of the court requiring security to be posted.

While authorizing provisional court measures in the cases concerned, the Convention is aimed at minimizing the use of judicial procedures to interfere in undertakings by limiting the granting of provisional court measures to those types of cases, with one additional type of case. Provisional court orders blocking payment or freezing proceeds are also authorized in the case of use of an undertaking for a criminal purpose.[4]

§ 7.11

1. Article 19(1), CIGSLC.
2. Article 19(2), CIGSLC.
3. Article 19(2), CIGSLC.
4. Article 20(3), CIGSLC.

*

Chapter 8

INTERNATIONAL ELECTRONIC COMMERCE

Table of Sections

---

§ 8.1   Introduction

Today's confluence of computerization, the Internet, and a variety of other communications technologies, is altering the historic business models and traditional contracting practices. With E–Commerce one is dealing with an intangible, digital, world. Thus, the traditional relationships among the parties to a transaction are affected, and concerns regarding the management, communication, and security of the digital information involved rise to a new level.[1]

The recent phenomenal growth of E–Commerce caught the legal regimes of the world unprepared. None was ready for the legal

---

§ 8.1

1. The phenomenon is not new. Consider the following statement:

"The businessman of the present day must be continually on the jump, the slow express train will not answer his purpose, and the poor merchant has no other way in which to work to secure a living for his family. He *must* use the telegraph." (Emphasis in the original.) Statement in 1868 by W.E. Dodge *quoted in* Tom Standage, THE VICTORIAN INTERNET (1999) at 166.

175

problems caused by the new forms of contract-making, payment, performance, and information exchange brought about by the application of new technologies. The law also adapts to changing technologies, however it commonly takes some time for legal rules and principles to adjust to new circumstances, and consequently there is often a lag between the time new business practices are created and changes in the legal rules. They have done their best to adapt traditional rules to new business patterns, but each legal regime has adapted in a different manner. Thus, there is little consistency in the rules applicable to E–Commerce transactions which cross national borders.

Such a lack of consistency is not new, but the problems are magnified by two practical aspects of E–Commerce. One is that the parties often do not know when an E–Commerce transaction involves dealings across national boundaries. A website with a ".com" address may literally be located anywhere in the world. Thus, the website address of each party, which may be the only information each has of the other, may not reveal the transborder nature of the transaction. The second aspect is that the amount of writing on a screen—and the attention span of parties acting at "Internet speed"—is limited. Accordingly, long sophisticated contracts with lots of form-pad clauses are "out" in E–Commerce. In particular, most E–Merchants believe that too many other terms have priority over choice of law and choice of forum clauses, for example, so they do not appear in the terms of many E–Commerce contracts. Thus, a second potential device for revealing the transborder nature of the transaction is usually missing.

There are a variety of new contract issues created by E–Commerce, including how to satisfy requirements for agreements in writing and signatures, authentication and attribution of communications without personal contact, security and integrity of electronic messages, and express and implied terms and conditions for both commercial and consumer contracts. E–Commerce also raises jurisdictional issues, ranging from choice of law to presence in a jurisdiction for purposes of being sued in a civil action to presence in a jurisdiction for purposes of regulation by public authorities. The public authorities not only wish to prevent fraud and deception by E–Merchants, but also to regulate privacy, intellectual property and taxation issues, among others. In all these areas, there are very few statutory rules or decided cases; and, where there are, the existing rules and approaches to E–Commerce differ from one legal regime to another.

Thus, there is a perceived need, not only for statutory rules to facilitate E–Commerce, but for such rules to be similar across national borders, since it is not usually clear where the parties are located. In the absence of clear rules, parties have attempted to address many of these issues through their private contractual dealings, with varying degrees of success. Additionally, attempts to legislatively create similar rules in different jurisdictions, through international treaties, regional directives, or model legislation, continue to be proposed from time to time. The concerns over *whether* a contract can be formed electronically in recent years led to a burst of legislative activity at the state, federal and international levels. At the international level, UNCITRAL has issued two Model Laws: The UNCITRAL Model Law on Electronic Commerce,[2] and the UNCITRAL Model Law on Electronic Signatures[3]. The European Union has similarly been active in addressing these issues on a regional level. At the U.S. federal level, Congress has enacted the E–Sign law. At the state level, there have been many enactments of state laws, and the National Conference of Commissioners is also proposing uniform acts in the field. In addressing the various issues raised by E–Commerce, the parties' private contractual solutions and those enabled or facilitated by these new statutory measures are interrelated and interdependent, and must be considered together.

§ 8.2 Private Contractual Measures Enabling E–Commerce—Trading Partner Agreements

Trading Partner or EDI Agreements were among the first tools used to address the issues raised by E–Commerce, and continue to serve that role to day in a number of different types of business relationships. EDI Agreements are used to facilitate electronic information exchange and to regulate many aspects of the relationship between the parties who do business with each other through electronic communication. The agreement may be just between two parties, or it may encompass a whole network of interrelated businesses either with a master agreement covering all parties or a series of standardized individual contracts. However, trading partner agreements could only be used in "closed systems," where every party was a member of the network and could not be used for "open" E–Commerce transactions on the internet.

§ 8.3 Legislative Measures Enabling E–Commerce

Given the speed with which technology is changing business practices related to E–Commerce, the gradual adaptation of existing legal rules to the new modes of doing business through caselaw is viewed by many as simply being too slow. Just as E–Merchants clamor for more legal certainty in the rules surrounding their

---

2. UNCITRAL Model Law on Electronic Commerce, U.N. Doc. A/RES/ 51/162, 16 December, 1996.

3. UNCITRAL Model Law on Electronic Signatures, U.N. Doc. A/CN.9/WG.IV/WP.88, January 30, 2001.

enterprises; legislatures and academicians on the national, regional, and international levels also want to demonstrate their receptiveness to these new ways of doing business. This has led to an explosion of new statutes, codes, and model laws on E–Commerce around the world.

These new statutory schemes have multiple purposes. Several of them are pure "enabling" measures, aimed simply at clarifying and confirming the ability to form contractual agreements electronically, for example. This is the most basic function for any statutory e-commerce measure, and one which deals with many of the same issues which underlie the private contractual approaches to E–Commerce. However, as legal systems generally get more comfortable with the notion of entering into binding agreements electronically, many of these e-commerce statutory measure are pushing ahead to deal with substantive issues beyond merely contract formation in cyberspace. Many of the statutory schemes deal with the terms found in "standard" electronic contracts, and raise the types of issues which might cause concern in any form contract. Are any of the standard terms unconscionable? Are they sufficiently clear and conspicuous so as to fully bind the user? Do the existing approaches to warranties and consumer protection measures need to be altered when dealing with E–Commerce? Are there particular public policy issues, such as privacy issues, associated with E–Commerce transactions? Do existing contractual and legal remedies work with E–Commerce transactions? And even at the most fundamental level, are there particular problems with choice of law and choice of forum in the global marketplaces found in cyberspace?

Whatever the scope of their coverage, the national regional, and international statutory schemes and the private contractual solutions devised for these issues are inextricably intertwined. Private contractual approaches and statutory measure borrow freely from one another in all jurisdictions, and their interplay helps inform the debate over what approaches will be most successful in the global marketplace for E–Commerce transactions.

§ 8.4 UNCITRAL Model Law on Electronic Commerce—In General

UNCITRAL (the organization which developed CISG) developed a Model Law on Electronic Commerce, which it adopted in 1996.[1] The Model Law is a minimalist approach to legislation, seeking to facilitate E–Commerce transactions and not to regulate

---

§ 8.4

1. General Assembly Resolution 51/162 of 16 December 1996; Y.B. Int'l Trade L. Comm'n 237, Vol. XXVII.

them. This Model Law is now available to all legal regimes for enactment to provide guidance for E–Merchants and their customers. The UNCITRAL Model Law is intended to provide a legal guide in order to facilitate modern business transactions in the electronic environment. The fundamental principle of this Model Law is that data messages should not be discriminated against, in other words, that there should be no disparity of treatment between data messages and paper documents. Under this basic principle, Articles 5 to 10 address the issues of legal recognition of data messages,[2] admissibility and evidential weight of data message,[3] the concepts of "writing," "signature" and "original" in the aspect of electronic commerce,[4] and retention of data messages.[5] Articles 11 to 15 furnish a set of provisions dealing with formation of electronic contracts and the communication of data messages. As of jan. 1, 2005, legislation based on the UNCITRAL Model Law on Electronic Commerce has been enacted by Australia, Bermuda, Columbia, France, India, Hong Kong, Ireland, Jordan, Mauritius, Mexico, New Zealand, Pakistan, Panama, the Philippines, the Republic of Korea, Singapore, Slovenia, South Africa, Thailand and Venezuela and the state of Illinois. Further enactments are expected.[6]

§ 8.5   UNCITRAL Model Law on Electronic Commerce—Non–Discrimination

In its non-discrimination provisions, the UNCITRAL Model Law provides for equality of treatment between paper documents and electronic messages.[1] It provides that "data messages" are not to be denied legal effect because they are electronic,[2] and that any "writing" requirement is satisfied by a data message which is acceptable for subsequent reference.[3] Legal requirements for a "signature" are met by a data message if there is a method which is "reasonable for the circumstances" to identify both the identity of the person sending the message and that person's approval of the message.[4] An electronic data message is allowed to satisfy evidentiary requirements, and an evidentiary requirement for "an original document" is satisfied by an electronic data message whose information integrity can be assured, and whose information can be displayed.[5] Finally, record retention requirements may be satisfied for data messages by appropriate electronic retention.[6]

2. Electronic Commerce Model Law, supra § 8.1, note 2, Article 5.

3. *Id.*, at Article 9.

4. *Id.*, at Articles 6, 7, 8.

5. *Id.*, at Article 10.

6. See http:www.uncitral.org/en-index.html.

§ 8.5

1. Electronic Commerce Model Law, arts. 5–10.

2. *Id.*, at art. 5.

3. *Id.*, at art. 6(1).

4. *Id.*, at art. 7(1)(b).

5. *Id.*, at art. 8(1).

6. *Id.*, at art. 9.

Article 5 provides that a party of the transaction cannot solely rely on the ground that the information is in the form of a data message to deny its legal effect.[7] At the same time, however, information contained in a data message is not necessarily valid on the sole ground that it is in the form of part of a data message.[8]

The Model Law on Electronic Commerce also addresses the issue of legal recognition of data message, in terms of the admissibility and evidential weight of data message in legal proceedings.[9] According to Article 9, the fact that an information is in the form of data message cannot be used as the sole ground to deny the admissibility as evidence of that data message. In case the data message is the best evidence one party could obtain, the fact that it is not in its original form may not be used as the ground to deny the admissibility of the data message. The evidential value depends on whether the data message was generated, stored or communicated in a reliable manner.

Information meets the requirement of writing in the applicable State law, if the information is accessible so one can use it at some later time as reference.[10] The word "accessible" implies that the information in the form of data message should be retrievable, reproducible, readable and interpretable.

Any legal requirement of signature is met if a reliable method is used to identify the person and, at the same time, to identify that person's approval of the information contained in the data message.[11] There are three statutory requirements for an effective electronic signature: the method used must be able to identify the person himself; the method used must also identify the person's approval the data massage, and the method must be reliable. Only after these criteria are met, will the data message be regarded as authenticated with sufficient credibility and therefore be enforceable in legal proceedings under the statute.

§ 8.6   UNCITRAL Model Law on Electronic Commerce—Contract Formation

Articles 11 to 15 of the UNCITRAL Model Law on Electronic Commerce address issues relating the contract formation and communication of data messages. These more specialized rules may be varied by agreement between the parties.[1] These rules concern

---

7. *Id.*, at art. 5.

8. UNICTRAL Model Law on Electronic Commerce, Guide to Enactment (hereafter Guide) ¶ 46.

9. Electronic Commerce Model Law, art. 9.

10. *Id.*, at art. 6.

11. *Id.*, at art. 7.

§ 8.6

1. Electronic Commerce Model Law, art. 11. This provision also allows the parties to agree that they will be bound only by paper-based communications,

formation, attribution of messages, and acknowledgment and time of receipt of data messages. As to attribution, a message is deemed to be sent by a designated originator if it is sent either by an authorized person or by a machine that is programmed by the originator to operate automatically. The addressee of the data message is authorized to rely on it as being from the originator if either an agreed-upon security procedure has been used or the originator enabled the actual sender to gain access to a message identification method.

Article 11 concerns the issue of the validity of contract formed by exchange of data messages. It establishes the legal effectiveness of data messages by stating that a contract shall not be denied validity on the sole ground that it was formed by exchange of data messages.[2] This article covers not only the case in which both the offer and the acceptance are communicated by electronic means but also the case in which only the offer or only the acceptance is communicated electronically.

The Model Law also establishes a set of rules on attribution of data messages.[3] The underlying issues are under what circumstances should a data message be considered as a message of the originator, and under what circumstances should the originator be bound by the addressee's response or action.

First, a party is bound as an originator by a data message if it has actually sent that message.[4]

Second, a party is deemed to be bound by a message if the sender had the authority to act on behalf of the originator in respect of that data message,[5] or if the data message was sent automatically by an information system programmed by or on behalf of the originator.[6] In such circumstances, the data message is deemed to be sent by the originator.

Third, the addressee "is entitled" to rely on a data message as being that of the originator: if the addressee properly applied an authentication procedure previously agreed to by the originator for that purpose.[7] The addressee is also "entitled" to rely on a data message which results from the action of an unauthorized person who nevertheless had access to the originator's authentication procedure.[8] Under both circumstances, the originator would be stopped if the addressee relies and acts on the data message.

such as a formally-signed written document, prepared by attorneys and signed by corporate executives, to conclude the contracts.

2. *Id.*

3. *Id.*, at art. 13.

4. *Id.*, at art. 13(1).

5. *Id.*, at art. 13(2)(a).

6. *Id.*, at art. 13(2)(b).

7. *Id.*, at art. 13(3)(a).

8. *Id.*, at art. 13(3)(b).

If the data message is deemed to be binding or the addressee is entitled to rely upon the message, and the addressee is entitled to action it.[9] However, the addressee is never entitled to act on a message if it knew or should have known that the data message was not from the originator.[10]

A major problem with electronic data messages is that they get lost much more often than messages sent through the U.S. Post Office. Thus, acknowledgment of receipt of electronic message is much more important to the parties than is acknowledgment of paper-based messages, and the parties often stipulate in their agreements that data messages must be acknowledged. If they so agree, under the UNCITRAL Model Law, acknowledgment can be accomplished either by the method agreed upon or, where no specific acknowledgment method has been agreed, any communication or conduct can be sufficient.[11] Even where the parties have not agreed to require acknowledgment, the originator of a data message may unilaterally require it by stating in the body of the message that it is conditional on acknowledgment.[12] Such a message is deemed "never been sent" until acknowledgment is received. Receipt of a message generally requires that the message enter an information system outside the control of the originator or its agents.[13]

§ 8.7   United States—Federal Laws

The Electronic Signatures In Global and National Commerce Act (E–SIGN Act),[1] implements a national uniform standard for all electronic transactions. Its provisions cover electronic signatures, electronic contracts and electronic records. The E–SIGN Act includes several key provisions that address its: (1) scope; (2) application; (3) consumer consent requirements; (4) validity requirements for electronic signatures, electronic contracts and electronic records; (5) retention requirements for electronic contracts and records; (6) notarization rules; and (7) national uniform standards for the banking, insurance and stock industries.

The E–SIGN Act regulates any transaction in interstate and foreign commerce. In this regard, the E–SIGN Act applies to any transaction "relating to the conduct of business, consumer or commercial affairs between two or more persons." The provisions of the E–SIGN Act may be superceded by a state statute, so long as

9. *Id.*, at art. 13(5).

10. *Id.*, last sentence.

11. *Id.*, at art. 14(2).

12. *Id.*, at art. 14(3).

13. Id., at art. 15(1).

§ 8.7

1. Electronic Signatures in Global and National Commerce Act of 2000 (hereafter E–SIGN Act) Pub.L. No. 106–229, 114 Stat. 464, 15 U.S.C. § 7000–7006, 7021, 7031 (West. Supp. 2000).

that state statute is the Uniform Electronic Transaction Act (UETA) as adopted by the National Conference of Commissioners on Uniform State Laws.[2] Otherwise, the E–SIGN Act does not alter the obligations of persons under any requirements imposed by statute, regulation or other rule of law. In this regard, the E–SIGN Act does not restrict the scope or availability of any other federal or state statute, regulation and other rule of law that requires, authorizes or otherwise allows for the use of electronic signatures or electronic records if it is consistent with the provisions of this Act.

"Electronic signatures" are defined very broadly under the E–Sign Act. The statutory definition is "an electronic sound, symbol or process attached to or logically associated with a contract or other record and executed or adopted by a person with the intent to sign the record."[3] It thus as intended to include telephone keypad agreements (e.g., "press 9 to agree or press to 7 to hear this menu again") and click wrap agreements. Moreover, a contract or other record may not be denied legal effect because its is in an electronic format and a contract may not be denied legal effect solely because an electronic signature was used in its formation. Consistent with the UNCITRAL Model Law on Electronic Commerce,[4] the E–SIGN Act does not require the use of electronic signatures, electronic contracts or electronic record. Instead, it seeks to facilitate the use of these electronic communications by upholding their legal effect. The E–SIGN Act is also technology-neutral and does not require a specific type or method that businesses and consumers must use or accept in order to conduct their electronic transaction.

There are special provisions for consumer contracts. The E–SIGN Act assumes that many consumers will want a paper (hardcopy) record of the transaction, while others prefer not to be bothered with paper. The Act provides that a consumer may elect to receive an electronic record in substitution of a required written record if: "(1) the consumer affirmatively consents to receive an electronic record" and (2) before consent "is provided with a clear and conspicuous statement informing the consumer of rights or options to have the record provided or made available on paper." However, the pre-consent notice may state that the seller will refuse to deal if the consumer wants paper. The consumer must also have some ability to access the electronic records to which the consent applies. However, this requirement may be met if the consumer confirms electronically that he or she can access the electronic records in the specified formats, or the consumer acknowledges or responds affirmatively to an electronic query that asks whether the consumer can access the electronic record. Any consent of a consumer applies only

---

2. See discussion at § 8.8, infra.

3. E–SIGN Act, § 106(5).

4. See discussion at § 8.4, supra.

to the particular transaction that gave rise to the obligation to provide the record.

The E–SIGN Act does not alter the existing contract law as to the validity and enforceability of an electronic contract. Instead, it provides substitute methods of satisfying the requirements of contract law. Where a Statute of Frauds provision requires a contract to be in writing, then an electronic contract must be in a form that is capable of being retained and accurately reproduced at the time of entering into the contract. If an electronic contract meets the validity requirement of a writing under existing substantive contract law, it is then legally enforceable. "If a customer chooses to use a device, such as a Palm Pilot or cellular phone, that does not have a printer or a disk drive allowing the customer to make a copy of the contract at the time of contracting, the contract will only be valid and legally enforceable if it was capable of being retained and reproduced" at the time of entering into the contract. In addition, an electronic signature is only valid under the E–SIGN Act if the signatory intends to sign the contract. Thus, the person or entity accepting an electronic signature has a duty of care to determine whether the electronic signature was really created by the person to whom it is attributed.

§ 8.8   United States—State Laws

In the United States, the National Conference of Commissioners on Uniform State Laws has adopted two different proposed uniform acts to facilitate electronic commerce. One is the Uniform Electronic Transactions Act (UETA), which is similar in scope and substance to the UNCITRAL Model Law on Electronic Commerce[1] and the federal E–SIGN Act.[2] It applies to all types of electronic messages and contracts, and seeks to validate and facilitate their use at a very basic level. As of Jan., 2005, UETA was enacted in 46 states.[3]

The second is the Uniform Computer Information Transactions Act (UCITA) which applies only to software licensing transactions, and incorporates very detailed provisions concerning every aspect of the transaction. Its format is similar to UCC Article 2 on sales of goods, and at one time was intended to be UCC Article 2B, until it was rejected by the American Law Institute as not sufficiently balanced. As of Jan., 2005, UCITA was enacted in two states,[4] and

---

§ 8.8

1. See discussion at § 8.4, supra.

2. See discussion at § 8.7, supra.

3. California, Hawaii, Indiana Kansas, Kentucky, Maryland, Minnesota, Nebraska, Ohio, Oklahoma, Pennsylvania, South Dakota, Utah, and Virginia. See http://www.mbc.com/ecommerce/legis.ucvue.htm for a current list of States where UETA has been adopted.

4. Maryland, Oklahoma and Virginia. See http://www.mbc.com/ecommerce/legis/ucvue.htm for a current list

four states had enacted "bomb shelter" statutes, which allowed courts in the "bomb shelter" state to void any provision in a contract that specifies UCITA as the law to be applied, or a UCITA state as tthe chosen forum.[5] As of 2003, the Uniform Commissioners stated that they would not seek further enactments of UCITA, but they did not withdraw their previous adoption.

UCITA rejects many of the concepts in both the UNCITRAL Model Law and UETA. Thus, the Uniform Commissioners have proposed two different uniform acts whose provisions conflict on such basic terms as authentication and attribution.

§ 8.9   European Union—Background to the eEurope Initiative

The EU efforts through the eEurope Initiative to develop an European Information Society.[1] Were an attempt to coherently address the impact of technology on European society as a whole. It resulted in a very different approach to many of the issues raised by E–Commerce than that seen in the United States for example. It provides legal rules throughout the different member countries in the EU. At the same time it consciously seeks to regulate and channel the development of E–Commerce and other Information Society services. Measures related to E–Commerce include the 1997 European Initiative on Electronic Commerce,[2] which focused on primarily on developing infrastructure and protecting consumers' economic and legal interests; the related 1997 Distance Selling Directive;[3] the 1999 Electronic Signature Directive;[4] and most recently the Electronic Commerce Directive in 2000.[5] There are also several other important measures aimed at particular issues, such as the Privacy Directive,[6] which have a significant impact upon online transactions but which would not themselves be considered as "enabling" legislation for E–Commerce transactions. Unlike the

of States where UCITA has been adopted.

5. Iowa, North Carolina, Vermont and West Virginia. *Id.*

§ 8.9

1. "eEurope—An Information Society for All," COM(99) 687 final, 8.12.1999.

2. "A European Initiative on Electronic Commerce," COM(97) 157 final, 16.6.1997.

3. Directive 1997/7/EC of the European Parliament and of the Council of 20 May 1997 on the Protection of Consumers in respect of Distance Contracts, *Official Journal L 144, 04/06/1997.*

4. Directive 1999/93/EC of the European Parliament and of the Council of

13 December 1999 on a Community framework for Electronic Signatures, *Official Journal L 013, 19/01/2000.*

5. Directive 2000/31/EC of the European Parliament and of the Council of 8 June 2000 on certain legal aspects of information society services, in particular electronic commerce, in the Internal Market, *Official Journal L 178, 17/07/2000.*

6. Directive 95/46/EC of 24 October 1995 on the protection of individuals with regard to the processing of personal data and on the free movement of such data., *Official Journal L 281, 23.11.1995.*

UNICTRAL Model Law, however, all these measures have immediate legal impact within the European Union.

§ 8.10   European Union—Distance Selling Directive

The Distance Selling Directive is intended to promote European consumer confidence in E–Commerce, by guaranteeing that the local consumer protection laws will apply to contracts concluded at a distance.[1] By relying upon the protections of local laws, presumably concerns over the nature and amount of information provided by sellers, the privacy accorded to information provided by consumers, aggressive marketing techniques, and payment fraud resulting from online transactions would be ameliorated. The Directive, however, applies to all types of contracts concluded by any means where the supplier and consumer are not in each others physical presence including those created by mail, telephone, videophone, radio, fax, and email, for example, and is not confined just to online transactions.[2] Each member state in the EU was required to implement the Directive's requirements in their national law, in this manner the various national laws on distance contracts through the EU "approximate" one another and achieve the same objectives.[3]

The Directive imposes a number of requirements. Certain types of technologies, such as automated calling machines or faxes, may not be used for unsolicited marketing without prior consent, and others may not be employed over the consumer's objection.[4] Prior to concluding the contract, consumers are to be provided with certain information in "clear and comprehensible form" covering a variety of basic details about the supplier; the cost, terms, and conditions of the transaction; and, significantly, the consumer's right to withdraw or cancel the transaction.[5] This information must be provided either in writing or in some other "durable" media accessible to the consumer prior to delivery or completion of performance of the contract.[6] Orders placed through distance selling must ordinarily be filled within 30 days.[7] Consumers are typically given 7 business days to withdraw from a distance contract for any reason, with no penalty, and the consumer's reimbursement following withdrawal must be processed within 30 days.[8] If the supplier failed to provide the requisite information in advance of the trans-

§ 8.10

1. Directive 1997/7/EC of the European Parliament and of the Council of 20 May 1997 on the Protection of Consumers in respect of Distance Contracts, *Official Journal L 144, 04/06/1997.*

2. *Id.*, Art. 2 & Annex1.

3. *Id.*, Art. 15. EU member nations were given until the end of 2000 to implement the Directive.

4. *Id.*, Art. 10.

5. *Id.*, Art. 4.

6. *Id.*, Art. 5.

7. *Id.*, Art. 7.

8. *Id.*, Art. 6.

action, the time period for the consumer to exercise this right of withdrawal expands to three months.[9]

§ 8.11   European   Union—Electronic   Signature Directive

The Electronic Signature Directive,[1] establishes that a signature may not be denied legal effect of validity solely on the grounds that it is in electronic form.[2] Additionally, member states within the EU are prohibited from imposing obligations which would restrict the free flow of electronic signature services across national borders.[3] In accord with the emphasis on consumer protection in many European measures, the Directive imposes a number of obligations upon general providers of electronic signature services, but not upon those who use electronic signature technologies within their own closed or proprietary systems.[4] In particular, Certification Service Providers (CSPs), those who provide an "electronic attestation which links signature-verification data to a person and confirms the identity of that person," are to be supervised and regulated in the country where they are established[5] and are liable for the certifications they issue.[6] The establishment of national voluntary accreditation schemes to bolster public confidence in electronic signatures is encouraged,[7] and intended to promote the cross border acceptability of electronic signatures and their accompanying certifications.[8]

§ 8.12   European   Union—Personal   Data   Protection Directive

The European Union has adopted a personal data protection directive that applies to international electronic commerce. Council Directive 95/46 requires each member EU state to protect the processing of personal data. Under this directive, any information relating to natural persons must be secure, current, relevant and not excessive in content. In most cases, personal data may be processed only with the consent of the individual involved. Processing data revealing racial or ethnic origin, political opinions, religious beliefs, philosophical or ethical persuasion, and health or sexual life is rarely permitted without written consent.

9. *Id.*

§ 8.11

1. Directive 1999/93/EC of the European Parliament and of the Council of 13 December 1999 on a Community framework for Electronic Signatures, *Official Journal L 013, 19/01/2000.*

2. *Id.,* Art. 5.

3. *Id.,* Art. 4.

4. *Id.,* Preamble (16).

5. *Id.,* Art. 3.

6. *Id.,* Art. 6.

7. *Id.,* Art. 3.

8. *Id.,* Art. 7.

Directive 95/46 guarantees individual access to processed information and notice of its use. Individuals may object at any time to the legitimacy of personal data processing. They may also demand erasure without cost of personal data before it is disclosed to or used by third parties for direct mail marketing.

Data processors are required to make extensive disclosures to individuals and to governments. Such disclosure duties, for example, apply to virtually all web sites that invite registration. National authorities are empowered where appropriate to access, erase or block information held by data processors. Private civil liability and public penalty remedies are administered under member state laws, which allow electronic commerce consumers to sue in their countries of residence.

Article 25 of Directive 95/46 mandates a prohibition against the transfer of personal data to non-member states (like the United States) unless they offer an "adequate level of protection." Exemptions from this scrutiny exist for "unambiguous" consents, when the data is necessary for contract performance between individuals and data processors (e.g., billing), the transfer is legally required or serves "important public interests," the transfer is necessary to protect the individual's "vital interests," or the transfer comes from an open, public register.

Practically speaking, Directive 95/46 governs most global businesses since it is very difficult to segregate European Union data from that collected elsewhere. Both online and offline data processors fall within its scope. The directive's impact has been felt, for example, in restrictive orders denying U.S. direct mail companies access to European mailing lists. More broadly, the European Commission and the U.S. Department of Commerce have sought to defuse the potentially explosive issue of the "adequacy" of U.S. law on personal data privacy. Early in 2000, agreement was reached to create a "safe harbor" for U.S. firms from EU data privacy litigation or prosecution. To qualify for the safe harbor, a data processing organization can voluntarily (1) join a self-regulatory privacy program that adheres to the safe harbor's requirements: or (2) develop its own self regulatory privacy policy that conforms to the safe harbor. The organization can self certify annually to the department of Commerce in writing that it agrees to adhere to the safe harbor's requirements, which includes elements such as notice, choice, access, and enforcement. It must also state in its published privacy policy statement that it adheres to the safe harbor. The Department of Commerce maintains a list of all organizations that file self certification letters and makes both the list and the self certification letters publicly available.

In general, enforcement of the safe harbor takes place in the United States in accordance with U.S. law and is carried out primarily by the private sector. As part of their safe harbor obligations, organizations must have a dispute resolution system that will investigate and resolve individual complaints and disputes, and procedures for verifying compliance. They must also remedy problems arising out of a failure to comply with the principles. Under the Federal Trade Commission Act, a company's failure to abide by commitments to implement the safe harbor principles might be considered deceptive and actionable by the Federal Trade Commission.

To date, only a handful of U.S. companies have signed up with self-regulatory privacy groups (such as BBBOnline) to obtain shelter from Directive 95/46. The Department of Commerce has found the number of businesses signing up for the plan to be disappointingly small. Many companies use pop-up screens which state the purpose for collection of data, then rely upon the customer's check on a box that they could have viewed this information as creating a record of consent. Many organizations in the EU have developed an array of contract clauses. Some U.S. companies (e.g., Amazon.com) assert that they are in compliance. Others (e.g., DoubleClick.com) have selectively curtailed their use of "cookies" to track online users. Many seem blissfully unaware of the scope and intensity of Directive 95/46.

*

Chapter 9

AN INTRODUCTION TO THE WTO, IMF AND U.S. TRADE AUTHORITIES

Table of Sections

The need to balance the protection of local industries from harm by foreign competitors and the encouragement of trade across national borders is a recurrent theme in the law of international business transactions. There has been a shift in recent years toward freer international trade because of diminished restrictions on imported goods. However, trade problems associated with the movement of goods across national borders still arise because of restrictive trade devices which impede or distort trade. Common devices include tariff barriers (e.g., import duties and export duties) as well as certain nontariff trade barriers (NTBs) such as import quotas, import licensing procedures, safety, environmental and

191

other minimum manufacturing standards, import testing requirements, complex customs procedures (including valuation), government procurement policies, and government subsidies or countervailing measures. For example, during a part of 1982, France
required that all video recorders entering France had to do so
through a small customs post at Poitiers and carry documentation
written in French. Product distribution practices have been an
effective NTB in Japan. The Japanese have also banned from
importation a food preservative which is essential to preserve the
edibility of certain agricultural products from abroad.

Efforts by countries to limit disruptive trade practices are
commonly found in bilateral treaties of friendship, commerce and
navigation (FCN), which open the territory of each signatory nation
to imports arriving from the other signatory nation. Such bilateral
FCN treaty clauses are usually linked to other preferential trade
agreements. In a bilateral arrangement, such linkage will most
often be through a reciprocal "most favored nation" (MFN) clause.
In a MFN clause, both parties agree not to extend to any other
nation trade arrangements which are more favorable than available
under the bilateral treaty, unless the more favorable trade arrangements are immediately *also* available to the signatory of the bilateral treaty.

In various parts of the world, two or more countries have
joined in customs unions or free trade areas in order to facilitate
trade between those countries and to acquire increased bargaining
power in trade discussions with countries which already enjoy a
strong trade position.

The General Agreement on Tariffs and Trade (GATT), now
replaced by the new World Trade Organization (WTO), was an
international arrangement with over one hundred countries as
Contracting States which regularly held multilateral trade negotiations (MTN) seeking ways of making international trade more
open. These periodic negotiations cumulatively reduced tariff barriers by an average of up to eighty percent below those existing three
decades before. After the most recent multilateral negotiations, the
Uruguay Round, average tariff rates of developed countries on
dutiable manufactured imports were cut from 6.3 percent to 3.9
percent. Tariff reductions are one of the success stories of GATT.
But not all nations participated in the GATT or are members of its
replacement, the WTO. For example, both Russia and Vietnam are
seeking membership in the WTO, but are not yet Members. China
joined in 2001. Nontariff trade barriers (NTBs) are also addressed
in the WTO Covered Agreements, which include agreements designed to lessen or to eliminate NTBs such as complex customs
valuation procedures, import licensing systems, product standards,
subsidies and countervailing duties, and dumping practices.

§ 9.1　The General Agreement on Tariffs and Trade: History and Provisions

Participants in the Bretton Woods meetings in 1944 recognized a post-War need to reduce trade obstacles in order to foster freer trade. They envisioned the creation of an International Trade Organization (ITO) to achieve the desired result. Fifty-three countries met in Havana in 1948 to complete drafting the Charter of an ITO that would be the international organizational umbrella underneath which negotiations could occur periodically to deal with tariff reductions. A framework for such negotiations had already been staked out in Geneva in 1947, in a document entitled the General Agreement on Tariffs and Trade (GATT). Twenty-three nations participated in that first GATT session, India, Chile, Cuba and Brazil representing the developing world. China participated; Japan and West Germany did not. Stringent trading rules were adopted only where there were no special interests of major participants to alter them. The developing nations objected to many of the strict rules, arguing for special treatment justified on development needs, but they achieved few successes in drafting GATT.

The ITO Charter was never ratified. The United States Congress in the late 1940s was unwilling to join more new international organizations, thus U.S. ratification of the ITO Charter could not be secured. Nonetheless, and moving by way of the President's power to make executive agreements, the United States did join twenty-one other countries, as Contracting Parties, in signing a Protocol of Provisional Application of the General Agreement on Tariffs and Trade (61 Stat.Pts. 5, 6) (popularly called the "GATT Agreement").

From 1947 to 1986, GATT was concerned primarily with international trade of goods. The central features of GATT, as reflected by the Articles of the Agreement, include Article I, which makes a general commitment to the long standing practice of most favored nation treatment (MFN) by requiring each Contracting Party to accord unconditional MFN status to all other Contracting Parties. Thus, any privilege granted by any Contracting Party to any product imported from any other country must also be "immediately and unconditionally" granted to any "like product" imported from any Contracting Parties.

Although addressed to national treatment regarding internal taxation and regulation, GATT Article III incorporates the practice of according national treatment to imported goods by providing, with enumerated exceptions, that the products of one Contracting State, when imported into any other Contracting State, shall receive most favored nation (MFN) treatment. In this context, MFN treatment requires that the products of the exporting GATT Contracting State be treated no less favorably than domestic products of the importing Contracting State under its laws and regulations concerning sale, internal resale, purchase, transportation and use.

In addition to requiring MFN treatment, GATT prohibits any use of certain kinds of quantitative restrictions. Although GATT does permit "duties, taxes or other charges", Article XI prohibits the use of other "prohibitions or restrictions" on imports from Contracting Parties. It specifically prohibits the use of "quotas, import or export licenses or other measures" to restrict imports from a Contracting Party. Article XIII requires non-discrimination in quantitative trade restrictions, by barring an importing Contracting State from applying any prohibition or restriction to the products of another Contracting State, "unless the importation of the like product of *all* third countries ... is similarly prohibited or restricted." (emphasis added).

While GATT does permit nondiscriminatory "duties, taxes and other charges," the powers of a Contracting Party are limited even as to these devices. First, GATT Article X requires that notice be given of any new or changed national regulations which affect international trade, by requiring the prompt publication by any Contracting Party of those "laws, regulations, judicial decisions and administrative rulings of general application"

> which pertain to the classification or the valuation of products for customs purposes, or to rates of duty, taxes or other charges, or to requirements, restrictions or prohibitions on imports or exports or on the transfer of payments therefor, or affecting their sale, distribution, transportation, insurance, warehousing, inspection, exhibitions, processing, mixing or other use. . . .

Second, the Contracting Parties commit themselves, under GATT Article XXVIII to a continuing series of MTN ("from time to time") to seek further reductions in tariff levels and other barriers to international trade. Such negotiations are to be "on a reciprocal and mutually advantageous basis." GATT negotiated tariff rates (called "concessions" or "bindings"), which are listed in the "tariff Schedules", are deposited with GATT by each participating country. These concessions must be granted to imports from any Contracting Party, both because of the GATT required MFN treatment, and also because Article II specifically requires use of the negotiated rates.

Framers of GATT were well aware that a commitment to freer trade could cause serious, adverse economic consequences from time to time within part or all of a country's domestic economy, particularly its labor sector. The GATT contains at least seven safety valves (in nine clauses of the Agreement) to permit a country, in appropriate circumstances, to respond to domestic pressures while remaining a participant in GATT. Two safety valves deal with antidumping duties and countervailing subsidies. See Chapters 12 and 13.

§ 9.2   The GATT/WTO Multinational Trade Negotiations (Rounds)

Under the auspices of GATT Article XXVIII, the Contracting Parties committed themselves to hold periodic multinational trade negotiations (MTN or "Rounds"). They have completed eight such Rounds to date, and the WTO Doha Round is ongoing.

While the first five Rounds concentrated on item by item tariff reductions, the "Kennedy Round" (1964–1967) was noted for its achievement of across-the-board tariff reductions. In 1961, GATT began to consider how to approach the increasing trade disparity with the developing world. In 1964, GATT adopted Part IV, which introduced a principle of "diminished expectations of reciprocity". Reciprocity remained a goal, but developed nations would not expect concessions from developing nations which were inconsistent with developmental needs. For the developing nations, nonreciprocity meant freedom to protect domestic markets from import competition. Import substitution was a major focus of developmental theory in the 1960s, and developing nations saw keeping their markets closed as a way to save these domestic industries. Although they also sought preferential treatment of their exports, that was a demand which would remain unsatisfied for another decade.

The "Tokyo Round" (1973–1979) engendered agreements about several areas of nontariff barrier (NTB) trade restraints. Nearly a dozen major agreements on nontariff barrier issues were produced in the Tokyo Round. In the early 1970s, national and regional generalized preference schemes developed to favor the exports of developing nations. The foreign debt payment problems of the developing nations suggest that they need to generate revenue to pay these debts, and that developmental theory must shift from import substitution to export promotion.

In 1986, the "Uruguay Round" of multilateral trade negotiations began at a Special Session of the GATT Contracting States. This Uruguay Round included separate negotiations on trade in goods and on trade in services, with separate groups of negotiators dealing with each topic. Subtopics for negotiation by subgroups included nontariff barriers, agriculture, subsidies and countervailing duties, intellectual property rights and counterfeit goods, safeguards, tropical products, textiles, investment policies, and dispute resolution. The negotiating sessions were extraordinarily complex, but were able to achieve a successful conclusion at the end of 1993.

Because protectionist barriers to international trade in services were stifling, the United States and several other countries insisted that there should be a General Agreement on Trade in Services (GATS). In the United States, trade in services accounts for two-thirds of the Nation's GNP; services provide work for nearly two-thirds of the work force. Services account for almost one-third of U.S. trade abroad.

The 1947 GATT Agreement and its subsequent multinational negotiating rounds were quite successful in reducing tariff duty levels on trade in goods. This was its original purpose, and the mechanism was well-adapted to accomplishing that purpose. However, its effectiveness was also limited to trade in goods, and primarily to reduction of tariffs in such trade. It was not designed to affect trade in services, trade-related intellectual property rights or trade-related investment measures. As tariff duty rates declined, the trade-distorting effects of these other issues became relatively more important.

Even within "trade in goods," the 1947 GATT had limitations. It included a Protocol of Provisional Application which allowed numerous grandfathered exceptions to Members' obligations under the GATT Agreement. The Protocol exempted from GATT disciplines the national laws of Member States which were already enacted and in force at the time of adoption of the Protocol. Further, the 1947 GATT did not have an institutional charter, and was not intended to become an international organization on trade. It did later develop institutional structures and acquired quasi-organizational status, but there was always a lack of a recognized organizational structure. This lack was most often perceived in the inability of GATT to resolve disputes which were brought to it. Dispute settlement procedures were dependent upon the acquiescence of the individual Member States.

§ 9.3 The World Trade Organization (WTO) and GATT 1994

The WTO is the product of the Uruguay Round of GATT negotiations, which was successfully completed in 1994. The Uruguay Round produced a package of agreements, the Agreement Establishing the World Trade Organization and its Annexes, which include the General Agreement on Tariffs and Trade 1994 (GATT 1994) and a series of Multilateral Trade Agreements (the Covered Agreements), and a series of Plurilateral Trade Agreements.[1]

§ 9.3

1. *See* 33 Int. Legal Mat. 1130 (1994).

GATT 1947 and GATT 1994 are two distinct agreements. GATT 1994 incorporates the provisions of GATT 1947, except for the Protocol of Provisional Application, which is expressly excluded. Thus, the problems created by exempting the existing national laws at the time of the adoption of the Protocol will now be avoided by this exclusion in the Covered Agreements. Otherwise, in cases involving a conflict between GATT 1947 and GATT 1994, GATT 1947 controls. The WTO will be guided by the decisions, procedures and customary practices under GATT.

Annexed to the WTO Agreement are several Multilateral Trade Agreements. As to trade in goods, they include Agreements on Agriculture, Textiles, Antidumping, Subsidies and Countervailing Measures, Safeguards, Technical Barriers to Trade, Sanitary and Phytosanitary Measures, Pre-shipment Inspection, Rules of Origin, and Import License Procedures. In addition to trade in goods, they include a General Agreement on Trade in Services and Agreements on Trade–Related Aspects of Intellectual Property Rights and Trade–Related Investment Measures. Affecting all of these agreements is the Understanding on Rules and Procedures Governing the Settlement of Disputes. All of the Multilateral Trade Agreements are binding on all Members of the World Trade Organization.

In addition to the Multilateral Trade Agreements, there are also Plurilateral Trade Agreements which are also annexed to the WTO Agreement. These agreements, however, are not binding on all WTO Members, and Members can choose to adhere to them or not. They include Agreements on Government Procurement, Trade in Civil Aircraft, International Dairy and an Arrangement Regarding Bovine Meat. States which do not join the plurilateral trade agreements do not receive reciprocal benefits under them.

The duties of the World Trade Organization are to facilitate the implementation, administer the operations and further the objectives of all these agreements. Its duties also include the resolution of disputes under the agreements, reviews of trade policy and cooperation with the International Monetary Fund (IMF) and the World Bank. To achieve these goals, the WTO Agreement does provide a charter for the new organization, but provides for only a minimalist institution, with institutional and procedural capabilities, but with no substantive competence being given to the organization itself. Thus, there is a unified administration of pre-existing and new obligations under all agreements concerning trade in goods, including the Uruguay Round Agreements. In addition, the administration of the new obligations on trade in services and intellectual property are brought under the same roof.

On the other hand, both the International Monetary Fund (IMF) and the World Bank have executive powers for their institutions, which the WTO does not have. The WTO as an institution has no power to bring actions on its own initiative. Under the provisions of the WTO Agreement, only the Members of WTO can initiate actions under the Dispute Settlement Understanding. Enforcement of WTO obligations is primarily through permitting Members to retaliate or cross retaliate against other members, rather than by execution of WTO institutional orders. However, the WTO has an internationally recognized organizational structure, which is a step forward from the status of GATT as an organization.

§ 9.4   WTO Decision–Making

The World Trade Organization is structured in three tiers. One tier is the Ministerial Conference, which meets biennially and is composed of representatives of all WTO Members. Each Member has an equal voting weight, which is unlike the representation in the IMF and World Bank where there is weighted voting, and financially powerful states have more power over the decision-making process. The Ministerial Conference is responsible for all WTO functions, and is able to make any decisions necessary. It has the power to authorize new multilateral negotiations and to adopt the results of such negotiations. The Ministerial Conference, by a three-fourths vote, is authorized to grant waivers of obligations to Members in exceptional circumstances. It also has the power to adopt interpretations of Covered Agreements. When the Ministerial Conference is in recess, its functions are performed by the General Council.

The second tier is the General Council which has executive authority over the day to day operations and functions of the WTO. It is composed of representatives of all WTO Members, and each member has an equal voting weight. It meets whenever it is appropriate. The General Council also has the power to adopt interpretations of Covered Agreements.

The third tier comprises the councils, bodies and committees which are accountable to the Ministerial Conference or General Council. Ministerial Conference committees include Committees on Trade and Development, Balance of Payment Restrictions, Budget, Finance and Administration. General Council bodies include the Dispute Settlement Body, the Trade Policy Review Body, and Councils for Trade in Goods, Trade in Services and Trade–Related Intellectual Property Rights. The Councils are all created by the WTO Agreement and are open to representatives of all Member States. The Councils also have the authority to create subordinate organizations. Other committees, such as the Committee on Subsidies and Countervailing Measures are created by specific individual agreements.

Of the General Council bodies, the two which are likely to be most important are the Dispute Settlement Body (DSB) and the Trade Policy Review Body (TPRB). The DSB is a special meeting of the General Council, and therefore includes all WTO Members. It has responsibility for resolution of disputes under all the Covered Agreements, and will be discussed in more detail below, under Dispute Resolution.

The purpose of the Trade Policy Review–Mechanism (TPRM) is to improve adherence to the WTO agreements and obligations, and to obtain greater transparency. Individual Members of WTO each prepare a "Country Report" on their trade policies and perceived adherence to the WTO Covered Agreements. The WTO Secretariat also prepares a report on each Member, but from the perspective of the Secretariat. The Trade Policy Review Body (TPRB) then reviews the trade policies of each Member based on these two reports. At the end of the review, the TPRB issues its own report concerning the adherence of the Member's trade policy to the WTO Covered Agreements. The TPRB has no enforcement capability, but the report is sent to the next meeting of the WTO Ministerial Conference. It is then up to the Ministerial Conference to evaluate the trade practices and policies of the Member.

The process of decision-making in the WTO Ministerial Conference and General Council relies upon "consensus" as the norm, just as it did for decision-making under GATT 1947. "Consensus", in this context means that no Member formally objects to a proposed decision. Thus, consensus is not obtained if any one Member formally objects, and has often been very difficult to obtain, which proved to be a weakness in the operation of GATT. However, there are many exceptions to the consensus formula under WTO, and some new concepts (such as "inverted consensus", discussed below) which are designed to ease the process of decision-making under WTO.

Article IX(1) of the WTO Agreement first provides that "the practice of decision-making by consensus" followed under GATT shall be continued. The next sentence of that provision, however, states that "where a decision cannot be arrived at by consensus, the matter at issue shall be decided by voting", except where otherwise provided. The ultimate resolution of the conflict between these two sentences is not completely clear.

There are a number of exceptions to the requirement for consensus that are expressly created under the WTO Agreement. One such exception is decisions by the Dispute Settlement Body, which has its own rules (see below). Another set of exceptions concerns decisions on waivers, interpretations and amendments of the Covered Agreements. Waivers of obligations may be granted and amendments adopted to Covered Agreements only by the Ministerial Conference. Amendments of Multilateral Trade Agreements usually require a consensus, but where a decision on a proposed amendment cannot obtain consensus, the decision on that amendment is to be made in certain circumstances by a two-thirds majority vote. In "exceptional circumstances", the Ministerial Conference is authorized to grant waivers of obligations under a Covered Agreement by a three-fourths vote. Another exception to the consensus requirement allows procedural rules in both the Ministerial Conference and the General Council to be decided by a majority vote of the Members, unless otherwise provided.

However, in addition to these express exceptions, Article IX (1) seems to indicate that where a decision would normally be made by consensus, but consensus cannot be obtained, the matter will then be decided "by voting." Whether this provision destroys the basic consensus requirement whenever there is an impasse is not yet clear. It is possible that any issue which fails to obtain a consensus, but has majority support, can be determined "by voting", as long as there is no other express provision. It is also not completely clear what procedure is to be used to satisfy the "by voting" standard. It is also possible, however, that this provision is only to be applied to decisions which the Ministerial Conference must make to assure the continuance of a workable WTO system. An illustration of such a decision could be the continuation, modification or termination of the dispute settlement procedure.

§ 9.5   WTO Agreements and U.S. Law

The WTO Covered Agreements concern not only trade in goods, but also trade in services (GATS), and trade-related aspects of intellectual property (TRIPS). The basic concepts that GATT applied to trade in goods (described above) are now applied to these areas through GATS and TRIPS. In the WTO Covered Agreements, the basic concepts of GATT 1947 and its associated agreements are elaborated and clarified. In addition, there is an attempt to transform all protectionist measures relating to agriculture (such as import bans and quotas, etc.) into only tariff barriers, which can then be lowered in subsequent MTN Rounds (a process known as "tariffication"). WTO also contains some superficial provisions on trade-related investment measures (TRIMS). Some of the WTO provisions, particularly those concerning trade in goods, will be discussed in more detail below in relation to United States trade law.

As of 2005, there were about 150 Member States of the World Trade Organization. Russia, Vietnam, Saudi Arabia and Iran are notable non-members, some actively seeking to join. The United States enacted legislation to implement WTO and the Covered Agreements on December 3, 1994. The implementing legislation was submitted to Congress under the "fast track" procedures of 19 U.S.C.A. § 2112, which required that the agreement and its implementing legislation be considered as a whole by Congress, and which also prohibits Congressional amendments to the implementing legislation. The Congressional authority for "fast track" procedures also required that the President give ninety days notice of his intention to enter into such an agreement. Similar fast track procedures are in place for the Doha Round of WTO negotiations under the Trade Promotion Authority Act of 2002.

Neither GATT 1947 nor the WTO Agreement, GATT 1994 and the other Covered Agreements have been ratified as treaties, and therefore comprise international obligations of the United States only to the extent that they are incorporated in United States' implementing legislation. GATT 1947 was not considered controlling by the courts of the United States, and these courts have always held themselves bound to the U.S. legislation actually enacted.[1] The WTO Covered Agreements will be considered to have a non-self-executed status, and therefore are likely to be regarded in the same manner as GATT 1947.

§ 9.6　WTO Dispute Settlement/U.S. Disputes

WTO provides a unified system for settling international trade disputes through the Dispute Settlement Understanding (DSU) and using the Dispute Settlement Body (DSB). The DSB is a special assembly of the WTO General Council, and includes all WTO Members. There are five stages in the resolution of disputes under WTO: 1) Consultation; 2) Panel establishment, investigation and report; 3) Appellate review of the panel report; 4) Adoption of the panel and appellate decision; and 5) Implementation of the decision adopted. There is also a parallel process for binding arbitration, if both parties agree to submit this dispute to arbitration, rather than to a DSB panel. In addition, during the implementation phase (5), the party subject to an adverse decision may seek arbitration as a matter of right on issues of compliance and authorized retaliation.

Although the DSU offers a unified dispute resolution system that is applicable across all sectors and all WTO Covered Agreements, there are many specialized rules for disputes which arise under them. Such specialized rules appear in the Agreements on

§ 9.5

1. *See, e.g.*, Suramerica de Aleaciones Laminadas, C.A. v. United States, 966 F.2d 660 (Fed.Cir.1992).

Textiles, Antidumping, Subsidies and Countervailing Measures, Technical Barriers to Trade, Sanitary and Phytosanitary Measures, Customs Valuation, General Agreement on Trade in Services, Financial Services and Air Transport Services. The special provisions in these individual Covered Agreements govern, where applicable, and prevail in any conflict with the general provisions of the DSU.

Under WTO, unlike under GATT 1947, the DSU practically assures that panels will be established upon request by a Member. Further, under WTO, unlike under GATT 1947, the DSU virtually ensures the adoption of unmodified panel and appellate body decisions. It accomplishes this by requiring the DSB to adopt panel reports and appellate body decisions automatically and without amendment unless they are rejected by a consensus of all Members. This "inverted consensus" requires that all Members of the DSB, including the Member who prevailed in the dispute, decide to reject the dispute resolution decision; and that no Member formally favor that decision. Such an outcome seems unlikely. This inverted consensus requirement is imposed on both the adoption of panel reports or appellate body decisions and also on the decision to establish a panel.

The potential resolutions of a dispute under DSU range from a "mutually satisfactory solution" agreed to by the parties under the first, or consultation phase, to authorized retaliation under the last, or implementation, phase. The preferred solution is always any resolution that is mutually satisfactory to the parties. After a panel decision, there are three types of remedies available to the prevailing party, if a mutually satisfactory solution cannot be obtained. One is for the respondent to bring the measure found to violate a Covered Agreement into conformity with the Agreement. A second is for the prevailing Member to receive compensation from the respondent which both parties agree is sufficient to compensate for any injury caused by the measure found to violate a Covered Agreement. Finally, if no such agreement can be reached, a prevailing party can be authorized to suspend some of its concessions under the Covered Agreements to the respondent. These suspended concessions, called "retaliation," can be authorized within the same trade sector and agreement; or, if that will not create sufficient compensation, can be authorized across trade sectors and agreements.

Consultation

Any WTO Member who believes that the Measures of another Member are not in conformity with the Covered Agreements may call for consultations on those measures. The respondent has ten days to reply to the call for consultations and must agree to enter into consultation within 30 days. If the respondent does not enter into consultations within the 30 day period, the party seeking consultations can immediately request the establishment of a panel under DSU, which puts the dispute into Phase 2.

Once consultations begin, the parties have 60 days to achieve a settlement. The goal is to seek a positive solution to the dispute, and the preferred resolution is to reach whatever solution is mutually satisfactory to the parties. If such a settlement cannot be obtained after 60 days of consultations, the party seeking consultations may request the establishment of a panel under DSU, which moves the dispute into Phase 2.

Third parties with an interest in the subject-matter of the consultations may seek to be included in them. If such inclusion is rejected, they may seek their own consultations with the other Member. Alternatives to consultations may be provided through the use of conciliation, mediation or good offices, where all parties agree to use the alternative process. Any party can terminate the use of conciliation, mediation or good offices and then seek the establishment of a panel under DSU, which will move the dispute into Phase 2.

Panel establishment, investigation and report

If consultations between the parties fail, the party seeking the consultations (the complainant) may request the DSB to establish a panel to investigate, report and resolve the dispute. The DSB must establish such a panel upon request, unless the DSB expressly decides by consensus not to establish the panel. Since an "inverted consensus" is required to reject the establishment of the panel and the complainant Member must be part of that consensus, it is very likely that a panel will be established. Roughly 100 panels were established in the first five years of operation of the DSU.

The WTO Secretariat is to maintain a list of well-qualified persons who are available to serve as panelists. The panels are usually composed of three individuals from that list who are not citizens of either party. If the parties agree, a panel can be composed of five such individuals. The parties can also agree to appoint citizens of a party to a panel. Panelists may be either nongovernmental individuals or governmental officials, but they are to be selected so as to ensure their independence. Thus, there is a bias towards independent individuals who are not citizens of any party. If a citizen of a party is appointed, his government may not instruct that citizen how to vote, for the panelist must be independent. By the same reasoning, a governmental official of a non-party Member who is subject to instructions from his government would not seem to fit the profile of an independent panelist.

The WTO Secretariat proposes nominations of the panelists. Parties may not normally oppose the nominations, except for "compelling reasons." The parties are given twenty days to agree on the panelists and the composition of the panel. If such agreement is not forthcoming, the WTO Director–General is authorized to appoint the panelists, in consultation with other persons in the Secretariat.

Complaints brought to DSB panels can involve either violations of Covered Agreements or nonviolation nullification and impairment of benefits under the Covered Agreements. A prima facie case of nullification impairment arises when one Member infringes upon the "obligations assumed under a Covered Agreement." Such infringement creates a presumption against the infringing Member, but the presumption can be rebutted by a showing that the complaining Member has suffered no adverse effect from the infringement.

The panels receive pleadings and rebuttals and hear oral arguments. Panels can also engage in fact development from sources outside those presented by the parties. Thus, the procedure has aspects familiar to civil law courts. A panel can, on its own initiative, request information from any body, including experts selected by the panel. It can also obtain confidential information in some circumstances from an administrative body which is part of the government of a Member, without any prior consent from that Member. A panel can establish its own group of experts to provide reports to it on factual or scientific issues. In a series of rulings commencing with the *Shrimp-Turtles* decision in 1998, the WTO Appellate Body has affirmed the right of panels and itself to elect to receive unsolicited informational and argumentative briefs or letters from non-governmental organizations (NGOs), business groups and law firms.

A panel is obligated to produce two written reports—an interim and a final report. A panel is supposed to submit a final written report to the DSB within six months of its establishment. The report will contain its findings of fact, findings of law, decision and the rationale for its decision. Before the final report is issued, the panel is supposed to provide an interim report to the parties. The purpose of this interim report is to apprize the parties of the panel's current analysis of the issues and to permit the parties to comment on that analysis. The final report of the panel need not change any of the findings or conclusions in its interim report unless it is persuaded to do so by a party's comments. However, if it is not so persuaded, it is obligated to explain in its final report why it is not so persuaded.

The decisions in panel reports are final as to issues of fact. The decisions in panel reports are not necessarily final as to issues of law. Panel decisions on issues of law are subject to review by the Appellate Body, which is Phase 3, and explained below. Any party can appeal a panel report, and as is explained below it is expected that appeals will usually be taken.

Appellate review of the panel report

Appellate review of panel reports is available at the request of any party, unless the DSB rejects that request by an "inverted consensus." There is no threshold requirement for an appellant to present a substantial substantive legal issue. Thus, most panel decisions are appealed as a matter of course. However, the Appellate Body can only review the panel reports on questions of law or legal interpretation.

The Appellate Body is a new institution in the international trade organization and its process. GATT 1947 had nothing comparable to it. The Appellate Body is composed of seven members (or judges) who are appointed by the DSB to four year terms. Each judge may be reappointed, but only once, to a second four year term. Each judge is to be a recognized authority on international trade law and the Covered Agreements. To date, Appellate Body members have been drawn mostly from the academe and retired justices. They have come from Germany, Japan, Egypt, India, New Zealand, the Philippines, Argentina and the United States. The review of any panel decision is performed by three judges out of the seven. The parties do not, however, have any influence on which judges are selected to review a particular panel report. There is a schedule, created by the Appellate Body itself, for the rotation for sitting of each of the judges. Thus, a party might try to appear before a favored judge by timing the start of the dispute settlement process to arrive at the Appellate Body at the right moment on the rotation schedule, but even this limited approach has difficulties.

The Appellate Body receives written submissions from the parties and has 60, or in some cases 90, days in which to render its decision. The Appellate Body review is limited to issues of law and legal interpretation. The panel decision may be upheld, modified, or reversed by the Appellate Body decision. Appellate Body decisions will be anonymous, and ex parte communications are not permitted, which will make judge-shopping by parties more than usually difficult.

Adoption of the panel or Appellate Body decision

Appellate Body determinations are submitted to the DSB. Panel decisions which are not appealed are also submitted to the DSB. Once either type of decision is submitted to the DSB, the DSB must automatically adopt them without modification or amendment at its next meeting unless the decision is rejected by all Members of the DSB through the form of "inverted consensus" discussed previously.

An alternative to Phases 2 through 4 is arbitration, if both parties agree. The arbitration must be binding on the parties, and there is no appeal from the arbitral tribunal's decision to the DSB Appellate Body.

Implementation of the decision adopted; Compensation; Retaliation

Once a panel or Appellate Body decision is adopted by the DSB, implementation is a three-step process. In the first step, the Member found to have a measure which violates its WTO obligations has "a reasonable time" (usually 15 months) to bring those measures into conformity with the WTO obligations. That remedy is the preferred one, and this form of implementation is the principal goal of the WTO implementation system. To date, most disputes have resulted in compliance in this manner. If the adequacy of compliance is disputed, such disputes typically return to the WTO panel that rendered decision on the merits which also determines, acting as an arbitrator, the amount (if any) of authorized retaliation. The retaliation process is discussed below.

If the violating measures are not brought into conformity within a reasonable time, the parties proceed to the second step. In that second step, the parties negotiate to reach an agreement upon a form of compensation which will be granted by the party in violation to the injured party. Such compensation will usually comprise trade concessions by the violating party to the injured party, which are over and above those already available under the WTO and Covered Agreements. The nature, scope, amount and duration of these additional concessions is at the negotiating parties' discretion, but each side must agree that the final compensation package is fair and is properly related to the injury caused by the violating measures. Presumably, any such concessions need not be extended under MFN principles to all WTO members.

If the parties cannot agree on an appropriate amount of compensation within twenty days, the complainant may proceed to the third step. In the third step, the party injured by the violating measures seeks authority from the DSB to retaliate against the party whose measures violated its WTO obligations. Thus complainant seeks authority to suspend some of its WTO obligations in regard to the respondent. The retaliation must ordinarily be within the same sector and agreement as the violating measure. "Sector" is sometimes broadly defined, as all trade in goods, and sometimes narrowly defined, as in individual services in the Services Sectoral Classification List. "Agreement" is also broadly defined. All the agreements listed in Annex IA to the WTO Agreement are considered a single agreement. If retaliation within the sector and agreement of the violating measure is considered insufficient compensation, the complainant may seek suspension of its obligations across sectors and agreements.

The DSB must grant the complainant's request to retaliate within 30 days unless all WTO members reject it through an "inverted consensus." (Article 22.6, D.S.U.) However, the respondent may object to the level or scope of the retaliation. The issues raised by the objection will be examined by either the Appellate Body or by an arbitrator. The respondent has a right, even if arbitration was not used in Phases 2 through 4, to have an arbitrator review in Phase 5 the appropriateness of the complainant's proposed level and scope of retaliation. The arbitrator will also examine whether the proper procedures and criteria to establish retaliation have been followed. The Phase 5 arbitration is final and binding and the arbitrator's decision is not subject to DSB review.

In addition to objecting to the level of authorized retaliation, the responding WTO member may simultaneously challenge the assertion of noncompliance (Article 21.5, D.S.U.). This challenge will ordinarily be heard by the original panel and must be resolved within 90 days. Thus the request for authorized retaliation and objections thereto could conceivably be accomplished before noncompliance is formally determined. In practice, WTO dispute settlement has melded these conflicting procedures such that compliance and retaliation issues are decided together, typically by the original panel.

The amount of a U.S. retaliation permitted against the EU after the WTO *Bananas* and *Beef Hormones* decisions were not implemented by the EU was contested. The arbitration tribunals for this issue were the original WTO panels, which did not allow the entire amount of the almost $700 million in retaliatory tariffs proposed by the United States. The U.S. was authorized and has levied retaliatory tariffs amounting to about $300 million against European goods because of the EU failure to implement those WTO decisions. Since 2000, Congress has authorized rotating these tariffs in "carousel" fashion upon different European goods. The threat of carousel retaliation contributed to an April 2001 settlement of the *Bananas* dispute.

In a landmark ruling, a WTO panel acting as an arbitrator has authorized Ecuador to remove protection of intellectual property rights regarding geographical indicators, copyrights and industrial designs on European Union goods for sale in Ecuador. This authorization is part of Ecuador's $200 million compensation in the *Bananas* dispute. The WTO panel acknowledged that Ecuador imports mostly capital goods and raw materials from the European Union and that imposing retaliatory tariffs on them would adversely harm its manufacturing industries. This risk supported "cross-retaliation" under Article 22.3 of the DSU outside the sector of the EU trade violation.

Both "compensation" in the second step and "retaliation" in the third step of implementation provide only for indirect enforcement of DSB decisions. There is no mechanism for direct enforcement by the WTO of its decisions through WTO orders to suspend trade obligations. Some commentators believe that retaliation will be an effective implementation device; others believe that it will prove ineffective. The division represented by these conflicting views represents two different approaches to the nature of both international law and international trade law. One approach seeks a rule-oriented use of the "rule of law"; the other seeks a power-oriented use of diplomacy. The United States and less developed countries have traditionally sought to develop a rule-oriented approach to international trade disputes. The European Union and Japan have traditionally sought to use the GATT/WTO primarily as a forum for diplomatic negotiations, although the EU has begun to file more formal complaints.

U.S. Involvement in WTO Dispute Resolution

The WTO dispute resolution process has been invoked more frequently than many expected. The United States has been a complainant or a respondent in dozens of disputes. It lost a dispute initiated by Venezuela and Brazil (WT/DS 2 and 4) concerning U.S. standards for reformulated and conventional gasoline. The offending U.S. law was amended to conform to the WTO ruling. It won on a complaint initiated jointly with Canada and the European Union (WT/DS 8, 10 and 11) regarding Japanese taxes on alcoholic beverages. Japan subsequently changed its law. When Costa Rica complained about U.S. restraints on imports of underwear (WT/DS 24), the U.S. let the restraints expire prior to any formal DSB ruling at the WTO. Similar results were reached when India complained of U.S. restraints on wool shirts and blouses (WT/DS 23). The United States won a major dispute with Canada concerning trade and subsidies for periodicals (WT/DS 31). This celebrated *Sports Illustrated* dispute proved that WTO remedies can be used to avoid Canada's cultural industries exclusion under NAFTA.

In the longstanding *Bananas* dispute (WT/DS 27) noted above, the United States joined Ecuador, Guatemala, Honduras and Mexico in successfully challenging EU import restraints against so-called "dollar bananas." The EU failed to comply with the Appellate Body's ruling, and retaliatory measures were authorized and imposed. In April 2001, the *Bananas* dispute was settled on terms that convert EU quotas to tariffs by 2006. A patent law complaint by the U.S. against India (WT/DS 50) prevailed in the DSB and ultimately brought changes in Indian law regarding pharmaceuticals and agricultural chemicals. In *Beef Hormones* (WT/DS 26 and 48), also noted above, the European Union once again lost before the Appellate Body. It refused to alter its import restraints and presently faces retaliatory tariffs on selected exports to Canada and the United States.

The United States prevailed against Argentina regarding tariffs and taxes on footwear, textiles and apparel (WT/DS 56). It lost a challenge (strongly supported by Kodak) to Japan's distribution rules regarding photo film and paper (WT/DS 44). In this dispute the U.S. elected *not* to appeal the adverse WTO panel ruling to the Appellate Body. In contrast, the European Union took an appeal which reversed an adverse panel ruling on its customs classification of computer equipment (WT/DS 62, 67 and 68). The U.S. had commenced this proceeding. Opponents in many disputes, Japan, the United States and the European Union united to complain in WT/DS 54, 55, 59 and 64 that Indonesia's National Car Programme was discriminatory and in breach of several WTO agreements. They prevailed and Indonesia altered its program.

India, Malaysia, Pakistan and Thailand teamed up to challenge U.S. shrimp import restraints enacted to protect endangered sea turtles (WT/DS 58). The WTO Appellate Body generally upheld their complaint and the U.S. has moved to comply. The adequacy of U.S. compliance is being challenged by Malaysia. The European Union and the United States jointly opposed Korea's discriminatory taxes on alcoholic beverages (WT/DS 75 and 84). This challenge was successful and Korea now imposes flat non-discriminatory taxes. The United States also complained of Japan's quarantine, testing and other agricultural import rules (WT/DS 76/1). The U.S. won at the WTO and Japan has changed its procedures.

In a semiconductor dumping dispute, Korea successfully argued that the U.S. was not in compliance with the WTO Antidumping Agreement (WT/DS 99/1). The United States amended its law, but Korea has instituted further proceedings alleging that these amendments are inadequate. The United States did likewise after Australia lost a subsidies dispute relating to auto leather exports (WT/DS 126/1). The reconvened WTO panel ruled that Australia had indeed failed to conform to the original adverse DSB decision. A U.S. challenge concerning India's quotas on imports of agricultural, textile and industrial products was upheld (WT/DS 90/1). India and the United States subsequently reached agreement on a timeline for removal of these restraints.

Closer to home, New Zealand and the United States complained of Canada's import/export rules regarding milk (WT/DS 103/1). Losing at the WTO, Canada agreed to a phased removal of the offending measures. The United States also won against Mexico in an antidumping dispute involving corn syrup (WT/DS 132/1), but lost a "big one" when the DSB determined that export tax preferences granted to "Foreign Sales Corporations" of U.S. companies were illegal (WT/DS 108/1). Another "big one" went in favor of the United States. The European Union challenged the validity under the DSU of unilateral retaliation under Section 301 of the Trade Act of 1974 (WT/DS 152/1). Section 301 has been something of a bete noire in U.S. trade law, but the WTO panel affirmed its legality in light of Presidential undertakings to administer it in accordance with U.S. obligations to adhere to multilateral WTO dispute settlement.

U.S. involvement in WTO dispute settlement continues to be extensive. The Appellate Body ruled that U.S. countervailing duties against British steel based upon pre-privitization subsidies were unlawful (WT/DS 138/1). The European Union prevailed before a WTO panel in its challenge of the U.S. Antidumping Act of 1916 (WT/DS 136), since repealed. U.S. complaints against Korean beef import restraints and procurement practices were upheld (WT/DS 161/1, 163/1). Canada's patent protection term was also invalidated by the WTO under a U.S. complaint (WT/DS 170/1). European Union complaints concerning U.S. wheat gluten quotas (WT/DS 166/1) and the royalty free small business provisions of the Fairness in Music Licensing Act of 1998 (WT/DS 160/1) have been sustained. The *Wheat Gluten* dispute questions the legality of U.S. "causation" rules in escape clause proceedings under Section 201 of the Trade Act of 1974.

A WTO Panel ruled in 2002 that the Byrd Amendment violates the WTO antidumping and subsidy codes. The Byrd Amendment (Continued Dumping and Subsidy Act of 2000) authorizes the Customs Service to forward AD and CVD duties to affected domestic producers for qualified expenses. Eleven WTO members including the EU, Canada and Mexico challenged the Amendment. This ruling was affirmed by the WTO Appellate Body and retaliation has been authorized. The Appellate Body also ruled against Section 211 of the Omnibus Appropriations Act of 1998 denying trademark protection in connection with confiscated assets (the "HAVANA CLUB" dispute). U.S. compliance with these rulings has been slow in forthcoming. The United States and other complainants prevailed in a 2002 WTO proceeding against Indian local content and trade balancing requirements for foreign auto manufacturers. These requirements violated the TRIMs agreement.

In March of 2004, the European Union commenced raising tariffs against U.S. goods under the WTO retaliation authorized out of the FSC/export tax subsidy dispute. Monthly increments were planned until either the U.S. complied or the EU reached the maximum of roughly $4 billion annually it was authorized to retaliate. In the Fall of 2004, the United States repealed the extraterritorial income exclusion and the EU subsequently removed its retaliatory tariffs. In 2004, also, Antigua–Barbuda won a WTO panel ruling under the GATS against U.S. Internet gambling restraints. The U.S. won a panel decision against Mexico's exorbitant telecom interconnection rates, but lost a 2004 cotton subsidy challenge by Brazil. It also lost a second dispute with the EU about pre-privatization countervailable subsidies, in particular the legality of the U.S. "same person" methodology. (WT/DS212/AB/R). The U.S. won an SPS dispute against Japanese quarantine of U.S. apples (WT/DS245/AB/R), while losing an important softwood lumber "zeroing" methodology complaint brought by Canada. (WT/DS257/AB/R).

The United States has also settled a number of disputes prior to WTO panel decisions, and remains in consultation on other disputes that may be decided by a WTO panel. For the latest summary of all WTO disputes, including many not involving the United States, see www.wto.org

§ 9.7 Import Quotas and Licenses Under the WTO

Quantity restrictions, such as numerical quotas on the importation of an item or upon a type of item, continue to exist, despite GATT Article XI which calls for their elimination. Import quotas may be "global" limitations (applying to items originating from anywhere in the world), "bilateral" limitations (applying to items originating from a particular country) and "discretionary" limitations. Quantitative limitations may have arisen from a Treaty of Friendship, Commerce and Navigation or from a narrow international agreement, such as agreements on trade in textiles and textile products. Discretionary limitations, when coupled with a requirement that importation of items must be licensed in advance by local authorities, provide an effective vehicle for gathering statistical data and for raising local revenues. "Tariff-rate quotas" admit a specified quantity of goods at a preferential rate of duty. Once imports reach that quantity, tariffs are normally increased.

The WTO has significantly reduced the number of trade quotas. The Agreement on Textiles eliminates in 2005 the quotas long maintained under the Multi–Fibre Arrangement. The demise of MFA textile quotas in 2005 is widely expected to accelerate Chinese and other Asian textile exports to the United States. Responding to domestic pressures, President Bush set temporary quotas in the Fall of 2004 against surges of Chinese bras, bathrobes and knit fabrics. More such restraints are permitted until 2008. Voluntary export restraints (quotas) are severely limited by the Safeguards Agreement. In addition, the WTO removes trade quotas by pressuring for "tariffication," or replacing them with tariffs—sometimes even at extraordinarily high tariff rates. Tariffication is the approach adopted in the Agriculture Agreement. It is expected that such high tariff rates will be reduced in subsequent negotiating Rounds. Import licensing schemes are also being phased out under WTO agreements.

§ 9.8 GATT/WTO Nontariff Trade Barrier Codes

There are numerous nontariff trade barriers applicable to imports. Many of these barriers arise out of safety and health regulations. Others concern the environment, consumer protection, product standards and government procurement. Many of the relevant rules were created for legitimate consumer and public protection reasons. They were often created without extensive consideration of their international impact as potential nontariff trade barriers. Nevertheless, the practical impact of legislation of this type is to ban the importation of nonconforming products. Thus, unlike tariffs which can always be paid, and unlike quotas which permit a certain amount of goods to enter the market, nontariff trade barriers have the potential to totally exclude foreign exports.

Multilateral GATT negotiations since the end of World War II have led to a significant decline in world tariff levels, particularly on trade with developed nations. As steadily as tariff barriers have disappeared, nontariff trade barriers (NTBs) have emerged. Health and safety regulations, environmental laws, rules regulating products standards, procurement legislation and customs procedures are often said to present NTB problems. Negotiations over nontariff trade barriers dominated the Tokyo Round of the GATT negotiations during the late 1970s. A number of NTB "codes" (sometimes called "side agreements") emerged from the Tokyo Round. These concerned subsidies, dumping, government procurement, technical barriers (products standards), customs valuation and import licensing. In addition, specific agreements regarding trade in bovine meats, dairy products and civil aircraft were also reached. The United States accepted all of these NTB codes and agreements except the one on dairy products. Most of the necessary implementation of these agreements was accomplished in the Trade Agreements Act of 1979.

Additional GATT codes were agreed upon under the Uruguay Round ending in late 1993. They revisit all of the NTB areas covered by the Tokyo Round Codes and create new codes for sanitary and phyto-sanitary measures (SPS), trade-related investment measures (TRIMs), preshipment inspection, rules of origin, escape clause safeguards and trade-related intellectual property rights (TRIPs). The United States Congress approved and implemented these Codes in December of 1994 under the Uruguay Round Agreements Act.

One problem with nontariff trade barriers is that they are so numerous. Intergovernmental negotiation intended to reduce their trade restricting impact is both tedious and difficult. There are continuing attempts through the World Trade Organization to come to grips with additional specific NTB problems. Furthermore, various trade agreements of the United States have been undertaken in this field. For example, the Canadian–United States Free Trade Area Agreement and the NAFTA built upon the existing GATT agreements to further reduce NTB problems between the United States, Canada and Mexico.

In the *EU Beef Hormones* case, the EU banned imports of growth-enhancing hormone-treated beef from the U.S. and Canada as a health hazard. The Appellate Body ruled that, since the ban was more strict than international standards, the EU needed scientific evidence to back it up. However, the EU had failed to undertake a scientific risk assessment, and the EU's scientific reports did not provide any rational basis to uphold the ban. In fact, the primary EU study had found no evidence of harm to humans from the growth-enhancing-hormones. The Appellate Body ruled that the ban violated the EU's SPS obligations and required the EU to produce scientific evidence to justify the ban within a reasonable time, or to revoke the ban. Arbitrators later determined that 15 months was a reasonable time, but the EU has failed to produce such evidence and the U.S. has retaliated. Late in 2004, the EU commenced new WTO proceedings asserting that more recent scientific studies and precaution justified its ban and require removal of U.S. retaliation.

§ 9.9　The WTO Agreement on Agriculture

Agricultural issues played a central role in the Uruguay Round GATT negotiations. More than any other issue, they delayed completion of the Round from 1990 to 1993. The agreement reached in December of 1993 is a trade liberalizing, market-oriented effort. Each country has made a number of commitments on market access, reduced domestic agricultural support levels and export subsidies. The United States Congress approved of these commitments in December of 1994 by adopting the Uruguay Round Agreements Act.

Broadly speaking nontariff barriers (NTBs) to international agricultural trade are replaced by tariffs that provide substantially the same level of protection. This is known as "tariffication." It applies to virtually all NTBs, including variable levies, import bans, voluntary export restraints and import quotas. Tariffication applies specifically to U.S. agricultural quotas adopted under Section 22 of the Agricultural Adjustment Act. All agricultural tariffs, including those converted from NTBs, are to be reduced by 36 and 24 percent by developed and developing countries, respectively, over 6 and 10 year periods. Certain minimum access tariff quotas apply when imports amount to less than 3 to 5 percent of domestic consumption. An escape clause exists for tariffed imports at low prices or upon a surge of importation depending upon the existing degree of import penetration.

Regarding domestic support for agriculture, some programs with minimal impact on trade are exempt from change. These programs are known as "green box policies." They include governmental support for agricultural research, disease control, infrastructure and food security. Green box policies were also exempt from GATT/WTO challenge or countervailing duties for 9 years. Direct payments to producers that are not linked to production are also generally exempt. This will include income support, adjustment assistance, and environmental and regional assistance payments. Furthermore, direct payments to support crop reductions and *de minimis* payments are exempted in most cases.

After removing all of the exempted domestic agricultural support programs, the agreement on agriculture arrives at a calculation known as the Total Aggregate Measurement of Support (Total AMS). This measure is the basis for agricultural support reductions under the agreement. Developed nations must reduce their Total AMS by 20 percent over 6 years, developing nations by 13.3 percent over 10 years. United States reductions undertaken in 1985 and 1990 suggest that little or no U.S. action will be required to meet this obligation.

Agricultural export subsidies of developed nations must be reduced by 36 percent below 1986–1990 levels over 6 years and the quantity of subsidized agricultural exports by 21 percent. Developing nations must meet corresponding 24 and 14 percent reductions over 10 years.

All conforming tariffications, reductions in domestic support for agriculture and export subsidy alterations were essentially exempt from challenge for 9 years within the GATT/WTO on grounds such as serious prejudice in export markets or nullification and impairment of agreement benefits. However, countervailing duties could be levied against all unlawfully subsidized exports of agricultural goods except for subsidies derived from so-called national "green box policies" (discussed above).

§ 9.10 The WTO Public Procurement Code

Where public procurement is involved, and the taxpayer's money is at issue, virtually every nation has some form of legislation or tradition that favors buying from domestic suppliers. The Tokyo Round GATT Procurement Code was not particularly successful at opening up government purchasing. Only Austria, Canada, the twelve European Union states, Finland, Hong Kong, Israel, Japan, Norway, Singapore, Sweden, Switzerland and the United States adhered to that Procurement Code. This was also partly the result of the 1979 Code's many exceptions. For example, the Code did not apply to contracts below its threshold amount of $150,000 SDR (about $171,000 since 1988), service contracts, and procurement by entities on each country's reserve list (including most national defense items). Because procurement in the European Union and Japan is often decentralized, many contracts fell below the SDR threshold and were therefore GATT exempt. By dividing up procurement into smaller contracts national preferences were retained. United States government procurement tends to be more centralized and thus more likely to be covered by the GATT Code. This pattern may help explain why Congress restrictively amended the Buy American Act in 1988.

Chapter 13 of the North American Free Trade Area Agreement opened government procurement to U.S., Canadian and Mexican suppliers on contracts as small as $25,000. However, the goods supplied must have at least 50 percent North American content. These special procurement rules effectively created an exception to the GATT Procurement Code which otherwise applied. The thresholds are $50,000 for goods and services provided to federal agencies and $250,000 for government-owned enterprises (notably PEMEX and CFE). These regulations are particularly important because Mexico, unlike Canada, has not traditionally joined in GATT procurement codes.

The Uruguay Round Procurement Code took effect in 1996 and replaced the 1979 Tokyo Round GATT Procurement Code. The Uruguay Round (WTO) Code expanded the coverage of the prior GATT Code to include procurement of services, construction, government-owned utilities, and some state and local (subcentral) contracts. The U.S. and the European Union applied the new Code's provisions on government-owned utilities and subcentral contracts as early as April 15, 1994.

Various improvements to the procedural rules surrounding procurement practices and dispute settlement under the WTO Code attempt to reduce tensions in this difficult area. For example, an elaborate system for bid protests is established. Bidders who believe the 1979 Code's procedural rules have been abused will be able to lodge, litigate and appeal their protests. The WTO Procurement Code became part of U.S. law in December of 1994 under the Uruguay Round Agreements Act. The United States has made, with few exceptions, all procurement by executive agencies subject to the

Federal Acquisition Regulations under the Code's coverage (i.e., to suspend application of the normal Buy American preferences to such procurement).

§ 9.11   The General Agreement on Trade in Services (GATS)

Market access for services is a major focus of the General Agreement on Trade in Services (GATS), a product of the Uruguay Round of Negotiations. The U.S. Congress approved and implemented the GATS agreement in December of 1994 under the Uruguay Round Agreements Act. Subsequently, early in 1995, the United States refused to extend most-favored-nation treatment to financial services. The European Union, Japan and other GATS nations then entered into an interim 2–year agreement which operated on MFN principles. Financial services was revisited in 1996–97 with further negotiations aimed at bringing the United States into the fold. These negotiations bore fruit late in 1997 with 70 nations (including the United States) joining in an agreement that covers 95 percent of trade in banking, insurance, securities and financial information. This agreement took effect March 1, 1999.

National laws that restrict the number of firms in a market, that are dependent upon local "needs tests" or that mandate local incorporation are regulated by the GATS. Various "transparency" rules require disclosure of all relevant laws and regulations, and these must be administered reasonably, objectively and impartially. Specific service market access and national treatment commitments are made by various governments in schedules attached to the agreement. These commitments may be modified or withdrawn after 3 years, subject to a right of compensation that can be arbitrated. Certain mutual recognition of education and training for service-sector licensing will occur. State monopolies or exclusive service providers may continue, but must not abuse their positions. Detailed rules are created in annexes to the GATS on financial, telecommunications and air transport services. A general right of most-favored-nation treatment in the services sector has been established.

The GATS has reduced unilateral U.S. action under Section 301 to gain access to foreign markets for U.S. service providers. This reduction flows from U.S. adherence to the Dispute Settlement Understanding (DSU) that accompanies the Uruguay Round accords. The DSU obligates its signatories to follow streamlined dispute settlement procedures under which unilateral retaliation is restrained until the offending nation has failed to conform to a World Trade Organization ruling.

§ 9.12   The WTO and Rules of Origin

The Uruguay Round accord on rules of origin is, in reality, an agreement to agree. A negotiations schedule was established along with a WTO Committee to work with the Customs Cooperation Council on harmonized rules of origin. Certain broad guiding principles for the negotiations are given and considered binding until agreement is reached. These principles are:

● rules of origin applied to foreign trade must not be more stringent than applied to domestic goods.

● rules of origin must be administered consistently, uniformly, impartially and reasonably.

● origin assessments must be issued within 150 days of a request and remain valid for three years.

● new or modified rules or origin may not be applied retroactively.

● strict confidentiality rules apply to information submitted confidentially for rule of origin determinations.

§ 9.13   The WTO TRIPs Agreement

The Uruguay Round accords of late 1993 include an agreement on trade-related intellectual property rights (TRIPs). This agreement is binding upon the over 140 nations that are members of the World Trade Organization. In the United States, the TRIPs agreement must be ratified and implemented by Congress. There is a general requirement of national and most-favored-nation treatment among the parties.

The TRIPs Code covers the gamut of intellectual property. On copyrights, there is protection for computer programs and databases, rental authorization controls for owners of computer software and sound recordings, a 50–year motion picture and sound recording copyright term, and a general obligation to comply with the Berne Convention (except for its provisions on moral rights).

On patents, the Paris Convention prevails, product and process patents are to be available for pharmaceuticals and agricultural chemicals, limits are placed on compulsory licensing, and a general 20–year patent term is created. For trademarks, service marks become registrable, internationally prominent marks receive enhanced protection, the linking of local marks with foreign trademarks is prohibited, and compulsory licensing is banned. In addition, trade secret protection is assisted by TRIPs rules enabling owners to prevent unauthorized use or disclosure. Integrated circuits are covered by rules intended to improve upon the Washington Treaty. Lastly, industrial designs and geographic indicators of alcoholic beverages (e.g., Canadian Whiskey) are also part of the TRIPs regime.

Infringement and anticounterfeiting remedies are included in the TRIPs, for both domestic and international trade protection. There are specific provisions governing injunctions, damages, customs seizures, and discovery of evidence.

* * *

The international trade of the United States is regulated by a number of different governmental bodies. The International Trade Administration is part of the Commerce Department, which in turn is part of the Executive Branch of the federal government. The Commerce Department also contains the Office of Export Licensing and the Office of Anti-boycott Compliance. The International Trade Commission is an independent federal government agency, and the Court of International Trade is part of the Judicial Branch of the United States government. Lastly, the Office of the United States Trade Representative works directly under the President.

§ 9.14   U.S. International Trade Administration (ITA)

The International Trade Administration (ITA) is an administrative agency. In broadest terms, the ITA is to foster, promote and develop world trade, and to bring U.S. companies into the business of selling overseas. At a practical level, the ITA is designed to be helpful to the individual business by providing it with information concerning the "what, where, how and when" of imports and exports, such as information sources, requirements for a particular trade license, forms for an international license agreement or procedures to start a business in a foreign country. The ITA provides business data and educational programs to United States businesses. In addition to these duties, the ITA also decides whether there are subsidies in countervailing duty (CVD)[1] cases or sales at less than fair value in antidumping duty (AD) cases.[2] Prior to 1980, such decisions were made by the Treasury Department. The ITA is not, however, involved in decision-making in escape clause (Section 201), market disruption (Section 406) and unfair import practices (Section 337) proceedings.

§ 9.15   U.S. International Trade Commission (ITC)

The United States International Trade Commission (ITC) is an independent bipartisan agency created in 1916 by an act of Congress. The ITC is the successor to the United States Tariff Commission. In 1974, the name was changed and the ITC was given

---

§ 9.14   2. See Chapter 12.
1. See Chapter 13.

additional authority, powers and responsibilities. The Commission's present powers and duties include preparing reports pertaining to international economics and foreign trade for the Executive Branch, the Congress, other government agencies and the public. To carry out this responsibility, the ITC conducts investigations which entail extensive research, specialized studies and a high degree of expertise in all matters relating to the commercial and international trade policies of the United States. Statutory investigations conducted by the ITC include unfair import trade practice determinations (Section 337 proceedings),[1] domestic industry injury determinations in antidumping and countervailing duty cases,[2] and escape clause and market disruption import relief recommendations.[3] The ITC also advises the President about probable economic effects on domestic industries and consumers of modifications on duties and other trade barriers incident to proposed trade agreements with foreign countries.

The ITC is intended to be a quasi-judicial, bipartisan, independent agency providing trade expertise to both Congress and the Executive. Congress went to great lengths to create a bipartisan body to conduct international trade studies and provide reliable expert information. The six Commissioners of the ITC are appointed by the President and confirmed by the United States Senate for nine year terms, unless appointed to fill an unexpired term. The presence of entrenched points of view is inhibited because a Commissioner who has served for more than five years is not eligible for reappointment. Not more than three Commissioners may be members of the same political party. The Chairman and Vice–Chairman are designated by the President for two year terms. No Chairman may be of the same political party as the preceding Chairman, nor may the President designate two Commissioners of the same political party as Chairman and Vice–Chairman. Congress further guaranteed the independence of the ITC from the Executive Branch by having its budget submitted directly to the Congress. This means that its budget is not subject to review by the Office of Management and Budget.

§ 9.16 U.S. Court of International Trade (CIT)

The United States Court of International Trade (CIT) is an Article III court under the United States Constitution for judicial review of civil actions arising out of import transactions and certain federal statutes affecting international trade. It grew out of the Board of General Appraisers (a quasi-judicial administrative unit within the Treasury Department which reviewed decisions by Unit-

---

§ 9.15

1. See Chapter 24.

2. See Chapters 12 and 13.

3. See Chapter 15.

ed States Customs officials concerning the amount of duties to be paid on imports in actions arising under the tariff acts) and the United States Customs Court which had essentially the same jurisdiction and powers. The President, with the advice and consent of the Senate, appoints the nine judges who constitute the Court of International Trade. Not more than five of the nine judges may belong to any one political party.

The geographical jurisdiction of the Court of International Trade extends throughout the United States, and it is also authorized to hold hearings in foreign countries. The court has exclusive subject-matter jurisdiction to decide any civil action commenced against the United States, its agencies or its officers arising from any law pertaining to revenue from imports, tariffs, duties or embargoes or enforcement of these and other customs regulations. This includes disputes regarding trade embargoes, quotas, customs classification and valuation, country of origin determinations and denials of protests by the U.S. Customs Service. The court's exclusive jurisdiction also includes any civil action commenced by the United States that arises out of an import transaction, and authority to review final agency decisions concerning antidumping and countervailing duty matters, the eligibility of workers, firms and communities who are economically harmed by foreign imports for trade adjustment assistance, disputes concerning the release of confidential business information, and decisions to deny, revoke or suspend the licenses of customs brokers. However, the CIT does *not* have jurisdiction over disputes involving restrictions on imported merchandise where public safety or health issues are raised. This limitation on CIT jurisdiction arises because such issues involving domestic goods would be determined by other regulatory bodies, and only referral to United States District Courts can ensure uniform treatment of both imports and domestically produced goods.

The standard for the judicial review exercised by the CIT varies from case to case. In some instances, such as confidentiality orders, a *de novo* trial is undertaken. In others, notably antidumping and countervailing duty cases, the standard is one of substantial evidence or arbitrary, capricious or unlawful action or an abuse of discretion. In trade adjustment assistance litigation, the administrative determinations are considered conclusive absent substantial evidentiary support in the record with the CIT empowered to order the taking of further evidence. Unless otherwise specified by statute, the Administrative Procedure Act governs the judicial review by the CIT of U.S. international trade law. The CIT possesses all the remedial powers, legal and equitable, of a United States District Court, including authority to enter money judgments for or against the United States, but with three limitations. First, in an action challenging a trade adjustment ruling, the court may not issue an injunction or writ of mandamus. Second, the CIT may order disclosure of confidential information only as specified in Section 777(c)(2) of the Tariff Act of 1930. Third, the CIT may order only declaratory relief for suits brought under the provision allowing the court accelerated review because of a showing of irreparable harm.

The CIT must give due deference to Customs Service regulations under *Chevron* rules[1] even when undertaking *de novo* review.[2] CIT decisions are first appealed to the Court of Appeals for the Federal Circuit (formerly to the Court of Customs and Patent Appeals), and ultimately to the United States Supreme Court.

§ 9.17 United States Trade Representative (USTR)

Removing trade barriers is usually done on a reciprocal basis, and requires lengthy bargaining and negotiations between the sovereigns. Congress is not adapted to carry on such negotiations, so it routinely delegates limited authority to the President to negotiate agreements reducing trade restrictions. Recent efforts to reduce trade restrictions have been multilateral, bilateral and trilateral. In all cases, Congress has given quite broad authority to the President, or his representative, to reduce or eliminate United States tariffs on a reciprocal basis.

The power to negotiate for international trade advantage within the framework of GATT or elsewhere was summarized in a 1975 letter by the (then) Acting Assistant Secretary of State for Congressional Relations, Mr. Kempton Jenkins, to a Congressional committee:[1]

> The Trade Act of 1974, [19 U.S.C. § 2101 et seq.] which became law on January 3, 1975, provides the President with substantial new authority in the area of trade negotiations. He may, under certain circumstances, enter into trade agreements, and, as a result thereof, decrease existing tariffs or harmonize, reduce or eliminate nontariff barriers to and other distortions of trade. This authority may be exercised through both multilateral and bilateral trade agreements. Agreements regarding nontariff barriers are subject to congressional approval.... Finally, Title IV of the Trade Act contains a number of limitations on the President's authority to make commercial agreements with nonmarket economy countries, including provisions

§ 9.16

1. Chevron, U.S.A., Inc. v. Natural Resources Defense Council, Inc., 467 U.S. 837, 104 S.Ct. 2778, 81 L.Ed.2d 694 (1984).

2. United States v. Haggar Apparel Co., 526 U.S. 380, 119 S.Ct. 1392, 143 L.Ed.2d 480 (1999).

§ 9.17

1. See 69 Am.J.Int'l Law 651–52 (1975).

relating to congressional approval or disapproval of such agreements.[2]

In response to Section 1104 of the Trade Agreements Act of 1979,[3] the President reviewed the structure of the international trade functions of the Executive Branch. Although this did not lead to the establishment of a new Department of International Trade and Investment, it did lead to enhancement of the Office of the Special Representative for Trade Negotiations,[4] which has since been renamed the United States Trade Representative (USTR). The powers of the USTR were expanded and its authority given a legislative foundation.

The USTR is appointed by the President, with the advice and consent of the Senate.[5] The Office of the USTR has been the principal vehicle through which trade negotiations have been conducted on behalf of the United States. Among other things, the USTR has had continuing responsibility in connection with implementation of the WTO Agreements and U.S. free trade agreements. The USTR is the contact point for persons who desire an investigation of instances of noncompliance with any trade agreement. The USTR also negotiates "orderly marketing agreements" and "voluntary restraint agreements" with foreign governments that are willing to restrict the flow of goods into the United States.

In 1988, the duties of the USTR were significantly expanded in conjunction with an overhaul of Section 301 of the Trade Act of 1974.[6] Section 301 creates a controversial unilateral trade remedy which principally has been used to obtain foreign market access for U.S. exports. Prior to 1988, the President directly administered Section 301. Thereafter, as amended by the Omnibus Trade and Competitiveness Act, the USTR assumed this role along with new duties governing the Super 301 and Special 301 procedures created in 1988. Moreover, since the 1988 Act expanded the coverage of Section 301 and introduced mandatory (not discretionary) remedies, the USTR has been in the spotlight of many domestic industry complaints about foreign governments. Such complaints can reach breaches of international agreements as well as unjustifiable, unreasonable or discriminatory foreign country practices.

§ 9.18   An Introduction to the IMF

Most nations have a national currency and pursue an internal monetary policy to meet their own political and economic goals.

---

2. Section 1102 of the Omnibus Trade and Competitiveness Act of 1988 (P.L. 100–418) extended until June 1, 1993 the President's authority under the Trade Act of 1974.

3. P.L. 96–39.

4. The office had been established by an Executive Order in 1963.

5. 19 U.S.C.A. § 2171.

6. See Chapter 19.

Twelve EU nations have joined in a common currency, the Euro, managed by the European Central Bank. No central authority controls a world monetary system; monetary policy is decentralized. Since 1944, nations have coordinated national monetary policies principally through the International Monetary Fund (IMF).

Both the IMF and the International Bank for Reconstruction and Development (the "World Bank") arose out of the Bretton Woods Conference in 1944. The World Bank was to facilitate loans by capital surplus countries (e.g., then the United States) to countries needing foreign investment for economic redevelopment after World War II. The IMF was to stabilize currency exchange rates, assist countries in their balance of payments, and repair other war damage to the international monetary system. Twenty-nine countries including the United States became party to the IMF Articles of Agreement in 1945. Today, over 150 countries are members of the IMF.

The IMF goals are to facilitate the expansion and balanced growth of international trade, to assist in the elimination of foreign exchange restrictions which hamper the growth of international trade, and to shorten the duration and lessen the disequilibrium in the international balances of payments of members. The mitigation of wide currency fluctuations is achieved through a complex lending system which permits a country to borrow money from other Fund members or from the Fund (by way of "Special Drawing Rights" or "SDRs") for the purpose of stabilizing the relationship of its currency to other world currencies. These monetary drawing arrangements permit a member country to support its national currency's relative value when compared with national currencies of other countries, especially the "hard" ("reserve") currencies such as the Swiss franc, the Euro, Japanese yen, and United States dollar.

In recent years, IMF loans have normally been "conditioned" upon adoption of specific economic reforms by debtor states, especially in Asia and Latin America. This has led to the perception that the IMF is the world's "sheriff", setting the terms for refinancing national debts and protecting the interests of commercial bank creditors. The IMF does function as the first line of negotiation in an international "debt crisis," and commercial and national banks often conform their loans to IMF conditions. These IMF conditions can have dramatic political and social repercussions in debtor nations.

An American trader who incurs expenses and pays bills in U.S. dollars wishes to be paid in U.S. dollars—even for goods or services which are sold outside of the United States. Similarly, a French business person wishes to have Euros. Both have a need for, and must rely upon, the convertibility of currencies (e.g., dollars for Euros and vice versa) so that payments can be made abroad or foreign income can be used to pay bills at home. Convertibility in the international setting has been achieved at different times by using, as a common reference point or standard, different forms of "international money". Gold has been an international money for centuries. The U.S. dollar is both a national currency and a primary form of international money. The Europeans hope to challenge the dollar's supremacy with the Euro.

The International Monetary Fund has established a form of international money which is not a national currency and is called a Special Drawing Right (SDR). Certificates of deposit are denominated in SDRs; short-term SDR loans may be obtained commercially; and some OPEC nations have begun to value their national currencies in SDRs. Mechanically, an SDR is an international medium of exchange having a 1991 composite value based 39 percent on the U.S. dollar, 32 percent on the Euro, 18 percent on the Japanese yen, and 11 percent on the British pound. Each exchange rate fluctuation in any one of these "basket currencies" produces commensurately only a smaller, fractional fluctuation in the value of an SDR.

Although the SDR has been talked about as if it is a supranational currency, the SD "Right" is more technically a "unit of account" created by an IMF process. When an IMF member country, having a negative balance of payments position, runs short of its currency "reserves" (which may be its stocks of "hard" "reserve" currencies or gold), the member country may exercise its "Right" to make a "Special Drawing" from the IMF Special Drawing Account (e.g., the country may exercise its Special Drawing Right to ask the IMF to arrange for that country to receive $40 million (U.S.) worth of currency other than gold). Upon receipt of the Drawing "request", the IMF approaches another member country having a fuller stock of "reserves" (which "back up" its national currency), and requests that country to provide currency to the requesting country (e.g. to provide $40 million worth of currency other than gold). In return for having supplied the currency, the supplying country acquires additional Special Drawing Rights (e.g. worth $40 million) which it may revoke if ever its currency "reserves" get too low. Each IMF Member Country participating in the SDR scheme has a finite allocation of SDRs available for its possible use. A net result of the SDR scheme is that countries "swap" currencies to help other countries from time to time in maintaining existing, relative values between their national currency and other currencies of the world.

There have also been regional efforts to use the "unit of account" to stabilize relationships among currencies within a region and thereby to promote regularity of currency settlements. Of these regional efforts the "Ecu" of the European Monetary System (EMS) was the most successful. The Ecu was used by EU countries to establish relative values of Member Country currencies. The Ecu, however, has been succeeded by the Euro, which is a "regional," rather than a national, currency. The Euro is issued by the European Central Bank. On January 1, 1999 the Euro became the currency of the 11 Member States of the EMS, replacing the German mark, the French franc and the national currencies of Austria, Belgium, Finland, Ireland, Italy, Luxembourg, the Netherlands, Portugal and Spain. Greece subsequently joined the Euro zone, while Denmark and Sweden rejected participation in national referendums. Euro banknotes and coins were issued on January 1, 2002 and are now widely circulated. After an initially steep fall against the U.S. dollar, the Euro bounced back to above its opening exchange rate of $1.18 per Euro.

*

Chapter 10

UNITED STATES TARIFFS AND DUTY FREE IMPORTS

Table of Sections

§ 10.1 Introduction

This chapter focuses on United States tariffs under the Harmonized Tariff Schedule (HTS). Column 1 tariffs, known as most-favored-nation (MFN) tariffs, are the lower and most likely to be applicable. Column 2 tariffs, originating in the Smoot–Hawley Tariff Act of 1930, are the higher and least likely to be applicable. In addition, there are a variety of duty free entry programs to which the U.S. subscribes. This chapter selectively reviews duty free entry under the Generalized System of Tariff Preferences of the United States (GSP), the Caribbean Basin Initiative, the Andean Trade Preference Act and Section 9802.00.80 of the HTS. Duty

227

free entry is, of course, the ultimate goal of all exporters and importers involved in United States trade. The Israeli and Canadian–American Free Trade Area Agreements, as well as the North American Free Trade Agreement (NAFTA), are treated separately in Chapter 15.

United States tariffs generally take one of three forms. The most common is an ad valorem rate. Such tariffs are assessed in proportion to the value of the article. Tariffs may also be assessed at specific rates or compound rates. Specific rates may be measured by the pound or other weight. A compound rate is a mixture of an ad valorem and specific rate tariff. Tariff rate quotas involve limitations on imports at a specific tariff up to a certain amount. Imports in excess of that amount are not prohibited, but are subject to a higher rate of tariff. Thus tariff rate quotas tend to restrict imports that are in excess of the specified quota for the lower tariff level.

§ 10.2   The Origins of United States Tariffs

Article I, Section 8, of the United States Constitution authorizes Congress to levy uniform tariffs on imports. Tariff legislation must originate in the House of Representatives. Although tariffs were primarily viewed as revenue-raising measures at the founding of the nation, it was not long before tariffs became used for openly protectionist purposes. The Tariff Act of 1816 initiated this change in outlook. During much of the Nineteenth Century, the United States legislated heavy protective tariffs. These were justified as necessary to protect the country's infant industries and to force the South to engage in more trade with the North (not with Europe). Exceptions were made to the high level of tariffs for selected United States imports. These typically flowed from conditional most-favored-nation reciprocity treaties. The first of these treaties involved Canada (1854) and Hawaii (1875).

As the United States moved into the 20th Century, additional tariffs in excess of the already high level of protection were authorized. "Countervailing duty" tariffs were created in 1890 to combat export subsidies of European nations, particularly Germany. After 1916, additional duties could also be assessed if "dumping practices" were involved. Early American dumping legislation was largely a reaction to marketplace competition from foreign cartels. Throughout all of these years the constitutionality of protective tariffs was never clearly resolved. In 1928, however, the United States Supreme Court firmly ruled that the enactment of protective tariffs was constitutional.[1] This decision, followed by the crash of

§ 10.2

1. J.W. Hampton, Jr. & Co. v. United States, 276 U.S. 394, 48 S.Ct. 348, 72 L.Ed. 624 (1928).

the stock market in 1929, led to the enactment of the Smoot–Hawley Tariff Act of 1930. This Act set some of the highest rates of tariff duties in the history of the United States. It represents the last piece of tariff legislation that Congress passed without international negotiations. These tariffs remain part of United States law and are generally referred to as "Column 2 tariffs" under the Harmonized Tariff Schedule (HTS).

Since 1930, changes in the levels of tariffs applicable to goods entering the United States have chiefly been achieved through international trade agreements negotiated by the President and affirmed by Congress. During the 1930s and 40s, the Smoot–Hawley tariffs generally applied unless altered through bilateral trade agreements. The Reciprocal Trade Agreements Act of 1934[2] gives the President the authority to enter into such agreements, and under various extensions this authority remains in effect today. An early agreement of this type was the Canadian Reciprocal Trade Agreement of 1935.

§ 10.3   Column 1 Tariffs and the GATT/WTO

The Trade Agreements Extension Act of 1945 authorized the President to conduct multilateral negotiations in the trade field. It was out of this authority that the General Agreement on Tariffs and Trade (GATT) was negotiated. The GATT became effective on January 1, 1948 and was implemented in the United States by executive order. Indeed, despite its wide-ranging impact on United States tariff levels since 1948, the GATT has never been ratified by the United States Congress. Nevertheless, it is the source of the principal tariffs assessed today on imports into the United States. These duties, known as most-favored-nation (MFN) tariffs or "Column 1 tariffs," have been dramatically reduced over the years through successive rounds of trade negotiations. They are unconditional MFN tariffs, meaning that reciprocity is not required in order for them to apply. Multilateral tariff agreements have predominated over bilateral negotiations since 1948.

The term "most-favored-nation" is misleading in its suggestion of special tariff arrangements. It is more appropriate and since 1998 officially correct to think of MFN tariffs as the normal level of U.S. tariffs, to which there are exceptions resulting in the application of higher or lower tariffs. After the Tokyo Round of GATT negotiations in 1978, the average MFN tariff applied to manufactured imports into the United States was approximately 5.6 percent. Reductions in this level to approximately 3.5 percent have been accomplished under the Uruguay Round of 1994.

---

2.   48 Stat. 943 (1934).

Tariff cuts on a wide range of information technology products were agreed to late in 1996. The United States, the European Union and most of East Asia agreed to abolish tariffs on computers, electrical capacitors, calculators, ATM's, fax and answering machines, digital copiers and video cameras, computer diskettes, CD-ROM drives, computer software, fiber optical cables and hundreds of other items by the year 2000. This agreement covers more than 90 percent of all information technology trade.

In early 1997, agreement on liberalizing trade and reducing tariffs on basic telecommunications equipment was reached by 69 nations. This agreement took effect Feb. 5, 1998. Later that year, a WTO declaration imposed standstill obligations on all members to continue to refrain from applying customs duties to electronic commerce while negotiations are underway for more permanent rules in this area.

§ 10.4   Column 2 Tariffs

Between 1948 and 1951 the United States granted Column 1 most-favored-nation tariff treatment to goods originating from virtually every part of the world. Commencing in 1951, goods originating in nations controlled by communists were withdrawn from such tariff treatment. This had, and to some degree continues to have, the effect of treating the importation of goods from communist nations under Column 2 United States tariff headings. As a practical matter, very few such imports can overcome the high Smoot-Hawley tariffs embodied in Column 2.

The designation of which nations are "communist" for these purposes has varied over time. Yugoslavia was generally not treated as a communist country and its goods therefore entered under Column 1 MFN tariffs. Goods from Slovenia, Croatia, Macedonia and Bosnia–Hercegovina presently do so as well. Central and Eastern European nations were sometimes treated as communist countries, particularly during the 1950s and 1960s. This is no longer the case, and at this point nearly every European and Baltic nation has been granted MFN status under United States tariff law. Belarus, Kazakhstan, Turkmenistan, Georgia, Azerbaijan, Tajikstan, Moldava, Kyrgyszstan, Armenia, Uzbekistan, the Russian Federation and Ukraine are also MFN beneficiaries. It is perhaps more useful, therefore, to indicate those nations that do not presently benefit from most-favored-nation tariff treatment. These include Cuba and North Korea. Goods from some of these nations are totally embargoed as a matter of national security; the law in this area is covered in Chapter 8. The most current listing of those nations whose products are subject to Column 2 tariffs can be found in General Headnote 3(b) to the HTS.

§ 10.5   The Jackson–Vanik Amendment

Section 402 of the 1974 Trade Act presently governs American grants of most-favored-nation tariff status.[1] This is commonly known as the "Jackson–Vanik Amendment." Under its terms, no products from a nonmarket economy nation may receive MFN treatment, nor may that country participate in U.S. financial credit or guaranty programs, whenever the President determines that it denies its citizens the right or opportunity to emigrate, imposes more than nominal taxes on visas or other emigration documents, or imposes more than nominal charges on its citizens as a result of their desire to leave. These statutory conditions are widely thought to have been the product of United States desires to have the Soviet Union permit greater exodus of its Jewish population during the early 1970s. However, the passage of the Jackson–Vanik Amendment was an important factor in the Soviet decision to withdraw from a broad trade agreement with the United States at that time, and led to sharply curtailed Jewish emigration from the Soviet Union.

The application of Jackson–Vanik by the President is subject to a waiver by executive order whenever the President determines that such a waiver will substantially promote the objectives of freedom of emigration and the President has received assurances that the emigration practices of a particular nonmarket economy nation will lead substantially to the achievement of those objectives. If the President decides to exercise this waiver authority, the waiver must be renewed annually and reported to Congress. These reports and the exercise of presidential waivers have over the years been contentious. At one point Congress had the power to veto presidential waivers under the Jackson–Vanik Amendment. However, a 1983 decision of the United States Supreme Court strongly suggested that these veto powers were unconstitutional.[2] The Customs and Trade Act of 1990 amended the Trade Act of 1974 so as to permit Congress to jointly resolve against presidential Jackson–Vanik waivers. These resolutions can be vetoed by the President, and the President's veto can in turn by overridden by Congress. It is thought that these amendments resolved the constitutional problems associated with Congressional vetoes of presidential action.

Congress and the President have disagreed significantly over the renewal of most-favored-nation treatment for Chinese goods. Questions surrounding China's emigration policies, and its general human rights record, were downplayed by U.S. authorities for many years prior to Tiananmen Square. As internal discord within

§ 10.5

1. 19 U.S.C.A. § 2432.

2. See Immigration and Naturalization Service v. Chadha, 462 U.S. 919, 103 S.Ct. 2764, 77 L.Ed.2d 317 (1983).

China increased, especially in Tibet and more generally in connection with the Democracy Movement, the Jackson–Vanik amendment came to the forefront of Sino–American trade relations. President Bush's renewal of China's most favored nation status in June of 1990, 1991 and 1992 was heavily criticized.

Jackson–Vanik became the political fulcrum of Sino–American trade relations. Congress threatened but did not achieve a veto of the President's renewal of MFN tariffs for Chinese goods. Early in 1992, Congress adopted the United States–China Act of 1991. This law would have prohibited the President from recommending further extensions of MFN status to China unless he reports that the PRC has accounted for citizens detained or accused in connection with Tiananmen Square and has made significant progress in achieving specified objectives on human rights, trade and weapons proliferation. President Bush vetoed the Act and the Congress was unable to override that veto.

In 1993, President Clinton renewed China's MFN status subject to some general human-rights conditions, including "significant progress" in releasing political prisoners, allowing international groups access to prisons and respect for human rights in Tibet. This seemed to pacify Congress for the moment. But it engendered hostility and resistance in China. Less publicly, the United States business community opposed the linkage of human rights to MFN tariffs as its PRC trade and investment commitments and opportunities were endangered. China, meanwhile, had developed the world's fastest growing economy and it decided to force the issue. If anything, abuse of human rights in the PRC actually increased early in 1994, notably prior to a well-publicized visit of the U.S. Secretary of State. With Congress increasingly split on the issue, President Clinton made what will probably prove to be an historic reversal in policy. In June of 1994, he renewed China's MFN tariff status without human rights conditions, limiting its coverage only as regards Chinese-made ammunition and guns.

President Clinton renewed China's MFN tariff status each year after 1994. Congress did not seek to override these decisions. In 1998, for the first time, President Clinton waived the Jackson–Vanik requirements for Vietnam. President George W. Bush has done likewise. This waiver survived Congressional scrutiny. It opens the door to EXIMBANK and OPIC programs, as well as Column 1 MFN tariffs on Vietnamese goods entering the United States.

Should Vietnam join the World Trade Organization, the Jackson–Vanik amendment will no longer apply. WTO members like China since 2001 receive MFN tariff status automatically and unconditionally.

§ 10.6 U.S. Generalized System of Tariff Preferences—Statutory Authorization

The Generalized System of Preferences (GSP) originated in United Nations dialogues between the developed and the developing world. The third world successfully argued that it needed special access to industrial markets in order to improve and advance their economies. One problem with this approach is that it is contrary to the unconditional most-favored-nation principle contained in the GATT. Nevertheless, in 1971 the GATT authorized its parties to establish generalized systems of tariff preferences for developing nations. The European Union, Japan and nearly all other developed nations adopted GSP systems before the United States. Although similar in purpose, each of these systems is governed by a unique body of law of the "donor" country.

It was not until the Trade Act of 1974 that a GSP system was incorporated into United States tariff law. The Trade Act authorized GSP tariff preferences for ten years. The program was renewed in the Trade Act of 1984 for an additional nine years ending in July 1993. Incremental extensions have since been made pending a program review. The Trade Promotion Authority–Trade Adjustment Assistance Act of 2002 (TPA–TAA) renewed the GSP program through 2006 retroactive to its expiration on Sept. 30, 2001. At this point, tens of billions of dollars worth of goods enter the U.S. market duty free under the GSP program, but it is estimated that more imports could achieve this status if traders better understood the GSP.

Title V of the Trade Act of 1974 contains the provisions authorizing the United States GSP program.[1] The United States GSP system, as presently operated, designates certain nations as "beneficiary developing countries." Unless a country is so designated, none of its imports can enter duty free under the GSP program. In addition, only selected goods are designated "eligible articles" for purposes of the GSP program. Thus, for duty free entry under the GSP program to occur, the goods must originate from a beneficiary nation and qualify as eligible articles.

§ 10.7 U.S. Generalized System of Tariff Preferences—USTR Petition Procedures

Any United States producer of an article that competes with GSP imports can file a petition with the United States Trade Representative (USTR) to have a country or particular products withdrawn from the program. This petitioning procedure can also be used in the reverse by importers and exporters to obtain product

§ 10.6
1. 19 U.S.C.A. §§ 501–506.

or beneficiary country status under the United States GSP program. The President is given broad authority to withdraw, suspend or limit the application of duty free entry under the GSP system.[1] Specific products from specific countries may be excluded from GSP benefits. In one case, for example, the President's decision to withdraw GSP benefits for "buffalo leather and goat and kid leather (not fancy)" from India was affirmed.[2] In another decision, the President's discretionary authority to deny GSP benefits to cut flowers from Colombia was similarly upheld.[3]

The President is required to take into consideration the impact of duty free entry on U.S. producers of like or directly competitive products. There is a set of regulations, codified at 15 C.F.R. Part 2007, which details the petitioning procedures used in connection with the certification of GSP eligible products or countries. These regulations require the domestic competitor to cite injury caused by duty free GSP imports. Within 6 months after the petition is filed, and a review by the United States Trade Representative (USTR) acting with the advice of the International Trade Commission (ITC) has been undertaken, a decision on the petition will be rendered by the USTR.

§ 10.8 U.S. Generalized System of Tariff Preferences—Competitive Need Limitations

There are two statutory limitations on the applicability of duty free GSP entry. These are known as the "competitive need" limitations. They are found in Section 504 of the Trade Act of 1974, codified at 19 U.S.C.A. § 2464(c). The first statutory limitation focuses upon dollar volumes. Duty free entry is not permitted to any eligible product from a beneficiary country if during the preceding that country exported to the United States more than a designated dollar volume of the article in question. There is a statutory formula for establishing this dollar volume limitation. In recent years, the maximum dollar volume limitation has ranged between 75 and 80 million dollars. The second statutory limitation on duty free GSP entry is framed in terms of percentages. Duty free entry is denied to products if during the preceding year the beneficiary country exported to the United States 50 percent or more of the total U.S. imports of that particular product.[1]

§ 10.7

1. See 19 U.S.C.A. § 2464(a).

2. Florsheim Shoe Co. v. United States, 744 F.2d 787 (Fed.Cir.1984).

3. Sunburst Farms, Inc. v. United States, 797 F.2d 973 (Fed.Cir.1986).

§ 10.8

1. See West Bend Co. v. United States, 10 C.I.T. 146 (1986) (competitive impact still must be proven).

A complex system of waivers applies to the competitive need formulae. These are administered by the USTR and the President acting on advice of the International Trade Commission.[2] Basically, there are five possibilities for waivers of the competitive need limitations. The first can occur if the President decides that there is no like or directly competitive article produced in the United States and the imported product is exempt from the percentage but not the dollar value competitive need limitation. The second can occur under circumstances where the President determines that the imports in question are de minimis. The third possibility involves imports from the least developed developing nations, after notice to Congress. A list of these countries can be found in HTS General Note 3(c)(ii)(B). A fourth opportunity for a competitive need waiver exists when there has been an historical preferential trade relationship between the United States and the source country, and there is a trade agreement between that country and the United States, and the source country does not discriminate against or otherwise impose unjustifiable or unreasonable barriers to United States commerce.

Lastly, the President is authorized to waive the competitive need requirements of the GSP program if the International Trade Commission decides that the imports in question are not likely to have an adverse effect on the United States industry with which they compete, and the President determines that such a waiver is in the national economic interest.[3] In making waiver determinations, the President must consider generally the extent to which the beneficiary country has assured the United States that it will provide equitable and reasonable access to its markets and basic commodity resources. The President must also consider the extent to which the country provides adequate and effective means for foreigners to secure and exercise intellectual property rights. Once a waiver of the competitive need limitations is granted, it remains in effect until circumstances change and the President decides that it is no longer justified. Attorneys can play a useful role in monitoring Department of Commerce trade statistics to determine how close imports are coming under the competitive need formulae to restriction. By shifting to purchases of similar goods from another country, importers can preserve duty free entry and avoid the affects of these statutory restraints.

§ 10.9 U.S. Generalized System of Tariff Preferences—Country Eligibility

At present, thousands of products from over one hundred countries benefit from duty free GSP entry into the United States.[1]

---

2. See 19 U.S.C.A. § 2464(c).

3. See 19 U.S.C.A. § 2464(c)(3)(A).

§ 10.9

1. See Executive Order 11888 (Nov. 24, 1975, 40 F.R. 55276, extensively amended, for a detailed listing of eligible products and countries).

A list of GSP qualified nations and territories is presented in HTS General Note 3(c)(ii). Goods from insular possessions of the United States (e.g., American Samoa and the U.S. Virgin Islands) ordinarily receive duty free GSP entry "no less favorable" than allowed GSP beneficiary nations.[2] The President's power over the list of eligible countries and eligible products is wide and politically sensitive. For example, the President is required to evaluate, in determining whether a country is eligible under the U.S. GSP program, if it is upholding "internationally recognized workers' rights." Such rights include the right of association, the right to organize and bargain collectively, a prohibition against forced or compulsory labor, a minimum age for employment of children, and acceptable working conditions (minimum wages, hours of work, and occupational safety and health.)[3] In 2002, the definition of "core worker rights" for GSP country eligibility purposes was updated to include the ILO prohibition on the worst forms of child labor. The President must report annually to the Congress on the status of internationally recognized workers' rights in every GSP beneficiary country, but the issue is not open to private challenge.[4]

The President must also consider whether the foreign country is adequately protecting United States owners of intellectual property, (compliance with TRIPs is not necessarily sufficient), and whether its investment laws adversely affect U.S. exports. In addition, when designating GSP beneficiary nations, the Trade Act requires the President to take into account various factors which amount to a U.S. agenda on international economic relations:

(1) the desires of the country;

(2) its level of economic development;

(3) whether the EU, Japan or others extend GSP treatment to it;

(4) the extent to which the country provides equitable and reasonable access to its markets and its basic commodity resources, and the extent to which it will refrain from unreasonable export practices;

(5) the extent to which it provides adequate and effective intellectual property rights; and

2. 19 U.S.C.A. § 2462(d).

3. 19 U.S.C.A. 2462(a).

4. See International Labor Rights Education & Research Fund v. Bush,

752 F.Supp. 495 (D.D.C.1990), *affirmed* 954 F.2d 745 (D.C.Cir.1992).

(6) the extent to which it has taken action to reduce trade distorting investment practices (including export performance requirements) and reduced barriers to trade in services.[5]

No communist nations and no oil restraining OPEC nations (Indonesia, Ecuador and Venezuela are excepted) may benefit from the GSP program. Furthermore, the President must not designate countries that grant trade preferences to other *developed* nations. The President must also consider, in making GSP decisions, whether beneficiary countries are cooperative on drug enforcement, whether they are expropriators of U.S. property interests, whether they offer assistance to terrorists, and whether they are willing to recognize international arbitration awards. The President may waive the expropriation requirement if it is determined that the country in question has paid prompt, adequate and effective compensation or entered into good faith negotiations or arbitration with the intent to do so.

The statutory bar against communist, oil restricting OPEC and preferentially trading countries as GSP beneficiaries is absolute. The bar against expropriating, drug dealing, arbitration award unenforcement, terrorist aiding and workers rights nonrecognition beneficiaries is discretionary with the President. The goods of such nations may still qualify if the President determines that GSP duty free entry would be in the national economic interest of the United States.[6] In applying these country eligibility criteria, past Presidents have disqualified a variety of nations from the U.S. GSP program. For example, Romania, Nicaragua, Paraguay, Chile, Burma, the Central African Republic and Liberia have all been disqualified in the past for failure to meet the workers' rights standards. Argentina and Honduras have lost GSP benefits for perceived failures to adequately protect U.S. pharmaceutical patents. Panama under General Noriega was rendered ineligible in 1988 because of the failure to cooperate on narcotics. Intellectual property piracy led in 2001 to the suspension of Ukraine's country eligibility in the GSP program. The President's review of a country's eligibility under the GSP program is ongoing. This has led to the reinstatement of GSP beneficiary nations. Russia was made a GSP beneficiary by President Clinton in the Fall of 1993. Any country designated as a beneficiary nation under the GSP program that is subsequently disqualified by exercise of Presidential discretion, or graduated, must receive 60 days notice from the President with an explanation of this decision.[7] This, in effect, presents the opportunity to reply and negotiate.

---

5. 19 U.S.C.A. § 2462(c).   **7.** 19 U.S.C.A. § 2462(a).

6. 19 U.S.C.A. § 2462(b).

Since the GSP program originated within the GATT/WTO nearly all the beneficiary countries are members of that organization. It is not, however, mandatory for a developing nation to be a member of the WTO in order to receive GSP trade benefits from the United States. China is a WTO member, but for other reasons its goods do not qualify for GSP duty free entry. Other nations whose goods are not eligible are specifically listed in the Trade Act: Australia, Austria, Canada, European Union States, Finland, Iceland, Japan, Monaco, New Zealand, Norway, Republic of South Africa, Sweden, and Switzerland.[8]

§ 10.10 U.S. Generalized System of Tariff Preferences—Product Eligibility

For each designated GSP beneficiary country, the President also issues a list of products from that country that qualify for duty free entry into the United States. The statutory authorization for the United States GSP program generally excludes leather products, textiles and apparel,[1] watches,[2] selected electronics and, certain steel, footwear and categories of glass from being designated as eligible articles.[3] All these goods are thought to involve particular "import sensitivity."

The UNCTAD Certificate of Origin Form A is ordinarily required of the foreign exporter when GSP eligible merchandise is involved. A complex body of "rules of origin" determine where goods are from for purposes of the United States GSP program. Basically, for goods to originate in a beneficiary country, at least 35 percent of the appraised value of those goods must be added in that nation.[4] The statutory rules of origin for GSP eligible goods are found in 19 U.S.C.A. § 2463(b).[5] A federal Circuit Court of Appeals

---

8. 19 U.S.C.A. § 2462(b).

§ 10.10

1. See Luggage and Leather Goods Mfrs. of America, Inc. v. United States, 588 F.Supp. 1413 (C.I.T.1984) (man-made fiber flat goods are textile and apparel articles).

2. See North American Foreign Trading Corp. v. United States, 600 F.Supp. 226 (C.I.T.1984), *affirmed* 783 F.2d 1031 (Fed.Cir.1986) (exemption for watches includes solid-state digital watches).

3. 19 U.S.C.A. § 2463(c).

4. See Madison Galleries, Ltd. v. United States, 870 F.2d 627 (Fed.Cir. 1989).

5. 19 U.S.C.A. § 2463(b). Eligible articles qualifying for duty-free treatment:

(b)(1) The duty-free treatment provided under section 501 shall apply to any eligible article which is the growth, product, or manufacture of a beneficiary developing country if—

(A) that article is imported directly from a beneficiary developing country into the customs territory of the United States; and

(B) the sum of (i) the cost or value of the materials produced in the beneficiary developing country or any 2 or more countries which are members of the same association of countries which is treated as one country under section 502(a)(3), plus (ii) the direct costs of processing operations performed in such beneficiary developing country or such member countries is not less than 35 percent of the appraised value of such

has ruled that a "two-stage" substantial transformation process must also occur in order to qualify goods for GSP purposes.[6] Thus, the value of U.S.-grown corn did not count towards meeting the 35 percent requirement because the intermediate products into which it was turned did not qualify as Mexican in origin for lack of substantial transformation into a new and different article of commerce.[7] But the assembly of integrated circuits in Taiwan from slices containing many integrated circuit chips, gold wire, lead frame strips, molding compound and epoxy (all of which were U.S. in origin) did constitute a substantial transformation of such items into a new article of commerce. Thus the circuits could be deemed from Taiwan for purposes of the 35 percent value added GSP rule.[8]

One unusual feature of the rules of origin for the United States GSP program is that which favors selected regional economic groups. Goods made in the ANDEAN pact, ASEAN or CARICOM may be designated as "one country" for purposes of origin. So too may goods produced in the East African Community, the West African Economic and Monetary Union and the Southern African Development Community. This means that the value added requirement as applied in these regions is met if 35 percent of the value added has been created inside each group as opposed to inside any one nation of the group. It is notable that many other third world regional economic groups are not similarly treated, e.g. the Central American Common Market, MERCOSUR, and the Gulf Council of the Middle East.

article at the time of its entry into the customs territory of the United States.

(2) The Secretary of the Treasury, after consulting with the United States Trade Representative, shall prescribe such regulations as may be necessary to carry out this subsection, including, but not limited to, regulations providing that, in order to be eligible for duty-free treatment under this title, an article must be wholly the growth, product, or manufacture of a beneficiary developing country, or must be a new or different article of commerce which has been grown, produced, or manufactured in the beneficiary developing country; but no article or material of a beneficiary developing country shall be eligible for such treatment by virtue of having merely undergone—

(A) simple combining or packaging operations, or

(B) mere dilution with water or mere dilution with another substance that does not materially alter the characteristics of the article.

6. See Torrington Company v. United States, 764 F.2d 1563 (Fed.Cir.1985). See generally Cutler, United States Generalized System of Preferences: the Problem of Substantial Transformation, 5 North Carolina Journal of International Law & Commercial Regulation, 393 (1980).

7. Azteca Mill. Co. v. United States, 890 F.2d 1150 (Fed.Cir.1989).

8. Texas Instruments Inc. v. United States, 681 F.2d 778 (C.C.P.A.1982). See Madison Galleries, Ltd. v. United States, 688 F.Supp. 1544 (C.I.T.1988) (blank porcelain from Taiwan substantially transformed when painted and fired in Hong Kong).

§ 10.11   U.S. Generalized System of Tariff Preferences—Graduation

As nations develop, U.S. law either bars their participation in the GSP program absolutely or vests discretion in the President to remove nations or products from its scope. Since 1984, developing nations with a per capita gross national product in excess of $8,500 are totally ineligible for GSP duty free entry. The Bahamas, Bahrain, Brunei, Israel, Nauru and Bermuda have been disqualified under this rule. In addition, the President has a broad authority to "graduate" countries from the United States GSP program. The basic concept here is that certain nations are sufficiently developed so as to not need the benefits of duty free entry into the United States market. Discretionary graduation is based on an assessment of the economic development level of the beneficiary country, the competitive position of the imports and the overall national economic interests of the United States.[1]

In recent years, Presidents have been graduating more and more products from countries like India and Brazil. In January of 1989, President Reagan graduated all products from Hong Kong, Singapore, South Korea and Taiwan. At that time, these countries were the source of about 60 percent of all goods benefiting from the United States GSP program. Mexico then emerged as the chief beneficiary country under the program until late in 1993 when all of its products were removed from the GSP treatment in anticipation of the North American Free Trade Agreement. In 1997, President Clinton graduated Malaysia entirely from the GSP program.

§ 10.12   U.S. Generalized System of Tariff Preferences—Judicial and Administrative Remedies

Legal challenges to presidential revocations of duty free GSP treatment were originally filed with the U.S. Customs Court. This was the case despite contentions of inadequate legal remedies in that court and the fact that plaintiff could not pursue class action relief except in federal district court.[1] Litigation involving the GSP program is now commenced in the U.S. Court of International Trade.

The goods entering the United States duty free through the GSP program remain subject to the possibility of escape clause relief under Section 201 of the Trade Act of 1974.[2] Moreover, such

---

§ 10.11

1. See 47 Fed.Reg. 31,099, 31,000 (July 16, 1982).

§ 10.12

1. Barclay Industries, Inc. v. Carter, 494 F.Supp. 912 (D.D.C.1980).

2. See 19 U.S.C.A. § 2251.

goods may also be restrained pursuant to Section 232 of the Trade Expansion Act of 1962 in the name of the national security of the United States.[3]

§ 10.13 Caribbean Basin Initiative (CBI)

The European Union has had for many years a policy which grants substantial duty free entry into its market for goods originating in Mediterranean Basin countries. The United States has duplicated this approach for the Caribbean Basin. This is accomplished through the Caribbean Basin Economic Recovery Act of 1983.[1] For these purposes, the Caribbean Basin is broadly defined to include nearly all of the islands in that Sea, and a significant number of Central and South American nations bordering the Caribbean. So defined, there are 28 nations which could qualify for purposes of the United States Caribbean Basin Initiative. As with the GSP program, the Caribbean Basin Initiative (CBI) involves presidential determinations to confer beneficiary status upon any of these eligible countries. However, unlike the GSP, there are no presidential determinations as to which specific products of these countries shall be allowed into the United States on a duty free basis. All Caribbean products except those excluded by statute are eligible. Moreover, there are no "competitive need" or annual per capita income limits under the CBI. Lastly, unlike the GSP program which must be renewed periodically, the Caribbean Basin Initiative is a permanent part of the U.S. tariff system.

The United States has maintained a steady trade surplus with Caribbean Basin countries. Leading export items under the CBI are typically beef, raw cane sugar, medical instruments, cigars, fruits and rum. The leading source countries have often been the Dominican Republic, Costa Rica and Guatemala. The value of all CBI duty free imports now exceeds $1 billion annually, but the CBI countries fear a diversion of trade and investment to Mexico as the North American Free Trade Agreement (NAFTA) matures.

§ 10.14 CBI Country Eligibility

The President is forbidden from designating Caribbean Basin Initiative beneficiaries if they are communist, have engaged in expropriation activities, nullified contracts or intellectual property rights of the U.S. citizens, failed to recognize and enforce arbitral awards, given preferential treatment to products of another developed nation, broadcast through a government-owned entity United

---

3. See 19 U.S.C.A. § 2463(c)(2).

§ 10.13

1. Public Law 98–67, 97 Stat. 384 codified at 19 U.S.C.A. § 2701 et seq.

States copyrighted material without consent, failed to sign a treaty or other agreement regarding extradition of United States citizens, failed to cooperate on narcotics enforcement, or failed to afford internationally recognized workers rights. For these purposes, the definition of workers rights enacted in connection with the GSP program applies.[1] Since 2000, CBI countries must also show a commitment to implementing WTO pledges.

These prohibitions notwithstanding, the President can still designate a Caribbean Basin country as a beneficiary if he or she determines that this will be in the national economic or security interest of the United States. However, this can be done only in connection with countries that are disqualified as being communist, expropriators, contract or intellectual property nullifiers, nonenforcers of arbitral awards, unauthorized broadcasters, or those who fail to provide for internationally recognized workers rights. Thus, if a Caribbean nation is disqualified because it grants preferential trade treatment to products of another developed nation or refuses to sign an extradition treaty with the United States, there is no possibility of its designation as a beneficiary nation under the Caribbean Basin Initiative. As with the GSP statutory requirements, if the basis for the disqualification is expropriation or nullification of benefits, the President may override this disqualification if that nation is engaged in payment of prompt, adequate and effective compensation or good faith negotiations intended to lead to such compensation.

In addition, the President is required to take various factors into account in designating beneficiary countries under the Caribbean Basin Initiative. These include:

(1) the desire of that country to participate;

(2) the economic conditions and living standards of that nation;

(3) the extent to which the country has promised to provide equitable and reasonable access to its markets and basic commodity resources;

(4) the degree to which it follows accepted GATT rules on international trade;

(5) the degree to which it uses export subsidies or imposes export performance requirements or local content requirements which distort international trade;

(6) the degree to which its trade policies help revitalize the region;

§ 10.14
1.   See § 10.9, supra.

(7) the degree to which it is undertaking self-help measures to promote its own economic development;

(8) whether it has taken steps to provide internationally recognized workers rights;

(9) the extent to which it provides adequate and effective means for foreigners to secure and enforce exclusive intellectual property rights;

(10) the extent to which the country prohibits unauthorized broadcasts of copyrighted material belonging to U.S. owners; and

(11) the extent to which it is prepared to cooperate with the United States in connection with the Caribbean Basin Initiative, particularly by signing a tax information exchange agreement.

Under these criteria, the President has designated a large number of the 28 eligible nations as beneficiary countries under the Caribbean Basin Initiative. These include Antigua and Barbuda, Aruba, the Bahamas, Barbados, Belize, the British Virgin Islands, Costa Rica, Dominica, the Dominican Republic, El Salvador, Grenada, Guatemala, Guinea, Haiti, Honduras, Jamaica, Monserrat, the Netherlands Antilles, Nicaragua, Panama, St. Christopher–Nevis, St. Lucia, St. Vincent and the Grenadines, and Trinidad and Tobago. The nations not designated as beneficiary countries under the Caribbean Basin Initiative to date include Anguilla, Suriname, the Cayman Islands and the Turks and Caicos Islands. Cuba is not even listed among the nations eligible for consideration in connection with the Caribbean Basin Initiative.

U.S. Presidents have typically required of each potential beneficiary a concise written presentation of its policies and practices directly related to the issues raised by the country designation criteria listed in the Caribbean Basin Economic Recovery Act. Wherever measures were in effect which were inconsistent with the objectives of these criteria, U.S. presidents have sought assurances that such measures would be progressively eliminated or modified. For example, the Dominican Republic promised to take steps to reduce the degree of book piracy and the Jamaican and Bahamian governments promised to stop the unauthorized broadcast of U.S. films and television programs.[2]

§ 10.15   CBI Product Eligibility

Unless specifically excluded, all products of Caribbean Basin nations are eligible for duty free entry into the United States market. Certain goods are absolutely excluded from such treat-

2.   19 U.S.C.A. § 2702.

ment.[1] These include footwear, canned tuna, petroleum and petroleum derivatives, watches, and certain leather products. It should be noted that this listing of "import sensitive" products is different from but overlaps with that used in connection with the United States GSP program. Since 2000, products ineligible for CBI benefits enter at reduced tariff levels corresponding to Mexican goods under NAFTA . . . so-called "NAFTA parity".

One of the most critical of the products that may enter the United States on a duty free basis is sugar. But the President is given the authority to suspend duty free treatment for both sugar and beef products originating in the Caribbean Basin or to impose quotas in order to protect United States domestic price support programs for these products.[2] Sugar exports have traditionally been critical to many Caribbean Basin economies. Nevertheless, sugar import quotas into the United States from the Caribbean have been steadily reduced in recent years. For example, by 1988 the sugar quota allocations for some CBI countries reached a low of 25 percent of their 1983 pre-Caribbean Basin Initiative allocations.[3] Many consider the few duty free import benefits obtained under the Initiative to be more than counterbalanced by the loss in sugar exports to the United States market.

The rules of origin for determining product eligibility in connection with the Caribbean Basin Initiative are virtually the same as discussed previously under the GSP.[4] As a general rule, a substantial transformation must occur and a 35 percent value added requirement is imposed (but 15 percent may come from the United States). This percentage is calculated by adding the sum of the cost or value of the materials produced in the beneficiary country or two or more beneficiary countries plus the direct cost of processing operations performed in those countries.[5] It should be noted that this approach effectively treats all of the CBI-eligible nations as a regional beneficiary since the 35 percent required value can be cumulated among them.

As under the GSP program, the President is given broad powers to suspend duty free treatment with reference to any eligible product or any designated beneficiary country.[6] Import injury relief under Section 201 of the Trade Act of 1974 can be invoked in connection with Caribbean Basin imports. And the equivalent of that relief is authorized specifically for agricultural

---

§ 10.15

1. See 19 U.S.C.A. § 2703(b).

2. 19 U.S.C.A. § 2073(c) and (d).

3. See Fox, Interaction of the Caribbean Basin Initiative and U.S. Domestic Sugar Price Support: A Political Contra-

diction, 8 Mississippi College Law Review 197 (1988).

4. See HTS General Note 3(c)(v).

5. 19 U.S.C.A. § 2703(a).

6. 19 U.S.C.A. § 2702(e).

imports upon similar determinations by the Secretary of Agriculture.[7] The effects of these protective proceedings may be diminished in the context of Caribbean Basin imports. Whenever the International Trade Commission is studying whether increased imports are a substantial cause of serious injury to a domestic industry under Section 201 or its agricultural equivalent, the ITC is required to break out the Caribbean Basin beneficiary countries. The President is given the discretion if he or she decides to impose escape clause relief to suspend that relief relative to Caribbean Basin imports. A similar discretion is granted to the President in connection with national security import restraints under Section 232 of the Trade Expansion Act of 1962. However, these discretionary provisions relate only to those goods that are eligible for duty free entry under the Caribbean Basin Initiative.[8]

In 1986, President Reagan initiated a special program for textiles produced in the Caribbean. Essentially, this program increases the opportunity to sell Caribbean textile products when the fabric involved has been previously formed and cut in the United States. If this is the case, there are minimum guaranteed access levels that are different from those quotas which traditionally apply under the Multi–Fiber Arrangement. This program is run in conjunction with Section 9802.00.80 of the Harmonized Tariff Schedule of the United States.[9]

The U.S.–Caribbean Basin Trade Partnership Act of 2000 grants duty-free and quota-free access to the U.S. market for apparel made from U.S. fabric and yarn. Apparel made from CBI fabric is capped for duty free into the United States. CBI textiles and apparel are subject to market surge safeguards comparable to those under NAFTA.

§ 10.16 Andean Trade Preferences

The Andean Trade Preference Act (ATPA) of 1991[1] authorizes the President to grant duty free treatment to imports of eligible articles from Colombia, Peru, Bolivia and Ecuador. Venezuela is not included as a beneficiary country under this Act. The Andean Trade Preference Act is patterned after the Caribbean Basin Economic Recovery Act of 1983. Goods that ordinarily enter duty free into the United States from Caribbean Basin nations will also enter duty free from these four Andean countries. The same exceptions and exclusions discussed above in connection with the Caribbean Basin Initiative generally apply. However, while the CBI is a permanent

7. 19 U.S.C.A. § 2703(f).

8. See 29 U.S.C.A. § 2703(e).

9. See 51 Fed.Reg. 21,208 (June 11, 1986).

§ 10.16

1. Public Law 102–82, 19 U.S.C.A. § 3201 et seq.

part of United States Customs law, the ATPA was only authorized initially for a period of ten years. Furthermore, the guaranteed access levels for Caribbean Basin textile products, separate cumulation for antidumping and countervailing duty investigations, and the waiver of the Buy American Act for procurement purposes are not authorized by the ATPA. The Andean Trade Preference Act was renewed by the TPA–TAA through February 2006 retroactive to its expiry Dec. 4, 2001. Textile and apparel products, and most other products previously excluded, are now included under the ATPA. Country eligibility for enhanced benefits includes consideration of steps taken to comply with WTO obligations, the protection of worker rights and combating corruption. Broadly speaking, the passage of the ATPA represents fulfillment of the elder President Bush's commitment to assist these nations economically in return for their help in containing narcotics.

§ 10.17   African Trade Preferences

The Africa Growth and Opportunity Act of 2000[1] granted duty-free and quota-free access to the U.S. market for apparel made from U.S. fabric and yarn. Apparel made from African fabric is capped for duty free entry. The least developed sub-Saharan countries enjoy duty-free and quota-free apparel access regardless of the origin of the fabric.

The Act also altered U.S. GSP rules to admit certain previously excluded African products on a duty-free basis, including petroleum, watches and flat goods. Sub–Saharan countries can export almost all products duty-free to the United States. These countries are encouraged to create a free trade area with U.S. support.

African exports are subject to import surge (escape clause) protection and stringent rules against transshipments between countries for purposes of taking advantage of U.S. trade benefits.

§ 10.18   Section 9802.00.80 of the HTS

Section 9802.00.80 of the Harmonized Tariff Schedule of the United States (formerly Section 807.00 of the Tariff Schedule of the United States) is an unusual "duty free" provision. This section allows for the duty free importation of United States fabricated components that were exported ready for assembly abroad. If qualified, goods assembled abroad containing U.S. components are subject only to a duty upon the value added through foreign assembly operations. In order for this to be the case, Section 9802.00.80 requires that the components be fabricated and a prod-

§ 10.17
1. Public Law No. 106–200, 114 Stat.
252.

uct of the United States, that they be exported in a condition ready for assembly without further fabrication, that they not lose their physical identity by change in form, shape or otherwise, and that they not be advanced in value or improved in condition abroad except by being assembled and except by operations incidental to the assembly process such as cleaning, lubricating and painting.

The regulations issued in connection with Section 9802.00.80 indicate that there are other incidental operations which will not disqualify components from duty free re-entry into the United States. These include removing rust, grease, paint or other preservative coatings, the application of similar preservative coatings, the trimming or other removal of small amounts of excess material, adjustments in the shape or form of a component required by the assembly that is being undertaken, the cutting to length of wire, thread, tape, foil or similar products, the separation by cutting of finished components (such as integrated circuits exported in strips), and the calibration, testing, marking, sorting, pressing and folding and assembly of the final product.[1] In contrast, the regulations also provide examples of operations that are not considered incidental to assembly for these purposes. These examples include the melting of ingots to produce cast metal parts, the cutting of garments according to patterns, painting which is intended to enhance the appearance or impart distinctive features to the product, chemical treatment so as to realize new characteristics (such as moisture-proofing), and the machining, polishing or other treatment of metals which create significant new characteristics or qualities.[2]

If all of the Section 9802.00.80 criteria are met, the tariff that will be assessed upon the imported assembled product will be limited to a duty upon the full value of that product less the cost or value of U.S. made components that have been incorporated into it.[3] Those who seek to take advantage of Section 9802.00.80 must provide the United States Customs Service with a Foreign Assembler's Declaration and Certification. This is known as Form 3317. The assembly plant operator certifies that the requirements of Section 9802.00.80 are met, and the importer declares that this certification is correct. Billions of dollars of ordinarily tariffed value have been excluded as a result of this Customs law provision. Motor vehicles, semiconductors, office machines, textiles and apparel, and furniture are good examples of the kinds of products assembled abroad with fabricated U.S. components so as to meet the requirements of Section 9802.00.80. Historically, many of these products

§ 10.18
1. 19 C.F.R. § 10.16(b).
2. 19 C.F.R. § 10.16(c).

3. See generally 19 C.F.R. § 10.14 et seq.

have been assembled in Japan, Germany or Canada. In more recent times, the assembly operations to which Section 9802.00.80 frequently applies have more commonly been found in the developing world.

§ 10.19   Mexican Maquiladoras

Section 9802.00.80 is applicable to goods imported into the United States from anywhere in the world. However, it is most frequently associated and used in connection with Mexican maquiladoras. Maquiladoras are "in-bond" assembly plants located in Mexico that often take advantage of the duty free potential of Section 9802.00.80. Maquiladoras have enjoyed a phenomenal popularity since 1982 when the Mexican peso was dramatically devalued. This had the practical effect of rendering Mexican labor costs lower than those of Taiwan, Hong Kong, Singapore and South Korea. These Asian nations were traditionally low-cost assembly plant centers. Since 1982, thousands of maquiladoras have been established in Tijuana, Ciudad Juarez, Neuvo Laredo and other border cities. They provide Mexico with hundreds of thousands of jobs and are a major source of foreign currency earnings. Electronics, apparel, toys, medical supplies, transport equipment, furniture and sporting goods are examples of the types of industries that have been attracted south of the border. United States components, when assembled in maquiladoras and qualifying under Section 9802.00.80, are exported and then reimported on a duty free basis.

The maquiladora industry has enjoyed explosive growth. Mexican law, like Section 9802.00.80, supports this growth. Various decrees permit goods to enter Mexico on a duty free basis *under bond* for purposes of assembly in maquiladoras. Mexican law permits duty free importation of equipment, technology and components for six months. At the end of that period the goods must be exported from Mexico, typically back to the United States. Except with special permission, which has been increasingly granted by the authorities, maquiladora-assembled goods may not enter the Mexican market. Investors may own maquiladoras, typically using 30–year land trusts (fideicomiso) and Mexican subsidiaries. Alternatively, they may lease assembly plant space from a Mexican company and operate a maquiladora from that space. The simplest way to enter into maquiladora assembly operations is to contract with a Mexican company to assemble the goods in question.

In 1998, Mexico's Ministry of Commerce and Industry Development (SECOFI) published an amended Maquiladora Decree. The revised Decree streamlines regulation of maquiladoras in Mexico, notably reducing SECOFI's discretion to deny, suspend or cancel maquila programs. A translation of the new Decree can be found at www.natlaw.com.

The net result of the United States and Mexican law in this area is to create an interdependent legal framework mutually supportive of maquiladora operations. Many have characterized this legal framework as a "co-production" or "production sharing" arrangement between the two countries. However, utilization of maquiladoras is not limited to U.S. firms nor United States' components. Japanese and Korean companies have become major investors in maquiladora industries. To the extent that they utilize U.S. components, they may benefit from the duty free entry provisions of Section 9802.00.80.

Until late in 1993, there was also a link between the United States System of Generalized Preferences (GSP) and Mexican maquiladoras. Under the rules of origin that govern the GSP program, if at least 35 percent of the value of a maquiladora product was of Mexican origin, it could qualify entirely for duty free entry into the United States. The possibility of this result caused many users of maquiladoras to seek out Mexican suppliers in order to try to meet the 35 percent rule of origin. This incentive was enhanced by the fact that South Korea, Singapore, Taiwan and Hong Kong were all graduated from the United States GSP program in 1989. Mexico was the largest source of GSP qualified goods entering the United States market prior to December, 1993 when all of its products were removed from the GSP program.

The North American Free Trade Area incorporating Mexico, Canada and the United States furthers the investment trend in Mexico. Nearly all Mexican-made goods are able to enter the United States market on a duty free basis. NAFTA phased out over seven years the duty free entry Section 9802.00.80 benefits applied to Mexican maquiladoras, but not as regards goods assembled with United States components outside North America.

§ 10.20   Section 9802.00.80 Case Law

There is a surprisingly large body of case law interpreting Section 9802.00.80. Much of it was developed when this provision was formally known as Section 807 of the Tariff Schedule of the United States. One issue is whether the United States components have been advanced in value or improved in condition abroad. If this is the case, duty free re-entry into the United States is prohibited. An early decision of the Court of Customs and Patent Appeals held that the export of U.S. fish hooks, which were assembled abroad into individually packaged assortments so as to meet the requirements of retail purchasers in the United States, were not advanced in value or improved in condition so as to be disqualified.[1] In another decision, U.S. revolvers were rechambered in

§ 10.20

1. United States v. John V. Carr & Son, Inc., 496 F.2d 1225 (C.C.P.A.1974).

Canada such that they no longer fired with accuracy .38 caliber bullets as originally designed. This change in condition caused the revolvers to be disqualified under Section 9802.00.80.[2] United States tomatoes shipped to Canada in bulk and sorted, graded as to color and size, and repackaged in smaller cartons were not changed, advanced in value or improved in condition so as to be disqualified from duty free re-entry.[3]

The buttonholing in Mexico of U.S. shirt components (cuffs and collar-bands) did not advance them in value nor improve their condition as a result of this incidental operation.[4] But polyester fabric exported from the United States to Canada where it was dyed and processed, and then exported back to the United States as finished fabric did involve an advancement in value and changing of the condition of the U.S. component so as to disqualify it from duty free entry.[5] Similarly, glass pieces produced in annealled form in the United States which were sent to Canada for heat treatment and returned for use as pieces of tempered glass were not capable of benefiting from duty free entry.[6] Terminal pins of U.S. origin were shipped to Mexico and incorporated into header assemblies and relays. This operation constituted an assembly which did not advance the value of the terminals nor improve their condition.[7]

Another requirement of Section 9802.00.80 is that the United States component be fabricated and ready for assembly without further fabrication. Circuit boards for computers made in the United States from foreign and U.S. parts qualify as fabricated components for these purposes.[8] In this case, the programmable read only memory (PROM) was programmed in the United States causing it to undergo a substantial transformation and become a United States product. Aluminum foil, tabs, tape, paper and mylar made in the United States and shipped to Taiwan in role form where they were used together with other articles of U.S. origin to produce aluminum electrolytic capacitors were not eligible for duty free entry because they were not "fabricated components" upon departure from the United States to Taiwan.[9] The fact that gold

---

2. A.D. Deringer, Inc. v. United States, 386 F.Supp. 518, 73 Cust.Ct. 144 (1974).

3. Border Brokerage Co., Inc. v. United States, 314 F.Supp. 788, 65 Cust. Ct. 50 (1970).

4. United States v. Oxford Industries, Inc., 668 F.2d 507 (C.C.P.A.1981). See United States v. Mast Industries, Inc., 668 F.2d 501 (C.C.P.A.1981) (buttonholing and pocket slitting operations incidental to assembly process do not lead to duty free entry disqualification.)

5. Dolliff & Co., Inc. v. United States, 455 F.Supp. 618 (Cust.Ct.1978), *affirmed* 599 F.2d 1015 (C.C.P.A.1979).

6. Guardian Industries Corp. v. United States, 3 C.I.T. 9 (1982).

7. Sigma Instruments, Inc. v. United States, 565 F.Supp. 1036 (C.I.T.), *affirmed* 724 F.2d 930 (Fed.Cir.1983).

8. Data General Corp. v. United States, 4 C.I.T. 182 (1982).

9. General Instrument Corp. v. United States, 67 Cust.Ct. 127 (1971).

wire made in the United States was not cut until used for transistors assembled in Taiwan did not make it a U.S. component that was not ready for assembly abroad without further fabrication. The cutting of the gold wire was an incident of the assembly process.[10] But the assembly in Ecuador of flattened cylinders and ends into tunafish cans which were then packed with tuna and shipped back to the United States did not qualify under Section 9802.00.80.[11]

The failure to lock knitting loops to keep the knitting from unravelling in the United States meant that knitted glove shelves were not exported in a condition ready for assembly without further fabrication. The importer of those gloves was not entitled to duty free entry for the value of the shelves.[12] On the other hand, pantyhose tubes made in the United States were fully constructed and secured from unravelling by stitches. A closing operation did not create a new toe portion and the goods were permitted the benefits of Section 9802.00.80.[13] Likewise the joinder of molten plastic to the upper portion of a shoe abroad did not prevent the shoe vamp from duty free entry upon return to the United States. This operation did not constitute further fabrication of the vamp.[14]

The scoring and breaking of silicon slices along designated "streets" was an incidental operation to the assembly of transistors and therefore the slices were entitled to duty free entry into the United States.[15] Magnet and lead wire made in the U.S. and exported to Taiwan where it was wound into coils and cable harness put into television deflection yolks were entitled to duty free entry.[16] The two-step assembly process in this case did not defeat the application of Section 9802.00.80. The burning of slots and holes in steel Z-beams in order to incorporate them into railroad cars was an operation incidental to the assembly process and therefore the beams were not dutiable.[17]

For Section 9802.00.80 to apply the components must be assembled abroad. It has been held that a needling operation causing fibers to be entwined with exported fabric in order to create papermaker's felts constituted an assembly abroad for these purposes.[18] Likewise the adhesion of Canadian chemicals to sheets of

10. General Instrument Corp. v. United States, 462 F.2d 1156 (C.C.P.A. 1972).

11. Van Camp Sea Food Co. v. United States, 73 Cust.Ct. 35 (1974).

12. Zwicker Knitting Mills v. United States, 613 F.2d 295 (C.C.P.A.1980).

13. L'Eggs Products, Inc. v. United States, 704 F.Supp. 1127 (C.I.T.1989).

14. Carter Footwear, Inc. v. United States, 669 F.Supp. 439 (C.I.T.1987).

15. United States v. Texas Instruments, Inc., 545 F.2d 739 (C.C.P.A. 1976).

16. General Instrument Corp. v. United States, 499 F.2d 1318 (C.C.P.A. 1974).

17. Miles v. United States, 567 F.2d 979 (C.C.P.A.1978).

18. E. Dillingham, Inc. v. United States, 470 F.2d 629 (C.C.P.A.1972).

the United States polyester involved an assembly.[19] Another requirement of Section 9802.00.80 is that the components not lose their physical identity by change in form, shape or otherwise. Fabric components used to make papermaker's felts which were needled abroad and thus perforated with holes and changed in width did not lose their physical identity and therefore continued to qualify for duty free re-entry.[20] The absence of a loss of physical identity was apparently included as a requirement of Section 9802.00.80 in order to exclude U.S. components that are chemical products, food ingredients, liquids, gases, powders and the like. These products would presumably lose their physical identity when "assembled" abroad.[21]

19. C.J. Tower & Sons of Buffalo, Inc. v. United States, 304 F.Supp. 1187 (Cust.Ct.1969).

20. E. Dillingham, Inc. v. United States, 470 F.2d 629 (C.C.P.A.1972).

21. See United States v. Baylis Bros., Co., 451 F.2d 643 (C.C.P.A.1971).

Chapter 11

CUSTOMS CLASSIFICATION, VALUATION AND ORIGIN

Table of Sections

§ 11.1 Purpose of Classification and Valuation

What customs officials do is to classify and value imported merchandise. The importer (and the exporter) may disagree with the conclusions reached as to the classification of the merchandise, its country of origin, and its valuation. Where they disagree, there are avenues of appeal. This chapter concentrates on who plays a role in classification and valuation, and how they undertake their roles.

Foreign goods entering the United States must be identified and assigned a value. The identification process is called classification. There are actually two forms of classification. The first is classification to determine the nature of the product, such as whether an imported doll wig made from human hair should be classified as a wig of human hair, a part of a doll, or a toy.[1] The second is classification by country to determine in what country or countries the product was made. If the doll wig was made in Argentina from human hair from Cuba, is the doll wig a product of Argentina or Cuba? This form of classification by country is more commonly referred to as the determination of the country of origin, and may involve quite formal rules of origin.

Knowing the nature of the product will allow Customs to determine the proper tariff. But tariffs differ for each foreign nation. Consequently, knowing the country of origin informs Customs which tariff column to use, such as one for countries granted most favored nation (MFN) status, countries denied such status, or countries with special tariff levels such as Canada and Mexico under the North American Free Trade Agreement (NAFTA), Caribbean Basin beneficiaries under the Caribbean Basin Economic Recovery Act, or other such agreements. Furthermore, identification of the country of origin may mean the product cannot be imported because it is from a country whose products are embargoed by the United States for reasons of foreign policy, such as Cuba. But even if the product and its source has been identified, Customs must know the value of the product before the tariff may be determined.[2]

§ 11.2   The Actors Who Classify and Value—The Customs Service

The United States Customs Service is part of the Department of the Treasury. It is assigned the role of administering the entry of goods into the United States.[1] Extensive regulations governing such entry are outlined in Title 19 of the Code of Federal Regulations.[2]

§ 11.1

1. A hypothetical problem involving imported doll wigs and the process of classification and valuation was included in R. Folsom, M. Gordon & J. Spanogle, International Business Transactions: A Problem Oriented Coursebook 276 (2d ed. 1991). The hypothetical in the latest edition of this book involves classifying peanut butter-jelly swirl.

2. Assigning a value to an import is called valuation. Customs officials must be able to determine a value in order to calculate the appropriate import tariff.

The task is easier if the product is entitled to duty free entry. In such case the valuation is not needed for purposes of collecting a tariff. But valuation remains useful for gathering information regarding the value of various classes of imports for statistical purposes.

§ 11.2

1. 19 U.S.C.A. § 1500, granting Customs authority to appraise, classify and liquidate merchandise entering the United States.

2. Title 19 of the C.F.R. is divided into three chapters. Chapter I includes

A Customs Service official at the port of entry makes a determination regarding the correctness of the documentation presented by the importer. If the Customs official rejects the documentation, that official's decision may be appealed to the District Director (Regional Commissioner if for the port of New York), and to the Commissioner of Customs.[3]

Judicial review of the decisions of Customs regarding classification or valuation go to the United States Court of International Trade (CIT),[4] which has exclusive jurisdiction.[5] Appeals from the CIT may be made to the Court of Appeals for the Federal Circuit (CAFC).[6] From these specialized courts, appeals are ultimately made to the United States Supreme Court. The U.S. Supreme Court held in *United States v. Mead Corp.*[7] that Customs Service classification rulings are not entitled to full administrative deference. Rather, such rulings are entitled to limited deference depending on their "thoroughness, logic and expertness, fit with prior interpretations, and any other sources of weight."

On the international level there are other actors involved in classification and valuation. The most important follows:

Secretariat of the Customs Cooperation Council (CCC). This Brussels based organization is the administrative entity formed under the Convention on the Commodity Description and Coding System (the Convention). The CCC has sought since 1970 to develop an internationally accepted "Harmonized Commodity Coding and Description System" which nations would adopt as domestic law for classifying goods for all purposes, including the application of tariffs and gathering statistics. Its system, the Customs Cooperation Council Nomenclature (CCCN), was formerly known as the Brussels Tariff Nomenclature (BTN). The CCCN has evolved into the Harmonized Tariff Schedule (HTS), and is the system in use in the United States.

The Customs Cooperation Council (CCC) has been composed of four committees which have dealt with the HTS, one of which

parts 1–199 entitles United States Customs Service, Department of the Treasury. Chapter II and Chapter III include parts 200 to the end and are entitled United States International Trade Commission, and International Trade Administration, Department of Commerce, respectively.

3. 19 C.F.R. §§ 173–174. There is a process for omitting the review by the district director in certain instances, by application for "further review." See 19 C.F.R. § 174.23–174.27.

4. 19 C.F.R. § 176.

5. The CIT is the successor to the Customs Court.

6. The CAFC is the successor to the Court of Customs and Patent Appeals.

7. 533 U.S. 218, 121 S.Ct. 2164, 150 L.Ed.2d 292 (2001).

remains active. It is the Harmonized System Committee, which administers the Convention.

§ 11.3   The Sources of Law for Classification and Valuation

The process of classification (of the item and the country of origin) and valuation requires us to turn to separate rules. Classification of products or materials requires use of the Harmonized Tariff Schedule adopted by the enactment of the Omnibus Trade and Competitiveness Act of 1988, the HTS comprising extensive schedules of products. Classification of the country of origin tends to focus on theory developed in cases. Valuation requires use of provisions in the Tariff Act of 1930 which generally following the GATT Customs Valuation Code. The statutory development of classification of products and valuation follows.

Classification. Although most nations for many decades used the internationally accepted Brussels Tariff Nomenclature (BTN), the United States refused to participate. The United States long used its own system of classification, included in the Tariff Schedule of the United States (TSUS). This quite obviously created a very different set of classifications for United States exports destined to a nation using the BTN, in comparison to the classifications of products entering the United States from other nations. What might be very narrowly defined in one system might be very broadly defined in another. It made it quite difficult to achieve fairness in seeking to lower tariffs for certain products. What was called a widget in the foreign nation, might be a gadget in the United States. The United States was increasingly isolated in using its own system, and it became apparent that it was the United States TSUS which would have to give way to the BTN. In 1982, after much urging from other major trading partners, the United States began to convert to the HTS, the effective successor to the BTN. That conversion was completed by adoption of the HTS for all imports in the Omnibus Trade and Competitiveness Act of 1988, effective January 1, 1989.[1] Most United States exports enter other nations under the HTS, and now the same is true for products of those other nations which enter the United States.

The HTS has twenty sections, the majority of which group articles from similar branches of industry or commerce. Examples of sections are Section I which includes live animals and animal products, Section II which includes vegetable products, Section III

§ 11.3

1. P.L. 100–418, title I, §§ 1202–1217, Aug. 23, 1988, 102 Stat. 1107. The HTS is not published in the U.S.Code. The United States International Trade Commission maintains the current version, which is available from the Superintendent of Documents, U.S. Government Printing Office, Washington, D.C., 20402.

which includes animal or vegetable fats, Section IV prepared foodstuffs, Section V mineral products, etc. These twenty sections are divided into 96 chapters. Finally, the 96 chapters in total list approximately 5,000 article descriptions in the heading and subheading format, as discussed below. These provisions apply to all goods entering the customs territory of the United States, which includes the 50 states, the District of Columbia and the Commonwealth of Puerto Rico.

Valuation. For many years the United States used the American Selling Price (ASP) system to determine the value of an imported good. That system valued an imported good at the level of the usual wholesale price at which the same product was offered for sale if manufactured and sold in the United States. The valuation thus had no relation to the costs of production in the foreign nation. The ASP system was much criticised abroad.[2] Many other nations, especially in Europe, used a system based on the 1950 convention which established the Brussels Definition of Value. The Brussels Definition was thought to be too general by many, and it was not adopted by either the United States or Canada. Harmonization of customs valuation became one of the most important topics at the 1979 GATT Tokyo Round, which produced the GATT Customs Valuation Code.[3] The GATT Code adopted a very different approach to valuation than the ASP. Valuation is basically calculated by the "transaction" value, or if that cannot be determined, by several fall-back methods in a descending order of allowable application. The United States abandoned the ASP by adopting the GATT Customs Valuation Code in the Trade Agreements Act of 1979.[4]

Because of the replacement of the TSUS with the HTS for classification of imports, and the replacement of the ASP with the GATT Customs Valuation Code for valuation of imports, the United States uses classification and valuation systems harmonized with those of its major trading partners.

The next step in the development of customs valuation comes with the implementation of the Uruguay Round. The World Trade Organization replaces the GATT, and incorporates customs valuation provisions rather than having them exist as a separate external code. There were three principal amendments to the Customs Valuation Code, all discussed below. Of considerable importance to customs procedures was the addition of provisions allowing preship-

2. Such criticism was quite expected since United States domestic producers could indirectly control the valuation applied to foreign competitors' imports.

3. Its importance is reflected by its adoption by the European Union, Canada and the United States, plus such major trading nations as Australia, Japan, Spain (prior to joining the EU) and Sweden, and even important developing nations such as Argentina, Brazil, and India.

4. 19 U.S.C.A. § 1401a.

ment inspection.[5] These provisions attempt to balance the interests of some nations in contracting with outside companies to determine whether imports were fairly valued in the invoice, with the interest of exporting nations to reduce or remove impediments to trade, not to increase them.

§ 11.4   Classification—Sample Provisions of the Harmonized Tariff System

Immediately below is a very small part of the very large classification schedules of the United States.[1] These provisions help to illustrate two features of the HTS. First are the Notes which precede the chart and provide some comments on such areas as what the chapter does or does not not cover. Second is the schedule of tariffs with the various columns.

CHAPTER 67

PREPARED FEATHERS AND DOWN AND ARTICLES MADE OF FEATHERS OR OF DOWN; ARTIFICIAL FLOWERS; ARTICLES OF HUMAN HAIR

Notes

    1.   This chapter does not cover:

       (a) Straining cloth of human hair (heading 5911);

       (b) Floral motifs of lace, of embroidery or other textile fabric (section XI);

       (c) Footwear (chapter 64);

       (d) Headgear or hair-nets (chapter 65);

       (e) Toys, sports equipment, or carnival articles (chapter 95); or

       (f) Feather dusters, powder-puffs or hair sieves (chapter 96).

Heading Subheading	Stat. Suf. & cd	Article Description	Units of Quantity	Rates of Duty 1 General	Rates of Duty 1 Special	2
6703.00		Human hair, dressed, thinned, bleached or otherwise worked; wool or other animal hair or other textile materials, prepared for use in making wigs or the like:				
6703.00.30	00 1	Human hair	kg	3.1%	Free (A, E, I)	20%
6703.00.60	00 4	Other	kg	4.7%	Free (A, E*, I)	35%
6704		Wigs, false beards, eyebrows and eyelashes, switches and the like, of human or animal hair or of textile materials; articles of human hair not elsewhere				

5. See Creskoff, Pre–Shipment Inspection Programs: The Myth of Inconsistency with GATT Customs Valuation Provisions, 35 Fed.Bar News & J. 83 (1988).

§ 11.4

1. See Harmonized Tariff Schedule of the U.S., Annotated for Statistical Reporting Purposes (ITC Publ. 2030).

			specified or included: Of synthetic textile materials:				
6704.11.00	00	3	Complete wigs	No.	2.8%	Free (A*, E, I)	35%
6704.19.00	00	5	Other	X	2.8%	Free (A*, E, I)	35%
6704.20.00	00	2	Of human hair	X	2.8%	Free (A*, E, I)	35%
6704.90.00	00	7	Of other materials...............	X	2.8%	Free (A*, E, I)	35%

§ 11.5 Classification—The Meaning of the Headings in the HTS

The heading in the above excerpt is used under the General Rules of Interpretation to assist in determining the classification.[1] Thus, were the goods false eyelashes made of human hair for human adult use, it would appear that Chapter 67 is the correct chapter to apply. But more than one heading may seem appropriate for a commodity, as will be discussed below.

§ 11.6 Classification—The Meaning of the Notes in the HTS

The notes at the beginning of chapters in the HTS are often useful in classification. They are to be used along with the terms of the headings, under the General Rules of Interpretation.[1] For example, according to Note 1, Chapter 67 is not to be used for footwear, which is the subject of Chapter 64. These "chapter notes" should not be confused with the Explanatory Notes to the Harmonized System.[2] Nor should they be confused with the General Notes to the HTS.[3]

§ 11.7 Classification—The Meaning of the Columns in the HTS

Assuming one is not driven from the seemingly applicable chapter by the notes, the next step is to look at the columns. The United States HTS combines the international use of six digits by adding additional digits for even further subdivisions and for statistical use. Using the above excerpt the first column, titled "Heading/Subheading", has eight digits. The first six are the heart of the HTS, and must be adopted by all contracting nations. The first two (67 in the excerpt) repeat the chapter. The second two designate the heading (03 for Human hair, etc., 04 for Wigs, etc., in the

§ 11.5

1. General Rules of Interpretation are reproduced in the Selected Documents section.

§ 11.6

1. Id.

2. The Explanatory Notes to the Harmonized System are part of the documents of the Customs Cooperation Council in Brussels which may have

some influence on the classification. They are discussed in § 5.8, infra.

3. These General Notes identify the customs territory of the United States, list nations to which Column 2 rates of duty apply, define symbols for special treatment such as the Caribbean Basin nations, give definitions, abbreviations, items exempted from coverage and rules on commingled goods. See ITC Pub. 2333 (1991).

excerpt). The next two are subheadings. This completes the international system, but the United States in some cases adds two more further sub-subheadings (.30 for Human hair and .60 for Other in the excerpt).[1] Finally, in the columns titled "Stat. Suf. & cd", additional numbers help to maintain records for statistical purposes.

The three column section titled "Rates of Duty" is what finally discloses the rate of duty for the article which has been classified. Column 1 rates are those applied to nations which receive most favored nation (MFN) status. The "General" column applies to most MFN nations. The "Special" column applies to nations which have tariff preferences which make these nations even more favored than the most favored. They may be commodities which enter duty free or with tariffs less than the general MFN rate. The capital letters denote different special preferential tariff programs. For example, A means nations qualifying under the Generalized System of Preferences (GSP),[2] B means commodities under the Automotive Products Trade Act, C means products under the Agreement on Trade in Civil Aircraft, CA means commodities under the Canada–United States Free Trade Agreement, E means commodities under the Caribbean Basin Economic Recovery Act,[3] IL means commodities under the United States–Israel Free Trade Area, and NA means commodities under the North American Free Trade Agreement.

Column 2 applies to all nations which are not entitled to Column 1 rates of duty. These countries are listed in General Note 3(b). They include principally nations under communist or socialist rule. They are essentially "least" favored nations, although that term perhaps ought to be saved for those nations which are excluded from trading with the United States altogether.

While it might seem that the HTS offers a fairly easy resolution to classification, that is true only when a commodity clearly fits into only one chapter, one heading, and if present one sub-heading. Fortunately, that is often the case. But many commodities are not so clearly allocated within the system, and there may be multiple possibilities for their classification. That will be the subject of much of the remainder of this chapter.

§ 11.7

1. The use of an additional four digits is permitted by the Convention and other nations have adopted their own form of using these additional digits. Such use will lead to some lessening of the uniformity of the system.

2. An A* appears if a country is specifically ineligible.

3. The symbol E* appears if a country is ineligible.

§ 11.8   Classification—Applying the General Rules of Interpretation

Classifying goods is the job of the Customs Service. But the importer (also the foreign exporter) is obviously interested in the classification because if the goods are classified with a high rate of duty applicable, the transaction may not go forward. Thus, the United States importer will wish to consider the classification. If the importer's conclusion is not the same as the Customs Service (meaning undoubtedly that the later will be a classification at a higher rate of duty), the importer may (1) decide not to import the goods, (2) pay the higher duty, or (3) challenge the Customs determination.

The process of determination, whether conducted by Customs or the importer, must use the rules of interpretation of the United States. They are the General Rules of Interpretation and the Additional U.S. Rules of Interpretation. A walk through those rules ought to illustrate how difficult classification may be.

Headings and relevant section or chapter notes (Rule 1). The legal classification of a good is determined according to (1) the terms of the *headings,* and (2) any relative *section* and *chapter notes.*[1] This means the section, chapter and sub-headings are subordinated to the headings in importance. If the headings and notes do not otherwise require, one turns to the additional provisions of the General Rules,[2] and also to the Additional U.S. Rules of Interpretation.[3] The General Rules specifically note that the "table of contents, alphabetical index, and titles of sections, chapters and sub-chapters" are only for reference, not legal classification.[4]

Heading references to articles (Rule 2(a)). When any reference in a heading is to an *article,* as opposed to a material or substance, the reference is to be understood to mean that article incomplete or unfinished if the article in an incomplete or unfinished state "has the essential character" of the complete or finished article.[5] The reference to an article is also to mean that article unassembled or disassembled.[6] This emphasis on the *material* as well as on the *function* of the good replaces emphasis on how the goods are used under the TSUS.

Heading references to a material or substance. (Rule 2(b)). When the reference in a heading is to a *material* or *substance,* as opposed to

---

§ 11.8

1. General Rules of Interpretation 1.

2. Id.

3. The Additional U.S. Rules of Interpretation are found immediately following the General Rules in the HTS, as adopted in the United States. These additional rules often include methods of interpretation used under the prior classification system in the United States.

4. General Rules of Interpretation 1.

5. General Rules 2(a).

6. Id. Rule 2 generally follows the previous position under the TSUS.

an article, the reference is to be understood to mean mixtures or combinations of that material or substance with other materials or substances.[7] Furthermore, any reference to goods of a given material or substance should include a reference to goods consisting wholly or partly of such material or substance. The obvious problem with this is that when the goods are only partly of the material or substance, the other party may have its own classification. That is also true when there are mixtures or combinations. The Rules acknowledge this and require one to move on to Rule 3.

Classification under two or more headings—most specific description (Rule 3(a)). When goods may be classified under two or more headings,[8] the most specific description is preferred over the *more general description*.[9] But if each possibly applicable heading refers only to a *part* of the material or substances in mixed or composite goods, or of the items in a set for retail sale, the headings must be considered equally specific. That is so even if one heading provides a more complete or precise description of the goods.[10] In such case one must move on to Rule 3(b). This Rule 3(a) is somewhat parallel to the long used "rule of relative specificity" and decisions under that rule may continue to be of some use.[11]

Classification under two or more headings—essential character (Rule 3(b)). Inability to classify under the most specific description test in Rule 3(a) requires classification with regard to that material or component which gives the items their *essential character*.[12] There was no similar provision in the TSUS,[13] and "essential character" is not defined in the HTS. It has some parallel under the TSUS definition of the term "almost wholly of." One must turn to the cases as they develop, although some past United States cases defining "almost wholly of" may be useful when defining "essential character."

Classification under two or more headings—last in numerical order (Rule 3(c)). If classification is not possible using either the most specific description or essential character tests, the rules move from a substantive classification method to one based simply on location. The proper classification is to be the heading which occurs last in numerical order among those which might be applicable.[14]

---

7. General Rules 2(b).

8. This applies to Rule 2(b) discussed above and to any other situation where two or more headings seem possibly applicable.

9. General Rules 3(a).

10. Id.

11. That includes the doctrine that an *eo nomine* description prevails over headings having only general or functional descriptions.

12. General Rules 3(b).

13. A "chief value" determination applied, no less capable of exact determination.

14. General Rules 3(c).

Goods unclassifiable under Rules 1–3—most akin (Rule 4). When there are no headings which seem directly applicable, and which might lead to the use of Rules 1–3 above, the goods are to be classified under the heading to which the goods are *most akin.* It is not expected that this test will have to be used very frequently. This is essentially a "do the best the headings allow" test, and may result in two or more headings being equally "most akin." In such case one would seem to try to find which is "more" akin. If there is still uncertainty, move on to Rule 5.

Specially shaped or fitted cases for goods—classed with their contents (Rule 5(a)). Containers, such as camera cases, musical instrument cases, gun cases, drawing instrument cases, and necklace cases, which are "specially shaped or fitted" are to be classified with the goods they serve, if they enter with those goods and are suitable for long term.[15] But the rule does not apply if the containers give the whole its essential character.[16]

Packing materials and containers—classed with their contents (Rule 5(b)). Subject to the provisions of Rule 5(a) above, packing materials and containers which enter with the goods and classified with the goods if they are the normal kind used as packing or containers.[17] But this is not true when the materials or containers are suitable for repetitive use.

These above rules 5(a) & (b) are quite specific and apply only in a very limited situation. In most cases when one is going through the list and has not yet found a clear classification after using Rule 4, it will be necessary to go on to the final General Rule 6 for additional guidance.

Subheadings and subheading notes (Rule 6). Subheadings, which are found in the first "Heading/Subheading" column of each chapter in the tariff schedules, may more specifically define goods than the heading. When subheadings or subheading notes are used, and there are two or more subheadings on the same level which seem possibly applicable, the process follows the outline in the rules discussed above.[18]

§ 11.9 Classification—The Additional U.S. Rules of Interpretation

The above six General Rules of Interpretation are the contribution to classification provided by the HTS system. But when the

---

15. General Rules 5(a).

16. For example, expensive carved tea caddies containing tea would not be classified as tea, because the container is not shaped to fit the tea (as is a musical instrument case) and the container gives the whole (tea plus caddy) the essential character.

17. General Rules 5(b).

18. General Rules 6.

United States adopted that system, it added to the General Rules its own "Additional U.S. Rules of Interpretation." One thus must check these rules to determine whether in a given situation their use is (1) consistent with the General Rules, (2) helpful where the General Rules do not lead to a satisfactory conclusion, or (3) conflict with the conclusion reached under the General Rules. The additional U.S. Rules of Interpretation consist of a four part provision.

Classification controlled by use other than actual use (U.S. Rule 1(a)). If classification is controlled by use other than actual use, and there is no special language or context which mandates otherwise, the use must be the use in the United States. It is to be the use in the United States at or immediately prior to the time of importation. Furthermore, the controlling use must be the *principal* use (which exceeds any other single use).[1] This is a change from the past reference to chief use (which exceeds all other uses).

Classification controlled by actual use (U.S. Rule 1(b)). The rule is similar to the above, being the actual use in the United States and the use to which the goods are actually put with proof so provided within three years of the date of entry.[2]

Parts and accessories—general v. specific (U.S. Rule 1(c)). Where there is a provision specifically describing a part or accessory, that must be used over a general "parts and accessories" provision.[3] Thus, the import of bicycle chains would be classified as bicycle chains if such is described specifically, not under a "catch-all" "other parts and accessories" category. Such rule certainly is consistent with the preference for a specific description over a general description contained in the General Rules. The General Rules do not contain a rule for parts. Individual chapter and section notes, however, sometimes include parts rules.

Textile materials (U.S. Rule 1(d)). Principles of section XI, which govern mixtures of two or more *textile* materials, apply to goods in any provision which names a textile material.[4] Textiles have their own mystique, and are subject to many special trading rules throughout the world. This provision assures that special rules of classification for textile materials are applied throughout the tariff schedules wherever a textile material is mentioned.

What if a conflict arises between the application of the General Rules and the Additional U.S. Rules? There is no guidance in the rules, but it seems likely that the Additional U.S. Rules would be deemed to supplant as well as supplement. But the likelihood for

---

§ 11.9

1. U.S. Rules 1(a).
2. U.S. Rules 1(b).

3. U.S. Rules 1(c).
4. U.S. Rules 1(d).

such conflict is slim, the Additional U.S. Rules were not intended to set forth views where the United States differs with the HTS, but where it believes there are necessary supplementary rules to express.

Application of the above rules is not easy, and certainly does not mean that all reasonable minds (including those found in the Customs Service) will reach the same conclusion when applying the General and Additional U.S. Rules. But we have not exhausted the assistance provided. There is one important source to consider, the "United States Customs Service, Guidance for Interpretation of Harmonized System."

§ 11.10 Classification—United States Customs Service, Guidance for Interpretation of Harmonized System

When the HTS was adopted in 1989, there was some question as to how Customs would use some of the materials developed over the years as the HTS developed. Of specific concern was the use of the Explanatory Notes to the Harmonized System, and reports of the Nomenclature Committee which administered the Customs Cooperation Council (CCC) Nomenclature. Additionally unclear was how letters from the Secretariat of the CCC would be used, and also rulings and regulations from the customs administrations of other nations. The United States Customs Service soon issued the *Guidance for Interpretation of Harmonized System*.[1] The guide makes several points quite clear.

United States Customs Service does not seek uniformity of interpretation with other nations. Uniformity is considered to be the function of the Harmonized System Committee (HSC) under Article 7 of the Convention, not the function of the United States Customs Service. The United States is not to alter "sections, chapters, headings or subheadings" of the HTS, and will consider background documents to avoid such alterations. But the Customs Service will not attempt to make its interpretations of the HTS consistent with interpretations in other HTS member nations. If serious inconsistency in interpretation results, it is likely that the HTS will be modified to minimize the inconsistency, such as by further refining the classifications.

Use of Explanatory Notes to the Harmonized System. These notes are the official interpretation of the Harmonized System by the Customs Cooperation Council. They are considered useful for guidance by Customs, but are not treated as dispositive. That is the Custom Service's interpretation of the intention of Congress in

1. 54 Fed.Reg. 35127 (1989).

adopting the HTS.[2] The Explanatory Notes are amended from time to time and reflect changes in interpretation. They thus must be consulted periodically as changes are adopted. Status similar to the Explanatory Notes is to be given only, as Congress stated, to "similar publications of the Council." The only similar publication is the Compendium of Classification Opinions.

Use of the Compendium of Classification Opinions. These opinions are decisions of the Harmonized System Committee on the classification of different products. They result from requests presented to the HSC. They are considered to have the same weight as Explanatory Notes and are the official interpretation of the HSC on the particular issue decided.

Harmonized System Committee Reports. The HSC has periodically issued reports on various subjects. They do not have the weight of the Explanatory Notes or Compendium of Classification Opinions, but may be helpful in determining the intention of the HSC. Reports of committees of the HSC, such as the Nomenclature Committee, carry virtually no weight, but may nevertheless be of some assistance in interpretation. Of even less use are the "working documents" of the Nomenclature and Classification Directorate of the CCC. They are the basis of discussions in HSC sessions, but they may not reflect the intent of the HSC.

Rulings of Other Countries. Because other nations which have adopted the HTS use the same General Rules of Interpretation, Section and Chapter Notes, and first six digits in the classification tables, decisions of their customs administrations are sometimes presented to the United States Customs Service. Customs does not follow other nations' rulings because it believes that they "may have been subject to political realities or domestic regulations which are different from our own." What this means is not further defined, but may serve to illustrate that there may be political pressure to classify goods so as to more readily admit them to, or more readily exclude them from, the United States. In any event, these foreign rulings are considered "merely instructive of how others" classify imports.

Position papers. Before a session of the HSC, United States Customs, the International Trade Commission and the Bureau of Census prepare position papers for the session. These papers do not reflect the Customs position in the interpretation of the HTS and are considered to have no value, although they are occasionally circulated and obtained by importers or their counsel.

These notes, opinions, reports, rulings and papers all add to the process of interpretation a layer which did not exist before the

2. See Conf.Rep. No. 100–576, 100th Cong., 2d Sess. 549 (1988).

adopted of the HTS by the United States. Awareness of their use by the Customs Service may prove helpful to United States counsel, but they should not expect to be given weight beyond that announced by the Customs Service and described above.

§ 11.11   Classification—Decisions of United States Courts

While it may seem strange to suggest that decisions of United States courts may not be applicable in interpreting the HTS, that may be correct for decisions interpreting the prior TSUS.[1] Interpretations of the United States HTS are to follow the procedure outlined above. Certainly decisions rendered subsequent to the adoption of the HTS in 1988, which interpret the HTS, will be useful. But in so many cases decisions have very little usefulness since they apply to very narrow issues affecting specific goods where there are two or more classification possibilities. Some earlier decisions may be useful to understand the analytical process used by the courts.[2] Although the HTS has a different process, the approach used in the past may find use in the future.

One example is the application of General Rule of Interpretation 3(a), which uses a kind of "rule of relative specificity" under the wording "most specific description." United States decisions applying the rule of relative specificity may be used in interpreting Rule 3(a).[3]

§ 11.12   Rules of Origin—Substantial Transformation

A second form of classification is to determine the country of origin of the items to be imported. Determination of the proper classification discussed above does not disclose whether Column 1 or Column 2 rates of duty apply. Furthermore, if Column 1 rates of duty are applicable, the goods may qualify for preferential or duty free treatment if they are from a country of origin included by the code letters in the Special part of Column 1.[1] Finally, knowing the country of origin may invoke more general prohibitions of trade

---

§ 11.11

1. See JVC Company of America v. United States, 234 F.3d 1348 (Fed.Cir. 2000).

2. For example, the Mattel, Inc. v. United States decision, 287 F.Supp. 999 (Cust.Ct.1968), might be used when the issue involves priority of one classification over another.

3. See, e.g., Great Western Sugar Co. v. United States, 452 F.2d 1394 (C.C.P.A.1972).

§ 11.12

1. The Court of International Trade requires importers seeking preferential tariff treatment to verify the country of origin of their goods. "Reasonable care" must be exercised, not just simple reliance on the exporter's assertions of origin. Failures in this regard can result in collection of lost duties and penalties. United States v. Golden Ship Trading Co., 2001 WL 65751 (C.I.T.2001) (T-shirts imported from Dominican Republic under Caribbean Basin Act were from China).

with that country, since the United States nearly always has several nations with which it does not trade by legislative or presidential declaration.[2]

There are other reasons to wish to know the country of origin. The United States may limit the products which enter from a specific foreign nation. That limitation might be the result of a formal quota,[3] or an informal voluntary restraint agreement (VRA). VRAs have covered a great many products (i.e., steel, vehicles, electronics), and have been a major device adopted by the United States (and other areas such as the European Union) as executive policy in order to discourage legislative action to establish mandatory and involuntary quotas to reduce trade imbalances.[4] The WTO Safeguards Agreement has reduced the frequency of their utilization.

Counsel representing an importer must know the framework for determining the country of origin of articles.[5] Eligibility of entry often depends on country of origin determination.[6] Country of origin law is not found in as consolidated a framework as for classification of the goods discussed above. Such classification takes one exclusively to the HTS, although working within that system is not a simple matter. Determination of the country of origin requires the use of rules which may be applicable in quite different areas. The most fundamental rule for determining the country of origin is *substantial transformation*. While there are several references to various aspects of the rule of origin in different sources of law, the substantial transformation test, in its various costumes, is *the* test.

§ 11.13   Rules of Origin—Sources of Law

Tariff Act of 1930. Section 304 of the Tariff Act requires that every article of foreign origin or its container which is imported into the United States be marked in a conspicuous place with the English name of the country of origin.[1]

---

2. These prohibitions may extend to both exports and imports, but may have certain exceptions, such as medical supplies.

3. Quotas are regulated by the Customs Service. See 19 C.F.R. Part 132.

4. See, e.g., Note, Voluntary Restraint Agreements: Effects and Implications of the Steel and Auto Cases, 11 N.C.J. Int'l L. & Com.Reg. 101 (1986).

5. Counsel may wish to obtain a ruling from Customs in advance of importation. See 19 C.F.R. §§ 177.1–177.11.

6. The United States must know whether the country of origin is one entitled to most favored nation treatment.

§ 11.13

1. 19 U.S.C.A. § 1304. For example the product would have to say "Made in Spain" rather than "Made in Espana". The HTS governs treatment of containers and holders for imported merchandise. See 19 C.F.R. § 1202. The purpose of the rule is essentially to inform the public. The Trademark Act of 1946, 15 U.S.C.A. §§ 1051–1127, does not allow

Trade Agreements Act of 1979. Section 308,[2] provides various definitions, including a rule of origin for eligible products. The definition focuses on the substantial transformation concept,[3] leaving to the courts the meaning of substantial transformation.

The basic rule is that of substantial transformation, and it has origins both in this statute and much earlier case law. It is discussed below.

Code of Federal Regulations, Country of Origin Marking. Part 134 of 19 C.F.R. provides rules governing country of origin *marking.* These regulations implement or reflect the provisions noted above in both the Tariff Act of 1930 and the HTS. The regulations define articles that are subject to marking, with special rules for articles repacked or manipulated, and ones usually combined with another article.[4] Rules also specify how containers or holders must be marked,[5] exceptions to the marking requirements,[6] method and location of marking,[7] and the consequences of finding articles not legally marked.[8] The consequences are essentially (1) to properly mark the goods, or (2) to return the goods to the foreign nation, or (3) to destroy the goods.[9]

Generally, a single country of origin must be determined for labeling purposes, even though the product may have been made in several countries. The country of origin as determined by Customs may not disclose other nations which participated in the process. That may be important to the United States consumer, who may not wish to purchase products from a country substantially benefiting from the sale, but not the official country of origin. And it may be important to the United States government, which may not trade with the country which has substantially benefited, but which is not the official country of origin.

Special Rules—The North American Free Trade Agreement (NAFTA). In drafting the NAFTA, as in drafting the earlier Canada–United States Free Trade Agreement, there was considerable concern that products would enter into the United States as products of Canada or Mexico which actually had little fabrication or pro-

---

admission of goods of foreign origin if they have a mark or name intended to lead the United States public to believe the product was made in the United States, or any country other than its true country of origin.

2. 19 U.S.C.A. § 2518.

3. "An article is a product of a country or instrumentality only if (i) it is wholly the growth, product, or manufacture of that country or instrumentality, or (ii) in the case of an article which consists in whole or in part of materials from another country or instrumentali-

ty, it has been substantially transformed into a new and different article of commerce with a name, character, or use distinct from that of the article or articles from which it was so transformed." 19 U.S.C.A. § 2518(4)(B).

4. 19 C.F.R. §§ 134.13–134.14.

5. 19 C.F.R. §§ 134.21–134.26.

6. 19 C.F.R. §§ 134.31–134.36.

7. 19 C.F.R. §§ 134.41–134.47.

8. 19 C.F.R. §§ 134.51–134.55.

9. 19 C.F.C. § 134.51(a).

cessing in those countries. The result was the adoption of special NAFTA rules of origin (discussed in Chapter 21), which include articles governing customs procedures for the certification of origin. The procedures create a North American "Certificate of Origin" and extensive verification provisions. The Certificate of Origin is provided by the exporter when the importer wishes to claim the duty free tariff treatment offered by the NAFTA.[10] Certificates are not required for goods of a value of $1,000 or less or where the member state has waived their use.[11] A member state may conduct a verification by questionnaires or visits to the exporter, or by other procedures the member states establish.[12] Verification is of considerable concern to the United States, which does not wish Mexico to be used as a base for transshipping products from outside the NAFTA area, especially from Asia.

Decisions of United States Courts. There are several areas where Customs is required to determine the country of origin. Products from countries with which the United States does not trade may be transshipped through a country with which the United States does trade. Products from countries subject to high rates of duty in Column 2 may be transshipped through countries subject to lower rates of duty in Column 1. Products with most favored nation Column 1 rates of duty may be transshipped through a country with special access, such as a Caribbean nation. Exporters from a nation which has agreed to a voluntary restraint agreement may try to exceed the agreed upon numbers by having the products transshipped through a nation without any such quota. As the United States enters into free trade agreements such as NAFTA, other nations may attempt to take advantage of that relationship by having goods transshipped through Canada or Mexico into the United States.

Fortunately, some case law has evolved addressing the country of origin issue. Cases involving one specific area may be helpful in addressing another. For example a case which has attempted to identify the country of origin to determine whether the agreed amount under a voluntary restraint agreement has been exceeded,[13] may be helpful where products are alleged to be violating the rules of the generalized system of preferences. Thus, in attempting to deal with a country of origin issue, cases outside the scope of the form of entry (i.e., GSP, VRA, NAFTA, etc.) must be consulted. The sense of the cases is that the same test of substantial transforma-

---

10. NAFTA Art. 501.

11. NAFTA Art. 503.

12. NAFTA Art. 506.

13. See, e.g., Superior Wire, A Div. of Superior Products Co. v. United States, 669 F.Supp. 472 (C.I.T.1987), *affirmed* 867 F.2d 1409 (Fed.Cir.1989).

tion is applied, whether the matter involves quota restrictions or trade preferences.[14]

§ 11.14　Rules of Origin—Applicable Legal Theories

There is some consistency in the approach to identifying the country of origin. More is obviously needed than to read the label which states the country of origin. A nation may do little more to an item than sew on a label which states that the item is a product of the country. The label may well be a product of the country, but that may be the only part of the item which is. It is the product itself which must be measured. The tests tend to be product specific. Since there are so many product variations, there are also many variations in application.

Substantial transformation test. The principal focus in a country of origin determination is whether the product was substantially transformed in the country stated to be the country of origin.[1] One of the principal cases defining substantial transformation in the United States, an early United States Supreme Court decision, involved drawbacks.[2] Substantial transformation would occur if the product was transformed into a new and different article "having a distinctive *name, character or use.*"[3] But while this case may be a standard, it has been applied in many different ways.[4] A name change alone would not always be sufficient, such as from "wire" to "wire rod".[5] But changing heat treated steel to galvanizing steel was sufficient, because it involved a substantial manufacturing leading to the substantial transformation that had to occur.[6] The character of the steel was changed. The annealing process strengthened the steel, and the galvanizing process made it resistant to corrosion.

Courts have tended to concentrate more on changes in *character* or *use* than in name. They often develop subtests appropriate for a particular kind of article. For example, is *significant value*

---

14. See Ferrostaal Metals Corp. v. United States, 664 F.Supp. 535, 538 (C.I.T.1987) (case law does not suggest that the court should depart from "policy-neutral rules governing substantial transformation in order to achieve wider import restrictions in particular cases.").

§ 11.14

1. This test is in the Trade Agreements Act of 1979. See 19 U.S.C.A. § 2518(4)(B).

2. Anheuser–Busch Brewing Ass'n v. United States, 207 U.S. 556, 28 S.Ct. 204, 52 L.Ed. 336 (1908).

3. Id. at 562, 28 S.Ct. at 206.

4. But it is applied by the courts. See, e.g., Texas Instruments Inc. v. United States, 681 F.2d 778, 782 (C.C.P.A.1982).

5. See Superior Wire, A Div. of Superior Products Co. v. United States, 669 F.Supp. 472 (C.I.T.1987) (the court noted that in recent years the focus was on a change in use or character).

6. Ferrostaal Metals Corp. v. United States, 664 F.Supp. 535 (C.I.T.1987) (there was a "significant altering" of the "mechanical properties and chemical composition of the steel").

added, or how much *additional costs* are incurred? But each test creates some subjective evaluation, leading to a sort of sense of whether the product is really from the state country. While the substantial transformation test has been criticized,[7] it remains the applicable law.

Value added test. This test allows a more exacting process. How much value has been added as a percent of the value of the original product? There may be situations where there has been no substantial transformation, but there has been significant value added.[8] What if a completed shirt with K–Mart logo buttons has those buttons removed and buttons are added with the logo of the most prestigious (currently) designer? If the result is the retail price may be trebled would that satisfy the value added test? There has certainly been minimal processing. Was the added value any more than the cost of the new buttons and their application? Isn't the high price really added in the United States by the consumers' willingness to pay more for apparent prestige? It seems that there must be some real value, such as labor or capital equipment, added in the country claiming to be the country of origin.

Considerations. However a court reaches a decision in a country of origin question, it is likely to have considered most of the following changes:

    1.   Change in name (and change in tariff classification);

    2.   Change in physical appearance;

    3.   Change in material substance (at each stage of manufacture);

    4.   Change in apparent use;

    5.   Change in value of item in the mind of the consumer;

    6.   Additional capital vested in article;

    7.   Additional labor vested in article;

    8.   Type of processing;

    9.   Affect of processing; and

    10.   Change in method of distribution.

There is no secret formula for determining which factor, if any, will play the most significant role. The end result may seem much like a test parallel to pornography—"I'll know it when I see it."

---

7. Maxwell, Formulating Rules of Origin for Imported Merchandise: Transforming the Substantial Transformation Test, 23 J. Int'l L. & Econ. 669 (1990).

8. One may nevertheless claim this to be a substantial transformation of value, if not of substance.

§ 11.15 Valuation—United States Law

The law applicable to classification of products is quite clearly limited to the United States adoption of the HTS. The law applicable to classification of the country of origin tends to evolve in case law applying variations on the theme of substantial transformation. The law applicable to valuation is included in the United States Tariff Act of 1930, as amended, but within the confines of the United States commitment to the GATT Customs Valuation Code, and the successor World Trade Organization provisions regulating customs valuation evolving from the Uruguay Round.

The United States Tariff Act of 1930 for the most part incorporates the GATT Customs Valuation Code of 1979.[1] But because the United States adopted that GATT Code in 1979 amendments to the Tariff Act of 1930, some of the prior methods of interpretation of valuation may continue to be considered by courts.[2]

§ 11.16 Valuation—The Law of the GATT/WTO

Of the several codes adopted by the GATT in the Tokyo Round and renewed in the Uruguay WTO Round, the Agreement on the Implementation of Article VII of the General Agreement on Tariffs and Trade (GATT Customs Valuation Code) is of considerable importance to the United States.[1] Article VII of the GATT, titled "Valuation for Customs Purposes", had much earlier established a form of transaction value, but it was not until the Customs Valuation Code was adopted that the form of valuation by a descending order of tests was introduced. That form of valuation was incorporated into the United States law in 1979 and is the source of law to which one must turn for valuation of imports.

§ 11.17 Valuation—Appraisal of Imported Merchandise

Imports of merchandise are valued according to a series of alternative methods.[1] But they are not alternative methods in the

§ 11.15

1. 19 U.S.C.A. § 1401a. See Sherman, Reflections on the New Customs Valuation Code, 12 Law & Pol'y Int'l Bus. 119 (1980).

2. The same is true of other areas with pre-Code established procedures. See Snyder, Customs Valuation in the European Economic Community, 11 Georgia J. Int'l & Comp.L. 79 (1981).

§ 11.16

1. Geneve, 1979, GATT, 26th Supp. BISD 116 (1980). See Davey, Customs

Valuation: Commentary on the GATT Customs Valuation Code (1989).

§ 11.17

1. Merchandise is defined as of the same class or kind as other merchandise if within a group or range which is produced by a particular industry or industrial sector. 19 U.S.C.A. § 1401a(e)(2).

sense that Customs may use any method it chooses. Nor may Customs reject information provided if based on the use of generally accepted accounting procedures.[2] The methods of valuation are set forth in the order of use which must be followed. Most valuations never go beyond the first, the transaction value.

§ 11.18   Valuation—Transaction Value

Customs first considers the transaction value.[1] The transaction value is often referred to as the *invoice* value, since, in the absence of over or under invoicing, that would be the value of the transaction. The statute refers to the transaction value as the *price actually paid or payable.*[2] It is the price when sold for exportation to the United States and thus is usually a wholesale price.[3] It may be confusing where there are several contracts in addition to the actual contract between the buyer-seller, such as between a party to the sale and the party's parent entity,[4] or between a foreign seller and United States company acquiring items purchased by the foreign seller from a foreign manufacturer.[5] The transaction value may or may not include some elements about which there may be doubt as to application of duty. Rebates to the price actually paid or payable made after the merchandise has entered the United States are disregarded in determining the transaction value.[6] For example, quota charges clearly separated on the invoice are nevertheless includable.[7] Dividing the assembly (service) price from the consumer (sale of goods) price for made-to measure clothing does not relieve the importer from duty on the former portion, the full cost is subject to duty.[8]

Added to the transaction value are five other categories of associated costs. Some are costs which may be part of the price paid or payable and thus subject to valuation. But some are costs which, if not subject to tariffs, could be split off from the price of the goods

---

2. 19 U.S.C.A. § 1401a(g)(3).

§ 11.18

1. 19 U.S.C.A. § 1401a(a)(1)(A).

2. 19 U.S.C.A. § 1401a(b)(1). Price actually paid or payable is defined in 19 U.S.C.A. § 1401a(b)(4). Disbursements by the buyer for the benefit of the seller are included, as when the buyer disburses some funds to the agent's seller who assists in bringing about the sale. Moss Mfg. Co., Inc. v. United States, 714 F.Supp. 1223 (C.I.T.1989), *affirmed* 896 F.2d 535 (Fed.Cir.1990).

3. That would not be the case for direct purchases of large items, such as a United States customer directly purchasing a yacht from a German builder.

4. Nissho Iwai American Corp. v. United States, 786 F.Supp. 1002 (C.I.T. 1992), *aff'd in part, rev'd in part* 982 F.2d 505 (Fed.Cir.1992).

5. See Brosterhous, Coleman & Co. v. United States, 737 F.Supp. 1197 (C.I.T.1990).

6. 19 U.S.C.A. § 1401a(b)(4)(B). See Allied Int'l v. United States, 795 F.Supp. 449 (C.I.T.1992) (importer has the burden of showing that the rebate occurred on or before date of entry).

7. Generra Sportswear Co. v. United States, 905 F.2d 377 (Fed.Cir.1990).

8. E.C. McAfee Co. v. United States, 842 F.2d 314 (Fed.Cir.1988).

and paid separately, thus avoiding or evading proper duty.[9] These additional costs subject to duty are:

1. Packing costs incurred by the buyer.[10] If incurred by the seller they would be part of the price paid for the merchandise, probably buried in the price of the goods.

2. Selling commission incurred by the buyer.[11]

3. Any assist, apportioned as appropriate.[12] An assist includes a very broad range of benefits, and is the subject of an extensive definitional provision.[13]

4. Any royalty or license fee related to the goods which the buyer pays directly or indirectly as a condition of the sale.[14] This can be a difficult provision to interpret. If a buyer pays a flat fee per year directly to the designer of the goods, no matter how many are sold, the buyer may escape duty. But any payment which is related to the number sold seems subject to duty.

5. Any direct or indirect accrual to the seller from the subsequent resale, disposal, or use of the goods.[15] This prevents the sale at a low base price, with the buyer required to pass on a percentage to the seller after the goods are resold.

In order to include any of the above five additions it must be shown that they have not been included already in the price paid or payable by "sufficient" information.[16] The statute defines sufficient information as used in this section and others in the valuation provisions.[17] Where sufficient information is not available but there is a belief that one or more of the five additional amounts exist, the transaction value is considered not to be determinable.[18] One would have to move to the next section in the chronology of applicable provisions.

Where the transaction value is determinable under the above discussed provisions, it is to be considered the *appraised* value only

9. See All Channel Products v. United States, 787 F.Supp. 1457 (C.I.T. 1992), *judgment affirmed* 982 F.2d 513 (Fed.Cir.1992) (inland freight charges separately invoiced properly included in transaction value); United States v. Arnold Pickle & Olive Co., 659 F.2d 1049, 68 C.C.P.A. 85 (1981) (inspection costs).

10. 19 U.S.C.A. § 1401a(b)(1)(A).

11. 19 U.S.C.A. § 1401a(b)(1)(B). See Jay–Arr Slimwear Inc. v. United States, 681 F.Supp. 875 (C.I.T.1988).

12. 19 U.S.C.A. § 1401a(b)(1)(C).

13. 19 U.S.C.A. § 1401a(h)(1). See, e.g., Texas Apparel Co. v. United States,

883 F.2d 66 (Fed.Cir.1989), *cert. denied* 493 U.S. 1024, 110 S.Ct. 728, 107 L.Ed.2d 747 (1990) (sewing machine costs constitute an assist in manufacturing jeans). See Collins, The Concept of Assist as Applied to Customs Valuation of Imported Merchandise, 1991 Detroit Col.L.R. 239.

14. 19 U.S.C.A. § 1401a(b)(1)(D).

15. 19 U.S.C.A. § 1401a(b)(1)(E).

16. 19 U.S.C.A. § 1401a(b)(1).

17. 19 U.S.C.A. § 1401a(b)(5).

18. Id.

if certain further conditions exist. If they do not exist, one must also move to the next applicable method of valuation.[19]

First, the buyer must be able to dispose of or use the goods without restriction, except restrictions that (1) are required by law, (2) limit resale to a geographical area, or (3) do not substantially affect the value.[20]

Second, there may not be any condition or consideration affecting the sale of or the price paid or payable where the value of the condition or consideration cannot be determined.[21]

Third, no part of the proceeds from the use or resale may accrue directly or indirectly to the seller, unless that amount is calculable under the provisions noted above.[22]

Fourth, the buyer and seller are either unrelated, or if related the transaction is acceptable under the discussion below regarding related buyers and sellers.[23] The statutes define related persons under special rules.[24]

Often the buyers and sellers are related. The most common relationship is that of a parent and subsidiary. Intraorganization transfers are often conducted with prices that are not truly reflective of arm's length prices, sometimes to avoid taxes, sometimes to avoid tariff duties, sometimes for other purposes.[25] Because of the unique nature of related buyers and sellers, separate provisions apply. The transaction value in a sale from a related seller to buyer is the appraised value, as long as (1) the circumstances of the sale do not suggest the relationship influenced the price, and (2) the transaction value approximates either the transaction value in an unrelated parties transaction, or the deductive value or computed value for identical or similar merchandise.[26] This exception introduces the concept of *deductive* value and *computed* value, both alternative valuations methods discussed below. The exception also requires defining both *identical* merchandise and *similar* merchandise. Definitions of both are in the statutes.[27] The comparison values referred to above must be values for merchandise entering the United States at or about the same time as the merchandise in question.

19. In rejecting use of transaction value, there must be more than mere suspicion that the value is not fairly reflective of sales in the market. See Texas Instruments Inc. v. United States, 500 F.Supp. 922 (Cust.Ct.1980), *judgment vacated* 8 C.I.T. 1, 5 ITRD 2543 (C.I.T.1984).

20. 19 U.S.C.A. § 1401a(b)(2)(A)(i).

21. 19 U.S.C.A. § 1401a(b)(2)(A)(ii).

22. 19 U.S.C.A. § 1401a(b)(2)(A)(iii). The above provision is 19 U.S.C.A. § 1401a(b)(1)(E).

23. 19 U.S.C.A. § 1401a(b)(2)(A)(iv).

24. 19 U.S.C.A. § 1401a(g)(1).

25. Transfer pricing is discussed in chapter 24.

26. 19 U.S.C.A. § 1401a(b)(2)(B).

27. 19 U.S.C.A. § 1401a(h)(2) & (4).

Values used for comparison purposes may consist of identical or similar goods,[28] but differences in the method of sales may distort the comparison. Consequently, the values used must consider differences, if based on sufficient information, in commercial levels, quantity levels and any costs, commissions, values, fees and proceeds in § 1401a(b)(1), discussed above.[29]

While the above identifies provisions which designate the composition of the transaction value, there are also specific items which are not to be included in that value. They include two specific areas.

First, transaction value should not include any reasonable cost or charge for either (1) construction, erection, assembly, or maintenance of, or technical assistance to the merchandise after importation, or (2) transportation after importation.[30]

Second, transaction value should not include the customs duties or other federal taxes imposed upon importation, nor federal excise tax.[31]

Transaction value of identical and similar merchandise. This separate section largely draws from the above section those provisions applicable to determining transaction value where it is necessary to refer to identical or similar merchandise. The identical merchandise value method is used when the above transaction value cannot be determined or used, and if the identical merchandise value cannot be used the similar merchandise value is used.[32] Where the transaction value has been determined above for identical merchandise or for similar merchandise, as defined in the statute,[33] it is to be adjusted. That adjustment requires consideration of any different commercial level or quantity level of sales for the comparison identical or similar merchandise.[34] The adjustment must be based on sufficient information. Where there are two or more comparison transactions, the appraisal of the imported merchandise will be based on the lower or lowest of the comparison values, thus resulting in a favorable conclusion for the importer.[35]

§ 11.19   Valuation—Deductive Value

The most important question is when is the deductive method of valuation to be used? It is used when the above transaction value

28. See Walter Holm & Co. v. United States, 3 C.I.T. 119 (1982) (use of value of exports of cantaloupes through Laredo, Texas, to determine value of same items through Nogales, Arizona).

29. 19 U.S.C.A. § 1401a(b)(2)(C).

30. 19 U.S.C.A. § 1401a(b)(3)(A). International transportation is separately excluded in 19 U.S.C.A. § 1401a(b)(4)(A).

31. 19 U.S.C.A. § 1401a(b)(3)(B).

32. 19 U.S.C.A. §§ 1401a(a)(1)(B) & (C).

33. 19 U.S.C.A. § 1401a(h)(2) & (4).

34. 19 U.S.C.A. § 1401a(c)(2).

35. Id.

does not lead to a determination acceptable to Customs.[1] But the importer may request that the computed value discussed below be used in place of the deductive value.[2] If use of the computed value does not prove possible, the deductive value is next used.[3]

In using deductive value, it may be applied to the merchandise being appraised, or to either identical or similar merchandise.[4] The deductive value focuses on unit value,[5] and constitutes the most appropriate value as determined in one of three ways.

The first method of determining deductive value applies where the merchandise imported is sold (1) in the condition as imported and (2) at or about the date of importation. The deductive value is the unit price at which the merchandise is sold in the greatest quantity.[6]

The second method applies where the merchandise imported is sold in the condition as imported but not at or about the date of importation. The deductive value is the unit price at which the merchandise is sold in the greatest quantity, but within 90 days after importation.[7]

The third method is where the merchandise is neither sold in the condition imported nor within 90 days after importation. The deductive value is the unit price at which the merchandise, after further processing, is sold in the greatest quantity within 180 days of importation.[8] But this third method applies only at the election of the importer, upon notification to the customs officer.[9]

If none of these deductive methods apply, which also means the transaction value was first ruled inapplicable, the next test to apply will be the computed value method.

If the deductive method proves applicable, there may be some applicable reductions from the unit price. They include commissions, additions for profit and expenses, costs of domestic and international transportation, customs duties and other federal taxes on the merchandise, and where the third method of deductive value is used, the costs of additional processing.[10] Deductions for profits and expenses must be consistent with profits and expenses in the

§ 11.19

1. 19 U.S.C.A. § 1401a(a)(1)(D).

2. 19 U.S.C.A. § 1401a(a)(2).

3. Id.

4. 19 U.S.C.A. § 1401a(d)(1).

5. Unit value is the price the merchandise is sold (1) in the greatest aggregate quantity, (2) to unrelated persons, (3) at the first commercial level after importation (at level i and ii discussed below), or after further process-ing (at level iii discussed below), (4) in a total volume which is both greater than the total volume sold at any other unit price, and sufficient to establish the unit price. 19 U.S.C.A. § 1401a(d)(2)(B).

6. 19 U.S.C.A. § 1401a(d)(2)(A)(i).

7. 19 U.S.C.A. § 1401a(d)(2)(A)(ii).

8. 19 U.S.C.A. § 1401a(d)(2)(A)(iii).

9. Id.

10. 19 U.S.C.A. § 1401a(d)(3)(A).

United States for similar merchandise, and any state or local taxes on the importer relating to the sale of the merchandise is considered an expense.[11]

There may also be an increase to the unit price, if such costs have not already been included, amounting to the packing costs incurred by the importer or buyer.[12]

A final provision requires that in calculating deductive value one disregards any sale to a person who supplies an assist for use in connection with the merchandise.[13]

Where deductive value is inapplicable, or where the importer has chosen to pass over deductive value, the next method is computed value.

§ 11.20   Valuation—Computed Value

Computed value is used when transaction and deductive value methods have not provided an appropriate result. But the importer may skip over using deductive value and use the computed value.[1] The computed value constitutes the sum of four parts.[2]

First, the cost or value of materials and fabrication or processing.[3] It does not include any internal tax by the exporting country if the tax is remitted upon exportation.[4]

Second, profit and expenses of the amount usually associated with the same kind of merchandise.[5] They are based on producer's profits and expenses, unless inconsistent with those for sales of the same class or kind of merchandise by producers in the country exporting to the United States, in which case there is a calculation of such profits and expenses using the "sufficient information" procedure.[6] The foreign assembler's profit for integrated circuits and transistors assembled in Curacao were properly included, but Customs also should have applied same rationale in determining general expenses.[7] The costs of a warranty for aircraft should also

---

11. 19 U.S.C.A. § 1401a(d)(3)(B).

12. 19 U.S.C.A. § 1401a(d)(3)(C).

13. 19 U.S.C.A. § 1401a(d)(3)(D).

§ 11.20

1. 19 U.S.C.A. § 1401a(a).

2. 19 U.S.C.A. § 1401a(e)(1). For cases which have used the constructed value approach, see Texas Instruments, Inc. v. United States, 3 C.I.T. 114 (1982) (values of integrated circuits and transistors); New York Credit Men's Adjustment Bureau, Inc. v. United States, 314 F.Supp. 1246 (Cust.Ct.1970), *affirmed* 342 F.Supp. 745 (Cust.Ct.1972).

3. 19 U.S.C.A. § 1401a(e)(1)(A). See Texas Apparel Co. v. United States, 698

F.Supp. 932 (C.I.T.1988), *affirmed* 883 F.2d 66 (Fed.Cir.1989), *cert. denied* 493 U.S. 1024, 110 S.Ct. 728, 107 L.Ed.2d 747 (1990).

4. 19 U.S.C.A. § 1401a(e)(2)(A).

5. 19 U.S.C.A. § 1401a(e)(1)(B). See Texas Instruments Inc. v. United States, 500 F.Supp. 922 (Cust.Ct.1980), *judgment vacated* 8 C.I.T. 1, 5 ITRD 2543 (C.I.T.1984); Braniff Airways, Inc. v. United States, 2 C.I.T. 26 (1981).

6. 19 U.S.C.A. § 1401a(e)(2)(B).

7. Texas Instruments Inc. v. United States, 500 F.Supp. 922 (Cust.Ct.1980), *judgment vacated* 8 C.I.T. 1, 5 ITRD 2543 (C.I.T.1984).

be included as profit, less expenditures the manufacturer-seller may establish have been incurred by the warranty obligations in curing defects.[8]

Third, any assist if not included in the amount above.[9] Computing the value of jeans would allow the addition of the cost or value of the sewing machines used to produce the jeans.[10]

Fourth, packing costs.[11]

§ 11.21 Valuation—Value When Other Methods Are Not Effective

If the value cannot be determined under the above discussed methods, there is a final method of calculation of value. It is to derive a value using the methods set forth above, adjusting them to the extent necessary to achieve a reasonable result.[1] But in making such appraisal, the statute prohibits using any of seven items.[2] They are:

(1) United States selling price of United States produced merchandise,

(2) any system using the higher of two alternatives,

(3) domestic market price in country of exportation,

(4) cost of production for identical or similar merchandise which differs from such cost of production determined under the computed value method,

(5) price for export to a country other than the United States,

(6) minimum values, or

(7) arbitrary or fictitious values.

As first noted, transaction value expressed in the invoice is used in the vast majority of cases. When there is some challenge to transaction value, the procedure may become very complex. Any of the determinations of Customs may be challenged, but the cost of such challenge for all but the largest importers will often result in paying the Customs determined value, or not importing the goods.

---

8. Braniff Airways, Inc. v. United States, 2 C.I.T. 26 (1981).

9. 19 U.S.C.A. § 1401a(e)(1)(C).

10. Texas Apparel Co. v. United States, 698 F.Supp. 932 (C.I.T.1988), *affirmed* 883 F.2d 66 (Fed.Cir.1989), *cert. denied* 493 U.S. 1024, 110 S.Ct. 728, 107 L.Ed.2d 747 (1990).

11. 19 U.S.C.A. § 1401a(e)(1)(D).

§ 11.21

1. 19 U.S.C.A. § 1401a(f)(1).

2. 19 U.S.C.A. § 1401a(f)(2).

Counsel will calculate the possible rates of duty under all the possible alternatives and will only import the products if the rate of duty is acceptable and does not cause the price for resale to be either excessive, or more than would result from using United States products which may cost more to produce, but do not have added duty.

*

Chapter 12

ANTIDUMPING DUTIES

Table of Sections

§ 12.1 Dumping—What Is It and Why Is It Done?

Dumping involves selling abroad at a price that is less than the price used to sell the same goods at home (the "normal" or *"fair"* value). To be unlawful, dumping must threaten or cause material injury to an industry in the export market, the market where prices are lower. Dumping is recognized by most of the trading world as an unfair practice (akin to price discrimination as an antitrust offense). Dumping is the subject of a special GATT code which establishes the basic parameters for determining when dumping exists, what constitutes material injury and the remedy of antidumping tariffs. Such tariffs can amount to the margin of the dump, i.e. the difference in the price charged at home and (say) the European Union or the United States.

The economics of dumping as an unfair trade practice arise from a producer's opportunity to compartmentalize the global marketplace for its goods. Such opportunities permit it to offer the product for sale at different prices in different sectors and thereby maximize its revenues. Only if trade barriers or other factors insulate each market sector is there an opportunity to vary substantially the price in different sectors of the global market. For example, a producer can safely "dump" in an overseas market at cheap prices and a high volume only if it can be sure that the market in its home country is immune from penetration (arbitrage) by the products sold abroad. The objective of dumping may be to increase long term marginal revenues or to ruin a competitor's market position (predatory pricing). On the other hand, the dumping may not represent an unfair trade practice, but only short term interests related to distress sales, introductory offers or loss leaders. Dumping to develop a new foreign market or brand awareness in an existing market may make sense as a marketing technique. There is great difficulty in determining which type of dumping is being practiced in any particular case.

§ 12.2   The WTO Antidumping Code (1994)

Late in 1993, the Uruguay Round of GATT negotiations were concluded and President Clinton notified Congress of his intent to sign the many agreements involved. One of these agreements is yet another attempt at clarification of antidumping law. The WTO Antidumping Code focuses upon dumping determinations (particularly criteria for allocating costs) and material injury determinations (particularly causation). *De minimis* dumping, defined as less than 2 percent of the product's export price, is not subject to antidumping duties and signatories must terminate such investigations immediately. Cumulation of imports in injury determinations is permitted, as is the filing of petitions by unions and workers. When another signatory challenges the implementation of the Code, World Trade Organization dispute settlement panels will have binding authority to resolve the dispute without hearing new evidence and allowing for "competing, reasonable interpretations" of the Code under national laws.

§ 12.3   U.S. Implementation of and Compliance with the WTO Antidumping Code

Congress ratified and implemented the Uruguay Round accords in December of 1994 under the Uruguay Round Agreements Act.[1]

---

§ 12.3

1. Public Law No. 103–465, 108 Stat. 4809.

Section 733(b) of the Tariff Act (1930)[2] has been amended by the addition of a subparagraph providing for a de minimis dumping margin. The administrating authority, in making its preliminary determination, must disregard any weighted average dumping margin that is de minimis, i.e., any average dumping margin that is less than two percent ad valorem or the equivalent specific rate for the subject merchandise. Any weighted average dumping margin that is de minimis must also be disregarded by the administrating authority when making its final determinations.[3]

A significant effect of the Uruguay Round Agreements Act (URAA) is that it has reduced the discretion previously available to the administrating authorities by imposing strict statutory time limits. In the case of an antidumping petition, the administrative authority must make an initial determination within twenty days after the date on which a petition is filed. This time limit may be extended to forty days in any case where the administrative authority is required to poll or otherwise determine support for the petition by the industry and exceptional circumstances exist.[4] Time limits are also imposed on the Commission in their determination of whether there is a reasonable indication of injury.[5]

The Uruguay Round Agreements Act authorizes an adjustment to sales-below-cost calculations for start-up costs,[6] thought to be particularly beneficial to high-tech products. It adds a new "captive production" section[7] intended to remove such internal sales from ITC injury determinations. The URAA, however, fails to fully implement the average-to-average or transaction-to-transaction dumping calculations mandated by the Antidumping Code. Rather, weighted average approaches will only be used in the investigatory phase, not in subsequent administrative reviews where the traditional U.S. calculation of dumping margins by comparing individual U.S. sales to average home or third country sales will continue.[8] Adjustments for profits from further manufacturing, selling and distribution of products in the U.S. are authorized.[9] And the URAA strengthens existing U.S. anticircumvention provisions despite their absence from the Uruguay Round Antidumping Code.[10] It also reinforces U.S. law on exclusion of sales below cost from normal value calculations in the home market.[11]

2. 19 U.S.C.A. 1673b(b).

3. 19 U.S.C.A. 1673d(a).

4. 19 U.S.C.A. 1673a(c).

5. 19 U.S.C.A. 1673b(a).

6. 19 U.S.C. § 1671.

7. 19 U.S.C. § 1677b(f)(1)(c)(iii).

8. 9 U.S.C. § 1677a(d)(3).

9. 9 U.S.C. § 1677a(d)(3).

10. 19 U.S.C. § 1677j.

11. 19 U.S.C. § 1677b(d)(3).

The URAA requires that the International Trade Commission provide all parties to the proceeding with an opportunity to comment, prior to the Commission's vote, on *all* information collected in the investigation. The URAA also generally requires imports from a country subject to investigation to be deemed negligible if the imports amount to less than 3 percent of the volume of all such merchandise imported into the United States in the most recent 12–month period preceding the filing of the petition for which data are available. If imports from a country are deemed negligible, then the investigation regarding those imports must be terminated.

Under the URAA, the Commission is ordinarily required to consider cumulation of imports from two or more countries when the imports are subject to investigations as a result of petitions filed on the same day. The Commission must make any cumulative analysis on the basis of the same record, even if the simultaneously filed investigations end up with differing final deadlines.

The URAA requires the International Trade Commission to consider the magnitude of the dumping margin (although not the magnitude of the margin of subsidization) in making material injury determinations. Lastly, the Commission must conduct a review no later than five years after an antidumping or countervailing duty order is issued to determine whether revoking the order would likely lead to continuation or recurrence of dumping or subsidies and material injury. Known as the "sunset provision," this new requirement will result in review of all existing antidumping and countervailing duty orders.

The WTO Appellate Body has taken a restrictive view of what constitutes permissible antidumping duties. In the *EC-Bed Linen from India* dispute, for example, the Appellate Body ruled against "zeroing," a methodology used in dumping margin calculations by the United States and other countries. Both positive and negative dumping margins should be weighed in calculating weighted average dumping margins. However, the Federal Circuit Court of Appeals has held "zeroing" a reasonable interpretation of the U.S. antidumping statute, calling the Appellate Body opinion not "sufficiently persuasive."[12] In the *Thai-steel from Poland* dispute, the Appellate Body rejected a cursory material injury determination stressing that all relevant economic factors must be considered. In the *United States–Hot–Rolled Steel from Japan* dispute, the Appellate Body found bias in the determination of normal value when low-priced sales from a respondent to an exporter were automatically excluded. The Body also indicated that injury determinations must include an analysis of captive production markets in addition

---

12. See Timken Co. v. United States, 354 F.3d 1334 (Fed.Cir.2004), cert. denied ___ U.S. ___, 125 S.Ct. 412, 160 L.Ed.2d 352 (2004).

to merchant markets. Causation in such determinations must be rigorously scrutinized. A WTO panel has ruled that the Commerce Department's refusal to revoke an antidumping order against South Korean DRAMS was inconsistent with Article 11.2 of the Antidumping Code. Hence, U.S. regulations regarding the likelihood of continued dumping after a 3–year hiatus are suspect under the Code.[13] The Court of International Trade, on the other hand, found the U.S. regulations in question consistent with the WTO Antidumping Code.[14] The Court took the position that the WTO panel ruling was not binding precedent, merely informative.

§ 12.4   The Evolution of U.S. Antidumping Law

The United States was an early advocate of the perspective that dumping constitutes an unfair international trade practice. Indeed, United States objections to dumping were recorded as the subject of a protest by Secretary of the Treasury Alexander Hamilton in 1791. In general, United States antidumping statutes compare the price at which articles are imported or sold within the United States with their price in the country of their production at the time of their export to the United States. This approach was first established by the Antidumping Act of 1916, a rarely invoked criminal statute prohibiting "predatorily low price levels."[1] This statute, which also created a private remedy for treble damages, requires proof of an intent to seriously injure or destroy a U.S. industry. This burden of proof made it almost impossible to prevail as a treble damages dumping plaintiff.[2] The European Union, Japan and others have successfully challenged the 1916 Act in WTO dispute resolution proceedings as inconsistent with the Antidumping Code. The United States promised to repeal the Act, and finally did so late in 2004. The EU an Japan sought but did not receive authorization to retaliate by adopting "mirror image" antidumping laws.

The United States law on antidumping is now set forth in Title I of the Trade Agreements Act of 1979, codified at 19 U.S.C.A. §§ 1671–1677g (as amended). Prior noncriminal antidumping provisions, dating from the Antidumping Act of 1921,[3] were repealed. The new provisions are comparable to, but not always identical

---

13. See BNA–ATRR (12–16–98) at 2097.

14. Hyundai Electronics Co. v. United States, 53 F.Supp.2d 1334 (C.I.T. 1999).

§ 12.4

1. 39 Stat. 798, 15 U.S.C.A. §§ 71–77.

2. See In re Japanese Electronic Products Antitrust Litigation, 807 F.2d 44 (3d Cir.1986), *cert. denied* 481 U.S. 1029, 107 S.Ct. 1955, 95 L.Ed.2d 527 (1987). But see Goss International Corp. v. Tokyo Kikai Seisakusho, Ltd., 294 F.Supp.2d 1027 (N.D. Iowa 2003) (jury award of $10.5 million).

3. 42 Stat. 9.

with, the GATT and the Tokyo Round GATT Antidumping Code. The principal U.S. antidumping regulations are found in 19 C.F.R. Part 353.

Modern United States law on antidumping provides an increasingly used and effective private international trade remedy. Prior to 1974, the Treasury Department exercised great discretion over whether to impose antidumping duties. Domestic producers might complain, but the Treasury did not have to act at all or within any time limits and its negative decisions were not subject to judicial review. The Trade Act of 1974, by imposing time limits and clarifying judicial review, marked the arrival of U.S. antidumping law as private remedy.

Unlike early U.S. countervailing duty law, the Antidumping Act of 1921 required proof of injury or the threat thereof to a U.S. industry before duties could be levied. As a matter of practice, the Treasury had always interpreted the Act as requiring proof of *material* injury, an interpretation that eventually caused Congress to shift the determination of injury (but not the determination of dumping) to the U.S. Tariff Commission.[4] This bifurcation of the administration of U.S. antidumping law is now carried over in the roles played by the International Trade Administration (ITA) and International Trade Commission (ITC). On the issue of requiring proof of material injury, Congress remained adamantly opposed even to the point of rejecting this standard as part of the Kennedy Round GATT Antidumping Code.[5] It was not until the same standard was also incorporated in the Tokyo Round Antidumping Code that Congress finally relented and made proof of material injury necessary under the Trade Agreements Act of 1979.[6] This Act also transferred the dumping determination from the Treasury to the Commerce Department and continued the trend towards structured procedural rights in U.S. antidumping proceedings.

U.S. law places authority for administering antidumping (AD) law in two different governmental agencies. The "Administering Authority",[7] responsible for all administration except injury determinations, is the Secretary of Commerce,[8] who has designated the International Trade Administration (ITA) as the administering agency. Injury determinations are the responsibility of the International Trade Commission (ITC).[9]

---

4. Customs Simplification Act of 1954, 68 Stat. 1136, 1138.

5. See Renegotiations Amendments Act of 1968, 82 Stat. 1345.

6. 93 Stat. 148.

7. 19 U.S.C.A. § 1673(1).

8. Prior to 1980, the Treasury Department was the "administering au-

thority", but the Secretary of Commerce was so designated in 1980. See President's Reorganization Plan No. 3 of 1979, 44 Fed.Reg. 69,273 (1979); and Executive Order 12188, 45 Fed.Reg. 989 (1980).

9. 19 U.S.C.A. §§ 1673(2) and 1677(2).

Under current United States law, dumping occurs when foreign merchandise is sold in the United States at "less than its fair value" (LTFV).[10] "Fair value", in turn, is usually determined by the amount charged for the goods in the exporter's domestic market (the "home market").[11] If such sales are both at LTFV and cause or threaten "material injury" to a domestic industry, or retard its development, then an antidumping duty "shall" be imposed. Thus antidumping duties are a statutory remedy, one which the President cannot veto or affect except by negotiation of an international trade agreement. When this occurs, agreement is typically reached with foreign governments to restrain the flow of the offending goods into the U.S. market. These agreements are known as VERs ("voluntary" export restraints). If the complaining U.S. industry is not satisfied with such an agreement, it may generally pursue an antidumping proceeding to its conclusion in spite of the President by refusing to withdraw its complaint.[12] This gives the domestic industry substantial leverage and influence over VER negotiations.

The antidumping duty is in addition to the usual customs duties charged on such products, and is in the amount of the "dumping margin," the difference between the price at which the goods are sold for export to the United States ("United States price")[13] and the "home market" price.[14] The dumping margin may be different for similar merchandise from different foreign states, and may also be different for different manufacturers from the same foreign state.

§ 12.5   The Dumping Determination

The ITA determines whether foreign merchandise is or is likely to be sold in the United States at less than fair value (LTFV) by comparing the "foreign market value" (FMV) to the "United States price" (USP) for such merchandise. If the former exceeds the latter, dumping can be found, which places great stress on the definitions of these two terms. Since the FMV is normally calculated as an average price, and the USP is a transaction-specific price, dumping can be found despite the fact that the average USP exceeds the average FMV.

---

10. 19 U.S.C.A. § 1673(1). Thus, in place of the GATT formulation of "less than its normal value" (Tokyo Round GATT Antidumping Code, Art. 2(1)), the United States AD statute substitutes "fair" value. As is discussed below, no substantive difference is created however.

11. 19 U.S.C.A. §§ 1673, 1673b(b)(1)(A).

12. See 19 U.S.C.A. § 1673c(a).

13. 19 U.S.C.A. § 1677a.

14. 19 U.S.C.A. § 1677b.

§ 12.6   Foreign Market Value

"Foreign market value" is the weighted average wholesale F.O.B. shipment price of the merchandise in the exporter's home (foreign) market—after many adjustments to assure comparability.[1] If sales in the home market are nonexistent or too small to form an adequate basis for comparison, usually less than 5 percent, then export sales to other countries may be used.[2] Export sales to other countries may be used even when they comprise less than 5 percent of export sales to the United States.[3] Sales intended to establish fictitious markets in the source country cannot be considered.[4]

If comparable merchandise is not offered for sale either in the home market or for export to other countries, the ITA is authorized to calculate a "constructed" foreign market value.[5] Such constructed values are most often used when the ITA determines that the merchandise is being sold at less than the cost of production,[6] and also for imports from nonmarket economies.[7]

The time and place to be used in establishing the home market value is often crucial. The time is when the merchandise is first sold within the United States by the importer to a person who is not related to the importer.[8] That is also the date for determining the exchange rate to be used in converting prices in foreign currency into United States dollars.[9] When the goods are manufactured in one country and then shipped to another, from which they are exported to the United States, there is a question as to whether the foreign market value is to be determined according to prices in the country of manufacture or the country of transshipment. The statute does provide a partial answer. The prices in country of transshipment are to be used when:

> (1) the manufacturer sells to "a reseller" and the manufacturer does not know to what country the reseller intends to export the merchandise;

> (2) the merchandise is exported to a country other than the United States, enters into the commerce of that other country, but is not substantially transformed in that country; AND

> (3) the goods are later exported to the United States.[10]

§ 12.6

1. 19 U.S.C.A. § 1677b(a)(1)(A); 19 C.F.R. § 353.46.

2. 19 U.S.C.A. § 1677b(a)(1)(B); 19 C.F.R. § 353.48.

3. Certain Dried Salted Codfish from Canada, 50 Fed.Reg. 20,819 (1985), 7 ITRD 2121.

4. 19 U.S.C.A. § 1677b(a)(1), (5).

5. 19 U.S.C.A. § 1677b(a)(2); 19 C.F.R. § 353.50.

6. 19 C.F.R. § 353.51.

7. 19 U.S.C.A. § 1677b(c).

8. 19 U.S.C.A. § 1677b(a)(1). Prior to 1984, the time used was the time of export of the merchandise to the United States.

9. 19 C.F.R. § 353.60(a).

10. 19 U.S.C.A. § 1677b(g).

In determining foreign market value, averaging and generally recognized sampling techniques may be used whenever there is a significant volume of sales or number of adjustments. The samples are selected by the Secretary, but must be "appropriate" and "representative."[11] Insignificant adjustments "may" be disregarded, and will ordinarily be disregarded when their individual *ad valorem* effect is less than 0.33 percent, or when a group of adjustments has an *ad valorem* effect of less than 1.0 percent of the foreign market value.[12]

Other issues relating to the determination of foreign market value are discussed below. These problems include issues arising out of sales at less than costs of production, constructed values, imports from nonmarket economy countries, special rules for multinational corporations, and adjustments necessary to get comparable prices.

§ 12.7   United States Price

To determine whether dumping exists, it is necessary to compare the "foreign market value" to the "United States price," which is either the "purchase price" or the "exporter's sales price."[1] The "purchase price" is the price at which the goods were purchased in a foreign market prior to importation into the United States, if the purchase was from a producer or reseller of the merchandise to a non-related buyer for export to the United States.[2] The purchase price may, however, not be the price of the last sale before importation. Where the producer sells to a reseller knowing that the reseller will, prior to importation into the United States, resell the goods for export to the United States, the ITA has used the price between the producer and reseller as the purchase price.[3] The Federal Circuit has held that the location of sales determines whether sales are an export price or a constructed export price. This fundamental antidumping rule invalidated the "PQ Test" of the Court of International Trade.[4]

The "exporter's sales price" is the price at which the goods are sold or are likely to be sold in the United States, either before or after importation, by an "exporter."[5] "Exporter" is a defined term, and includes not only the actual exporter from or producer in a

---

11. 19 C.F.R. § 353.59(b).

12. 19 C.F.R. § 353.59(a).

§ 12.7

1. 19 U.S.C.A. § 1677a(a).

2. 19 U.S.C.A. § 1677a(b).

3. Sandvik AB v. United States, 721 F.Supp. 1322 (C.I.T.1989), *aff'd* 904 F.2d 46 (Fed.Cir.1990).

4. AK Steel Corp. v. United States, 226 F.3d 1361 (Fed.Cir. 2000) *invalidating* PQ Corp. v. United States, 652 F.Supp. 724 (C.I.T.1987).

5. 19 U.S.C.A. § 1677a(c).

foreign market, but also any agent or related entity in the United States which, directly or indirectly, is controlled by or controls that actual exporter or producer.[6] It also includes entities which are controlled (20 percent or more of voting power) by a third party which controls (20 percent or more of voting power) the actual exporter or producer. Thus, use of the "exporter's sale price" is an attempt to avoid transfer sale problems, and to prohibit use of prices arising out of sales between related parties.[7]

The determination of whether to compare the "purchase price" or the "exporter's sales price" to the "foreign market value" does not depend upon whether the sale occurred before or after the importation. Instead, the purchase price will be used for comparison only if the sale transaction resulted in the goods being shipped directly to a United States purchaser through customary commercial channels for the parties involved, and the exporter's related United States sales agents act only as communications links and documentation processors.[8]

§ 12.8   Sales Below Cost

Sales at less than cost of production are to be disregarded in determining "foreign market value;" but only if the below-cost sales have been over an extended time, in substantial quantities, and will not permit recovery of all costs within a reasonable time in the normal course of trade.[1] Thus, recovery of start up costs can properly be prorated over commercially normative periods. Omission of sales below cost from FMV calculations naturally raises the average FMV and increases the potential to find dumping. Inclusion has the opposite effect.

The central question in most antidumping proceedings is whether and to what degree the foreign producer or exporter is making a portion of its sales in its own market at below cost of production.[2] The ITA interprets "extended time" to mean the investigation period, usually the most recent six months.[3] More than ten percent of total sales, measured by volume, will meet the "substantial quantities" requirement, although fifty percent is sometimes required for fresh agricultural products. Sales are below cost is they do not recover total costs, both fixed and variable, over

---

6.   19 U.S.C.A. § 1677(13).

7.   PQ Corp. v. United States, 652 F.Supp. 724 (C.I.T.1987).

8.   Internal–Combustion Industrial Forklift Trucks from Japan, 52 Fed.Reg. 45,003 (1987).

§ 12.8

1.   19 U.S.C.A. § 1677b(b). See generally Timken Co. v. United States, 673

F.Supp. 495 (C.I.T.1987) (review of ITA practice on sales below cost).

2.   Palmeter, Antidumping Law: A Legal and Administrative Nontariff Barrier, in Down in the Dumps, at 73 (R. Boltuck and R.E. Litan, eds.) (Brookings, 1991).

3.   19 C.F.R. § 353.42(b).

a commercially normative period.[4] Thus, a significant volume of sales by a foreign producer at prices which cover only its variable costs can be disregarded by the ITA in its calculation of foreign market value.

§ 12.9 Nonmarket Economies Included

A constructed value is always used to determine the "foreign market value" of imports from nonmarket economy countries.[1] The actual prices used in the exporter's (home) foreign market are deemed irrelevant because they are assumed to be determined bureaucratically and not by market forces. They are not sufficiently subject to the forces of competition to form an accurate standard for comparison.[2]

The statute defines "nonmarket economy country" in terms of a determination by the ITA,[3] and insulates that administrative determination from judicial review.[4] Within that procedure, the statute gives the ITA a criterion—whether the country's economy operates on "market principles" so that (home market) sales reflect "fair value"—and five factors to consider.[5] The factors include the convertability of the foreign country's currency, the extent to which wages and prices are determined by government control or free bargaining, the extent of governmental ownership of the means of production and the receptivity to private foreign investment. Although the statute speaks in terms of a country by country decision, the ITA has more often analyzed the particular industrial segment involved.[6] In 1992, the ITA indicated that determinations regarding nonmarket economy status will follow its traditional practice and focus upon government involvement in fixing prices and production, private versus collective ownership and the degree of market pricing for industrial inputs. Under these criteria, many believe that the People's Republic of China or at least the Southern Coastal region thereof may be treated as a market economy source under U.S. antidumping law.[7]

§ 12.10 Nonmarket Economy Constructed Values

If the imports are from a nonmarket economy (NME) country, the statute directs the ITA to "construct" a foreign market value

---

4. Palmeter, supra Note 2.

§ 12.9

1. 19 U.S.C.A. § 1677b(c).

2. The courts came to the same conclusion before the enactment of the 1988 Omnibus Trade and Competitiveness Act. See Georgetown Steel Corp. v. United States, 801 F.2d 1308 (Fed.Cir.1986).

3. 19 U.S.C.A. § 1677(18)(A), (C).

4. 19 U.S.C.A. § 1677(18)(D).

5. 19 U.S.C.A. § 1677(18)(B).

6. See, e.g., Certain Headware from China, 54 Fed.Reg. 11,983, 54 Fed.Reg. 18,561 (1989); Natural Menthol from the People's Republic of China, 46 Fed. Reg. 3,258 (1981).

7. See Chrome–Plated Lug Nuts from China, 57 Fed.Reg. 15,052 (1992).

by determining the factors of production (labor, materials, energy, capital, etc.) actually used by the NME to produce the imported goods.[1] A value for each of those factors of production must then be determined according to the prices or costs in a market economy, but the ITA is directed to use countries "considered to be appropriate." Surrogate countries are appropriate if they are at the same level of economic development and are significant producers of comparable merchandise.[2]

To the cost of production, as constructed by this use of factors of production, the ITA is directed to add amounts for general expenses, profits, containers and packing for shipment to the United States. The amounts for general expenses and profits are to be derived from sales of the same class or kind of merchandise in the "country of exportation,"[3] but that really means the surrogate "appropriate" market economy country. The general expenses must be at least 10 percent of the cost of production, and profit must be at least 8 percent of the cost of production plus general expenses.

Several problems arise in the application of this scheme. First, "appropriate" market economy countries may be limited or not available. Second, the surrogate market economy countries selected may be obviously inappropriate, when compared to the level of economic development of the NME.[4] Third, producers in such countries may not furnish the necessary information, even though the ITA is authorized to use the "best available information."[5] Fourth, there is no necessary relationship between the price so constructed by the ITA and any price which the NME producer may decide to charge. This leaves the NME producer or exporter always open to dumping charges, and there is no pre-transaction analytical path for avoiding the dumping charges.

In recognition of some of these difficulties, the statute provides an exception to the construction method outlined above, allowing the use of a different method of constructing a foreign market value for imports from a NME. This second method may be used if the ITA finds that the best available information on factors of production is not adequate. The second, less preferred method of constructing foreign market value of exports from NMEs, is to find a "surrogate" market economy country that produces the same or goods similar to the merchandise imported from the NME, and base

---

§ 12.10

1. 19 U.S.C.A. § 1677b(c)(1).

2. 19 U.S.C.A. § 1677b(c)(4).

3. 19 U.S.C.A. § 1677b(e)(1)(B).

4. The statutory language has, in the past, allowed Canadian prices to be applied to goods produced in Poland, and Paraguayan prices to commodities from China. See Natural Menthol from the People's Republic of China, 46 Fed.Reg. 3,258 (1981); Electric Golf Cars from Poland, 40 Fed.Reg. 25,497 (1975).

5. 19 U.S.C.A. § 1677b(c)(1).

the foreign market value on the price of the goods imported from the surrogate country.[6] Such a construction methodology does not require the ITA to break the pricing of the goods into factors of production.

§ 12.11   Market Economy Constructed Values

The ITA may use constructed values not only for imports from NME countries, but in other circumstances as well. It is directed to construct a foreign market value whenever merchandise comparable to the imported merchandise is not offered for sale either in the home market of the foreign producer or exporter or for export from that home market to other countries.[1] A constructed foreign market value is also to be used when so many sales in the home market are below cost of production, and therefore are disregarded, that the remaining sales provide an inadequate basis for determining foreign market value.[2]

In the circumstances above (not involving NME merchandise), foreign market value is constructed by calculating the actual producer variable costs of production (materials, labor, energy, etc.), then adding industry-normative amounts for general overhead, profit, containers and packing.[3] The "general expenses" usually include a portion of all fixed costs fully allocated to the portion of merchandise exported to the United States, and must be at least ten percent of variable costs, and may be higher if that is done by other producers in the exporting country in the ordinary course of trade. A minimum profit of eight percent is also added, but again may be higher if other producers in the exporting country generally seek higher percentage profits in the ordinary course of their trade.

Actual costs of inputs purchased by the producer from third parties "may be disregarded" if the producer and the third party are related in any way, including the common ownership of five percent of voting stock by any third party.[4] If the actual cost of the input is disregarded, the ITA is directed to look first at other transactions in the market, and if none to use the best evidence available. Where a "major input" is provided by a related person, and there are reasonable grounds to believe it was furnished at

6. 19 U.S.C.A. § 1677b(c)(2). Until 1988, this method of construction was the normal method for constructing a foreign market value for imports from a NME.

§ 12.11

1. 19 U.S.C.A. § 1677b(a)(2); 19 C.F.R. § 353.50.

2. 19 U.S.C.A. § 1677b(b); 19 C.F.R. § 353.51(b).

3. 19 U.S.C.A. § 1677b(e)(1).

4. 19 U.S.C.A. § 1677b(e)(2), (4).

below the cost of production, the ITA is authorized to consult the best evidence available.[5]

There is a special rule for determining the foreign market value of merchandise produced by a corporation having production facilities in two or more countries, where there are insufficient sales by that producer in its home market on which to base a comparison of its export sales to the United States.[6] If the foreign market value of the goods produced in the country of exportation is less than the price of the goods produced in the corporation's facilities in another country, the ITA "shall" construct a foreign market value which reflects the price of the goods produced in the nonexporting country.

§ 12.12   Similar Merchandise and Price Adjustments

All of the analysis above depends upon a comparison of the prices of "such or similar merchandise."[1] Since merchandise sold in foreign markets is often different, due to cultural, technical or legal constraints, the determination of comparability of merchandise sold in the foreign market to the imported merchandise is often a crucial one. The statute provides a definition, with a hierarchy of criteria.[2] Thus, merchandise which is identical in physical characteristics, and produced in the same country by the same person as the imported merchandise is to be categorized as such or similar merchandise.[3]

If such identical merchandise is not available, the ITA next looks for merchandise which is produced in the same country by the same person which has component materials and is approximately equal in value to the imported merchandise.[4] If neither of the above is available, the ITA is to look at merchandise produced in the same country by the same person, used for the same purpose and "may reasonably be compared with" the imported merchandise.[5] In practice, the ITA considers similarities in the physical characteristics, use and expectations of ultimate purchasers, including advertising of the product, and distribution channels.[6]

A considerable number of adjustments are necessary to obtain comparable prices for goods sold in home markets and for export to the United States. To obtain the United States price, packing costs and container costs are added to the purchase price or exporter's

---

5. 19 U.S.C.A. § 1677b(e)(3).

6. 19 U.S.C.A. § 1677b(d).

§ 12.12

1. 19 U.S.C.A. § 1677b(a)(1)(A).

2. 19 U.S.C.A. § 1677(16).

3. 19 U.S.C.A. § 1677(16)(A).

4. 19 U.S.C.A. § 1677(16)(B).

5. 19 U.S.C.A. § 1677(16)(C).

6. 3.5 inch Microdisks and Coated Media from Japan, 54 Fed.Reg. 6433, 11 ITRD 1767 (1989); Antifriction Bearings from West Germany, 54 Fed.Reg. 18,992, 11 ITRD 2204 (1989).

sales price, if they are not already included in that price.[7] Other amounts added to obtain the United States price include any import duties or other taxes which are rebated or not collected by the country of exportation, and which are imposed on similar merchandise sold in the country of exportation.

Adjustments deducted from the purchase price or exporter's sales price include any expenses, such as freight or insurance, included in that price and attributable to the costs of bringing the goods from the country of export to the United States and most export taxes of the exporting country.[8] There are also deductions for any commissions and other expenses for selling in the United States and the costs of additional processing or assembly in the United States after importation and before sale.[9] But the additional cost of U.S. product liability insurance is not an allowable adjustment.[10]

Adjustments and exchange rate conversions are also made to determine the foreign market value of the goods. Exchange rate conversions are required whenever the USP or FMV sales are not in U.S. dollars. The rates for the relevant sales period as determined quarterly by the Federal Reserve Bank of New York are ordinarily used except when those rates are fluctuating rapidly.[11] In such cases, the ITA will test whether the dumping margin remains if the rates from the prior quarter are used. If the margin disappears, the dumping is attributed to exchange rate fluctuations and the ITA may determine that no dumping occurred.

To obtain an equivalent of the conditions of the United States price, an amount equal to the packing costs and container costs for shipment to the United States is added to the foreign market value.[12] Allowances may be made for sales at different trade levels (wholesale versus retail), quantity or production cost justified discounts, differences in the circumstances of sale and for physical differences in the merchandise.[13] Differences in the circumstances of the sale include credit terms, warranties, servicing, technical assistance, and advertising allowances. Adjustments for cost differences in the circumstances of sale are allowable even if they do not

---

7. 19 U.S.C.A. § 1677a(d)(1).

8. 19 U.S.C.A. § 1677a(d)(2). See Zenith Electronics Corp. v. United States, 755 F.Supp. 397 (C.I.T.1990) *affirmed* 988 F.2d 1573 (Fed.Cir.1993).

9. 19 U.S.C.A. § 1677a(e).

10. See Carlisle Tire & Rubber Co. v. United States, 622 F.Supp. 1071 (C.I.T. 1985).

11. 19 C.F.R. § 353.60(b); see Washington Red Raspberry Commission v.

United States, 859 F.2d 898 (Fed.Cir. 1988).

12. 19 U.S.C.A. § 1677b(a)(1).

13. 19 U.S.C. § 1677b(a)(4). See Smith–Corona Group v. United States, 713 F.2d 1568 (Fed.Cir.1983), *cert. denied* 465 U.S. 1022, 104 S.Ct. 1274, 79 L.Ed.2d 679 (1984) (advertising and rebate sale adjustments upheld) (physically different accessory adjustments upheld).

give rise to comparable price increases in the foreign market.[14] And even if they involve rebates or discounts not made available to all purchasers.[15] These decisions reflect the substantial deference given by the Court of International Trade and appellate courts to the ITA on the important issue of adjustments to its FMV and United States Price calculations.

§ 12.13 The Injury Determination

Antidumping proceedings in the United States are conducted in two stages. In the second stage, the International Trade Commission (ITC) must determine whether the dumping has caused material injury to concerned domestic industries.[1] This section reviews the material injury determination under United States law, including market definition, injury factors and causation.

The Tariff Act provides that an affirmative injury determination should be made when an industry in the United States is "materially" injured or is threatened with material injury by reason of dumped imports, or the establishment of an industry in the United States is materially retarded.[2] The "material injury" standard is applied to established industries, and is defined in the statute.[3] The "threat of material injury" standard is separately stated, but has a substantial overlap with the material injury criteria.[4] The standard for "material retardation" of the establishment of an industry is applied to new industries which have made a substantial commitment to begin production, or have recently begun production.[5]

§ 12.14 Like Domestic Products

Both the ITA and the ITC must determine what constitute "like products" in performing their duties under U.S. antidumping law. The ITA necessarily focuses upon which foreign products are like those alleged to be dumped in the United States. And the ITC must define the relevant domestic industry producing like products in making its injury assessment. The term "like products" is defined by statute as one which is "like, or in the absence of like, most similar in characteristics and uses" to the foreign product

14. See Atlantic Steel Co. v. United States, 636 F.Supp. 917 (C.I.T.1986) (credit and warehousing costs).

15. Zenith Radio Corp. v. United States, 783 F.2d 184 (Fed.Cir.1986).

§ 12.13

1. See 19 U.S.C.A. § 1673(2).

2. 19 U.S.C.A. § 1673(2).

3. 19 U.S.C.A. § 1677(7).

4. 19 U.S.C.A. § 1677(7)(F).

5. BMT Commodity Corp. v. United States, 667 F.Supp. 880 (C.I.T.1987), affirmed 852 F.2d 1285 (Fed.Cir.1988), cert. denied, 489 U.S. 1012, 109 S.Ct. 1120, 103 L.Ed.2d 183 (1989).

under investigation. Although this definition applies to both the ITA and the ITC, they do not always agree on the outcome.[1]

The determination of like products can be influential to ITA dumping and particularly ITC injury decision-making. In one case, for example, the ITC excluded large screen TVs from the U.S. domestic industry definition. This had the effect of giving Japanese TV exports a much larger market share in the U.S., thus supporting an affirmative injury determination.[2] In another decision, the ITC defined the U.S. industry as canned mushrooms, noting that fresh mushrooms were not always interchangeable. This narrow market definition again supported a preliminary injury determination.[3] Variations on the theme of defining "like products" can occur if the ITC decides it is appropriate to exclude domestic companies that also import the allegedly dumped goods or are related to the importer or foreign producer.[4] The ITC may also define the domestic industry regionally in situations where that reflects market realities.[5] Thus, which U.S. firms (and their relative state of economic health) are included or excluded in the ITC's like products definition of the domestic industry is an important threshold issue in material injury analysis.

§ 12.15　Material Injury

There are two potential positions on the meaning of "material." The first is that the term material means any economic harm that is more than trivial, inconsequential or *de minimis*. The second is that material injury means a higher threshold, something not quite as hurtful as the "serious injury" required for escape clause relief,[1] but yet still serious in the ordinary sense of that word. The consensus was that the spirit of Article VI of the GATT was intended to procure the higher standard.[2]

The Tariff Act incorporated the concept of materiality when the Act was amended by the Trade Agreements Act of 1979 in an effort to bring United States law into conformity with the Tokyo Round GATT Antidumping Code. Before the amendment, the ITC used a standard of injury known as the *"de minimis"* standard[3]

§ 12.14

1. See Tantalum Electrolytic Fixed Capacitors from Japan, U.S.I.T.C. Publ. No. 789 (Oct. 1976).

2. Television Sets from Japan, U.S.I.T.C. Publ. No. 367 (March 1971).

3. Canned Mushrooms from the People's Republic of China, U.S.I.T.C. Publ. No. 1324 (Dec. 1982).

4. 19 U.S.C.A. § 1677(4)(B).

5. 19 U.S.C.A. § 1677(4)(C). See National Pork Producers Council v. United States, 661 F.Supp. 633 (C.I.T.1987).

§ 12.15

1. See Chapter 8.

2. Hudec, United States Compliance with the 1967 GATT Antidumping Code, in 1 Antidumping Law; Policy and Implementation 217 (Michigan Yearbook of International Legal Studies 1979).

3. See Titanium Sponge from the U.S.S.R., 33 Fed.Reg. 10,769, 10,772 (1968).

with congressional approval.[4] Under that standard, antidumping duties could be imposed if the injury was more than *de minimis*.[5]

The Tariff Act defines material injury as "harm which is not inconsequential, immaterial, or unimportant."[6] This is the same standard that applies in CVD proceedings "under the Agreement"[7] and much of the law in the area may therefore be treated as interchangeable. Although the material injury definition seems to require a higher standard than a mere injury requirement, the Senate Finance Committee report did not consider them inconsistent. It stated that the material injury standard was nothing more than a codification of the *de minimis* standard as it had been construed by the ITC.[8] The ITC's subsequent interpretations suggest that it understood the material injury requirement to codify the *de minimis* rule.[9]

After the development of the Tokyo Round GATT Antidumping Code, however, the United States amended its statutes to incorporate the Code's principles. The Tariff Act requires the ITC to consider three basic economic aspects in applying the injury standard:

(1) The volume of imports of the merchandise subject to investigation;

(2) The effect of these imports on prices in the United States for like products; and

(3) The impact of these imports on domestic producers of like products, but only in the context of domestic United States production operations.[10]

The Commission is required to explain its analysis of each factor considered and explain its relevance to the agency's determination. The Tariff Act, however, also provides that the "presence or absence" of any of these three factors should "not necessarily give decisive guidance" to the ITC in its material injury determination, and the Commission is not required to give any particular weight to any one factor.[11] The factors are examined through extensive statis-

4. See S.Rep. No. 1298, 93d Cong., 1st Sess. 180 (1974).

5. See, e.g., Cast Iron Soil Pipe from Poland, USTC 214 (AA 1921–50) (1967).

6. 19 U.S.C.A. § 1677(7)(A).

7. See Chapter 13.

8. Senate Comm. on Finance, Trade Agreements Act of 1979, S.Rep. No. 249, 96th Cong., 1st Sess. 87.

9. Vermulst, supra Note 2, § 6.3, at 364–76.

10. 19 U.S.C.A. § 1677(7)(B). See Angus Chemical Co. v. United States,

140 F.3d 1478 (Fed.Cir.1998) (three factors are mandatory for ITC to consider).

11. 19 U.S.C.A. § 1677(7)(E)(ii). See e.g., Iwatsu Elec. Co. v. United States, 758 F.Supp. 1506, 13 ITRD 1120 (C.I.T. 1991) (ITC may weigh each factor in light of circumstances and need not find all economic factors negative before it makes a finding of injury). Compare Tokyo Round GATT Antidumping Code Art. 3(2).

tical analyses. The analysis is performed for the domestic industry as a whole, and not on a company-by-company basis.[12] The ITC may select whatever time period best represents the business cycle and competitive conditions in the industry, and most reasonably allows it to determine whether an injury exists.[13]

Volume of Imports

In compliance with Tokyo Round GATT Antidumping Code Article 3(2), the Tariff Act requires the ITC to consider the absolute volume of imports or any increase in volume of imports in evaluating the volume of imports subject to investigation. This assessment may be made in relation to production or consumption in the United States. The standard in this evaluation is whether the volume of imports, viewed in any of the above ways, is significant.[14]

Data relating to the volume of imports are an important factor in the ITC's injury determinations.[15] In particular, the ITC is more concerned with the dynamics of the market share, such as a significant rise in market penetration, than it is with the size of market share.[16] It is also primarily concerned with the effects that market share changes might have on profits and lost sales.[17] Injury can be found when an importer has a small market share, but imports from a single country are increasing rapidly and the domestic industry reduces its prices during the period of investigation.[18] On the other hand, a large market share for the importer, coupled with increases in production, domestic shipments, exports, employment and profits of the domestic industry, may indicate no injury.

Price Effects

While price issues are obviously crucial to any determination of dumping margins, they have no strict correlation to injury determinations. However, under the Tariff Act, the ITC when making an

---

12. Copperweld Corp. v. United States, 682 F.Supp. 552 (C.I.T.1988).

13. 19 U.S.C.A. § 1677(7)(C)(iii); Kenda Rubber Industrial Co., Ltd. v. United States, 630 F.Supp. 354 (C.I.T. 1986).

14. 19 U.S.C.A. § 1677(7)(C)(i).

15. See, e.g., Certain Seamless Steel Pipes and Tubes from Japan, 47 Fed. Reg. 11,331 (1982) (affirmative preliminary injury determination) (Japanese import tonnage in the heat-resisting category almost tripled during the period of investigation and import penetration nearly doubled).

16. *J. Pattison,* Antidumping and Countervailing Duty Laws 4–2 (1992).

17. See, e.g., Tubeless Tire Valves from Federal Republic of Germany, 46 Fed.Reg. 29,794 (1981) (dumped imports of tubeless tire valves from West Germany caused United States producers to lose sales).

18. Barbed Wire and Barbless Wire Strand from Argentina, 7 ITRD 2610, I.T.C. Pub. No. 1770 (October 1985) (increase from 0.5 to 4.0 percent of market). However, import penetration of only 0.2 percent has been found incapable of causing material injury. Alberta Pork Producers' Marketing Board v. United States, 669 F.Supp. 445 (C.I.T. 1987), *appeal after remand* 683 F.Supp. 1398 (C.I.T.1988).

injury determination may consider the effect of the dumped imports upon prices for like products in the domestic market. This is done to the extent that such a consideration assists in evaluating whether (1) there is significant price underselling by the imported merchandise as compared with the price of like products of the United States,[19] and (2) whether the effect of the imported merchandise is otherwise to depress domestic prices to a significant degree or prevent price increases, which otherwise would have occurred to a significant degree.[20] If there is no price underselling, but instead the exporters cut their U.S. prices to effectively meet price competition from U.S. producers, this is traditionally considered only "technical dumping" and precludes a finding of material injury.[21] The rationale for this approach focuses upon the purposes behind AD law; to prevent unfair not procompetitive trade practices. Thus, technical dumping constitutes a defense to U.S. material injury determinations.

Price underselling is not a *per se* basis for a finding of injury. For example, if the demand for the product is not price sensitive, price underselling will not be a central consideration in any injury finding. There may be no injury from price underselling, even though the domestic producers lost sales in the United States, if the domestic producers' inability to sell goods was not caused by dumped imports. For example, the industry's decline may have been caused by its failure to develop, produce and market a competitive product. A more extensive analysis of causation issues appears in the next subsection.

Substantial underselling, on the other hand, will lead to an affirmative injury finding, where the market is price sensitive.[22] The ITC looks for a pervasive pattern of underselling, which can occur even where there are instances of overselling as well.[23] When the ITC finds that demand for a specific product is price sensitive and importers are engaging in price underselling, it further examines whether domestic producers are being forced into price suppression[24] or actual price cutting[25] due to this price underselling.

19. 19 U.S.C.A. § 1677(7)(C)(ii)(I).

20. 19 U.S.C.A. § 1677(7)(C)(ii)(II).

21. Asphalt Roofing Shingles from Canada, 2 ITRD 5171 (Oct. 1980); Rayon Staple Fibers from France and Belgium, U.S.I.T.C. Inv. No. AA1921–17 and 18 (1961).

22. The ITC views a product as price sensitive when its price is the most important factor in purchasing the product. In Tubeless Tire Valves from the Federal Republic of Germany, 46 Fed. Reg. 29,794 (1981), the ITC relied upon the testimony of buyers who had switched their sourcing from domestic producers to the imports that price was the most important factor in purchasing decisions, with availability a secondary but often critical factor. Id. at 29,795.

23. Metallverken Nederland B.V. v. United States, 728 F.Supp. 730 (C.I.T. 1989), *on remand* 12 ITRD 1784 (1990), action *dismissed* 744 F.Supp. 281 (C.I.T. 1990).

24. Price suppression arises when the domestic industry can affect smaller price increases on those articles directly competitive with dumped imports than

25. See note 25 on page 303.

Since price suppression can be as severe a burden to domestic producers as can an actual price cutting, the ITC will find an injury if it determines that because of the less-than-fair-value price of the dumped imports, domestic producers have lowered or have been unable to raise their prices to accommodate rising costs.[26]

Domestic Industry Impact

The impact on a domestic industry of an allegedly dumped product is probably the most important factor in any injury analysis. The Tariff Act employs the same criteria as are set out in the Tokyo Round GATT Antidumping Code.[27] It then provides supplemental factors for ITC consideration, adding the actual and potential negative effects on the existing development and production efforts of the domestic industry, including efforts to develop a derivative or more advanced version of the like product.[28] The ITC relies primarily on two of these factors in making this determination. First, the industry must be in a distressed or a stagnant condition. Second, the ITC analyzes whether low domestic price levels are a factor in the industry's difficulties (e.g., high unemployment or low capacity utilization rate), and whether the low prices are causing low profits.[29]

The ITC will often base an affirmative determination of material injury on severe downward trends in profitability among domestic producers. For example, a drop in the ratio of net profit to sales from 5.55 percent to 1.05 percent over a three year period, coupled with a 75 percent decline in the aggregate profit in the relevant industry in the same period, has resulted in an affirmative determination of material injury.[30] Thus, it is not necessary that an

it can on those articles that directly compete with non-dumped imports. Tapered Roller bearings from Japan, 40 Fed.Reg. 26,312, 26,314–26,315 (1975).

25. Price cutting arises when the domestic industry is compelled to lower its prices to meet the prices of dumped imports in an attempt to protect its market share.

26. See, e.g., Unrefined Montan Wax from East Germany, 46 Fed.Reg. 45,223, 45,224 (1981).

27. 19 U.S.C.A. § 1677(C)(iii) provides:

In examining the impact required to be considered under subparagraph (B)(iii), the Commission shall evaluate all relevant economic factors which have a bearing on the state of the industry in the United States, including, but not limited to—

(I) actual and potential decline in output, sales, market share, profits, produc-

tivity, return on investments, and utilization of capacity,

(II) factors affecting domestic prices,

(III) actual and potential negative effects on cash flow, inventories, employment, wages, growth, ability to raise capital, and investment, and

(IV) actual and potential negative effects on the existing development and production efforts of the of the domestic industry, including efforts to develop a derivative or more advanced version of the like product.

28. 19 U.S.C.A. § 1677(7)(C)(iii)(IV).

29. Vermulst, supra Note 2, § 6.3, at 369.

30. Sugars and Syrups from Canada, 46 Fed.Reg. 51,086 (1981).

industry suffer an actual loss as a prerequisite to a finding of material injury.

When a negative injury determination has been made despite the industry's declining profitability, the ITC may find alternative injury factors such as general economic conditions and industry overexpansion, which are unrelated to dumping or subsidization of foreign goods.[31] On the other hand, absent other severe injury factors, a general upward trend and strong profitability of domestic firms is likely to result in a negative determination.[32]

The effect of dumped imports on employment in the relevant domestic industry is also considered. Employment data are not dispositive due to the broad spectrum of economic factors related to such data, and many of those factors may not be attributable to dumping. However, changes in domestic employment during the period of dumping are one factor to be considered. For example, the ITC has found a 35 percent drop in employment during the period of dumping to be a reasonable indication of material injury.[33] On the other hand, where employment and man-hours worked have increased in the domestic industry, this data will be cited by the ITC as a factor in its determination that there has been no material injury.[34] But such negative determinations are usually made only when other factors also indicate no material injury is present.

The utilization of plant capacity has been considered a factor in many determinations, but such capacity utilization data is treated ambiguously because it is dependent upon diverse factors. For example, a reasonable indication of material injury has been found when capacity utilization fell from 88 percent to 77 percent in two years.[35] However, no material injury has been found when capacity utilization went from 85 to 77 percent and the decline was found to be caused by frequent equipment breakdowns and quality control disruptions.[36]

§ 12.16   Threat of Material Injury

A good example of the analysis of the *threat* of material injury standard before the Court of International Trade (CIT) is found in

---

31. See, e.g., Silicon Metal from Canada, 44 Fed.Reg. 13,590 (1981).

32. Motorcycle Batteries from Taiwan, 46 Fed.Reg. 53,235 (1981) (negative final injury determination) (data regarding profitability data showed the industry as a whole to be prosperous during times of greatest import penetration).

33. Montan Wax from the German Democratic Republic, 45 Fed.Reg. 73,821 (1980).

34. Portable Electric Nibblers from Switzerland, 45 Fed.Reg. 80,209 (1980).

35. Carbon Steel Wire Rod from Brazil, Belgium, France, and Venezuela, 47 Fed.Reg. 13,927 (1982).

36. Crystal from Austria and Italy, 45 Fed.Reg. 31,830 (1980).

Rhone Poulenc, S.A. v. United States.[1] This case involved the shipment of package anhydrous sodium metasilicate (ASM) from France to the United States. The U.S. industry was comprised of four companies, only one of which was demonstrably injured. *Rhone Poulenc* was an appeal to the CIT from an ITC decision concerning the "threat of material injury" standard. The court first determines the relevant market, then rejects the importers argument that present market penetration by imports is the crucial fact in determining whether such a threat exists. Instead, the court states that it is proper for the ITC to consider, in determining the likelihood of future injury, the developing trends in all the indicators used to determine whether actual injury has occurred. These indicators of actual injury include the volume of imports, the effect of imports on prices, and the impact of the imports on the domestic industry. The ITC is permitted, however, to look at likely future conduct of producers.

In *Rhone Poulenc,* the court finds that the volume of imports, although now only 4.4 percent, had increased rapidly, and that fact was significant. The importer argued that this rapid increase had leveled off but the court determined that the leveling off was primarily due to the cash bond requirement imposed after the ITA Preliminary Decision on sales at LTFV. The facts also showed that the foreign source operated at less than its maximum capacity, and that its efficiency would improve if it operated at maximum capacity. Thus, the importers could expand their foreign supply quickly to increase market penetration.

The ITC and CIT also found that there was price undercutting by the importers, which caused lost sales. These lost sales, in turn, had a negative effect on domestic industry prices. Because ASM is a fungible good, there is decreasing demand for it, and ASM buyers are price sensitive. A direct causal relation between the lost sales and present injury to the domestic injury does not need to be proven, so long as the ITC finds that the lost sales "indicate" a threat to future sales, production and profit.

The importers raised the question of whether the ITC can look at the injury to each producer separately, or can look only at the domestic injury as a whole. The court responded that enough producers must be threatened such that their collective output is a major proportion of domestic production. Further, different domestic producers can be subject to different kinds of threats, as long as the single source of all such threats is imports. The CIT holds that this burden was met, and threat of material injury proved.

§ 12.16
1.   592 F.Supp. 1318 (C.I.T.1984).

§ 12.17 Causation

Causation of material injury by dumping is a required element which must be found independently of the finding of material injury, threat of material injury or the material retardation of the establishment of a domestic industry. However, there is a tendency to enter an affirmative injury determination when dumping and material injury to a concerned industry are found, without a lengthy analysis of the causal link between them. In a negative injury determination, on the other hand, the ITC may engage in a rather detailed analysis of causation.

The Tariff Act requires a simple causation element, stating that material injury must be caused "by reason of" the dumped imports.[1] The same standard applies in CVD proceedings "under the Agreement" and once again the law in this area is largely interchangeable. The causation requirement is not a high one. Imports need only be *a* cause material injury, and need not be the most substantial or primary cause of injury being suffered by domestic industry. This causation element of an affirmative injury determination can be satisfied if the subsidized imports contribute even minimally to the conditions of the domestic injury.[2] Under this "contributing cause" standard, causation of injuries may be found despite the absence of correlation between dumped imports and the alleged injuries if there is substantial evidence that the volume of dumped imports was a contributing factor to the price depression experienced by the domestic injury.[3]

In examining the causal link between the dumped imports and the material injury, the ITC is willing to recognize that there can be causal factors other than dumping which can be responsible for the alleged injury in a particular proceeding.[4] For example, the ITC has found no causal link between dumped imports and the condition of the industry when the industry prospered during times of

---

1. 128. 19 U.S.C.A. § 1673(2): If ... (2) the Commission determines that—

(A) an industry in the United States—

(i) is materially injured, or

(ii) is threatened with material injury, or

(B) the establishment of an industry in the United States is materially retarded, by reason of imports of that merchandise ... , then there shall be imposed upon such merchandise an antidumping duty....

2. British Steel Corp. v. United States, 593 F.Supp. 405, 413 (C.I.T. 1984).

3. Id.

4. Such extraneous factors include:

(1) Volume and prices of imports not sold at less than fair value;

(2) Contraction in demand or changes in patterns of consumption;

(3) Trade restrictive practices of and competition between foreign and domestic producers;

(4) Developments in technology; and

(5) The export performance and productivity of the domestic industry.

S.Rep. No. 249, 96th Cong., 1st Sess. 57 (1979).

greatest import penetration and did less well during times of decreased imports.[5] The existence of extraneous injury factors will not, however, necessarily preclude an affirmative finding of material injury for purposes of the Tariff Act[6] as long as the dumping is a contributing cause to the material injury of the domestic industry. The ITC is not required to weigh the effects from the dumped imports against the effects associated with other factors. For example, in evaluating causation, the ITC may uncover other major causes for the problems of the domestic industry. These may include huge unnecessary expenses, chronic excess capacity, inefficiency, poor quality, price sensitivity or increased domestic competition. Nevertheless, the presence of such major alternative causes of injury does not foreclose the possibility that imports have been *a* contributing cause of the industry's problems.[7]

The ITC may, but is not required to, consider the margin of dumping when evaluating causation. In practice the margin of dumping is an important factor in the ITC's causation analysis.[8] The ITC may also include or exclude sales at fair value in calculating the dumping margin for this purpose.[9] If the dumping margin is slight or substantially lower than the margin of underselling,[10] this may indicate that the injury was not caused by the dumped imports. The imports will still be able to undersell domestic producers, even if the prices of the imports are raised to their fair values. If, on the other hand, the dumping margin is higher than the margin of underselling, thereby enabling the foreign exporters to undersell domestic producers, material injury may be said to have been caused by the dumping because the foreign exporters were

5. Motorcycle Batteries from Taiwan, 47 Fed.Reg. 13,619 (1982).

6. At least one Commissioner has argued that although this traditional analysis may be useful in determining material injury, it is not a proper tool to resolve the issue of causation because it does not do well in separating the effects of dumped imports from the effects of other factors operating in the marketplace. Instead she advocates what is termed the elasticity analysis. This new approach analyses the elasticity of domestic demand for the product under investigation to determine the effect on the domestic injury of unfair imports, as separated from many other factors that affect the concerned industry. See H. Blinn, The Injury–Test under United States Antidumping and Countervailing Duty Laws as Interpreted by the International Trade Commission and the Department of Commerce: A Comparison Study of the Conventional "Trend–Analysis" and the "Elasticity-test" 23–30 (1991).

7. Iwatsu Electric Co., Ltd. v. United States, 758 F.Supp. 1506 (C.I.T.1991) (small telephone systems); United Engineering & Forging v. United States, 779 F.Supp. 1375 (C.I.T.1991), *opinion after remand* 14 ITRD 1748 (C.I.T.1992) (crankshafts).

8. Hyundai Pipe Co., Ltd. v. United States Intern. Trade Com'n, 670 F.Supp. 357, 8 ITRD 2044 (C.I.T.1987).

9. Algoma Steel Corp. v. United States, 865 F.2d 240 (Fed.Cir.1989), *cert. denied* 492 U.S. 919, 109 S.Ct. 3244, 106 L.Ed.2d 590 (1989); Floral Trade Council of Davis, Cal. v. United States, 704 F.Supp. 233 (C.I.T.1988).

10. Certain Spirits from Ireland, 46 Fed.Reg. 38,780 (1981) (negative injury determination) (subsidy was so small as to have a "minuscule possible price effect").

able to undersell only because of the higher dumping margin. Though it may be useful as one factor in determining causation, the size of the dumping margin is usually not determinative in injury determinations. For example, the ITC has found no causation of injury despite dumping margins of 50 percent and 36 percent.[11]

§ 12.18   Cumulative Causation

Can "material injury" be caused by imports from several exporters in more than one country through the cumulative effect of many small injuries? There are arguments against cumulating each source of dumping to determine whether it is a cause of injury. Such cumulation could penalize small suppliers who would not have caused injury if their dumping had been examined in isolation.[1] Nevertheless, the injury to a domestic industry is measured by the cumulated results of dumping on the ground that injury caused by "many nibbles" is just as harmful as that caused through "one large bite." Cumulation provides administrative ease, since the antidumping agency is not required to allocate the amount of injury caused by each individual exporter. A decision of the Court of Appeals for the Federal Circuit strongly upholds cumulative causation in U.S. anti-dumping injury determinations.[2]

The GATT and the Tokyo Round Antidumping Code are ambiguous on the propriety of cumulation. While GATT Article VI seems to contemplate a country-by-country approach by referring repeatedly to the singular term "country,"[3] the Antidumping Code uses the term "dumped imports," which implicitly permits an aggregate approach.[4] The use of cumulation doctrines in determining material injury in dumping cases has never been criticized by the Committee on Antidumping practices, which is further evidence that the practice of cumulation has been accepted by the signatories to the Tokyo Round GATT Antidumping Code.[5] The Uruguay Round Code expressly permits cumulation.

The Tariff Act requires that the ITC cumulatively assess the volume and effect of reasonably coincident dumped imports from two or more countries of like products subject to investigation if the imports compete with each other and with like United States products.[6] There is, however, an exception for imports from benefi-

---

11. Fall Potatoes from Canada, 48 Fed.Reg. 43,412 (1983).

§ 12.18

1. Horlick, The United States Antidumping System, in Antidumping Law and Practice: A Comparative Study 102 (1989).

2. See Hosiden Corp. v. Advanced Display Mfrs. of America, 85 F.3d 1561 (Fed.Cir.1996).

3. GATT Art. 6(1), 6(6).

4. Antidumping Code, Arts. 3(1), 3(2), 3(4), 3(5) and 3(7).

5. Vermulst, supra Note 2, § 6.3, at 401.

6. 19 U.S.C.A. § 1677(7)(C)(iv). This statutory provision settled a pre–1984

ciary countries of the Caribbean Basin Initiative.[7] The ITC has held cumulation to be proper if the factors and conditions of trade in the particular case show its relevance to the determination of injury, and has given a nonexhaustive list of such factors.[8] The list includes the volume of imports, the trend of import volume, the fungibility of imports, competition in the markets for the same end users, common channels of distribution, pricing similarity, simultaneous impact, and any coordinated action by importers. From these factors, the ITC determines whether the imports compete with each other and like domestic products. Surprisingly, the ITC found that French and Italian wines do not compete with each other.[9] But an ITC ruling that steel imports from Spain, Brazil and Korea competed with each other was overturned by the Court of International Trade,[10] which also refused to require the ITC to cumulate steel plate imports from Brazil, Korea and Argentina.[11] The ITC has also ruled that, when cumulating, it is not necessary to find for each country a separate causal link between its imports and U.S. material injury.[12] Such multiple country cumulation should be distinguished from the "cross cumulation" allowed by the Tariff Act. Cross cumulation involves consideration by the ITC of both dumped and subsidized imports into the United States.[13] The net effect of U.S. rules on cumulation of import injury is to encourage petitioners to name as many countries as possible as the source of their problems.

§ 12.19 Antidumping Procedures—Petition and Response

In an antidumping proceeding, the ITA determines whether the imports are being sold at less than fair value (LTFV), and the ITC makes a separate determination concerning injury to the domestic industry making like or similar products.

United States antidumping proceedings may be initiated by either the Commerce Department, a union or an aggrieved business—or by a group association of aggrieved workers or businesses.[1]

conflict within the Commission concerning whether to cumulate or not.

7. 19 U.S.C.A. § 1677(7)(C)(iv)(II).

8. Certain Steel Products from Belgium, Brazil, France, Italy, Luxembourg, the Netherlands, Romania, the United Kingdom, and West Germany, ITC Pub. 1221, Inv. No. 701–TA–86–144 (February 1986).

9. See American Grape Growers Alliance v. United States, 615 F.Supp. 603 (C.I.T.1985).

10. Republic Steel Corp. v. United States, 591 F.Supp. 640 (C.I.T.1984).

11. USX Corp. v. United States, 698 F.Supp. 234 (C.I.T.1988).

12. Fundicao Tupy S.A. v. United States, 678 F.Supp. 898 (C.I.T.1988), *affirmed* 859 F.2d 915 (Fed.Cir.1988).

13. See especially Bingham & Taylor Div., Virginia Industries, Inc. v. United States, 815 F.2d 1482 (Fed.Cir.1987).

§ 12.19

1. 19 U.S.C.A. § 1673a.

However, the petition must be filed "on behalf of" the entire domestic industry.[2] Unless a majority of the industry actively opposes the petition,[3] such representation is presumed.[4] However, the Commerce Department may commence an antidumping proceeding even if a majority of the industry opposes it.[5]

It has become increasingly difficult to ascertain which firms are part of the domestic industry and thus entitled to file a dumping petition. The Court of International Trade reversed an ITA ruling that a U.S. subsidiary of a Japanese company assembling Brother typewriters in Tennessee was not a member of the domestic industry.[6] The Japanese subsidiary was thus permitted to file its petition alleging the dumping of typewriters made in Singapore by Smith–Corona, a U.S. firm. And, at least preliminarily, Brother prevailed before the ITA which found a Smith–Corona dumping margin of 16.02 percent.[7] In another proceeding, however, Smith–Corona was also treated as a member of the U.S. domestic industry. Smith–Corona requested an anticircumvention order against Brother under an antidumping order outstanding against the Japanese parent.[8] It does not appear, from these cases, that a significant amount of value must be added in the U.S.A. for a company to be treated as domestic and thus capable of seeking antidumping relief.

The information that must be provided in an antidumping petition is set forth in 19 C.F.R. § 353.12, which is reproduced in Section 6.30 of this chapter. Contact in advance with the ITA and the ITC can often resolve any petitioning issues. The ITA determines whether the petition "alleges the elements necessary for the imposition of a duty," based on the "best information available at the time."[9] Such information cannot include any information furnished by respondents or a respondent's government.[10] In other words, the ITA accepts or rejects the petition almost entirely on the basis of the information supplied by the petitioner.

Once the petition is accepted, the proceeding becomes genuinely adversarial if (as is commonly the case) the parties alleged to be dumping respond to the questionnaires on sales volumes and prices that the ITA creates and later verifies through on-the-spot investigations. It is rare for the "defense" to have more than one month to respond. Any failure to respond or permit verification risks an

---

2.   19 U.S.C.A. § 1673a(b).

3.   See Gilmore Steel Corp. v. United States, 585 F.Supp. 670 (C.I.T.1984).

4.   NTN Bearing Corp. v. United States, 757 F.Supp. 1425 (C.I.T.1991); Suramericana de Aleaciones Laminadas, C.A. v. United States, 746 F.Supp. 139 (C.I.T.1990), *reversed* 966 F.2d 660 (Fed. Cir.1992).

5.   Id.

6.   Brother Industries (USA), Inc. v. United States, 801 F.Supp. 751 (C.I.T. 1992).

7.   58 Fed.Reg. 7537 (1993).

8.   56 Fed.Reg. 46594 (1991).

9.   19 U.S.C.A. § 1673a(c).

10.   United States v. Roses Inc., 706 F.2d 1563 (Fed.Cir.1983).

ITA dumping decision on the "best information available," i.e. most likely the petitioner's or other respondent's submissions.[11] Since this is obviously an undesirable result, the best information available rule functions like a subpoena. Most respondents answer the ITA's questionnaires. Protective orders preserve the confidentiality of the often strategically valuable information submitted to the ITA and ITC in dumping proceedings.[12] Such orders ordinarily preclude release to corporate counsel engaged in competitive decision-making, but permit release to outside counsel and outside experts.[13]

§ 12.20 Administrative Determinations

Antidumping proceedings under U.S. law involve four stages. The ITC first makes a "preliminary determination" that there is reason to believe injury is occurring, again based on the best information available at that time.[1] If the ITC makes such a finding, the ITA then makes a preliminary determination whether there is a reasonable basis to believe that goods are being sold at LTFV.[2] If the ITA makes such a preliminary determination, it proceeds to make a "final determination" concerning sales at LTFV.[3] If sales at LTFV are found by the ITA, the ITC then must make a final determination concerning injury.[4] Thus the chain of decision-making in antidumping proceedings runs as follows:

ITC Preliminary Injury Determination

ITA Preliminary Dumping Determination

ITA Final Dumping Determination

ITC Final Injury Determination

Congress has repeatedly amended U.S. antidumping law so as to accelerate the rate at which these determinations are made. The chart presented in Section 6.32 details U.S. antidumping investigation procedures. At this point, it is common for the proceeding to be completed within one year. U.S. antidumping duties are then and in the future assessed retrospectively for each importation such that the amount payable varies for each importer and transaction.

Any goods imported after an ITA preliminary determination of sales at LTFV (Stage Two) will be subject to any antidumping duties imposed later, after final determinations are made.[5] In customs law parlance, liquidation of the goods is suspended. In

---

11. See 19 U.S.C.A. § 1677e(b).

12. 19 U.S.C.A. § 1677f.

13. See Sacilor, Acieries et Laminoirs De Lorraine v. United States, 542 F.Supp. 1020 (C.I.T.1982); Matsushita Electrical Industrial Co., Ltd. v. United States, 929 F.2d 1577 (Fed.Cir.1991).

§ 12.20

1. 19 U.S.C.A. § 1673b(a).

2. 19 U.S.C.A. § 1673b(b).

3. 19 U.S.C.A. § 1673d(a).

4. 19 U.S.C.A. § 1673d(b).

5. 19 U.S.C.A. § 1673b(d).

"critical circumstances," the antidumping duties will also be imposed on goods entered 90 days *before* suspension of liquidation.[6] Critical circumstances exist when there is a prior history of dumping or the importer knew or should have known that the sales were below fair value, and there have been massive imports over a relatively short period of time.[7] Since the ITA has demonstrated a willingness to order retroactive antidumping duties and need not find injury as a result of the massive imports,[8] the importer's risks may be substantial.

§ 12.21 The Importance of the ITA Preliminary Dumping Determination

Clearly, the ITA's preliminary determination of sales at LTFV tends to discourage imports. Importers do not know what their liabilities for duties will be and must post an expensive bond in the meantime to gain entry. Foreign exporters frequently raise their "United States prices" to the level of home market prices soon after such a preliminary determination. They may also reduce their home market prices to USP levels. If they do, the antidumping law will have accomplished its purpose in eliminating dumping. However, unlike European law and the Tokyo Round GATT Antidumping Code, the U.S. antidumping statute disfavors termination of the proceeding on the basis of voluntary undertakings of compliance.[1]

United States antidumping proceedings may be settled by the ITA if the respondents formally agree to cease exporting to the United States within six months or agree to revise their prices so as to eliminate the margin of the dump.[2] Since price revision agreements are hard to monitor, they are disfavored by the ITA. But an agreement to cease exports also cancels any outstanding suspension of liquidation. The total time secured in this manner may allow foreigners a window of opportunity to establish market presence prior to shifting production to the U.S. If requested, final ITA and ITC determinations are reached after settlement is agreed with normal trading resumed if respondents prevail. If petitioners prevail, the settlement agreement remains in effect. All settlement agreements are monitored by the ITA and civil penalties (in addition to antidumping duties) may be assessed if they are breached.[3] The only other settlement alternative involves withdrawal of the petition, something the petitioners may do if the President secures an international trade agreement in their favor.

---

6. 19 U.S.C.A. 1673b(e).

7. Id.

8. See ICC Industries, Inc. v. United States, 812 F.2d 694 (Fed.Cir.1987).

§ 12.21

1. See 19 U.S.C.A. § 1673c.

2. 19 U.S.C.A. § 1673c(b)(1).

3. 19 U.S.C.A. § 1673c(i)(2).

§ 12.22　AD Duties and Anticircumvention

The ITA final determination of sales at LTFV establishes the amount of any antidumping duties. Since duties are not imposed to support any specific domestic price, they are set at the "margin of dumping" (the amount the foreign market value exceeds the United States price).[1] In the ordinary case, antidumping duties are retroactive to the date of the suspension of liquidation that occurred when the ITA preliminarily found dumping. However, if the ITC final determination is one of threatened (not actual) domestic injury, the duties usually apply as from the ITC's final decision and not retroactively to the suspension date. The antidumping duty remains in force only as long as the dumping occurs. Upon request, annual ITA reviews are conducted. The ITA may review and revoke or modify any antidumping order if changed circumstances warrant such a revocation, but the burden of proof is on the party seeking revocation.[2]

Problems in assessing and collecting antidumping duties may occur because the antidumping duty order applies to goods that do not exactly correspond to normal United States HTS tariff classifications.[3] While the ITA is given some leeway to modify an antidumping order to accommodate such problems, it may not use them as an excuse to exclude merchandise falling within the scope of the order.[4] Where, on the other hand, merchandise was deliberately excluded from the original antidumping order, the ITA may not subsequently include that merchandise in an anticircumvention order.[5]

Important amendments to U.S. dumping law undertaken in 1988 focused on the circumvention of antidumping duties. "Anticircumvention" law was at that time being debated within the GATT Uruguay Round. Meanwhile, both the EU and the U.S. incorporated such rules into their dumping statutes. The U.S. anticircumvention provisions are part of the Tariff Act of 1930. They allow, for example, the ITA to ignore fictitious markets in the source nation when calculating foreign market value.[6] Components may be included in the scope of an antidumping duty order when subsequently imported into the U.S. for assembly if there is only a "small" difference between their value and that of the dumped product.[7] This rule is explored in an ITA investigation involving Brother

§ 12.22

1. 19 U.S.C.A. § 1673e.

2. 19 U.S.C.A. § 1675(b), (c); See Electric Golf Cars—Poland, 1 I.T.R.D. 5511 (1980).

3. See Chapter 5.

4. Alsthom Atlantique and Cogenel, Inc. v. United States, 787 F.2d 565 (Fed. Cir.1986).

5. Wheatland Tube Co. v. United States, 161 F.3d 1365 (Fed.Cir.1998).

6. 19 U.S.C.A. § 1677b(a)(5).

7. 19 U.S.C.A. § 1677j.

typewriters reaching the conclusion that the value added in the U.S. was not small.[8]

Similarly, when the exporter ships the components to a third country for assembly and subsequent exportation to the U.S., such circumvention efforts can be defeated by imposing the antidumping duties on these goods.[9] Product alterations that are minor and product innovations that result in essentially similar merchandise will not escape a U.S. antidumping order.[10] Even under pre–1988 law, the extension of antidumping duties to imported electric typewriters with new features was upheld.[11] Anticircumvention rules are not precluded by the Uruguay Round WTO Antidumping Code. No substantive WTO anticircumvention rules were agreed upon.

In 2000, the United States adopted the so-called "Byrd amendment." Under this provision of H.R. 4461, antidumping and countervailing tariff duties collected by the U.S. government may be passed on to injured U.S. companies. The Byrd amendment was lobbied heavily by the U.S. steel industry, which has been a major complainant in AD and CVD proceedings. The European Union, Japan and South Korea assert that this provision violates WTO rules and are preparing to challenge it.

§ 12.23   Appeals

The United States—Canada FTA and the NAFTA provide for resolution of antidumping and countervailing duty disputes through binational or trinational panels. Such panels apply the domestic law of the importing country, and provide a substitute for judicial review of the decisions of administrative agencies of the importing country. They are discussed in Chapter 21. Apart from panel review of this kind, final (not preliminary) U.S. dumping determinations of the ITA and injury determinations of the ITC are challenged "on the record" first before the Court of International Trade (CIT). The CIT has demonstrated a willingness to reverse the findings of the ITA and ITC for lack of support by substantial evidence or arbitrariness.[1] Appeals may subsequently be lodged with the Federal Circuit Court of Appeals and ultimately the U.S. Supreme Court.

8. Brother Industries (USA), Inc., 56 Fed.Reg. 46594 (1991).

9. 19 U.S.C.A. § 1677j.

10. Id.

11. Smith Corona Corp. v. United States, 698 F.Supp. 240 (C.I.T.1988).

§ 12.23

1. See 19 U.S.C.A. § 1516a and cases discussed in this chapter.

Chapter 13

SUBSIDIES AND
COUNTERVAILING DUTIES

Table of Sections

§ 13.1   Subsidies and International Trade

The duty payable on an item may be increased above that normally required by the posted tariff schedule because "countervailing duties" (CVD) have been imposed by the country of importation. Countervailing duties are a trade response to unfair "subsidies", typically given by another country to position its exports more competitively in the international marketplace. Thus, a "countervailing duty" is levied as an offset by the country of importation upon goods the production or export of which have been helped by an unfair "subsidy" in the country of origin.

Subsidies come in many forms (e.g. tax rebates, investment tax credits, other tax holidays, subsidized financing). Rapidly developing countries often offer to give some form of subsidy for initial foreign investments intended to generate exports. In the United States, the Eximbank offers low cost loans to overseas buyers of products exported from the United States; other countries have similar programs. Many U.S. export incentives could attract the CVD of nations importing U.S. goods.

In theory, the countervailing duty exactly offsets the unfair subsidy. Proponents of countervailing duties argue that they are necessary to keep imports from being unfairly competitive; there must be a level playing field for international trade. Opponents of countervailing duties argue that there is no coherent standard of "fairness" vs. "unfairness" to justify rational application of such duties. They point out that, absent a predatory motive by a foreign government, there is no more reason to justify intervention in favor of a producer disadvantaged by foreign competition than one disadvantaged by domestic competition. The result in each case is that the domestic resources used by the disadvantaged producer are shifted to their next highest value use. Viewing the world market as a unity, production efficiency worldwide is increased. Opponents of countervailing duties also point out that it is often difficult to identify a subsidy.

Countervailing duties (CVD) complement antidumping duties (AD). Unfair international trade practices can arise either through practices of producers or exporters, or through unfair practices of foreign governments. The former are subject to AD law; the latter are subject to CVD law. Either can be equally harmful to domestic industries.

§ 13.2   Uruguay Round WTO Subsidies Code (1994)

Late in 1993, the Uruguay Round of multilateral trade negotiations were concluded. One of the many agreements reached at that time concerns subsidies and countervailing duties. The Uruguay Round Subsidies Code was approved and implemented by Congress in December of 1994 under the Uruguay Round Agreements Act (URAA).[1] The 1994 Code involves a substantial overhaul of prior law.

Subsidies are defined as financial contributions that confer benefits. The Uruguay Round Code distinguishes and provides international trade rules for three categories of subsidies ... prohibited ("red light"), actionable ("yellow light") and nonactionable

§ 13.2

1. Pub. L. No. 103–465, 108 Stat. 4809.

("green light") (lapsed in 2000). Export subsidies, including so-called de facto export subsidies, are prohibited. Domestic subsidies that have adverse effects on industries in other countries are actionable when specific in character. Domestic subsidies that are non-specific are not actionable. Specific or non-specific subsidies granted to economically disadvantaged regions, to meet environmental requirements, and for research and precompetitive development are also not actionable.

The Uruguay Round Subsidies Code also creates rules for CVD procedures. The commencement of CVD proceedings, the conduct of CVD investigations, the calculation of the amount of subsidy, and the right of all interested parties to present information are covered. Dispute settlement in the subsidies area will focus upon whether another country's trade interests have been seriously prejudiced. A presumption of such prejudice will exist whenever the total *ad valorem* subsidization of a product exceeds 5 percent, and when the subsidy is by way of debt forgiveness or to cover operating losses.

§ 13.3   Historical Introduction to U.S. Law

The United States considers the use by a foreign nation of a subsidy granted to exporters from that nation to be an unfair trade practice. Unfair subsidy practices have been subject to United States countervailing duty (CVD) laws since 1897, long before the creation of the GATT. The origin of U.S. laws against export "bounties" or "grants" can be traced to Section 5 of the Tariff Act of 1897.[1] For many years, this law vested almost complete discretion in the Treasury Department to levy CVD as it saw fit. Several early CVD tariffs were targeted at tax subsidies on sugar exports.[2] And the U.S. Supreme Court essentially gave the Treasury Department *carte blanche* to impose CVD whenever foreign government regulations favored exports reaching the United States.[3] Prior to the Trade Act of 1974, U.S. law on CVD was largely administered as a branch of U.S. foreign policy, not as a private international trade remedy.[4] It was not until 1974, for example, that negative bounty or grant determinations by the Treasury Department became subject to judicial review. In 1974, also, private parties

---

§ 13.3

1. 30 Stat. 205.

2. United States v. Hills Bros., 107 Fed. 107 (2d Cir.1901) (Holland); Downs v. United States, 187 U.S. 496, 23 S.Ct. 222, 47 L.Ed. 275 (1903) (Russia).

3. G.S. Nicholas & Co. v. United States, 249 U.S. 34, 39 S.Ct. 218, 63 L.Ed. 461 (1919).

4. See Energetic Worsted Corp. v. United States, 53 C.C.P.A. 36 (1966) (Uruguay wool); United States v. Hammond Lead Products, 440 F.2d 1024 (C.C.P.A.1971), *cert. denied* 404 U.S. 1005, 92 S.Ct. 565, 30 L.Ed.2d 558 (1971) (Mexican lead).

obtained a number of statutory procedural rights, notably time limits for Treasury decisions on their petitions for CVD relief and mandatory publication of Treasury rulings. It is from this point, therefore, that a systematic body of case law interpreting and applying U.S. bounty, grant and CVD provisions commences.

The next major development in the United States statutes governing this field arrived in the Trade Agreements Act of 1979. This Act, *inter alia,* codified the rules on use of CVDs to counteract unfair "export subsidies" as agreed in the Tokyo Round GATT Subsidies Code. In addition, the 1979 Act authorized limited use of CVDs against foreign *domestic* subsidies, an authorization for which there was no distinct provision in the GATT Subsidies Code. Furthermore, the 1979 Act adopted the GATT requirement of proof of domestic industry injury or the threat or retardation thereof. This requirement had been, and remains for some imports, totally absent from U.S. law on countervailing duties.

The Uruguay Round Agreements Act of 1994 adapted the WTO Subsidies Code to U.S. law. Most importantly, Section 1677(5) of the Tariff Act of 1930 was amended to reflect the "red light," "yellow light" and "green light" (now lapsed) categories of subsidies defined in the WTO Code. The Tokyo Round amendments relating to material injury were substantially retained.

§ 13.4   Two Statutory Regimes

The U.S. currently has two statutes on countervailing duties: Section 1671 of the Tariff Act of 1930 for products imported from countries that participate in the WTO Subsidies Code or its equivalent,[1] and Section 1303 for products imported from other nations.[2] Most importantly, duties may be imposed under the latter *without* any finding of injury to a domestic industry (unless the product enters duty free); but may not be imposed under the former without a determination that a U.S. industry is "materially" injured, or threatened with such injury, or its development is materially retarded. As implemented by the United States, the GATT/WTO-derived Section 1671 imposes two conditions on the creation of countervailing duties. First, the International Trade Administration (ITA) in the Department of Commerce must determine that a nation is providing a subsidy to its exporters. Second, the International Trade Commission (ITC) must determine that imports benefiting from the subsidy injure, threaten to injure, or retard the establishment of a domestic industry.[3] This second condition embraces proof of causation, a difficult CVD issue. If these conditions

§ **13.4**

1. 19 U.S.C.A. § 1671 et seq.

2. 19 U.S.C.A. § 1303.

3. 19 U.S.C.A. § 1671(a).

are met, a duty equal to the net subsidy "shall be imposed" upon the imports.

Like antidumping duties, countervailing duties are a statutory remedy, one which the President cannot veto or affect except in Section 1671 (but not Section 1303) proceedings by negotiation of an international trade agreement. If the complaining U.S. industry is not satisfied with such an agreement, it may generally pursue CVD proceedings to their conclusion in spite of the President by refusing to withdraw its complaint. This refusal power typically gives U.S. industries seeking CVD relief substantial leverage over Commerce Department subsidy complaint negotiations. The steel industry, for example, has repeatedly exercised such leverage to its advantage when various Presidents have negotiated voluntary export restraint (VER) agreements with foreign governments.[4] In accepting VERs, the Commerce Department must find them to be in the public interest and consider whether the costs to U.S. consumers will exceed the benefits of protection to U.S. industries.

CVD proceedings under Section 1671 can also be suspended if the foreign government or exporters accounting for substantially all of the exports agree to cease exporting to the U.S. or to eliminate the subsidy within six months.[5] The subsidy may be eliminated by imposition of an export tax or price increases amounting to the net subsidy. In complex "extraordinary circumstances" benefiting the domestic industry, a settlement agreement reducing the subsidy by at least 85 percent and preventing price cutting in the U.S. can be negotiated.[6] These approaches, which are increasingly common, may effectively give exporters a brief window of opportunity to enter the U.S. market at subsidized price levels prior to shifting production to the United States.

Although the subsidy may arise from either public or private sources, all U.S. determinations to date have involved foreign governmental subsidies. Thus, these cases are usually determined on a country-wide basis (automobiles from Germany), and CVD orders usually apply to all imported goods of a particular tariff classification from a particular country—including indirect imports shipped via other countries. Note that this is one of the few instances in which the GATT/WTO allows an importing nation to engage in discriminatory conduct. In a CVD proceeding involving imports from "a Subsidies Agreement Country" (generally the WTO Subsidies Code), there are at least three separate issues for analysis under U.S. law: the extent of the concept "subsidy," the

---

4. See especially Note, International Trade: Countervailing Duties and European Steel Imports, 23 Harv.Int'l L.J. 443 (1983) and discussion of "escape clause" relief for steel in Chapter 14.

5. 19 U.S.C.A. § 1671(c)(b).

6. 19 U.S.C.A. § 1671(c)(4).

amount of injury suffered by the domestic industry, and the procedure to be followed by one who wishes to induce the application of countervailing duties.

§ 13.5   U.S. Implementation of the WTO Subsidies Code—Countervailable Subsidies

International concern with unfair subsidies and countervailing duties is reflected in Articles VI, XVI, and XXIII of the GATT 1947 and in the "Agreement on Subsidies and Countervailing Measures" (the SCM Agreement), which is part of the Covered Agreements under WTO. The United States legislation implementing the SCM Agreement changed many concepts under U.S. law. Under the SCM Agreement, the authorities of the importing signatory have the power to impose a countervailing duty (CVD) in the amount of the subsidy for as long as the subsidy continues. The CVD may only be imposed after an investigation, begun on the request of the affected industry, has "demonstrated" the existence of (1) a subsidy; (2) adverse trade effects, such as injury to a domestic industry, and (3) a causal link between the subsidy and the alleged injury.

Under the SCM Agreement there is an attempt to shift the focus of subsidy rules from a national forum, as it was exclusively under GATT, to the multinational forum provided by the Subsidies Committee under WTO and the SCM Agreement. Subsidies complaints can now be brought either in the national forum or the WTO. There are two remaining classes of subsidies: (1) prohibited ("red light"); and (2) permissible, but actionable if they cause adverse trade effects ("yellow light"). A third category of non-actionable and non-countervailable ("green light") subsidies lapsed in 2000. There are special rules which require LDCs to phase out their export subsidies and local content rules, but over eight and five years respectively. Transitional economies are also required to phase out both export subsidies and local content rules, but over a 7 year period.

The U.S. statutory provisions on countervailing duties on products imported from WTO Members is set forth in 19 U.S.C.A. § 1671, et seq. Duties may be imposed if it is found that the product is subsidized and that a U.S. industry is materially injured or threatened with such injury or its development is materially retarded.

A "subsidy" is defined as a "financial contribution" by a government entity which confers a benefit to the manufacturer of the subsidized product.[1] It includes governmental grants, loans, equity infusions and loan guarantees, as well as tax credits and the

§ 13.5
1.   19 U.S.C.A. § 1677(5).

failure to collect taxes. It can also include the governmental purchase or providing of goods or services on advantageous terms. Further, direct governmental action is not required; a subsidy can also be created if any of the above are provided through a private body. In addition to a "financial contribution" and a "benefit," a subsidy must be specific to a particular industry or enterprise.[2] Red light subsidies are "deemed" to be specific in WTO proceedings, and this concept is incorporated into the provisions on U.S. domestic proceedings for countervailing duties.[3] However, specificity must be proven for other types of actionable subsidies.

"Red light" (prohibited) subsidies include financial contributions which are conditioned upon the export performance of the beneficiary, even where that condition is only one of several criteria (export subsidies). It includes both subsidies legally conditioned on expert performance and also those which are in fact tied to actual or anticipated exportation or export earnings. It does not include, however, all financial contributions to all enterprises which happen to export. "Red light" subsidies also include financial contributions which are conditioned on the use of local goods (import substitutions subsidies).

"Yellow light" (permissible, but actionable) subsidies are permissible under the SCM Agreement, but only so long as they do not cause "adverse trade effects." These subsidies include "financial contributions" which benefit specific enterprises or industries, but are not contingent upon export performance and are not insulated under "green light" criteria. Under U.S. law, such subsidies are subject to countervailing duties if they cause or threaten material injury to an industry in the United States, or materially retard the establishment of an industry in the United States. The definition of "material injury," or a threat thereof, or material retardation of establishment, is the same as in anti-dumping proceedings.[4] However, there are references in that U.S. definition to two provisions in the SCM Agreement—those dealing with "red light" subsidies—with instructions that the ITC consider the nature of the subsidy in determining whether the subsidy imposes a material threat to an industry.[5]

§ 13.6 National or WTO Proceedings

If a subsidy is either prohibited ("red light") or actionable ("yellow light"), it may be subject to either national or multinational actions. It will be subject to action within the U.S. legal system to impose a countervailing duty on imports of the subsidized

2. 19 U.S.C.A. § 1677(5)(A).   **4.** 19 U.S.C.A. § 1677(7).

3. 19 U.S.C.A. § 1677(5)(A)(A).   **5.** 19 U.S.C.A. § 1677(7)(E)(1).

product. It will also be subject to multilateral process within the WTO to obtain the withdrawal of the subsidy by the subsidizing Member.

The procedure for deciding whether to impose countervailing duties under domestic U.S. law is the same as that for antidumping duties, described previously, and involving both the ITA and ITC making both preliminary and final determinations. An ITA preliminary determination that a countervailable subsidy exists subjects any goods imported after that date to any countervailing duties imposed later, and therefore usually has the effect of reducing imports of such goods.

The multilateral procedure under WTO first provides for consultations between the complaining Member and the Subsidizing Member. If these do not resolve the dispute within 30 days for a "red light" subsidy, or 60 days for a "yellow light" subsidy, either party is entitled to request that the DSB establish a panel to investigate the dispute and make a written report on it. The DSB panel will have 90 days (red light), or 120 days (yellow light), to investigate and prepare its report. The panel report is appealable on issues of law to the Appellate Body. The Appellate Body has 30 days (red light), or 60 days (yellow light), to decide the appeal. Panel and Appellate Body decisions are adopted without modification by the DSB unless rejected by an "inverted consensus."

If a prohibited or actionable subsidy is found to exist, the subsidizing Member is obligated under WTO to withdraw the subsidy. If the subsidy is not withdrawn within a six month period, the complaining Member can be authorized to take countermeasures. Such countermeasures may not be countervailing duties, but may instead comprise increased tariffs by the complaining Member on exports from the subsidizing Member to the complaining Member.

§ 13.7   Export Subsidies

The clearest examples of export subsidies are export incentives, including export credit and loan guarantees at less than commercial rates and differential governmentally set freight tariffs.[1] Governmental infusion of equity into the British Steel Co. after its nationalization was also held to be a subsidy.[2] Where benefits, such as

§ 13.7

1. ASG Industries, Inc. v. United States, 610 F.2d 770 (C.C.P.A.1979), *on remand* 519 F.Supp. 909 (C.I.T.1981), *order vacated* 657 F.2d 1226 (C.C.P.A. 1981).

2. British Steel Corp. v. United States, 605 F.Supp. 286 (C.I.T.1985), *ap-*

peal after remand 632 F.Supp. 59 (1986). For important decisions upholding the current Commerce Department method of valuing the amount of past nonrecurring subsidies repaid in privatizations, see British Steel PLC v. United States, 127 F.3d 1471 (Fed.Cir.1997); Inland

loans with below market interest rates and uncompensated deferrals of payments of the principal, are used to induce the building of a plant with a capacity too large for the local market, such benefits may also be subject to CVDs.[3] Outright cash payments to exporters,[4] export tax credits,[5] and accelerated depreciation benefits for exporters[6] provide additional examples of clearly countervailable export subsidies.

More difficulties are presented in analyzing whether tax rebates confer benefits which should be subject to CVDs. Remission or deferral of, or exemption from, a direct tax on exports is a countervailable subsidy. But the remission of an indirect tax (sales tax, value added tax, etc.) is not subject to a CVD, as long as it is not excessive (the amount remitted is no greater than the amount actually paid).[7] However, the foreign government which makes payments to exporters must show a clear link between the amount, eligibility and purpose of the payments and actual payment of indirect taxes, and then document the links. This is less difficult if the indirect taxes have been paid by the exporter, but is much more difficult if they have been paid by several prior producers of the goods and their components. In the latter case ("prior stage cumulative indirect taxes"), the burden of documentation is formidable.[8] The Court of International Trade has held that such a remission of domestic taxes on exported goods can still be subject to countervailing duties, *unless* the exporter can prove that the domestic tax is actually passed on to domestic purchasers of the product—which most authorities believe will be a difficult burden of proof to sustain.[9]

At one time, the amount of a U.S. CVD would be reduced by the "nonexcessive" amount of the remission of an indirect tax. However, the statute now provides a definition of "net subsidy" which includes an exclusive list of permissible offsets,[10] and the prior practice is terminated. The only offsets now permitted under the statutory definition are: 1) application fees to qualify for the subsidy, 2) any reduction in the value of the subsidy due to a

Steel Bar Co. v. United States, 155 F.3d 1370 (Fed.Cir.1998).

3. Michelin Tire Corp. v. United States, 3 ITRD 1177 (C.I.T.1981), *decision vacated* 9 C.I.T. 38 (1985).

4. See Cotton Shop Towels from Pakistan, 49 Fed.Reg. 1408 (1984).

5. See Carbon Steel Products from Brazil, 49 Fed.Reg. 1788 (1984).

6. See Oil Country Tubular Goods from Korea, 49 Fed.Reg. 46776 (1984).

7. Zenith Radio Corp. v. United States, 437 U.S. 443, 98 S.Ct. 2441, 57 L.Ed.2d 337 (1978) (commodity tax).

8. Industrial Fasteners Group v. United States, 525 F.Supp. 885 (C.I.T. 1981), *appeal after remand* 542 F.Supp. 1019 (C.I.T.1982), *rehearing denied* 3 C.I.T. 104 (1982).

9. Zenith Electronics Corp. v. United States, 633 F.Supp. 1382 (C.I.T.1986).

10. 19 U.S.C.A. § 1677(6).

governmentally mandated deferral in payment, and 3) export taxes intended to offset the subsidy.

The benefit of tax credits and allowances is usually considered to accrue at the time the exporter receives the benefit on a cash accounting basis. However, when a grant is used to acquire a long-life capital asset, the benefit will be allocated over the useful life of the asset, using data from the company if available.[11]

§ 13.8   Upstream Subsidies

A foreign government may subsidize the product actually exported. Alternatively, it may subsidize component parts or raw materials which are incorporated into the final product or services used in prior production stages. The latter are called "upstream subsidies" and are subject to CVD if they both bestow a competitive benefit on the product exported to the U.S. and have a significant effect on its cost of production.[1] A competitive benefit is bestowed if the price of the subsidized "input" (component or material) to the producer of the final product is less than it would have been "in an arms length transaction."[2] Countervailing duties may be applied to upstream subsidies only if the inputs are granted certain specified domestic subsidies.[3] As in other countervailable domestic subsidies, the benefit cannot be generally available; but the availability of the subsidized input need not be restricted to any special group.[4]

The amount of the benefit is determined by calculating the subsidy rate on the input and then determining what percentage of the cost of the final product is represented by the subsidized input. The ITA has stated that, if the subsidy so calculated represents more than 5 percent of the total cost, it will presume that there is a "significant effect;" and if it is less than 1 percent, it will presume no significant effect.[5] However, both presumptions are rebuttable, and the ITA will also analyze the importance of price in the competitiveness of the final product.[6]

There are more special rules for processed agricultural products. A subsidy provided to producers of a "raw agricultural product" is deemed to be provided to the producer of the processed agricultural product if (1) the demand for the "raw" product is substantially dependent upon the demand for the processed prod-

11. Ipsco, Inc. v. United States, 710 F.Supp. 1581 (C.I.T.1989), *affirmed* 899 F.2d 1192 (Fed.Cir.1990) (remanded on other grounds).

§ 13.8

1. 19 U.S.C.A. § 1677–1(a).

2. 19 U.S.C.A. § 1677–1(b).

3. 19 U.S.C.A. § 1677–1(a), citing the domestic subsidies specified in 19 U.S.C.A. § 1677(5)(B)(i)–(iii).

4. Steel Wheels from Brazil, 54 Fed. Reg. 15,523 (1989).

5. Agricultural Tillage Tools from Brazil, 50 Fed.Reg. 34,525 (1985).

6. *Id.*

uct, and (2) the processing adds only limited value to the raw product.[7]

§ 13.9   De Minimis Subsidies

De minimis subsidies, defined in U.S. law as subsidies of "less than 0.5 percent *ad valorem*," are disregarded and no CVD is imposed.[1] However, when the ITA calculates country-wide CVD rates, it uses a fair average of aggregate subsidy benefits to exports of all firms from that country. In making such calculations, the ITA must include not only sales by exporters who receive substantial subsidy benefits, but also sales by exporters who receive zero or *de minimis* subsidies, when calculating the weighted average benefit conferred.[2] Thus, in such circumstances, the CVD imposed may not exceed the weighted average benefit received by all exporters of the goods subject to the CVD proceeding.

§ 13.10   Nonmarket Economies Excluded

The Federal Circuit Court of Appeals has ruled that economic incentives given to encourage exportation by the government of a nonmarket economy (NME) cannot create a countervailable "subsidy."[1] The court's rationale was that, even though an NME government provides export-oriented benefits, the NME can direct sales to be set at any price, so the benefits themselves do not distort competition. The court also suggested that imports from NMEs with unreasonably low prices should be analyzed under antidumping duty provisions. It is believed that this reasoning was implicitly approved by Congress when it enacted the 1988 amendments to the Tariff Act of 1930, without adding provisions for CVDs on exports from NMEs, and adding several amendments to the antidumping provisions concerning exports from NMEs.[2] Thus, it is expected that unfair trade practices by NMEs will be subjected to AD but not generally to CVD analysis.[3]

The criteria used to determine whether a country has a nonmarket economy in antidumping proceedings[4] are also used by the ITA in deciding NME status for purposes of exclusion under the *Georgetown Steel* precedent from coverage by U.S. countervailing duty law. These criteria focus principally upon government involve-

---

7. 19 U.S.C.A. § 1677–2. This section codified prior ITA practice. See Live Swine and Fresh, Chilled and Frozen Pork Products from Canada, 50 Fed. Reg. 13,264 and 25,097 (1985).

§ 13.9

1. 19 C.F.R. § 355.7.

2. Ipsco, Inc. v. United States, 899 F.2d 1192 (Fed.Cir.1990).

§ 13.10

1. Georgetown Steel Corp. v. United States, 801 F.2d 1308 (Fed.Cir.1986).

2. See, e.g. 19 U.S.C.A. §§ 1677b(c) and 1677(18).

3. See Chapter 12.

4. See Chapter 12.

ment in setting prices or production, private versus collective ownership and market pricing of inputs.[5] Note that such an approach suggests that particular industries and products from countries deemed NMEs may be countervailable if "market-oriented."[6]

§ 13.11   The Injury Determination

CVD proceedings in the United States for Subsidies Agreement countries and only such countries, are conducted in two stages. In the second stage, the International Trade Commission (ITC) must determine whether the subsidization of the imported merchandise has caused or threatens material injury to concerned domestic industries.[1] The ITC's review constitutes the material injury determination under United States law, including injury factors and causation.

The Tariff Act provides that an affirmative injury determination should be made when an industry in the United States is "materially" injured or is threatened with material injury by reason of subsidized imports, or the establishment of an industry in the United States is materially retarded.[2] The "material injury" standard is applied to established industries, and is defined in the statute.[3] The "threat of material injury" standard is separately stated, but has a substantial overlap with the material injury criteria.[4] The standard for "material retardation" of the establishment of an industry is applied to new industries which have made a substantial commitment to begin production, or have recently begun production.[5]

§ 13.12   Like Domestic Products

In a CVD proceeding, it is important to define the relevant industry for injury investigation purposes. In both AD and CVD proceedings, the "industry" means domestic producers of "a like product."[1] However, in AD proceedings, such like products will have been identified in determining a foreign market value for the imported merchandise and in AD injury determinations.[2] In CVD proceedings, the like product identification is used primarily in determining injury. Since the concept of "like product" is used for a

---

5. See, e.g., Final Negative CVD Determination: Oscillating and Ceiling Fans from China, 57 Fed.Reg. 24018 (1992).

6. Id.

§ 13.11

1. See 19 U.S.C.A. § 1671(2)

2. 19 U.S.C.A. § 1671(2).

3. 19 U.S.C.A. § 1677(7).

4. 19 U.S.C.A. § 1677(7)(F).

5. BMT Commodity Corp. v. United States, 667 F.Supp. 880 (C.I.T.1987), affirmed 852 F.2d 1285 (Fed.Cir.1988), cert. denied 489 U.S. 1012, 109 S.Ct. 1120, 103 L.Ed.2d 183 (1989).

§ 13.12

1. 19 U.S.C.A. § 1677(4).

2. See Chapter 12.

different purpose, its definition need not necessarily be the same as that used by the ITA in determining whether dumping has occurred.[3]

The ITC considers a number of factors in determining what are "like products," and what is therefore the relevant domestic injury. These factors include (1) physical appearance, (2) interchangeability, (3) channels of distribution, (4) customer perception, (5) common manufacturing facilities and production employees, and (6) price.[4] Domestic producers who import the foreign products in question or who are related to exporters or importers can be excluded from the industry as defined by the ITC.[5] The ITC is to analyze U.S. production of the domestic like product in terms of production process and profits if useable data is present. If such data is not available, the ITC is to analyze data from "the narrowest range of products which includes the like product" and for which data can be provided.[6]

In addition, the ITC may create regional geographic product markets if the local producers sell most of their production in the regional market, and the demand in the regional market is not supplied by other U.S. producers outside that region.[7] If the relevant domestic injury in such a region is harmed, then there is material injury to a domestic industry. Such analysis of material injury to regional producers or industries is permitted under the Tokyo Round GATT Subsidies Code.[8]

§ 13.13 Material Injury

The Tariff Act defines material injury as "harm which is not inconsequential, immaterial, or unimportant."[1] This is the same standard that applies in AD proceedings and much of the law in the area may therefore be treated as interchangeable. Although the material injury definition seems to require a higher standard than a mere injury requirement, the Senate Finance Committee report did not consider them inconsistent. It stated that the material injury

---

3. Mitsubishi Elec. Corp. v. United States, 898 F.2d 1577 (Fed.Cir.1990).

4. Asociacion Colombiana de Exportadores de Flores v. United States, 693 F.Supp. 1165, 1169–70 (C.I.T.1988), *appeal after remand* 704 F.Supp. 1068 (1988); Torrington Co. v. United States, 747 F.Supp. 744, 749 (C.I.T.1990), *judgment affirmed* 938 F.2d 1278 (Fed.Cir. 1991).

On the other hand, the ITA relies upon factors which include (1) general and physical characteristics of the merchandise, (2) the expectations of the ultimate purchasers, (3) the channels of trade in which the merchandise moves, (4) the ultimate use of the merchandise, and (5) cost. Diversified Prods. Corp. v. United States, 572 F.Supp. 883, 889 (C.I.T. 1983).

5. 19 U.S.C.A. § 1677(4)(B).

6. 19 U.S.C.A. § 1677(4)(D).

7. 19 U.S.C.A. § 1677(4)(C).

8. Tokyo Round GATT Subsidies Code, Art. 6(7).

§ 13.13

1. 19 U.S.C.A. § 1677(7)(A).

standard was nothing more than a codification of the de minimis standard as it had been construed by the ITC.[2] The ITC's subsequent interpretations suggest that it understood the material injury requirement to codify the de minimis rule.[3]

After the development of the Tokyo Round GATT Subsidies Code, however, the United States amended its statutes to incorporate the Code's principles. The Tariff Act requires the ITC to consider three basic economic aspects in applying the injury standard:

> (1) The volume of imports of the merchandise subject to investigation;

> (2) The effect of these imports on prices in the United States for like products; and

> (3) The impact of these imports on domestic producers of like products, but only in the context of domestic United States production operations.[4]

The Commission is required to explain its analysis of each factor considered and explain its relevance to the agency's determination. The Tariff Act, however, also provides that the "presence or absence" of any of these three factors should "not necessarily give decisive guidance" to the ITC in its material injury determination, and the Commission is not required to give any particular weight to any one factor.[5] The factors are examined through extensive statistical analyses. The analysis is performed for the domestic industry as a whole, and not on a company-by-company basis, and the analysis is industry specific.[6] The ITC may select whatever time period best represents the business cycle and competitive conditions in the industry, and most reasonably allows it to determine whether an injury exists.

Volume of Imports

In compliance with Tokyo Round GATT Subsidies Code Article 6(2), the Tariff Act requires the ITC to consider the absolute volume of imports or any increases in volume in evaluating the volume of imports subject to investigation. This assessment may be made in relation to production or consumption in the United States. The standard in this evaluation is whether the volume of imports, viewed in any of the above ways, is significant.[7]

2. Senate Comm. on Finance, Trade Agreements Act of 1979, S.Rep. No. 249, 96th Cong., 1st Sess. 87.

3. Vermulst, supra Note 10, § 7.2, at 364–76.

4. 19 U.S.C.A. § 1677(7)(B).

5. 19 U.S.C.A. § 1677(7)(E)(ii). Compare Tokyo Round GATT Subsidies Code Art. 6(2).

6. Alberta Pork Producers' Marketing Board v. United States, 669 F.Supp. 445 (C.I.T.1987), *appeal after remand* 683 F.Supp. 1398 (1988).

7. 19 U.S.C.A. § 1677(7)(C)(i).

Data relating to the volume of imports are an important factor in the ITC's injury determinations. In particular, the ITC is more concerned with the dynamics of market share, such as a significant rise in market penetration, than it is with the size of market share.[8] It is also primarily concerned with the effects that market share changes might have on profits and lost sales. Significant injury has been found when an importer has less than a 2 percent market share, but the imports market share has increased eightfold,[9] while market shares of greater than 2 percent for the subsidized imports have been found to be insignificant.[10] A large market share for the importer may still indicate no injury when coupled with increases in production, domestic shipments, exports, employment and profits of the domestic industry.

Price Effects

Under the Tariff Act, the ITC when making an injury determination may consider the effect of the subsidized imports upon prices for like products in the domestic market. This is done to the extent that such a consideration assists in evaluating whether (1) there is significant price underselling by the imported merchandise as compared with the price of like products of the United States,[11] and (2) whether the effect of the imported merchandise is otherwise to depress domestic prices to a significant degree or prevent price increases, which otherwise would have occurred to a significant degree.[12]

Price underselling is not a *per se* basis for a finding of injury. For example, if the demand for the product is not price sensitive, price underselling will not be a central consideration in any injury finding. There may be no injury from price underselling, even though the domestic producers lost sales in the United States, if the domestic producers' inability to sell goods was not caused by subsidized imports. For example, the industry's decline may have been caused by its failure to develop, produce and market competitive merchandise. A more extensive analysis of causation issues appears in the next section.

Substantial underselling, on the other hand, will lead to an affirmative injury finding, where the market is price sensitive.[13]

---

8. J. E. Pattison, Antidumping and Countervailing Duty Laws 4–2 (1992).

9. Alberta Pork Producers' Marketing Board v. United States, 669 F.Supp. 445 (C.I.T.1987), *appeal after remand* 683 F.Supp. 1398 (1988).

10. Cast–Iron Pipe Fittings from Brazil, 7 ITRD 1823 (ITC Final, 1985).

11. 19 U.S.C.A. § 1677(7)(C)(ii)(I).

12. 19 U.S.C.A. § 1677(7)(C)(ii)(II).

13. The ITC views a product as price sensitive when its price is the most important factor in purchasing the product. In Tubeless Tire Valves from the Federal Republic of Germany, 46 Fed. Reg. 29,794 (1981), the ITC relied upon the testimony of buyers who had switched their sourcing from domestic producers to the imports that price was the most important factor in purchasing

When the ITC finds that demand for a specific product is price sensitive and importers are engaging in price underselling, it further examines whether domestic producers are being forced into price suppression[14] or actual price cutting[15] due to this price underselling. Since either price suppression or price cutting can be a severe burden to domestic producers, the ITC will find an injury if it determines that because of the subsidization of the imports, domestic producers have lowered or have been unable to raise their prices to accommodate rising costs.[16]

Domestic Industry Impact

The impact on a domestic industry of an allegedly subsidized product is probably the most important factor in any injury analysis. The Tariff Act employs the same criteria as are set out in the Tokyo Round GATT Subsidies Code.[17] It then provides supplemental factors for ITC consideration, adding the actual and potential negative effects on the existing development and production efforts of the domestic industry, including efforts to develop a derivative or more advanced version of the like product.[18] The ITC relies primarily on two of these factors in making this determination. First, the industry must be in a distressed or a stagnant condition. Second, the ITC analyzes whether low domestic price levels are a factor in the industry's difficulties (e.g., high unemployment or low capacity utilization rate), and whether the low prices are causing low profits.[19]

The ITC will often base an affirmative action determination of material injury on severe downward trends in profitability among

decisions, with availability a secondary but often critical factor. Id. at 29,795.

14. Price suppression arises when the domestic industry can affect smaller price increases directly competitive with subsidized imports than it can on those articles that directly compete with non-subsidized imports. Tapered Roller bearings from Japan, 40 Fed.Reg. 26,312, 26,314–26,315 (1975).

15. Price cutting arises when the domestic industry is compelled to lower its prices to meet the prices of subsidized imports in an attempt to protect its market share.

16. See, e.g., Unrefined Montan Wax from East Germany, 46 Fed.Reg. 45,223, 45,224 (1981).

17. 19 U.S.C.A. § 1677(C)(iii) provides:

In examining the impact required to be considered under subparagraph (B)(iii), the Commission shall evaluate all relevant economic factors which have a bearing on the state of the industry in the United States, including, but not limited to—

(I) actual and potential decline in output, sales, market share, profits, productivity, return on investments, and utilization of capacity,

(II) factors affecting domestic prices,

(III) actual and potential negative effects on cash flow, inventories, employment, wages, growth, ability to raise capital, and investment, and

(IV) actual and potential negative effects on the existing development and production efforts of the domestic industry, including efforts to develop a derivative or more advanced version of the like product.

18. 19 U.S.C.A. § 1677(7)(C)(iii)(IV).

19. Vermulst, supra Note 10, § 7.2, at 369.

domestic producers. For example, loss of profitability in the face of increasing imports can indicate material injury.[20] Thus, it is not necessary that an industry suffer an actual loss as a prerequisite to a finding of material injury.

When a negative determination has been made despite the industry's declining profitability, the ITC has generally indicated that the industry was still in a healthy state, increasing production, shipments, capacity and market share despite losses in profitability.[21] Thus, the ITC can make a negative determination concerning material injury, even though the industry has suffered profitability losses.

The effect of subsidized imports on employment in the relevant domestic industry is also considered. Employment data are not dispositive due to the broad spectrum of economic factors related to such data, and many of those factors may not be attributable to foreign subsidization. However, changes in domestic employment during the period under investigation are one factor to be considered. A drop in employment during the period of investigation may be an indication of injury, and an increase in employment and man-hours worked in the domestic industry may be cited by the ITC as one factor in a determination that there has been no material injury. But increasing employment usually is a factor in determinations of no injury only when other factors also indicate that no material injury is present.

The utilization of plant capacity has been considered a factor in many determinations, but such capacity utilization data is treated ambiguously because it is dependent upon diverse factors. Falling capacity utilization may indicate material injury if there is no other explanation, but the ITC can make negative injury determinations despite falling capacity utilization, if the decline is caused by other factors, such as frequent equipment breakdowns and quality control disruptions.

§ 13.14   Causation

Causation of material injury by subsidization is a required element which must be found independently of the finding of material injury, threat of material injury or the material retardation of the establishment of a domestic industry. However, there is a tendency to enter an affirmative injury determination when subsidization and material injury to a concerned industry are found, without a lengthy analysis of the causal link between them.

---

20. Cotton Shop Towels from Pakistan, 6 ITRD 1494 (ITC Final, 1984).

21. See, e.g., American Spring Wire Corp. v. United States, 590 F.Supp. 1273

(C.I.T.1984), *affirmed sub nom.* Armco, Inc. et al. v. United States, 760 F.2d 249 (Fed.Cir.1985).

In a negative injury determination, on the other hand, the ITC may engage in a rather detailed analysis of causation.

The Tariff Act requires a simple causation element, stating that material injury must be caused "by reason of" the subsidization of the imports.[1] The same standard applies in AD proceedings and once again the law in this area is largely interchangeable. The causation requirement is not a high one. Imports need only cause material injury, and need not be the most substantial or primary cause of injury being suffered by domestic industry. This causation element of an affirmative injury determination can be satisfied if the subsidized imports contribute, even minimally, to the conditions of the domestic injury.[2] Under this "contributing cause" standard, causation of injuries may be found despite the absence of correlation between subsidized imports and the alleged injuries, if there is substantial evidence that the volume of subsidized imports was a contributing factor to the price depression experienced by the domestic injury.[3]

In examining the causal link between the subsidized imports and the material injury, the ITC is willing to recognize that there can be causal factors other than subsidies which can be responsible for the alleged injury in a particular proceeding.[4] An industry which prospers during times of greater import penetration will find it difficult to persuade the ITC that subsidized imports cause material injury to it. The existence of extraneous injury factors will not, however, necessarily preclude an affirmative finding of material injury for purposes of the Tariff Act,[5] as long as the subsidies are a

§ 13.14

1. 19 U.S.C.A. § 1671(a):

If—

. . .

(2) the Commission determines that—

(A) an industry in the United States—

(i) is materially injured, or

(ii) is threatened with material injury, or

(B) the establishment of an industry in the United States is materially retarded,

by reason of imports of that merchandise . . . , then there shall be imposed upon such merchandise a countervailing duty. . . .

2. British Steel Corp. v. United States, 593 F.Supp. 405, 413 (C.I.T. 1984).

3. Id.

4. Such extraneous factors include:

(1) Volume and prices of non-subsidized imports;

(2) Contraction in demand or changes in patterns of consumption;

(3) Trade restrictive practices of and competition between foreign and domestic producers;

(4) Developments in technology; and

(5) The export performance and productivity of the domestic industry.

S.Rep. No. 249 96th Cong., 1st Sess. 57 (1979).

5. At least one Commissioner has argued that although this traditional analysis may be useful in determining material injury, it is not a proper tool to resolve the issue of causation because it does not do well in separating the effects of subsidized imports from the effects of other factors operating in the marketplace. Instead she advocates what is termed the elasticity analysis. This new

contributing cause to the material injury of the domestic industry. The ITC is not required to weigh the effects from the subsidized imports against the effects associated with other factors, if the subsidization is a contributing cause of the injury. For example, in evaluating causation, the ITC may uncover other major causes for the problems of the domestic industry. These may include huge unnecessary expenses, chronic excess capacity, inefficiency, poor quality, price sensitivity or increased domestic competition. Nevertheless, the presence of such major alternative causes of injury does not foreclose the possibility that imports have been *a* contributing cause of the industry's problems.[6]

§ 13.15   Cumulative Causation

Can a "material injury" be caused by imports from several exporters in more than one country through the cumulative effect of many small injuries? There are arguments against cumulating each source of subsidized imports to determine whether it is a cause of injury. Such cumulation could penalize small suppliers who would not have caused injury if their subsidization had been examined in isolation.[1] Nevertheless, the injury to a domestic industry is measured by the cumulated results of all subsidies on the ground that injury caused by "many nibbles" is just as harmful as that caused through "one large bite." Cumulation provides administrative ease, since the countervailing duty agency is not required to allocate the amount of injury caused by each individual exporter.

The GATT and the Tokyo Round GATT Subsidies Code were ambiguous on the propriety of cumulation. While GATT Article VI seems to contemplate a country-by-country approach by referring repeatedly to the singular term "country,"[2] the Tokyo Round Subsidies Code used the term "subsidized imports," which implicitly permits an aggregate approach.[3] The Uruguay round expressly permits cumulation.

approach analyzes the elasticity of domestic demand for the product under investigation to determine the effect on the domestic injury of unfair imports, as separated from many other factors that affect the concerned industry. See H. Blinn, The Injury–Test under United States Antidumping and Countervailing Duty Laws as Interpreted by the International Trade Commission and the Department of Commerce: A Comparison Study of the Conventional "Trend–Analysis" and the "Elasticity-test" 23–30 (1991).

  6. Iwatsu Electric Co., Ltd. v. United States, 758 F.Supp. 1506 (C.I.T.1991)

(small telephone systems); United Engineering & Forging v. United States, 779 F.Supp. 1375 (C.I.T.1991), *opinion after remand* 14 ITRD 1748 (1992) (crankshafts).

§ 13.15

  1. For a comparable argument, see Horlick, The United States Antidumping System, in Antidumping Law and Practice: A Comparative Study 102 (1989).

  2. GATT Art. VI(1), VI(6).

  3. Tokyo Round GATT Subsidies Code, Arts. 6(1), 6(2), 6(4), 6(6) and 6(7).

The Tariff Act requires that the ITC cumulatively assess the volume and effect of reasonably coincident subsidized imports from two or more countries of like products subject to investigation if the imports compete with each other and with like United States products.[4] There is, however, an exception for imports from beneficiary countries of the Caribbean Basin Initiative.[5] The ITC has held multicountry cumulation to be proper if the factors and conditions of trade in the particular case show its relevance to the determination of injury, and has given a nonexhaustive list of such factors.[6] The list includes the volume of imports, the trend of import volume, the fungibility of imports, competition in the markets for the same end users, common channels of distribution, pricing similarity, simultaneous impact, and any coordinated action by importers. From these factors, the ITC determines whether the imports compete with each other and like domestic products. Surprisingly, the ITC found that French and Italian wines do not compete with each other.[7] But an ITC ruling that steel imports from Spain, Brazil and Korea competed with each other was overturned by the Court of International Trade,[8] which also refused to require the ITC to cumulate steel plate imports from Brazil, Korea and Argentina.[9]

The ITC has also ruled that, when cumulating, it is not necessary to find for each country a separate causal link between its imports and U.S. material injury.[10] Such multiple country cumulation should be distinguished form the "cross cumulation" allowed by the Tariff Act. Cross cumulation involves consideration by the ITC of both dumped and subsidized imports into the United States.[11] The net effect of U.S. rules on cumulation of import injury is to encourage petitioners to name as many countries as possible as the source of their problems.

§ 13.16 Countervailing Duty Procedures

For a "Subsidies Agreement Country," the procedures governing the applicability of countervailing duties to its goods will be determined under 19 U.S.C.A. § 1671, not 19 U.S.C.A. § 1303.

4. 19 U.S.C.A. § 1677(7)(C)(iv). This statutory provision settled a pre–1984 conflict within the Commission concerning whether to cumulate or not.

5. 19 U.S.C.A. § 1677(7)(C)(iv)(II).

6. Certain Steel Products Belgium, Brazil, etc., ITC Pub. No. 1221, U.S.I.T.C. Inv. No. 701–TA–86–144 (February 1986).

7. See American Grape Growers Alliance v. United States, 615 F.Supp. 603 (C.I.T.1985).

8. Republic Steel Corp. v. United States, 591 F.Supp. 640 (C.I.T.1984).

9. USX Corp. v. United States, 698 F.Supp. 234 (C.I.T.1988).

10. Fundicao Tupy S.A. v. United States, 678 F.Supp. 898 (C.I.T.1988), *decision affirmed* 859 F.2d 915 (Fed.Cir. 1988).

11. See especially Bingham & Taylor Div., Virginia Industries, Inc. v. United States, 815 F.2d 1482 (Fed.Cir.1987).

Section 1671 proceedings can be settled by international agreement; Section 1303 proceedings cannot.[1] Section 1303 CVD can be applied retroactively without limitation whereas Section 1671 CVD can be applied retroactively only in "critical circumstances." The major difference between the two sections is that only a determination that a subsidy exists is necessary under Section 1303, while Section 1671 requires both a determination of a subsidy and an injury determination. Thus the administrative procedure for deciding whether to impose countervailing duties under Section 1671 is the same as that for antidumping duties[2] and involves the ITA and ITC making both preliminary and final determinations. Under either Section 1671 or 1303, an ITA preliminary determination that a countervailable subsidy exists subjects all goods imported after that date to any countervailing duties imposed later. This usually has the effect of immediately reducing imports of such goods.

§ 13.17 Administrative Determinations

Two different governmental agencies are involved in regulating, through countervailing duties, imports into the United States. The International Trade Administration (ITA) is part of the Commerce Department, which in turn is part of the Executive Branch of the government. The International Trade Commission (ITC) is an independent agency.

The chain of decision-making in CVD proceedings depends upon which statutory section controls. If Section 1303 governs, which petitioners (the domestic industry) will ordinarily favor, the proceeding is totally before the ITA with the ITC excluded. This will be a two-stage proceeding:

ITA Preliminary Countervailable Subsidy Determination

ITA Final Countervailable Subsidy Determination

If, however, a "country under the Agreement" is the source of the goods, then Section 1671 controls. Respondents (the importers) will generally prefer this because a four-stage proceeding allowing argument over the alleged domestic industry injury will follow:

ITC Preliminary Injury Determination

ITA Preliminary Countervailable Subsidy Determination

ITA Final Countervailable Subsidy Determination

ITC Final Injury Determination

The CVD process may be initiated by either the Department of Commerce, a union or business, or by a group or association of

---

§ 13.16   2. See Chapter 12.

1. See Section 13.4.

aggrieved workers or businesses—an aggrieved "industry."[1] The required contents of the petition are stipulated at 19 C.F.R. § 355.12 (reproduced in the Selected Documents section of this chapter). Pre-filing contact with the ITA and (if needed) the ITC can often resolve any problems regarding the contents of the petition. Petitioners may also access the ITA's library of information on foreign subsidy practices. The ITA determines whether the petition alleges the elements necessary for the imposition of a duty, based on the best information available at the time.[2] In other words, the ITA accepts or rejects the petition.

Once the petition is accepted, the ITC makes a preliminary determination as to a real or threatened material injury within 45 days of the date the petition was filed based on the best information available to it at that time.[3] If the ITC makes such a finding, the ITA must then make a preliminary determination whether there is "a reasonable basis to believe" based on the best information available that there is a countervailable subsidy with respect to the exported merchandise.[4] The time for making this decision may be extended if the petitioner so requests, or the ITA determines both that the parties are cooperating and that it is an extraordinarily complicated case.[5] The time period may also be extended for "upstream subsidy" investigations.[6]

If the ITA makes a preliminary determination that a countervailable subsidy exists, within 75 days it must make a "final determination" concerning the existence of a countervailable subsidy and calculate the amount of the proposed CVD.[7] If subsidization is found by the ITA, the ITC then must make a final determination concerning material injury within 120 days after the ITA has made an affirmative preliminary determination,[8] or within 75 days after an affirmative final determination by the ITA if its preliminary determination was negative.[9] The chart presented in Section 6.32 details U.S. countervailing duty investigation procedures. As with antidumping, most CVD proceedings are done within a year.

In reaching their determinations, both the ITA and the ITC frequently circulate questionnaires to interested parties, including foreign governments and exporters. Since any failure to respond risks a determination on the "best information available," this results in the flow of significant and often strategically valuable business information to the government. Amendments adopted in

§ 13.17

1. 19 U.S.C.A. § 1671a(a) and (b).
2. 19 U.S.C.A. § 1671a(b).
3. 19 U.S.C.A. § 1671b(a).
4. 19 U.S.C.A. § 1671b(b).
5. 19 U.S.C.A. § 1671b(c).

6. 19 U.S.C.A. § 1671b(h).
7. 19 U.S.C.A. § 1671d(a).
8. 19 U.S.C.A. § 1671d(b)(2).
9. 19 U.S.C.A. § 1671d(b)(3).

1988 now require release under protective order of all confidential business information to counsel for interested parties.[10] This protection is particularly important because not all domestic producers may support the CVD petition, but they are generally able to access the submissions of others who do. Confidentiality is defined in the regulations at 19 C.F.R. § 355.4 and 19 C.F.R. § 207.6.

§ 13.18   The Importance of the ITA Preliminary Subsidy Determination

An ITA preliminary determination that a countervailable subsidy exists places great pressure on the importers of the foreign goods. Liquidation (entry at a determined rate of tariff) of all such merchandise is suspended by order of customs. Goods imported after an ITA preliminary determination of a countervailable subsidy will be subject to any CVD imposed later, after final determinations are made.[1] Such a preliminary determination, although subject to final determinations by the ITA and the ITC and appealable to the CIT, will effectively cut off further importation of the disputed goods unless an expensive bond is posted until the process has been completed. In this process the respondent importer often wants a speedy resolution as its total costs for the imports are unknown. The statute is replete with time provisions established to protect the importer by requiring action to be completed and decisions to be made within specified time limits. Many CVD proceedings are concluded within a year.

At one level, then, a useful intermediate goal in representing a petitioner is to obtain an ITA preliminary determination concerning a "subsidy" or "bounty" which meets the statutory requirements. The respondent's "defense" to such efforts must be organized quickly, usually within 30 days of the filing of a CVD petition. The importer's ability to present a defense is handicapped by the nature of CVD proceedings ... the complaint is really lodged against the subsidy practices of foreign governments. Unlike most foreign exporters whose pricing decisions are the focus in AD proceedings, many foreign governments are loath to provide information necessary to an adequate response to a CVD complaint. Since the ITA and ITC are authorized to make decisions on the basis of the best information available, any failure to adequately respond to a CVD complaint can contribute to adverse rulings. Moreover, responses by foreign governments and exporters to ITA questionnaires that cannot be verified by on the spot investigations are ignored and thus removed from the best information available for decision-making. This may leave only the petitioner's or other

---

10.   See 19 U.S.C.A. § 1677f(c)(1).

1.   19 U.S.C.A. § 1671b(d).

respondent's submissions for review, a one-sided proceeding almost sure to result in affirmative determinations.

The respondent importer's uncertainties over the amount of duty owed after a preliminary ITA determination that a countervailable subsidy exists can increase in Section 1671 (GATT-derived) proceedings if the ITA decides that "critical circumstances" are present. In such cases, the suspension of liquidation of the goods applies not only prospectively from the date of such determination, but also retrospectively for 90 days.[2] Moreover, in traditional Section 1303 proceedings against bounties or grants, there is *no* time limit to the ability to retroactively apply CVD against any unliquidated entries and there need not be any determination that critical circumstances are present.

§ 13.19 CVD Duties and Anticircumvention

The ITA final determination of the existence of a subsidy establishes the amount of any CVD. Since duties are not imposed to support any specific domestic price, they are set only to equal the amount of the net subsidy.[1] The CVD remains in force as long as the subsidization occurs. The ITA may modify or revoke a CVD order if changed circumstances warrant, but the burden of proof is on the party seeking alteration of the CVD order.[2] Circumvention of an existing CVD order, on the other hand, can trigger anticircumvention orders. The statutes authorize such relief when goods subject to a CVD are "downstreamed" (incorporated as a component in another product)[3] or shipped as components for assembly in the United States or a third country.[4]

Another circumvention issue of growing importance is whether subsidies received by a firm that is subsequently sold or privatized pass through to benefit the new owner's exports. The Commerce Department generally has denied the existence of a countervailable subsidy after private sector arm's length acquisitions, but recently sought to impose CVD after steel industry privatization sales by the British and German governments. This effort was strongly rebuked by the Court of International Trade.[5] The CIT declared that the Commerce Department's approach in these cases was in "direct contravention" of the guiding principles of U.S. countervailing duty law, namely to ensure a level playing field. Purchasers in arm's length transactions, whether private or public, do not receive any countervailable benefits since what they have paid includes the

---

2. 19 U.S.C.A. § 1781(b)(e)(1)(B).

§ 13.19

1. 19 U.S.C.A. § 1671e.

2. 19 U.S.C.A. § 1675.

3. 19 U.S.C.A. § 1677i.

4. 19 U.S.C.A. § 1677j.

5. [See Saarstahl, AG v. United States, Inland Steel Bar Co., 858 F.Supp. 187, 11 BNA ATRR 961 (1994).]

value of past subsidies received. The past subsidies either remain with the seller, the shareholders of the selling corporation upon dissolution, or revert to the state if a privatization sale is involved. If subsidies passed through on arm's length transactions, buyers would have great trouble evaluating the potential CVD liabilities of the firm they purchase. Critics see in this decision the possibility of considerable circumvention through acquisitions of U.S. countervailing duty law.

In 2000, the United States adopted the so-called "Byrd amendment." Under this provision of H.R. 4461, antidumping and countervailing tariff duties collected by the U.S. government may be passed on to injured U.S. companies. The Byrd amendment was lobbied heavily by the U.S. steel industry, which has been a major complainant in AD and CVD proceedings. The European Union, Japan and South Korea asserted that this provision violates WTO SCM rules and won a WTO challenge to it. The United States is under an obligation to repeal the Byrd amendment.

Many petitioners in countervailing duty cases also seek antidumping duties[6] and other relief through escape clause or market disruption proceedings.[7] Thus, domestic producers seeking relief from import competition will often use a "shotgun" approach to obtain protective relief.

§ 13.20   Appeals

Judicial review "on the record" of final (not preliminary) decisions by the ITA and the ITC in both CVD and AD proceedings may be sought before the Court of International Trade (CIT). However, for proceedings arising out of exports from Canada and Mexico, the United States—Canada FTA and the NAFTA provide for resolution of antidumping and countervailing duty disputes through binational panels.[1] Such panels apply the domestic law of the importing country, and provide a substitute for judicial review of the decisions of administrative agencies of the importing country.

---

6. See Chapter 12.

7. See Chapter 15.

§ 13.20

1. Canada–United States Free Trade Agreement (1989), Chapter 19; NAFTA (1994), Chapter 19.

*

Chapter 14

UNITED STATES IMPORT CONTROLS AND NONTARIFF TRADE BARRIERS

Table of Sections

§ 14.1 Import Quotas and Licenses

Goods imported into the United States may have to qualify within numerical quota limitations imposed upon importation of that item or upon that kind of item. Import quotas may be "global" limitations (applying to items originating from anywhere in the world), "bilateral" limitations (applying to items originating from a particular country) and "discretionary" limitations. Bilateral limitations may be found in an applicable Treaty of Friendship, Commerce and Navigation or in a more narrow international agreement, such as the 1978 Poland–United States Importation Agreement on Trade in Textiles and Textile Products.[1] Discretionary limitations, when coupled with a requirement that importation of items must be licensed in advance by local authorities, provide an effective vehicle for gathering statistical data and for raising local revenues. "Tariff-rate quotas" admit a specified quantity of goods at a preferential rate of duty. Once imports reach that quantity, tariffs are normally increased.

If a quota system is created, a fundamental subsidiary issue is: How will the quotas be allocated? The Customs Service generally administers quotas on a first-come, first-served basis. This approach creates a race to enter goods into the United States. One potential allocation method is through the use of licenses, which would be the documentation for administration of such quantitative restrictions. Licensing of imports can work a trade restrictive effect.

§ 14.1

1. TIAS 9064.

International concern about delays which result from cumbersome licensing procedures was manifested in the 1979 Tokyo Round MTN Import Licensing Code (which most developing countries refused to sign). The United States adhered to this Code, as did a reasonable number of other nations. The Uruguay Round made an Agreement on Import Licensing Procedures (1994) binding on all World Trade Organization members. The Agreement's objectives include facilitating the simplification and harmonization of import licensing and licensing renewal procedures, ensuring adequate publication of rules governing licensing procedures, and reducing the practice of refusing importation because of minor variations in quantity, value or weight of the import item under license.

The President is authorized to sell import licenses at public auctions.[2] One advantage of an auction system is its revenue raising potential. The U.S. Tariff Act of 1930 also provides that to the extent practicable and consistent with efficient and fair administration, the President is to insure against inequitable sharing of imports by a relatively small number of the larger importers.[3] In fact, allocating quotas among U.S. importers rarely happens. Rather, in the past, quotas have been part of a "voluntary restraint" or orderly market agreement between the U.S. and one or more foreign governments, and represent adherence by those governments to U.S. initiatives. The negotiations have typically concentrated on obtaining foreign government agreement to limitations on exportation of their products into the U.S. market, and have not pursued limitations on who might use the resulting allocations. Thus, instead of an auction system, the U.S. has usually used a Presidentially managed system of import allocations, especially in regard to agricultural import quotas.

§ 14.2   U.S. Import Restraints

In addition to NTBs, the United States has employed import quotas for many years. Tariff-rate quotas have been applied to dairy products, olives, tuna fish, anchovies, brooms, and sugar, syrups and molasses. Quite a few absolute quotas originate under Section 22 of the Agricultural Adjustment Act.[1] These quotas are undertaken when necessary to United States farm price supports or similar agricultural programs. They have used on animals feeds, dairy products, chocolate, cotton, peanuts, and selected syrups and sugars. Some U.S. agricultural quotas are being "tariffied" under the WTO Agreement on Agriculture. Some quotas imposed by the U.S. are sanctions for unfair trade practices, as against tungsten from China. Other quotas originate in international commodity

2. 19 U.S.C.A. § 2581.   § **14.2**

3. Id.   1.   7 U.S.C.A. § 624.

agreements, and important restraints on textile imports are achieved as a result of the international Multi–Fiber Arrangement (phased out under the WTO Textiles Agreement).

The Agricultural Act of 1949 requires the President to impose global import quotas on Upland Cotton whenever the Secretary of Agriculture determines that its average price exceeds certain statutory limits.[2] Whenever this is the case, unlike the ordinary restrictive import quota, the importation of Upland Cotton is duty free. Like the Meat Import Act, this provision tends to be countercyclical to market forces for cotton in the United States.

Lastly, the United States sometimes imposes import restraints for national security or foreign policy reasons. Many of these restraints originate from Section 232 of the Trade Expansion Act of 1962. This provision authorizes the President to "adjust imports" whenever necessary to the national security of the country. Trade embargoes are sometimes imposed on all the goods from politically incorrect nations (e.g., Cuba). Product-specific import bans also exist for selected goods, e.g., narcotic drugs and books urging insurrection against the United States.[3] The importation of "immoral" goods is generally prohibited[4], even for private use, and the obscenity of such items is decided by reviewing the community standards at the port of entry.[5] Generally, as well, goods produced with forced, convict, indentured or bonded child labor are excluded from the United States.[6] This ban has been applied to certain goods from the People's Republic of China.[7]

The materials that follow selectively present United States law governing import controls and nontariff trade barriers. A parallel discussion of "voluntary" export restraints (VERs) and orderly marketing agreements (OMAs) limiting exports into the U.S. market can be found in Chapter 9. VERs and OMAs have been applied

---

2.   7 U.S.C.A. § 1444.

3.   21 U.S.C.A. § 171 and 19 U.S.C.A. § 1305.

4.   19 U.S.C.A. § 1305.

5.   United States v. Various Articles of Obscene Merchandise, 536 F.Supp. 50 (S.D.N.Y.1981).

6.   19 U.S.C.A. § 1307. The 1997 Bonded Child Labor Elimination Act amended 19 U.S.C. § 1307 to prohibit the U.S. importation of goods produced by "bonded child labor." Such labor is defined as work or service exacted by confinement against his or her will from persons under age 15 in payment for debts of parents, relatives or guardians, or drawn under false pretexts. Section 307 bans products of convict, forced and indentured labor. See China Diesel Imports, Inc. v. United States, 870 F.Supp. 347 (C.I.T. 1994) (Chinese government documents referring to factory as "Reform through Labor Facility" probative of convict labor origin of goods; exclusion order affirmed; U.S. consumption demand exception applies only to forced and indentured labor). On standing to sue to block importation of prohibited labor goods, see McKinney v. U.S. Department of Treasury, 799 F.2d 1544 (Fed.Cir.1986) (causal link between imports and clear economic injury must be shown).

7.   See, e.g., 57 Fed.Reg. 9469 (March 18, 1992).

to textiles, autos, steel, machine tools and semiconductors. Their use is now severely limited by the WTO Agreement on Safeguards.[8]

§ 14.3 Nontariff Trade Barriers

There are numerous nontariff trade barriers applicable to United States imports. Many of these barriers arise out of federal or state safety and health regulations. Others concern the environment, consumer protection, product standards and government procurement. Many of the relevant rules were created for legitimate consumer and public protection reasons. They were often created without extensive consideration of their international impact as potential nontariff trade barriers. Nevertheless, the practical impact of legislation of this type is to ban the importation of nonconforming products from the United States market. Thus, unlike tariffs which can always be paid and unlike quotas which permit a certain amount of goods to enter the United States market, nontariff trade barriers have the potential to totally exclude foreign exports.

The diversity of regulatory approaches to products and the environment makes it extremely difficult to generalize about nontariff trade barriers. The material below concerns health restrictions relating to food, safety restrictions relating to consumer products, environmental auto emissions standards and selected other NTBs. These areas have been chosen merely as examples of the types of NTB barriers to the United States market, and are by no means exhaustive. Special NTB rules apply in the context of the Canada–U.S. Free Trade Agreement and the NAFTA.[1] Sanitary and phytosanitary (SPS) measures dealing with food safety and animal and plant health regulations are the subject of a Uruguay Round WTO accord.

The European Union and the United States, and (separately) Canada and the U.S., have agreed to Mutual Recognition Agreements on certain product standards. Each side will test their exports according to the other's standards. A second test in the country of importation will no longer be necessary. The Agreements should reduce the trade restraining potential of regulations applicable to telecommunications equipment, medical devices, pharmaceuticals, recreational craft, electrical safety and electromagnetic compatibility.

§ 14.4 Public Procurement

Where public procurement is involved, and the taxpayer's money is at issue, virtually every nation has some form of legisla-

---

8. See Chapter 15.

1. See Chapter 21.

tion or tradition that favors buying from domestic suppliers. In federal nations like the United States, these rules can extend to state and local purchasing requirements. The principal United States statute affecting imports in connection with government procurement is the Buy American Act of 1933.[1] This Act requires the government to buy American unless the acquisition is for use outside the U.S.,[2] there are insufficient quantities of satisfactory quality available in the U.S., or domestic purchases would be inconsistent with the public interest or result in unreasonable costs.

As currently applied, the United States Buy American Act requires federal agencies to treat a domestic bid as unreasonable or inconsistent with the public interest only if it exceeds a foreign bid by more than six percent (customs duties included) or ten percent (customs duties and specific costs excluded). Exceptions to this general approach exist for reasons of national interest, certain designated small business purchases, domestic suppliers operating in areas of substantial unemployment and demonstrated national security needs. Bids by small businesses and companies located in labor surplus areas are generally protected by a 12 percent margin of preference. Bids from U.S. companies are considered foreign rather than domestic when the materials used in the products concerned are below 50 percent American in origin. These rules apply to civil purchasing by the United States government,[3] but are suspended for purchasing subject to the GATT/WTO Procurement Codes as implemented by the Trade Agreements Act of 1979 and the Uruguay Round Agreements Act of 1994.

The Department of Defense has its own Buy American rules. Generally speaking, a 50 percent price preference (customs duties excluded) or a 6 or 12 percent preference (customs duties included) whichever is more protective to domestic suppliers is applied. However, intergovernmental "Memoranda of Understanding" (MOU) on defense procurement provide important exceptions to the standard Department of Defense procurement rules.[4] Additional procurement preferences are established by the Small Business Act of 1953.[5] Under this Act, federal agencies may set-aside certain procurement exclusively for small U.S. businesses. In practice, the

---

§ 14.4

1. 41 U.S.C.A. §§ 10a–10d.

2. See the U.S. Balance of Payments Program, 48 C.F.R. § 225.302 et seq., creating procurement preferences for materials used outside the U.S. but suspended if the Code on Procurement applies.

3. See Executive Order No. 10582 (Dec. 17, 1954), 19 Fed.Reg. 8723 *as* amended by Exec. Order No. 11051 (Sept. 27, 1962), 27 Fed.Reg. 9683 and Exec. Order No. 12148, July 20, 1979, 44 Fed.Reg. 43239.

4. See Self–Powered Lighting, Ltd. v. United States, 492 F.Supp. 1267 (S.D.N.Y.1980).

5. 15 U.S.C.A. §§ 631–648. See 48 C.F.R. §§ 19.000–.902.

federal government normally sets aside about 30 percent of its procurement needs in this fashion. Special set-aside rules apply to benefit socially and economically disadvantaged minority-owned businesses. These preferences are excepted from U.S. adherence to the GATT/WTO Procurement Codes under a U.S. reservation.

A number of federal statutes also contain specific Buy American requirements. These include various GSA, NASA and TVA appropriations' bills, the AMTRAK Improvement Act of 1978,[6] the Public Works Employment Act of 1977,[7] various highway and transport acts,[8] the Clean Water Act of 1977,[9] and the Rural Electrification Acts of 1936 and 1938.[10] Many of these statutes involve federal funding of state and local procurement. Most are generally excepted from the GATT/WTO Procurement Codes as applied by the United States.

The Buy American Act generally conformed to the GATT Code on Government Procurement negotiated during the Tokyo Round. However, Congress expressed its displeasure with the degree to which that Code opened up sales opportunities for United States firms abroad. It therefore amended the Buy American Act in 1988 to deny the benefits of the Procurement Code when foreign governments are not in good standing under it. United States government procurement contracts are also denied to suppliers from countries whose governments "maintain ... a significant and persistent pattern of practice or discrimination against U.S. products or services which results in identifiable harm to U.S. businesses."[11] Presidential waivers of these statutory denials may occur in the public interest, to avoid single supply situations or to assure sufficient bidders to provide supplies of requisite quality and competitive prices.

The European Union was one of the first to be identified as a persistent procurement discriminator by the USTR. This identification concerns longstanding heavy electrical and telecommunications disputes that were partly settled by negotiation in 1993. The remaining disputes led to U.S. trade sanctions and European retaliation. This did not occur with Greece, Spain and Portugal (where the EU procurement rules do not apply), and with Germany which broke ranks and negotiated a pathbreaking bilateral settlement with the U.S. In 1993, also, Japan was identified as a persistent procurement discriminator in the construction, architectural and engineering areas.

---

6. Pub.L. 95–421.

7. 42 U.S.C.A. § 6705.

8. See, e.g., Highway Improvement Act of 1982, Pub.L. 97–424.

9. 33 U.S.C.A. § 1295.

10. 7 U.S.C.A. § 903.

11. 41 U.S.C.A. § 10d.

The Tokyo Round GATT Procurement Code was not particularly successful at opening up government purchasing. Only Austria, Canada, the twelve European Union states, Finland, Hong Kong, Israel, Japan, Norway, Singapore, Sweden, Switzerland and the United States adhered to the Procurement Code. This was also partly the result of the 1979 Code's many exceptions. For example, the Code did not apply to contracts below its threshold amount of $150,000 SDR (about $171,000 since 1988), service contracts, and procurement by entities on each country's reserve list (including most national defense items). Because procurement in the European Union and Japan is often decentralized, many contracts fall below the SDR threshold and were therefore exempt. By dividing up procurement into smaller contracts national preferences were retained. U.S. government procurement tends to be more centralized and thus more likely covered by the Code. This pattern helps explain why Congress restrictively amended the Buy American Act in 1988.

In addition to the Buy American Act, state and local purchasing requirements may inhibit import competition in the procurement field. For example, California once had a law which made it mandatory to purchase American products. This law was declared unconstitutional as an encroachment upon the federal power to conduct foreign affairs.[12] A Massachusetts ban on contracts with companies invested in Burma was preempted by federal sanctions adopted in 1997 against Burma.[13] State statutes which have copied the federal Buy American Act, on the other hand, and incorporated public interest and unreasonable cost exceptions to procurement preferences, have generally withstood constitutional challenge.[14] A Pennsylvania statute requiring state and local agencies to ensure that contractors do not provide products containing foreign steel was upheld by the Third Circuit Court of Appeals.[15] This case illustrates the inapplicability of the Tokyo Round Procurement Code to state and local purchasing requirements.[16]

A practice known as "unbalanced bidding" has arisen in connection with the Buy American Act. Unbalanced bidding involves the use of United States labor and parts by foreigners in sufficient

12. Bethlehem Steel Corp. v. Board of Commissioners of the Department of Water and Power of the City of Los Angeles, 276 Cal.App.2d 221, 80 Cal. Rptr. 800 (1969).

13. Crosby v. National Foreign Trade Council, 530 U.S. 363, 120 S.Ct. 2288, 147 L.Ed.2d 352 (2000).

14. See K.S.B. Technical Sales Corp. v. North Jersey District Water Supply Commission of the State of New Jersey, 75 N.J. 272, 381 A.2d 774 (1977), *appeal*

dismissed 435 U.S. 982, 98 S.Ct. 1635, 56 L.Ed.2d 76 (1978).

15. Trojan Technologies, Inc. v. Pennsylvania, 916 F.2d 903 (3d Cir. 1990), *cert. denied* 501 U.S. 1212, 111 S.Ct. 2814, 115 L.Ed.2d 986 (1991).

16. See Southwick, Binding the States: A Survey of State Law Conformance with Standards of the GATT Procurement Code, 13 U.Pa.J.Int'l Bus.L. 57 (1992).

degree so as to overcome the bidding preferences established by law for U.S. suppliers. This occurs because the United States value added is *not* included in the calculations of the margin of preference for the U.S. firms. Thus foreign bids minus the value of work done in the U.S. are multiplied by the 6, 12 or 50 percent Buy American Act preference. If the U.S. bids are above the foreign bids but within the margin of preference, the U.S. company gets the contract. If the U.S. bids are higher than the foreign bids plus the margin of preference, the foreigners get the contract.[17]

Chapter 13 of the 1989 Canada–United States Free Trade Area Agreement opens government procurement to U.S. and Canadian suppliers on contracts as small as $25,000. However, the goods supplied must have at least 50 percent U.S. and Canadian content. The NAFTA also establishes distinct procurement regulations. The thresholds are $50,000 for goods and services provided to federal agencies and $250,000 for government-owned enterprises (notably PEMEX and CFE). These regulations are particularly important because Mexico, unlike Canada, has not traditionally joined in GATT/WTO procurement codes.[18]

The Uruguay Round Procurement Code replaced the Tokyo Round agreement. It is one of very few WTO agreements that is optional. The WTO Code expands coverage to include procurement of services, construction, government-owned utilities, and some state and local (subcentral) contracts. Various improvements to the procedural rules surrounding procurement practices and dispute settlement attempt to reduce tensions in this difficult area. For example, an elaborate system for bid protests is established. Bidders who believe the Code's procedural rules have been abused will be able to lodge, litigate and appeal their protests. The United States has agreed, with few exceptions, to bring all procurement by executive agencies subject to the Federal Acquisition Regulations under the Code's coverage (i.e., to suspend application of the normal Buy American preferences to such procurement).

§ 14.5   Product Standards

Widespread use of "standards" requirements as NTB import restraints resulted in 1979 in the GATT Agreement on Technical Barriers to Trade (called the "Standards Code").[1] This Code was made operative in the United States by the Trade Agreements Act of 1979,[2] and was followed by a reasonable number of other nations. Its successor is the Uruguay Round Agreement on Technical Barri-

---

17. See Allis–Chalmers Corp. v. Friedkin, 635 F.2d 248 (3d Cir.1980).

18. See generally Chapter 15 on free trade agreements of the United States.

§ 14.5

1. See 18 Int'l Legal Mat. 1079.

2. 19 U.S.C.A. § 1531 et seq.

ers to Trade (1994). This agreement is binding on all WTO members. In general, this Code deals with the problem of countries' manipulation of product standards, product testing procedures, and product certifications in order to slow or stop imported goods. The Code provides, in part and subject to some exceptions, that imported products shall be accorded treatment (including testing treatment and certification) no less favorable than that accorded to like products of national origin or those originating in any other country. It also requires that participating nations establish a central office for standards inquiries, publish advance and reasonable notice of requirements that are applicable to imported goods, and provide an opportunity for commentary by those who may be affected adversely. The Code establishes an international committee to deal with alleged instances of noncompliance.

Under United States law,[3] state and federal agencies may create standards which specify the characteristics of a product, such as levels of quality, safety, performance or dimensions, or its packaging and labelling. However, these "standards-related activities" must not create "unnecessary obstacles to U.S. foreign trade," and must be demonstrably related to "a legitimate domestic objective" such as protection of health and safety, security, environmental or consumer interests. Sometimes there is a conflict between federal and state standards. For example, federal law licensing endangered species' articles preempted California's absolute ban on trade in such goods.[4] The Office of the USTR is charged with responsibility for implementation of the Standards Code within the United States.[5]

The Secretary of Commerce maintains a "standards information center" (National Bureau of Standards, National Center for Standards and Certification Information), in part to "serve as the central national collection facility for information relating to standards, certification systems, and standards-related activities, whether such standards, systems or activities are public or private, domestic or foreign, or international, regional, national, or local [and to] make available to the public at ... reasonable fee ... copies of information required to be collected."[6]

United States standards have been attacked in international tribunals as violating international obligations. Sometimes the standards have been upheld, sometimes not. For example, a binational arbitration panel established under Chapter 18 of the Canada–U.S. FTA issued a decision upholding a United States law

---

3. 19 U.S.C.A. § 2531.

4. Man Hing Ivory and Imports, Inc. v. Deukmejian, 702 F.2d 760 (9th Cir. 1983).

5. 19 U.S.C.A. §§ 2541, 2552.

6. 19 U.S.C.A. § 2544.

setting a minimum size on lobsters sold in interstate commerce. The panel found that, since the law applied to both domestic and foreign lobsters, it was not a disguised trade restriction. On the other hand, in 1991, a GATT panel found that United States import restrictions designed to protect dolphin from tuna fishers did violate the GATT. The panel ruled that GATT did not permit any import restrictions based on environmental concerns, whether they were considered disguised trade restrictions or not. This decision suggested repeal of a number of United States laws which concern health, safety and environmental conditions in exporting nations. A 1994 decision by a second GATT panel recognized the legitimacy of extraterritorial environmental regulations, but ruled against the tuna boycott of the U.S. because of its focus on production methods. In 1998, the WTO Appellate Body ruled against a U.S. ban on shrimp imports from nations that fail to use turtle exclusion devises comparable to those required under U.S. law. The Appellate Body found the U.S. ban "arbitrary" and "unjustifiable".

The standards of other nations have also been challenged as violations of GATT obligations. For example, the United States has criticized European Union bans of imports of meat from the United States, first for containing certain hormones, later for unsanitary conditions in U.S. meatpacking facilities. In 1997, the WTO Appellate Body ruled against the EU hormone-treated beef ban, citing lack of an adequate scientific basis as required under the WTO SPS Code. Future disputes with the EU are sure to arise regarding genetically modified food organisms (GMOs).

§ 14.6 Product Markings (Origin, Labels)

The United States requires clear markings of countries of origin on imports. This can be perceived, especially by those abroad, as a nontariff trade barrier intended to promote domestic purchases. Section 304 of the Tariff act of 1930 establishes the basic rules for origin markings.[1] Every imported article of foreign origin (or its container) must be marked conspicuously, legibly, indelibly and as permanently as practical in English so as to indicate to ultimate purchasers its country of origin.[2]

The principle sanction for failure to properly mark imports is the imposition of statutory tariffs of 10 percent ad valorem, which are imposed in addition to regular duties and even if the goods would ordinarily enter the U.S. duty free. Importers ordinarily receive notice from the Customs Service and an opportunity to comply with marking requirements. Any untimely failure to comply

§ 14.6

1. 19 U.S.C.A. § 1304.

2. See Precision Specialty Metals, Inc. v. United States, 116 F.Supp.2d 1350 (C.I.T.2000).

can result in liquidated damages proceedings by Customs against the importer. The amount of damages assessed will vary with the frequency and circumstances of the offense, and will be assessed as a percentage of the appraised value of the merchandise. In severe cases, Customs may seek civil penalties under Section 592 of the Tariff Act of 1930.[3] This provision generally sanctions imports under false documents. Furthermore, criminal sanctions are also possible, either for use of false documents[4] or altering a required marking with concealment intended.[5] The latter penalties can rise to $250,000 or one year imprisonment or both. The severity of these sanctions must be measured against the temptation of traders to alter country of origin markings so as to obtain duty free or quota free entry of goods into the United States.

Various exceptions apply to the U.S. country of origin marking requirements.[6] These include goods that are incapable of being marked, goods economically prohibitive to mark (unless the failure to do so was a deliberate attempt at avoiding the law), or goods that will be injured if marked. If the containers will reasonably indicate origin to the ultimate consumer, or the import circumstances or character of the goods necessarily convey knowledge of their source, no marking is required. Nor is it mandatory to mark goods not intended for resale, goods which when processed will obliterate the mark, goods over twenty years old and goods intended for export without entering U.S. commerce. Certain United States fishery products, products of U.S. possessions and products that originally came from the U.S. and are being imported are likewise exempt. Lastly, there is a "J-list" of specific goods that have been individually ruled exempt by the Secretary of the Treasury.[7] These include items like cordage, buttons, nails, etc., all of which must be marked by container.

Special regulations govern the marking requirements for imported textiles. These are created by the Textile Fiber Products Identification Act.[8] This Act is enforced by the U.S. Federal Trade Commission. It mandates disclosure of country of origin, generic fiber contents and the name or identification number of the manufacturer or marketer. Violation of the Textile Fiber Products Identification Act amounts to a violation of Section 5 of the Federal Trade Commission Act.[9] This means that F.T.C. cease and desist order proceedings, injunction actions, civil penalties and consumer redress relief can follow. Similar but not identical labelling require-

---

3. 19 U.S.C.A. § 1592.

4. 18 U.S.C.A. § 1001.

5. 19 U.S.C.A. § 1304.

6. See 19 C.F.R. § 134.32.

7. See 19 C.F.R. § 134.33.

8. 15 U.S.C.A. § 70–70K.

9. 15 U.S.C.A. § 45.

ments are established by the Wool Products Labelling Act[10] (country of origin required) and the Fur Products Labelling Act[11] (country of origin not required). These laws are also enforced by the Federal Trade Commission.

Significant litigation has ensued under the Tariff Act country of origin requirements regarding when a U.S. manufacturer is to be deemed the "ultimate purchaser" which may render the goods exempt from marking. In a major decision by the Court of Customs and Patent Appeals, wooden brush handles from Japan were processed in the U.S. by inserting bristles which obliterated the marking. The CCPA, adopting a common rationale in U.S. customs law, held that the handles had undergone a "substantial transformation" into a new product in the United States and were thus subject only to container marking obligations.[12] In contrast, when leather uppers for shoes were imported from Indonesia, the Court of International Trade required individual markings despite the attachment of soles in the U.S. and argument that a "substantial transformation" had taken place.[13] Gifts of products to ordinary consumers (umbrellas to racetrack patrons) may still require origin markings even if the donor would be exempt.[14]

Other litigation has focused on the duty to mark origin "conspicuously." The Court of International Trade initially reversed a "plainly erroneous" Customs Service position that frozen food markings at the rear of the package (Made in Mexico) were conspicuous.[15] The Court took the position that such markings did not give U.S. consumers realistic choices when shopping and noted the health risks associated with such goods. Subsequently, the Court of International Trade vacated this opinion.

10.   15 U.S.C.A. § 68–68j.

11.   15 U.S.C.A. § 69–69j.

12.   United States v. Gibson–Thomsen Co., 27 C.C.P.A. 267 (1940), *superseded by regulation as stated in* Cumins Engine Co. v. United States, 83 F.Supp.2d 1366 (C.I.T.1999).

13.   Uniroyal, Inc. v. United States, 542 F.Supp. 1026 (C.I.T.1982), *affirmed* 702 F.2d 1022 (Fed.Cir.1983).

14.   Pabrini, Inc. v. United States, 630 F.Supp. 360 (C.I.T.1986).

15.   Norcal/Crosetti Foods, Inc. v. United States Customs Service, 758 F.Supp. 729 (C.I.T.1991), *opinion vac'd* 790 F.Supp. 302 (C.I.T.1992).

Chapter 15

ESCAPE CLAUSE PROCEEDINGS; TRADE ADJUSTMENT ASSISTANCE

Table of Sections

§ 15.1   Prospects for Relief

One way that United States businesses may seek protection from import competition is by initiating what are known as escape clause or market disruption proceedings under the Trade Act of 1974. In contrast to most other statutory trade law remedies, these "safeguard" proceedings are not targeted at unfair practices. Rather, the goods are assumed to be fairly traded but in such volume that domestic industry relief is temporarily appropriate while adjustments are undertaken. Escape clause proceedings can involve imports from anywhere in the world and are authorized by Section

201 of the Trade Act.[1] Escape clause proceedings are also typically found in the bilateral trade agreements of the United States.

Market disruption proceedings concern imports from communist nations and are authorized by Section 406 of the 1974 Trade Act.[2] These proceedings are similar but not identical. Either may result in the imposition of U.S. import restraints or presidential negotiation of export restraints from the source country. Escape clause and market disruption proceedings are anticipated by Article XIX of the General Agreement on Tariffs and Trade. There has been an ongoing dialogue within the GATT about reforming the law of Article XIX. A WTO "Safeguards Agreement" emerged from the Uruguay Round of negotiations and is outlined below.

Import injury relief available under the Trade Act of 1974 is basically of two kinds: (1) Presidential relief designed to temporarily protect domestic producers of like or directly competitive products; and/or (2) governmental assistance to workers and firms economically displaced by import competition. This assistance is intended to enhance job opportunities and competitiveness. Protective relief tends to be awarded when the President believes that U.S. industry needs sometime to adjust, while governmental assistance is seen as a means to accommodate the injury caused by import competition. Adjustment to import competition is the longer term goal, resulting in competitive U.S. industries and markets.

One reason why protective escape clause relief is difficult to obtain is the fact that most trading partners of the United States are entitled to take compensatory action if the President decides to provide such relief. They are authorized to do this by the General Agreement on Tariffs and Trade. This is the case because escape clause proceedings do not concern any unfair trade practice. Rather, they are simply a reaction to the fact of increased import competition. This perspective helps explain why the President frequently decides that it is not in the national economic interest of the United States to impose escape clause relief. The same factors are much less relevant to market disruption relief because so few communist countries are WTO members.

§ 15.2   The Impact of Limited Judicial Review

Judicial review of escape clause and market disruption proceedings and remedies is limited to procedural irregularities or clear misconstruction of a statute.[1] This flows from the President's broad constitutional powers over foreign affairs. Derivatively, the actions

§ 15.1

1. 19 U.S.C.A. § 2251.

2. 19 U.S.C.A. § 2436.

§ 15.2

1. Sneaker Circus, Inc. v. Carter, 566 F.2d 396 (2d Cir.1977), *on remand* 457 F.Supp. 771 (E.D.N.Y.1978).

of the International Trade Commission (ITC) in these proceedings are likewise sheltered from extensive judicial review.[2] This means that the decisions of the ITC are critical to obtaining escape clause relief. For example, between 1984 and 1990 the Commission reviewed 14 escape clause petitions. In ten of these petitions, the ITC decided that the statutory criteria for import injury relief were not present. In four of these petitions, the Commission recommended import relief. However, the President refused relief in three of these four cases. Only in a decision concerning wood shakes and shingles imported from Canada did the petitioner actually obtain protective escape clause relief.[3]

GATT compensation duties, U.S. free trade agreements, Presidential prerogatives and the 1988 amendments to Section 201 have significantly reduced the potential for success under these proceedings. During the 1990s, there were very few Section 201 or Section 406 proceedings. The main focus of U.S. escape clause relief has become trade adjustment assistance, which is discussed below.

§ 15.3   The WTO Safeguards Agreement

A "Safeguards Agreement" on escape clause and related "gray area" protective measures was agreed upon during the Uruguay Round. One of its more important prohibitions is against seeking, undertaking or maintaining voluntary export or import restraint agreements with the exception of one such agreement which could last through 1999.[1] Substantive and procedural escape clause rules are also established, notably on proof of "serious domestic injury," opportunities to present evidence and a maximum 4–year period of protection (extendable to 8 years). The right to retaliate when another country invokes escape clause relief is suspended for the first 3 years of such invocation. Special rules limit the use of escape clause measures to exports from developing nations and extend the potential for their use on imports by such nations.

§ 15.4   U.S. Implementation of and Compliance with the WTO Safeguards Agreement

Congress ratified and implemented the Uruguay Round accords in December of 1994 under the Uruguay round Agreements Act.[1] The ITC has summarized the URAA changes to United States escape clause proceedings as follows:

2. Maple Leaf Fish Co. v. United States, 762 F.2d 86 (Fed.Cir.1985).

3. See U.S. International Trade Commission Publication 1826 (March 1986) and 51 Fed.Reg. 19157 (May 28, 1986).

§ 15.3

1. See Section 15.12.

§ 15.4

1. Public Law No. 103–465, 108 Stat. 4809.

The legislation amends section 202 of the Trade Act to require the ITC to disclose confidential business information under administrative protective order to authorized representatives of interested parties who are parties to an investigation. As directed in both the legislation and in the accompanying Statement of Administrative Action, the ITC has issued interim regulations that provide for such disclosure in a manner similar to that provided for in the case of investigations under Title VII of the Tariff Act of 1930 and the regulations issued thereunder.

The legislation also amends section 202 to provide for a new and faster critical circumstances investigation procedure. If a petitioner alleges critical circumstances in a petition, the ITC must, within 60 days of receipt of the petition, make a determination concerning the existence of such circumstances and report to the President its determination and any recommendation concerning provisional relief. Under prior law, the Commission did not make a determination concerning critical circumstances until the end of the 120–day injury phase of an investigation. After receiving an affirmative Commission report, the President has 30 days in which to decide what, if any, action to take, with any such action generally to remain in effect until completion of the ITC investigation and consideration by the President of the ITC recommendation for longer term relief, but in no event longer than 200 days.

The legislation amends section 202 of the Trade Act to clarify the meaning of the term "domestic industry" and to define the terms "serious injury" and "threat of serious injury," tracking definitions in the Safeguards Agreement. Because the definitions reflect prior law and ITC practice, the Statement of Administrative Action indicated that the incorporation of these definitions into U.S. law "should not affect the outcome of ITC decisions."

The legislation makes several technical changes in the relief provisions in section 203 of the Trade Act. Under the new law, relief may be provided for an initial period of up to four years, and may be extended one *or more* times, with the overall duration of relief not to exceed eight years. Under prior law, the overall limitation on relief actions were also eight years; however, only one extension of a relief action was permitted, and there was no limitation (short of the full eight years) on the duration of the initial period of relief. Under the new law, relief actions that exceed one year must be "phased down at regular intervals" during the relief period. The law does not specify the degree of phase-down period or interval. Under prior law, phase down was required "to the extent feasible" after three years. The term "orderly marketing agreement" has been changed simply to "agreement" to avoid confusion with "orderly marketing arrangements," which are prohibited by the Safeguards Agreement.

The legislation amends Section 204 of the Trade Act to provide for ITC investigations at the request of the President or on petition by industry concerning whether relief action continues to be necessary to prevent or remedy serious injury and whether there is evidence that the industry is making a positive adjustment to import competition. The ITC must transmit its report to the President no later than 60 days before the relief action terminates.[2]

The WTO Appellate Body rulings concerning the Safeguards Agreement stringently limit use of escape clause remedies. In 2001, three rulings went against U.S. safeguard measures. In *U.S.-Wheat Gluten from the EC*, the Appellate Body emphasized the critical issue of causation. The U.S. International Trade Commission's analysis of factors other than imports that may have caused domestic industry injury lacked clarity and was inadequate. In addition, U.S. notice of intent to impose safeguards had to be "immediate," sufficient to allow a "meaningful exchange" of consultations. In *U.S.-Lamb Meat from New Zealand*, the Appellate Body reiterated that all causation factors must be isolated and examined. Further, it rejected the "domestic industry" definition adopted by the ITC because growers were included. Exclusion of free trade partners (Canada, Mexico) from escape clause remedies is not permissible if their imports were included in the injury determination. Both of these decisions emphasize the need for the ITC to find "unforseen developments" in its injury determinations. No guidance is given by the Appellate Body on this term.

The third 2001 Appellate Body ruling against U.S. safeguards concerned cotton yarn from Pakistan. This decision came under the Agreement on Textiles and Clothing. The Appellate Body rejected exclusion of vertically integrated yarn producers from the definition of "domestic industry." Similarly, exclusion of Mexican yarn from the relief was not permissible. In 2002, the Appellate Body ruled against U.S. safeguards on line pipe from Korea, finding under strict scrutiny a number of substantive and procedural errors.

In March of 2002, President Bush imposed tariffs of up to 30 percent on imported steel over three years. This escape clause relief was tempered by exclusions for selected steel from selected countries. Most Australian and Japanese steel products, for example, were not subject to these U.S. tariffs. About half of all EU steel imports were exempt. Canada and Mexico were fully exempt. Nu-

---

2. ITC Annual Report, (1995).

merous WTO members commenced dispute proceedings under the WTO Safeguards Agreement. In 2003, the Appellate Body ruled the U.S. tariffs on steel illegal under the WTO Safeguards Agreement. The Appellate Body held that the U.S. erred in utilizing the protective tariffs some four years after the surge of steel imports during the Asian economic meltdown, and that exclusion of NAFTA partners Canada and Mexico was improper. The European Union threatened over $2 billion annually in retaliatory tariffs on U.S. exports of clothing, citrus and boats, products thought to be politically damaging to the Bush Administration. In November 2003, the United States lifted its escape clause steel tariffs.

§ 15.5   Escape Clause Proceedings—Petitions

Escape clause proceedings may be initiated by the President, the United States Trade Representative, Congress, and any interested trade association, union or company. It is reasonably common for both labor and management to petition for escape clause relief. Such petitions are filed with the International Trade Commission. Their requirements are detailed in the Selected Documents section of this chapter. Ordinarily the Commission will not commence a second escape clause investigation of the same subject matter unless at least one year has passed since the previous investigation. However, the Commission can waive this rule for good cause.[1] Since 1988, if escape clause relief is imposed, no new investigation regarding the same imports will be initiated until after that relief has expired plus an additional period of time representing the length of the relief originally granted.[2]

The petition must include a statement describing the specific purposes for which relief is being sought. Petitions under Section 201 must show that a substantial number of the companies or workers in the industry support the petition. In this sense, the petitioner is like a class action representative. While it is not necessary for all companies or workers in the industry to support the petition, a substantial proportion must do so since Section 201 is focused upon industry-wide relief.[3]

The statute suggests that the facilitation of the orderly transfer of resources to more productive pursuits, enhancing competitiveness, or other means of adjustment to new conditions of competition are legitimate purposes for seeking Section 201 relief.[4] The petition may request provisional relief pending the outcome of an escape clause proceeding. The petitioner has the option of submitting a plan "to facilitate positive adjustment to import competi-

---

§ 15.5

1. See 19 U.S.C.A. § 2251(e).

2. 19 U.S.C.A. § 2252(h).

3. 19 C.F.R. § 206.9.

4. 19 U.S.C.A. § 2252(a)(2).

tion." This is often done because the Commission is required in conducting its escape clause investigation to seek information on actions being taken or planned by the firms and workers in the industry to make a positive adjustment to import competition. Moreover, the Commission is authorized to accept "commitments" regarding such action if it affirmatively determines that the statutory criteria of Section 201 are met.[5]

§ 15.6 Escape Clause Proceedings—ITC Investigations

If the industry is unable to adequately document its case for escape clause relief, it may be possible to essentially have the Commission do this under what is known as a Section 332 investigation.[1] If successful, a Section 332 investigation will shift the burden and the cost of preparing for a Section 201 proceeding from the industry or its representatives to the Commission.

As the Commission's investigation proceeds, it will develop an extensive questionnaire to send to domestic producers. This questionnaire focuses on the kinds of information the Commission needs to obtain in order to rule under the statutory criteria for escape clause proceedings. Although industry members typically support escape clause relief, they may not wish to reveal all the information requested in the questionnaire. In this case, the International Trade Commission can obtain subpoena enforcement from the District Court for the District of Columbia.[2] The hearings held by the ITC in connection with escape clause proceedings involve testimony under oath with the right of cross examination by opposing parties. Thus, for example, importers who do not wish to see restrictive measures undertaken, may oppose the domestic industry and its witnesses seeking such relief. The various procedures governing escape clause investigations and proceedings before the International Trade Commission are provided in 19 C.F.R. Parts 201 and 206. The entire ITC investigation normally takes about six months.

§ 15.7 Escape Clause Proceedings—Statutory Criteria

Section 201 of the Trade Act of 1974 requires proof of an increase in imports which substantially cause or threaten to cause serious injury to domestic industries producing like or directly competitive articles before protective trade relief will be considered.

---

5. 19 U.S.C.A. § 2252(a)(4)–(7).   **2.** 19 U.S.C.A. § 1333.

§ 15.6

1. See 19 U.S.C.A. § 1332.

It should be noted that the increase in imports can be actual or relative to domestic production. Relative increases occur when domestic production declines when measured against imports. Imports could thus decline but be relatively increasing if domestic production declined at an even faster rate.[1] Prior to 1974, escape clause law required the increase in imports to be caused by tariff concessions under trade agreements. This linkage was removed by the 1974 Act.

In conducting its escape clause investigation, Section 201 guides and controls the International Trade Commission's decision making. It defines, for example, the term "substantial cause" to mean a cause which is important and not less than any other cause.[2] In making its determinations with reference to serious injury or the threat of serious injury to a domestic industry producing like or directly competitive articles, the Commission must take into account all economic factors which it considers relevant including (but not limited to):

(1) the significant idling of productive facilities;

(2) the inability of a significant number of firms to carry out domestic production at a reasonable level of profit;

(3) significant unemployment or underemployment within the domestic industry;

(4) declines in sales or market share and higher and growing inventories as well as downward trends in production, profits, wages or employment in the domestic industry;

(5) the extent to which the industry is unable to generate adequate capital to finance modernization or maintain existing levels of research and development; and

(6) the extent to which the United States market is the focal point for the diversion of exports of the article in question by reason of trade restraints in other countries.

In making its determinations in connection with escape clause proceedings, the International Trade Commission must also consider the condition of the domestic industry over the course of its relevant business cycle. However, the Commission may not aggregate the cause of declining demand associated with a recession or economic downturn into a single cause of serious injury or threat of injury.[3] The Commission must also examine factors other than imports which may be a cause of serious injury or the threat of serious injury to the domestic industry. Specifically with reference

---

§ 15.7

1. See 19 U.S.C.A. § 2252(c).

2. 19 U.S.C.A. § 2252(b).

3. 19 U.S.C.A. § 2252(c)(2). Compare Certain Motor Vehicles and Certain Chassis and Bodies Thereof, USITC Inv. No. TA–201–44, 2 ITRD 5241 (1980).

to the question of "substantial cause," the statutes provide that an increase in imports (either actual or relative to domestic production) and a decline in the proportion of the domestic market supplied by domestic producers must be considered.[4] The term "significant idling of productive facility" includes the closing of plants or underutilization of production capacity.[5]

In order to determine the existence of a domestic industry producing an article like or directly competitive with the import competition, the ITC must consider only domestic production, may limit its consideration to specific articles of particular producers, and may limit the industry geographically where the imports are focused into a particular part of the United States.[6] For these purposes, a domestic industry includes producers located in the United States as well as its insular possessions.

Escape clause petitions can involved disputes as to the nature of the imported article. Typically, domestic producers will want to define the imported article broadly so as to enhance the possibility of proving domestic injury as well as obtaining broader relief. Importers of the product in question will want to define the imported article narrowly or in terms of separate categories so as to minimize the potential for escape clause remedies. For example, in the non-rubber footwear case,[7] the domestic producers succeeded in persuading the International Trade Commission that the imported competition constituted all non-rubber footwear. They did so over the objection of the importers of this footwear who wished to have the Commission distinguish between athletic and non-athletic footwear.

§ 15.8   Escape Clause Proceedings—Substantial Causation

Despite the elaborate nature of the statutory requirements for ITC determinations of import injury under Section 201, substantial latitude in reaching these decisions still remains. A number of cases turn upon the issue of substantial causation. Restrictive interpretations of escape clause causation under the Trade Expansion Act of 1962 were widely criticized and a major reason for the amended causation criteria of the Trade Act of 1974. The 1962 Act focused on whether the imports were "the major factor" in causing domestic injury, whereas the 1974 Act considers substantial causation (important and not less than any other cause) sufficient. One of the better known decisions in this area under the 1974 Act involves the

---

4. 19 U.S.C.A. § 2252(c)(1)–(2).

5. 19 U.S.C.A. § 2252(c)(6).

6. 19 U.S.C.A. § 2252(c)(4).

7. U.S. International Trade Commission Publication 1545 (July, 1984).

importation of automobiles from Japan.[1] In this decision, the ITC held that there was an increase in imports of Japanese automobiles which was directly competitive with U.S. production but that other factors were more important to the explanation of the serious injury being suffered by the U.S. auto industry. In particular, the general economic recession of the times was held by the majority to be a more substantial cause of this injury.

In most escape clause proceedings there are often arguably other causes for injury to the domestic industry. Management may be inept, labor underproductive, general economic trends predominantly negative, technological innovations affecting competition adversely and so forth. Whether one cause is more substantial than the other is often very difficult to pinpoint with any kind of administrative expertise. The issue of causation may be affected by political currents at the ITC. For example, in a later decision involving the importation of motorcycles, the ITC specifically refused to treat recessionary elements in the United States economy as a more substantial cause for industry injury.[2] It is difficult to reconcile this decision with that concerning auto imports. Congress has since made a recession or an economic downturn incapable of being an aggregate cause of domestic injury for escape clause proceedings.[3]

In evaluating substantial causation under Section 201 of the Trade Act of 1974, the International Trade Commission has considered the following alternative causes of injury to domestic industries:

(1) Consumer cycles that affect product purchases;

(2) fundamental changes in consumption;

(3) governmental regulation;

(4) industry competition;

(5) management decision making;

(6) trends in imports, domestic consumption and production;

(7) price changes in the product market;

(8) business cycle changes;

§ 15.8

1. Certain Motor Vehicles and Certain Chassis and Bodies Thereof, U.S. International Trade Commission Investigation No. TA–201–44, 2 ITRD 5241 (1980).

2. Heavy Weight Motorcycles, & Engines & Power Train Subassemblies Therefor, U.S. International Trade Commission Investigation No. TA–201–47, 4 ITRD 2469 (1983).

3. See 19 U.S.C.A. § 2252(c).

(9) labor contract negotiations; and

(10) world price and competitive conditions.[4]

In evaluating declines in domestic consumption, there may be a variety of factors at work. These could include, for example, technological innovation, product substitution or interest rate shifts. It is not clear whether the International Trade Commission will consider these as possible separate and independent causation factors.[5]

§ 15.9   Escape Clause Proceedings—Serious Injury

A less developed but potentially controversial area of ITC determinations under Section 201 involves the question of what constitutes serious injury to the domestic industry. The statutory criteria indicate that loss of production should be the relevant inquiry, whereas loss of market share is relevant primarily to causation. Whether there is serious injury will of course depend upon the definition of the domestic industry. This is a bit like deciding what is the relevant market in United States antitrust litigation. Sub-markets, including sub-product markets and sub-geographic markets can clearly be domestic industries for purposes of Section 201. In the auto industry case referenced above, the ITC used tariff classifications of the United States in order to determine the domestic industry. Using such classifications has the practical feature of allowing identifiable tariff relief if that is ultimately granted. It is important to remember that the mere threat of serious injury is sufficient to satisfy the statute. There must be a reasonable degree of imminence to the projected import injury.[1]

The International Trade Commission has interpreted the term "serious injury" to mean damage or hurt of a grave or important proportion.[2] In a decision denying relief to U.S. cigar producers, the Commission determined that a marked decline in U.S. consumption of large cigars was a more important cause of injury than import competition.[3] A decline in housing construction was determined to be more important to the injury suffered by door manufacturers than import competition.[4] In most of its decisions concerning causa-

---

4. For a review of these alternative causation factors, see especially Carbon & Certain Alloy Steel Products, U.S. International Trade Commission Publication 1553, 6 ITRD 2236 (July 1984).

5. See Stainless Steel and Alloy Tool Steel, U.S. International Trade Commission Publication 1377, 5 ITRD 1411 (May 1983).

§ 15.9

1. See Heavy Weight Motorcycles, U.S. International Trade Investigation No. TA–201–47, 4 ITRD 2469, Publication No. 1342 (Feb.1983).

2. Bolts, Nuts & Screws of Iron or Steel, U.S. International Trade Commission Publication 747, 1 ITRD 5142 (November 1975).

3. Wrapper Tobacco, U.S. International Trade Commission Publication 746, 1 ITRD 5137 (November 1975).

4. Birch Plywood Door Skins, U.S. International Trade Commission Publication 743, 1 ITRD 5121 (October 1975).

tion and serious injury, the Commission ordinarily reviews the economic trends over the past five years so as to screen out temporary problems.

In one decision, the Commission excluded domestic production of certain pigments because they were inorganic in contrast to iron blue pigments which are organic and against which import relief was sought. The different pigments had contrasting commercial uses and were markedly apart in terms of cost. Under these conditions, organic and inorganic pigments were held not to be like or directly competitive products.[5] In determining whether products are competitive with each other, the Commission may consider earlier or later stages of processing.[6] Imports of raw sugar were considered directly competitive with U.S. sugarcane and sugar beets even though these products were not yet processed into sugar. Moreover, U.S. produced refined or processed sugar, even though at a later stage than the imports in questions, could be considered directly competitive with the raw sugar.[7]

In defining the nature of the domestic industry for escape clause purposes, the parties typically engage in argument which seeks to promote either a broader or narrower definition. Importers may contest the definition initially offered by the domestic industry so as to decrease the perception that like or directly competitive products are at risk or reduce the measurement of increase in imports. The definition of the industry will also impact on the question of causation. All of these issues were raised in the *Heavy Weight Motorcycles* case. In this decision, the Commission ruled that imported sub-assemblies were not directly competitive with domestic sub-assemblies because the imports were captively consumed.[8] Similar issues were raised in the automobile investigation. The domestic industry argued that passenger cars should be defined as a single industry producing automobiles and light trucks. Importers who opposed the escape clause proceeding sought to subdivide the industry into large automobiles and small automobiles. The Commission's ultimate determination found three different industries, passenger automobiles, light trucks and medium-heavy weight trucks.[9]

5. Ferrocyanide and Ferrocyanide Pigments, U.S. International Trade Commission Publication 767 (April 1976).

6. 19 U.S.C.A. § 2481(5).

7. Sugar Imports, U.S. International Trade Commission Publication 807 (March 1977).

8. See Heavy Weight Motorcycles, U.S. International Trade Investigation No. TA–201–47, 4 ITRD 2469, Publication No. 1342 (Feb. 1983).

9. See Certain Motor Vehicles and Certain Chassis and Bodies Thereof, Investigation No. TA–201–44, 2 ITRD 5241 Publication No. 1110 (December 1980).

Having defined the industry, the Commission then must decide which particular companies belong to it. This is not always easy. In the automobile case, for example, the Commission had to decide whether dealers and independent parts suppliers were part of the domestic industry. It decided that neither were part of the domestic industry because the dealers did not produce any article, and the independent suppliers of parts did not produce products that were like or directly competitive with the final product. If a domestic company is also an importer, the Commission can only consider that part of its business that relates to domestic production to be part of the domestic industry.[10] This legislative provision effectively reverses earlier decisions, such as in *Heavy Weight Motorcycles,* where the Commission found that domestic subsidiaries of Japanese companies were also domestic producers even when the parts they imported comprised more than 50 percent of the final product.

One definition of serious injury is that the industry is "in danger of disappearing or suffering major shrinkage."[11] Section 202 now requires the Commission to specifically consider the significant idling of productive facilities, the inability of a significant number of firms to carry out production at reasonable levels of profit and significant unemployment or underemployment within the industry when determining serious injury.[12] When evaluating the threat of serious injury as opposed to actual injury, the Commission must consider declines in sales or market share, growing inventories, downward trends in production, profits, wages or employment, the inadequacy of capital to finance modernization or maintain existing expenditures for research and development, and the extent to which the United States is the focal point for a diversion of exports into other markets.[13] In actual practice, there may be little difference between evaluating potential and actual injury in escape clause proceedings.

One issue concerning the definition of the domestic industry is whether it can involve various stages of processing. In other words, the issue is whether the imports must be at the same level of processing as the domestic industry. The International Trade Commission has indicated that when several stages are involved in the production of goods, the domestic industry includes the facilities involved in all of the various stages.[14] For example, the Commission held that the copper refining industry in the United States includes four stages. For purposes of determining injury to that industry, it

---

10. 19 U.S.C.A. § 2252(c).

11. See Certain Canned Tuna Fish, U.S. International Trade Commission Publication No. 1558, 6 ITRD 2464 (August 1984).

12. 19 U.S.C.A. § 2252(c).

13. Id.

14. U.S. International Trade Commission Publication 1558 (August, 1984).

was appropriate to consider all four stages of copper production when gauging the impact of import competition.[15] The Trade Act of 1974 specifically indicates that various stages of processing can be considered in defining the imported product. This has the practical effect of allowing the imported article to be at a different level of process from that which causes injury to the domestic industry.[16]

§ 15.10 Escape Clause Proceedings—Relief Recommendations of the Commission

If the International Trade Commission affirmatively decides that the statutory criteria of Section 301 are met, it must make recommendations to address the serious injury or threat thereof to the domestic industry as well as consider the most effective means to allow that industry to make a positive adjustment to import competition.[1] The Commission is authorized to choose from a menu of relief options. It may recommend an increase in or the imposition of a tariff or a tariff rate quota, modification or imposition of an import quota, various trade adjustment measures including trade adjustment assistance, or any combination of these possibilities.[2] No recommended relief may exceed an eight-year time limit. In addition, the Commission may also recommend that the President initiate international negotiations to address the underlying cause of the increase in imports. Interestingly, only those members of the ITC who voted affirmatively to find a breach of Section 201 are eligible to vote on recommendations to the President. Dissenting members appear to have no input on relief recommendations.

The Commission's report to the President will also include any adjustment plans submitted by the domestic industry in its petition and any commitments made by firms and workers in that industry in order to facilitate positive adjustment to import competition. The Commission's report must also analyze the long and short term economic effects of the relief it recommends.

The Commission's Report to the President is advisory, but if the President decides not to follow any recommended import relief, Congress may pass a joint resolution by majority vote of both houses disapproving of the President's action. This joint resolution may be vetoed by the President, and the veto may in turn be overridden by Congress. If this were to occur, then the Commission's original relief recommendations would be implemented.[3]

---

15. U.S. International Trade Commission Publication 1549 (July, 1984).

16. See 19 U.S.C.A. § 2481(5).

§ 15.10

1. 19 U.S.C.A. § 2252(e).

2. Id.

3. See 19 U.S.C.A. § 2253(c).

§ 15.11   Escape Clause Proceedings—Presidential Relief Decisions

After receiving the recommendations and report of the International Trade Commission, the President is required to take all appropriate and feasible action that he or she determines will facilitate efforts by the domestic industry to make a positive adjustment to import competition and which provide greater economic and social benefits than costs. The latter requirement, essentially a cost-benefit analysis, was added to the statute by 1988 amendments.[1] The President need not take any action at all. If the President decides to provide escape clause relief, this may be in the form of a tariff, a tariff rate quota, an import quota, adjustment assistance, orderly marketing agreements with foreign countries, an allocation among importers by auction of import licenses, international negotiations, legislative proposals, or any combination thereof.[2] Duty free treatment under the Generalized System of Tariff Preferences of the United States is automatically suspended if the President decides to impose an escape clause proceeding tariff. No increase in tariff resulting from escape clause proceedings can exceed 50 percent ad valorem of the rate existing at the time of the escape clause proceeding.[3]

Since all escape clause relief is intended to be temporary, no relief ordered by the President may exceed eight years.[4] President Carter denied relief against stainless steel flatware in part because a tariff rate quota had been in effect for more than 13 of the previous 20 years. The President determined that escape clause relief would be inconsistent with the basic concept that this kind of relief is supposed to be temporary in nature.[5]

Petitioners in escape clause proceedings should consider in advance which form of relief they hope to receive. Tariffs may not provide effective relief because of floating currency values. For example, if the dollar declines in value, imports get cheaper and the negative impact of tariffs might be offset. On the other hand, if dollar values are rising, this will cause tariffs to be an effective form of protection because imports become notably more expensive. The point to be made is that the result in connection with tariff relief is uncertain. In either case, tariffs can always be just simply paid if the economics of the transaction support payment. In the *Heavy Weight Motorcycles* case, for example, the relief ultimately determined by the President was a tariff increase with an automatic termination date five years later. In fact, the industry requested

---

§ 15.11

1. See 19 U.S.C.A. § 2253(a).

2. 19 U.S.C.A. § 2253(a)(3).

3. 19 U.S.C.A. § 2254(e).

4. 19 U.S.C.A. § 2253(e).

5. Certain Stainless Steel Table Flatware, 43 Fed.Reg. 29259 (July 7, 1978).

an earlier termination and many believe that this is one of the few examples of successful adjustment to import competition under escape clause relief.

The President has provided escape clause relief in relatively few instances.[6] Congress can (but never has) override any presidential denial of escape clause or market disruption relief recommended by the International Trade Commission, and it may override any decision of the President that differs from the type of relief recommended by the Commission. Congress can do so by adopting a joint resolution of disapproval. Once this is enacted, the President is required to adopt the import relief previously recommended by the Commission. However, the President may veto this joint resolution, in which case an override of the President's veto is required to obtain relief.[7]

If the President decides to impose protective escape clause relief, subsequent proceedings concerning extension, reduction or termination of that relief may be held. The level of the relief granted however cannot be increased. In the subsequent proceedings, the Commission's role is advisory, and it will report upon its monitoring of the existing relief relative to continuing injury and the progress of the domestic industry to adjust to import competition.[8] The President may alter existing escape clause relief if he or she finds that the domestic industry has failed to make adequate efforts to adjust to import competition, the circumstances have sufficiently changed to warrant a reduction or termination in relief, or upon the request of the domestic industry.[9]

In deciding whether to undertake escape clause relief, the President is directed to take into account the report of the Commission, the extent to which the workers and firms in the industry are benefiting from adjustment assistance, the efforts being made by the industry to make a positive adjustment to import competition, the likelihood of effectiveness of relief in facilitating such adjustment, and the short and long term economic and social costs of the relief relative to their short and long term economic and social benefits. The President must also consider other factors related to the national economic interest of the United States including but not limited to the economic and social costs if relief is not granted, the impact on consumers and on competition in domestic markets, and the impact on United States industries if other nations take compensatory action. Consumer interests have sometimes been critical to the President's decision to deny escape clause relief.

---

6. See particularly the remedies challenged in WTO dispute settlement, Section 15.5, supra.

7. See 19 U.S.C.A. § 2253(b).

8. See Color Television Receivers and Subassemblies Thereof, U.S. International Trade Commission Publication 1068, 2 ITRD 5046 (May 1980).

9. 19 U.S.C.A. § 2253(a).

Various presidents have noted that such relief can as a practical matter increase prices to consumers and that this would be adverse to the national economic interests of the United States.[10] The argument that escape clause relief may cause inflation in the United States is a variation on this theme.[11] The fact that the imposition of escape clause relief may provoke retaliation has also been used to justify denial of such relief by several Presidents.[12]

The President is further directed to consider the extent to which there is a diversion of foreign exports to the U.S. markets by reason of foreign restraints, the potential for circumvention of any relief taken, the national security interests of the United States, and those factors that the Commission is required to consider in reaching its recommendations.[13] These considerations have frequently in the past caused presidents to deny escape clause relief. This is consistent with the President's primary role in the foreign affairs of the nation. Thus, for example, the President decided not to grant escape clause relief regarding imports of honey because it might have an adverse effect on the bargaining position of the United States in international trade negotiations.[14] Similar results were achieved in connection with imports of copper when there were ongoing GATT negotiations as well as UNCTAD negotiations about commodities trade.[15] Later rejections of other efforts to obtain import relief in connection with copper were based upon considerations of the need for the exporters of copper to obtain adequate export earnings.[16]

Amendments to the Trade Act of 1974 adopted in 1988 promote the goal of adjustment to import competition instead of trade restrictive relief. This has been sought by strongly encouraging the submission of adjustment plans and commitments by petitioners for Section 201 relief, and by expanding the range of remedies the Commission can recommend to the President in escape clause proceedings to *any* action that will facilitate adjustment. Furthermore, the standards for presidential relief mandate a determination that such relief will facilitate efforts by the domestic industry to make a positive adjustment to import competition. Finally there is increased monitoring of Section 201 relief plans and limitations on the right to petition for further relief. Thus, Section 201 of the

---

10. See Certain Stainless Steel Flatware, supra.

11. See Nonrubber Footwear, U.S. International Trade Commission Publication No. 1717, 7 ITRD 2125 (July 1985).

12. See High Carbon Verochrominium, 43 Fed.Reg. 4245 (November 6, 1978).

13. 19 U.S.C.A. § 2253(a).

14. Honey, 41 Fed.Reg. 3787 (Sept. 1, 1976).

15. Domestic Copper Industry, 43 Fed.Reg. 49523 (October 24, 1978).

16. Copper Import Relief Determination, 49 Fed.Reg. 35609 (1984).

Trade Act is now considerably less protectionist and more adjustment oriented than previously.

§ 15.12 Trade   Adjustment   Assistance—Individual and Company Assistance Criteria

The idea of trade adjustment assistance has its origins in programs intended to assist people who were dislocated when the European Community (now Union) was established. Its adoption in the United States has had a checkered history, particularly as regards Congressional willingness to fund trade adjustment assistance. The first authority for such assistance was provided in the Trade Expansion Act of 1962. However, no assistance was actually provided until 1969. The Trade Act of 1974 made trade adjustment assistance a greater possibility. But dramatic increases in payments to workers under the program during the early 1980s caused the Reagan Administration to actively seek to repeal the Trade Adjustment Assistance Program. During the 1980s, tighter eligibility requirements and shrinking budgetary allocations reduced the scope of the program. It was not until the Omnibus Trade and Competitiveness Act of 1988 that significant funds were committed to trade adjustment assistance and the program was reauthorized through 1993. Even so, actual payment of adjustment assistance to workers has occurred slowly, and assistance to companies has been extremely difficult to obtain.

Trade adjustment assistance programs of the United States were expanded in 2002, including for the first time worker assistance with health insurance, coverage of "secondary workers," a new pilot program on wage insurance for older workers, benefits for family farmers and ranchers, and expanded training and income support. This expansion came in conjunction with the Trade Promotion Authority ("fast track") granted by Congress to the President. See the Trade Act of 2002, Public Law 107–210.

There is a growing trend in escape clause law to provide adjustment assistance to workers and companies impacted by import competition rather than protective relief through presidential action. The Trade Act of 1974 facilitates the provision of such assistance either as an alternative to or in addition to protective presidential relief under Sections 201 or 406 of the Trade Act of 1974. Workers, for example, may petition the Secretary of Labor for trade adjustment assistance.[1] In order for such relief to be granted, the Secretary must certify that (1) a significant number or proportion of the workers have become totally or partially separated or threatened to become so separated, (2) that sales or production or both of the firm in question have decreased absolutely, and (3) that

§ 15.12

1. 19 U.S.C.A. § 2271.

increased imports of articles like or directly competitive with those made by the workers or the firm for which the workers provide essential goods or services "contributed importantly" to such separation and decline.[2]

All three criteria must be met.[3] These criteria are related but not identical to those considered by the International Trade Commission in connection with escape clause proceedings. For example, the term "contributed importantly" means a cause which is important but not necessarily more important than any other cause. This is a lesser standard than substantial causation in connection with Section 201 proceedings. Whether imports are "like or directly competitive" with domestic products is a question of interchangeability or substitutability.[4] The fact that imports are actually decreasing does not per se eliminate the possibility of trade adjustment assistance. The critical issue is whether those imports have contributed importantly to unemployment.[5]

Adjustment assistance for workers, when granted, often resembles supplemental cash unemployment compensation. Such benefits are now conditioned upon participation in job training and job search programs. Adjustment assistance for companies has sometimes involved income maintenance through loans like the Chrysler bail-out. At this point, assistance to companies is primarily limited to technical aid.[6] Companies may receive adjustment assistance only if the Secretary of Commerce finds that a significant number of their workers have been separated or threatened with separation, that sales or production have decreased absolutely, and increased importation of like or directly competitive articles contributed importantly to these results.[7] Agricultural firms may apply for adjustment assistance. Although once authorized by statute, Congress has not been willing to fund trade adjustment assistance for communities impacted by import competition.

It should be emphasized that it is not necessary for the ITC to determine that import injury has occurred under the criteria of Section 201 or Section 406 in order for adjustment assistance to be rendered. Such assistance flows from the separate determinations by the Secretaries of Labor and Commerce under the Trade Act of 1974. One important difference is the fact that in adjustment assistance proceedings the effect of imports on the industry as a whole is not at issue. The focus is on specific workers and specific

2. 19 U.S.C.A. § 2272.

3. Former Employees of Asarco's Amarillo Copper Refinery v. United States, 675 F.Supp. 647 (C.I.T.1987).

4. International Union, UAW v. Donovan, 592 F.Supp. 673 (C.I.T.1984).

5. United Rubber, Cork, Linoleum and Plastic Workers of America, Local 798 v. Donovan, 652 F.2d 702 (7th Cir. 1981).

6. See 19 U.S.C.A. § 2431.

7. 19 U.S.C.A. § 2341(c).

companies. Whenever the International Trade Commission commences an investigation for purposes of Section 201 escape clause proceedings, the Secretary of Labor is required to begin a parallel investigation as to the likelihood and number of workers who may be certified as eligible for trade adjustment assistance. The Secretary of Labor then compiles a report which is forwarded to the President along with the report of the International Trade Commission concerning the escape clause petition.

§ 15.13   Trade Adjustment Assistance—Secretary of Labor Determinations

The Circuit Court of Appeals for the District of Columbia has indicated that when the Secretary of Labor determines worker eligibility for trade adjustment assistance, it is appropriate to ask whether the buyers of the imports alleged to have caused injury have decreased their purchases from the employer in question. Such decreases, combined with evidence of increases in purchases of imported glass, supported the conclusion that imports contributed importantly to unemployment at a glass plant.[1] When deciding whether imports have increased for purposes of making these determinations, the Secretary of Labor can limit consideration to the immediate preceding year as a base period in the absence of any valid reason to consider a different year.[2] The Secretary of Labor cannot deviate from past practices focusing on the immediate preceding year. To do so may result in reversible error.[3] In deciding what constitutes "an appropriate subdivision" for purposes of worker eligibility, the Secretary of Labor must demonstrate clear reasons for such decisions. In a case where the Secretary took the position that a subdivision could never be larger than a plant, this decision upon review was remanded for clarification of the underlying reasons.[4] On the other hand, the Secretary's determination that the appropriate subdivision could only be that which produces articles which are like or directly competitive with imports was not erroneous and withstood challenge on appeal.[5]

In making determinations as to worker eligibility, the Secretary of Labor is given a subpoena power.[6] It is no defense to such

§ 15.13

1. United Glass and Ceramic Workers of North America, AFL–CIO v. Marshall, 584 F.2d 398 (D.C.Cir.1978).

2. Paden v. U.S. Department of Labor, 562 F.2d 470 (7th Cir.1977).

3. Katunich v. Donovan, 594 F.Supp. 744 (C.I.T.1984), *appeal after remand* 599 F.Supp. 985 (1984).

4. International Union, United Auto., Aerospace and Agricultural Implement Workers of America, UAW v. Marshall, 584 F.2d 390 (D.C.Cir.1978), *appeal after remand* 627 F.2d 559 (D.C.Cir.1980).

5. Paden v. U.S. Department of Labor, 562 F.2d 470 (7th Cir.1977).

6. 19 U.S.C.A. § 2321.

subpoenas that the information requested is confidential.[7] No prior judicial determination of the nature of the materials and their possible exemption from disclosure under the Freedom of Information Act is permissible.[8] Judicial review of worker eligibility determinations by the Secretary of Labor are now filed in the Court of International Trade. On review, the question is whether the findings of fact by the Secretary are supported by substantial evidence.[9] It has been said the Secretary's determinations will be reversed only if arbitrary or not based on substantial evidence.[10]

The Secretary of Labor may conduct investigations by mail rather than in the field when determining worker eligibility. This is not an abuse of discretion.[11] The Secretary of Labor is absolutely required to publish notice of the fact that he or she has received petitions for certification for eligibility for trade adjustment assistance benefits, and must publish a summary of the determinations on that petition in the Federal Register.[12] Any failure to do so will amount to substantial prejudice to the petitioners and a court order requiring further action by the Secretary.[13] However, a petition filed by only one worker where the record does not indicate that that person was an official or certified representative of a union or other worker representative does not impose upon the Secretary of Labor the duty to commence an investigation.[14] Once an investigation is commenced, the nature and the extent of the investigations are discretionary matters for the Secretary.[15] This means, for example, that petitioners do not have a right to a trial-type hearing with cross examination of the witnesses of the Department of Labor as part of the process of determining eligibility for trade adjustment assistance.[16]

The importation of fully manufactured televisions sets was held not directly competitive with a manufacturer of printed circuit boards and other parts used in televisions. The workers at a plant which produced those parts were therefore not entitled to trade adjustment assistance.[17] Shipyard workers who customized various

7. Usery v. Whitin Machine Works, Inc., 554 F.2d 498 (1st Cir.1977).

8. Id.

9. Id.

10. United Glass and Ceramic Workers of North America, AFL–CIO v. Marshall, 584 F.2d 398 (D.C.Cir.1978).

11. Abbott v. Donovan, 570 F.Supp. 41 (C.I.T.1983), *appeal after remand* 588 F.Supp. 1438 (1984).

12. Woodrum v. Donovan, 544 F.Supp. 202 (C.I.T.1982), *rehearing denied* 4 C.I.T. 130 (1982).

13. Id.

14. Former Employees of USX Corp. v. United States, 660 F.Supp. 961 (C.I.T. 1987).

15. Cherlin v. Donovan, 585 F.Supp. 644 (C.I.T.1984).

16. United Electric, Radio and Machine Workers of America v. Brock, 731 F.Supp. 1082 (C.I.T.1990), *appeal after remand* 14 C.I.T. 818 (1990).

17. Morristown Magnavox Former Employees v. Marshall, 671 F.2d 194 (6th Cir.1982), *cert. denied* 459 U.S. 1041, 103 S.Ct. 458, 74 L.Ed.2d 610 (1982).

parts failed to show an increase in imports of such articles causing a decrease in their business and therefore were ineligible for trade adjustment assistance.[18] The question of whether imports contribute importantly to worker unemployment is a critical one in trade adjustment proceedings. A large number of the cases taken up on judicial review suggest that the Secretary's determinations on these questions will be ordinarily upheld.[19] Coal miners, for example, were ineligible to receive trade adjustment assistance as a result of increased importation of steel into the United States. Coal could not be regarded as a substitute or directly competitive with steel.[20] Likewise, handknitting yarn was held not like or directly competitive with cotton and synthetic sewing thread. This caused the workers in question to be ineligible for trade adjustment assistance.[21]

Services do not appear to be covered by worker adjustment assistance programs. Thus it was held that airline services are not "articles" within the meaning of the statute.[22] Likewise, former employees of an independently owned automobile dealership were not entitled to assistance since they were engaged in service activities that did not produce an import-impacted article.[23] Workers at a shipyard who were mainly involved in repair and maintenance and thus did not produce or create articles as required for trade adjustment assistance were similarly ineligible.[24]

---

18. Pemberton v. Marshall, 639 F.2d 798 (D.C.Cir.1981).

19. See Local 167, International Molders and Allied Workers' Union, AFL–CIO v. Marshall, 643 F.2d 26 (1st Cir.1981); International Union, United Auto., Aerospace and Agricultural Implement Workers of America v. Marshall, 627 F.2d 559 (D.C.Cir.1980); Former Employees of CSX Oil and Gas Corp. v. United States, 720 F.Supp. 1002 (C.I.T.1989); Former Employees of Asarco's Amarillo Copper Refinery v. United States, 675 F.Supp. 647 (C.I.T.1987).

20. United Mine Workers of America v. Brock, 664 F.Supp. 543 (C.I.T.1987).

21. Kelley v. Secretary, 626 F.Supp. 398 (C.I.T.1985).

22. Fortin v. Marshall, 608 F.2d 525 (1st Cir.1979).

23. Miller v. Donovan, 568 F.Supp. 760 (C.I.T.1983). Accord Woodrum v. United States, 737 F.2d 1575 (Fed.Cir. 1984).

24. Pemberton v. Marshall, 639 F.2d 798 (D.C.Cir.1981).

Chapter 16

UNITED STATES EXPORT CONTROLS

Table of Sections

§ 16.1   Governance of Exports

Unlike the control of imports, the law regulating exports is briefer and relies on the issuance of extensive regulations. For example, the statutes prohibiting U.S. persons from assisting boycotts against friendly nations fill only a few pages. But the regulations and examples of prohibited and permissible conduct fill many pages in the Code of Federal Regulations. The control of exports, meaning their limitation, quite expectantly creates some conflict by way of the diminished economic benefit to the United States that may be gained from export trade. Indeed, the Export Administration Act in its statement of policy indicates that it is only after consideration of the impact of restrictions on the economy that export restrictions are adopted, and only to the extent necessary.[1]

Exports are controlled for three reasons stated in the governing rules—(1) to protect against the drain of scarce materials and reduce inflation from foreign demand, (2) to further U.S. foreign policy and (3) to assure national security.[2] These goals are expressed in the principal export enactment, the Export Administration Act (EAA), and are implemented by means of licensing requirements.[3] But the EAA does not contain many substantive provisions regulating exports. They are contained in the Export Administration Regulations (EAR). These regulations constitute an extensive set of provisions detailing the governance of exports.

§ 16.2   The Meaning of a "License"

Prior to 1996 changes, exporters sent items abroad under either a "general" license or a "validated" license. The general license was used for most exports and it did not require prior Department of Commerce approval. When most goods were shipped and a "Shipper's Export Declaration (SED)" was filled out, the SED constituted a general license. Validated licenses were issued upon application to the Department of Commerce.

The current regulations eliminate the terms "general license" and "validated license". "License" refers to an authorization to export granted by the Department of Commerce. The change is to some degree a matter of semantics. General licenses, which were in a sense "self-granted", are abolished in favor of referring to such exports as exports permitted without any license. The new "license" replaces the old "validated license." But much more was accomplished in the rearrangement of the regulations. The myriad

---

§ 16.1

1. 50 U.S.C.A.App. § 2402.

2. 15 C.F.R. § 730.6.

3. The EAA of 1979 has been amended several times. It expired in 1994 but has been kept in force ever since by the President declaring a state of emergency under the International Emergency Economic Powers Act (IEEPA). 50 U.S.C.A. §§ 1701–1706. The President is required to report to Congress every six months on the national emergency. The report is more an outline of changes in export rules and actions taken than a disclosure of any conditions which any "reasonable man" might conclude constitute a national emergency.

The Congress and the President have allowed the EAA to expire because of the continuing conflict regarding control over export trade between the Congress and the President. Unhappy with what Congress presents as a new framework, that often grants little discretion to the President, the President may veto the new act and allow the provisions of the old act to remain in force under the International Emergency Economic Powers Act, while waiting for a "better" new law from Congress which does not so severely limit discretionary power of the President to curtail exports to countries for U.S. foreign policy reasons. Legislators annually predict that it will be passed "this year".

of "special" licenses has been redone. There are now ten general prohibitions making up Part 736, rather than the previous scattering of the prohibitions throughout the regulations. These prohibitions indicate the circumstances where a license must be obtained.

§ 16.3   Export Administration Regulations

The Export Administration Regulations[1] govern most export activity, including the issuance of licenses. The regulations are implemented and enforced by the Bureau of Industry and Security (BIS). The regulations include helpful provisions for the exporter, that attempt to explain the regulations in simple terms. The regulations introduce the exporter to considerable new terminology.[2] The export of some commodities and technical data is absolutely prohibited, while other commodities are permitted to be exported under a range of lenient to severe restrictions. Special provisions of the EAA apply to further control the proliferation of missiles, and chemical and biological weapons.[3] The EAR has integrated the role of the former Coordinating Committee for Multilateral Export Controls (COCOM), a group of nations which sought to keep sensitive material from communist dominated nations. COCOM was abolished soon after the Soviet Union was dismantled.[4] The United States enacted the Enhanced Proliferation Control Initiative (EPCI), motivated by the Iraq conflict. This enactment seeks to establish greater control where commodities or technical data are destined for a prohibited nuclear, chemical or biological weapons or missile development use or end user. Considerable emphasis is placed on making the exporter aware of the nature of the buyer and where the items are going.

The Department of Commerce has considerable discretion to allow or block exports where they are subject to licensing. In addition, certain *items* may be subject to mandatory controls, just as certain *destinations* may be subject to mandatory controls (e.g., a boycott that disallows most or all exports). Actually these mandatory controls allow some deviation, usually by the President rather than an agency exercising discretion. Some examples of mandatory controls include the Nuclear Non–Proliferation Act regulations governing exports that have nuclear explosive capability, unprocessed timber under the Forest Resources Conservation and Shortage Relief Act (FRCSRA 1990), oil for purposes of conservation or to establish reserves, and oil from certain locations such as the North Slope of Alaska. Exports are thus subject to a mix of

§ 16.3

1. 15 C.F.R. §§ 730–774.

2. Terms are defined in 50 U.S.C.A.App. § 2415, and in 15 C.F.R. § 772.

3. 50 U.S.C.A.App. §§ 2410b and c.

4. COCOM expired in 1994. It has been replaced by the Wassenaar Arrangement, discussed below in § 16.34.

regulations *by* different persons or agencies, *of* different products, *for* different purposes, and *to* different places.

§ 16.4 Steps for Using the Export Administration Regulations

Part 730 provides a general introduction to the EAR. It outlines the scope of the regulations, statutory authority, defines "dual use" exports (generally civil versus military), other agencies which participate in the regulation of exports, extraterritorial application of regulations, purposes of control, and limited situations requiring licenses. Part 732 includes the 29 steps for using the EAR. They include an overview, steps regarding the scope of the EAR, the ten general prohibitions, License Exceptions, Shipper's Export Declaration and other documents and records, and other requirements.

The overview notes some important questions to which the exporter must give thought, such as—What is the item?, Where is it going?, Who will actually receive and use it?, and What will it be used for?[1] This will help the exporter determine whether the EAR are applicable. The first six steps regarding the scope of the EAR cover (1) items subject to the exclusive jurisdiction of another federal agency; (2) publicly available technology and software; (3) reexport of U.S. origin items; (4) foreign made items incorporating less than a de minimis level of U.S. parts, components and materials; (5) foreign made items incorporating more than a de minimis level of U.S. parts, components and materials, and (6) foreign made items produced with certain U.S. technology for export to specified destinations.

§ 16.5 General Prohibitions[1]

If an export is subject to the EAR, the general prohibitions, as well as the License Exceptions, must be reviewed to determine if a license is necessary. This part informs the exporter of both the facts that make the proposed transaction subject to the general prohibitions, and the nature of the general prohibitions.

§ 16.6 Determination of the Applicability of the General Prohibitions

Five factors help determine the obligations of the exporter under the ten general prohibitions.[1] They are:

    1. Classification of the item using the CCL.

§ 16.4
1. 15 C.F.R. § 732.1

§ 16.5
1. 15 C.F.R. Part 736.

§ 16.6
1. 15 C.F.R. § 736.2.

2. Destination of the item using the CCL and Country Chart.

3. End-user referring to a list of persons the exporter may not deal with.

4. End-use.

5. Conduct such as contracting, financing and freight forwarding in support of a proliferation project.

The ten general prohibitions follow, with commentary under the following headings:

1. General Prohibition One—Export and reexport of controlled items to listed countries (Exports and Reexports).

2. General Prohibition Two—Reexport and export from abroad of foreign-made items incorporating more than a de minimis amount of controlled U.S. content (Parts and Components Reexports).

3. General Prohibition Three—Reexport and export from abroad of the foreign-produced direct product of U.S. technology and software (Foreign–Produced Direct Product Reexports).

4. General Prohibition Four—Engaging in actions prohibited by a denial order (Denial Orders).

5. General Prohibition Five—Export or reexport to prohibited end-uses or end-users (End–Use End–User).

6. General Prohibition Six—Export or reexport to embargoed destinations (Embargo).

7. General Prohibition Seven—Support of Proliferation Activities (U.S. Person Proliferation Activity).

8. General Prohibition Eight—In transit shipments and items to be unladen from vessels or aircraft (Intransit).

9. General Prohibition Nine—Violation of any order, terms, and conditions (Orders, Terms, and Conditions).

10. General Prohibition Ten—Proceeding with transactions with knowledge that a violation has occurred or is about to occur (Knowledge Violation to Occur).

In preparing these prohibitions, the Commerce Department rejected a number of suggestions to liberalize existing reexport controls, such as to create a separate part for reexports. Reexports create a problem with the nation from which the item may be reexported, which nation may object to any extraterritorial application of the U.S. rules. Some comments noted that the new regulations were intended to be easier to use and less complex than the old, but that the new regulations created a system just as complex.

§ 16.7   Overview of Export Controls

The Commerce Control List (CCL—Part 774) is maintained by the BIS. The CCL includes all items (i.e., commodities, software, and technology) subject to BIS controls. The CCL does not include items exclusively governed by other agencies. But where there is shared governance, the CCL will note other agency participation. Knowing the Harmonized Code (customs classification for tariff purposes) Schedule B number does not help to determine whether or not an export license is required. That number is used by the Census Bureau for trade statistics. It is only the ECCN that will indicate whether or not an export license is required.

§ 16.8   The Commerce Control List (CCL)

The CCL is contained in Supplement No. 1 to Part 774. Supplement No. 2 to Part 774 contains the General Technology and Software Notes relevant to entries in the CCL. The CCL basic structure includes the following ten general categories:

0. Nuclear Materials, Facilities and Equipment and Miscellaneous

1. Materials, Chemicals, "Microorganisms," and Toxins

2. Materials Processing

3. Electronics

4. Computers

5. Telecommunications and Information Security

6. Lasers and Sensors

7. Navigation and Avionics

8. Marine

9. Propulsion Systems, Space Vehicles and Related Equipment

Within each of the above ten categories are five different groups of items, identified by the letters A through E, as follows:

A. Systems, Equipment and Components

B. Test, Inspection and Production Equipment

C. Material

D. Software

E. Technology

To classify an item the exporter determines the general characteristics that will usually be expressed by one of the categories. Having the appropriate category, the next step is to match the characteristics and functions with one of the groups. For example, a common television would be in category 3 and group A. The first digit and letter of the ECCN would thus be 3A.

This is followed by another digit that differentiates individual entries by the types of controls associated with the second digit. The Reasons for Control are as follows:

> *0.* National Security reasons (including Dual Use and International Munitions List) and Items on the NSG Dual Use Annex and Trigger List
>
> *1.* Missile Technology reasons
>
> *2.* Nuclear Nonproliferation reasons
>
> *3.* Chemical & Biological Weapons reasons
>
> *9.* Anti-terrorism, Crime Control, Regional Stability, Short Supply, UN Sanctions, etc.

There may be more than one reason for control of a particular item. If so the first digit in the above list would appear as the second digit in the ECCN. The third digit in the ECCN reflects the possible unilateral and multilateral controls.

§ 16.9 License Requirements, License Exceptions and List of Items Controlled Sections

Next to each ECCN is a brief description, followed by "License Requirements", "License Exceptions", and "List of Items Controlled" sections.

"License Requirements" identifies all possible Reasons for Control in order of precedence. Items within a particular ECCN number may be controlled for more than one reason. All the possible Reasons for Control are as follows:[1]

AT Anti–Terrorism

CB Chemical & Biological Weapons

CC Crime Control

EI Encryption Items

MT Missile Technology

NS National Security

NP Nuclear Nonproliferation

RS Regional Stability

SS Short Supply

XP Computers

SI Significant Items

§ 16.9
1. 15 C.F.R. § 738.2(d)(2)(i).

The applicable reasons appear in one of two columns in the License Requirements, entitled "Control(s)". The second column, entitled "Country Chart", identifies a column name and number for each applicable Reason for Control (e.g., CB Column 1). Once the exporter has determined that the item is controlled by a specific ECCN, information contained in the "License Requirements" section of the ECCN in combination with the Country Chart will allow a decision regarding the need for a license.

"License Exceptions" is used after it is determined that a license is required. It provides a brief eligibility statement for each ECCN-driven License Exception that may be applicable to the transaction. This is intended to help the exporter decide which ECCN-driven License Exception should be considered before submitting an application.[2] License Exceptions, the subject of Part 740, includes numerous categories. In the interim regulations, several exceptions were "bundled" under the grouping symbol LST (limited value shipments (LVS), shipments to group B countries (GBS), civil end-users (CIV), technology and software under restriction (TSR) and computers (CTP)). But objections by exporters with automated processes, who complained that an additional step was created, resulted in December 1996 changes which dropped the LST, "debundled" the process, putting each exception into its own section. This makes them similar to other separated exceptions (i.e., temporary imports and exports (TMP), servicing and parts replacement (RPL), governments and international organizations (GOV), gift parcels and humanitarian donations (GFT), some technology and software (TSU), baggage (BAG), aircraft and vessels (AVS) and additional permissive reexports (APR)). Part 740 is an extensive and important part of the EAR. It is followed by Supplement No. 1 to Part 740, which is the Country Group listing countries under A,B,D, or E, allowing the above exceptions to be limited to certain country groups.

"List of Items Controlled" defines the unit of measure applicable to the entry, may add definitions, notes related controls by other agencies or departments, and lists all items controlled by an entry.

§ 16.10   The Commerce Country Chart

The Country Chart is essential in determining the need for a license. It is useful in all cases except where short-supply reasons apply, or where there are unique entries.[1] The Country Chart is Supplement No. 1 to Part 738, and over several pages lists countries alphabetically. Territories, possessions and departments are

---

2.   15 C.F.R. § 738.2(d)(2)(ii).   § **16.10**

1.   15 C.F.R. § 738.3

not listed, but are subject to the same rules as the governing country. On the right of the listed countries are the numerous columns identifying the various Reasons for Control. There may be one, two or three columns under a particular Reason for Control. They correlate to references in the License Requirements section of the applicable ECCN. There may be an "x" in one or more of the cells. Where it appears in more than one cell, there will be multiple reviews.

§ 16.11   Determining the Need for a License[1]

Having determined that the item to be exported is controlled by a specific ECCN number, the exporter uses information in the "License Requirements" section of the ECCN entry in combination with the Country Chart. The need for a license is thus determined. Using the CCL "Controls" the exporter learns the reasons for control. Turning to the Country Chart and finding the appropriate country and the heading(s) for the reason(s), and with the column identifiers from the ECCN, the exporter looks for an "x". If found in the cell on the Country Chart, the exporter knows a license is required. A license application must be submitted unless a License Exception applies. Turning to the License Exceptions in the ECCN entry list, if a "yes" appears a further search of Part 740 will disclose whether an exception is available. Where there is no "x" in the cell on the Country Chart, a license is not required for control and destination, but one or more of General Prohibitions Four through Ten may prohibit the export. One can thus go to Parts 758 and 762 for information on export clearance procedures and record keeping.

§ 16.12   Advisory Opinions

A party who wishes to know whether a license is required may obtain an Advisory Opinion from the BIS.[1] Receipt of an opinion does not mean the subsequent application will be granted, opinions are not binding. But the BIS is likely to help the applicant in the preparation of an application which will meet the Advisory Opinion's requirements. An applicant may wish to avoid asking for an Advisory Opinion for fear that the opinion will be unfavorable. But if an export is made without an opinion and is in violation of the law, the sanctions may be severe.[2] Certainly, obtaining an unfavorable opinion and then exporting without a license creates a rather clear case of intent to disregard the law. But the Advisory Opinion

§ 16.11
1. 15 C.F.R. § 738.4.

§ 16.12
1. 15 C.F.R. § 748.3.

2. Persons convicted of a violation of any statute specified in § 11(h) of the EAA may not apply for any export license for ten years. 15 C.F.R. § 748.4(c).

is a good route to follow. If an unfavorable opinion is received, the BIS may explain what is required to obtain permission, unless the case is a clear one where no exports are permitted.

Support documents may be required along with an application.[3] Numerous countries are exempt from the need of support documents, mostly (1) any exports or reexports in the Western Hemisphere, (2) sales to government purchasers, and licenses submitted under special procedures, such as by A.I.D., or under the Special Comprehensive License procedure. When support documentation is required, the required data is to gain information about the disposition of the items, and to answer questions about national security controls and certain destinations. The transaction may require an End–User Certificate, or a Statement of Ultimate Consignee and Purchaser.[4]

§ 16.13   Issuance and/or Denial of Applications[1]

Part 750 describes the BIS's process for reviewing a license application, including processing times, denials, revocations, issuance, duplicates, transfers, and shipping tolerances on approved licenses. The part also includes information on processing Advisory Opinion requests.

The BIS undertakes a complete review of the application, including an analysis of the license and support documentation, plus a consideration of the reliability of each party to the transaction, including any intelligence information. The Departments of Defense, Energy, State and the Arms Control and Disarmament Agency may also have review authority. Furthermore, the BIS may request review by other departments or agencies, which may agree to review, or waive review.

If there are disputes between or among agencies within the U.S. government,[2] they are dealt with by various internal groups initially. Appeals are made to the Export Administration Review Board, chaired by the Secretary of Commerce. The Secretary may discuss the most difficult cases with the Secretaries of Defense, State or Energy. Final review goes to the President.

There has been a continuing dispute between Commerce and State over control of technology that seems to fall within the jurisdiction of each department. While the Arms Export Control Act gives State exclusive authority to issue jurisdiction determinations,

---

3. 15 C.F.R. § 748.9.

4. See also 15 C.F.R. § 748.10–13, and Supplements.

§ 16.13

1. 15 C.F.R. Part 750.

2. Where there is initial disagreement, some 85% are settled by informal discussion.

Commerce has attempted to obtain concurrent authority to issue commodity jurisdiction determinations. Hearings were held in 1995 by the Senate Armed Services Committee after complaints that Commerce had issued export licenses for stealth technology that was under the jurisdiction of State. State intervened to stop the shipments, determined that they had jurisdiction, and denied the license. This kind of dispute has made it difficult to reach agreement on a new Export Administration Act. With proposals to abolish Commerce and transfer much of its export jurisdiction to State, the issue could become moot. There is little likelihood that State will agree to the transfer of any authority to Commerce.

Delay has been used by the government, especially by the Department of Defense, as a means of discouraging exports which might be permissible, but to which the Department objects. The *Daedalus Enterprises, Inc. v. Baldrige* case is an example.[3] Twenty-nine months after the filing of an application, the Department of Commerce had not reached a decision. The company had to seek a court order that the Secretary comply with the statutory timetable. There is little a company can do. It may not export the goods when the time period has expired if no response has been made by the government. It must go to court at each stage when the government fails to comply with the statute. Fortunately, the *Daedalus* case is an exception, and this kind of delay has been much diminished. The filing process is considerably improved. Furthermore, the President in 1996 made a major transfer of authority over encryption devices from the Department of State to the Department of Commerce.

§ 16.14 Timetable for Application Review

The BIS is required to resolve all applications, or refer them to the President, within 90 calendar days from the date of registration by the BIS. That is the date the BIS enters the application into the electronic license processing system.[1] Where there are deficiencies, the BIS tries to contact the applicant to obtain needed information. If no contact is made, the license is returned with notations of the deficiencies. This may cause a suspension in the processing time. If another department or agency is involved, or if government-to-government assurances or consultations are involved, there are additional time requirements for making requests and analyzing their results. When certain countries are involved, such as Congressional designated terrorist supporting nations, Congress may have to be notified, delaying the application for another 60 days.

---

3. 563 F.Supp. 1345 (D.D.C.1983).

§ 16.14
1. 15 C.F.R. § 750.4.

§ 16.15   Issuance of a License[1]

A license is issued for a transaction, or series of transactions. The application may be approved in whole or in part. A license number is issued and a validation date. The license number must be used when preparing a Shipper's Export Declaration (SED), and in discussing the license with the Department of Commerce. Non-material changes may be made without obtaining a "Replacement" license.

§ 16.16   Revocation or Suspension of a License[1]

All licenses may be revised, suspended, or revoked. This may occur without notice when the BIS learns that the EAR have been violated or are about to be violated. The exporter may have to stop a shipment about to be made, or if possible one that is already en route. When revocation or suspension occurs, the exporter is required to return the license to the BIS. Appeals from actions taken under the EAA or the EAR by the BIS are allowed for most actions.[2] There is an internal appeal process prior to appealing to the federal courts.

§ 16.17   Review of Export Applications by International Agencies

In December, 1995, 28 nations,[1] including the United States, agreed to establish a new export control regime that would assume some of the functions of the expired COCOM. The Wassenaar Arrangement on Export Controls for Conventional Arms and Dual–Use Goods and Technologies (the organizational meeting was in Wassenaar, the Netherlands; the secretariat was established in Vienna) fell short of U.S. expectations, not containing a requirement of prior notification of sales by one country to other countries in the group. A second concern is the lack of agreement on prohibiting dual-use goods and conventional weapons to civilian as well as military end-users in such nations as Iran, Iraq, Libya and North Korea. An additional concern is the lack of transparency in exchanging information on exports of dual use goods and conventional arms.

§ 16.15

1.   15 C.F.R. § 750.7.

§ 16.16

1.   15 C.F.R. § 750.8.
2.   15 C.F.R. § 756.1.

§ 16.17

1.   Australia, Austria, Belgium, Canada, the Czech Republic, Denmark, Finland, France, Germany, Greece, Hunga-ry, Iceland, Italy, Japan, Luxembourg, the Netherlands, New Zealand, Norway, Poland, Portugal, the Russian Federation, the Slovak Republic, Spain, Sweden, Switzerland, Turkey, the United Kingdom, and the United States. Several other nations have since joined.

§ 16.18   Shipper's Export Declaration (SED)

The exporter is responsible for following the regulations that govern carrying out the export.[1] This is so whether a license is issued or the exporter relies on a License Exception. The most important responsibility is the proper preparation of the Shipper's Export Declaration (SED). The SED is a statement to the U.S. government used for gathering information to prepare trade statistics. Most exports require an SED, but most to Canada do not. Limited value (not over $500) mail shipments do not require an SED. As many as one-half the SEDs contain errors of omission or commission, according to the Bureau of Census and U.S. Customs Service. The two organizations have compared SEDs with outboard vessel manifests and discovered numerous inaccuracies in the vessel manifests as well as the SEDs. Cargo is often manifested not on the vessel actually carrying the goods, but on the manifest of a later departing vessel. The reason is the failure of exporters (and forwarders) to supply SEDs with complete and accurate information when the goods are shipped. This causes difficulties for Customs in detecting export law violations, and creates inaccurate trade statistics. The usual fine is up to $1,000, but sometimes shipments are detained. Unless voluntary compliance improves, Customs may delay or detain an increasing number of shipments unless SEDs are presented with complete and accurate information.

The Commerce Department conducts audits of SEDs to disclose violations of the export laws. The Customs Service screens SEDs and compares commodities and values. An internal compliance program is a common procedure within companies selling abroad to assure SEDs are proper. A single program is often useful to assure compliance with general export laws, antiboycott laws, specific country prohibitions (Cuba, Libya, etc.) and the Foreign Corrupt Practices Act.

§ 16.19   Fines, Suspensions and Revocation of Export Authority

Some means of enforcement is necessary to assure compliance with rules. The export laws and regulations are no exception. Violation of laws and regulations governing exports brings into play both the basic law and the regulations. The EAA contains provisions governing violations of both the EAA and EAR.[1] The Export Administrative Regulations contain supplementary provisions.[2] The general sanction for violations of the export laws, where the conduct was entered into *knowingly,* is a fine of the higher of $50,000

§ 16.18

1.   15 C.F.R. § 758.3.

§ 16.19

1.   50 U.S.C.A.App. § 2410.
2.   15 C.F.R. Part 764.

or five times the value of the exports.[3] This can obviously be *very* substantial.[4] *Willful* violations, with knowledge that the commodities or technology will be used to benefit, or are destined for, a controlled country, may result in a fine for business entities of the higher of $1 million or five times the value of the exports.[5] For individuals who engage in such willful violations the fine is $250,000 and/or 10 years imprisonment. This provision covers misuse of licenses. Cases involving violations of the licensing requirements tend to be quite complex.[6] If the party exported to a controlled country commodities or technology under a license with knowledge that the commodities or technology were being used for military or intelligence gathering purposes, and willfully fails to report this use, the business entity fine is the same as above, the higher of $1 million or five times the value of the exports, but for the individual the imprisonment drops to five years, with the fine remaining the same, $250,000.[7] Even possession of goods or technology either with the intent to export in violation of the law, or knowing that the goods might be so exported, can result in a fine.

Perhaps the most severe statutory penalty in the EAA is in the civil penalty section. The Department of Commerce may impose a fine of $10,000 for violations (in certain cases up to $100,000), and they may *suspend or revoke the authority to export.*[8] This is a most severe sanction, used only in extreme cases. It was used in the Toshiba dispute, where Toshiba (Japan) and Köngsberg (Norway) enterprises sold the Soviet Union technology allegedly useful for developing submarine propellers which would be sufficiently silent to avoid detection.[9] The result was enactment of the Multilateral Export Control Enhancements Act in 1988,[10] amending the EAA and providing trade prohibition sanctions for two to five years.[11] These sanctions are applied whether or not the other nations take action against their companies. The EAR repeat and expand upon these statutory sanctions. They further add provisions dealing with "causing, aiding, or abetting" a violation,[12] and "solicitation and attempt", and "conspiracy."[13] Further details are provided address-

3. 50 U.S.C.A. App. § 2410(a).

4. See United States v. Ortiz de Zevallos, 748 F.Supp. 1569, 1573 (S.D.Fla. 1990), *judgment reversed* 994 F.2d 1526 (11th Cir.1993).

5. 50 U.S.C.A. App. § 2410(b)(1).

6. United States v. Pervez, 871 F.2d 310 (3d Cir.1989); *cert. denied* 492 U.S. 925, 109 S.Ct. 3258, 106 L.Ed.2d 603 (1989).

7. 50 U.S.C.A. App. § 2410(b)(2).

8. 50 U.S.C.A. § 2410(c).

9. See Robert van den Hoven van Genderen, Cooperation on Export Control Between the United States and Europe: A Cradle of Conflict in Technology Transfer? 14 N.C.J.Int'l L. & Com.Reg. 391 (1989).

10. It was part of the 1988 Omnibus Trade and Competitiveness Act. See 50 U.S.C.A.App. § 2410a.

11. 50 U.S.C.A.App. § 2410a.

12. 15 C.F.R. § 764(2)(b).

13. 15 C.F.R. § 764(2)(c) & (d).

ing misrepresentation and concealment of facts, or evasion,[14] failing to comply with reporting and record keeping requirements',[15] alterations of documents,[16] and acting contrary to the terms of a denial order.[17]

The political nature of export controls is emphasized by judicial refusal to agree to a settlement negotiated between a company accused of violations of the export laws and the Justice Department. In one instance a bargained for $1 million fine was rejected by the court, which imposed a $3 million fine.[18]

§ 16.20 Administrative Proceedings and Denial Orders

Administrative procedures which supplement the Administrative Procedures Act, are the subject of a separate Part of the EAA and EAR.[1] They provide the framework for proceedings dealing largely with denial of export privileges and civil penalties. Appeals are the subject of several parts of the regulations.[2] The denial of export rights occurs principally either as an administrative sanction for violation of the EAR; or as a temporary measure when there is evidence of an imminent violation of the EAR. A denial order prohibits the party from any exports, unless there are exceptions in the order. The denial order states the extent to which exports are restricted. Because all denial orders are not the same, it is important to read carefully any specific denial order to determine the extent of the denial.

The denial order also affects persons dealing with the denied party.[3] The denied party may not be part of a transaction nor receive any benefit from a transaction. What are subject to regulation are essentially items of U.S. origin, or foreign items which require reexport permission. A person who deals with a denied party is not innocent if there is no knowledge of the denial status; everyone is responsible for knowing that any person with whom they engage in transactions is *not* on the denial list.

14. 15 C.F.R. § 764.2(g) & (h).

15. 15 C.F.R. § 764.2(i).

16. 15 C.F.R. § 764.2(j).

17. 15 C.F.R. § 764.2(k).

18. United States v. Datasaab Contracting A.B., (D.D.C.Criminal No. § 84–00130, 4–27–84).

§ 16.20

1. 50 U.S.C.A.App. § 2412; 15 C.F.R. Parts 756, 764, and 766. One court has held that attorneys' fees of a prevailing defendant are not allowable under § 2412, because Congress did not make the equal Access to Justice Act part of the EAA. See Dart v. United States, 961 F.2d 284 (D.C.Cir.1992).

2. 15 C.F.R. Part 764. See Iran Air v. Kugelman, 996 F.2d 1253 (D.C.Cir. 1993).

3. It could even limit employment of a denied party, to the extent that the party could not engage in transactions subject to the EAR.

Licensed items to be shipped to a denied party may place the exporter at risk. The denial order must be checked to determine the extent of the loss of export privileges *if* the sale to the denied party is a product to be reexported, or it releases controlled technical data to a denied foreign national. A person may buy products from a denied party in the United States, however, unless the intention is to subsequently export the product, which would give a "benefit" to the denied party. A transaction within a foreign country may be prohibited, as the foreign recipient of U.S. origin items may not sell them to a denied party even if the sale occurs within the foreign nation.[4] This purportedly applies whether the foreign firm is a U.S. subsidiary or not.

4. This is not likely to be acceptable to the foreign country, which is likely to consider the prohibition an unreason- able extension of U.S. laws into its territory. A foreign court might order the transaction to take place.

Chapter 17

THE FOREIGN CORRUPT PRAC-
TICES ACT AND ILLEGAL
PAYMENTS ABROAD

Table of Sections

§ 17.1 Foreign Policy–Based Laws—The Antiboycott Laws and the FCPA

Two special sets of laws that affect exports and foreign investments address specific foreign policy issues. First, the antiboycott laws and regulations (chapter 18) were enacted to reduce U.S. participation in the Arab nations' boycott of Israel. Second, the Foreign Corrupt Practices Act of 1977 (FCPA) was enacted to reduce U.S. participation in making certain payments or giving of items of value to foreign government officials in an attempt to influence government decisions. These are two examples of laws enacted to achieve political, as opposed to international trade, goals.

§ 17.2 History of the FCPA

The FCPA resulted from disclosures made to the Special Investigator of the Watergate investigations that many U.S. corporations had made payments to foreign officials to influence official government decisions affecting the companies. The FCPA is a response to real and perceived harm to U.S. foreign relations with important, developed friendly nations, and the interest of the United States to prevent U.S. persons from making payments which might embarrass the United States in conducting foreign policy. SEC investigations disclosed a large number of payments by U.S. corporations to foreign officials. Names of alleged recipients were disclosed, causing considerable embarrassment (Prince Bernard of the Netherlands), and even withdrawal or removal from office (Prime Minister Tanaka of Japan[1]), of national leaders. Ultimately, many consent agreements were concluded between the U.S. government and U.S. companies charged with making questionable payments. The agreements usually provided that names of foreign officials who received payments would be held confidential if the companies would disclose the payments. Considerable debate ensued in the press, generally attacking the U.S. companies and including little about the way business was conducted in many other nations, where bribes were not only commonplace but a precondition to doing business. There were legitimate concerns that several large U.S. corporations' payments had been extremely harmful to U.S. foreign relations. Some new legislation was inevitable. Morality was at stake. Many foreign observers, especially from other major exporting nations, did not object to the proposed legislation. Preventing U.S. persons from

§ 17.2

1. Lockheed was alleged to have paid $1.4 million to Prime Minister Tanaka, which led to his removal and imprison-ment. See 134 Cong. Rec. S9617–18 (July 14, 1988)(quoting statement of Senator Proxmire).

making such payments would give foreign businesses a competitive advantage. Some foreign observers wondered why Americans needed to make such public disclosure of their moments of transgression. The inevitable legislation occurred in 1977 with the enactment of the FCPA.[2] It has had two principal amendments: in 1988 and 1998.

§ 17.3　Amendments in 1988

The 1988 amendments removed some of the strictness of the initial act.[1] The level of conduct required to violate the Act was altered in favor of U.S. business by substantial elimination of the "reason to know" standard when payments made to agents might be passed on to foreign officials. The amendment requires that payments to agents must have been knowingly made, and includes a definition of such knowledge. One leading proponent of the original provision in the Senate was so incensed at the change that he suggested that the new loophole established by the amendment was "big enough to fly a Lockheed through."

§ 17.4　Amendments in 1998

The FCPA was again amended in 1998, to comply with U.S. obligations under the 1997 OECD Convention on Combating Bribery of Foreign Officials in International Business Transactions.[1] The Convention included language, added to the FCPA, making it unlawful to make payments to gain "any improper advantage" in order to obtain or renew business. The FCPA was further amended to expand its scope to cover prohibited acts by "any person." The 1998 amendments both significantly expand who is covered and add an alternate jurisdiction provision. Domestic concerns other than issuers and "other" persons are now included, the latter making the FCPA cover all *foreign* natural and legal persons who commit acts while in the United States.[2] The amendments also reach payments by U.S. businesses and persons taking place wholly outside the United States, and payments to officials of international agencies. Finally, penalties for non-U.S. citizen employees and agents of U.S. employers and principals, previously limited to civil sanctions, now include the same criminal sanctions as for U.S. citizen employees and agents.

2. Pub.L. 95–213, 91 Stat. 1494, Dec. 19, 1977 (amending the Securities Exchange Act of 1934, 15 U.S.C.A. §§ 78q(b), 78dd, 78ff(a)).

§ 17.3

1. 15 U.S.C.A. §§ 78q(b), 78dd, 78ff(a).

§ 17.4

1. Pub.L. 105–366, Nov 10, 1998 (International Anti-bribery & Fair Competition Act).

2. 15 U.S.C.A. §§ 78dd–2, 78dd–3.

§ 17.5   Responses From Other Nations

Following the conclusion of the OECD Convention in 1997, several nations adopted domestic antibribery laws. But the number has been disappointing to the Convention's advocates. In the first year of the Convention, only 12 of 34 signatories enacted domestic laws to implement the Convention. But Japan's Ministry of International Trade and Industry (MITI) began immediately to adopt measures consistent with the OECD guidelines, and Canada enacted an antibribery law that adopted the OECD recommendation to prohibit tax deductions for bribes.

§ 17.6   Definitional Challenges

One difficulty with the FCPA is defining what constitutes a wrongful payment. Because the payment is made to a foreign official, cultural standards of that official's nation may affect the payment. Conflicts of interest by government officials are governed by very different notions in each countries. While apparently no foreign country has written laws permitting foreign officials to accept bribes to influence their conduct, the "operational code" or unwritten law of many countries makes that very conduct commonplace. The FCPA imposes a U.S. ethic on conduct in the United States and abroad by U.S. persons, and to conduct within the United States by foreign persons. But the FCPA does not prohibit bribes qua bribes: it prohibits only actions that violate the express language of the Act.

§ 17.7   Exempting Minor Payments

In defining conduct that violates the FCPA it was understood that certain minor payments to minor foreign officials for minor activities should not be condemned. The original act defined "foreign official" to exclude foreign employees "whose duties are essentially ministerial or clerical."[1] But the 1988 amendments altered this to specifically exclude acts that were "routine government action."[2] Only a few court decisions interpret the language of the FCPA, making the often uncertain meaning of the definitions in the amended law very important.

§ 17.8   Who Is Covered?

In addition to limiting prohibited payments to certain kinds of payments, the drafters of the Act also had to consider the scope of coverage regarding who would fall within the prohibitions of the Act. That meant both which persons would be subject to an action

---

§ 17.7

1.   15 U.S.C.A. § 78dd–1(b) (1977).

2.   15 U.S.C.A. § 78dd–1(b).

for making prohibited payments, and which persons abroad had to be the recipients of the payments for the transaction to be unlawful. The amendments in 1998 expanded the scope of coverage of payors, extending to "any person", natural or legal, United States or foreign, acting within United States territory. Omitted are foreign persons acting outside the United States. But as to payees the Convention mandates are quite narrow, and required no amendments to the FCPA. The Convention, for example, does not cover payments to political parties, party officials, or candidates (except in some one-party states). Such payments, however, are covered under the FCPA.

§ 17.9   Prohibited Payments

The FCPA made it unlawful for an issuer of registered securities under § 12 of the SEA, or an issuer required to file reports under § 15(d) of the SEA, to make certain payments to foreign officials or other persons. The FCPA also requires those issuers to maintain accurate financial records which would disclose such payments. The Act additionally extends the scope of prohibited payments to any issuer *or domestic concern* making use of the mails or any means or instrumentality of interstate commerce,[1] thus effectively extending the liability to all corporations, in a manner not unlike the insider trading provisions of § 10 of the SEA. These rules allegedly were based on a shareholder's right to know if its corporation books were inaccurate, if management used corporate money to violate U.S. or foreign laws, if bribes were paid with corporate funds, or if payments were made to consultants with no accountability as to the disbursements by the consultants.

The 1988 amendments retained much of the 1977 act's structure, but made very important changes and additions. The most significant and controversial change was removing the "reason to know" language from the provision regulating payments to third persons that might be passed on to government officials.[2] This language was replaced with a "knowing" standard for liability, and a complex definition of "knowing" violations.[3] The amendments in 1998 expanded the scope of prohibited payments by including payments made to secure "any improper advantage."

The current FCPA remains relatively concise. After establishing accounting standards,[4] it prohibits payments to certain foreign officials directly, or by way of third persons, when such payments

---

§ 17.9

1. 15 U.S.C.A. §§ 78dd–1(a), 78dd–2(a). The latter part also defines both "domestic concern" and "interstate commerce." See § 78dd–2(h)(1) and (5).

2. 15 U.S.C.A. §§ 78dd–1(a)(3), 78dd–2(a)(3) (1977).

3. 15 U.S.C.A. § 78dd–1(f)2.

4. 15 U.S.C.A. § 78m(b).

are for the purpose of influencing any act or decision of the foreign official,[5] inducing the foreign official to act or refrain from acting in violation of the official's duty,[6] inducing the foreign official to use influence with a foreign government or instrumentality to influence that government's or instrumentality's act or decision,[7] or to secure any improper advantage.[8] There is next an important exception for routine government action,[9] which is further defined in a separate section.[10] The Act then establishes as an affirmative defense, cases where the payment was lawful under the *written* laws of the foreign country, or was a "reasonable and bona fide expenditure."[11] The Act also defines of "foreign official", "public international organization", "knowing" and "routine governmental action."[12] Added in 1998 is a provision for alternative jurisdiction.[13] This provision extends jurisdiction to issuers and U.S. persons who are officers, directors, employees or agents (and shareholders acting on behalf) of issuers acting corruptly *outside* the United States, regardless of whether the act involved the use of the mails or any means or instrumentality of interstate commerce. "U.S. person" is defined. Concluding provisions of the Act consist of a penalty section with some exceptionally severe sanctions, including fines up to $1 million and ten years' imprisonment for individuals, and fines to $2.5 million for enterprises.[14]

§ 17.10   Accounting Standards

One approach used in the FCPA to discourage illegal payments is to require issuers subject to the SEA to maintain certain accounting records that assist in disclosing payments that might violate the other substantive sections of the FCPA. The original law generated considerable criticism about standards that threatened harsh penalties for even slight, incorrect accounting entries. The standards further required considerable documentation of foreign transactions. The 1988 amendments addressed what was a concern for "reasonable detail" and "reasonable assurances" in internal accounting controls, and indicate that the Act does not cover technical or insignificant errors in record keeping. Liability is to be imposed on persons who "knowingly circumvent or knowingly fail

---

5. 15 U.S.C.A. § 78dd–1(a)(1)(A)(i).

6. 15 U.S.C.A. § 78dd–1(a)(1)(A)(ii).

7. 15 U.S.C.A. § 78dd–1(a)(1)(B).

8. 15 U.S.C.A.§§ 78dd–1(a)(1)(A)(iii), 78dd–1(a)(2)(A)(iii), 78dd–1(a)(3)(A)(iii). The content of these provisions is essentially repeated in sections 78dd–2 and 78dd–3.

9. 15 U.S.C.A. § 78dd–1(b).

10. 15 U.S.C.A. § 78dd–1(f)(2).

11. 15 U.S.C.A. § 78dd–1(c).

12. 15 U.S.C.A. §§ 78dd–1(f), 78dd–2(h). Section 78dd–2(h) also defines "domestic concern" and "interstate commerce."

13. 15 U.S.C.A. § 78dd–1(g).

14. 15 U.S.C.A. § 78ff.

to implement a system of internal controls or knowingly falsify any book, record or account."[1]

§ 17.11   What Is Given?

The persons described above who are subject to the Act may not "make use of the mails or any means or instrumentality of interstate commerce *corruptly*" where the act is "in furtherance of" any one of several actions, including an:

1. offer,
2. payment,
3. promise to pay, or
4. authorization of the payment

"of any money", or an:

1. offer,
2. gift,
3. promise to give, or
4. authorization of the giving

"of anything of value."[1]

Thus, the Act divides numerous "giving" actions between giving either money or anything of value. The fact that something offered, promised or given has a very small value does not remove it from the Act. There is no *de minimis* exemption. The exemptions exist in *to whom* the item is offered, promised or given, or *for what purpose* the item is offered, promised or given.

§ 17.12   Acting "Corruptly"

The act of offering, promising or giving must be done *corruptly*. "Corruptly" is not defined in the Act. If all of the provisions are met, i.e., a payment is made to a defined foreign official and there is no statutory affirmative defense, does the government nevertheless have to prove that the act was done corruptly. Or does the giving to a foreign official where there is no statutory defense constitute a corrupt act? The word "corruptly" seems unnecessary; the FCPA prohibits certain conduct, about which persons might debate endlessly regarding whether it is corrupt conduct. One decision suggests that the word "corruptly" means that the court or jury determines whether the conduct violates the provisions of the Act, rather than meeting some external definition of "corrupt".[1] The

§ 17.10

1. 15 U.S.C.A. § 78m(b)5.

§ 17.11

1. 15 U.S.C.A. §§ 78dd–1(a), 78dd–2(a).

§ 17.12

1. See United States v. Liebo, 923 F.2d 1308 (8th Cir.1991).

party charged must be the one who acts corruptly; carrying out an employer's instructions might not be acting corruptly.[2] Thus, an employee of a U.S. aircraft-maintenance contractor who made a "gesture" to the chief of maintenance for Nigerian Air Force cargo planes, in the form of purchasing airline tickets for the official's honeymoon, after the contract was awarded to the U.S. company, was entitled to a new trial to determine whether the employee met the "corrupt" standard.[3]

An unusual comment in the Senate Committee Report on the 1977 Act stated:

> That the payment may have been first proposed by the recipient rather than the U.S. company does not alter the corrupt purpose on the part of the person paying the bribe. On the other hand true extortion situations would not be covered by this provision since a payment to an official to keep an oil rig from being dynamited should not be held to be made with the requisite corrupt purpose.[4]

This would be a useful defense where there is clearly an attempt to extort money from the company or individual. But it may be very difficult to prove, and may require the kind of dramatic case noted in the Senate Report.

§ 17.13 Foreign Official

The offer, promise or gift may not be made to any person in any one of three classes. One class is a payment to any *foreign official* if the offer, promise or gift is either (1) to influence an official act or decision, induce an act or omission in violation of lawful duty, or secure any advantage, or (2) to induce the use of the official's influence with a foreign government or instrumentality in order to "affect or influence" any act thereof, and where the ultimate purpose is assisting the issuer in either obtaining or retaining business, or directing business to any person.[1] The "obtaining or retaining" business language was discussed in *United States v. Liebo,* where the court held the standard had been met.[2] It later came before the court in *United States v. Kay,* where the Fifth Circuit found the "obtaining or retaining" business to mean more than bribes beyond payments sufficient only to "obtain or retain government contracts."[3] But it also held that bribes did not have to rise to the level of influencing awarding contracts to violate the Act.

---

2. Id.

3. Id.

4. Senate Report No. 114, 95th Cong. 10 (1977).

§ 17.13

1. 15 U.S.C.A. §§ 78dd–1(a)(1), 78dd–2(a)(1).

2. 923 F.2d 1308 (8th Cir.1991).

3. 359 F.3d 738 (5th Cir.2004).

In addition to defining "knowing", the Act offers some help in defining the term "foreign official."[4] A foreign official is any "officer or employee" of any foreign government, or department, agency or instrumentality thereof. "Official" is thus very broadly defined to include the lowest-level employee.[5] Also included are persons acting in an *official capacity* for or on behalf of a government or international organization. Added in 1998 were officers or employees of international organizations. The addition of international organizations substantially expands the scope of the FCPA. When payments to only foreign *government* officials were covered, it was necessary to define "government." That is not always easy. Some entities, such as the Vatican, the PLO, or a territory over which there is some government control, may or may not be considered governments.

§ 17.14 Foreign Political Party, Official or Candidate

An offer, promise or gift may not be made to any *foreign political party* or *official of that party* or *candidate for political office,* if it is (1) to influence such party in an official act or decision, induce an act or omission in violation of lawful duty, or secure any improper advantage, or (2) to induce the use of that party's influence with a foreign government or instrumentality to "affect or influence" any act thereof. The ultimate purpose must be to assist the issuer in either obtaining or retaining business, or directing business to any person.[1] "Candidate" may be difficult to define, since it may not be clear that a person is a candidate at the time of making a payment. The act does not specifically cover a person intending to become a candidate.

§ 17.15 Any Person "While Knowing"

An offer, promise or gift may not be made to any *person,* while *knowing* it will be offered, promised or given to (1) a foreign official, (2) a foreign political party, (3) an official of a foreign political party, or (4) a candidate for foreign political office, where the purpose is the same as in the first two sections above.[1] This third category of persons to whom payments are prohibited governs payments to persons hired as agents or consultants, but adds the very important requirement that a payment to such third party be

---

4. 15 U.S.C.A. §§ 78dd–1(f)(1), 78dd–2(h)(2).

5. But the exceptions for routine government actions are most likely to apply to payments to relatively low-level employees.

§ 17.14

1. 15 U.S.C.A. §§ 78dd–1(a)(3), 78dd–2(a)(3).

§ 17.15

1. 15 U.S.C.A. §§ 78dd–1(a)(3), 78dd–2(a)(3).

made "while knowing" that the money or item of value will be
passed on to a prohibited person. In the original Act, the language
was "knowing or having reason to know."[2] The "having reason to
know" language was the subject of continual criticism by business
persons, who believed it created an unfair and ambiguous standard
that placed the burden on the business to prove that its conduct
was proper. Although proponents of the original language lost the
fight to retain it in the 1988 amendments, added to the Act was a
broad definition of "knowing". The definition seems to be so broad
to possibly include within the definition of the word "knowing"
some actual "reason to know" criteria. The definition of "knowing"
states that knowing conduct is where either (1) the person is *aware*
of the conduct, that "such circumstance" exists, or the result is
"substantially certain" to occur, or (2) the person has a "firm
belief" that such circumstance exists or the result is substantially
certain to occur.[3] The provision then adds that the knowing standard is met if the person is "aware of a high probability" of the
existence of such circumstance, *unless* the person "actually believes" that such circumstance does not exist.[4] Does the "high
probability" language carry the knowing standard into the territory
of a reason to know standard? The definition certainly modifies
what might normally be considered a knowing standard, and will be
the subject of considerable debate when it comes to an argument
before the courts.

§ 17.16   De Minimis or "Grease" Payments

The FCPA might leave one with the sense that the Act extended far beyond what Congress initially wished to label as corrupt,
into the area of the myriad of minor "grease" payments made to
government officials (usually too nominal in amount to have a third
party involved) to do what they are supposed to do, but to do it in a
shorter period of time. Probably few persons who have crossed a
border into Mexico or further South driving a car filled with
personal belongings (but no illegal items) have not paid the customs
officials a few dollars to avoid having to unload every item, and to
speed the car on its way without a lengthy inspection. Probably
many business persons have paid a small amount to a customs
official to expedite the processing of goods needed for an impatient
customer. The FCPA needed some exception for "minor" payments,
without compromising its premise that "corrupt" payments ought
not be allowed. The result is that corruption has a *de minimis*
element, but it is not defined by dollar amount. Payments made to

2. 15 U.S.C.A. §§ 78dd–1(a)(3), 78dd–2(a)(3) (1977).

3. 15 U.S.C.A. §§ 78dd–1(f)(2)(A), 78dd–2(h)(3)(A).

4. 15 U.S.C.A. §§ 78dd–1(f)(2)(B), 78dd–2(h)(3)(B).

obtain or retain business are not minor payments. Furthermore, even *de minimis* payments may be subject to the accounting requirements.

§ 17.17 "Facilitating or Expediting Routine Governmental Action"

The original Act exempted payments to minor government officials for acts that were ministerial, using language to exempt payments to foreign government employees "whose duties are essentially ministerial or clerical."[1] The 1988 amendments changed that to create an exception for "facilitating or expediting" payments when the purpose is to "expedite or to secure the performance of a routine governmental action."[2] A "routine governmental action" is defined in the Act,[3] in four specific sections and one general subsection. Specifically allowed are payments made when:

1. obtaining permits, licenses or other official documents which are part of the process of qualifying to do business in the country,

2. processing such papers as visas and work orders,

3. providing police protection, mail pick-up and delivery, or scheduling inspections which are associated with the performance of a contract or related to transit of goods across country, and

4. providing telephone service, power and water supply, loading and unloading cargo, or protecting perishables from deterioration.

A final, fifth class encompasses "actions of a similar nature."

Specifically exempted from being considered a "routine governmental action" is any decision by a foreign official about the terms of a new contract, the awarding of such contract, continuing business, or any action by any official involved in the process of new or renewal business.[4]

There is a very large gap between what is specifically allowed and what is specifically disallowed. One of the least clear areas involves the extent to which foreign officials may be entertained. Entertaining is not always motivated solely by courtesy. Foreign officials are usually entertained as part of the process of receiving the award of a contract, or establishing or continuing a business. The line of legitimacy must fall somewhere between reasonable

---

§ 17.17

1. 15 U.S.C.A. § 77dd–1(b) (1977).

2. 15 U.S.C.A. §§ 78dd–1(b), 78dd–2(b).

3. 15 U.S.C.A. §§ 78dd–1(f)(3), 78dd–2(h)(4).

4. 15 U.S.C.A. §§ 78dd–1(f)(3)(B), 78dd–2(h)(4)(B).

expenses associated with normal business, and unreasonable expenses associated with unreasonable influence. Finding that line is helped by the special provisions providing affirmative defenses.[5]

§ 17.18   Lawful Under "Written" Laws

The FCPA establishes two basic classes of affirmative defenses. The first is when the payment, gift, offer or promise is lawful under the *written* laws and regulations of the foreign country.[1] Since nations uncommonly enact laws giving legitimacy to what may be common but corrupt practices of its officials, this section is likely to be of little use. Were it to allow payments where the *unwritten* laws, i.e., the expected and common practice, mandate payments, the loophole would be considerably wider than merely enough to fly a Lockheed through. To be safe, counsel should obtain an opinion in writing from foreign local counsel that identifies the written law or regulation that allows a payment. It is of course possible that payments may be allowed to political campaigns under local written law, but not personally to serving officials to influence their official decisions.

§ 17.19   "Reasonable and Bona Fide Expenditures"

The second specific affirmative defense is when the payment, gift, offer or promise is a "reasonable and bona fide expenditure, such as travel and lodging expenses" that a foreign official incurs, and which is related to either (1) the promotion, demonstration or explanation of products or services, or (2) the execution or performance of a contract.[1] While the first part of this section broadens the permissible payments, the second part narrows it. Noticeably excluded are such payments when the contract is being considered, either initially or for renewal. But a carefully crafted corporate policy might provide that even in the advance of obtaining a contract or having it renewed, payments to foreign officials are exclusively based on promotions, demonstrations and/or explanations relating to the performance of the contract if granted or renewed.

§ 17.20   Enforcement Authority

The severity of penalties for violations of the FCPA mandates close consideration of its provisions by all persons doing business abroad. Violations of the FCPA are dealt with principally by the SEC (which monitors the record keeping) and the Department of

---

5. 15 U.S.C.A. §§ 78dd–1(c), 78dd–2(c).

§ 17.18

1. 15 U.S.C.A. § 77dd–1(c)(1).

§ 17.19

1. 15 U.S.C.A. § 77dd–1(c)(2).

Justice (which enforces the antibribery provisions). Comparatively few actions have been brought by the Department of Justice and reached the appellate courts. One example, involving the International Harvester Company, alleged participation in a series of charges relating to dealings with officials of Petroleos Mexicanos (PEMEX), the national oil company.[1] But it is not only the largest U.S. corporations which have been the subject of actions. Another action involved an individual who owned a postage stamp concession for a Caribbean island and who paid for flights for citizens to return to the island to vote for the reelection of the president, allegedly to influence the government to renew the concession.[2]

Investigations are often reported in the news, suggesting that U.S. persons and companies have not ceased making payments to foreign officials.[3] Some of the most controversial allegations in the past few years involved IBM and Mexico in 1993, during the sensitive negotiations for the North American Free Trade Agreement.[4] An Iranian-born British businessman was retained by IBM to be its agent in a tender bid for a new air-control system in Mexico City. The agent alleged that soon after a meeting with several Mexican officials at which they tried to obtain a $1 million bribe, IBM's bid was rejected and the contract given to the French Thomson Company. The agents' subsequent public disclosure and numerous newspaper articles led nowhere, but caused a sensation in Mexico early in 1993. The Minister of Communications was ousted in a cabinet reorganization. The agent alleged that the Mexican government later tried to buy him off. IBM did not support the agent in his claims, and settled with the agent out of court. The whole episode illustrates many problems. The U.S. government showed no inclination to become involved or investigate the matter. There were foreign policy problems, NAFTA priorities, perhaps a sense that the whole story was not implausible, but a realization that this is how things work. Aliases or no names, secret meetings, finger pointing, and leaks to the press are all part of the game. No one seems to have asked how the French Thomson Company got the bid so quickly after IBM was rejected.

§ 17.20

1. The company pleaded guilty to conspiracy to violate the FCPA. See McLean v. International Harvester Co., 902 F.2d 372 (5th Cir.1990); McLean v. International Harvester Co., 817 F.2d 1214 (5th Cir.1987); Executive Legal Summary No. 5, Business Laws, Inc. 100.03 (Hancock ed., Oct. 1988).

2. Executive Legal Summary No. 5, Business Laws, Inc., 100.03, 100.04 (Hancock ed., Oct. 1988).

3. See, e.g., Some Weapons Makers Are Said To Continue Illicit Foreign Outlays, Wall St.J., Nov. 5, 1993, at 1, discussing GE, Teledyne Inc., Litton Industries, Inc., Loral Corp., and United Technologies Corp. problems.

4. See The Independent, August 29, 1993, Sunday Review at 2; The Financial Post, Oct. 27, 1993, at 13.

IBM was later again in the news regarding an investigation of bribes in Argentina to obtain a $250 million contract to modernize the computer system for the Banco de la Nación.[5] IBM allegedly paid bribes to CCR, a computer systems company, in connection with obtaining a contract with Nación, money which soon found its way into Swiss accounts.[6]

§ 17.21   Consent Decrees

Few of the cases investigated ever come to court.[1] Most cases are resolved by consent decrees. Corporations prefer to accept a negotiated fine rather than litigate in the federal courts.[2] Furthermore, corporations usually prefer to avoid the publicity accompanying charges of making foreign payments corruptly. There is also the problem that the payment usually occurs in a foreign country and proof of the payment is difficult to establish. The foreign country is not likely to assist in allowing discovery or taking depositions.

§ 17.22   Charges of Accounting and Illegal Payment Violations

More actions have been brought charging violations of the accounting provisions as opposed to making illegal payments. The proof of accounting violations is mostly available in the United States, where the corporate books are located. But the books often disclose little to auditors, since payments may be made to persons who appear to be legitimate foreign consultants, and thus are listed only as payments made to consultants, not to foreign officials.

§ 17.23   Additional Charges

Persons charged by the government with violations of either the accounting requirements or the payments provisions may face other charges. Competitors may brings claims under RICO, antitrust or direct FCPA theories. Employees who are dismissed for refusing to comply with orders to make foreign payments may bring unlawful discharge suits, usually in the form of a breach of contract action, or become whistle-blowers and tell all to the government.[1] Shareholders may initiate derivative suits. Finally, a

---

5. National Law Journal, Mar. 3, 1997, at B16.

6. Financial Times, Oct. 19, 1995, at 5.

§ 17.21

1. See United States v. McLean, 738 F.2d 655 (5th Cir.1984), *cert. denied* 470 U.S. 1050, 105 S.Ct. 1748, 84 L.Ed.2d 813 (1985).

2. The FCPA Reporter includes information regarding consent decrees and

guilty pleas. The names of corporations charged are well known, including such companies as Ashland Oil, General Electric, Goodyear International, International Harvester, and Lockheed Martin.

§ 17.23

1. A whistle-blower's experience at GE is described in Some Weapons Makers Are Said To Continue Illicit Foreign Outlays, Wall St.J., Nov. 5, 1993, at 1.

foreign government whose officials are offered bribes may take action.

§ 17.24   Penalties: Record Keeping and Accounting Violations

Section 78m(b) violations, the record-keeping and internal accounting-control standards section, may lead to penalties of $100 per day during the period in which the company fails to comply with the requirements. These are civil rather than criminal penalties. But where there is (1) a willful violation of the provisions, or (2) a willful and knowing making of a false or misleading statement in filed applications, statements or reports, a criminal penalty may be imposed of not more than $1,000,000, or not more than ten years imprisonment, or both.[1]

§ 17.25   Penalties: Illegal Payment Violations

Section 78dd–1 and § 78dd–2 violations for making illegal payments are governed in these two different provisions, for issuers and domestic concerns, respectively, and their officers, directors, agents and shareholders acting on behalf of the entity. Each section leads to the same levels of penalties.[1] The entities are subject to fines of not more than $2 million, and civil penalties of not more than $10,000. The officers, directors, employees, agents, and shareholders acting on behalf of the concerns are subject to fines up to $100,000, or five years' imprisonment, or both, if the violation was willful.[2] They are also subject to civil penalties up to $10,000, without the willful requirement. Any fine imposed on a person under the above provisions, criminal or civil, may not be paid by the company, directly or indirectly. These penalties illustrate that the government is serious about violations of the FCPA.[3]

§ 17.26   Review Process

The FCPA requires the Department of Justice to establish a procedure allowing persons to request an opinion about proposed activity that might create some FPCA concern.[1] The first step is for

§ 17.24

1. 15 U.S.C.A. § 78ff(a). An exchange may be fined up to $2,500,000. Proof of no knowledge of the rule or regulation will avoid imprisonment. Id.

§ 17.25

1. 15 U.S.C.A. §§ 78ff(c) and 78dd–2(g).

2. Only willful violations are subject to criminal penalties. See Trane Co. v. O'Connor Securities, 718 F.2d 26 (2d Cir.1983).

3. Two units of Litton Industries pleaded guilty in 1999 to fraud and conspiracy in making payments to obtain defense business in Greece and Taiwan. Litton agreed to pay $18.5 million to settle the matter (including an amount to reimburse the Department of Justice for the costs of the investigation).

§ 17.26

1. 15 U.S.C.A. §§ 78dd–1(e), 78dd–2(f). The review procedure is contained in 28 C.F.R. § 50.18.

the person or company to present to the Department of Justice details of the proposed transaction. The person or company may only rely upon a review letter signed by the Assistant Attorney General (or delegate) in charge of the criminal division. The procedure has not been used very often, possibly because of concern about identifying foreign officials and the consequences if the review request information is not held confidential.[2] The 1988 amendments provide more definitional information of what may be allowed, and may lead to even less use of the review procedure.

§ 17.27   When to Use Review Process?

The review process should be used when a company is clearly uncertain about the lawfulness of the proposed payments, and believes that the information it will provide to the Department will not be disclosed, or will not cause injury if disclosed, and that the protection afforded by the request outweighs the potential harm to the company if it does not disclose and is later challenged.

§ 17.28   Actions by the Government

The FCPA was drafted with the intent that the Department of Justice and the SEC would enforce the law. The former would challenge illegal payments and the latter record keeping and accounting procedures. That is the way the Act has functioned. But, as in the case of many federal laws, questions have been raised regarding the extent to which the FCPA creates private rights of action and other suits.

§ 17.29   Private Right of Action

There have not been many suits charging violations of the FCPA initiated by private individuals or companies against other private parties. One federal circuit court has held that there is no private right of action under the FCPA.[1] The case involved donations Philip Morris allegedly promised a Venezuelan Children's Foundation (the wife of the President of Venezuela was the president of the Foundation) for benefits to Philip Morris in obtaining

---

2. Furthermore, information provided in a review request might be used against the person in a criminal prosecution. See John W. Bagby, Enforcement of the Accounting Standards in the Foreign Corrupt Practices Act, 21 Am.Bus. L.J. 213 (1983).

§ 17.29

1. Lamb v. Phillip Morris, Inc., 915 F.2d 1024 (6th Cir.1990), *cert. denied* 498 U.S. 1086, 111 S.Ct. 961, 112 L.Ed.2d 1048 (1991). See also Citicorp

Int'l Trading Co., Inc. v. Western Oil & Refining Co., 771 F.Supp. 600 (S.D.N.Y. 1991) (applying the well established four-part Cort v. Ash test to determine that there is no private cause of action); Shields on Behalf of Sundstrand Corp. v. Erickson, 710 F.Supp. 686 (N.D.Ill.1989) (violations of financial and accounting controls do not give rise to private right); Lewis v. Sporck, 612 F.Supp. 1316 (N.D.Cal.1985) (same conclusion).

Venezuelan tobacco. Two U.S. tobacco producers sued Philip Morris for harm caused by the alleged violation of the FCPA (and antitrust law). The *Lamb* decision is influential and law in the Sixth Circuit, but may not be the last word on the issue.

§ 17.30   Employee Suits

If a company intends to make payments to foreign officials that appear likely to be in violation of the FCPA, the payments will obviously require acts by company employees. Very large payments are likely to be authorized and possibly made directly by senior officers. Other payments may be authorized by senior officials but be made by lower level employees who are in more frequent contact with the foreign officials. In some cases, the lower-level employees, such as sales or purchasing agents, decided upon and make the payments on their own. If executives have made a decision to make payments and delegate making those payments to another employee, the decision-makers are in jeopardy of the employee refusing to participate and, if dismissed for the refusal, bringing a lawsuit. The FCPA itself does not provide any basis for a corporate employee to bring a claim against the corporation where the corporation appears to have made the employee the scapegoat for allegedly unlawful payments.[1] The original 1977 Act included what was known as the Eckhardt provision, which did not allow actions to be brought against employees without first going against the employer. The amendments in 1988 reversed this and allow such actions. An employer may now urge the government to bring suit directly against the employee who made the payment, even if the payment was authorized by other higher-level officers. The possibility of a scapegoat is back. But the scapegoat employee may not be without a remedy. That employee is likely to be or soon become a *former* employee, and may have an action against the company.

Ashland Oil Inc., learned that firing an employee for refusing to make an illegal payment abroad is costly.[2] Ashland's vice-president William McKay was instructed but refused to make an illegal payment to an official in Oman. McKay later cooperated with SEC and IRS investigations of the payment. Another executive, Harry Williams, was sympathetic to McKay's attempt to change the corporate policy at Ashland. Both were soon no longer employed. They sued Ashland for wrongful discharge and received a verdict of nearly $70 million, later settled for $25 million. A key to the settlement was a provision in McKay's employment contract that

§ 17.30

1. McLean v. International Harvester Co., 817 F.2d 1214 (5th Cir.1987), *appeal after remand* 902 F.2d 372 (5th Cir.1990).

2. See Marshall Sella, More Big Bucks in Jury Verdicts, 75 A.B.A. Journal 69 (July 1989). See also Williams v. Hall, 683 F.Supp. 639 (E.D.Ky.1988).

he would not be compelled to make unlawful payments. It is an appropriate employment contract provision for an officer, because many states do not allow suits for termination in the absence of a contractual provision. Any suit commenced under such a contract provision would be based on the contract and not the FCPA. It would therefore not face the uncertain issue noted above of bringing private suits under the Act. Because it is a suit based on breach of the employment contract, it requires inquiry only regarding the company's act of demanding a payment that, if made, would be a violation.[3]

Teledyne Systems faced another possible use of the FCPA: whistle-blower suits. A significant military contractor, Teledyne became involved in several whistle-blower suits in the early 1990s. One filed by a former program manager for Teledyne in the Middle East alleged a payment to an Egyptian general to help obtain Air Force contracts.[4]

§ 17.31   Suits Charging Competitor With Violation of FCPA

A person or company believing that a competitor violated the FCPA and obtained business at the company's expense has several choices. First, a direct suit charging a violation of the FCPA may fail as in the case of the Philip Morris experience discussed above, because it is an attempt to bring a private cause of action.[1] Second, a suit might be based on violations of antitrust laws. A third choice is a violation of the Racketeer Influenced and Corrupt Organizations Act (RICO).[2] In each of the latter two actions, the corrupt payment would be *evidence* of the wrong alleged, but not used as the basis of the suit, and thus the suit would not fail as a disallowed private right of action. A fourth possible cause of action would be for tortious interference with a current or prospective business relationship.[3]

A RICO action was brought in *W.S. Kirkpatrick & Co., Inc. v. Environmental Tectonics Corp., Int'l.*[4] Environmental Tectonics was

---

3. See also Pratt v. Caterpillar Tractor Co., 149 Ill.App.3d 588, 102 Ill.Dec. 900, 500 N.E.2d 1001 (1986), *appeal denied* 114 Ill.2d 556, 107 Ill.Dec. 68, 506 N.E.2d 959 (1987), holding that the FCPA did not create a basis for a state claim of retaliatory discharge.

4. See At Teledyne, A Chorus of Whistle–Blowers, Business Week, Dec. 14, 1992, at 40.

§ 17.31

1. Lamb v. Phillip Morris, Inc., 915 F.2d 1024 (6th Cir.1990), *cert. denied*

498 U.S. 1086, 111 S.Ct. 961, 112 L.Ed.2d 1048 (1991).

2. 18 U.S.C.A. §§ 1961–1968.

3. See discussion in Citicorp Int'l Trading Co., Inc. v. Western Oil & Refining Co., Inc., 771 F.Supp. 600 (S.D.N.Y.1991).

4. 493 U.S. 400, 110 S.Ct. 701, 107 L.Ed.2d 816 (1990).

an unsuccessful bidder for a contract with the Nigerian Air Force. The company complained that Kirkpatrick had paid unlawful bribes to Nigerian officials. The company sued under the federal RICO statute. The court ruled that the act of state doctrine did not apply because the lawfulness of acts of a foreign government in its own territory were not at issue, but only the motives of foreign officials in accepting payments. The case was remanded. RICO thus may be an effective method for private suits involving violations of the FCPA, unless RICO is amended to diminish its scope.

As the incidents of such cases as the above, involving Ashland and Environmental Tectonics, become more common, companies may be more inclined to develop serious internal policies which are intended both to prevent company officials from making such payments abroad and to assure that they are in fact not made. Facing litigation by dismissed employees who refused to make illegal payments, and by competitors injured by such payments, companies may find it better to stop such payments rather than to attempt to hide them.

*

Chapter 18

UNITED STATES BOYCOTT AND ANTI–BOYCOTT LAW

Table of Sections

---

§ 18.1   Boycott and Antiboycott Laws

The United States engages in both boycott and antiboycott practices. In the past few decades the United States has boycotted or embargoed goods from or to such countries as Cuba, Iran, Iraq, Libya, Nicaragua, North Korea, South Africa, Rhodesia and Vietnam. The effectiveness of these boycotts in achieving political goals has been widely debated.[1] The U.S. boycotts have not all been unilateral. It has engaged in collective sanctions when many others

§ 18.1

1. See Gary C. Hufbauer, Jeffrey J. Schott & Kimberly Ann Elliot, Economic Sanctions Reconsidered (1990).

have joined, such as the U.N. trade boycott against Iraq after the invasion of Kuwait,[2] or against Serbia and Montenegro after the Serbian-promoted invasion of Bosnia.[3] Less "collective" were the trade sanctions imposed on Argentina by the United States and the European Economic Community after the Argentine invasion of the Falklands/Malvinas Islands.[4]

The United States has engaged in boycotts when many have participated, such as the U.N. collective sanctions, and it has sometimes stood nearly alone among major nations in implementing boycotts, such as that directed to Cuba. Additionally, the United States has engaged in long term boycotts, notably against Cuba, and very brief boycotts, such as limits on exports to Europe which might be used in the construction of a gas pipeline from the USSR after the Soviet invasion of Poland. There is little doubt that in the future unilateral or collective boycotts will continue to be part of U.S. foreign policy.

The United States has only one significant experience with the use of antiboycott law. That is the Arab boycott of Israel. The law was adopted exclusively because of the Arab boycott of Israel. But nowhere does the law specifically mention either Arabs or Israel. Furthermore, the law is likely to remain on the books long after the Arab boycott ends. The law is directed to prohibiting U.S. persons from participating in or supporting boycotts by foreign nations against other foreign nations friendly to the United States.

§ 18.2   Boycott Laws and International Law

International law scholars have long debated whether boycotts violate international law.[1] But boycotts have been used frequently as an instrument of international law to achieve political goals,[2] such as actions by the United Nations. A primary boycott, which involves a curtailment of trade with another nation, generally is regarded as not constituting a violation of international law. But that view may differ when the boycotted nation is little more than

2. See United Nations Security Council Resolution 661 (1990).

3. See United Nations Security Council Resolution 757 (1992).

4. See Domingo E. Acevedo, The U.S. Measures Against Argentina Resulting from the Malvinas Conflict, 78 Am.J.Int'l L. 323 (1984).

§ 18.2

1. See, e.g., Margaret P. Doxey, Economic Sanctions and International Enforcement (1980); Christopher C. Joyner, The Transnational Boycott as Economic Coercion in International

Law: Policy, Place and Practice, 17 Vand.J.Transnat'l L. 205 (1984).

2. They may be referred to as "self-help" or unilateral measures. The Restatement (Third) of Foreign Relations Law addresses unilateral measures in § 905, as does the International Law Commission's Draft Articles on State Responsibility (Part Two), in Articles 12–14. Both assume similar approaches. Neither constitute law; they reflect the perceptions (and sometimes goals) of their drafters.

an economic dependent of the boycotting nation. Even when the boycott assumes secondary or tertiary characteristics, international law may not be violated. It is when the boycotting nation carries the boycott to a stage of economic warfare, such as a blockade, that it more readily conflicts with international law, especially when human rights issues arise. Further obscuring the issue is whether there must be some act by the nation boycotted which justifies the boycotting action of the other.[3]

A *blockade* of another nation may constitute a violation of international law, but some may be reluctant in labeling a blockade such a violation when it appears to be the only likely alternative to armed conflict. Few disagree as to the less harmful alternative, but that does not reject the idea that both may be violations of acceptable international conduct.

However elevated the argument over the norms of international law may soar to academic heights, nations will continue to use boycotts as instruments of foreign policy. The use of boycotts by the United States illustrates that it is quite an extensive, although perhaps not always effective, instrument of that policy.

§ 18.3   The Structure of United States Boycott Law

With whom the United States does not trade tends to be the decision of the President, although the Congress may act in special situations to deny trade benefits. Trade embargoes or other sanctions are often imposed quickly following some act which the U.S. President finds politically unacceptable. The Department of Commerce participates in the process of enforcing trade sanctions by controls on exports to various nations. Although the Congress governs foreign commerce and specifically *exports* by means of the Export Administration Act, Congress tends to leave to presidential discretion the imposition of sanctions against specific countries. This is not always the case, however. Congress may enact specific laws targeting particular nations. An example is the Cuban Democracy Act of 1992, which placed severe limitations on trade with Cuba, including trade by U.S. controlled subsidiaries abroad.[1] When Congress does act, it usually provides that its law will be carried out with additional regulations. The Export Administration Act has substantial regulations that are enforced largely by the Department of Commerce.

When the United States wishes to go further than to simply deny most favored nation status to a foreign nation, it may totally

---

3. A critical point is whether the boycotted state must have committed an illegal act. The majority view seems to be that the act need not be illegal, it may simply be "unfriendly."

§ 18.3

1. Pub.L. No. 102–484, §§ 1706–12, 106 Stat. 2315, 2578–81 (1992).

prohibit trade. Congressional action is likely to target a specific nation. When Congress prohibits trade, or delegates such authority to the President, there is a shift of much of the enforcement (and enactment of regulations) responsibility from the Department of Commerce to the Department of the Treasury. Part of the reason is that Treasury has an extensive framework of regulations governing the control of foreign assets.[2] The Office of Foreign Assets Control of Treasury has jurisdiction over a broad range of controls on transactions between U.S. persons and persons in foreign countries.[3] When those latter persons are in certain foreign countries, the controls may prohibit nearly any form of "transaction" or "transfer". A transaction or transfer may involve money or goods or services. Certain transactions or transfers may be absolutely prohibited, others may be subject to special licensing.[4]

The general regulations governing foreign assets control are followed by a series of mostly country-specific regulations.[5] These regulations vary in intensity of restrictiveness, but follow a general format including (1) the relation of the regulations to other laws and regulations, (2) what transactions are prohibited, (3) definitions, (4) interpretations, (5) licensing process, (6) reports, (7) penalties and (8) procedures. Some of the provisions are brief, others extensive. To give an idea of how these restrictions function, the experience of Cuba is outlined in the following section.

The Office of Foreign Assets Control has two forms of sanctions. One is financial sanctions and asset freezes. The second is trade and commercial embargoes. They may be used selectively or quite comprehensively. Selective sanctions may include blocking assets held in the United States, limitations on engaging in contracts, in travel, in transportation or even in exporting any goods or services. Selective sanctions have been used against various countries, including former "communist bloc" nations, South Africa, Iran and Angola. Comprehensive sanctions usually involve all the available options, and have been used against Cuba, Iran, Iraq, Libya, North Korea and parts of the former Yugoslavia.

The Cuban sanctions discussed immediately below represent the most severe sanctions yet adopted. They were partly used as a model for the 1996 Iran and Libya Sanctions Act, often referred to

---

2. 31 C.F.R. Parts 500–585.

3. For a clash of OFAC and the Constitution see Looper v. Morgan, 1995 WL 499816 (S.D.Tex.1995) (regarding the search of an attorney's briefcase upon entry to the United States in search of documents supporting violations of the Libyan sanctions).

4. Licensing is in 31 C.F.R. Part 500, subpart E.

5. The consolidation of regulations as of July 10, 2000, included specific regulations for Angola, Burma, Cuba, Iran (two parts), Iraq, Libya, Sudan and Yugoslavia (two parts: Bosnian Serb-controlled areas of Republic [part 585] and Kosovo [part 586]).

as the D'Amato Act.[6] This Act, following the Libertad Act, requires the President to impose sanctions against *foreign* companies that invest more than $20 million a year in the development of petroleum resource production in Iran, or more than $40 million in Libya. The proposed $2 billion investment in Iran by the French Total company in the late 1990s generated a conflict between France and the United States over possible sanctions, which the U.S. President did not impose, although he was under pressure to do so. If sanctions had been imposed, this matter quickly would have been taken to the WTO by the European Union on behalf of France.

Although the focus of this chapter is on federal law, in the past few years a number of state and local governments have adopted boycott provisions. The provisions for the most part limit government procurement for reasons of perceived violations of human rights (a principal target is Burma (Myanmar)), religious freedom (many countries), and the failure to deal with the return of Holocaust assets (Switzerland). These laws have created a separate (from federal sanctions) opposition among some foreign nations. The EU initiated a challenge under the WTO government procurement rules against a 1996 Massachusetts law addressed to Burma. Federal sanctions were authorized against Burma in 1997,[7] but the law did not discuss preemption. In a case against the Massachusetts law brought by the National Foreign Trade Council, the federal district court, the federal circuit court and the U.S. Supreme Court all held for the NFTC.[8] The federal ruling caused the EU to withdraw its action under the WTO dispute resolution procedures.

§ 18.4   Trade Restrictions: The Case of Cuba

The trade boycott of Cuba illustrates how the United States carries out a unilateral boycott. The Cuban boycott has endured longer than current sanctions against other nations. Furthermore, Cuba has received attention by Congress and the U.S. President of varying levels of forcefulness over the past three decades, often in direct relation to political campaigns.

The boycott of Cuba began as a response to the Cuban nationalization of all U.S. citizens' properties in 1959 and 1960,[1] and to

---

6. Pub.L. No. 104–172, 110 Stat. 1541 (1996).

7. Omnibus Consolidated Appropriations Act, Pub.L. No. 104–208, § 570, 110 Stat. 3009, 3009–166–167, on September 30, 1996.

8. National Foreign Trade Council v. Baker, 26 F.Supp.2d 287 (D.Mass.1998), *aff'd*, National Foreign Trade Council v. Natsios, 181 F.3d 38 (1st Cir.1999), *aff'd sub nom.*, Crosby v. National Foreign

Trade Council, 530 U.S. 363, 120 S.Ct. 2288, 147 L.Ed.2d 352 (2000)(holding Massachusetts' Burma law invalid under the Supremacy Clause because it threatens to frustrate federal statutory objectives).

§ 18.4

1. The expropriations effectively commenced under the Agrarian Reform Law on June 1, 1959, but did not reach

the trade agreement concluded by Cuba with the USSR in February, 1960. The U.S. Congress amended the Sugar Act of 1948 giving the President authority to alter the Cuban sugar quota. The President used this authority during the height of the July, 1960, bitterness to nearly totally remove the extensive quotas, leaving Cuba with no access to the U.S. sugar market. In October, 1960, the President imposed an extensive embargo on shipments of goods to Cuba, except for nonsubsidized food, medicines and medical supplies. With the cessation of diplomatic relations, the United States has continued the boycott without a break, but the intensity of the boycott has varied. The boycott provisions were amended in 1975 to allow foreign subsidiaries of U.S. companies to trade with Cuba. These amendments followed U.S. threats to tighten controls on foreign subsidiaries that caused several foreign governments to angrily denounce the policy, and even threaten nationalization of the companies. After 1975, U.S. subsidiaries abroad developed significant trade with Cuba. This trade angered anti-Castro groups in the United States, and led to the enactment of the Cuban Democracy Act in 1992. The Cuban Assets Control Regulations were amended to reflect the Act's strict provisions.

Proponents of the Cuban Democracy Act were also urging adoption of a much harsher act, which would allow litigation by current U.S. citizens who were Cuban nationals at the time of the Castro expropriations, seeking compensation from persons currently using expropriated properties. This became the Cuban Liberty and Democratic Solidarity (Libertad) Act (more commonly known as Helms–Burton), enacted in March, 1996,[2] only because of the emotions aroused due to the shooting down of two U.S. civilian aircraft by Cuba near Cuban territory. The Act included two very controversial sections. The first, Title III, created a right of action in U.S. courts for a U.S. national with a claim that Cuba expropriated property after January 1, 1959, against any person who is "trafficking" in such property. Trafficking is quite broadly defined, including not only such actions as selling, buying, leasing or transferring, but also engaging in a "commercial activity using or otherwise benefitting from confiscated property."[3] The Act authorizes the President to suspend the effectiveness of Title III actions for successive periods of six months. President Clinton issued such suspension every six months since August, 1996, throughout his term. These suspensions were the only reason the European Union kept on hold its request for a panel under the WTO to challenge the

---

their zenith until the resolutions issued under the authority of the major nationalization law of July, 1960. See Michael Wallace Gordon, The Cuban Nationalizations: The Demise of Foreign Private Property (1976).

2. Pub.L. No. 104–114, 110 Stat. 785 (Mar. 12, 1996).

3. Libertad Act § 4(13).

extraterritorial effects of the Libertad Act. The United States has stated that it would use the national-security defense under the WTO, and also in response to any similar challenge brought by Canada or Mexico under the NAFTA.[4] The second important part of the Act, Title IV, requires that the Secretary of State deny visas for entry into the United States to corporate officers, principals, shareholders and even the spouse, minor children or agents of such persons, if they are trafficking in or have confiscated property.[5] This authority has been used against officials of Canadian, Israeli and Mexican companies. Other nations and organizations have responded in very strong terms against the Libertad Act by adopting blocking laws and enacting resolutions.[6] Cuba enacted its own response to the Libertad Act, which, *inter alia*, denies any possible compensation in a future settlement with the government of Cuba to anyone attempting to take advantage of the Libertad Act by using the U.S. courts under Title III.[7]

The Cuban Assets Control Regulations, approximately four dozen pages and nearly 150 separate provisions, are the principal regulations which govern trade with Cuba. The application of the Regulations is limited by the Cuban Democracy Act, which removed administrative discretion in allowing some trade with Cuba from foreign subsidiaries. Furthermore, the Regulations may not conflict with the Trading with the Enemy Act,[8] or the Foreign Assistance Act of 1961, both as amended.[9] The administration of the Regulations is delegated to the Office of Foreign Assets Control (OFAC) of the Department of the Treasury.

The Regulations prohibit certain transactions and transfers, where Cuba or a Cuban national is involved. The scope is very wide, including various transfers involving (1) currency, securities, and

---

4. The use of the national security defense was strongly criticized in such a case, where there was no foreseeable security threat.

5. Id. at § 401.

6. See, e.g., Peter Glossop, Canada's Foreign Extraterritorial Measures Act and U.S. Restrictions on Trade with Cuba, 32 Int'l Lawyer 93 (1998); Mexico: Act to Protect Trade and Investment from Foreign Statutes which Contravene International Law, with Introductory note by Jorge Vargas, 36 Int'l Legal Materials 133 (1997); Douglas H. Forsythe, Introductory Note, Canada: Foreign Extraterritorial Measures Act Incorporating the Amendments Countering the U.S. Helms–Burton Act, 36 Int'l Legal Materials 111 (1997); Protecting Against the Effects of the Extraterritorial Application of Legislation

Adopted by the Third Country, E.U. Council Regulation 2271/96, 1996 O.J. (L 309), reprinted in 36 Int'l Legal Materials 127 (1997).

7. Ley de Reafirmacion de la Dignidad y Soberania Cubana (Ley No. 80), Dec. 24, 1996.

8. The original powers of the President were in the Trading With the Enemy Act (TWEA) of 1917. The President delegated authority to Treasury in accordance with the TWEA. The International Emergency Economic Powers Act (IEEPA) was enacted in 1988 and substantially replaced the TWEA. The authority of the President continues under the IEEPA.

9. 31 C.F.R. § 515.101.

gold or silver coin or bullion; (2) property or indebtedness; and (3) any form where the transfer is one which attempts to evade or avoid the first two prohibitions.[10] But the Secretary of the Treasury is given authority to authorize such transfers. Imports are prohibited if (1) Cuban in origin,[11] (2) the goods have been in Cuba (including transported through), or (3) made from any Cuban parts.[12] There are few exceptions to the trade restrictions. One is a limited exception allowing trade in informational materials, such as some books.[13] More recently cash sales of certain agricultural products have been allowed. The trade prohibitions conclude with a restriction that disallows (1) any vessel which has entered a Cuban port for trade purposes from entering a U.S. port for 180 days after the departure from Cuba, or (2) any vessel carrying goods or passengers to or from Cuba (or goods in which a Cuban has any interest) from entering any U.S. port with such goods or passengers on board.[14]

The prohibitions are followed by quite extensive definitions.[15] While nearly all of the definitions create little problem, one is of considerable importance to U.S. businesses with subsidiaries. A "person subject to the jurisdiction of the United States," upon whom the Regulations impose trade restrictions, includes, "any corporation, partnership, or association, wherever organized or doing business, that is owned or controlled by persons" citizen or resident of the United States or where an entity is organized under the laws of the United States.[16] The meaning of "owned" or "controlled" is not included in the Regulations. The focus of the Cuban Democracy Act is to limit trade with Cuba from foreign subsidiaries of U.S. corporations. It has brought negative responses from the European Union (and separately from member states of the EU), Canada, Argentina, Mexico and the U.N. General Assembly. It is one more example of the extraterritorial application of U.S. laws, and one more example of foreign rejection of such application.

Until this point, the Regulations are mostly prohibitory. But the next section contains important provisions covering "licenses, authorizations, and statements of licensing policy."[17] These provisions authorize the Secretary of the Treasury to issue licenses in a wide variety of circumstances, including (1) for certain judicial proceedings to take place, (2) to determine persons to be unblocked

---

10. 31 C.F.R. § 515.201.

11. See, e.g., United States v. Plummer, 221 F.3d 1298 (11th Cir.2000).

12. 31 C.F.R. § 515.204.

13. 31 C.F.R. § 515.206.

14. 31 C.F.R. § 515.207. These vessel restrictions were added to comply

with § 1706(b) of the Cuban Democracy Act.

15. 31 C.F.R. Subpart C.

16. 31 C.F.R. § 515.329(d).

17. 31 C.F.R. Subpart E.

nationals, (3) and to allow transfers by operations of law. The provisions of most importance for U.S. business interests allow some limited trade with Cuba by U.S. owned or controlled firms.[18] But it was this provision which was the principal focus of the Cuban Democracy Act, which reversed a decade old policy allowing Treasury to license foreign subsidiaries to trade with Cuba.[19] The current law prohibits the issuance of any such licenses to contracts entered into after the enactment of the Cuban Democracy Act. The governments of the foreign nations in which many U.S. subsidiaries are located, however, have enacted laws which mandate that the subsidiaries disregard the U.S. restrictions. It must be assumed that some trade continues, without any attempt to obtain a license.

The subsequent subpart governs reports, and requires reports by any person engaging in any transaction subject to the Regulations.[20] Thus, a U.S. company trading through a subsidiary may twice violate the law, first by trading and second by failing to report the trade. Penalties are contained in the next provisions,[21] and are severe. Fines may reach $1 million for willful violations, with a maximum of $500,000 as civil penalties. If experience with the antiboycott Regulations discussed below offers any parallel, consent decrees are likely to be the method used to respond to investigated violations. Just as the antiboycott provisions have not eliminated violations, these boycott provisions are unlikely to eliminate violations. That becomes even more clear when it is realized that with antiboycott violations there is no violation of foreign law when the violation of the U.S. law occurs. But in the case of these boycott Regulations, a U.S. firm in violation of some of the provisions may have a mitigating argument not present in the antiboycott situation—to comply with the U.S. law means violation of the law of the nation in which the U.S. subsidiary is incorporated and operating.

§ 18.5   United States Reaction to the Arab Boycott of Israel: The Antiboycott Laws

Two important historic events surrounding the conflict between businesses' freedom to export and the government's political goals led to special rules governing exports. The first was the Arab nations' extensive international primary, secondary and tertiary boycott of Israel.[1] The boycott is inconsistently applied by the Arab

---

18.   31 C.F.R. § 515.559.

19.   Cuban Democracy Act § 1706(a).

20.   31 C.F.R. § 515.601.

21.   31 C.F.R. Subpart F.

§ 18.5

1. A primary boycott is where one nation, for example, Oman, refuses to

deal with another, for example, Israel. The boycott is secondary when the boycotting nation (Oman) refuses to deal with any third party nation, such as the United States, if that nation deals with the boycotted nation, Israel. The tertiary boycott arises when the boycotting nation (Oman) refuses to deal with the third party nation (the United States), if

nations. Where the product or project is of high priority, the Arab nations either ignore their own boycott or grant a waiver.[2]

The Arab boycott of Israel led to the adoption of U.S. laws and regulations essentially prohibiting U.S. persons from complying with or supporting any boycott by a foreign nation against a nation friendly to the United States.[3] Nowhere in the law is there any direct reference to either Israel or any specific Arab nation, but these provisions owe their existence to a long and bitter struggle within Congress, and between Congress and the administration, over the creation of rules that would prohibit U.S. companies from assisting the Arab nations in their attempts to harm Israel.[4] Prior to the enactment of federal export laws dealing with the Arab boycott of Israel, several states enacted similar laws, and the federal tax and antitrust laws were used to deter U.S. companies from compliance with boycott requests. Although the boycott of Israel by the Arab nations is the reason the federal law exists, there has been some question raised about the applicability of the law to foreign boycotts against South Africa. The Department of Commerce interpreted the law as not applicable to the (since terminated) boycotts against South Africa. The law does affect many commercial relationships between U.S. persons and Middle Eastern governments, private individuals and banks.

The second event leading to special rules governing exports evolved from the discovery during the Watergate investigations that many U.S. companies had made payments to foreign officials to encourage those officials to purchase the goods of the company making the payments or extend other favors, such as allowing a foreign investment. Congressional reaction was much swifter than in the case of the Arab boycott. Congress adopted amendments to the securities laws to prohibit certain payments and regulate reporting of payments, in legislation called the Foreign Corrupt Practices Act.[5] Congress instead might have further amended the Export Administration Act to prohibit such payments, but the securities laws already addressed reporting and accounting requirements and that was one method used to regulate payments abroad.

---

any of the elements of its products are from a fourth party nation company (e.g., The Netherlands) which trades with the boycotted nation (e.g., Israel).

2. See Abrams v. Baylor College of Medicine, 581 F.Supp. 1570, 1576 n. 3, (S.D.Tex.1984) for an example of a waiver of the boycott regarding medical equipment from a blacklisted company.

3. Export Administration Act of 1979, 50 App.U.S.C.A. § 2407; Export Administrative Regulations, 15 C.F.R. Part 769.

4. The history of the boycott provisions is contained in Trane Co. v. Baldrige, 552 F.Supp. 1378 (W.D.Wis.1983). There are numerous references to Arab nations in the Supplements to 15 C.F.R. Part 769, which include interpretations of the regulations.

5. Foreign Corrupt Practices Act of 1977 (as amended in 1988 and 1998), 15 U.S.C.A. §§ 78q(b), 78dd, 78ff(a). The FCPA is the subject of the previous chapter.

The FCPA added new reporting and accounting requirements which would help identify payments abroad. Prohibiting certain payments abroad, the second part of the FCPA, could be monitored by a company's records of payments. Use of the securities laws additionally meant that the Department of Justice would be the agency to pursue violations. The antiboycott provisions were under the jurisdiction of the Department of Commerce, thought to be somewhat more lenient than Justice.[6]

§ 18.6   Export Administration Act

The Export Administration Act (EAA) governs the export of goods from the United States, including the antiboycott provisions. These antiboycott provisions, and the regulations, prohibit U.S. persons from participating in boycotts by a foreign nation against third nations that are friendly towards the United States. The statutory language is very broad, not unlike the concept of the U.S. antitrust laws. The EAA structure requires the President to issue regulations that prohibit any U.S. person from engaging principally in two different areas of activity, *refusals to deal* and *furnishing information*, if such actions further or support a boycott by one foreign nation against another foreign nation that is friendly to the United States.[1] There is a further provision that applies particularly to banks, that prohibits certain actions with regard to letters of credit which also may further or support a boycott. These prohibitions are included in six sections of the law.[2] The law subsequently states that the regulations should provide exceptions governing some six classes of activity.[3] Further mandated is reporting to the Secretary of Commerce any request to furnish information.[4] Violations of these provisions are subject to the same statutes that govern other violations of the export laws.

§ 18.7   Export Administration Regulations

Supplementing the EAA are Export Administration Regulations (EAR).[1] They include very extensive examples of conduct which provide guidance in determining whether specific conduct may constitute a violation of the EAA and EAR. Many of the examples are of common occurrences where companies are in jeopardy of refusing to deal or furnishing prohibited information. Use of these examples is essential to determining both the sense of

---

6. There have been attempts by businesses to shift the jurisdiction of the FCPA from Justice to Commerce.

§ 18.6

1. 50 App.U.S.C.A. § 2407(a)(1).

2. 50 App.U.S.C.A. § 2407(a)(1)(A)–(F).

3. 50 App.U.S.C.A. § 2407(a)(2)(A)–(F).

4. 50 App.U.S.C.A. § 2407(b)(2).

§ 18.7

1. 15 C.F.R. Part 769.

the administration in interpreting the law, and the likelihood that the conduct in question may be challenged. The examples in the regulations follow the pattern of the principal statute. Thus, the regulations begin (after a section with definitions[2]) with examples of the six classes of prohibited conduct,[3] and are followed by examples of the six classes of exceptions.[4] Following the regulations are a series of 16 Supplements that include Department of Commerce interpretations of various provisions, with some suggested contractual provisions that may avoid challenges by the Department.

§ 18.8   Prohibited Actions Must Be Done Intentionally

The purpose of the antiboycott provisions is to prohibit any U.S. person "from taking or knowingly agreeing to take [certain actions] with intent to comply with, further, or support any boycott" against a country friendly to the United States.[1] It specifically exempts boycotts pursuant to U.S. law. The requirement of intent is essential, but what constitutes intent may seem marginal. In *United States v. Meyer*,[2] the defendant Meyer was held to have knowledge that a form required by Saudi Arabia to have a trademark registered in that country was not used to obtain information needed for the registration, but to further the boycott of Israel. Meyer claimed that his actions were inadvertent and not intentional, but Meyer's knowledge and intention were rather clearly illustrated by his receipt of information from the Department of State that it could not notarize the form because of the boycott, and his subsequent acquisition of a notarization through the U.S.–Arab Chamber of Commerce.[3] The *Meyer* decision involves a rather clear attempt to find a way past the law. It is thus not very helpful for a case where the intent is based on less apparent criteria. But it does emphasize that *inadvertent* compliance is not a violation.

§ 18.9   Refusals to Deal

The first prohibition in the EAA is against directly refusing to do business with or in the boycotted country, or with a national or resident of that country. Also prohibited is any refusal to do business with the boycotted country by agreement with or response to requests from any other person.[1] This means a U.S. company

2.   15 C.F.R. § 769.1.

3.   15 C.F.R. § 769.2.

4.   15 C.F.R. § 769.3.

§ 18.8

1.   50 App.U.S.C.A. § 2407(a)(1).

2.   864 F.2d 214 (1st Cir.1988).

3.   A strong dissent inappropriately relied on an inapplicable case to argue that the required level of intent was not met.

§ 18.9

1.   50 App.U.S.C.A. § 2407(a)(1)(A).

may not refuse to do business with Israel at the request of the central boycott office of the Arab nations in Damascus. Intent to refuse to do business is not established by the absence of any business relationship with the boycotted country.

The Export Administration Regulations, which include ten subsections further defining the meaning of refusing to do business, expand upon this prohibition.[2] The regulations make it clear that a refusal to do business may be established by a course of conduct as well as a specific refusal, or by a use of any "blacklist" or "white-list". They emphasize, nevertheless, that intent to comply with or support a boycott is required. The regulations also suggest what does *not* constitute a refusal to do business, such as an agreement to comply generally with the laws of the boycotting country. There does not have to be an agreement not to do business. Compliance with a request, or a unilateral decision, if for boycott reasons, will suffice. These regulations raise one especially difficult issue—the use of a list of suppliers. The regulations give a specific example, although specific examples are usually left for the "examples" section.[3] A U.S. person under contract to provide management services for a construction contract may provide a list of qualified bidders for the client if the service is customary, and if qualified persons are not excluded because they are blacklisted.

The regulations and especially the examples disclose the nearly unlimited possible configurations of fact situations that may give rise to problems. Consider only a few possible variations, from which numerous additional variations may be easily considered:

1. A U.S. company is doing business in Israel, but wants to do business in Arab nations while retaining the Israel business. This creates a problem if the Arab nations have alternative sources for the goods, especially from companies in nations which do not have antiboycott laws, meaning essentially all other nations in the world.

2. Same as above but the company would like to terminate the business in Israel because:

   a. it believes in or doesn't really care about the boycott. The company is in danger of challenge by the Department of Commerce. But is a business likely to state that it believes in or doesn't care about the boycott?

   b. the Israel business is not as large as the potential Arab nations business and the company does not have the capacity to do business in both. As long as the decision is not boycott

---

2. 15 C.F.R. § 769.2(a). See also Supplements No. 6(a), 7, and 15(a) to Part 769.

3. 15 C.F.R. § 769.2(a)(6).

based, it is proper to drop the Israel business. But it may have to prove that its motives were business and not boycott based.

c. the company had planned to close the Israel business because it has been losing money. It had best be able to prove that loss.

3. The company trades with Arab nations and would also like to do business with Israel. It knows if it does do business with Israel it may lose the business with the Arab nations.

4. The same but the company is willing to drop the business with the Arab nations. It may do so without violating the boycott rules because Israel is not boycotting the Arab nations.

5. The company is doing business in both Israel and Arab nations. The Arabs do not know this. The company wants to drop the Israel business because it fears that the Arabs will learn of that business and terminate very profitable Arab business.

Prior to 1985–86, the focus of the Department of Commerce was on reporting violations. But in 1986 the Department, concerned with its limited resources, began to concentrate on the blacklist, religious discrimination and refusals to deal. These are viewed by the Department as the most serious violations.

The regulations attempt to cover many variations, but obviously cannot offer an example for each possible situation. Refusals to deal arise for reasons both directly related and totally unrelated to the boycott. When normally justified business reasons for refusing to deal begin to show a pattern of not dealing for reasons consistent with a boycott, however, the party is in some danger of a challenge from Commerce. But the law does include language of intent, which is most difficult to show from a pattern of conduct that indicates good business reasons for refusing to deal.

§ 18.10 Discriminatory Actions

The second statutorily prohibited conduct is refusing to employ or otherwise discriminating against any U.S. person on the basis of race, religion, sex or national origin, where such conduct is intentional and in furtherance of an unlawful boycott.[1] This section addresses the Arab nations' attempts to injure Jewish people wherever they may live, rather than to harm Israel as a nation. Thus, a company may not refuse to employ Jewish persons so that it may gain favor with Arab clients. In one of the few court decisions involving the antiboycott provisions, Baylor College of Medicine was

---

§ 18.10

1. 50   App.U.S.C.A.   § 2407(a)(B). Even if employment discrimination is

not boycott based, and thus not a violation of the EAA, it may violate other laws, such as civil rights legislation.

found to have persistently appointed non-Jewish persons for a project with Saudi Arabia.[2]

The antidiscrimination section of the EAA includes both refusals to employ and *other discrimination.* For example, a requirement that a U.S. company not use a six-pointed star on its packaging of products to be sent to the Arab nation would be a violation because it is part of the enforcement effort of the boycott. But it is not a violation if the demand is that no symbol of Israel be included on the packaging. The former is a religious symbol generally, the latter an acceptable request which does not include reference to any person's religion.[3] This illustrates a general attempt to acknowledge that the boycotting nations are entitled to have *some* control over what comes into their nation. They are entitled to say no imports may be stamped "Products of Israel", but they may not attack the Jewish religion more broadly by requiring certification that no religious symbols appear on any packages. The United States is attempting to say that the Arab nations may have a right to engage in a primary boycott against Israel, but they may not draw U.S. persons into supporting that boycott.

The regulations governing discriminatory actions make it clear that such actions must involve "intent to comply with, further or support an unsanctioned foreign boycott."[4] The regulations further state that the boycott provisions do not supersede or limit U.S. civil rights laws.[5]

§ 18.11   Furnishing Information Regarding Race, Religion, Sex or National Origin

The third specific prohibition relates to the refusal to hire for reasons of race, religion, sex or national origin, discussed immediately above. This provision prohibits furnishing information with respect to race, religion, sex or national origin.[1] This brief provision is supplemented by regulations that state that it shall apply whether the information is specifically requested or offered voluntarily and whether stated in the affirmative or negative.[2] Furthermore, prohibited information includes place of birth or nationality of the parents, and information in code words or symbols that would

2. Abrams v. Baylor College of Medicine, 581 F.Supp. 1570 (S.D.Tex.1984), *aff'd*, 805 F.2d 528 (5th Cir.1986). The case also deals with the issue of the right to bring a private action. Using the Cort v. Ash factors test the court held that there is an implied right under the EAA.

3. These are examples included in 15 C.F.R. § 769.2(b), examples (viii) and

(ix). See Supplement No. 6(b) & (c) to Part 769.

4. 15 C.F.R. § 769.2(b)(2).

5. 15 C.F.R. § 769.2(b)(3).

§ 18.11

1. 50 App.U.S.C.A. § 2407(a)(C).

2. 15 C.F.R. § 769.2(c)(2).

identify a person's race, religion, sex or national origin.[3] The regulations also reaffirm the element of intent.[4]

The examples in the regulations illustrate the difficulty of clearly defining "prohibited information". If the boycotting nation requests a U.S. company to give all employees who will work in the boycotting nation visa forms, and these visa forms request otherwise prohibited information, the company is not in violation for giving the forms to its employees or for sending the forms back to the boycotting country party. This is considered a ministerial function and not support of the boycott. But the company may not itself provide the information on race, religion, sex or nationality of its employees, if it meets the intent requirement. The company might certify that none of its employees to be sent to the boycotting nation are women, where the laws of the boycotting country prohibit women from working. The reason for the submission has nothing to do with the boycott.

§ 18.12 Furnishing Information Regarding Business Relationships—The Use of "Blacklists"

The fourth prohibition is one that is often at issue. It involves the use of blacklists. The Arab nations maintain a blacklist of persons and companies with whom they will not do business. Arab nations often ask a prospective commercial agreement party to certify that none of the goods will include components obtained from any companies on the blacklist.

Persons are prohibited from furnishing information about an extensive list of business activities ("including a relationship by way of sale, purchase, legal or commercial representation, shipping or other transport, insurance, investment, or supply"[1]), with an equally extensive list of business relationships ("with or in the boycotted country, with any business concern organized under the laws of the boycotted country, with any national or resident of the boycotted country, or with any other person which is known or believed to be restricted from having any business relationship with or in the boycotting country"[2]). At the end is a statement that the section does not prohibit furnishing "normal business information in a commercial context as defined by the Secretary." Thus, clients are very extensively governed with regard to the flow of information between the company and the boycotting country.

The regulations develop this already expansive section.[3] The prohibited information may not be given whether directly or indi-

---

3. 15 C.F.R. § 769.2(c)(3).

4. 15 C.F.R. § 769.2(c)(4).

§ 18.12

1. 50 App.U.S.C.A. § 2407(a)(D).

2. Id.

3. 15 C.F.R. § 769.2(d).

rectly requested or furnished on the initiative of the U.S. person.[4] The Secretary's definition of normal business in a commercial context is that related "to factors such as financial fitness, technical competence, or professional experience" as might be normally found in documents available to the public, such as "annual reports, disclosure statements concerning securities, catalogues, promotional brochures, and trade and business handbooks."[5] Such public information may not be supplied if in response to a boycott request.[6] But it may be supplied if it could be used by the boycotting country to further the boycott—knowledge and intent on the part of the U.S. person is the key to making the furnishing of the information unlawful. There are numerous examples of this prohibition, many referring to use of blacklists. For example, a person may not certify that its suppliers are not on a furnished blacklist.[7] If a company is on the blacklist, or if it wishes to know whether it is on the blacklist, it may request such information.[8] That is not furnishing information. But if it furnishes information in order to be removed, it may be in violation. If a company believes it is on the blacklist but no longer would be listed were the Arab nations to know the true facts, supplying those facts may constitute a violation.[9] The same may occur when a company believes it is mistakenly listed, and wishes to make this known to the Arab nations. Companies have removed their names, but it must be done with great care.

The most publicized blacklist case involved Baxter International Inc., a large U.S. medical supply company.[10] As a result of an informant's disclosure, Baxter was investigated and charged with violating the EAA because of the way in which it attempted to have its name removed from the Arab blacklist.[11] Commerce was prepared to charge Baxter and a senior officer with providing over 300 items of prohibited information to Syrian authorities and a Saudi Arabian firm. The company and the officer admitted civil and criminal violations and were assessed total civil penalties of $6,060,-600—the highest at the time. The case would not have succeeded without the informant providing substantial documentation of the violations.

4. 15 C.F.R. § 769.2(d)(2)(ii).

5. 15 C.F.R. § 769.2(d)(3).

6. 15 C.F.R. § 769.2(d)(4).

7. 15 C.F.R. § 769.2(d) example (x).

8. 15 C.F.R. § 769.2(d) example (xv).

9. A U.S. subsidiary of the French cosmetics company L'Oreal provided the parent information to assist in removal from the blacklist. Providing this information and failing to report to the Commerce department led to L'Oreal agreeing to pay $1.4 million in civil penalties. See, e.g, Los Angeles Times, August 30, 1995, at Part D.

10. See, e.g., The Case Against Baxter International, Business Week, Oct. 7, 1991, pg. 106.

11. See 5 OEL Insider 7 (Dec. 1993).

§ 18.13 Prohibition of Intentional Evasion

The EAA and the regulations each include a section that states that no U.S. person may take any action with intent to evade the law.[1] Permitted activities are not to be considered an evasion of the law. An example of an evasion is placing a person at a commercial disadvantage or imposing on that person special burdens because that person is blacklisted or otherwise restricted from business relations for boycott reasons.[2] Another evasion may be use of risk-of-loss provisions that expressly impose a financial risk on another because of the import laws of a boycotting country, unless customarily used.[3] Two final suggested evasions are the use of dummy corporations or other devices to mask prohibited activities, or diverting boycotting country orders to a foreign subsidiary.[4]

§ 18.14 Reporting Requirements

Under the title "Foreign policy controls," the EAA includes very important provisions that require the reporting of the receipt of any request for the "furnishing of information, the entering into or implementing of agreements, or the taking of any other action" outlined in the policy section[1] of the EAA.[2] The receipt of any such request must be reported to the Secretary of Commerce. Failure to report boycott-associated requests is perhaps the most frequent violation of the EAA. The report must include any information the Secretary deems appropriate and must state whether the person intends to comply or has complied with the request. These reports are public records, except to the extent that certain confidential information is included that would cause a competitive disadvantage to the reporting person.

The regulations include quite extensive provisions, covering (a) the scope of reporting requirements, (b) the manner of reporting, and (c) the disclosure of information.

Scope of reporting requirements. Whenever a person receives a written or oral request to take any action in furtherance or support of a boycott against a friendly foreign country it must be reported. The request may be to enter into or implement an agreement. It may involve a solicitation, directive, legend or instruction asking for information or action (or inaction). The request must be reported whether or not the action requested is prohibited, except as the

---

§ 18.13

1. 50 App. U.S.C.A. § 2407(a)(5); 15 C.F.R. § 769.4; see also Supplement No. 12 to Part 769 for an interpretation dealing with use of an agent.

2. 15 C.F.R. § 769.4(c).

3. 15 C.F.R. § 769.4(d).

4. 15 C.F.R. § 769.4(e).

§ 18.14

1. 50 App. U.S.C.A. § 2402(5).

2. 50 App. U.S.C.A. § 2407(b).

regulations provide.[3] That essentially means reporting is required if the person knows or has reason to know that the purpose of the request is to enforce, implement or otherwise support, further or secure compliance with the boycott.[4]

When a request is received by a U.S. person located outside the United States (subsidiary, branch, partnership, affiliate, office or other controlled permanent foreign establishment), it is reportable if received in connection with a transaction in interstate or foreign commerce.[5] A general boycott questionnaire, unrelated to any specific transaction, must be reported when that person has or anticipates a business relationship with or in the boycotting country, also in interstate or foreign commerce.

The reporting requirements apply whether the U.S. person is an exporter, bank or other financial institution, insurer, freight forwarder, manufacturer, or other person.[6] If the information about a country's boycotting requirements is learned by means of the receipt or review of books, pamphlets, legal texts, exporter's guidebooks and other similar publications, it is not considered a reportable request. The same is true of receipt of an unsolicited bid where there is no intention to respond.[7]

The regulations including ten specific requests that are not reportable. They were added because of the customary use of certain terms for boycott and non-boycott purposes, Congressional mandates for clear guidelines in uncertain areas, and the Department of Commerce's desire to reduce paperwork and costs. They are:[8]

   (i) request to refrain from shipping goods on a carrier flying the flag of a particular country, or that is owned, chartered, leased or operated by a particular country or its nationals or residents; or a request for certification to such effect;

   (ii) request to ship goods, or refrain from shipping goods, on a prescribed route, or a certification request of either;

   (iii) request for an affirmative statement or certification regarding the country of origin of goods;

   (iv) request for an affirmative statement or certification of supplier's or manufacturer's or service provider's name;

---

3. 15 C.F.R. § 769.6(a)(1).

4. 15 C.F.R. § 769.6(a)(2).

5. Id., citing 15 C.F.R. §§ 769.1(c) and (d). The definition of "interstate or foreign commerce" is the subject of a Department of Commerce interpretation in Supplement No. 8 to Part 769.

6. 15 C.F.R. § 769.6(a)(3).

7. 15 C.F.R. § 769.6(a)(4). A definition of "unsolicited invitation to bid" is included in Supplement No. 11 to Part 769.

8. 15 C.F.R. § 769.6(a)(5); see also Supplement No. 10(b) to Part 769.

(v) request to comply with laws of another country except where it requires compliance with that country's boycott laws;

(vi) request to individual for personal information about himself or family for immigration, passport, visa or employment requirements;

(vii) request for an affirmative statement or certification stating destination of exports or confirming or indicating the cargo will be unloaded at a particular destination;

(viii) request for certification from owner, master, charterer, or any employee thereof, that a vessel, aircraft, truck or other transport is eligible, permitted, nor restricted from or allowed to enter, a particular port, country or group of countries under the laws, rules, or regulations of that port, country or countries;

(ix) request for certification from insurance company stating the issuing company has an agent or representative (plus name and address) in a boycotting country; or

(x) request to comply with term or condition that vendor bears the risk of loss and indemnify the purchaser if goods are denied entry for any reason if this clause was in use by the purchaser prior to January 18, 1978.

The Department of Commerce periodically is to survey domestic concerns to determine the worldwide scope of boycott requests received by U.S. subsidiaries and controlled affiliates regarding activities outside U.S. commerce.[9] This is to cover requests that would be required to be reported but for the fact that they involve commerce outside the United States. Information collected from U.S. persons will include the number and nature of non-reportable requests received, action requested, action taken, and countries making such requests.

Manner of reporting requests. Every request must be reported; however, only the first need be reported when the same request is received in several forms.[10] But each different request regarding the same transaction must be reported. Each U.S. person receiving a request must report the request, but one person may designate another to make the report, such as a parent reporting on behalf of a subsidiary.[11]

Disclosure of information. The third part of the regulations applying to reporting states that the reports shall become public records, except for "certain proprietary information."[12] The reporting party may certify that the disclosure of information relating to the (1)

---

9. 15 C.F.R. § 769.6(a)(7).

10. 15 C.F.R. § 769.6(b)(1).

11. 15 C.F.R. § 769.6(b)(2).

12. 15 C.F.R. § 769.6(c)(1).

quantity, (2) description, or (3) value of any articles, materials or supplies (including technical data and other information), may place the company at a competitive disadvantage. In such case the information will not be made public. But the reporting party must edit the public inspection copy of the accompanying documents as noted below, and the Secretary may reject the request for confidentiality for reasons either of disagreement regarding the competitive disadvantage, or of national interest in not withholding the information.[13] If such decision is made, the party must be given an opportunity to comment.

Because the report is made public, one copy must be submitted intact and the other may be edited in accordance with the above limitations. Any additional material considered confidential may also be deleted, as may be any material not required to be reported.[14] The copy is to be marked "Public Inspection Copy."

§ 18.15 Violations and Enforcement

Violations and enforcement of the antiboycott laws are subject to the same provisions as violations and enforcement of the export laws.[1] The enforcement of the antiboycott laws has generated few court decisions. Most have involved issues of constitutionality, creation of private rights of action, or the statute of limitations.[2] Several persons have had licenses suspended and fines exceeding $5 million have been levied. Most of these cases involved the receipt of requests for information from Arab countries. In instances where the companies had complied with the request, the Department of Commerce and the company usually agreed on a fine as part of a consent decree. The procedures were dealt with administratively, and the decisions are found only in some private reporters.[3] One of the largest civil penalties was imposed in a settlement with Baxter International Inc., in 1993. Baxter, a Swiss subsidiary, and an officer paid a penalty of $6,060,600.

The Department of Commerce began in 1986 to emphasize what it considered the most serious violations, involving the blacklist, religious discrimination and refusals to deal. The number of reported court decisions remains very small. Although in the early

---

13. Id.

14. 15 C.F.R. § 769.6(c)(2).

§ 18.15

1. 50 App.U.S.C.A. §§ 2410, 2411 and 2412. See supra, chapter 17.

2. United States v. Core Laboratories, Inc., No. 3–54–09 51–C (N.D.Tex. July 24, 1984), aff'd 759 F.2d 480 (5th Cir.1985) (EAA and the statute of limitations); Abrams v. Baylor College of Medicine, 581 F.Supp. 1570 (S.D.Tex.

1984), aff'd 805 F.2d 528 (5th Cir.1986) (EAA and affirming private right of action); Bulk Oil (ZUG) A.G. v. Sun Co., Inc., 583 F.Supp. 1134 (S.D.N.Y.1983), aff'd 742 F.2d 1431 (2d Cir.1984), cert. denied 469 U.S. 835, 105 S.Ct. 129, 83 L.Ed.2d 70 (1984) (EAA and rejecting private right).

3. See Int'l Boycotts (Business Law Inc.); Boycott L. Bull.

1990s the number of reported Arab requests for information had diminished, cases such as Baxter illustrate that violations continue to occur.

U.S. subsidiaries that carry out boycott activities of foreign parents are within the reach of the provisions. The French L'Oreal, S.A. cosmetics company requested information from two U.S. subsidiaries, Parbel of Florida, Inc. (formerly Helena Rubenstein, Inc.) and Cosmair, Inc., about their business relationships in or with Israel. More than 100 items of information were provided, and no report of the request was made to Commerce. The two subsidiaries (and individual corporate counsel for Cosmair) agreed to fines exceeding $1.4 million in 1995.

§ 18.16   Private Right of Action

As is the case with so many laws, there is no clear indication whether the EAA includes a private right of action. A federal district court in Texas, in *Abrams v. Baylor College of Medicine,*[1] addressing a claim by two Jewish medical students that Baylor University denied them opportunities when it excluded Jews from medical teams it sent to Saudi Arabia, found an implied right of action by applying the factors in the *Cort v. Ash* decision of the U.S. Supreme Court.[2] The Fifth Circuit upheld the decision. But in *Bulk Oil (ZUG) A.G. v. Sun Co.,* the Second Circuit rejected the existence of a private right of action, affirming a New York federal district court decision involving an accusation of violation of the antiboycott provisions by failing to deliver oil to Israel.[3]

§ 18.16

1. 581 F.Supp. 1570 (S.D.Tex.1984), *aff'd* 805 F.2d 528 (5th Cir.1986).

2. 422 U.S. 66, 95 S.Ct. 2080, 45 L.Ed.2d 26 (1975).

3. 583 F.Supp. 1134 (S.D.N.Y.1983), *aff'd* 742 F.2d 1431 (2d Cir.1984), *cert. denied* 469 U.S. 835, 105 S.Ct. 129, 83 L.Ed.2d 70 (1984).

Chapter 19

UNITED STATES SECTION 301 PROCEEDINGS—SUPER 301 AND SPECIAL 301 PROCEDURES

Table of Sections

§ 19.1 Foreign Country Practices and Market Access

Section 301 of the Trade Act of 1974 is one of the most highly political remedies concerning United States trade relations. Basically, this section applies when United States rights or benefits under international trade agreements are at risk or when foreign nations engage in unjustifiable, unreasonable or discriminatory conduct. Thus Section 301 is primarily focused on the activities of foreign governments. Although it has been used to protect United States markets from foreign imports, Section 301 has been most notably applied to open up foreign markets to United States exports, investments and intellectual property rights. The focus has been on foreign market access for U.S. goods and services.

Most Section 301 proceedings have been resolved through negotiations leading to alteration of foreign country practices. Ultimately, if the President or United States Trade Representative (USTR) is not satisfied with any negotiated result in connection with a Section 301 complaint, the United States may undertake unilateral retaliatory trade measures. Unlike subsidy, dumping, escape clause and market disruption proceedings, Section 301 of the Trade Act of 1974 has no origins in or other imprimatur of legitimacy from the GATT/WTO. Indeed, the unilateral nature of Section 301 is thought by many to run counter to the multilateral approach to trade relations. Brazil lodged but did not actively pursue a complaint about Section 301 during the Uruguay Round negotiations.

Although the U.S. has been a strong supporter of the GATT over the years, Section 301 reflects U.S. frustration with multilateral methods and procedures. It has received hostile responses from United States trade partners, especially after the amendments to Section 301 implemented in 1988 through the Omnibus Trade and Competitiveness Act. These amendments include the so-called "Super 301 Procedures" and the "Special 301 Procedures" discussed below. The offenses under Section 301 are now primarily subject to the authority of the United States Trade Representative as opposed to the President. The 1988 Act also introduces the concept of mandatory versus discretionary retaliation. Offenses for which retaliation is mandatory involve the breach of international agreements to which the United States is a party and unjustifiable trade practices. The USTR has discretionary authority to retaliate under Section 301 regarding unreasonable or discriminatory practices of foreign countries.

Late in 1999, a panel of the World Trade Commission concluded that Section 301 was not inconsistent with U.S. obligations under the WTO (WTO/DS 152/1). The panel relied heavily on President Clinton's Congressionally approved statement that the U.S. would refrain from Section 301 retaliation until the WTO has ruled on disputes falling within its domain. Should some future U.S. administration fail to adhere to this policy, the WTO panel indicated that Section 301 would violate the WTO Dispute Settlement Understanding.

§ 19.2   The Evolution of Section 301

The origins of Section 301 can be traced to a trade dispute between the United States and the European Community (now Union) during the 1960s. This dispute became known as "the Chicken War." Basically, United States chicken producers had mechanized and developed a large export market in the European Union. The Union sought to protect its smaller chicken producers and did so by establishing a minimum price for imported chicken. This had the effect of drastically curtailing United States exports into the European market. At that time, there was no vehicle through which the United States growers could express their complaints over this practice. Nevertheless, the United States government sought to resolve the dispute through the nullification and impairment provisions of Article XXIII of the GATT. These attempts failed and ultimately the United States imposed unilateral trade restraints upon European Union exports as a matter of compensation for the minimum import price program. In the Chicken War, the retaliatory tariffs concerned brandy, trucks and potato starch. These trade restraints, while arguably compensating the United States as a nation, did little to satisfy the chicken exporters. In other words, the remedy was not linked to the source of the complaint, a reality that remains in Section 301 law.

As the Chicken War was in progress, the Trade Expansion Act of 1962 was adopted. Section 252 of that Act specifically authorized the President to retaliate against foreign import restrictions imposed in breach of GATT obligations. Furthermore, the President was authorized to impose higher tariffs or other import restraints on the products of countries that established burdensome restraints upon U.S. exports of agricultural goods. The latter could be imposed regardless of whether the import restraints of the foreign country constituted a breach of the GATT. Section 252 of the Trade Expansion Act of 1962 thus preceded and anticipated Section 301 of the Trade Act of 1974.

The President exercised retaliatory authority under Section 252 only twice. Both cases involved the imposition of import restraints because of agricultural disputes. Between 1974 and 1979, the first of the private petitions for Section 301 action were considered. However the typical result was to refer the dispute to the GATT organization which deliberated at length and effectively turned the disputes into issues for review during the Tokyo Round of GATT negotiations concluded in 1979. Congress was not happy with these results, and in the Trade Agreements Act of 1979 imposed a variety of time limitations in connection with Section 301 complaints. Congress also expanded the range of complaints that could be filed and on balance sought to rejuvenate Section 301.

From 1979 through the 1980s, the number of Section 301 investigations initiated by private complaints increased considerably. Through the Trade and Tariff Act of 1984, Congress continued to seek to make Section 301 an effective trade remedy. Its availability for complaints in the field of intellectual property rights and trade involving services was made clear. Nevertheless, a significant number of these complaints were still being referred to the GATT and its remarkably slow dispute settlement procedures. Through the Omnibus Trade and Competitiveness Act of 1988, Congress expressed its displeasure with GATT as a dispute settlement forum by indicating that under appropriate circumstances Section 301 investigations and remedies can proceed notwithstanding the fact that GATT dispute settlement has not run its full course. At the same time, Congress switched the ultimate authority for determining Section 301 offenses and Section 301 remedies from the President to the United States Trade Representative.

The bottom line after all of these legislative efforts on the part of Congress to invigorate Section 301 is that it has become a significant forum for opening up foreign markets to United States exports. This forum can be accessed by private initiative as well as governmental action.

§ 19.3   The Impact of WTO Dispute Settlement Understanding

United States membership in the World Trade Organization since 1995 has committed it to multilateral dispute settlement of disputes arising out of the numerous WTO agreements. If the dispute is covered by a WTO agreement, the United States is obliged to pursue remedies under the WTO Dispute Settlement Understanding.[1] Section 301 petitions falling within the scope of the WTO routinely trigger USTR complaints with the multilateral Dispute Settlement Body. The United States has been involved in more WTO disputes (as a complaining and responding party) than any other member country. The DSU creates procedures under which unilateral retaliation is restrained until the offending nation has failed to conform to a WTO panel or Appellate Body ruling. Unilateral retaliation is then authorized by the WTO in an amount equal to the damages incurred.

However, when a petition concerns subject matter not covered by a WTO agreement or a country that is not a WTO member, Section 301 and its unilateral remedies remain in full force and effect.

§ 19.4   Mandatory versus Discretionary Offenses and Remedies

Section 301 of the Trade Act of 1974 vests in the United States Trade Representative the power to determine when the *rights* of the United States under any trade agreement are being denied, when foreign country practices are inconsistent with or otherwise denying the *benefits* to the United States of trade agreements, or foreign countries are engaged in unjustifiable practices that burden or restrict United States commerce. An affirmative finding by the USTR in connection with any of the above now requires mandatory retaliation on the part of the United States "subject to Presidential direction."[1]

---

§ 19.3   § 19.4

1. See Chapter 9.   1. 19 U.S.C.A. § 2411.

The USTR is not required to take action whenever the dispute has been adjudicated within the GATT/WTO and there has been a finding that United States rights under a trade agreement are not being denied or that the foreign country practices under dispute are not in violation of nor impair the benefits of the United States under any trade agreement. In addition, the USTR does not have to take retaliatory action if he or she determines that the foreign country in question is taking satisfactory measures to grant the rights of the United States under a trade agreement or has agreed to eliminate or phase out the practices that are in dispute. If this is not possible, but the foreign country agrees to provide the United States with compensatory trade benefits satisfactory to the USTR, no mandatory retaliation will take place. In extraordinary cases, the USTR need not undertake retaliatory action if that would have an adverse impact on the United States economy substantially out of proportion to the benefits of that action or would cause serious harm to the national security of the United States.[2]

Section 301 also authorizes the USTR to determine when foreign countries are engaged in unreasonable or discriminatory practices that burden or restrict United States commerce. If such findings are reached, the Trade Representative (subject to directives from the President) may decide to undertake retaliatory action.[3] Hence, these offenses do not require mandatory retaliation; they are discretionary.

With reference to both mandatory and discretionary actions under Section 301, the USTR is authorized to withdraw the benefits of trade agreements enjoyed by the foreign country engaging in the offending activities, impose tariffs or other import restrictions upon the goods of those nations, and enter into binding international agreements to eliminate or phase out the unfair practices or to provide the United States with compensatory trade benefits. If the dispute concerns services, and many recent Section 301 disputes have been focused upon services, the USTR may restrict any "service sector access authorization" under United States law. Presumably, for example, the USTR subject to presidential directives could deny access to foreign banks by withholding licenses from federal authorities. It is less clear, but appears possible, that the USTR could order state authorities to deny similar access to the services sector.[4]

One problem with Section 301 remedies is that they need not necessarily benefit those who have been injured by foreign country practices. Thus, for example, if the complaint concerns European Union export subsidies on sugar, the ultimate retaliatory action

---

2.   19 U.S.C.A. § 2411(a)(2).   **4.**   19 U.S.C.A. § 2411(c)(2).

3.   19 U.S.C.A. § 2411(b).

taken by the United States may involve the imposition of tariffs upon European wine. Similarly, if the dispute concerns the intellectual property rights afforded pharmaceuticals in Brazil, the ultimate Section 301 remedy may impose quotas or other trade restraints upon Brazilian hardwoods.

§ 19.5   Statutory Definitions

The provisions of Section 301 are remarkably broad and open-ended in language. The statute therefore seeks to define with greater specificity some of the important terms involved. These definitions are found in Section 301(d) of the Trade Act of 1974.[1] One important definition provides an expansive interpretation of the appropriate international commerce to which Section 301 applies. For these purposes, commerce includes trade in goods and services, and foreign direct investment by United States persons with implications for trade in goods or services.

Foreign country practices are "unreasonable" if they are unfair and inequitable, regardless of whether they are in violation of or inconsistent with the international legal rights of the United States. Unreasonable practices include those which deny fair and equitable opportunities for the establishment of a business abroad, those which provide inadequate or ineffective protection of intellectual property rights, those which deny market opportunities as a result of systematic anticompetitive activities of private firms, and those which constitute export targeting (defined to mean any government scheme designed to assist its exporters in becoming more competitive). Unreasonable practices include those which constitute a persistent pattern of conduct that denies workers the right to associate, organize or bargain collectively. They also include practices which tolerate forced or compulsory labor, fail to provide a minimum working age for children, or fail to provide general standards on minimum wages, hours of work and occupational safety and health requirements. However, Section 301(d) indicates that foreign country practices are not to be treated as unreasonable if the USTR determines that nation is taking action which demonstrates a significant and tangible advancement towards providing the rights and standards discussed above or that the practices in question are not inconsistent with the level of economic development of the foreign country. Where appropriate, the absence or presence of reciprocal opportunities in the United States for foreign nationals shall be taken into account in determining whether any particular practice is unreasonable.

It is important to bear in mind that this lengthy definition of unreasonable foreign country practices coincides with discretionary

§ 19.5
1.   19 U.S.C.A. § 2411(d).

USTR action if such practices are found. The other discretionary category under Section 301 includes foreign country practices which are "discriminatory." Section 301(d) defines discriminatory as any practice which denies national or most favored nation treatment to United States goods, services or investment. The prohibition against "unjustifiable" foreign country practices is expanded by a definition which indicates that such practices must violate or be inconsistent with the international legal rights of the United States. These include those which deny national or most favored nation treatment, the right of establishment or the protection of intellectual property rights. Unjustifiable practices, if determined to exist by the USTR, mandate retaliatory action by the United States.

Perhaps the most critical difference in the Section 301(d) definitions of Section 301 offenses concerns international legal rights. This is part of the definition of unjustifiable practices, but not found in connection with unreasonable or discriminatory practices. There is no requirement that unreasonable, discriminatory or unjustifiable practices violate or contradict any international agreement to which the United States is a party. Thus the international legal rights which must be breached in order to find an unjustifiable practice may turn upon customary international law of trade. The statutory definitions of unreasonableness reviewed above were greatly expanded in 1988. This suggests that the most likely avenue of success under Section 301 is in pleading unreasonable practices.

§ 19.6 Petitioning and Consultation Procedures

Section 302 of the Trade Act of 1974 permits any interested person to file a petition with the United States Trade Representative requesting action under Section 301. Complaints from U.S. industries have in fact driven most Section 301 proceedings, and they can be screened by the USTR before filing. The USTR is given 45 days within which to determine whether to initiate an investigation. Interested parties may include but are not limited to domestic companies and workers, representatives of consumer interests, U.S. exporters, and any industrial users of goods or services potentially affected by Section 301 actions.[1] The Trade Representative's powers to initiate investigations under Section 301 appear to be completely discretionary. That is to say, if the USTR is not persuaded by the petition and supporting documents, no Section 301 procedures will be commenced. This is true for both mandatory and discretionary action under Section 301. However, if the USTR decides not to initiate an investigation, he or she must inform the petitioner of

§ 19.6
1. 19 U.S.C.A. § 2411(d)(9).

the reasons why and publish notice of that determination together with its reasons in the Federal Register.[2]

If the USTR decides to initiate an investigation under Section 301, he or she then publishes a summary of the petition and is required to provide an opportunity for the presentation of views including a public hearing. The USTR may self-initiate Section 301 investigations.[3] The USTR is not required to initiate any investigation if he or she determines that to do so would be detrimental to United States economic interests.[4] Once an investigation under Section 301 is launched, either by petition or self-initiation, the USTR must consult with the foreign country alleged to have engaged in unfair trade practices. If a mutually acceptable solution is not reached, and the complaint concerns a breach of an international agreement to which the United States is a party, the USTR is obliged to commence dispute settlement procedures as provided for in that agreement.[5]

The regulations which detail the procedures and conduct of investigations in connection with Section 301 are found at 15 C.F.R. 2006 et seq. An interagency committee composed of staff from the Departments of State, Treasury, Commerce, Justice, Agriculture, Labor and the Council of Economic Advisors is involved in the decisionmaking under Section 301. This Committee is sometimes called the "Section 301 Committee" and its report and advice will be considered by the USTR in making Section 301 determinations. The input of this Committee does not diminish the discretion of the USTR in deciding whether to commence a Section 301 investigation. When a petition is received from the private sector alleging a Section 301 offense, the USTR typically notifies the country that is the object of the complaint. That country may supply any relevant information it chooses. In the absence of such a response, the USTR is entitled to proceed on the basis of the "best information available."[6] This will often as a practical matter be the information submitted by the petitioner or otherwise derived from the Section 301 Committee or other independent sources. Thus the procedures utilized in Section 301 make it imperative that private petitioners properly document the nature of their complaint.

The rules require that a private petition for Section 301 action describe the petitioner's interest that is allegedly impacted by the foreign country practice about which the petitioner is complaining. If the complaint is based upon international agreements to which the United States is a party and the denial of rights thereunder, this must be clearly cited and documented. The petition must

---

2. 19 U.S.C.A. § 2412(a).

3. 19 U.S.C.A. § 2412(b).

4. 19 U.S.C.A. § 2412(b).

5. 19 U.S.C.A. § 2413(a).

6. 15 C.F.R. § 2006.4.

specifically identify the foreign country alleged to be engaging in a Section 301 offense. It must identify the specific product or service which is the subject of the complaint. Most importantly, the petition must show exactly how the practice in question is inconsistent with a trade agreement or is otherwise unjustifiable, unreasonable or discriminatory and that it burdens or restricts United States commerce. Lastly, the petitioner must indicate whether any other requests for relief under the Trade Act of 1974 or other United States law have been filed.

Once the USTR determines to initiate an investigation under Section 301, the petitioner has 30 days to submit a written request for a public hearing.[7] Any other interested person can also submit an application for such a hearing. Section 305 of the Trade Act of 1974 allows U.S. companies and other interested persons to essentially request of the USTR information necessary to substantiate a Section 301 complaint. Such requests have the practical effect of obliging the USTR to provide any such available information, and perhaps even to require the USTR to contact foreign governments in order to satisfy this request for information. Such requests can amount to a kind of preliminary Section 301 investigation before formal investigations are initiated.[8]

§ 19.7 USTR Determinations

Since the amendments of 1988, the USTR is required to make a determination of whether foreign country practices are actionable under Section 301 regardless of whether any retaliatory action is taken. For many years disputes concerning export subsidies, particularly export subsidies of the European Union, dominated Section 301 proceedings.[1] Whenever Section 301 complaints involve an alleged breach of United States benefits under an existing international agreement, such as the package of WTO agreements, the USTR must initiate the dispute settlement procedures of that agreement.

Since 1988, the USTR is required to determine whether unfair practices have occurred under Section 301 within certain time limits. These are 12 months in cases involving export subsidies and practices not covered by trade agreements, 18 months in trade agreement cases other than subsidies unless the dispute settlement procedures of the relevant agreement are concluded earlier. Generally speaking, the USTR must determine whether a Section 301

---

7. 19 U.S.C.A. § 2414(b).
8. See 19 U.S.C.A. § 2411(d)(2).

Great Plains Wheat Case, 16 International Lawyer 339 (1982).

§ 19.7

1. See Bishop, The Multilateral Trade Negotiations, Subsidies and the

offense has occurred in all instances where an investigation has been commenced within a 12–month deadline. These time limits could pressure the USTR into making a determination before the international dispute settlement procedures of the WTO or other trade agreements are concluded.[2]

§ 19.8   Section 301 in Action

There have been a large number of complaints and investigations under Section 301 of the Trade Act of 1974. In some instances, complaints under Section 301 have been dismissed by the President or USTR as without merit. In other instances, the complaints led to a GATT/WTO dispute settlement panel which decided against the position of the United States. This has the effect of terminating the Section 301 proceeding. Many Section 301 complaints have been resolved to the satisfaction of those concerned through international negotiations. For example, in the early 1970s, a shipping company complained about the discriminatory practices of the government of Guatemala. The United States undertook negotiations with that government and reached an agreement satisfactory to the complainant.[1] In the same year, Canada had been imposing a quota on the importation of eggs from the United States. A trade association complaint to the USTR led to negotiations and an increase in this quota.[2] An exporter of thrown silk to Japan complained about the difficulties in obtaining import licenses for such silk. This complaint led to the threat of retaliatory action against Japanese-made silk products. However, subsequent negotiations resulted in an agreement which caused the Japanese to remove their import licensing restraints.[3]

A lengthy Section 301 complaint concerned European Union tariff restraints in connection with the export of Florida citrus products. In this case, the GATT (pre-WTO) did not provide an adequate dispute resolution forum, and the United States decided to retaliate by imposing substantial tariffs on European pasta products. Europe in turn retaliated with tariff increases on U.S. walnuts and lemons. Ultimately the United States and the European Union agreed to mutual elimination of the tariffs in question. This result did not really resolve the underlying dispute concerning the export of citrus products from the United States to Europe.[4] One Section 301 complaint involved the Cigar Association of America. This complaint was against Japanese practices which had the

---

2. See generally Bliss, The Amendments to Section 301: An Overview and Suggested Strategies for Foreign Response, 20 Law & Policy of International Business 501 (1989).

§ 19.8

1. See 41 Fed.Reg. 26758 (1976).

2. 41 Fed.Reg. 9430 (1976).

3. 43 Fed.Reg. 8876 (1978).

4. See 50 Fed.Reg. 26143 (1985).

effect of raising the price on U.S. cigars and making them difficult to market in Japan. International negotiations led to the formation of a GATT dispute settlement panel. However, this panel did not need to complete its task because the Japanese government agreed to substantial reductions in the relevant tariffs and retail requirements.[5]

While many Section 301 complaints have concerned export opportunities for United States firms, some have involved import competition. For example, a complaint was filed against Taiwanese subsidies of rice exports. International negotiations led to an agreement limiting these subsidized exports such that the Section 301 complaint was withdrawn.[6]

The United States Trade Representative has occasionally commenced Section 301 proceedings on its own initiative. For example, the Brazilian "informatics policy" was challenged in this manner. This policy discriminated against foreign computer and high technology imports principally through local content requirements and the grant of exclusive monopolies. International negotiations, backed up by a threat by the United States to suspend the benefits for Brazil under the U.S. Generalized System of Tariff Preferences, eventually resulted in an opening of the Brazilian informatics market.[7] Another example of a self-initiated Section 301 proceeding concerned Korea's restraints on foreign insurance companies. Korean law was discriminatory and failed to give foreign companies the same benefits that domestic firms obtained. An international settlement was reached between the United States and Korea which gave access to that market for life and non-life insurance.[8] Korea was also the object of another Section 301 investigation concerning its intellectual property rights. These were thought to be inadequate, particularly in the copyright area. International negotiations led to the creation of a comprehensive copyright system for Korea, including coverage of computer software. Amendments were also made to the Korean patent laws and the country joined the Universal Copyright Convention.[9]

Several Section 301 disputes have been resolved with Thailand. Following Section 301 success at opening the Japanese, Taiwanese and South Korean markets to United States cigarettes, the first dispute concerned Thai tariffs on U.S. cigarettes. United States producers petitioned under Section 301, and a lengthy investigation resulted in the formation of a GATT dispute settlement panel. This

---

5. See 44 Fed.Reg. 19083 (1979), 44 Fed.Reg. 64938 (1979) and 46 Fed.Reg. 1388, 1389 (1981).

6. See 48 Fed.Reg. 56289 (1983), 49 Fed.Reg. 10761 (1984).

7. See 51 Fed.Reg. 35993.

8. See 51 Fed.Reg. 29443.

9. See 51 Fed.Reg. 29445.

panel ruled against the tariffs and Thailand removed them.[10] A second Section 301 complaint by the International Intellectual Property Alliance and others led to an investigation focused on Thai piracy of audio and video cassettes. A substantial Thai industry had developed around such activities. The USTR threatened removal of Thailand's GSP duty free tariff entry benefits and the imposition of a total U.S. barrier to Thai imports. Thailand capitulated and announced copyright reforms targeted at cassette piracy.[11]

A longstanding dispute between the United States and Japan concerning semiconductor products resulted in a Section 301 complaint in the late 1980s. The essence of the complaint was that a prior agreement concerning trade in such products between the two nations had been breached and therefore the United States intended to impose tariffs on certain imports from Japan.[12] The United States argued that Japan had not opened up its market sufficiently to foreign semiconductor manufacturers and had not avoided dumping of Japanese-made semiconductors in various markets around the world. Thus the heart of this complaint was that the benefits of an international agreement previously made were being denied to the United States and that this constituted a burden or restraint on U.S. commerce. The United States did impose additional duties on Japanese data processing machines, rotary drills and color television sets. However, these duties were suspended when the USTR found improved compliance by the Japanese with the semiconductor agreement.[13]

Section 307 of the Trade and Tariff Act of 1984 focuses specifically on export performance requirements created by foreign countries. Such requirements are thought by many United States investors to be unreasonable. Section 307 requires the USTR to enter into consultations with any foreign country imposing export performance requirements in an effort to seek to alleviate them when they adversely the economic interests of the United States. If such consultations do not result in a settlement, the USTR is authorized to impose import restraints on the products or services of the country in question.[14] In one instance, for example, the USTR was able to successfully negotiate away export performance requirements maintained by the Taiwanese relative to automobiles.[15]

The Telecommunications Trade Act of 1988[16] focuses upon foreign market opportunities in the telecommunication field. It is integrated into Section 301 procedures and administrative determi-

10.   55 Fed.Reg. 49724 (USTR 1990).

11.   56 Fed.Reg. 67114 (USTR 1991).

12.   See 52 Fed.Reg. 13412 (1987).

13.   See 52 Fed.Reg. 22693 (1987).

14.   See 19 U.S.C.A. § 2112(g)(3).

15.   See 51 Fed.Reg. 41558.

16.   Pub.L. 100–418.

nations. In undertaking retaliation, however, the USTR is directed to target telecommunications industry exports to the U.S. unless other action would be more effective in opening up foreign export markets. Section 1374 of the 1988 Act requires the USTR to identify priority countries whose practices cause the greatest telecommunications trade barriers. South Korea and the European Union were so identified in 1989. Ensuing negotiations resulted in a market-opening telecommunications agreement with South Korea and the European Union.

In the fall of 1991, the USTR initiated a prominent investigation of restrictive trade practices of the People's Republic of China. This investigation was undertaken in part to mitigate Congressional frustration over President Bush's continued willingness to grant most-favored-nation tariff status to Chinese goods despite record U.S. trade deficits with the PRC (second only to Japan). The Section 301 investigation focused upon PRC import quotas, prohibitions and licensing procedures, and PRC technical barriers to trade (e.g., standards, testing and certification requirements). It also challenged the failure to publish PRC laws, regulations, judicial decisions and administrative rulings relating to import restraints. Additional discussions regarding PRC tariffs (ranging up to 200 percent) and import taxes were held. The main thrust of the proceeding was to open up China's markets to U.S. exports.

Since China was not a member of the GATT, and in spite of U.S. bilateral trade agreements with the PRC, the USTR proceeded with this investigation on an unfair practices' basis. This meant that no trade agreement dispute settlement procedures were triggered. The Section 301 investigation was in addition to the Special 301 priority country investigation of PRC practices in the intellectual property field.

In October of 1992 the United States and China signed a memorandum of understanding that narrowly avoided massive, unilateral Section 301 trade sanctions. The People's Republic agreed to phase out by the end of 1977 numerous nontariff trade barriers, including import licenses, quotas and bans as well as regulatory restraints. The removal of these barriers will improve U.S. export possibilities for telecommunications equipment, airplanes, machinery, agricultural goods, electrical appliances, computers, auto parts and pharmaceuticals. Furthermore, China promised to undertake a series of significant tariff cuts no later than the end of 1993. All of China's import-substitution regulations and policies are to be eliminated. In particular, the PRC will not condition entry into its market upon technology transfers. All laws, regulations, policies and decrees dealing with China's import and export system will be published on a regular basis and no such rules can be enforced unless they have been made readily available to foreign traders and governments. The goal is complete "transparency" of PRC trade law and an end to the use of secret internal directives. For its part, the United States committed itself to full GATT/WTO membership for the PRC, which was finally realized in 2001.

§ 19.9 Special 301—Prioritization of U.S. Intellectual Property Rights Disputes With Foreign Countries

Unlike the Super 301 procedures, which expired in 1991, the Special 301 procedures established by the 1988 Omnibus Trade and Competitiveness Act are permanent features of United States trade legislation. These procedures are located in Section 182 of the Trade Act of 1974.[1] Under these procedures the United States Trade Representative is required to identify foreign countries that deny adequate and effective protection of intellectual property rights, or deny fair and equitable access to United States persons that rely upon intellectual property protection. As with the Super 301 procedures, the USTR is given discretion to determine whether to designate certain of these countries to be "priority countries." If so designated, a mandatory Section 301 investigation must follow in the absence of a determination that this would be detrimental to U.S. economic interests or a negotiated settlement of the intellectual property dispute. Once designated, Special 301 investigations and retaliations against priority countries must ordinarily be decided within 6 months by the USTR. This is a fast track when compared with Super 301 procedures. Whether to retaliate or not is discretionary with the USTR, but retaliation is not authorized if the country in question enters into good faith negotiations or makes "significant progress" in bilateral or multilateral negotiations towards increased protection for intellectual property rights.

In identifying priority foreign countries in the intellectual property field, Section 182 indicates that the USTR is to prioritize only those countries that have the most "onerous or egregious" practices, whose practices have the greatest adverse impact on United States products, and are not entering into good faith negotiations bilaterally or multilaterally to provide adequate and effective protection of intellectual property rights.[2] For these purposes, the term "persons that rely on intellectual protection" covers those involved in copyrighted works of authorship or those involved in the manufacture of products that are patented or subject to process patents.[3] Interestingly, this definition does not include those who rely on United States trademarks. However, the relevant definitions include trademarks in connection with the denial by foreign

---

§ **19.9**

1. 19 U.S.C.A. § 2242.

2. 19 U.S.C.A. § 2422(b).

3. 19 U.S.C.A. § 2242(d).

countries of adequate and effective protection of intellectual property rights. The definition of practices that deny fair and equitable market access in connection with intellectual property rights appear to be limited to copyrights and patents. This denial must constitute a violation of provisions of international law or international agreements to which both the United States and that country are parties or otherwise constitute a discriminatory nontariff trade barrier.[4]

Regular reports to Congress are required of the USTR by Section 182. As with the Super 301 procedures, the USTR has chiefly placed foreign country intellectual property practices on watch lists rather than formally designating priority countries. These watch lists are divided as between "priority watch lists" and "secondary watch lists." Many nations have been listed by the USTR since 1989 in this fashion. This has the practical effect of placing pressure on those nations to enter negotiations with the United States that will improve their protection of intellectual property rights. The use of these lists gives the USTR more room to negotiate settlements with the countries concerned. In April of 1991, the USTR formally named China, India and Thailand as the first "priority countries" for Special 301 purposes. Thus the formal process of negotiation backed up by a mandatory Section 301 investigation and potential sanctions was begun. Thailand was cited for its failure to enforce copyrights and for the absence of patent protection for pharmaceuticals. India was named because its patent laws are deficient from the U.S. perspective, particularly on compulsory licensing and the absence of pharmaceutical protection. Extensive book, video, sound recording and computer software piracy in India was also cited.

The United States Trade Representative has been skeptical of the PRC commitment to intellectual property rights. In 1991 she commenced a Special 301 investigation into the adequacy of China's computer software and other intellectual property regulations. Absent satisfaction through negotiations, the U.S. threatened massive retaliatory trade sanctions blocking Chinese exports to America. Early in 1992, a last minute agreement was reached on significant reform of China's copyright, patent and trade secret laws. In the copyright area, China agreed to join the Berne Convention and the Geneva Convention on Phonograms, to extend protection to existing as well as new works, and to treat computer programs as literary works protected for 50 years. Accession to the Berne Convention will remove the barrier to Chinese copyright protection of works by most foreigners, including U.S. citizens, first published outside the PRC.

4. Id.

Regarding patents, China promised full protection for pharmaceuticals and agricultural chemicals with a 20–year patent term. It also promised a substantial waiver of the risk of compulsory licensing for all U.S. holders of Chinese patents, including a ban on such licensing if the U.S. holder does not manufacture the product in the PRC. This promise does not appear to apply to European or Japanese owners of Chinese patents. Trade secrets will be protected by legislation against unauthorized use or disclosure, including that by third parties.

China and the United States reached another crisis-ridden agreement on intellectual property early in 1995. This agreement emphasizes enforcement issues in the PRC, particularly regarding pirate CD plants. It does not preclude Section 301 action by the United States. In 1996, China was identified as a priority foreign country under Special 301. Shortly thereafter yet another crisis-ridden agreement on intellectual property was reached by the United States and the PRC. This agreement, once again, avoided massive mutual trade sanctions.

United States Special 301 investigations and watch lists have continued relentlessly in spite of the TRIPs agreement. By 2004, the USTR had filed over 30 TRIPs complaints with the WTO. These filings were against Denmark, Sweden, Ireland, Ecuador, Greece, Portugal, India, Pakistan and Turkey (among others).

Chapter 20

ANTITRUST LAWS (U.S. AND EUROPE)

Table of Sections

§ 20.1   Sherman Act Prohibitions and Remedies

The first federal antitrust statute was the Sherman Act of 1890. The early state statutes and the Sherman Act reflected a "populist" movement in United States society in the late 19th Century. This movement opposed the formation of large and economically powerful "trusts" by the captains of the American industrial revolution. Perhaps the most famous of all trusts was that put together by the Rockefellers to control the oil industry. Some assert that Microsoft's market power exceeds that of Rockfeller. Microsoft

449

is currently the subject of a major federal/state antitrust prosecution.

The Sherman Act contains two basic prohibitions. Section 1 prohibits every contract, combination or conspiracy in restraint of trade. Section 2 prohibits monopolization, attempts to monopolize, and combinations or conspiracies to monopolize. Both of these prohibitions extend to interstate commerce within the United States and, under Section 7 of the Sherman Act, to United States foreign commerce. Section 7 concerns the "extraterritorial" application of the Sherman Act to foreign enterprises and restraints of trade undertaken outside the limits of the United States which have "direct, substantial and reasonably foreseeable" effects on U.S. commerce. Extraterritorial U.S. antitrust jurisdiction has always been controversial and is discussed separately in this chapter.

Originally enacted as misdemeanors, the Sherman Act prohibitions have now become felony criminal offenses. Among the family of nations with antitrust-type laws, the United States is almost unique in criminally sanctioning anticompetitive behavior. Persons violating either Section 1 or Section 2 of the Sherman Act may be imprisoned up to three years or fined up to $350,000. Corporations held to violate those sections may be fined up to $10,000,000. In fact, criminal prosecutions under the Sherman Act are rare. Perhaps the most common kind of activity which is criminally prosecuted is bidrigging on government contracts.

The Sherman Act also created a powerful private remedy, treble the actual damages suffered as a result of an antitrust violation. This remedy has been carried forward and is now found in Section 4 of the Clayton Act. When combined with class action and parens patriae procedures before federal and state courts, and the constitutional right to a jury trial in civil litigation, treble damages is transformed into an incredibly powerful remedy. Private treble damages actions account for approximately 85 percent of all antitrust litigation. No other nation permits the bulk of its antitrust law enforcement to be accomplished by private parties. In the United States, this result is rationalized as promoting the enforcement of extremely important, almost quasi-constitutional law. The Supreme Court has repeatedly referred to the Sherman Act as "the economic constitution of the United States" or the "Magna Carta of free enterprise." Private antitrust litigants are often said to function as "attorneys general" when seeking to obtain treble damages relief.

§ 20.2 Reasonable and Unreasonable (Per Se) Restraints of Trade

After a period of "trust busting" led by President Theodore Roosevelt at the turn of the century, the Supreme Court of the

United States rendered its famous decision in *Standard Oil Company of New Jersey v. United States.*[1] In this decision, the Supreme Court held that Sections 1 and 2 of the Sherman Act apply only to *unreasonable* restraints of trade and monopolization activities. The *Standard Oil* case thus stands for the well-known proposition that the "rule of reason" governs Sherman Act law. In applying this approach to the Rockefellers and the Standard Oil Company of New Jersey, the Supreme Court ordered dissolution of this "trust" into approximately 30 oil companies. Whether a comparable remedy will be applied to Microsoft remains to be seen.

The courts have created categories of restraint of trade offenses which are treated as *per se* unreasonable, that is to say presumptively illegal. These categories presently include: (1) horizontal price fixing;[2] (2) vertical price fixing or minimum resale price maintenance;[3] (3) horizontal market division or customer allocation;[4] (4) certain tying arrangements;[5] and (5) certain commercial group boycotts.[6] The term "horizontal" applies to the activities of persons who operate at the same economic level, e.g., manufacturers, wholesalers, etc. Thus a horizontal price fixing, market division or customer allocation conspiracy would be among manufacturers, wholesalers or retailers, but not as between them. Such conspiracies are often referred to as cartels. The term "vertical" applies to relationships between actors who function at different economic levels, e.g., wholesalers and retailers. Thus a vertical price fixing conspiracy could be reflected in contracts between manufacturers and wholesalers or as between wholesalers and retailers. The

§ 20.2

1. 221 U.S. 1, 31 S.Ct. 502, 55 L.Ed. 619 (1911).

2. United States v. Trenton Potteries Co., 273 U.S. 392, 47 S.Ct. 377, 71 L.Ed. 700 (1927); Catalano, Inc. v. Target Sales, Inc., 446 U.S. 643, 100 S.Ct. 1925, 64 L.Ed.2d 580 (1980). Compare Broadcast Music, Inc. v. Columbia Broadcasting System, Inc., 441 U.S. 1, 99 S.Ct. 1551, 60 L.Ed.2d 1 (1979); Arizona v. Maricopa County Medical Society, 457 U.S. 332, 102 S.Ct. 2466, 73 L.Ed.2d 48 (1982); N.C.A.A. v. Board of Regents of University of Oklahoma, 468 U.S. 85, 104 S.Ct. 2948, 82 L.Ed.2d 70 (1984) (Rule of Reason cases).

3. Dr. Miles Medical Co. v. John D. Park & Sons Co., 220 U.S. 373, 31 S.Ct. 376, 55 L.Ed. 502 (1911); California Retail Liquor Dealers Ass'n v. Midcal Aluminum, Inc., 445 U.S. 97, 100 S.Ct. 937, 63 L.Ed.2d 233 (1980).

4. United States v. Topco Associates, 405 U.S. 596, 92 S.Ct. 1126, 31 L.Ed.2d 515 (1972); Palmer v. BRG of Georgia,

Inc., 498 U.S. 46, 111 S.Ct. 401, 112 L.Ed.2d 349 (1990).

5. Jefferson Parish Hospital District No. 2 v. Hyde, 466 U.S. 2, 104 S.Ct. 1551, 80 L.Ed.2d 2 (1984); Eastman Kodak Co. v. Image Technical Services, Inc., 504 U.S. 451, 112 S.Ct. 2072, 119 L.Ed.2d 265 (1992).

6. Klor's, Inc. v. Broadway–Hale Stores, 359 U.S. 207, 79 S.Ct. 705, 3 L.Ed.2d 741 (1959); FTC v. Superior Court Trial Lawyers Association, 493 U.S. 411, 110 S.Ct. 768, 107 L.Ed.2d 851 (1990). Compare NCAA v. Board of Regents of the University of Oklahoma, 468 U.S. 85, 104 S.Ct. 2948, 82 L.Ed.2d 70 (1984); Northwest Wholesale Stationers, Inc. v. Pacific Stationery and Printing Co., 472 U.S. 284, 105 S.Ct. 2613, 86 L.Ed.2d 202 (1985); FTC v. Indiana Federation of Dentists, 476 U.S. 447, 106 S.Ct. 2009, 90 L.Ed.2d 445 (1986) (Rule of Reason cases).

Supreme Court in recent years has indicated that none of these *per se* rules is absolute, and that in special circumstances the rule of reason will prevail. For example, the *per se* rule against resale price maintenance (RPM) has been tempered by an exception for most consignment sales,[7] by removing maximum RPM from *per se* treatment,[8] and by allowing manufacturers to suggest resale prices and unilaterally refuse to deal with distributors who do not comply (the "*Colgate* doctrine").[9]

These trends have revived interest in just exactly what the rule of reason is all about. The classic statement of the rule appears in *Board of Trade of Chicago v. United States*[10] where Justice Brandeis stressed analysis of the competitive significance or competitive impact of the restraints at issue. Recent cases sometimes also allow economic efficiency and noncompetitive business justifications to be weighed in the rule of reason calculus, and it is clear that nonprice vertical restraints are to be judged under such an approach.[11] Thus, most territorial and customer allocations by manufacturers among their distributors are evaluated in terms of their intrabrand versus interbrand competitive effects and marketing efficiency. These decisions, and others, suggest that the traditional distinction in U.S. antitrust law between rule of reason analysis and *per se* treatment of restraints of trade is breaking down and that a new synthesis, the contours of which are not yet clear, is emerging.

§ 20.3 Monopolization

Section 2 of the Sherman Act is primarily concerned with single firm market power. Attempts to monopolize have never been easily proved because the Supreme Court has required a "dangerous probability of success" in addition to proof of specific intent and acts undertaken to monopolize.[1] The typical analysis in monopolization cases first involves a definition of the market in which the defendant is alleged to have monopoly power and engaged in monopolization. This is known in antitrust parlance as "defining the relevant market." Each market for purposes of Section 2 will be

---

7. But see Simpson v. Union Oil Co., 377 U.S. 13, 84 S.Ct. 1051, 12 L.Ed.2d 98 (1964).

8. Atlantic Richfield Co. v. USA Petroleum Co., 495 U.S. 328, 110 S.Ct. 1884, 109 L.Ed.2d 333 (1990); State Oil Co. v. Kahn, 522 U.S. 3, 118 S.Ct. 275, 139 L.Ed.2d 199 (1997).

9. Monsanto Co. v. Spray–Rite Service Corp., 465 U.S. 752, 104 S.Ct. 1464, 79 L.Ed.2d 775 (1984); Business Electronics Corp. v. Sharp Electronics Corp., 485 U.S. 717, 108 S.Ct. 1515, 99 L.Ed.2d 808 (1988).

10. 246 U.S. 231, 38 S.Ct. 242, 62 L.Ed. 683 (1918). See National Society of Professional Engineers v. United States, 435 U.S. 679, 98 S.Ct. 1355, 55 L.Ed.2d 637 (1978).

11. Continental T.V., Inc. v. GTE Sylvania Inc., 433 U.S. 36, 97 S.Ct. 2549, 53 L.Ed.2d 568 (1977).

§ 20.3

1. Swift & Co. v. United States, 196 U.S. 375, 25 S.Ct. 276, 49 L.Ed. 518 (1905).

defined in terms of product and geographic scope. In *United States v. E.I. du Pont de Nemours & Co.,*[2] the Court emphasized that all "reasonably interchangeable" products should be included in defining the relevant product market. Geographically, markets are defined for purposes of Section 2 in terms of the area of effective competition faced by the alleged monopolist. Typically, this is the whole or part of the United States, but may exclude Hawaii or Alaska. Market shares are the beginning of an analysis of market power necessary to the monopolization offense under Section 2.

Assuming that the defendant in a Section 2 case has monopoly power in the relevant market, the next step is to examine whether exclusionary practices were used in obtaining this power or maintaining it. Such practices are referred to as "acts of monopolization." Common allegations of acts of monopolization have involved predatory pricing, price discrimination, tying practices, refusals to deal and mergers and acquisitions. In the famous *Alcoa* decision, Judge Learned Hand emphasized that the creation of new plants designed to meet market needs constituted an act by Alcoa of monopolization of the U.S. virgin aluminum ingot market.[3]

In recent years, other language in Judge Hand's opinion has been used to defeat allegations of monopolization when monopoly power has been achieved as a result of superior foresight, skill and industry. Thus, for example, Eastman Kodak Co. was held not to have monopolized under Section 2 as a result of its product market innovations which were not disclosed in advance to competing companies.[4] In 1982, partly because of the internationalization of the computer market, the government dropped its longstanding monopolization case against IBM. Shortly thereafter, it also settled another large monopolization case against American Telephone & Telegraph. This settlement, somewhat like the famous dissolutions under *Standard Oil of New Jersey,* resulted in the creation of a number of regional telecommunications companies and the breakup of the world's largest corporation.

§ 20.4   Clayton Act Prohibitions

Critics of the Sherman Act and the *Standard Oil* decision mounted a legislative campaign which resulted in two major federal antitrust statutes in 1914. The first of these statutes was the Clayton Act of 1914, and the second was the Federal Trade Commission Act, also of 1914. The Clayton Act prohibits four kinds of

2. 351 U.S. 377, 76 S.Ct. 994, 100 L.Ed. 1264 (1956).

3. United States v. Aluminum Co. of America, 148 F.2d 416 (2d Cir.1945).

4. Berkey Photo, Inc. v. Eastman Kodak Co., 603 F.2d 263 (2d Cir.1979).

activities if they involve commodities (not services) and may tend to substantially lessen competition in any line of commerce:

(1) price discrimination, subject to "cost justification" and "meeting competition" defenses (Section 2);

(2) exclusive dealing and tying arrangements (Section 3);

(3) mergers and acquisitions (Section 7); and

(4) interlocking company boards of directors (Section 8) (rarely invoked).

§ 20.5 Mergers and Acquisitions

The statutory prohibitions found in the Clayton Act are drafted in detailed language that has often led to narrow interpretations following the literal language of the statute. For example, initial interpretation of Section 7 did not permit coverage of assets acquisitions as distinct from stock mergers. It took, instead, an amendment in 1951 for asset acquisitions to fall under the jurisdictional scope of Section 7 of the Clayton Act. Section 7 is, since 1975, subject to "premerger notification." These requirements (sometimes known as "Hart–Scott–Rodino" notifications) stipulate that parties to large mergers and acquisitions must give the Justice Department and the Federal Trade Commission advance notice of their intentions. This advance notice allows the government antitrust authorities to review proposed mergers and acquisitions from the perspective of their potential to violate Section 7 of the Clayton Act and the desirability of challenging them in court. Of all the mergers that take place in the United States annually, including those involving takeovers by foreign firms, probably less than 1 percent are required to be notified to the federal antitrust authorities.

Under the Reagan and Bush administrations, vertical mergers were almost never challenged and very few horizontal mergers were subject to court proceedings under Section 7. Some mergers approved by the federal authorities have been subsequently challenged by a state Attorney General.[1] The states have, in general, become quite active in the mergers area and have adopted their own set of Horizontal Mergers Guidelines through the National Association of Attorneys General (NAAG).[2] Private challenges to mergers can also occur, and did so notably in the hostile takeover of British Consolidated Gold Fields by Minorco (a Luxembourg company controlled by the two leading South African gold producers).

---

§ 20.5

1. See California v. American Stores Co., 495 U.S. 271, 110 S.Ct. 1853, 109 L.Ed.2d 240 (1990).

2. The NAAG guidelines are reproduced in R. Folsom, State Antitrust Laws (Matthew Bender).

Gold Fields sought to block the takeover on antitrust grounds in the United States, Britain, South Africa, Australia and the European Union. These efforts failed everywhere except before a U.S. federal district court judge who issued an injunction against the takeover which was upheld by the Second Circuit Court of Appeals.[3]

§ 20.6 Price Discrimination, Exclusive Dealing and Tying Offenses

The price discrimination prohibition found in Section 2 of the Clayton Act was once the source of considerable public prosecution by the Federal Trade Commission. It was amended in the 1930s in an attempt to protect small retailers from the growing competitive pressures of chain stores. These amendments were undertaken in the Robinson–Patman Act of 1936. In this effort, Section 2 has largely proved unsuccessful. Chain stores are now a prominent form of merchandising in the United States. However, the prohibition against price discrimination remains law, despite considerable efforts at repeal. Its primary significance today is to permit private parties to sue for treble damages as victims of price discrimination practices. Thus, for example, small retailers of liquor may join together in a lawsuit which charges manufacturers with discriminating in price in favor of chain stores to their detriment. These small retailers often succeed in settling for or recovering at judgment substantial sums.

Section 3 of the Clayton Act concerns sales and distribution agreements. In general, exclusive dealing contracts have not been frequently challenged by the government or private parties. This is because the government now takes the position that exclusive dealing contracts are a variation on vertical integration, which may permit desirable economic efficiencies. Exclusive dealing arrangements are generally treated under the "rule of reason."

Section 3 also prohibits what are known as "tying arrangements." A tying arrangement must involve two separate products: the tying product and the tied product. The essence of the arrangement is coercion. The seller forces the buyer to take the tied product in order to get the tying product. If such activities may substantially lessen competition in any line of commerce, there is a violation of Section 3. Tying practices are also extensively litigated under Section 1 of the Sherman Act as restraints of trade. Under Section 1, the Supreme Court has traditionally viewed tying arrangements as a "per se offense." Per se offenses are those activities which the courts have treated as without redeeming virtues

---

3. Consolidated Gold Fields v. Anglo American Corp., 698 F.Supp. 487 (S.D.N.Y.1988), *affirmed* 871 F.2d 252 (2d Cir.1989), *cert. dismissed* 492 U.S. 939, 110 S.Ct. 29, 106 L.Ed.2d 639 (1989).

and therefore presumptively unreasonable. The case law on tying arrangements under Section 1 of the Sherman Act and Section 3 of the Clayton Act is extensive, complex, and not entirely consistent. Although the Supreme Court has recently affirmed the appropriateness of *per se* treatment for tying arrangements,[1] a number of lower court decisions indicate that it is a rather soft *per se* rule.

§ 20.7   The Federal Trade Commission Act

The second statute enacted in 1914 was the Federal Trade Commission Act. Under Section 5 of that Act, "unfair methods of competition" are prohibited. A number of leading cases of the United States Supreme Court indicate that Section 5 covers all of the types of activities prohibited by the Sherman and Clayton Acts. The FTC Act can also be construed to reach anticompetitive methods that are not clearly prohibited by those statutes, but which the Commission in its administrative wisdom determines unfair. Thus the Federal Trade Commission Act is said to "fill in the gaps" of federal antitrust law.

While Section 5 is arguably the most vague of all federal antitrust statutes, it is enforced exclusively by an administrative agency, the Federal Trade Commission. Over the years, the Commission has had a sporadic record in accomplishing its mission. The Commission is composed of five persons nominated by the President and confirmed by the Senate, no more than three of whom can be from the same political party. Despite the political nature of the appointment process to the Federal Trade Commission, the Commission is "an independent agency." It is supposed to exercise its statutory authority to act against unfair methods of competition without influence from the President or the Congress. In recent years, this supposition has been called into question as Congress, through its budget powers, has increasingly involved itself in policy and enforcement decisions of the Federal Trade Commission. A favorite method of control is to deny the Commission the power to spend money on specified law enforcement proceedings.

The antitrust remedies available to the Commission are limited to issuance of "cease and desist orders" against parties found to violate Section 5. Additional remedies can follow, including civil penalties and restitution, only if there is noncompliance with such orders. There is no private right of action to enforce Section 5 of the Federal Trade Commission Act. Because the only remedies available are public remedies, and the Commission inevitably has

---

§ 20.6

1. See Jefferson Parish Hospital District No. 2 v. Hyde, 466 U.S. 2, 104 S.Ct. 1551, 80 L.Ed.2d 2 (1984); Eastman Kodak Co. v. Image Technical Services, Inc., 504 U.S. 451, 112 S.Ct. 2072, 119 L.Ed.2d 265 (1992).

scarce resources, the ability to monitor and regulate unfair methods of competition under the FTC Act is limited.

The Federal Trade Commission can also enforce all of the prohibitions found in the Clayton Act. However, it cannot enforce Sections 1 or 2 of the Sherman Act. Today, the Commission's primary activity is evaluating mergers under the premerger notification rules of Section 7 of the Clayton Act. It is hard to see that the Commission's efforts since 1914 have lent much precision to the field of antitrust law. It has instead become a variable agency often swinging from periods of inaction to dramatic enforcement proceedings along with the tides of United States politics and the prevailing winds of antitrust.

§ 20.8   Extraterritorial U.S. Antitrust in Perspective—Blocking Statutes

After some initial hesitation,[1] United States courts have long asserted the right to apply the Sherman Antitrust Act to foreign commerce intended to or affecting the United States market. Perhaps the most famous application of this approach was by Judge Learned Hand in the *Alcoa* case.[2] This decision is the origin of the "effects test" governing extraterritorial U.S. antitrust jurisdiction. It was affirmatively applied in *Alcoa* to a foreign cartel acting almost entirely outside the United States but with clear restraint upon U.S. imports. In some cases, this approach has been tempered to allow consideration and balancing of the interests of comity and foreign countries in the outcome.[3] This results in a kind of jurisdictional "rule of reason" and is supported by the American Law Institute's Third Restatement of Foreign Relations Law.[4]

The extraterritorial reach of the antitrust laws was addressed by the U.S. Supreme Court in a divided decision in *Hartford Fire Insurance Co. v. California*.[5] The majority opted for an extraterritorial application unless there was a "true conflict." What a true conflict means was left to future debate, but it appeared to mean that the Sherman Act would be applied unless the foreign law required the American party to act in a manner which is in violation of U.S. law, or compliance with the laws of both nations is

§ 20.8

1. See especially, American Banana Co. v. United Fruit Co., 213 U.S. 347, 29 S.Ct. 511, 53 L.Ed. 826 (1909).

2. United States v. Aluminum Co. of America, 148 F.2d 416 (2d Cir.1945).

3. See especially Timberlane Lumber Co. v. Bank of America, 549 F.2d 597 (9th Cir.1976); Mannington Mills, Inc. v. Congoleum Corp., 595 F.2d 1287 (3d Cir.

1979); Compare Laker Airways Ltd. v. Sabena, Belgian World Airlines, 731 F.2d 909 (D.C.Cir.1984) and Uranium Antitrust Litigation, 617 F.2d 1248 (7th Cir.1980) (jurisdictional rule of reason rejected).

4. Section 403 (1987).

5. 509 U.S. 764, 113 S.Ct. 2891, 125 L.Ed.2d 612 (1993).

impossible. The case raises doubt about the status of interest balancing in any situation where U.S. laws are applied extraterritorially and create a conflict.[6]

The Circuit Courts have been divided on the impact of *Hartford Fire* on comity analysis. Predictably, the Ninth Circuit has resisted abandonment of its *Timberlane* approach.[7] The Second Circuit, on the other hand, has fully embraced the true conflict doctrine.[8] Most courts and commentators see comity as "more an aspiration than a fixed rule" after *Hartford Fire*.[9]

Some limits on the extraterritorial reach of the Sherman Act are created by the act of state doctrine and the Foreign Sovereign Immunities Act.[10] But in the main, United States antitrust law has been applied to foreigners and overseas activities with a zeal sometimes approaching religious fervor. Amendments to the Sherman Act in 1984 stress the "direct, substantial and reasonably foreseeable" nature of effects on United States foreign commerce as a prerequisite to antitrust jurisdiction. Nevertheless, the potential for conflict in this field is enormous. For example, a multinational enterprise (MNE) headquartered in the U.S. but doing business in England could be constrained by United States antitrust law from fixing prices, yet permitted by EU competition law to do exactly that. Assuming that the price fixing in question has effects in both markets, what course of action is to be followed? There is no easy answer. When the MNE is located within a country other than one of the Member States of the EU or the United States, but engages in activity having effects within those markets, the problem potential of extraterritoriality may be even more acute. Reconciling a conflict of antitrust laws applied extraterritorially by these two jurisdictions could become a flashpoint in international business transactions.

6. For a debate regarding the meaning of the decision, see Andreas F. Lowenfeld, Conflict, Balancing of Interests, and the Exercise of Jurisdiction to Prescribe: Reflections on the Insurance Antitrust Case, 89 Am.J. Int'l L. 42 (1995); Phillip R. Trimble, The Supreme Court and International Law: The Demise of Restatement Section 403, 89 Am.J.Int'l L. 53 (1995); Larry Kramer, Extraterritorial Application of American Law after the Insurance Antitrust Case: a Reply to Professors Lowenfeld and Trimble, 89 Am.J.Int'l L. 750 (1995).

7. Metro Industries, Inc. v. Sammi Corp., 82 F.3d 839 (9th Cir.1996), *cert. denied* 519 U.S. 868, 117 S.Ct. 181, 136 L.Ed.2d 120 (1996).

8. In re Maxwell Communication Corp., 93 F.3d 1036 (2d Cir.1996).

9. United States v. Nippon Paper Indus. Co., Ltd., 109 F.3d 1 (1st Cir.1997), *cert. denied* 522 U.S. 1044, 118 S.Ct. 685, 139 L.Ed.2d 632 (1998) (*criminal* extraterritorial antitrust jurisdiction affirmed).

10. Even when there are effects in the U.S.A., extraterritorial antitrust conspiracies are not actionable unless those effects "give rise" to the plaintiff's antitrust claim. No subject matter jurisdiction exists. See Den Norske Stats Oljeselskap As v. HeereMac Vof, 241 F.3d 420 (5th Cir.2001), *cert. denied* 534 U.S. 1127, 122 S.Ct. 1059, 151 L.Ed.2d 967 (2002), *rehearing denied* 535 U.S. 1012, 122 S.Ct. 1597, 152 L.Ed.2d 512 (2002) (Norwegian oil company claims fail).

Extraterritoriality is a matter of balance. The executive, legislative, and judicial branches of government in the United States have reached out extraterritorially in the law of admiralty, antitrust, crime, labor, securities regulation, taxation, torts, trademarks and wildlife management. A balance drawn wrongly by one nation invites retaliatory action by others. In the case of antitrust judgments emanating from courts in the United States, most notably the "Uranium Cartel" treble damages litigation of the late 1970s,[11] many nations consider that the balance has been wrongly drawn. At least nine nations (Australia, Canada, France, Germany, Netherlands, New Zealand, Philippines, South Africa and the United Kingdom) have taken retaliatory action by enacting "blocking statutes." In addition, the 41 Commonwealth nations have resolved general support for a position similar to that of the United Kingdom.

The United Kingdom blocking statute is the Protection of Trading Interests Act of 1980. This Act (without specifying United States antitrust law) makes it difficult to depose witnesses, obtain documents or enforce multiple liability judgments extraterritorially in the U.K. Violation of the 1980 Act may result in criminal penalties. Furthermore, under the "clawback" provision of the Act, parties with outstanding multiple liabilities in foreign jurisdictions (e.g., U.S. treble damages defendants) may recoup the punitive element of such awards in Britain against assets of the successful plaintiff. The British Act invites other nations to adopt clawback provisions by offering clawback reciprocity. United States attorneys confronted with a blocking statute need to understand that multiple liability judgments combined with contingency fee arrangements are virtually unknown elsewhere.

The extensive array of pre-trial discovery mechanisms allowed in U.S. civil litigation rarely, if ever, have a counterpart in foreign law. Discovery subpoenas originating in United States litigation are often "shocking" to many foreign defendants. And the U.S. Supreme Court has ruled that use of letters rogatory under the Hague Convention is not obligatory.[12] It is the blocking of discovery that potentially most threatens the extraterritorial application of United States laws, especially antitrust. Since U.S. courts may sanction parties who in bad faith fail to respond to discovery requests, foreign defendants requesting help from their home governments under blocking statutes are especially at risk. On the other hand, good faith efforts to modify or work around discovery blockades may favor foreign defendants. Such defendants are often caught in a "no win" situation. Either way they will be penalized.

---

11. See Uranium Antitrust Litigation (Westinghouse Electric Corp. v. Rio Algom Limited), 617 F.2d 1248 (7th Cir. 1980).

12. Société National Industrielle Aérospatiale v. U.S. District Court, 482 U.S. 522, 107 S.Ct. 2542, 96 L.Ed.2d 461 (1987).

The reasons advanced to support an extraterritorial application of United States antitrust laws are founded on the idea that some extraterritorial extension is necessary to prevent their circumvention by multinational corporations which have the business sagacity to ensure that anticompetitive transactions are consummated beyond the territorial borders of the United States. An extraterritorial extension of antitrust laws can also help to ensure that the U.S. consumer receives the benefit of competing imports, which in turn may spur complacent domestic industries. The effect of foreign auto imports on the car manufacturers in the United States may be cited as an example. In an increasingly internationalized world, extraterritorial antitrust may merely reflect economic reality.

On the other hand, the British argue that extraterritoriality permits the United States to unjustifiably "mold the international economic and trading world to its own image." In particular, the "effects test" doctrine creates legal uncertainty for international traders, and U.S. courts pay little attention to the competing policies (interests) of other concerned governments. As the House of Lords has stated: "It is axiomatic that in anti-trust matters the policy of one state may be to defend what it is the policy of another state to attack."[13] The British also argue, not without some support, that customary international law does not permit extraterritorial application of national laws. In making this argument, the British have a convenient way of forgetting about the extraterritorial scope of Articles 81 and 82 of the Treaty of Rome,[14] which are now part of their law. Moreover, in a curious reversal of roles illustrating the extremes of the debate, the British government applied the Protection of Trading Interests Act to block the pursuit of treble damages in U.S. courts by the liquidator of Laker Airway against British Airways and other defendants. A House of Lords decision reversed this ban but retained government restrictions on discovery related to the case.[15]

§ 20.9   The Goals of European Union Competition Policy

In Europe, the field of law that Americans call "antitrust" is generally referred to as "competition law." Although some nations in Europe have active competition law policies (notably Britain and Germany), none surpass the embracement of competition as a public good by the European Community.

The primary purpose of competition policy in Europe is preservation of the trade and other benefits of economic integration. The

13. Rio Tinto Zinc Corp. v. Westinghouse Electric Corp., 2 W.L.R. 81 (1978).

14. See Section 32.27.

15. British Airways Board v. Laker Airways, 3 W.L.R. 413 (1984).

removal of governmental trade barriers unaccompanied by measures to ensure that businesses do not recreate those barriers would be an incomplete effort. Competing enterprises might agree to geographically allocate markets to each other, making the elimination of national tariffs and quotas by the Treaty of Rome irrelevant. Similarly, a dominant enterprise in one state might tie up all important distributors or purchasers of its goods through long-term exclusive dealing contracts. The result could make entry into that market by another business exceedingly difficult. By assisting in the formation and maintenance of an economic community, business competition law is an important component in competition policy. It prevents enterprise behavior from becoming a substantial nontariff trade barrier to economic integration.

The secondary purpose of European competition policy is not unique to regional integration. This purpose is the attainment of the economic benefits generally thought to accrue in any economy organized on a competitive basis. These benefits are many. Perhaps most important of all, an economy characterized by competitive enterprise answers the questions of economic organization by maximizing the market desires of its human constituents. A genuinely competitive market is responsive to individual choice in a way that acknowledges and promotes diversity. Competition among businesses protects the public interest in having its cumulative demand for goods and services provided at the lowest possible prices and with the greatest possible degree of responsivity to public tastes. It is in this sense that a competitive economy is said to be guided by the principle of "consumer welfare" or "consumer sovereignty." When, for example, European law prevents competing enterprises from fixing prices for their goods or prevents a dominant enterprise from charging monopoly prices at the consumers' expense, such law helps to realize the economic benefits of competition within the Euro-economy.

§ 20.10   Article 81—Restraints of Trade

Article 81(1)(formerly 85(1)) of the Treaty of Rome deals with concerted business practices, business agreements and trade association decisions. When they have the potential to affect trade between member states *and* have the object or effect of preventing, restricting or distorting competition *within* Europe, such business activities are deemed incompatible with the Common Market and are prohibited. The focus of Article 81(1) is thus on cartels. By way of example, Article 81(1) lists certain prohibited activities:

(1) the fixing of prices or trading conditions;

(2) the limitation of production, markets, technical development or investment;

(3) the sharing of markets or sources of supply;

(4) the application of unequal terms to equivalent transactions, creating competitive disadvantages; and

(5) the conditioning of a contract on the acceptance of commercially unrelated additional supplies.

Article 81(2) voids agreements and decisions (or severable parts thereof) prohibited by Article 81(1). Thus the prohibitions of Article 81(1) against anticompetitive activity are absolute and immediately effective under 81(2) without prior judicial or administrative action. The open-ended text of 81(1) gives considerable leeway for interpretation and enforcement purposes. It has, for example, been interpreted to cover nonbinding "gentlemen's agreements."[1] Trade association "recommendations" influencing competition are caught.[2] It also generates considerable uncertainty as to the validity of many business agreements, since full market analyses of their competitive and trade impact are often required. However, Article 81(3) permits Article 81(1) to be declared inapplicable when agreements, decisions, concerted practices or classes thereof:

(1) contribute to the improvement of the production or distribution of goods, or to the promotion of technical or economic progress; while

(2) reserving to consumers an equitable share of the resulting benefits; and neither

(3) impose any restrictions not indispensable to objectives 1 and 2 (i.e., least restrictive means must be used); nor

(4) make it possible for the businesses concerned to substantially eliminate competition.

The prohibitions of Article 81(1) may be tempered by "declarations of inapplicability" (exemptions) only when the circumstances of Article 81(3) are present. As befits exemptions from broad prohibitions, the terms of 81(3) are more narrow and specific. Such legal issues are often considered simultaneously in the process of analyzing the market impact of restrictive agreements, decisions and concerted practices. The net result is not unlike the "rule of reason" approach found in United States antitrust law.

§ 20.11 Commission Investigations, Attorney–Client Privilege, Shared Prosecutorial Powers

In March of 1962 the Council of Ministers adopted Regulation 17 on the basis of proposals from the Commission. Regulation 17

§ 20.10

1. ACF Chemiefarma v. Commission (1970) Eur.Comm.Rep. 661.

2. Re ANSEAU–NAVEWA (1983) Eur.Comm.Rep. 3369.

has been the major piece of secondary law under Articles 81 and 82. Effective May 1, 2004, Regulation 17 is replaced by Regulation 1/2003. These regulations establish the scheme of enforcement for competition law. The Commission, for the most part its Competition Directorate–General or department, has a wide range of powers.

The regulations confer investigatory powers in the Commission to conduct general studies into economic sectors and to review the affairs of individual businesses and trade associations. The Commission may investigate in response to a complaint or upon its own initiative. These powers are particularly significant because (except in the case of mergers) notification of restrictive agreements, decisions and practices to the Commission, although at times beneficial, is not mandatory. The Commission may request all information *it* considers necessary, and examine and make copies of record books and business documents.

Written communications with external EU-licensed lawyers undertaken for defense purposes are confidential and need not be disclosed.[1] Written communications with in-house lawyers are *not* exempt from disclosure, nor are communications with external *non*-EU counsel.[2] Thus communications with North American attorneys (who are not also EU-licensed attorneys) are generally discoverable. For example, the Commission obtained in-house counsel documents from John Deere, Inc., a Belgian subsidiary of the United States multinational. These documents were drafted as advice to management on how to avoid competition law liability for export prohibition restraints. They were used by the Commission to justify the finding of an intentional Article 81 violation and a fine of 2 million ECUs.[3] United States attorneys have followed these developments with amazement and trepidation. Disclaimers of possible nonconfidentiality are one option to consider in dealing with clients. At a minimum, U.S. attorneys ought to advise their clients that the usual rules on attorney-client privilege may not apply.

In conducting its investigations, the Commission may ask for verbal explanations on the spot and have access to premises. One author refers to these powers as "dawn raids and other nightmares." Nevertheless, the Court of Justice has affirmed this right of hostile access.[4] Effective May 1, 2004, subject to the issuance of a local court warrant, this right of access will extend to private homes

§ 20.11

1. AM & S Europe Ltd. v. Commission (1982) Eur.Comm.Rep. 1575.

2. *Id.*

3. John Deere v. Commission (1985) 28 Off.J.Eur.Comm. L/35, 58.

4. Hoechst v. Commission (1987) Eur.Comm.Rep. 1549; Dow Chemical Nederland BV v. Commission (1987) Eur.Comm.Rep. 4367; NV Samenwerkende Elektriciteits-produktiebedrijven (SEP) v. Commission (1991) Eur.Comm. Rep. II–1497 (Case T–39/90).

and motor vehicles of corporate directors, managers and other staff. In these matters the Commission acts on its own authority provided there are reasonable grounds to believe that relevant books or records are kept in these locations. It must, however, inform member states prior to taking such steps and may request their assistance. The member states must render assistance when businesses fail to comply with competition law investigations of the Commission.

Businesses involved in the Commission's investigatory process have limited rights to notice and hearing.[5] They do not have access to the Commission's files. Any failure on the part of an enterprise to provide information requested by the Commission or to submit to its investigation can result in the imposition of considerable fines and penalties. For example, the Belgian and French subsidiaries of the Japanese electrical and electronic group, Matsushita, were fined by the Commission for supplying it with false information about whether Matsushita recommended retail prices for its products. These sanctions are civil in nature and run against the corporation, not its directors or management.

The Commission has increased the use of its investigatory powers. Several procedural requirements for Commission investigations and hearings have been discussed by the Court of Justice. One notable Court decision upheld the authority of the Commission to conduct searches of corporate offices without notice or warrant when it has reason to believe that pertinent evidence may be lost.[6] Another notable decision permitted a Swiss "whistle blower" who once worked for Hoffmann–La Roche (a defendant in competition law proceedings) to sue the Community in tort for disclosure of his identity as an informant.[7]

Regulation 17 and Regulation 1 envision significant cooperation and information sharing between European and national authorities in the field of competition law. Effective May 1, 2004, enforcement of Articles 81 and 82 will be shared with the competition agencies and national courts of the member states. A new European Competition Network will be established to facilitate cooperative law enforcement and minimize divergent application of competition law principles, with the Commission to act as final arbiter on substantive matters. The principal reason for this sharing of enforcement duties is to allow the Commission to focus its energies on price fixing, cartel arrangements and other serious violations of Articles 81 and 82.

5. Commission Regulation 99/63. See generally Hoffmann–La Roche v. Commission (1979) Eur.Comm.Rep. 461.

6. Re National Panasonic (1980) Eur.Comm.Rep. 2033.

7. Adams v. Commission (1985) Eur. Comm.Rep. 3539.

The Court of First Instance has ruled that the Commission can refuse to pursue a competition law complaint if an adequate remedy is available from a national court.[8] This decision supports the Commission's customary practice of decentralized "subsidiarity" in the competition law field. Starting May 1, 2004, national courts may ask the Commission for support regarding Article 81 or 82, with the Commission and national authorities empowered to file opinions with the national courts. Moreover, in all cases affecting member state trade, Regulation 1/ 2003 permits the Commission to issue ex ante binding decisions determining that a particular agreement or practice does not infringe European competition law. Such decisions would preclude different results at the national level.

§ 20.12   Commission Prosecutions and Sanctions

In addition to its investigatory powers, the Commission is authorized to determine when violations of the competition law provisions occur. This is the source of the Commission's power to render enforcement decisions. A regulation limits the time period in which the Commission may render a decision in competition law cases to five years. All Commission decisions, including enforcement decisions and decisions to investigate, fine or penalize must be published and are subject to judicial review. Since 1989, these appeals are heard by the Court of First Instance.

During interim periods, the Commission has the power to order measures indispensable to its functions.[1] Interim relief should be granted when there is prima facie evidence of a violation and an urgent need to prevent serious and irreparable private damage or intolerable damage to the public interest. La Cinq, a private television service twice denied membership in the European Broadcasting Union, successfully met these criteria. The Court of First Instance rebuked the Commission's refusal to grant provisional Article 82 protection.[2]

Before deciding that a competition law breach has occurred, the Commission issues a statement of "objections." This statement must reveal which facts the Commission intends to rely upon in reaching a decision that a violation has occurred.[3] A hearing can then be requested by the alleged violator(s) or any interested person. These hearings are conducted in private, with separate reviews of complainants and witnesses. The Commission must

8. Automec SRL v. Commission (1992) Eur.Comm.Rep. 2223 (Case T–24/90).

§ 20.12

1. Camera Care v. Commission (1980) Eur.Comm.Rep. 119.

2. La Cinq v. Commission (1992) Eur.Comm.Rep. 1 (Case T–44/90).

3. AEG v. Commission (1983) Eur. Comm.Rep. 3151.

disclose only those non-confidential documents in its file upon which it intends to rely and are necessary to prepare an adequate defense.[4] After the hearing, the Commission consults with the Advisory Committee on Restrictive Practices and Monopolies, which is composed of one civil servant expert from each member state. The results of this consultation are not made public. Having consulted the Committee, the Commission is then free to render an enforcement decision.

In its enforcement decision, the Commission may require businesses to "cease and desist" their infringing activities. In practice, this power has sufficed to permit the Commission to order infringing enterprises to come up with their own remedial solutions. However, the Commission may not, at least in an Article 81 proceeding, require a violator to contract with the complainant.[5] Daily penalties may be imposed to compel adherence to the order to cease and desist. Commission decisions on violations are also accompanied by a capacity to substantially fine any intentionally or negligently infringing enterprise. When appeals are lodged against Commission decisions imposing fines and penalties, payment is suspended but interest is charged and a bank guarantee for the amounts concerned must be provided.[6]

In the early years, fines and penalties actually levied by the Commission were few, relatively small in amount and frequently reduced on appeal to the Court of Justice. As competition law doctrine has become clearer, these trends have all been reversed. In its more recent decisions, the Court has upheld substantial fines and penalties imposed by the Commission in competition law proceedings and recognized their deterrent value.[7] In 2001, for example, the Commission imposed competition law fines of more than $850 million on European companies for conspiring to fix prices and divide up the vitamins market.

Any complete picture of the development of Article 81 must account for the Commission's informal negotiations as well as its decisions to prosecute infringing activities. Business compliance with Articles 81 and 82 is often achieved short of a formal Commission decision. Word of informal file-closings is occasionally revealed. In *Re Eurofima,*[8] for example, the Commission terminated proceedings without issuing a decision. In the process of responding to complaints from suppliers, the Commission was able to secure

---

4. VBVB and VBBB v. Commission (1984) Eur.Comm.Rep. 19.

5. Automec SRL v. Commission (1992) Eur.Comm.Rep. 2223 (Case T–24/90). Compare Article 82 case law on refusals to deal by dominant firms.

6. Hasselblad v. Commission (1982) Eur.Comm.Rep. 1555.

7. See Musique Diffusion Francaise SA v. Commission (1983) Eur. Comm.Rep. 1825.

8. (1973) Common Mkt.L.Rep. D217.

termination of infringing conduct from Eurofima, the most important buyer of railway rolling stock in the Common Market. Eurofima also undertook to continue to comply with competition law. The Commission announced these results in a press release.

§ 20.13   Article 81—Group Exemptions

The Commission received an onslaught of ... Article 81(3) notifications in 1962 when Regulation 17 took effect. The vast majority of the business activities involved in this deluge were in the distribution and licensing areas. As a result, the Commission sought and obtained authorization in 1965 from the Council to formulate, for limited time periods, group "declarations of inapplicability" under Article 81(3). These are commonly known as "group or block exemptions." The Council granted this authorization, noting that Article 81(3) allows "classes" of exempt agreements.

Group exemptions, guidelines and policy announcements by the Commission in areas where group exemptions have not yet been promulgated, invite businesses to conform their agreements and behavior to their terms and conditions. In other words, group exemptions rely upon confidential business self-regulation.

After a number of test enforcement decisions and definitive rulings by the Court of Justice, the Commission issued Regulation 67 in 1967. It became the first of a series of group exemptions from Article 81(1). Regulation 67/67 was replaced in 1983 by Regulation 1983/83. These regulations concerned exclusive dealing methods of distribution. Exclusive dealing agreements ordinarily involve restrictions on manufacturers and independent distributors of goods. These restraints concern who the manufacturer may supply, to whom the manufacturer or distributor may sell, and from whom the distributor may acquire the goods or similar goods. Exclusive dealing agreements should be distinguished from agency or consignment agreements where title and most risk remain with the manufacturer until the goods are sold by their retail agents to consumers. The announced policy position is that competition law will not require a manufacturer to compete with its agents. Exclusivity in genuine retail agency agreements is therefore legal.

The group exemptions for exclusive dealing, exclusive purchasing and franchise agreements were replaced in 2000 by Regulation 2790/99, known as the vertical restraints regulation. It is accompanied by lengthy vertical restraints guidelines. This regulation and its guidelines are more economic and less formalistic than the predecessors. Supply and distribution agreements of firms with less than 30 percent market shares are generally exempt; this is known as a "safe harbor." Companies whose market shares exceed 30 percent may or may not be exempt, depending upon the results of individual competition law reviews by the Commission under Article 81(3). In either case, no vertical agreements containing so-called "hard core restraints" are exempt. These restraints concern primarily resale price maintenance, territorial and customer protection leading to market allocation, and in most instances exclusive dealing covenants that last more than five years.

A series of Commission regulations have followed the pattern established by Regulation 67. Test cases are initiated by the Commission before the European Court prior to creating a group exemption. Group exemptions now exist for motor vehicle distribution and servicing agreements (Regulation 1400/2002), production specialization agreements among small firms (Regulation 2658/2000), and research and development agreements among small firms (Regulation 2659/2000). The formerly separate group exemptions for patent licensing and know-how licensing have been merged under the technology transfers Regulation 240/96, superceded by Regulation 772/2004 (See Chapter 23). Additional group exemptions are anticipated in light of the May 1, 2004 modernization reforms of Regulation 17 noted above.

§ 20.14   Article 82

Article 82 (formerly 86) of the Treaty of Rome prohibits abuses by one or more undertakings of a dominant position within a substantial part of the Common Market insofar as the abuses may affect trade between member states. The existence of a dominant position is not prohibited by European law. Only its abuse is proscribed.

Article 82 proceeds to list certain examples of what constitute abuses by dominant enterprises:

(1) the imposition of unfair prices or other trading conditions;

(2) the limitation of production, markets or technical development which prejudices consumers;

(3) the application of dissimilar conditions to equivalent transactions, thereby engendering competitive disadvantages; and

(4) the subjection of contracts to commercially unrelated supplementary obligations.

These examples are remarkably, although not exactly, similar to the examples of anticompetitive agreements, decisions and concerted practices provided in Article 81. Indeed, insofar as two or more enterprises are abusing their dominant market position under Article 82 they may well be simultaneously engaging in an Article 81(1) infringement. However, fines for the same conduct under both Articles 81 and 82 will not be permitted by the Court of Justice.[1]

Article 82 differs fundamentally from Article 81. There are no provisions to declare abuses by dominant enterprise(s) automatically void, nor to permit any exemptions from its prohibitions. Article 82 might be viewed as a *per se* rule of law. Thus, under the administrative framework of Regulation 17, no individual or group exemptions can be granted by the Commission for Article 82. The absence of exemptions from Article 82 means that there is little incentive for dominant firms to notify their abuses to the Commission. Negative clearances are obtainable, however, indicating that the Commission sees no grounds for intervention on the facts and law before it. Quite understandably, few requests for Article 82 clearances have been made. Regulation 17 grants the Commission the same powers with reference to Article 82 as it possesses under Article 81 to obtain information, investigate corporate affairs, render infringement decisions, and fine or penalize offenders.

A few Commission decisions concerning Article 82 have their origins in complaints to the Commission from competitors or those abused. Generally, however, the Commission has acted on its own initiative in Article 82 proceedings. Some of the Commission's decisions have been the subject of appeal to the Court of Justice, which occasionally has received Article 82 issues on reference from national courts under the preliminary ruling procedure. A limited number of Article 82 cases have been resolved informally through Commission negotiations. To highlight the more important developments in the interpretation of the language and scope of Article 82, a selection of cases and issues follows.

§ 20.15   Article 82—Dominant Positions

Unless an enterprise or group of enterprises possesses a dominant position within a substantial part of the Common Market, no questions of abuse can arise. A dominant position may exist on either the supply or demand side of the market.[1]

In establishing the existence of dominant positions, the Commission has tended to look at commercial realities, not technical legal distinctions. For example, the only two producers of sugar in Holland were legally and financially independent of each other. In practice they systematically cooperated in the joint purchase of raw

§ 20.14

1. ACF Chemiefarma v. Commission (1970) Eur.Comm.Rep. 661.

§ 20.15

1. Re Eurofima (1973) Common Mkt. L.Rep. D217 (dominant buyer). In 1997, the commission issued a "Notice on the Definition of Relevant Market For Purposes of Community Competition Law" (O.J. 1997 C372/5). This Notice covers Article 81 and 82 cases, as well as mergers and acquisitions.

materials, the adoption of production quotas, the use of by-products, the pooling of research, advertising and sales promotion, and the unification of prices and terms of sales. To other enterprises they appeared as if a single firm. They were involved in over 85 percent of the sales of sugar in Holland. The Commission and the Court of Justice held them to be a single enterprise for the purpose of assessing the existence of a dominant position under Article 82.[2] The Commission has recently found support for its "collective dominance" theory of liability under Article 82.[3] This theory may bear upon oligopolies within the Common Market.

A celebrated merger case involved Continental Can, a large U.S. corporation.[4] It is a leading case on the existence of a dominant position under Article 82 law. Evidence of Continental Can's worldwide and German national market strength in the supply of certain metal containers and tops, a concentrated market characterized by ineffective consumers and competitors, and strong technical and financial barriers to entry were sufficient for the Commission to find the existence of a dominant position in certain areas of Germany. In so doing, the Commission stressed that enterprises are in a dominant position:

> when they have the power to behave independently, which puts them in a position to act without taking into account their competitors, purchasers or suppliers ... This power does not necessarily have to derive from an absolute domination ... it is enough that they be strong enough as a whole to ensure to those enterprises an overall independence of behavior, even if there are differences in intensity in their influence on different partial markets.[5]

Power to behave independently of competitors, purchasers or suppliers amounting to a dominant position must be exercisable with reference to the supply or acquisition of particular goods or services, i.e., a market. In *Continental Can* the Commission distinguished between that enterprise's powerful position around the world and in Europe with reference to the generic market for light metal containers, and its dominant position in Germany with reference to the particular markets for preserved meat and shellfish tins and metal caps for glass jars. Thus, initial Commission selection of the appropriate geographic and product market is the key to its analysis of whether a dominant position exists or not. It is also

---

2. Re European Sugar Cartel (1973) Common Mkt.L.Rep. D65 (Commission); (1975) Eur.Comm.Rep. 1663 (Court of Justice).

3. See Societa Italiano Vetro SpA v. Commission (1992) Eur.Comm.Rep. 1403 (Cases T–68/89, 77/89, 78/89).

4. Europemballage Corporation and Continental Can Co., Inc. v. Commission (1972) Common Mkt.L.Rep. D11 (Commission); (1973) Eur.Comm.Rep. 215 (Court of Justice).

5. Id.

the key to the utility of its dominant position formula as set out in the *Continental Can* opinion. On such selection hinges the determination of the market power of the enterprise concerned. The broader the market for goods or services is defined (light metal cans versus cans for preserved meat, etc.), the less likely there will be overall independence of behavior from competitors, purchasers or suppliers. The same is true for broader geographic markets selected by the Commission (e.g., Europe versus Germany or parts thereof).

On appeal to the Court of Justice, the Commission's guiding principles for determining the existence of a dominant position under Article 82 were not seriously questioned. The Court did challenge the Commission's delineation of the relevant *product* market and its failure to explain in full how Continental Can had the power to behave independently in the preserved meat, shellfish, and metal top markets. Its German market shares were, by the Commission's calculation, 75, 85, and 55 percent respectively. Regarding the first criticism the Court said:

> The products in question have a special market only if they can be individualized not only by the mere fact that they are used for packaging certain products but also by special production characteristics which give them a specific suitability for this purpose.[6]

In other words the Commission failed to make clear, for the purpose of assessing the existence of a dominant position, why the markets for preserved meat tins, preserved fish tins, and metal tops for glass jars should be treated separately and independently of the general market for light metal containers.

The Commission's failure here overlapped with the Court's second point:

> A dominant position in the market for light metal containers for canned meat and fish cannot be decisive insofar as it is not proved that competitors in other fields but not in the market for light metal containers cannot, by mere adaptation, enter this market with sufficient strength to form a serious counter-weight.[7]

The Court felt that the existence or lack of competition from substitute materials such as plastic or glass as well as potential competition from new entrants to the metal container industry or purchasers who might produce their own tins were also aspects of market power insufficiently explored by the Commission. Under the Commission's own formula for establishing a dominant position,

6. Id.
7. Id.

the Court annulled the decision because it did not "sufficiently explain the facts and appraisals of which it [was] based."

The Court's emphasis in *Continental Can* on "special production characteristics," entry barriers and potential competition amounted to instructions to the Commission to do its homework a little better in future market power analyses under Article 82. Evaluating potential competition, of course, involves hypothetical calculations with which even an expert Commission would have difficulty. Yet these factors, as well as those considered by the Commission, made up the commercial realities of the German marketplace for canned meat and fish tins and metal tops for glass jars. What is clear from the Court's *Continental Can* opinion is that dominance can be found under Article 82 in sub-product markets such as these, provided the Commission is exhaustive in its research and analysis.

Subsequent opinions of the Court have elaborated upon the product market analysis presented in *Continental Can*. The "interchangeability" of products for specific uses is a critical factor in determining the relevant product market under Article 82.[8] Thus, bananas were a proper product market since their interchangeability with other fresh fruits was limited.[9] And the replacement market for tires (as distinct from original equipment) is another sub-market capable of sustaining a dominant position.[10] In exceptional circumstances, even a brand name product may be the relevant sub-market.[11]

The Court has held that a market share of 40 percent may constitute dominance under Article 82.[12] Such a percentage is well below the threshold market share associated with monopolization cases under Section 2 of the Sherman Antitrust Act. While the Court has said that a market share of 5 or 10 percent would ordinarily rule out the existence of a dominance, exceptional circumstances could show such a position. Moreover, a large market share (say 50 percent or more) is presumptive proof of a dominant position.[13]

Partial *geographic* markets can also be relevant to Article 82 market power analyses. A dominant position must exist within a

---

8. Hoffmann–La Roche v. Commission (1979) Eur.Comm.Rep. 461.

9. United Brands Co. v. Commission (1978) Eur.Comm.Rep. 207.

10. Michelin NV v. Commission (1983) Eur.Comm.Rep. 3461.

11. General Motors Continental NV v. Commission (1975) Eur.Comm.Rep. 1367 (legal monopoly over import certificates for which excessive prices were charged); Hugin Cash Registers Ltd. v. Commission (1979) Eur.Comm.Rep. 1869 (spare parts for brand name product must be supplied to service competitor.)

12. See United Brands v. Commission (1978) Eur.Comm.Rep. 207.

13. See Hoffmann–La Roche v. Commission (1979) Eur.Comm.Rep. 461.

"substantial" part of the Common Market. The Commission discussed geographic markets amounting to the whole of Germany in its opinion concerning tins and metal tops. Yet each of these products has different transport costs. The geographic commercial realities of competition in metal tops, given their relatively low level of transport costs, are likely to be much broader than that for tins. The same comparison can be made as between small and large tins. The Court held that the Commission's geographic delineation of the markets for large and small tins in *Continental Can* was at odds with some of its own evidence on their relative transport costs. The commercial realities of potential competition in small tins appeared to go beyond the national boundaries of Germany. Thus the Commission's delineation of the particular geographic markets in *Continental Can* was insufficiently explained and appraised. Later decisions have deferred to the Commission's expertise and discretion in selecting relevant geographic markets. Belgium, Holland, and Southern Germany, for example, have been held substantial parts of the Common Market for Article 82 purposes.[14]

When exclusive intellectual property rights are conferred by national states, the question of the existence of a dominant position remains vital. A patent, copyright or trademark for an individual product does not necessarily give an enterprise independent market power.[15] Other patented or nonpatented products of a similar nature may provide effective market competition and thereby protect suppliers and purchasers from abuse. The full market power analysis required in *Continental Can* must be undertaken. Similarly, the absence of patent rights is no barrier to finding a dominant position where know-how and costly and complex technology give former patent holders complete market power.[16]

§ 20.16   Article 82—Abuse

If the existence of a dominant position in the supply or acquisition of certain goods or services within a substantial part of the Common Market has been established, the next issue under Article 82 is whether an abuse or exploitation of that position has occurred. In *Commercial Solvents,* the Commission and the Court of Justice found abuse in the activities of the only producer in the world of aminobutanol, a chemical used in the making of the drug ethambutol. Commercial Solvents, a U.S. corporation, sold the chemical in Italy to its subsidiary, Istituto Chemioterapico, which

---

14. Re European Sugar Cartel (1975) Eur.Comm.Rep. 1663.

15. Parke, Davis v. Probel and Centrafarm (1968) Eur.Comm.Rep. 55; Sirena v. Eda GMBH (1971) Eur.Comm.Rep. 69. But see Radio Telefis Eireann v.

Commission (Magill TV Guide), 4 Common Mkt.L.Rep. 586 (1991).

16. Commercial Solvents Corp. v. Commission (1973) 12 Common Mkt. L.Rev. D50 (Commission); (1974) Eur. Comm.Rep. 223 (Court of Justice).

in turn sold it to Zoja, an Italian firm making the drug. After merger negotiations between Istituto and Zoja broke off, Zoja sought but failed to get supplies of the chemical from Istituto.

Upon receiving a complaint from Zoja, the Commission commenced Article 82 infringement proceedings. It eventually held that the refusal to deal of Commercial Solvents and Istituto (viewed as one enterprise) amounted to an abuse. Commercial Solvents, through its Italian subsidiary, was ordered to promptly make supplies of aminobutanol available to Zoja at a price no higher than the maximum which it normally charged.[1]

In *Re GEMA,* the only German authors' and composers' rights licensing society was in possession of a dominant position within a substantial part of the Common Market. This dominant position was reinforced by agreements with other societies in Europe granting exclusive rights to the various national markets. The societies were extremely advantageous and profitable to recording artists who otherwise faced formidable, if not impossible, tasks of distributing rights to their copyrighted goods on an individual basis to record manufacturers and other users. These commercial realities reinforced the Commission's conclusion that GEMA's market position was a dominant one.

The Commission instituted Article 82 infringement proceedings *sua sponte.*[2] It decided that the imposition of higher license fees on importers of records and tape recorders, compared with fees imposed on German manufacturers, was restrictive of competition between them and therefore an abuse of GEMA's dominant position relative to its purchasers. GEMA similarly abused its dominant position by extending its members' copyrights to noncopyrighted works through a system of package license fees that failed to distinguish between copyrighted and noncopyrighted works. By discriminating through loyalty rebates between German users and users from different member states, GEMA abusively helped to prevent the establishment of a single common market for the supply of recording services. In other words, it also abused its market power concerning potential competitors.

GEMA's discrimination against foreign members regarding management positions and a supplementary benefits scheme also constituted abuses of its dominant position. Requirements imposed on members to assign their rights to GEMA for the whole world and all marketing categories were deemed unnecessary to its operation and fell into the same category. GEMA members were also abusively excluded, by their contract terms, from recourse to the courts in the event of disputes as to distribution of GEMA funds.

By requiring a six-year term, by obliging assignment of all future works during that six-year period, and by establishing a lengthy period of waiting to be eligible for certain payments, GEMA abused its dominant position through agreements with its supplier-members. By generally curtailing their mobility to join other societies in the Common Market, GEMA inhibited the process of economic integration and the creation of a single market for music publishers.

Many of the abuses found in *GEMA* do not fall under the examples provided by the Treaty terms of Article 82. From this survey of some of the abuses found, it should be apparent that once a dominant position is established the Commission feels free to roam the whole of the behavior of the dominant enterprise. Anticompetitive aspects of contractual and noncontractual relations between GEMA and its members, GEMA's constitution, its general commercial practices, and its relations with record manufacturers and users of rights were reviewed and subjected to the Commission's regulation. Another decision involves a French society of musical composers' rights.[3]

Hoffmann–La Roche, the large multinational Swiss firm, was fined for abusing its dominant position in seven vitamin markets in Europe. It used a network of exclusive or preferential supply contracts, along with loyalty rebates, to reinforce its dominance by cornering retail markets.[4] United Brands, a U.S. multinational, abused its dominant position in bananas through discriminatory, predatory and excessive pricing in various countries. Its abuses also extended to refusals to deal with important past customers and prohibiting the resale of bananas. Excessive pricing occurred when its banana prices bore little relation to the economic value of the bananas supplied.[5] This particular finding of the Commission however, was quashed on appeal by the Court of Justice. Taking into account the "high profits" involved, the Commission fined United Brands 1,000,000 ECUs. In the Commission's opinion, this was a "moderate" fine under the circumstances.

The Court of Justice has held that predatory pricing can constitute an abuse of a dominant position in violation of Article 82. Predatory pricing below average total cost (as well as below average variable cost) may be abusive if undertaken to eliminate a competitor. Regarding the former, pricing below average total cost

---

3. See Greenwich Film Production, Paris v. SACEM (1979) Eur.Comm.Rep. 3275. See generally regarding copyright abuses, Radio Telefis Eireann v. Commission (Magill TV Guide), 4 Common Mkt.L.Rep. 586 (1991).

4. Hoffmann–La Roche v. Commission (1979) Eur.Comm.Rep. 461.

5. United Brands v. Commission (1976) Eur. Comm. Rep. 425, (1978) Eur.Comm.Rep. 207.

could drive out competitors as efficient as the dominant firm but lacking its extensive financial resources.[6]

§ 20.17   The Extraterritorial Reach of Articles 81 and 82

There is a question about the extent to which the competition rules of Europe extend to activity anywhere in the world, including activity occurring entirely or partly within the territorial limits of the United States, Mexico or Canada. Decisions by the Commission and the Court of Justice suggest that the territorial reach of Articles 81 and 82 is expanding and may extend to almost any international business transaction.

For an agreement to be incompatible with the Common Market and prohibited under Article 81(1), it must be "likely to affect trade between Member States" and have the object or effect of impairing "competition within the Common Market." Taken together, these requirements amount to an "effects test" for extraterritorial application of Article 81. This test is similar to that which operates under the Sherman Act of the United States.

The Court has repeatedly held that the fact that one of the parties to an agreement is domiciled in a third country does not preclude the applicability of Article 81(1). Swiss and British chemical companies, for example, argued that the Commission was not competent to impose competition law fines for acts committed in Switzerland and Britain (before joining the EU) by enterprises domiciled outside its scope even if the acts had effects within the Common Market.[1] Nevertheless, the Court held those companies in violation of Article 81 because they owned subsidiary companies within the Union and controlled their behavior. The foreign parent and its subsidiaries were treated as a "single enterprise" for purposes of service of process, judgment, and collection of fines and penalties. In doing so, the Court observed that the fact that a subsidiary company has its own legal personality does not rule out the possibility that its conduct is attributable to the parent company.

The Court has extended its reasoning to the extraterritorial application of Article 82. A United States parent company, for example, was held potentially liable for acquisitions by its subsidiary which affected market conditions within the Common Market.[2]

---

6. Akzo Chemie BV v. Commission (1991) Eur.Comm.Rep. 3359 (Case C–62/86).

§ 20.17

1. See ICI v. Commission (1972) Eur. Comm.Rep. 619.

2. See Europemballage Corp. and Continental Can Co., Inc. v. Commission (1973) Eur.Comm.Rep. 215.

In another decision, the Court held that a Maryland company's refusal to sell its product to a competitor of its affiliate company was a result of united "single enterprise" action.[3] It proceeded to state that extraterritorial conduct merely having "repercussions on competitive structures" in the Common Market fell within the parameters of Article 82. The Court ordered Commercial Solvents, through its Italian affiliate, to supply the competitor at reasonable prices.

In 1988, the Court of Justice widened the extraterritorial reach of Article 81 in a case where wood pulp producers from the U.S., Canada, Sweden and Finland were fined for price fixing activities affecting Union trade and competition. These firms did not have substantial operations within Common Market; they were primarily exporters to it. This decision's utilization of a place of implementation "effects test" is quite similar to that used under the Sherman Act.[4] And the reliance by the U.S. exporters upon a traditional Webb–Pomerene export cartel exemption from United States antitrust law carried no weight in European law. The Court has also affirmed the extraterritorial reach of Articles 81 and 82 to airfares in and out of Europe.[5]

§ 20.18   United States Antitrust Cooperation Agreements

Some evidence of international antitrust cooperation is contained in a 1976 recommendation of the OECD which provides for notification of antitrust actions, exchanges of information to the extent that the disclosure is domestically permissible, and where practical, coordination of antitrust enforcement. The OECD resolution served as a model for the 1972 "Antitrust Notification and Consultation Procedure" between Canada and the United States, and the 1976 antitrust cooperation agreement with the Federal Republic of Germany. Following the "Uranium Cartel" litigation, Australia and the United States reached an Agreement on Cooperation in Antitrust Matters (1982) to minimize jurisdictional conflicts. Australia has taken the position that United States courts are not proper institutions to balance interests of concerned countries within the context of private antitrust litigation. The Agreement on Cooperation provides that when the Government of Australia is concerned with private antitrust proceedings pending in a United States court, the Government of Australia may request the Government of the United States to participate in the litigation. The United States must report to the court on the substance and

3. See Commercial Solvents Corp. v. Commission (1974) Eur.Comm.Rep. 223.
4. Woodpulp Producers v. Commission (1988) Eur.Comm.Rep. 5193.

5. Ahmed Saeed Flugreisen v. Zentrale zur Bekämpfung unlauteren Wettbewerbs (1989) Eur.Comm.Rep. 838.

outcome of consultations with Australia on the matter concerned. In this way, Australia's views and interests in the litigation and its potential outcome are made known to the court. The court is not required to defer to those views, or even to openly consider them. It merely receives the "report." Australia, in turn, has indicated a willingness to be more receptive to discovery requests in United States antitrust litigation and to consult before invoking its blocking statute.

Similar arrangements have been made in the Memorandum of Understanding Between the U.S. and Canada With Respect to the Application of National Antitrust Laws (1984) and more generally in the context of NAFTA. No such agreement has been reached with the United Kingdom, with whom the extraterritoriality issue remains contentious, a fact which has led some to wonder whether the United States ought to have its own blocking statute against extraterritorial European competition law.

The International Antitrust Enforcement Assistance Act of 1994 (P.L. 103–438) authorizes mutual assistance agreements between the DOJ and FTC and their foreign counterparts. Such assistance includes the disclosure and sharing of evidence. The first International Antitrust Enforcement Assistance Agreement was completed between Australia and the United States in 1997. Its focus is on mutual assistance for criminal investigations. The agreement is especially notable in light of a 1997 decision of the First Circuit Court of Appeals that the Sherman Act applies criminally to foreign companies (in this case, Nippon Paper Industries). Additional antitrust cooperation agreements were negotiated with Israel, Japan and Brazil in 1999, and Mexico in 2000.

In August of 1995, the United States and Canada signed an antitrust and deceptive practices cooperation agreement, followed by a "comity" agreement in 2004 not unlike that between the EU and the United States (see below).

§ 20.19 United States–European Antitrust Cooperation

In 1991 the European Community (of which Britain is still a member) and the United States reached an antitrust cooperation agreement. This accord commits the parties to notify each other of imminent enforcement action, to share relevant information and consult on potential policy changes. It was prominently used in 1994 to jointly settle charges of restrictive trade practices with the Microsoft Corporation. An innovative feature is the inclusion of "comity" principles, each side promising to take the other's interests into account when considering antitrust prosecutions. Since the Commission has traditionally permitted U.S. lawyers to appear before it on competition law matters, the FTC announced on the same day as the signing of the antitrust cooperation agreement that European lawyers would be permitted to appear before it on a reciprocal basis.

The agreement has had a significant effect on mergers of firms doing business in North America and Europe. Each side has agreed to notify and consult with the other regarding antitrust matters, including mergers and acquisitions, that "may affect important interests." In its first six months of operation, about 45 notifications were exchanged between the Commission, the U.S. Federal Trade Commission, and the Antitrust Division of the U.S. Justice Department. A large portion of these notifications concerned international mergers and acquisitions. Since both Europe and the U.S. have pre-merger notification systems, the exchange of such information has increased rapidly. In the first year after the cooperation agreement, U.S. antitrust enforcers sent 37 such notifications to the European Commission and received 15 in return. About 20 percent of all the mergers reviewed by the Commission under its competition law were simultaneously being reviewed by U.S. antitrust authorities.

In April of 1997 the Justice Department made its first "positive comity" request to the European Commission under the U.S.-E.U. Antitrust Cooperation Agreement. The Justice Department has asked the Commission to investigate alleged anticompetitive conduct by European airlines regarding U.S.-based airline computer reservation systems (CRS). In 1998, the European Union and the United States signed a "Positive Comity Agreement." This agreement reinforces the 1991 Cooperation Agreement by establishing procedures for positive comity requests and responses, including parallel investigations such as against Microsoft. The Agreement can be found at *www.usdoj.gov*.

*

Chapter 21

FREE TRADE AGREEMENTS OF THE UNITED STATES

Table of Sections

---

§ 21.1 U.S. Free Trade Agreements

The United States has entered into a growing number of major free trade agreements. The first was with Israel, enacted through the United States–Israel Free Trade Area Implementation Act of 1985.[1] The Israeli–U.S. Agreement (IFTA) was fully implemented by January 1, 1995. The second was with Canada, and this agreement was adopted through the United States–Canada Free Trade Area Agreement Implementation Act of 1988.[2] The Canada–U.S. Agreement (CFTA) was fully implemented by January 1, 1998. The United States negotiated along with Canada and Mexico a three-way North American Free Trade Area Agreement (NAFTA). The NAFTA took effect January 1, 1994 with full implementation in nearly all areas by the year 2003. NAFTA was incorporated into United States law by the North American Free Trade Agreement Implementation Act of 1993.[3]

§ 21.1

1. Public Law 99–47, 98 Stat. 3013, June 11, 1985.

2. Public Law 100–449, 102 Stat. 1851, 19 U.S.C.A. § 2112 Note.

3. Public Law 103–182, 107 Stat. 2057.

481

Late in 2001, Jordan and the United States agreed on free trade. In 2003, the United States reached free trade agreements with Chile and Singapore, notably incorporating coverage of E–Commerce and digital products. Early in 2004, free trade between the United States and five Central American states (CAFTA) plus the Dominican Republic, and with Australia and Morocco, was agreed. More bilateral free trade deals are on horizon with Bahrain, Southern Africa and other U.S. trade partners. Most importantly, the United States and 33 nations are negotiating a comprehensive Free Trade Area of the Americas (FTAA).

These trade agreements provide new duty free import opportunities into the U.S. market. Unlike the Generalized System of Preferences (GSP) program and the Caribbean Basin Initiative,[4] these agreements are reciprocal. That is to say they open up foreign markets to United States exports on a duty free basis. In addition, they establish detailed rules targeting nontariff trade barriers (NTBs) among the parties.

The evolutionary character of the free trade agreements of the United States is readily apparent. The first agreement in 1985 with Israel is noticeably narrower in scope and level of legal detail that in 1994 with Canada and Mexico on NAFTA. And the second with Canada in 1989 was nothing less than path breaking; the most sophisticated free trade agreement in the world. Yet, for full understanding, each agreement must be viewed in its own geopolitical and economic context.

The economic integration of Canada and the United States is a certainty. The blueprint is already there. For most Canadians and Americans, revising the design to include Mexico required considerably more effort and discomfort. The discomfort came from years of observing protectionist Mexican trade policies, uncontrolled national debt, corruption, and the sense, somehow, that Mexico just did not "fit." In the end, these perspectives were overcome.

Mexico under Presidents de la Madrid, Salinas, Zedillo, and Fox has been unobtrusively breaking down its trade barriers and reducing the role of government in its economy. More than half of the enterprises owned by the Mexican government a decade ago have been sold to private investors, and more are on the auction block. Tariffs have been slashed to a maximum of 20 percent and import licensing requirements widely removed. Export promotion, not import substitution, has become the highest priority. Like the U.S. and Canada, Mexico (since 1986) participates in the General Agreement on Tariffs and Trade (GATT) and World Trade Organization (WTO). This brings it into the mainstream of the world

---

4. See Chapter 10.

trading community on a wide range of fronts, including participation in nearly the full range of the Uruguay Round agreements.

Mexican debt, under the Brady Plan with its emphasis on loan forgiveness, hopefully promises to become a manageable problem, although the collapse of the peso in December of 1994 and Mexico's ensuing financial crisis casts doubt on this. One party rule has ended nationally and in several states, with signs of an ever more pluralistic democracy on the horizon. Admittedly, political and economic corruption still runs deep within Mexico, but the winds of change are blowing. Major prosecutions of leading police, union and business leaders are underway. Perhaps most significantly, the rapid privatization of the state-owned sector of the economy combined with increasing tolerance of international competition has reduced not only the need for government subsidies but also the opportunity for personal enrichment by public officials.

Presidents Bush and Salinas, and Prime Minister Mulroney, pushed hard in 1991 to open "fast track" negotiations for a free trade agreement. In 1992, these efforts reached fruition when a NAFTA agreement was signed by Canada, the United States and Mexico with a scheduled effective date of Jan. 1, 1994. President Bush submitted the agreement to Congress in December 1992. President Clinton supported NAFTA generally, but initiated negotiations upon taking office for supplemental agreements on the environment and labor. This delayed consideration of the NAFTA agreement in Congress until the Fall of 1993.

Ratification was considered under fast track procedures which essentially gave Congress 90 session days to either ratify or reject NAFTA without amendments. After a bruising national debate that fractured both Democrats and Republicans with each party doing its best to avoid Ross Perot's strident anti-NAFTA attacks, ratification was achieved in mid-November, just weeks before NAFTA's effective date. During this same period, Canada's Conservative Party suffered a devastating defeat at the polls. This defeat was partly a rejection by the Canadian people of the earlier ratification of NAFTA under Prime Minister Mulroney.

The United States is Mexico's largest trading partner, accounting for nearly 70 percent of all Mexican trade and more than 60 percent of its foreign direct investment. In contrast, trade with Mexico in 1994 totaled only 7 percent of all U.S. international trade. Those facts help explain why Mexico has been the major beneficiary of the NAFTA accord.

§ 21.2   The NAFTA Agreement in Outline—Goods

Although each partner affirmed its rights and obligations under the General Agreement on Tariffs and Trade (GATT), the

NAFTA generally takes priority over other international agreements in the event of conflict. The NAFTA, for example, prevails over the Multi–Fiber Arrangement on trade in textiles. Certain exceptions to this general rule of supremacy apply; the trade provisions of the international agreements on endangered species, ozone-depletion and hazardous wastes notably take precedence over the NAFTA (subject to a duty to minimize conflicts). Unlike the GATT, the NAFTA makes a general duty of national treatment binding on all states, provinces and local governments of the three countries.

Prior to NAFTA, Mexican tariffs on U.S. goods averaged about 10 percent; U.S. tariffs on Mexican imports averaged about 5 percent. Under NAFTA, Mexican tariffs will be eliminated on all U.S. exports within ten years except for corn and beans which are subject to a fifteen-year transition. United States tariffs on peanuts, sugar and orange juice from Mexico will also last 15 years. Immediate Mexican tariff removals under the "A" list covered about half the industrial products exported from the United States. Further tariff eliminations were made for the "B" list after 5 years, and will occur for the "C" list when the treaty matures in ten years. Accelerated tariff reduction may occur by bilateral accord. The existing Canada–U.S. tariff reduction schedule remained in place.

NAFTA trade is subject to "rules of origin" that determine which goods qualify for its tariff preferences. These include goods wholly originating in the free trade area. A general waiver of the NAFTA rules of origin requirements is granted if their non-regional value consists of no more than 7 percent of the price or total cost of the goods. Goods containing non-regional materials are considered North American if those materials are sufficiently transformed so as to undergo a specific change in tariff classification. Some goods, like autos and light trucks, must also have a specified North American content. Ultimately, 62.50 percent of the value of such vehicles must be North American in origin. A 60 percent regional content rule will apply to other vehicles and auto parts. After 10 years, U.S. auto producers will no longer need to manufacture in Mexico in order to sell there.

Regional value may be calculated in most cases either by a "transaction value" or a "net cost" method. The former avoids costly accountings. The latter is based upon the total cost of the goods less royalties, sales promotion, packing and shipping, and allowable interest. Either requires manufacturers to trace the source of non-NAFTA components and maintain source records. The net cost method must be used for regional value calculations concerning automotive goods. Uniformity of tariff classification and origin decisions is promoted by NAFTA regulations, a common Certificate of Origin, and a trilateral working group.

Special rules of origin apply to free trade in textiles and apparel under NAFTA. For most products, a "yarn forward" rule applies. This means that the goods must be produced from yarn made in a NAFTA country. A similar "fiber forward" rule applies to cotton and man-made fiber yarns. Silk, linen and certain other fabrics in short supply within NAFTA are treated preferentially, as are yarns, fabrics and apparel covered by special tariff rate quotas. Safeguard import quotas and tariffs may be imposed during the transition period if a rise in textile and apparel trade causes serious damage. Other special rules of origin have been created for electronics. For example, if the circuit board (motherboard) is made in North America and transformed in the region so as to change a tariff classification, the resulting computer may be freely traded.

Import and export quotas, licenses and other restrictions are gradually being eliminated under NAFTA subject to limited rights to restrain trade, e.g. to protect human, animal or plant health, or to protect the environment. Customs user fees on internal NAFTA trade were eliminated in 1999 and existing tariff drawback refunds or waivers were removed by January 1, 2001. These changes, it is thought, will discourage the creation of "export platforms" in one NAFTA country to serve markets in the other member states by insuring that non-NAFTA components and materials are tariffed. NAFTA essentially phased out maquiladora tariff preferences over 7 years, notably disadvantaging producers who source heavily outside North America.

Export taxes and new waivers of customs duties are banned with few exceptions. Once goods are freely traded under NAFTA, they are subject to nondiscriminatory national treatment, including at the provincial and state levels of government. Goods sent to another NAFTA country for repair or alteration may return duty free.

Distinct rules govern energy and petrochemical products. Perhaps most notably, Mexico reserved to its state (as its Constitution provides) the oil, gas, refining, basic petrochemical, nuclear and electricity sectors. A limited range of new investment opportunities were created for non-basic petrochemicals, proprietary electricity facilities, co-generation and independent power production. As under the GATT, minimum or maximum import or export price controls are prohibited on energy products, but licensing systems may be used. Trade quotas or other restraints are permissible only in limited circumstances, e.g. short supply conditions, and a general duty of national treatment applies. Mexico, unlike Canada, has not committed itself to energy sharing during times of shortage.

A second set of distinct rules apply to agricultural trade. These are undertaken principally through separate bilateral agreements between the U.S. and Mexico and Canada and Mexico. The United States–Mexico agreement converts all nontariff trade barriers to tariffs or tariff rate quotas. These will be phased out over a maximum of 15 years. Roughly half of the bilateral trade in agriculture was made duty-free immediately. Under special rules, trade in sugar will be gradually liberalized with all restraints removed over 15 years. Safeguard tariff action may be undertaken during the first 10 years when designated "trigger" levels of agriculture imports are reached. All three countries have agreed to combat agricultural export subsidies, including consultation and what amounts to joint action against third-country subsidies affecting any one of their markets. Special rules of origin apply in the agricultural sector and standards on pesticide residues and inspections are being harmonized.

Another food-related issue is sanitary and phytosanitary measures against health, diseases, contaminants or additives (collectively known as SPS protection). Each country retains the right to establish its own SPS levels of protection provided they are based upon scientific principles and a risk assessment, apply only as needed and do not result in unfair discrimination or disguised restrictions on trade. Each NAFTA nation is committed to accepting the SPS measures of the others as equivalent to its own provided the exporting country demonstrates that its measures achieve the importing country's chosen level of protection. This is facilitated by procedural transparency rules requiring public notice of any SPS measure that may affect NAFTA trade. A committee on SPS measures strives to facilitate all of these principles and to resolve disputes.

Technical standards and certification procedures for products are classic nontariff trade barriers. The NAFTA reaffirmed each country's commitment to the GATT Agreement on Technical Barriers to Trade (1979). In addition, each must provide national treatment and most favored nation treatment. As in the food products area, international standards are used whenever possible, but each country may have more stringent requirements. Procedural transparency rules and a committee on standards are also created. One innovation of note allows companies and other interested parties to participate directly in the development of new standards anywhere within NAFTA. All three countries have agreed not to lower existing environmental, health and safety standards and to attempt to "upwardly harmonize" them. States, provinces and localities can adopt more stringent requirements in these fields provided they are scientifically justifiable, transparent and applied equally to local and imported goods. All health, safety and environmental regulations must be necessary, represent the least trade restrictive way of achieving these goals, and based on scientific principles and risk assessment. Loans from the newly created North American Development Bank help finance the border cleanup by Mexico and the U.S.

Escape clause rules and procedures are generally applicable to United States–Mexico trade under the NAFTA. These permit temporary trade relief against import surges subject to a right of compensation in the exporting nation. During the 10–year transition period, escape clause relief may be undertaken as a result of NAFTA tariff reductions only once per product for a maximum in most cases of 3 years. The relief is the "snap-back" to pre-NAFTA tariffs. After the transition period, escape clause measures may only be undertaken by mutual consent. If a global escape clause proceeding is pursued by one NAFTA partner, the others must be excluded unless their exports account for a substantial share of the imports in question (top five suppliers) and contribute importantly to the serious injury or threat thereof (rate of growth of NAFTA imports must not be appreciably lower than total imports).

There are a variety of other areas of law impacted by the NAFTA accord. Government procurement, apart from defense and national security needs, generally follows nondiscriminatory principles on the supply of goods and services (including construction services) to federal governments. The threshold for the application of the NAFTA to such procurement is $50,000 U.S. for goods and services, and $6.5 million U.S. for construction services. When state enterprises (e.g. PEMEX and CFE), not agencies, are the buyers, thresholds of $250,000 U.S. and $8 million U.S. respectively apply. The use of offsets or other requirements for local purchases or suppliers are prohibited. Independent bid challenge mechanisms must be created by each member state and transparency in the bidding process promoted by timely release of information. These provisions are particularly important because Mexico, unlike Canada, is not a signatory to the GATT/WTO Procurement Code. They do not apply to state and local procurement.

§ 21.3   The NAFTA Agreement in Outline—Services

Cross-border trade in services is subject to national treatment, including no less favorable treatment than that most favorably given at federal, state or local levels. No member state may require that a service provider establish or maintain a residence, local office or branch in its country as a condition to cross-border provision of services. However, a general standstill on existing discriminatory or limiting laws affecting cross-border services has been adopted. Mutual recognition of professional licenses is encouraged (notably for legal consultants and engineers), but not made automatic. All citizenship or permanent residency requirements for professional licensing have been eliminated.

Additionally, a NAFTA country may deny the benefits of the rules on cross-border provision of services if their source is in reality a third country without substantial business activities within the free trade area. For transport services, these benefits may be denied if the services are provided with equipment that is not registered within a NAFTA nation. Most air, maritime, basic telecommunications and social services are not covered by these rules, nor are those that are subject to special treatment elsewhere in the NAFTA (e.g. procurement, financing and energy). Even so, the NAFTA considerably broadens the types of services covered by free trade principles: accounting, advertising, architecture, broadcasting, commercial education, construction, consulting, enhanced telecommunications, engineering, environmental science, health care, land transport, legal, publishing and tourism. Whereas the CFTA allowed free trade in services only for those sectors that were positively listed in the agreement, the NAFTA adopts a broader "negative listing" approach. All services sectors are subject to free trade principles unless the NAFTA specifies otherwise.

Unlike CFTA, the NAFTA creates a timetable for the removal of barriers to cross-border land transport services and the establishment of compatible technical, environmental and safety standards. This extends to bus, trucking, port and rail services. It should eliminate the historic need to switch trailers to Mexican transporters at the border. Cross-border truck deliveries in the border states were supposed to come on line late in 1995, but U.S. concerns about the standards of Mexican carriers and (one suspects) Teamsters Union influence have delayed this result. After 6 years, truckers were supposed to be able to move freely anywhere within NAFTA. In 2001, Mexico prevailed in a NAFTA arbitration panel on truck access to the United States. President George W. Bush has indicated that the U.S. will comply. Bus services should have been totally free within 3 years, and 100 percent investment in Mexican truck and bus companies will be possible after 10 years. The bus services dispute may go to arbitration. Investment in port services was immediately opened. However, national restraints upon domestic cargo carriage (cabotage) are retained and the commitment to harmonize technical and safety laws was made subject to a 6–year "endeavor."

Public telecommunications networks and services must be opened on reasonable and nondiscriminatory terms for firms and individuals who need the networks to conduct business, such as intracorporate communications or so-called enhanced telecommunications and information services. This means that cellular phone, data transmission, earth stations, fax, electronic mail, overlay networks and paging systems are open to Canadian and American investors, many of whom have entered the Mexican market. Each

NAFTA country must ensure reasonable access and use of leased private lines, terminal equipment attachments, private circuit interconnects, switching, signaling and processing functions and user-choice of operating protocols. Conditions on access and use may only be imposed to safeguard the public responsibilities of network operators or to protect technical network integrity. Rates for public telecommunications transport services should reflect economic costs and flat-rate pricing is required for leased circuits. However, cross-subsidization between public transport services is not prohibited, nor are monopoly providers of public networks or services. Such monopolies may not engage in anticompetitive conduct outside their monopoly areas with adverse affects on NAFTA nationals. Various rights of access to information on public networks and services are established, and the NAFTA limits the types of technical standards that can be imposed on the attachment of equipment to public networks.

§ 21.4 The NAFTA Agreement in Outline—Investment and Financial Services

Investment in the industrial and services sectors of the NAFTA nations is promoted through rules against nondiscriminatory and minimum standards of treatment that even benefit non-NAFTA investors with substantial business operations in a NAFTA nation. For example, an Asian or European subsidiary incorporated with substantial business operations in Canada will be treated as a Canadian investor for purposes of NAFTA. Investment, for these purposes, is broadly defined to cover virtually all forms of ownership and activity, including real estate, stocks, bonds, contracts and technologies. National and most favored treatment rights apply at the federal, state and local levels of government, and to state-owned enterprises (e.g. PEMEX, Canadian National Railway Corporation). Furthermore, each country is to treat NAFTA investors in accordance with "international law," including fair and equitable treatment and full protection and security. Performance requirements, e.g. specific export levels, minimum domestic content, domestic source preferences, trade balancing, technology transfer and product mandates are disallowed in all areas except government procurement, export promotion and foreign aid. Senior management positions may not be reserved by nationality, but NAFTA states may require that a majority of the board of directors or committees thereof be of a designated nationality or residence provided this does not impair the foreign investor's ability to exercise control.

A general right to convert and transfer local currency at prevailing market rates for earnings, sale proceeds, loan repayments and other investment transactions has been established. But this right does not prevent good faith and nondiscriminatory restraints upon monetary transfers arising out of bankruptcy, insolvency, securities dealings, crimes, satisfaction of judgments and currency reporting duties. Direct and indirect expropriations of investments by NAFTA investors are precluded except for public purposes and if done on a nondiscriminatory basis following due process of law. A right of compensation without delay at fair market value plus interest is created.

In the event of a dispute, a NAFTA investor may (and quite a few have)[1] elect as between monetary (but not punitive) damages through binding arbitration in the home state of the investor under the ICSID Convention if both nations are parties, the Additional Facility Rules of the ICSID if only one nation is a party to the Convention or the UNCITRAL arbitration rules. An arbitration tribunal for investment disputes will be established by the Secretary–General of ICSID if the parties are unable to select a panel by choosing one arbitrator each and having those arbitrators choose a third. However, there are no time limits for the arbitration and either side may appeal the award to the courts. Alternatively, the investor may pursue judicial remedies in courts of the host state.

The NAFTA investment code does not apply to Mexican constitutionally-reserved sectors (e.g. energy, railroads and boundary and coastal real estate) nor Canada's cultural industries. It does, however, remove Mexican foreign investment controls for U.S. and Canadian investors below an initial $25 million U.S. threshold phased-up to $150 million U.S. in ten years and opened new Mexican mining ventures to NAFTA investors after 5 years. Canadian review of direct U.S. investments in excess of $150 million U.S. and indirect investments in excess of $450 million (indexed for inflation from Jan. 1, 1993) continue. Maritime, airline, broadcasting, fishing, nuclear, basic telecommunications, and government-sponsored technology consortia are exempt from the NAFTA investment rules. All of the NAFTA countries have agreed not to lower environmental standards to attract investment and permit (as Mexico requires) environmental impact statements for foreign investments. However, apart from consultations, there was no retaliatory remedy in this area prior to the environmental side agreement discussed below.

Financial services provided by banking, insurance, securities and other firms are separately covered under the NAFTA. Trade in such services is generally subject to specific liberalization commitments and transition periods. Financial service providers, including non-NAFTA providers operating through subsidiaries in a NAFTA country, are entitled to establish themselves anywhere within NAFTA and service customers there (the right of "commercial pres-

§ 21.4
1. See Chapter 27.

ence"). Existing cross-border restraints on the provision of financial services were frozen and no new restraints may be imposed (subject to designated exceptions). Providers of financial services in each NAFTA nation receive both national and most favored nation treatment. This includes equality of competitive opportunity, which is defined as avoidance of measures that disadvantage foreign providers relative to domestic providers. Various procedural transparency rules are established to facilitate the entry and equal opportunity of NAFTA providers of financial services. The host nation may legislate reasonable prudential requirements for such companies and, under limited circumstances, protect their balance of payments in ways which restrain financial providers.

The following are some of the more notable country-specific commitments on financial service made in the NAFTA:

United States—A grace period allowed Mexican banks already operating a securities firm in the U.S. to continue to do so until July of 1997.

Canada—The exemption granted U.S. companies under the Canada–U.S. FTA to hold more than 25 percent of the shares of a federally regulated Canadian financial institution was extended to Mexican firms, as was the suspension of Canada's 12 percent asset ceiling rules. Multiple branches may be opened in Canada without Ministry of Finance approval.

Mexico—Banking, securities and insurance companies from the U.S. and Canada are able to enter the Mexican market through subsidiaries and joint ventures (but not branches) subject to market share limits during a transition period that ended in the year 2000 (insurance) or 2004 (banking and securities). Finance companies are able to establish separate subsidiaries in Mexico to provide consumer, commercial, mortgage lending or credit card services, subject to a 3 percent aggregate asset limitation (which does not apply to lending by affiliates of automotive companies). Existing U.S. and Canadian insurers could expand their ownership rights to 100 percent in 1996. No equity or market share requirements apply for warehousing and bonding, foreign exchange and mutual fund management enterprises.

§ 21.5   The NAFTA Agreement in Outline— Intellectual Property

The NAFTA mandates adequate and effective intellectual property rights in all countries, including national treatment and effective internal and external enforcement rights. Specific commitments are made for virtually all types of intellectual property, including patents, copyrights, trademarks, plant breeds, industrial designs, trade secrets, semiconductor chips (directly and in goods incorporating them) and geographical indicators.

For copyright, the NAFTA obligates protection for computer programs, databases, computer program and sound recording rentals, and a 50 year term of protection for sound recordings. For patents, the NAFTA mandates a minimum 20 years of coverage (from date of filing) of nearly all products and processes including pharmaceuticals and agricultural chemicals. It also requires removal of any special or discriminatory patent regimes or availability of rights. Compulsory licensing is limited. Service marks are treated equally with trademarks. Satellite signal poaching is illegal and trade secrets are generally protected (including from disclosure by governments). The NAFTA details member states' duties to provide damages, injunctive, antipiracy and general due process remedies in the intellectual property field. This has, for example, reinforced major changes in Mexican law.

§ 21.6 The NAFTA Agreement in Outline—Other Provisions

The provisions on temporary entry visas for business persons found in the CFTA are extended under the NAFTA. These entry rights cover business persons, traders, investors, intra-company transferees and 63 designated professionals. Installers, after-sales repair and maintenance staff and managers performing services under a warranty or other service contract incidental to the sale of equipment or machinery are included, as are sales representatives, buyers, market researchers and financial service providers. White collar business persons only need proof of citizenship and documentation of business purpose to work in another NAFTA country for up to 5 years. However, an annual limit of 5,500 additional Mexican professionals may temporarily enter the United States during the first 10 years of the NAFTA. Apart from these provisions, no common market for the free movement of labor is undertaken.

The NAFTA embraces a competition policy principally aimed at state enterprises and governmentally sanctioned monopolies, mostly found in Mexico. State owned or controlled businesses, at all levels of government, are required to act consistently with the NAFTA when exercising regulatory, administrative or governmental authority (e.g. when granting licenses). Governmentally-owned and privately-owned state-designated monopolies are obliged to follow commercial considerations in their transactions and avoid discrimination against goods or services of other NAFTA nations. Furthermore, each country must ensure that such monopolies do not use their positions to engage in anticompetitive practices in non-monopoly markets. Since each NAFTA nation must adopt laws against anticompetitive business practices and cooperate in their enforcement, Mexico has revived its historically weak "antitrust" laws. A consultative Trade and Competition Committee reviews competition policy issues under the NAFTA.

Other notable provisions in the NAFTA include a general duty of legal transparency, fairness and due process regarding all laws affecting traders and investors with independent administrative or judicial review of government action. Generalized exceptions to the agreement cover action to protect national security and national interests such as public morals, health, national treasures, natural resources, or to enforce laws against deceptive or anticompetitive practices, short of arbitrary discriminations or disguised restraints on trade. Balance of payments trade restraints are governed by the rules of the International Monetary Fund. Taxation issues are subject to bilateral double taxation treaties, including a new one between Mexico and the United States. The "cultural industry" reservations secured by the CFTA now cover Canada and Mexico, but are not extended to Mexican–U.S. trade. A right of compensatory retaliation through measures of equivalent commercial effect is granted when invocation of these reservations would have violated the Canada–U.S. FTA but for the cultural industries proviso.

The NAFTA is not forever. Any country may withdraw on 6 months notice. Other countries or groups of countries may be admitted to the NAFTA if Canada, Mexico and the United States agree and domestic ratification follows. In December of 1994, Chile was invited to become the next member of the NAFTA. Negotiations have stalled for want of U.S. Congressional fast track negotiating authority.

§ 21.7 Dispute Settlement Under NAFTA

The institutional dispute settlement arrangements accompanying the NAFTA are minimal. A trilateral Trade Commission (with Secretariat) comprised of ministerial or cabinet-level officials meets at least annually to ensure effective joint management of the NAFTA is established. The various intergovernmental committees established for specific areas of coverage of the NAFTA (e.g. competition policy) to oversee much of the work of making the free trade area function. These committees operate on the basis of consensus, referring contentious issues to the Trade Commission.

Investment, dumping and subsidy, financial services, environmental, labor and standards disputes are subject to special dispute resolution procedures. A general NAFTA dispute settlement procedure is also established (Chapter 20). A right of consultation exists when one country's rights are thought to be affected. If consultations do not resolve the issue within 45 days, the complainant may convene a meeting of the Trade Commission. The Commission must seek to promptly settle the dispute and may use its good offices, mediation, conciliation or any other alternative means. Absent resolution, the complaining country or countries ordinarily commence proceedings under the GATT/WTO or the NAFTA. Once selected, the chosen forum becomes exclusive. However, if the dispute concerns environmental, safety, health or conservation standards, or arises under specific environmental agreements, the responding nation may elect to have the dispute heard by a NAFTA panel.

Dispute settlement procedures under Chapter 20 involve non-binding arbitration by five persons chosen in most cases from a trilaterally agreed roster of experts (not limited to NAFTA citizens), with a special roster established for disputes about financial services. A "reverse selection" process is used. The chair of the panel is first chosen by agreement or, failing agreement, by designation of one side selected by lot. The chair cannot be a citizen of the selecting side but must be a NAFTA national. Each side then selects two additional arbitrators who are citizens of the country or countries on the *other* side. The Commission has approved rules of procedure including the opportunity for written submissions, rebuttals and at least one oral hearing. Expert advice on environmental and scientific matters may be given by special procedures accessing science boards. Strict time limits are created so as to keep the panel on track to a prompt resolution. Within 90 days an initial confidential report must be circulated, followed by 14 days for comment by the parties and 16 days for the final panel report to the Commission.

Early NAFTA Chapter 20 arbitrations have concerned Canadian tariffication of agricultural quotas (upheld), U.S. escape clause relief from Mexican corn broom exports (rejected) and a successful Mexican challenge of the U.S. failure to implement cross-border trucking. Once the Trade Commission receives a final arbitration panel report, the NAFTA requires the disputing nations to agree within 30 days on a resolution (normally by conforming to the panel's recommendations). If a mutually agreed resolution does not occur at this stage, the complaining country may retaliate by suspending the application of equivalent benefits under the NAFTA. Any NAFTA country may invoke the arbitration panel process if it perceives that this retaliation is excessive.

When NAFTA interpretational issues are disputed before domestic tribunals or courts, the Trade Commission (if it can agree) can submit an interpretation to that body. In the absence of agreement within the Commission, any NAFTA country may intervene and submit its views as to the proper interpretation or application of the NAFTA to the national court or tribunal.

The independent binational review panel mechanism established in the CFTA for dumping and subsidy duties is carried over into NAFTA, along with the extraordinary challenge procedure to deal with allegations about the integrity of the panel review process. Chapter 19 panels are substituted for traditional judicial review at the national level of administrative dumping and countervailing duty orders. Mexico has undertaken major improvements to its law in this area. The procedures and rules for such panels generally follow those found in the CFTA. They are limited to issues of the consistency of the national decisions with domestic law, and once again have been numerous.

In addition, a special committee may be requested by any country believing that another's domestic law has prevented the establishment, final decision or implementation of the decision by such a panel. A special committee may also be invoked if the opportunity for independent judicial review on a dumping or subsidy determination has been denied (a concern focused especially on Mexico). This committee's findings, if affirmative, will result in member state consultations. Absent resolution, the complainant may suspend the panel system or benefits under the NAFTA agreement.

§ 21.8   The Side Agreements on Labor and the Environment

The NAFTA side agreements on labor (NALC) and the environment (NAEC) do not create additional substantive regional rules. Rather the side agreements basically create law enforcement mechanisms. The side agreements commit each country to creation of environmental and labor bodies that monitor compliance with the adequacy and the enforcement of *domestic* law. The Commission for Environmental Cooperation (CEC)(Montreal) and three National Administrative Offices (NAO) concerning labor matters are empowered to receive complaints. Negotiations to resolve complaints first ensue.

In the absence of a negotiated solution, the NAEC establishes five environmental dispute settlement mechanisms. *First*, the CEC Secretariat may report on almost any environmental matter. *Second*, the Secretariat may develop a factual record in trade-related law enforcement disputes. *Third*, the CEC Council can release that record to the public. *Fourth*, if there is a persistent pattern of failure to enforce environmental law, the Council will mediate and conciliate. *Fifth*, if such efforts fail, the Council can send the matter to arbitration and awards can be enforced by monetary penalties.

The NALC labor law enforcement system is a calibrated four-tier series of dispute resolution mechanisms. *First*, the NAOs may review and report on eleven designated labor law enforcement matters that correspond to the NALC Labor Principles. *Second*, ministerial consultations may follow when recommended by the NAO. *Third*, an Evaluation Committee of Experts can report on trade-related mutually recognized labor law enforcement patterns of practice concerning eight of the NALC Labor Principles (excluding strikes, union organizing and collective bargaining). *Fourth*, persistent patterns of failure to enforce occupational health and safety, child labor or minimum wage laws can be arbitrated and awards enforced by monetary penalties.

The NAEC and NALC law enforcement mechanisms have been used more frequently than many expected. Quite a few labor law enforcement complaints have focused on the organization of "independent" unions in Mexico. United States plant closings and treatment of immigrant workers have also been reviewed. Regarding the environment, a wide range of complaints have been filed asserting inadequate Canadian, Mexican and U.S. law enforcement. None of these environmental disputes have proceeded beyond development of a factual record.

§ 21.9   Expanding NAFTA to Include Chile

When Canada and the United States agreed to free trade in 1989, there was no expectation of extension of that agreement to Mexico or any other country. The NAFTA agreement, on the other hand, specifically anticipates growth by accession. Article 2204 invites applications to join NAFTA by countries or groups of countries without regard to their geographic location or cultural background. This is unlike the European Union which only allows "European" nations to join. Australia, South Korea, New Zealand and Singapore have, for example, all expressed interest in NAFTA. Canada would also like to see European nations actively considered for membership.

The NAFTA Free Trade Commission is authorized to negotiate the terms and conditions of any new memberships. The resulting accession agreement must be approved and ratified by each NAFTA nation. Practically speaking, as in the European Union, this means that current members can veto NAFTA applicants.

In December of 1994, at the "Summit of the Americas" in Miami, Canada and Mexico joined the United States in formally inviting Chile to apply for NAFTA membership. This invitation went nowhere because Congress repeatedly refused to authorize "fast track" negotiations by President Clinton. Fast track negotiations provide assurance to all concerned that Congress would not be able to alter the terms and conditions of Chile's accession. Under fast track, Congress would have to approve or disapprove the agreement by majority vote. Apart from partisan politics, one thorny issue was whether there would be side agreements with Chile on labor and the environment.

Absent fast track authority, Chile, Canada and Mexico all steered different courses. Mexico and Chile renegotiated and expanded their pre-NAFTA free trade agreement. Canada and Chile reached agreement in 1997 on free trade along with side agreements that are similar to NAEC and NALC. Chile in 1996 became a free trade associate of MERCOSUR, the Southern Cone common market of Brazil, Argentina, Paraguay and Uruguay. All these free trade commitments flowed partly from want of U.S. fast track authority. They had an impact on trade and investment patterns. Some U.S. companies with Canadian subsidiaries, for example, shifted production and exports to Canada in order to take advantage of Canada–Chile free trade.

§ 21.10   Free Trade and the Americas, Bilateral Free Trade Agreements

The United States "Enterprise for the Americas Initiative" (EAI) under elder President Bush raised hopes of economic integration throughout the Americas against a background of competitive regionalism in trade relations, especially between the European Union and North America. At the Americas Summit in Miami, President Clinton and 33 Latin American heads of state (only Fidel Castro was absent) renewed this hope by agreeing to commence negotiations on a Free Trade Area of the Americas (FTAA). The year 2005 was targeted at the Summit for creation of the FTAA. Preparatory working groups have regularly met since 1995 to discuss the following topics: (1) Market Access; (2) Customs Procedures and Rules of Origin; (3) Investment; (4) Standards and Technical Barriers to Trade; (5) Sanitary and Phytosanitary Measures; (6) Subsidies, Antidumping and Countervailing Duties; (7) Smaller Economies; (8) Government Procurement; (9) Intellectual Property Rights; (10) Services; (11) Competition Policy; and (12) Dispute Settlement. It is expected that each of these areas would be covered in any FTAA agreement. Formal FTAA negotiations were delayed several times, particularly because of differences between Brazil-led MERCOSUR and U.S.-led NAFTA.

The absence of fast track authority and the general perception that political support for free trade in the United States is weak has clearly slowed FTAA developments. MERCOSUR and Brazil in particular have seized the opportunity to move towards a South American Free Trade Area (SAFTA). Presumably, SAFTA would be in a much better position to negotiate terms and conditions with NAFTA than individual countries or sub-groups within South

America. To that end, Bolivia and Chile are already MERCOSUR free trade associates and negotiations with virtually all South American nations are in progress. Late in 2003, MERCOSUR and the Andean Community (ANCOM) signed a free trade deal. Indeed, MERCOSUR is even negotiating along the same lines with Canada, Mexico, the Central American states, and the European Union. The EU, for its part, is expanding its European membership and in 2000 closed a free trade agreement with Mexico!

In 2002, a bipartisan Congress authorized President George W. Bush to negotiate free trade agreements on a fast track basis. This authorization is valid until June 1, 2005 subject to possible extension. President Bush, following the pattern established by Canada and Mexico, rapidly concluded a bilateral U.S. free trade agreement with Chile, including coverage of the environment and labor.

The 2002 Congressional authorization of fast track free trade negotiations covers the FTAA. President George W. Bush is actively seeking such an agreement, while simultaneously negotiating U.S. free trade deals with five Central American states (CAFTA, finalized early in 2004), the Dominican Republic (2004) and Panama. Bilateral U.S. free trade with the ANDEAN nations of Columbia, Bolivia, Ecuador and Peru, and possibly other Latin American countries, is also being pursued. Such a "divide and conquer" strategy undermines Brazil's hopes for a united South/Central American negotiating front for the FTAA. It also reflects the reality of the United States playing catch up with Canada (which has free trade agreements with Chile and Costa Rica) and Mexico (which has numerous Latin American free trade agreements).

Divisions were particularly evident during the November 2003 FTAA ministerial meeting in Miami. Lowered expectations, known as FTAA–Lite, reflect U.S. refusal to budge on agricultural protection and trade remedies, and Brazilian refusal to fully embrace investment, intellectual property, services and procurement "free trade." Absent successful resolution of these issues in the WTO Doha Round negotiations, an unlikely prospect at this writing, FTAA–Lite with different levels of country commitments and more bilateral free trade agreements are anticipated.

Chapter 22

FRANCHISING AND TRADEMARK LICENSING

Table of Sections

§ 22.1 Franchising Abroad

Franchising constitutes a rapidly expanding form of doing business abroad. Most franchisors have established fairly standard contracts and business formulae which are utilized in their home markets, and receive counsel on the myriad of laws relevant to their domestic business operations. Approaches to developing, defining and managing franchise relationships that have worked domestically may not work abroad. For example, agreements authorizing development of multiple locations within a given territory and, possibly, subfranchising by a master franchisee are often used overseas while infrequent in the United States. International franchising confronts the attorney with the need to research and evaluate a broad range of foreign laws which may apply in any particular jurisdiction. Such laws tend to focus on placing equity and control in the hands of local individuals and on regulating the franchise agreement to benefit the franchisees. In addition, counsel should be sensitive to the cultural impact of foreign franchising. For example, the appearance of a franchise building or trademark

499

symbol may conflict in a foreign setting with traditional architectural forms (such as in European cities) or nationalist feelings hostile to the appearance of foreign trademarks on franchised products (such as in India or Mexico). Cultural conflicts can diminish the value of international franchises. To anticipate and solve legal and cultural problems, foreign counsel is often chosen to assist in the task of franchising abroad.

This chapter explores some of the concerns a franchisor or prospective franchisee may encounter in opting for, negotiating, drafting or enforcing an international franchise agreement. Although patents, copyrights and trademarks may all be involved in international franchising, trademark licensing is at the core of most international franchise agreements. Many rightly consider franchising to be a U.S. invention, but foreigners have rapidly been developing international franchising systems. Thus, while the primary focus in this chapter is on the problems of United States franchisors who intend to go abroad, additional coverage is given to United States law relevant to franchising.

§ 22.2   Trademark Protection

Virtually all countries offer some legal protection to trademarks, even when they do not have trademark registration systems. Trademark rights derived from the use of marks on goods in commerce have long been recognized at common law and remain so today in countries as diverse as the United States and the United Arab Emirates. The latter nation, for example, had no trademark registration law in 1986, but this did not prevent McDonald's from obtaining an injunction against a local business using its famous name and golden arches without authorization.[1] However, obtaining international trademark protection normally involves separate registration under the law of each nation. Roughly 40,000 trademark applications are filed each year by United States citizens with the appropriate authorities in other countries. In the United States, trademarks are protected by state and federal registrations. Federal registration is permitted by the U.S. Trademark Office for all marks capable of distinguishing the goods on which they appear from other goods.[2] Unless the mark falls within a category of forbidden registrations (e.g., those that offend socialist morality in the People's Republic of China), a mark becomes valid for a term of years following registration.

In some countries (like the U.S. prior to 1989), marks must be used on goods before registration. In others, use is not required and speculative registration of marks can occur. It is said that ESSO

1. Case No. 823/85. See 76 Trademark Reports 356 (1986).

2. 15 U.S.C.A. § 1052.

was obliged to purchase trademark rights from such a speculator when it switched to EXXON in its search for the perfect global trademark. Since 1989, United States law has allowed applications when there is a bona fide intent to use a trademark within 12 months and, if there is good cause for the delay in actual usage, up to 24 additional months.[3] Such filings in effect reserve the mark for the applicant. The emphasis on bona fide intent and good cause represent an attempt to control any speculative use of U.S. trademark registrations.

In many countries trademarks (appearing on goods) may be distinguished from "service marks" used by providers of services (e.g., the Law Store), "trade names" (business names), "collective marks" (marks used by a group or organization), and "certificate marks" (marks which certify a certain quality, origin, or other fact). Although national trademark schemes differ, it can be said generally that a valid trademark (e.g., a mark not "canceled," "renounced," "abandoned," "waived" or "generic") will be protected against infringing use. A trademark can be valid in one country (ASPIRIN brand tablets in Canada), but invalid because generic in another (BAYER brand aspirin in the United States). A trademark can be valid, e.g., CHEVROLET NOVA brand automobiles in the United States and Mexico, but diminished in value because of reasons of language. If you were Mexican, would you buy a CHEVROLET promising to "no va"?

Unlike patents and copyrights, trademarks may be renewed in perpetuity. A valid mark may be licensed, perhaps to a "registered user" or it may be assigned, in some cases only with the sale of the goodwill of a business. A growing example of international licensing of trademarks can be found in franchise agreements taken abroad. And national trademark law sometimes accompanies international licensing. The principal U.S. trademark law, the Lanham Act of 1946, has been construed to apply extraterritorially (much like the Sherman Antitrust Act) to foreign licensees engaging in deceptive practices.[4] Foreigners who seek a registration may be required to prove a prior and valid "home registration," and a new registration in another country may not have an existence "independent" of the continuing validity of the home country registration. Foreigners are often assisted in their registration efforts by international and regional trademark treaties.

§ 22.3   Quality Controls

Because franchising links trademarks with business attributes, there is a broad duty in the law for the franchisor to maintain

---

3. 15 U.S.C.A. § 1051(b).

4. See especially Scotch Whiskey Association v. Barton Distilling Co., 489 F.2d 809 (7th Cir.1973).

quality controls over the franchisee, particularly in the business format franchise system. Any failure of the franchisor to maintain such quality controls could cause the trademark in question to be abandoned and lost to the franchisor.[1] In order to maintain adequate quality controls, the franchisor must typically police the operations of the franchisee.[2] Broadly speaking, the duty to maintain quality controls arises because a trademark is a source symbol. The public is entitled to rely upon that source symbol in making its purchasing decisions so as to obtain consistent product quality and attributes. International franchisors operating at a distance from their franchisees must be especially concerned with quality controls. On the other hand, excessive control or the public appearance of such control may give rise to an agency relationship between the franchisor and the franchisee. Such a relationship could be used to establish franchisor liability for franchisee conduct, including international product and other tort liabilities.[3] It may be possible to minimize these risks through disclaimer or indemnification clauses in the franchise agreement.

§ 22.4   Copyright Protection in Franchising

Although franchising primarily focuses upon trademarks and trademark licensing, the use of copyrights frequently parallels such activity. For example, the designs and logos of the franchisor may be copyrighted, and certainly its instruction manual and other such written communications to franchisees should be copyrighted. These copyrights benefit in many countries from the Universal Copyright Convention (UCC) of 1952 and the Berne Convention of 1886. The United States now adheres to both of these conventions. Under the UCC, copyright holders receive national treatment, translation rights and other benefits. This convention will excuse any national registration requirement provided a notice of a claim of copyright is adequately given. However, in the United States, a reservation was made such that registration of foreign copyrights is required if the only convention under which foreigners are seeking such protection is the Universal Copyright Convention of 1952.

On the other hand, if the foreigner comes from a nation which also adheres to the Berne Convention, national treatment and a release from registration formalities is obtained. The Berne Convention permits local copyright protection independent of protec-

---

§ 22.3

1. See, e.g., Yamamoto & Co. v. Victor United, Inc., 219 U.S.P.Q. 968 (C.D.Cal.1982).

2. See Dawn Donut Co. v. Hart's Food Stores, Inc., 267 F.2d 358 (2d Cir. 1959).

3. See Hanson, The Franchising Dilemma: Franchisor Liability for Actions of a Local Franchisee, 19 N.C.Central L.J. 190 (1991).

tion granted in the country of origin and does not require copyright notice. Prior to 1987, most United States copyright holders acquired Berne Convention benefits by simultaneously publishing their works in Canada, a member country. Since 1987 the United States has ratified the Berne Convention. This has the practical effect of eliminating registration requirements for foreign copyright holders. It also extends United States copyright relations to approximately 25 new nations.

§ 22.5 Protection of Franchise Trade Secrets

Franchise formulae often involve utilization of trade secrets. This may range from recipes and cooking techniques to customer lists, pricing formulas, market data or bookkeeping procedures. It is extremely difficult to protect such trade secrets under United States law. The first problem arises from the concept of what is a trade secret. Generally speaking, abstract ideas or business practices which do not involve an element of novelty are not considered trade secrets.[1] Even if franchise trade secrets are involved, maintaining such secrets can be difficult given the wide number of persons who may have access to the confidential information. Even though the franchisees may warrant to maintain such secrets, once released into the business public there may not be an effective way to recapture the secret or remedy the harm.[2]

The duty not to disclose trade secrets should be extended to employees of the franchisee. This can be done by permitting dissemination only on a need-to-know basis. However, it may be impossible not to permit certain employees from the knowledge of cooking procedures or recipes, for example. Once again the remedies and efforts to recapture the secret are likely to be inadequate.[3] Terminated employees and terminated franchisees are another fertile source of the loss of trade secrets. Tort remedies employing misappropriation theories may prevent the utilization or disclosure by such persons of trade secrets where there is a possibility of competition with the franchisor.[4] Damages are generally viewed as an inadequate remedy in the trade secret field because the harm of the loss of the secret is irreparable.

§ 22.6 The Franchise Agreement

International franchising raises a host of legal issues under intellectual property, antitrust, tax, licensing and other laws. The

§ 22.5

1. See Kewanee Oil Co. v. Bicron Corp., 416 U.S. 470, 94 S.Ct. 1879, 40 L.Ed.2d 315 (1974).

2. See Smith v. Dravo Corp., 203 F.2d 369 (7th Cir.1953).

3. See Shatterproof Glass Corp. v. Guardian Glass Co., 322 F.Supp. 854 (E.D.Mich.1970) *affirmed* 462 F.2d 1115 (6th Cir.1972).

4. See FMC Corp. v. Taiwan Tainan Giant Industrial Co., 730 F.2d 61 (2d Cir.1984).

significance of these issues is magnified by the rapid growth of international franchising. Hundreds of U.S. companies have, in total, tens of thousands of foreign franchises. Nearly 70 percent of these franchisors started in Canada, with Japan and Britain following. Some United States investors have found franchising the least risky and most popular way to enter Eastern Europe. But franchising is not just a United States export. Many foreign franchisors have entered the U.S. market.

Most franchisors have standard contracts which are used in their home markets and receive counsel on the myriad of laws relevant to their business operations. Such contracts need to be revised and adapted to international franchising without significantly altering the franchisor's successful business formula. Franchise fees and royalties must be specified, the provision of services, training, and control by the franchisor detailed, the term and area of the franchise negotiated ("master franchises" conveying rights in an entire country or region are common in international franchise agreements), accounting procedures agreed upon, business standards and advertising selected, insurance obtained, taxes and other liabilities allocated, default and dispute settlement procedures decided. At the heart of all franchise agreements lies a trademark licensing clause conveying local trademark rights of the franchisor to the franchisee in return for royalty payments.

§ 22.7 Regulation of International Franchising

Were franchising unaffected by regulation, the attorney's role would be limited to negotiation and drafting of the agreement. But international franchising is increasingly regulated by home and host jurisdictions, including regional groups like the European Union (EU). In third world countries, especially Latin America, technology transfer laws aimed principally at international patent and know-how licensing also regulate franchise agreements. These laws benefit franchisees and further development policies, e.g., the conservation of hard currencies by control of royalty levels. In 1986, the European Court of Justice issued its first major opinion on the legality of franchise agreements under EU competition law.[1] This decision indicates that Union law can depart significantly from leading United States antitrust law on market division arrangements for distributors.[2] The EU has since implemented a compre-

§ 22.7

1. Pronuptia de Paris GmbH v. Pronuptia de Paris Irmgard Schillgallis (1986) Eur.Comm.Rep. 353. See Section 18.11.

2. Compare Continental T.V., Inc. v. GTE Sylvania Inc., 433 U.S. 36, 97 S.Ct. 2549, 53 L.Ed.2d 568 (1977) (location clauses not per se illegal); American Motor Inns, Inc. v. Holiday Inns, Inc., 521 F.2d 1230 (3d Cir.1975) (allocation of franchisor/franchisee towns and territories *per se* illegal).

hensive regulation on franchise agreements.[3] There is often a perception of being invaded culturally that follows franchising. Local laws sometimes respond to the cultural impact of foreign franchises, but this did not stop McDonald's from opening in Moscow with great success.

In India and Mexico, nationalist feelings hostile to the appearance of foreign trademarks on franchised products have produced laws intended to remove such usage. For example, the Mexican Law of Inventions and Trademarks (1976) (repealed 1987) anticipated requiring use of culturally Mexican marks in addition to marks of foreign origin. Dual marks are now voluntary in Mexico and prohibited by NAFTA. Other nations require local materials (olive oil in the Mediterranean) to be substituted. This could, for example, alter the formula for success (and value) of fast food franchises. Still others (e.g., Alberta, Canada) mandate extensive disclosures by franchisors in a registered prospectus before agreements may be completed. Disclosure violations can trigger a range of franchisee remedies: recision, injunctions and damages. Such laws are also found in many of the states of the United States.

Franchise advertising must conform to local law. For example, regulations in the People's Republic of China prohibit ads which "have reactionary ... content." Antitrust and tax law are important in international franchising. Double taxation treaties, for example, will affect the level of taxation of royalties. Antitrust law will temper purchasing requirements of the franchisor, lest unlawful "tying arrangements" be undertaken. Tying arrangements involve coercion of franchisees to take supplies from the franchisor or designated sources as part of the franchise.

Such arrangements must, by definition, involve two products: the tying and tied products. They are subject to a complex and not entirely consistent body of case law under the U.S. Sherman Antitrust Act, Articles 81 and 82 of the Treaty of Rome and other laws. For example, one leading United States antitrust case treats the trademark licenses as a separate tying product and the requirement of the purchase by franchisees of non-essential cooking equipment and paper products unlawful.[4] Another case permits franchisors to require franchisees to purchase "core products" (e.g., chicken) subject to detailed specifications, or from a designated list of approved sources.[5] Sometimes the "core product" and the trademark license are treated as a single product incapable of

3. Commission Regulation No. 4087/88, discussed in Section 18.12.

4. Siegel v. Chicken Delight, Inc., 448 F.2d 43 (9th Cir.1971), *cert. denied* 405 U.S. 955, 92 S.Ct. 1172, 31 L.Ed.2d 232 (1972).

5. Kentucky Fried Chicken Corp. v. Diversified Packaging Corp., 549 F.2d 368 (5th Cir.1977).

being tied in violation of the law.[6] Still another leading case suggests that anything comprising the franchisor's "formula for success" may possibly be tied in the franchise contract.[7]

The premium placed on priority of use of a trademark is reflected in several international trademark treaties. These include the 1883 Paris Convention for the Protection of Industrial Property, the 1957 Arrangement of Nice Concerning the International Classification of Goods and Services, and the 1973 Trademark Registration Treaty. The treaties of widest international application are the Paris Convention and the Arrangement of Nice, to which the United States is a signatory. The International Bureau of the World Intellectual Property Organization (WIPO) in Geneva plays a central role in the administration of arrangements contemplated by these agreements.

§ 22.8   The Paris Convention as Applied to Trademarks

The Paris Convention reflects an effort to internationalize some trademark rules. In addition to extending the nondiscriminatory principal of national treatment and providing for a right of priority of six months for trademarks, the Convention mitigates the frequent national requirement that foreigners seeking trademark registration prove a pre-existing, valid and continuing home registration. This makes it easier to obtain foreign trademark registration, avoids the possibility that a lapse in registration at home will cause all foreign registrations to become invalid, and allows registration abroad of entirely different (and perhaps culturally adapted) marks. The Paris Convention right of priority eliminates the need to simultaneously file for trademark protection around the globe. Filings abroad that are undertaken within six months of the home country filing for trademark registration will take priority.

The Paris Convention has in excess of 100 member nations. Since the Convention provides that any domestic trademark registration filing gives rise to priority in all Paris Convention countries, this means that foreign marks registered in countries that do not require use of the mark on an actual product can be obtained in the United States. In other words, foreign trademarks that are not used are entitled under the Paris Convention to U.S. trademark registration. Since 1988, the foreign applicant must state a bona fide

---

6. Krehl v. Baskin–Robbins Ice Cream Co., 664 F.2d 1348 (9th Cir.1982) (franchisees must buy Baskin–Robbins ice cream).

7. Principe v. McDonald's Corp., 631 F.2d 303 (4th Cir.1980), *cert. denied* 451 U.S. 970, 101 S.Ct. 2047, 68 L.Ed.2d 349 (1981) (franchisees required to lease land and buildings from McDonald's).

intention to use the mark in commerce, but actual use is not required prior to registration.[1]

The Paris Convention also deals with unregistered trademarks. Article 6bis requires the member nations to refuse to register, to cancel an existing registration or to prohibit the use of a trademark which is considered by the trademark registration authorities of that country to be "well known" and owned by a person entitled to the benefits of the Paris Convention. This provision concerns what are called "famous marks" and prevents their infringement even if there has been no local registration of the mark. This is a remarkable development because it effectively creates trademark rights without registration. It has, for example, been successfully invoked in the People's Republic of China in order to protect against infringing use of Walt Disney and other well known trademarks.

§ 22.9   The Nice Agreement on Trademark Classification

The Nice Agreement addresses the question of registration by "class" or "classification" of goods. In order to simplify internal administrative procedures relating to marks, many countries classify and thereby identify goods (and sometimes services) which have the same or similar attributes. An applicant seeking registration of a mark often is required to specify the class or classes to which the product mark belongs. However, not all countries have the same classification system and some lack any such system. Article 1 of the Nice Agreement adopts, for the purposes of the registration of marks, a single classification system for goods and services. This has brought order out of chaos in the field.

§ 22.10   International Trademark Registration Treaties

The 1973 Vienna Trademark Registration Treaty (to which the United States is a signatory) contemplates an international filing and examination scheme like that in force for patents under the Patent Cooperation Treaty of 1970.[1] This treaty has not yet been fully implemented, but holds out the promise of reduced costs and greater uniformity when obtaining international trademark protection. The 1994 Trademark Law Treaty substantially harmonized trademark registration procedures. Numerous European and Mediterranean countries are parties to the 1891 Madrid Agreement for International Registration of Marks. Since 2002, the United States has joined in the Madrid Protocol of 1989. This agreement permits

§ 22.8   § 22.10

1. 15 U.S.C.A. § 1126(e).   1. See Chapter 23.

international filings to obtain national trademark rights and is administered by WIPO. A Common Market trademark can now be obtained in the European Community.

§ 22.11   The *Pronuptia* Case

The European Union (EU) has become an active regulator of franchise agreements. Prior to *Pronuptia*,[1] the Commission had never sought to apply Article 81 (formerly Article 85) of the Treaty of Rome to franchise agreements. *Pronuptia* arose from the refusal of a franchisee to pay license fees to the franchisor. The distribution of the Pronuptia brand wedding attire in the Federal Republic of Germany was handled by shops operated by the German franchisor and by independent retailers through franchise agreements with that franchisor. The franchisee had obtained franchises for three areas (Hamburg, Oldenburg and Hannover). The franchisor granted the franchisee exclusive rights to market and advertise under the name of "Pronuptia de Paris" in these specific territories. The franchisor promised not to open any shops or provide any goods or services to another person in those territories. The franchisor also agreed to assist the franchisee with business strategies and profitability.

The franchisee agreed to assume all the risk of opening a franchise as an independent retailer. The franchisee also agreed to the following: (1) To sell Pronuptia goods only in the store specified in the contract and to decorate and design the shop according to the franchisor's instructions; (2) to purchase 80 percent of wedding related attire and a proportion of evening dresses from the franchisor, and to purchase the rest of such merchandise only from sellers approved by the franchisor; (3) to pay a one time entrance fee for exclusive rights to the specified territory and a yearly royalty fee of 10 percent of the total sales of Pronuptia and all other products; (4) to advertise only with the franchisor's approval in a method which would enhance the international reputation of the franchise; (5) to make the sale of bridal fashions the franchisee's main business purpose; (6) to consider the retail price recommendations of the franchisor; (7) to refrain from competing directly or indirectly during the contract period or for one year afterward with any Pronuptia store; and (8) to obtain the franchisor's prior approval before assigning the rights and obligations arising under the contract to a third party.

§ 22.11

1. Pronuptia de Paris GmbH v. Pronuptia de Paris Irmgard Schillgallis (1986) Eur.Comm.Rep. 353.

In due course, the case was referred to the European Court of Justice. The Court's judgment concentrates on the crucial issue of whether franchise agreements come within Article 85. The Court draws a preliminary distinction between "distribution" franchises such as Pronuptia as opposed to "service" and "production" franchises. The Court concludes that a franchising system as such does not interfere with competition. Consequently, clauses essential to enable franchising to function are not prohibited. Thus, the franchisor can communicate know-how or assistance and help franchisees apply its methods. The franchisor can take reasonable steps to keep its know-how or assistance from becoming available to competitors. Location clauses forbidding the franchisee during the contract, or for a reasonable time thereafter, from opening a store with a similar or identical object in an area where it might compete with another member of the franchise network were necessary for distribution franchises and therefore permissible. The obligation of the franchisee not to sell a licensed store without prior consent of the franchisor was similarly allowable.

Clauses necessary to preserve the identity and reputation of the franchise network, such as decorations and trademark usage, were upheld. The reputation and identity of the network may also justify a clause requiring the franchisee to sell only products supplied by the franchisor or by approved sources, at least if it would be too expensive to monitor the quality of the stock otherwise. Nevertheless, each franchisee must be allowed to buy from other franchisees. The requirement of uniformity may also justify advertisement approvals by the franchisor, but the franchisee must be allowed to set and advertise resale prices. The Court rejected the view that clauses tending to divide the Common Market between franchisor and franchisee or between franchisees are always necessary to protect the knowhow or the identity and the reputation of the network.

The location clause in *Pronuptia* was seen as potentially supporting exclusive territories. In combination, location clauses and exclusive territories may divide markets and so restrict competition within the network. Even if a potential franchisee would not take the risk of joining the network by making its own investment because it could not expect a profitable business due to the absence of protection from competition from other franchisees, that consideration (in the Court's view) could be taken into account only under an Article 85(3) individual exemption review by the Commission. The Commission, in fact, ultimately granted such an exemption to Pronuptia.[2]

2. Re Pronuptia, 30 O.J.Eur.Comm. 39 (L13/1987).

§ 22.12   EU Regulations 4087/88 and 2790/1999

The Commission, following the European Court of Justice decision in *Pronuptia*,[1] adopted a group exemption regulation (No. 4087/88) for franchise agreements under Article 81(3).[2] This regulation detailed permissible franchise restraints (the "white list") and impermissible obligations (the "black list"). Its terms were widely followed in drafting European franchise agreements. Any failure to adhere to the regulation could result in serious competition law (antitrust) sanctions.[3] Regulation 4087/88 has been superceded by Regulation 2790/1999, the vertical agreements regulation. This regulation is more economic and less formalistic than Regulation 4087/88. Supply and distribution agreements of firms with less than 30 percent market shares are generally exempt; this is known as a "safe harbor." Companies whose market shares exceed 30 percent may or may not be exempt, depending upon the results of individual competition law reviews by the Commission under Article 81(3). In either case, no vertical agreements containing so-called "hard core restraints" are exempt. These restraints concern primarily resale price maintenance, territorial and customer protection leading to market allocation, and in most instances exclusive dealing covenants that last more than five years.

§ 22.12

1. Pronuptia de Paris GmbH v. Pronuptia de Paris Irmgard Schillgallis (1986) Eur.Comm.Rep. 353.

2. O.J. 1988 L539/46.

3. See Chapter 20.

Chapter 23

PATENT AND KNOWHOW LICENSING

Table of Sections

---

§ 23.1   Protecting Patents and Knowhow

This chapter concerns the most common form of lawful international technology transfer—patent and knowhow licensing. Before any patent licensing can take place, patents must be acquired in all countries in which the owner hopes there will be persons interested in purchasing the technology. Even in countries where the owner has no such hope, patent rights may still be obtained so as to foreclose future unlicensed competitors. Licensing is a middle ground alternative to exporting from the owner's home country and direct investment in host markets. It can often produce, with relatively little cost, immediate positive cash flows. After a brief introduction to patents and knowhow, the main themes of this chapter are standard licensing contract terms and the regulation of international licensing agreements.

511

§ 23.2   The Nature of Patents

For the most part, patents are granted to inventors according to national law. Thus, patents represent *territorial* grants of exclusive rights. The inventor receives Canadian patents, United States patents, Mexican patents, and so on. There are relatively few jurisdictions without some form of patent protection. However, legally protected intellectual property in one country may not be protected similarly in another country. For example, many third world nations *refuse* to grant patents on pharmaceuticals. These countries often assert that their public health needs require such a policy. Thailand has been one such country and unlicensed "generics" have been a growth industry there. Similarly, most European countries do not grant patents on medical and surgical therapeutic techniques for reasons of public policy.

Nominal patent protection in some developing nations may lack effective forms of relief—giving the appearance but not the reality of legal rights. Since international patent protection is expensive to obtain, some holders take a chance and limit their applications to those markets where they foresee demand or competition for their product. Nevertheless, U.S. nationals continue to receive tens of thousands of patents in other countries. But the reverse is also increasingly true. Residents of foreign countries now receive over 50 percent of the patents issued under United States law. In many countries, persons who deal with the issuance and protection of patents are called patent agents. In the United States, patent practice is a specialized branch of the legal profession. Obtaining international patent protection often involves retaining the services of specialists in each country.

What constitutes a "patent" and how it is protected in any country depends upon domestic law. In the United States, a patent issued by the U.S. Patent Office grants the right for 17 years to exclude everyone from making, using or selling the patented invention without the permission of the patentee.[1] Patent infringement can result in injunctive and damages relief in the U.S. courts. "Exclusion orders" against foreign-made patent infringing goods are also available. Such orders are frequently issued by the International Trade Commission under Section 337 of the Tariff Act of 1930,[2] and are enforced by the U.S. Customs Service. A U.S. patent thus provides a short-term legal, but not necessarily economic, monopoly. For example, the exclusive legal rights conveyed by the patents held by Xerox on its photocopying machines have not given it a monopoly in the marketplace. There are many other producers of non-infringing photocopy machines with whom Xerox competes.

---

§ 23.2   2.   See Chapter 24.
1.   35 U.S.C.A. § 154.

There are basically two types of patent systems in the world community, registration and examination. Some countries (e.g., France) grant a patent upon "registration" accompanied by appropriate documents and fees, without making an inquiry about the patentability of the invention. The validity of such a patent grant is most difficult to gauge until a time comes to defend the patent against alleged infringement in an appropriate tribunal. In other countries, the patent grant is made following a careful "examination" of the prior art and statutory criteria on patentability or a "deferred examination" is made following public notice given to permit an "opposition." The odds are increased that the validity of such a patent will be sustained in the face of an alleged infringement. The United States and Germany have examination systems. To obtain U.S. patents, applicants must demonstrate to the satisfaction of the Patent and Trademark Office that their inventions are novel, useful and nonobvious. Nevertheless, a significant number of U.S. patents have been subsequently held invalid in the courts and the Patent Office has frequently been criticized for a lax approach to issuance of patents. Much of this growth is centered in high-tech industries, including computer software and business methods patents.

The terms of a patent grant vary from country to country. For example, local law may provide for "confirmation," "importation," "introduction" or "revalidation" patents (which serve to extend limited protection to patents already existing in another country). "Inventor's certificates" and rewards are granted in some socialist countries where private ownership of the means of production is discouraged. The state owns the invention. This was the case in China, for example, but inventors now may obtain patents and exclusive private rights under the 1984 Patent Law. Some countries, such as Britain, require that a patent be "worked" (commercially applied) within a designated period of time. This requirement is so important that the British mandate a "compulsory license" to local persons if a patent is deemed unworked. Many developing nations have similar provisions in their patent laws ... the owner must use it or lose it.

§ 23.3   The Nature of Knowhow and Trade Secrets

Knowhow is commercially valuable knowledge. It may or may not be a trade secret, and may or may not be patentable. Though often technical or scientific, e.g., engineering services, knowhow can also be more general in character. Marketing and management skills as well as simply business advice can constitute knowhow. If someone is willing to pay for the information, it can be sold or licensed internationally.

Legal protection for knowhow varies from country to country and is, at best, limited. Unlike patents, copyrights and trademarks, you cannot by registration obtain exclusive legal rights to knowhow. Knowledge, like the air we breathe, is a public good. Once released in the community, knowhow can generally be used by anyone and is almost impossible to retrieve. In the absence of exclusive legal rights, preserving the confidentiality of knowhow becomes an important business strategy. If everyone knows it, who will pay for it? If your competitors have access to the knowledge, your market position is at risk. It is for these reasons that only a few people on earth ever know the Coca Cola formula, which is perhaps the world's best kept knowhow.

In the United States, the Economic Espionage Act of 1996 creates *criminal* penalties for misappropriation of trade secrets for the benefit of foreign governments or anyone. For these purposes, a "trade secret" is defined as "financial, business, scientific, technical, economic or engineering information" that the owner has taken reasonable measures to keep secret and whose "independent economic value derives from being closely held." In addition to criminal fines, forfeitures and jail terms, the Act authorizes seizure of all proceeds from the theft of trade secrets as well as property used or intended for use in the misappropriation (e.g., buildings and capital equipment).

Protecting knowhow is mostly a function of contract, tort and trade secrets law. Employers will surround their critical knowhow with employees bound by contract to confidentiality. But some valuable knowledge leaks from or moves with these employees, e.g., when a disgruntled retired or ex-employee sells or goes public with the knowhow. The remedies at law or in equity for breach of contract are unlikely to render the employer whole. Neither is tort relief likely to be sufficient since most employees are essentially judgment proof, although they may be of more use if a competitor induced the breach of contract. Likewise, even though genuine trade secrets are protected by criminal statutes in a few jurisdictions, persuading the prosecutor to take up your business problem is not easy and criminal penalties will not recoup the trade secrets (though they may make the revelation of others less likely in the future).

Despite all of these legal hazards, even when certain knowhow is patentable, a desire to prolong the commercial exploitation of that knowledge may result in no patent registrations. The international chemicals industry, for example, is said to prefer trade secrets to public disclosure and patent rights with time limitations. Licensing or selling such knowhow around the globe is risky, but lucrative.

§ 23.4   International Patent and Knowhow Licensing

International patent and knowhow licensing is the most critical form of technology transfer to third world development. From the owner's standpoint, it presents an alternative to and sometimes a first step towards foreign investment. Such licensing involves a transfer of patent rights or knowhow (commercially valuable knowledge, often falling short of a patentable invention) in return for payments, usually termed royalties. Unlike foreign investment, licensing does not have to involve a capital investment in a host jurisdiction and may be tax-advantaged. However, licensing of patents and knowhow is not without legal risks.

From the licensee's standpoint, and the perspective of its government, there is the risk that the licensed technology may be old or obsolete, not "state of the art." Goods produced under old technology will be hard to export and convey a certain "second class" status. On the other hand, older more labor intensive technologies may actually be sought (as sometimes done by the PRC) in the early stages of development. Excessive royalties may threaten the economic viability of the licensee and drain hard currencies from the country. The licensee typically is not in a sufficiently powerful position to bargain away restrictive features of standard international licenses. For all these reasons, and more, third world countries frequently regulate patent and knowhow licensing agreements. Such law is found in the Brazilian Normative Act No. 17 (1976) and the Mexican Technology Transfer Law (1982) (repealed 1991), among others. Royalty levels will be limited, certain clauses prohibited (e.g., export restraints, resale price maintenance, mandatory grantbacks to the licensor of improvements), and the desirability of the technology evaluated.

Regulation of licensing is not limited to the developing world. The European Union extensively regulates patent and knowhow licensing.[1] In the United States, there is a less direct form of licensing regulation via antitrust law.[2]

The licensor also faces legal risks. The flow of royalty payments may be stopped, suspended or reduced by currency exchange regulations. The taxation of the royalties, if not governed by double taxation treaties, may be confiscatory. The licensee may abscond with the technology or facilitate "gray market" goods[3] which eventually compete for sales in markets exclusively intended for the

---

§ 23.4

1. See Section 23.8.

2. See generally the *Antitrust Guidelines for the Licensing for Intellectual Property* issued by the U.S. Dept. of Justice and the Federal Trade Commission on April 6, 1995. BNA–ATRR, Vol. 68, No. 1708 (April 13, 1995), Special Supplement. These Guidelines are primarily domestic in orientation, but also apply to international licensing.

3. See Chapter 24.

licensor. In the end, patents expire and become part of the world domain. At that point, unless the technology is somehow tied to a protected trade secret, the licensee has effectively purchased the technology and becomes an independent competitor (though not necessarily an effective competitor if the licensor has made new technological advances).

Licensing is a kind of partnership. If the licensee succeeds, the licensor's royalties (often based on sales volumes) will increase and a continuing partnership through succeeding generations of technology may evolve. If not, the dispute settlement provisions of the agreement may be called upon as either party withdraws from the partnership. Licensing of patents and knowhow often is combined with, indeed essential to, foreign investments. A foreign subsidiary or joint venture will need technical assistance and knowhow to commence operations. When this occurs, the licensing terms are usually a part of the basic joint venture or investment agreement. Licensing may also be combined with a trade agreement, as where the licensor ships necessary supplies to the licensee, joint venturer, or subsidiary. Such supply agreements have sometimes been used to overcome royalty limitations through a form of "transfer pricing," the practice of marking up or down the price of goods so as to allocate revenues to preferred parties and jurisdictions (e.g., tax havens).

§ 23.5   International Acquisition of Patents

The principal treaties regarding patents are the 1970 Patent Cooperation Treaty and the 1883 Paris Convention for the Protection of Industrial Property, frequently revised and amended. To some extent, the Paris Convention also deals with trademarks, servicemarks, trade names, industrial designs, and unfair competition. Other recent treaties dealing with patents are the European Patent Convention (designed to permit offices at Munich and The Hague to issue patents of all countries party to the treaty), the European Community Patent Convention (designed to create a single patent valid throughout the EU) and the 1994 Eurasian Patent Convention (which does the same for Russia and the Central Asian states).

The Paris Convention,[1] to which over 140 countries including the U.S. are parties, remains the basic international agreement dealing with treatment of foreigners under national patent laws. It is administered by the International Bureau of the World Intellec-

§ 23.5

1.   21 U.S.T. 1583, T.I.A.S. No. 6295, 828 U.N.T.S. 305 (Stockholm revision).

tual Property Organization (WIPO) at Geneva. The "right of national treatment" (Article 2) prohibits discrimination against foreign holders of local patents and trademarks. Thus, for example, an American granted a Canadian patent must receive the same legal rights and remedies accorded Canadian nationals. Furthermore, important "rights of priority" are granted to patent holders provided they file in foreign jurisdictions within twelve months of their home country patent applications. Patent applications in foreign jurisdictions are not dependent upon success in the home country: Patentability criteria vary from country to country. Nevertheless, the Paris Convention obviates the need to file simultaneously in every country where intellectual property protection is sought. If an inventor elects not to obtain patent protection in other countries, anyone may make, use or sell the invention in that territory. The Paris Convention does not attempt to reduce the need for individual patent applications in all jurisdictions where patent protection is sought. Nor does it alter the various domestic criteria on patentability.

The Patent Cooperation Treaty (PCT),[2] to which about 120 countries including the U.S. are parties, is designed to achieve greater uniformity and less cost in the international patent filing process, and in the examination of prior art. Instead of filing patent applications individually in each nation, filings under the PCT are done in selected countries. The national patent offices of Japan, Sweden, the former Soviet Union and the United States have been designated International Searching Authorities (ISA), as have the European Patent Offices at Munich and The Hague. The international application, together with the international search report, is communicated by an ISA to each national patent office where protection is sought. Nothing in this Treaty limits the freedom of each nation to establish substantive conditions of patentability and determine infringement remedies. However, the Patent Cooperation Treaty also provides that the applicant may arrange for an international preliminary examination in order to formulate a nonbinding opinion on whether the claimed invention is novel, involves an inventive step (non-obvious) and is industrially applicable. In a country without sophisticated search facilities, the report of the international preliminary examination may largely determine whether a patent will be granted. For this reason alone, the Patent Cooperation Treaty may generate considerable uniformity in world patent law. In 1986 the United States ratified the PCT provisions on preliminary examination reports, thereby supporting such uniformity.

2. 28 U.S.T. 7645, T.I.A.S. No. 8733.

§ 23.6 European Patents

The 1973 European Patent Convention (EPC)[1] established the European Patent Offices (EPO) in Munich and The Hague. It allows applicants to simultaneously apply for national patent rights in any of the contracting countries. These include all of the EU nations save Spain, plus a number of other European states. The applicant must meet the requirements for patentability established by the EPC. Challenges to patentability decisions by the EPO may be made within 9 months after granting of the patent. Thereafter, challenges must be made in national courts subject to national patent laws. Thus, the EPC basically presents a one-stop opportunity to obtain a basket of national patents in Europe. It does not foreclose the option of individual national patent applications.

The 1975 Community Patent Convention (CPC) still has not come into force.[2] The Convention originally provided that it had to be ratified by all Community members before becoming effective. Ireland and Denmark have not ratified the CPC for constitutional reasons. However, a conference was held in December 1985. It produced a "Community Patent Agreement," a "Protocol" on the settlement of disputes regarding infringement and validity of Community patents, a "Protocol" amending the Community Patent Convention, and two "Protocols" on a Community Court of [Patent] Appeals. It was agreed in 1985 that if unanimous CPC ratification was not achieved by December 31, 1991, a lesser number of required ratifications would suffice. The Convention was therefore expected to come into force before the end of 1992, but there has been little concrete movement towards realization of this goal.

The CPC will allow applications for a Common Market patent valid in any contracting state. A Common Market patent may be granted, revoked or transferred throughout the Community as a whole. Licenses for part of the Community will be possible. It will be an alternative to (but not a replacement for) national patent rights. The CPC should be contrasted with the bundle of national rights obtained through the EPC. However, the CPC will require its signatories to harmonize national patent laws to conform to the Convention's rules on infringement, litigation procedures, exhaustion of rights and other issues. It will create a new European Court of Patent Appeals.

§ 23.7 European Patent and Knowhow Licensing

In its 1982 *Maize Seed* judgment, the European Court of Justice addressed patent license restrictions under the Communi-

---

§ 23.6

1. 13 Int'l Legal Mats. 268 (1974).

2. O.J.Eur.Comm. (No. L17/1) (1976).

ty's competition rules.[1] The Commission waited for this judgment before publishing the 1984 group exemption under Article 81(3) (formerly 85(3)) for patent licensing agreements. In this case, a research institute financed by the French government (INRA) bred varieties of basic seeds. In 1960, INRA assigned to Kurt Eisele plant breeder's rights for maize seed in the Federal Republic of Germany. Eisele agreed to apply for registration of these rights in accordance with German law. In 1965, a formal agreement was executed by the parties. This agreement consisted of five relevant clauses.

Clause 1 gave Eisele the exclusive rights to "organize" sales of six identified varieties of maize seed propagated from basic seeds provided by INRA. This enabled Eisele to exercise control over distribution outlets. Eisele undertook not to deal in maize varieties other than those provided by INRA. Clause 2 required Eisele to place no restriction on the supply of seed to technically suitable distributors except for rationing in conditions of shortage. The prices charged to the distributors by Eisele were fixed in consultation with INRA, according to a specified formula. Clause 3 obligated Eisele to import from France for sale in Germany at least two-thirds of that territory's requirements for the registered varieties. This restricted Eisele's own production and sale to only one-third of the German market. Clause 4 concerned the protection by Eisele of INRA's proprietary rights, including its trademark, from infringement and granted Eisele the power to take any action to that end. Clause 5 contained a promise by INRA that no experts to Germany of the relevant varieties would take place otherwise than through the agency of Eisele. This meant that INRA would ensure that its French marketing organization would prevent the relevant varieties from being exported to Germany to parallel importers.

In September 1972, it became apparent that dealers in France were selling the licensed varieties of maize seed directly to German traders who were marketing the products in breach of the breeder's rights claimed by Eisele. This resulted in an action by Eisele in the German courts against one of the traders. The parties reached a court approved settlement under which the French trader promised to refrain from offering for sale without permission any variety of maize seed within the rights held by Eisele, and to pay a fine. In February 1974, another breach took place, this time advertising in the German press by a French dealer. In response to threats of legal proceedings, this dealer lodged a complaint with the Commission alleging breach of the Treaty of Rome competition rules.

The Commission considered both the agreement and the settlement to violate Article 81(1) because they granted an exclusive license and provided absolute territorial protection. The Court of Justice reversed the Commission with respect to exclusivity, but upheld the Commission with respect to absolute territorial protection. The Court drew a distinction between "open" licenses which do not necessarily fall under Article 81(1), and "closed" licenses which do so.

Open license agreements are those which do not involve third parties. In *Maize Seed,* the obligation upon INRA or those deriving rights through INRA to refrain from producing or selling the relevant seeds in Germany was treated as an open license term. The Court held such clauses necessary to the dissemination of new technology inasmuch as potential licensees might otherwise be deterred from accepting the risk of cultivating and marketing new products. The Court defined closed licenses as those involving third parties. Thus, the obligation upon INRA or those deriving rights through INRA to prevent third parties from exporting the seeds into Germany without authorization, Eisele's concurrent use of his exclusive contractual rights, and his breeder's rights, to prevent all imports into Germany or exports to other member states were invalid under Article 81(1).

The Commission of the European Community adopted in 1984 a patent licensing group exemption regulation under Article 81(3).[2] It acknowledged that patent licensing improves the production of goods and promotes technical progress by allowing licensees to operate with the latest technology. The Commission also believes that patent licensing increases both the number of production facilities and the quantity and quality of goods in the Common Market. Commission Regulation 2349/84 covered patent licensing agreements and licensing agreements for both patents and knowhow. Commission Regulation 556/89 covered pure knowhow licensing agreements, also exempting them under the terms of Article 81(3). Knowhow was broadly conceived in this regulation. Nonpatented technical information (*e.g.,* descriptions of manufacturing processes, recipes, formulae, designs or drawings) was the focus of Regulation 556/89.

§ 23.8   European Transfer of Technology Regulation

In 1996 the Commission enacted Regulation 240/96 on the application of Article 81(3) of the Rome Treaty to transfer technology agreements. The intention of this Regulation was to combine the existing patent and knowhow block exemptions into a single regulation covering technology transfer agreements, and to simplify and

---

2.   Commission Regulation 2349/84.

harmonize the rules for patent and knowhow licensing. It was also intended to encourage dissemination of technological knowledge and promote the manufacture of more technologically advanced goods.

Transfer of Technology Regulation 772/2004

The detailed regulation of technology transfer agreement clauses contained in Regulation 240/96 was replaced by Regulation 772/2004, which applies to patent, know-how and software copyright licensing. The new Regulation distinguishes agreements between those of "competing" and "noncompeting" parties, the latter being treated less strictly than the former. Parties are deemed "competing" if they compete (without infringing each other's IP rights) in either the relevant technology or product market, determined in each instance by what buyers regard as substitutes.[1] If the competing parties have a *combined* market share of 20 percent or less, their licensing agreements are covered by group exemption under Regulation 772/2004.[2] Noncompeting parties, on the other hand, benefit from the group exemption so long as their *individual* market shares do not exceed 30 percent.[3] Agreements initially covered by Regulation 772/2004 that subsequently exceed the "safe harbor" thresholds noted above lose their exemption subject to a two-year grace period.[4] Outside these exemptions, a "rule of reason" approach applies.

Inclusion of certain "hardcore restraints" causes license agreement to lose their group exemption. For competing parties, such restraints include price fixing,[5] output limitations on both parties,[6] limits on the licensee's ability to exploit its own technology,[7] and allocation of markets or competitors (subject to exceptions).[8] Specifically, restraints on active and passive selling by the licensee in a territory reserved for the licensor are allowed, as are active (but not passive) selling restraints by licensees in territories of other licensees.[9] Licensing agreements between noncompeting parties may not contain the "hardcore" restraint of maximum price fixing.[10] Active selling restrictions on licensees can be utilized, along with passive selling restraints in territories reserved to the licensor or (for two years) another licensee.[11] For these purposes, the competitive status of the parties is decided at the outset of the agreement.[12]

§ 23.8

1. Regulation 772/2004, Article 1(1)j.
2. *Id.*, Article 3(1).
3. *Id.*, Article 3(2).
4. *Id.*, Article 8(2).
5. *Id.*, Article 4(1)(a).
6. *Id.*, Article 4(1)(b).
7. *Id.*, Article 4(1)(d).
8. *Id.*, Article 4(1)(c).
9. *Id.*, Article 4(1)(c)(iv) and (v).
10. *Id.*, Article 4(2)(a).
11. *Id.*, Article 4(2)(b).
12. *Id.*, Article 4(3).

Other license terms deemed "excluded restrictions" also cause a loss of exemption.[13] Such clauses include: (1) mandatory grant-backs or assignments of severable improvements by licensees, excepting nonexclusive license-backs;[14] (2) no-challenges by the licensee of the licensor's intellectual property rights, subject to the licensor's right to terminate upon challenge;[15] and (3) for noncompeting parties, restraints on the licensee's ability to exploit its own technology or either party's ability to carry out research and development (unless indispensable to prevent disclosure of the licensed Know-how).[16]

In all cases, exemption under Regulation 772/2004 may be withdrawn where in any particular case an agreement has effects that are incompatible with Article 81(3).[17]

§ 23.9 Technology Transfers

The process of transferring technology involves an agreement which outlines the relationship between the transferor and the transferee. The extent to which the agreement is detailed may depend upon the character of the transferee.

Subsidiary or affiliate as transferee. Even when the technology is transferred to a wholly owned subsidiary in a foreign nation, there is almost always some agreement, at the very least for tax purposes. The corporate structure using a parent and subsidiary (the latter being an entity incorporated under the laws of the foreign host nation) demands that the separate nature of the two entities be maintained. If not, the parent may be held responsible for the debts of the subsidiary under veil piercing theory. Consequently, the transfer of technology from a parent to a subsidiary should be at arms length and represented by a written agreement.[1] But if the parent is convinced that there is little likelihood that the subsidiary's management will adversely affect the value of the technology, or produce poor quality goods using the technology, there are likely to be fewer provisions in the agreement than where the transferee is an independent entity, unrelated to the transferor.

Independent transferee. When the agreement is to transfer technology to an entity which is not part of the transferor's corporate structure, such as a subsidiary or affiliate, there will be a sense that more detail ought to appear in the technology agreement. For example, disputes will not be settled "within" the company, as they may when the transfer of technology is to a subsidiary, but by

---

13. *Id.*, Article 5.

14. *Id.*, Article 5(1)(a).

15. *Id.*, Article 5(1)(b) and (c).

16. *Id.*, Article 5(2).

17. *Id.*, Article 6.

§ 23.9

1. If it is not an arms length transaction, there may be accusations that transfer pricing is involved.

judicial or arbitral tribunals. A transfer within a corporate structure is usually easily worked out, but a transfer to an independent transferee may involve considerable negotiation of many details.

§ 23.10   Regulations in the Country of the Transferee

When there are no transfer of technology rules in the country of the transferee, the technology transfer agreement is the conclusion of the bargaining of the two parties, the transferor and the transferee. The agreement will not be public; it will not be registered. But when the transfer of technology is to some nations, especially developing nations and nonmarket economy nations, there may be a third party, i.e., the government, involved both in the determination and regulation of what may and may not be included in the technology transfer agreement, and in approving the agreement. During the 1970s a number of developing nations enacted transfer of technology laws.[1] The laws were adopted both as part of the general attempt to control foreign investment and technology transfers, but also to preserve scarce hard currency at a time of severe balance of payment problems. The developing nations viewed technology transfers as an area of investment where there were serious abuses, and believed that their laws would adequately address these issues.[2] The principal abuses were thought to include the following:

1.   Transfer of obsolete technology;

2.   Excessive price paid for the technology;

3.   Limitations on use of new developments by the transferee by grantback provisions;

4.   Little research performed by the transferee;

5.   Too much intervention by the transferor in transferee activities;

6.   Limitations on where the transferee may market the product;

7.   Requirements that components be purchased from the transferor which are available locally or could be obtained from other foreign sources more cheaply;

8.   Inadequate training of transferee's personnel to do jobs performed by personnel of the transferor;

---

§ 23.10

1.   For example, Mexico adopted a transfer of technology law in 1972. It was amended in 1982 but remained restrictive. In 1991 it was replaced by a law which removed the focus on restrictions and replaced this focus with more investment encouraging and protecting provisions.

2.   See Radway, Antitrust, Technology Transfers and Joint Ventures in Latin American Development, 15 Lawyer Am. 47 (1983).

9. Transfer of technology which has adequate domestic substitutes and is therefore not needed;

10. Too long a duration of the agreement; and

11. Application of foreign law and use of foreign tribunals for dispute resolution.

These do not establish an exclusive list. Some nations had different reasons for wishing to more closely govern technology transfers. But these reasons provide an outline of what areas transfer of technology laws in the 1970s attempted to govern.

The result of these restrictive laws was the transfer of less technology, and of technology less valuable to the parent. It was often older technology over which the company was willing to relinquish some control. The bureaucracies established to register and approve or disapprove the agreements were often staffed with persons who knew little about technology, less about international business, but who possessed all of the inefficiency and incompetence of many developing nation government agencies. The laws did not bring in more technology, but less. The consequence was that they did not serve the purpose of helping the balance of payments. Furthermore, the nations which adopted strict rules regulating the transfer of technology often did not have laws which protected intellectual property.

In the 1980s, these restrictive laws were dismantled in many countries, whether by formal repeal or replacement by more transfer encouraging and intellectual property protecting laws, or by a relaxed interpretation of the laws and a general automatic approval of what the transferor and transferee agreed upon. In the 1990s transferring technology increased.[3] Ironically, some technology agreements which were used in the 1960s before the enactment of the strict laws, and which became unusable after such enactments, are now once again be used in the developing world but regulated in the European Union (above). Much of the remainder of this chapter will focus on the nature of modern transfer of technology agreements.

§ 23.11 Different Kinds of Agreements

There are many variations of technology transfer agreements. But they all in some way address the transfer of intellectual property. The agreement may be exclusively for that purpose, or the transfer may be part of a larger agreement, such as the creation of a joint venture. What is included within the definition of intellec-

---

3. But it has only increased when the nations not only dismantled their restrictive transfer of technology laws, but also adopted laws protecting intellectual property, including knowhow.

tual property or technology transfers tends to be quite broad. The transfer may involve property which is granted protection under such laws as those protecting and regulating patents, copyrights and trademarks, or the transfer may involve property which is not granted such protection, but where some protection is maintained by controlling who obtains the knowledge. The previous chapter discussed the licensing of two forms of property, franchises and trademarks. This chapter considers licensing patents, trade secrets and knowhow.

A comparatively new form of transferring technology is by way of a strategic alliance. It is a kind of joint venture where two firms (or more) from different nations agree to jointly exploit technology. The participants often make different contributions to the alliance– one may contribute technology, another capital, or a distribution network, or service facilities, etc. Perhaps the most important part of a strategic alliance is the technology license agreement. It is not always clear whether the alliance structure also transfers enforcement rights to the licensee of the technology.[1]

§ 23.12   Agreement to License a Patent

The agreement to license a patent is a common form of agreement. The transferor presumably owns a valid patent and wishes to transfer its exploitation. Exploiting the patent widely may gain the most return from the limited period the property is granted patent protection. The transferor will likely have sought patent protection in the transferee's nation, just as it has registered the patent in its home nation. Both prevent others from using the patent. Transferring the patent does not create this protection from the use by others; it may well place the patent at risk. The protection is gained by national or multinational permission or agreement included in treaties and laws. The patent is not transferred by the registration abroad, but by the transfer agreement. There are thus two stages which are important for counsel. The first is gaining protection of the patent under the laws of every nation where the patent might be transferred, or where one fears that local parties may try to exploit the property. The second is transferring its use to a firm abroad. It is the licensee which will exploit the patent, and may be required by the agreement, or by virtue of the agreement, to undertake considerable expenditure in such exploitation.

§ 23.11

1. See J. Atik, Technology and Distribution as Organizational Elements

Within International Strategic Alliances, 14 U. Pa. J. Int'l Bus. L. 273 (1993)

§ 23.13   Agreement to License Knowhow or Trade Secrets

This information, or intellectual property, is often not available to the public. It is safe in some nations only as long as it can be kept from others. But many nations, both developed and an increasing number of developing, protect knowhow. Knowhow and trade secrets may be related to patents, in that it may deal with how the products are used, the cost of production, where they can best be marketed, etc. For example, a product which is expensive to produce may be difficult to market without knowledge of those who may be able to afford its purchase. A list of names of persons with the money and inclination to make such purchase may be a precondition to successful production and sales. The value of knowhow will vary considerably from one form to another. Knowhow can be very tenuous in its capacity to be protected, making the agreement an important device to establish the rules for its use by a licensee. Much of the agreement will focus on the protection and limits of permitted use of the knowhow.

All WTO member-nations are obliged under the TRIPs agreement to protect trade secrets. Because some nations do not protect knowhow or other proprietary information, it must be protected in the transfer agreement. What becomes important is for the transferee to agree to the contractually stated conditions of its use, and to assume responsibility for its improper dissemination to the public or other persons, particularly competitors. In a country where no protection is granted by law, dissemination may cause a severe financial loss to the transferor. Protecting the knowhow from such loss is thus central to an agreement to license knowhow.

§ 23.14   Agreement as Part of a Foreign Direct Investment

Any foreign direct investment which includes the transfer of some technology may include the transfer in an agreement which also includes the direct investment, quite possibly in a joint venture contract. Whether there is such an agreement will depend on the laws of the host nation. Sometimes foreign direct investment requires nothing more than entering the host nation with a branch operation or establishing a local wholly owned subsidiary. The articles of incorporation of the subsidiary will not include anything relating to the transfer of technology to the subsidiary. There will be a separate transfer of technology agreement. But in many nations which restrict foreign investment, there may be an agreement which expresses the total relationship, including the transfer of technology.[1] Investment in nations which mandate joint ventures

---

§ 23.14
1. For example, the few foreign investments established in Cuba must comply with the broad and often vague

are the most likely situations where the investment agreement will also include the technology transfer provisions. There is nothing wrong with combining transfer of technology provisions in a larger scope agreement, but the agreement ought to be just as detailed regarding technology provisions as it would standing alone as a separate agreement.

Where technology is transferred within the context of a joint venture or other form of investment agreement, the agreement ought to be clear as to the access of the host nation joint venture partner to any sensitive technology. Particularly where there is knowhow transferred, the foreign investor may wish to control the local party's access to the technology.[2] India demanded in the 1970s that the Coca–Cola company alter its structure from a wholly foreign owned investment to a joint venture. While the Indian government did not expressly state that the foreign parent would have to share the secret formula, the government did say that such sharing would be the natural consequence of the partnership sense of the joint venture. Coca–Cola would not disclose the technology, and withdrew from India, not to return until the 1990s, when India had relaxed its previously strict foreign investment rules.

§ 23.15   Other Forms of Agreement

Transfers may assume other functions or address other matters than noted above. They sometimes apply to a particular area because of the frequent use of licensing for that area.

Franchises. An example of a special form of licensing is the licensing of a franchise abroad.[1] While some franchises own their outlets, many are franchised to local investors. The licensing may involve transfers of trade secrets, knowhow, trademarks, patents and copyrights. All will be included in the same franchise agreement.

Computer software. The laws of some nations do not recognize computer software as protectable property by copyright or as a trade secret, thus making a transfer particularly risky.[2] Even when there is legal recognition of computer software as protectable property, however, it may be best not to transfer it if the risk of

---

provisions of the out-of-date 1982 joint venture law. That law notes the need for foreign technology and that a formal agreement with the government for an investment must also outline the nature of any technology transfers. Little technology is being transferred because there is little protection to technology under Cuban law.

2. While the local party may be one trusted by the foreign investor, unless

there are restrictions on the transfer of ownership interests, that party may change and bring into the ownership and management persons less trusted.

§ 23.15

1. Franchises are discussed in chapter 18 which addresses trademarks.

2. It may be recognized as property protected by copyright.

loss is high. Where the computer technology is contained in the end product, such as the bar coding process for retail products, the software technology may be protected by retaining it in the home country and only transferring the end use product.

Management contracts. Many enterprises, especially in the hotel industry, function by means of management contracts. The transfer usually involves knowhow, the knowledge of how to operate a facility. Often the most important aspect of the transfer is the experience of the manager of the management company. That experience is reflected in the manager's day to day decisions. It is an experience which has proven that it has value. For example, many Cuban government organizations attempted to manage hotels to develop tourism beginning in the mid–1980s. But the hotels were inefficiently managed until foreign management was obtained.

Training contracts. Knowledge of how to undertake a particular function or functions has value. That knowledge may be transferred as any other knowhow. The management contract noted above may include training of host nation persons in hotel management.[3]

---

3. Even if the management contract is not also a training contract, there will be a certain amount of transfer of training involved, simply by the other employees viewing how a well managed unit functions.

Chapter 24

COUNTERFEIT, INFRINGING AND GRAY MARKET IMPORTS—UNITED STATES SECTION 337 PROCEEDINGS

Table of Sections

---

§ 24.1 Technology Transfers

The predominant vehicle for controlling technology transfers across national borders is the "license" or "franchise" contract. The holder of a patent, copyright or trademark in one country first acquires the legally protected right to the same in another country. This is a time consuming and expensive process. Convincing new

529

franchising operations or other holders of patents, trademarks and copyrights of the value of securing international protection is often a role which falls to counsel. The holder then licenses foreign rights, usually for a fee known as royalty, to a persons in those countries. Thus, the licensor typically conveys to the licensee rights to make, use or sell the technology. The very sharing of intellectual property rights across borders raises a risk that proprietary control of the technology may be lost, or at a minimum, that a competitor will be created. For these reasons, international licensing agreements are complex legal documents that need to be carefully negotiated and drafted. Absent licensed transfers, piracy of intellectual property is increasingly commonplace.

The developing nations (as a "Group of 77"), the industrialized nations, and the nonmarket economy nations have tried to agree in UNCTAD upon an international "Code of Conduct" for the transfer of technology. Wide disparities in attitudes toward such a Code, which has now gone through many drafts, have been reflected by the developing nations' insistence that it be "internationally legally binding," and the industrialized nations' position that it consist of "guidelines" for the international transfer of technology. Some economics of the debate are illustrated by the fact that persons in the United States pay millions of dollars in royalties for the use of imported technology, but received billions in royalty payments from technology sent abroad. Many considered development of an international technology transfer Code the most important feature of the North–South dialogue between developed and developing nations. But it was not to be. Instead to some degree the TRIPs Agreement from the Uruguay Round of GATT negotiations functions as such a code.

Among the industrialized countries, efforts often occur to acquire (even by way of stealing) "leading edge" technology. One example in the 1980s involved attempted theft of IBM computer technology by Japanese companies ultimately caught by the F.B.I. In the United States, the Office of Export Administration uses the export license procedure to control strategic technological "diversions." But in 1984 falsification of licensing documents by prominent Norwegian and Japanese companies allowed the Soviets to obtain the technology for making vastly quieter submarine propellers. In the ensuing scandal, "anti-Toshiba" trade sanctions were adopted in the United States. Leading Japanese executives resigned their positions, which is considered the highest form of apology in Japanese business circles.

Theft of intellectual property and use of counterfeit goods are rapidly increasing in developing and developed countries. Such theft is not limited to consumer goods (Pierre Cardin clothing, Rolex watches). Industrial products and parts (e.g., automotive brake pads) are now being counterfeited. Some countries see illegal technology transfers as part of their strategy for economic development. They encourage piracy or choose not to oppose it. Since unlicensed producers pay no royalties, they often have lower production costs than the original source. This practice fuels the fires of intellectual property piracy. Unlicensed low-cost reproduction of entire copyrighted books (may it not happen to this book) is said to be rampant in such diverse areas as Nigeria, Saudi Arabia, and South Korea. Apple computers have been inexpensively counterfeited in Hong Kong. General Motors estimates that about 40 percent of its auto parts are counterfeited in the Middle East. Recordings and tapes are duplicated almost everywhere without license or fee. And the list goes on.

§ 24.2   Counterfeit Goods, U.S. Remedies

Legal protection against intellectual property theft and counterfeit goods is not very effective. The four principal U.S. remedies are: (1) seizure of goods by Customs; (2) infringement actions in federal courts; (3) criminal prosecutions or treble damages actions under the Trademark Counterfeiting Act of 1984; and (4) Section 337 proceedings. Each of these is discussed below.

The Anticounterfeiting Consumer Protection Act of 1996, Public Law 104–153 (110 Stat. 1386), made a number of statutory changes intended to combat counterfeiting. Trafficking in counterfeit goods is now an offense under the RICO Act (Racketeer Influenced and Corrupt Organizations Act). Importers must disclose the identity of any trademark on imported merchandise, ex parte seizures by law enforcement officers of counterfeit goods and vehicles used to transport them are widely authorized, damages and civil penalties that can be recovered from counterfeiters and importers were increased, and the Customs Service's authority to return counterfeit merchandise to its source (and potential re-entry into commerce) has been repealed. Customs must now destroy all counterfeit merchandise that it seizes unless the trademark owner otherwise consents and the goods are not a health or safety threat.

In the United States, the Copyright Felony Act of 1992 criminalized all copyright infringements. The No Electronic Theft Act of 1997 (NET) removed the need to prove financial gain as element of copyright infringement law, thus ensuring coverage of copying done with intent to harm copyright owners or copying simply for personal use. The Digital Millennium Copyright Act of 1998 (DMCA) brought the United States into compliance with WIPO treaties and created two new copyright offenses; one for circumventing technological measures used by copyright owners to protect their works ("hacking") and a second for tampering with copyright management information (encryption). The DMCA also made it clear that "webmasters" digitally broadcasting music on the internet must pay performance royalties. Criminal and civil sanctions apply.[1]

§ 24.3 Customs Service Seizures

United States trademark and copyright holders may register with the Customs Service and seek the blockade of pirated items made abroad. Such exclusions are authorized in the Tariff Act of 1930 and the Copyright Act of 1976.[1] The thrust of these provisions is that unauthorized imports bearing U.S. registered trademarks or copyrights may be seized by the Customs Service. Trade names that have been used for at least six months can also be recorded with the Customs Service. Such recordation permits those names to receive the same relief accorded registered trademark and copyright holders when imports that counterfeit or simulate those trade names are found.[2] Since these trademark, copyright and trade name remedies are only available to United States citizens, distributors of foreign goods must ordinarily be assigned United States trademark rights held by foreigners. Such assignments would permit the distributor to seek a new registration from the Patent and Trademark Office so as to be able to invoke these trade remedies.

The importation of semiconductor chip products or equipment that contains a semiconductor chip design or "mask work" registered with the U.S. Copyright Office is prohibited.[3] As with trademarks, copyrights and trade names, the owner of such a mask work may register it with the U.S. Customs Service or the U.S. International Trade Commission so as to invoke trade remedies which will preclude infringing products and equipment from entering into the United States. The Customs Service also administers a high-tech copyright protection program specially targeted at pirated computer programs.[4] Generally, the Customs Service will seize infringing programs if there is proof of access by the infringer and a "substantial similarity" between the imports and the registered program.[5]

There are some differences in Customs Service seizure proceedings depending upon whether the product seized is alleged to be a trademark counterfeit or a copyright counterfeit. The Customs Service rules indicate that in administrative hearings the burden is

---

§ 24.2

1. See, e.g., Universal City Studios, Inc. v. Shawn C. Reimerdes, 111 F.Supp.2d 294 (2000) (injunction against anti-encryption software).

§ 24.3

1. See 19 U.S.C.A. § 1526(a) (trademarks) and 17 U.S.C.A. § 602(b) (copyrights). See also 19 C.F.R. § 133, Parts A, D.

2. See 19 C.F.R. § 133, Parts B, C.

3. See 17 U.S.C.A. § 601(a).

4. See 19 C.F.R. § 133.31 et seq.

5. See Webster and Pryor, Customs Administration of the High-tech Copyright Protection Program, 73 J. Pat. & Trademark Off. Society 538 (1991).

on the importer to demonstrate why allegedly counterfeit trademarked goods should be released, whereas the burden is on the copyright owner to prove that copyrighted goods are being pirated. These burdens are different because of the greater difficulties in proving copyright infringements. The Second Circuit has ruled that the Customs Service must employ the "average purchaser test" in determining whether imports are counterfeits subject to seizure and forfeiture.[6] In this case, the Service had used experts to determine differences in the trademark such that it was deemed not a counterfeit (merely infringing) and therefore admissible if the confusing mark was obliterated. The consumer test mandated by the Second Circuit should give greater protection from counterfeits.

Attorneys invoking the Customs Service process frequently sense the inadequacy of relief against counterfeit goods. The first problem is simply knowing when counterfeit goods are likely to enter the United States market. The Customs Service has enormous duties and can only pay limited attention to the possibility that certain goods are pirated. This is understandable. How is the Customs Service officer to know that the goods are pirated? Can the Customs Service do anything more than look at the invoice in a cursory way? Pirates often take great pains to imitate the logo and trademarks they are copying. This makes such piracy non-obvious.

Copyright piracy of sound recordings is even more difficult to ascertain. It cannot reasonably be expected of the Customs Service that they will play records and tapes in order to determine that they are counterfeit goods. To make customs relief effective it is necessary for private interests to notify the Customs Service that a suspected shipment of counterfeit goods is about to or has arrived in the United States. Companies are increasingly hiring private detectives in order to assist with this task. Private detectives might also be used to try to locate pirated copies and counterfeiting operations inside the United States.

A second frustration with Customs Service relief concerns narrow Customs Service interpretations, such as in the *ROMless Computers* case.[7] In that decision, the Customs Service refused to seize ROMless computers alleged to be in violation of Apple Computer Company copyrights. The practical effect of this decision was to permit ROMless computers to enter the U.S. market, and thereafter be altered in rather simple fashion so as to become effective competitors and arguably infringers of copyrights held by the Apple Computer Company. By removing the ROM (Read Only Memory operating system computer program) unit from the computers, the

---

6. Montres Rolex, S.A. v. Snyder, 718 F.2d 524 (2d Cir.1983), *cert. denied* 465 U.S. 1100, 104 S.Ct. 1594, 80 L.Ed.2d 126 (1984).

7. See 9 BNA U.S. Import Wkly 1062 (May 30, 1984).

importers eliminated the only copyrighted element in the computer and thereby nullified attempts at blocking importation of these goods:

> Assuming without deciding that the making of the "ROM-less" computers constitutes a contributory infringement against the copyright holder's copyrights, the importation of such merchandise is not prohibited by 17 U.S.C. 602(b). While the phrase "an infringement of copyright" arguably includes contributory copyright infringement, preventing the importation of "ROMless" computers would be inconsistent with other language in the statute. The objects against which the provisions of 17 U.S.C. 602(b) are directed are copies or phonorecords of a work that have been acquired outside the United States.

> With regard to the very computer programs in issue, the statutory copyright requirement of fixation has been held to be satisfied through the embodiment of these programs in ROM devices. ... Furthermore, computer programs contained in ROMs can be perceived, reproduced, or otherwise communicated therefrom with the aid of other computer equipment. Accordingly, the provisions of 17 U.S.C. 602(b) are operative against ROMs (or diskettes, tapes, or other devices for fixed storage of software) that contain unlawful reproductions of copyrighted computer software, for these items are copies within the meaning of that section. ... Therefore, inasmuch as "ROMless" computers do not include such copies upon arrival in the United States, they may enter the country without violation of 17 U.S.C. 602(b).

§ 24.4   Section 337 Proceedings (Intellectual Property)

This section focuses on the application of Section 337 of the Tariff Act of 1930 to imports that infringe U.S. intellectual property rights. A later section in this chapter focuses upon non-intellectual property rights' cases, and there are two additional sections discussing Section 337 procedures and remedies generally.

Patent piracy is most often challenged in proceedings against unfair import practices under Section 337 of the Tariff Act of 1930.[1] Section 337 proceedings traditionally have involved some relatively complicated statutory provisions. Prior to 1988, the basic prohibition was against: (1) unfair methods of competition and unfair acts in the importation of goods (2) the effect or tendency of which is to destroy or substantially injure (3) an industry efficiently and eco-

---

§ 24.4

1.   19 U.S.C.A. § 1337.

nomically operated in the U.S. Such importation was also prohibited when it prevented the establishment of an industry, or restrained or monopolized trade and commerce in the U.S. Section 337 proceedings are *in rem* which explains why they are preferable to a series of *in personam* actions for infringement in the federal courts.

The Omnibus Trade and Competitiveness Act of 1988 revised Section 337. The requirement that the U.S. industry be efficiently and economically operated was dropped. Proof of injury to a domestic industry is *not* required in intellectual property infringement cases. The importation of articles infringing U.S. patents, copyrights, trademarks or semiconductor chip mask works[2] is specifically prohibited provided a U.S. industry relating to such articles exists or is in the process of being established. Such an industry exists if there is significant plant and equipment investment, significant employment of labor or capital, or substantial investment in exploitation of the intellectual property rights (including research and development or licensing). This test has origins in prior ITC case law.[3] There is also prior case law on the question of whether an American industry is "in the process of being established."[4]

Determination of violations and the recommendation of remedies to the President under Section 337 are the exclusive province of the International Trade Commission (ITC). Most of the case law under Section 337 concerns the infringement of patents. Trademark, copyright and mask work infringements may also be pursued under Section 337.[5] In copyright cases, the petitioner must prove ownership of the copyright and the fact of copying.[6] While not quite

---

2. The Semiconductor Chip Protection Act of 1984 (17 U.S.C.A. §§ 901–914) provides a national system for the registration of original mask works. Only a mask work that was first commercially exploited in the United States, or which was owned by a national or domiciliary of the United States or a national, domiciliary, or sovereign authority of a foreign nation that is a party to a treaty affording protection to mask works to which the United States is also a party or a stateless person at the time of its first commercial exploitation outside the United States, is entitled to registration. The owner of a registered mask work has exclusive rights to reproduce the work by optical, electronic, or any other means and to import or distribute a semiconductor chip product in which the mask work is embodied. The violation of any of these exclusive rights would amount to infringement. However, the owner of a particular semicon-

ductor chip product made by the owner of the mask work, or by any person authorized by the owner of the mask work, may import, distribute, or otherwise dispose of or use, but not reproduce, that particular semiconductor chip product without the authority of the owner of the mask work. Reverse engineering of the mask work is permitted for the purpose of teaching, analysis or evaluation or for the purpose of making another original mask work.

3. See Airtight Cast–Iron Stoves, 3 ITRD 1158, U.S.I.T.C. Pub. No. 1126 (1981).

4. See Caulking Guns, 6 ITRD 1432, U.S.I.T.C. Pub. No. 1507 (1984).

5. 19 U.S.C.A. § 1337(a).

6. See Coin–Operated Audio–Visual Games and Components, 1981 WL 50518, U.S.I.T.C. Pub. No. 1160 (June 1981).

a per se rule, it is nearly axiomatic that any infringement of United States patent rights amounts to an unfair import practice for purposes of Section 337.[7] Both product and process patents are entitled to protection under Section 337. But in a major decision affecting biotechnology firms, the Federal Circuit Court of Appeals refused relief when the U.S. patent owner had no claim either to the final product or the process used to create it even though the foreign party had to use the patented product to create the product being imported into the United States.[8] Had the same activity been undertaken in the U.S., an infringement would most probably have been found.

All legal and equitable defenses (but not counterclaims) may be presented, including attacks upon the validity or enforceability of the patent.[9] A patent license term requiring all "litigation" to take place in California barred pursuit of Section 337 relief.[10] The ITC's refusal to entertain a Section 337 proceeding because the complainant's patent was unenforceable due to prior inequitable conduct was upheld by the Federal Circuit Court of Appeals.[11] This decision illustrates the power of the ITC, as a practical matter, to rule on patent validity. International Trade Commission decisions on patent validity, and Federal Circuit Court of Appeals opinions on appeal from the ITC, can be treated as preclusive fact findings under collateral estoppel principles in ordinary federal court proceedings.[12] Res judicata effect is ordinarily denied given the fundamental differences between ITC administrative and federal judicial proceedings concerning patent validity.[13]

Section 337 proceedings can result in general exclusion orders permitting seizure of patent counterfeits at any U.S. point of entry. Apple Computer, for example, was able to get such an order against computers sold under the label "Orange" that contained infringing programs and color display circuits.[14] However, as previously noted, the Customs Service finds it extremely difficult when inspecting invoices and occasionally opening boxes to ascertain which goods are counterfeit or infringing. Many counterfeits do look like "the real thing." For most seizure remedies to work, the holder must notify the Customs Service of an incoming shipment of patent offending goods. Such advance notice is hard to obtain.

7. See Synthetic Star Sapphires, § 316, No. 13 (Sept. 1954), *aff'd sub nom.* In re Von Clemm, 229 F.2d 441 (C.C.P.A.1955).

8. Amgen, Inc. v. U.S. Int'l Trade Comm., 902 F.2d 1532 (Fed.Cir.1990).

9. 19 U.S.C.A. § 1337(c).

10. Texas Instruments Inc. v. Tessera, Inc., 231 F.3d 1325 (Fed.Cir.2000).

11. LaBounty Manufacturing, Inc. v. U.S. ITC, 958 F.2d 1066 (Fed.Cir.1992).

12. In re Convertible Rowing Exerciser Patent Litigation, 814 F.Supp. 1197 (D.Del.1993).

13. Id.

14. In Re Certain Personal Computers and Components Thereof, 6 ITRD 1140, 1984 Copr.L.Dec. p 25651, U.S.I.T.C. Pub. No. 1504.

Section 337 exclusion orders can be used against gray market imports (see Part C below). In one decision, the Federal Circuit Court of Appeals upheld the ITC's order against used Kubota-brand tractors.[15] This decision relies heavily on the existence of material differences between the gray market tractors and those distributed by authorized Kubota dealers in the U.S. These differences included parts and the absence of English-language labels and instructions.

A 1989 decision by a General Agreement on Tariffs and Trade (GATT) panel ruled that Section 337 violates the national treatment provisions of Article III:4 of the GATT. The panel was persuaded that imported goods are treated less favorably (i.e., more severely) under Section 337 in terms of patent infringement remedies than domestic goods which are remedied in the federal courts. The panel's decision was ultimately adopted by the GATT Council and the U.S. indicated that it would consider ways to reach compliance after the TRIPs accord was finalized. The Uruguay Round Agreements Act of 1994 did not alter the substance of Section 337 law. It did make procedural changes (such as allowance of counterclaims in Section 337 proceedings) intended to address the issue of an imbalance in patent infringement remedies. The federal district courts must stay infringement proceedings at the request of the respondent to Section 337 actions.

§ 24.5   Infringement Actions

Another alternative available to counsel attempting to assist U.S. firms combating foreign counterfeiting of their products is infringement relief, including temporary restraining orders, injunctions, damages and an award of the defendant's profits. The major problem with infringement relief is the inability of United States trademark, patent and copyright owners to get effective jurisdiction over and relief from foreign counterfeiters. Infringement and contributory infringement actions can be used more effectively against the importers, distributors or retailers of counterfeit goods. But relief against one such party may merely shift counterfeit sales to another who must then be brought to court, and then another, and another, etc. While such proceedings can result in *ex parte* seizure orders of counterfeit goods already in the United States, they do not represent a long term solution to production of counterfeit goods in foreign jurisdictions. Most injunctive and damages relief remains illusory, but it can sometimes be useful. For example, it has been held that counterfeit goods seized *ex parte* under the Lanham Trademark Act can be destroyed upon court order.[1] Civil

15. Gamut Trading Co. v. U.S. I.T.C., 200 F.3d 775 (Fed.Cir.1999).

§ 24.5

1. Fendi S.a.s. Di Paola Fendi E Sorelle v. Cosmetic World, 642 F.Supp.

remedies are *not* limited to simply removing the offending trade-mark.[2]

§ 24.6   Criminal Prosecutions

Many states have enacted criminal statutes to combat in-creased counterfeiting of goods and services in the United States. After much debate, Congress enacted the Trademark Counterfeit-ing Act of 1984.[1] Criminal penalties are established for anyone who "intentionally traffics or attempts to traffic in goods or services and knowingly uses a counterfeit mark on or in connection with such goods or services." Treble damages or profits (whichever is greater) and attorney fees may be recovered in civil actions unless there are "extenuating circumstances." Ex parte seizure orders for counter-feit goods may be issued by the federal courts. Parallel imports of genuine or "gray market goods" (goods legitimately produced over-seas but imported into the United States via unauthorized distribu-tion channels, infra) and "overruns" (goods produced without au-thorization by a licensee) are expressly *excluded* from the Act's coverage. The real problem with criminal sanctions as a remedy for counterfeiting is to persuade public prosecutors to take these crimes seriously and to allocate law enforcement resources to them.

§ 24.7   International Solutions

International solutions to the problem of intellectual property piracy have been no less elusive. A draft "Anti–Counterfeiting Code" received close scrutiny in the Uruguay Round of negotia-tions. Although the TRIPs accord incorporates some coverage of counterfeiting, it is not the encompassing anti-counterfeiting code that the developed world sought. The TRIPs agreement does man-date border measures to block the release of counterfeit goods into domestic circulation. It also requires criminal penalties for willful trademark counterfeiting or copyright piracy undertaken on a com-mercial scale. However, the TRIPs agreement does not reject the practice of re-exportation of counterfeit merchandise. Re-exporta-tion has the practical effect of pushing the problem on some other jurisdiction and does not represent a final solution from the point of view of the infringed party.

Various United States statutes authorize the President to withhold trade benefits from or apply trade sanctions to nations inadequately protecting the intellectual property rights of U.S. citizens. This is true of the Caribbean Basin Economic Recovery Act

1143 (S.D.N.Y.1986).   **§ 24.6**

   2. Id.   **1.** 18 U.S.C.A. § 2320 et seq.

of 1983,[1] the Generalized System of Preferences Renewal Act of 1984,[2] the Trade and Tariff Act of 1984 (amending Section 301 of the 1974 Trade Act),[3] and Title IV of the 1974 Trade Act as it applies to most-favored-nation tariffs.[4] Slowly this carrot and stick approach has borne fruit. Under these pressures for example, Singapore drafted a new copyright law, Korea new patent and copyright laws, and Taiwan a new copyright, patent, fair trade and an amended trademark law. Brazil introduced legislation intended to allow copyrights on computer programs. Though these changes have been made, there is some doubt as to the rigor with which the new laws will be enforced when local jobs and national revenues are lost.

§ 24.8   Gray Market Goods

One of the most controversial areas of customs law concerns "gray market goods," goods produced abroad with authorization and payment but which are imported into unauthorized markets. Trade in gray market goods has dramatically increased in recent years, in part because fluctuating currency exchange rates create opportunities to import and sell such goods at a discount from local price levels. Licensors and their distributors suddenly find themselves competing in their home or other "reserved" markets with products made abroad by their own licensees. Or, in the reverse, startled licensees find their licensor's products intruding on their local market shares. In either case, third party importers and exporters are often the immediate source of the gray market goods, and they have little respect for who agreed to what in the licensing agreement. When pressed, such third parties will undoubtedly argue that any attempt through licensing at allocating markets or customers is an antitrust or competition law violation.

In times of floating exchange rates, importers have found that by shopping around the world for gray market goods they can undercut local prices with "parallel imports." This explains in large part the dramatic growth in trade in gray market goods in recent years. Gray market goods have become an important source of price competition in the United States marketplace, particularly in years when the U.S. dollar is strong. Some retail firms, like K–Mart, are major traders of gray market goods.

A decline of the dollar against the Japanese yen or EURO would reduce the flow of gray market *imports* from those sources, but perhaps increased the flow of gray market *exports* from the U.S. to those countries. For example, assume a Cadillac sells in the U.S.

§ 24.7

1. See Chapter 10.
2. See Chapter 10.

3. See Chapter 19.

4. See Chapter 10.

for $30,000 and a Mercedes in Germany for 30,000 EUROs. At exchange rate of .75 EUROs to the dollar, the dollar is very strong. Mercedes sells in Germany for $22,500, Cadillac sells in the U.S. for 40,000 EUROs. This encourages importing cars bought in Germany to the U.S. The cars are converted to U.S. specifications for $2,000 and sold for $24,500 by nonauthorized companies, often independent Mercedes repair shops. Then the dollar drops in value to 1.50 EUROs. Now you must pay $45,000 in Germany to buy a Mercedes, but need only 20,000 EUROs to buy a Cadillac. This encourages exporting cars bought in the U.S. to Germany.

In most cases, the manufacturer is not unhappy at selling the product, whether it is sold in the regular market or gray market. But the manufacturer may do better when its product is sold through the regular distributor. First, this lessens the need to face angry authorized distributors as in the above Mercedes situation. Furthermore, when the dollar is strong there is a very substantial price differential. This profit is effectively divided between the manufacturer and the U.S. distributor.

§ 24.9   The U.S. Customs Service Position

In the early part of the century, gray market litigation provoked a Supreme Court decision blocking French cosmetics from entering the United States.[1] A United States firm was assigned the U.S. trademark rights for French cosmetics as part of the sale of the United States business interests of the French producer. The assignee successfully obtained infringement relief in federal district court against Katzel, an importer of the French product benefiting from exchange rate fluctuations. On appeal, the Second Circuit vacated this relief in a holding which followed a line of cases allowing "genuine goods" to enter the U.S. market in competition with established sources. The Supreme Court ultimately reversed the Second Circuit emphasizing the trademark ownership (not license) and independent public good will of the assignee as reasons for its reversal.

Congress, before the Supreme Court reversal, passed the Genuine Goods Exclusion Act, now appearing as Section 526 of the Tariff Act of 1930.[2] This Act bars *unauthorized importation* of goods bearing trademarks of U.S. citizens. Registration of such marks with the Customs Service can result in the seizure of unauthorized imports. Persons dealing in such imports may be enjoined, required to export the goods, destroy them or obliterate the offending mark,

§ 24.9

1. A. Bourjois & Co. v. Katzel, 260 U.S. 689, 43 S.Ct. 244, 67 L.Ed. 464 (1923).

2. 19 U.S.C.A. § 1526.

as well as pay damages. The Act has had a checkered history in the courts and Customs Service. The Customs Service view (influenced by antitrust policy) was that genuine (gray market) goods may be excluded only when the foreign and U.S. trademark rights are not under common ownership or control, or those rights have been used without authorization. The practical effect of this position was to admit most gray market goods into the U.S., thereby providing substantial price competition, but uncertain coverage under manufacturers' warranty, service and rebate programs. Some firms, like K–Mart, excel at gray market importing and may provide independent warranty and repair service contracts. Since 1986, New York and California require disclosure that manufacturers' programs may not apply to sellers of gray market goods.

An attempt in 1985 by Duracell to exclude gray market batteries alternatively under Section 337 of the Tariff Act of 1930 as an unfair import practice was upheld by the U.S. International Trade Commission, but denied relief by President Reagan in deference to the Customs Service position.[3] Despite that position, injunctive relief under trademark or copyright law is sometimes available against gray market importers and distributors.[4] Injunctive relief, however, applies only to the parties and does not prohibit gray market imports or sales by others. This remedy is thus useful, but normally insufficient.

A split in the federal Courts of Appeal as to the legitimacy in light of the Genuine Goods Exclusion Act of the Customs Service position on gray market imports resulted in a U.S. Supreme Court ruling.[5] In an extremely technical, not very policy-oriented decision, the Supreme Court arrived at a compromise. The Customs Service can continue to permit entry of genuine goods when there is common ownership or control of the trademarks. The Service must seize such goods only when they were authorized (licensed), but the marks are not subject to common ownership or control. For these purposes, "common ownership or control" is defined as a 50 percent shareholding or the effective control of policy and operations. Gray market goods originating from such "affiliated companies" will still be allowed to enter the United States.[6] However, a Fifth Circuit decision indicates that close and profitable business ties between a foreign trademark owner and the foreign owner of

---

3. See Duracell, Inc. v. U.S. International Trade Commission, 778 F.2d 1578 (Fed.Cir.1985).

4. See especially, CBS, Inc. v. Scorpio Music Distributors, Inc., 569 F.Supp. 47 (E.D.Pa.1983), *affirmed* 738 F.2d 424 (3d Cir.1984) (copyright infringement relief granted); NEC Electronics, Inc. v. CAL Circuit Abco, Inc., 810 F.2d 1506 (9th Cir.1987), *cert. denied* 484 U.S. 851, 108 S.Ct. 152, 98 L.Ed.2d 108 (1987) (trademark infringement relief denied).

5. K Mart Corp. v. Cartier, Inc., 486 U.S. 281, 108 S.Ct. 1811, 100 L.Ed.2d 313 (1988).

6. See 19 C.F.R. §§ 133.21(c), 133.2(d).

U.S. trademark rights does not amount to "common control." Rolex was thus able to obtain a Customs Service forfeiture ruling against gray market imports of its watches by Wal–Mart. The court applied a strict common ownership test to Section 526.[7] The Tenth Circuit affirmed summary judgment in favor of an Oklahoma company owning U.S. trademark rights to "Vittoria" for bicycle tires. The rights were transferred by an Italian company, the maker of the tires. The "common control" exception to gray market trademark protection did not apply because there was at most "a close business relationship" between the two companies.[8]

Many believe that the bulk of U.S. imports of gray market goods have continued under the Supreme Court's *K Mart* ruling. However, this perspective is somewhat undermined by treatment of gray market imports under other statutory regimes.

§ 24.10   Trademark and Copyright Remedies

Section 42 of the Lanham Trademark Act prohibits the importation of goods that copy or simulate a registered U.S. trademark.[1] In *K Mart*, the U.S. Supreme Court specifically declined to review the legality of barring gray market goods under this provision. Some courts have denied relief under Section 42 against gray market imports. These cases stress the absence of consumer confusion when genuine goods are involved.[2] Other courts have reached conclusions that in the absence of adequate disclosure Section 42 is actionable against gray market goods that materially differ in physical content from those sold in the U.S.A.[3] However, when there are material differences, labeling suffices to avoid Section 42.[4] A Second Circuit decision relying upon Section 32 of the Lanham Act also supports blocking imports of materially different gray market goods.[5] In this case, Cabbage Patch dolls produced in Spain under license came with birth certificates, adoption papers and

7. United States v. Eighty–Three Rolex Watches, 992 F.2d 508 (5th Cir. 1993)., *cert. denied* 510 U.S. 991, 114 S.Ct. 547, 126 L.Ed.2d. 449 (1993).

8. Vittoria North America, LLC v. Euro–Asia Imports, Inc., 278 F.3d 1076 (10th Cir.2001).

§ 24.10

1. 15 U.S.C.A. § 1124.

2. See, e.g., Monte Carlo Shirt v. Daewoo International (America) Corp., 707 F.2d 1054 (9th Cir.1983); Bell & Howell: Mamiya Co. v. Masel Supply Co., Corp., 719 F.2d 42 (2d Cir.1983).

3. See Lever Bros. Co. v. United States, 877 F.2d 101 (D.C.Cir.1989); Ferrero U.S.A., Inc. v. Ozak Trading, Inc.,

753 F.Supp. 1240 (D.N.J.1991), *affirmed* 935 F.2d 1281 (3d Cir.1991); Société Des Produits Nestle, S.A. v. Casa Helvetia, Inc., 982 F.2d 633 (1st Cir.1992); Lever Bros. Co. v. United States, 981 F.2d 1330 (D.C.Cir.1993).

4. See the U.S. Customs Service Regulation at 19 C.F.R. § 133.23.

5. Original Appalachian Artworks v. Granada Electronics, Inc., 816 F.2d 68 (2d Cir.1987), *cert. denied* 484 U.S. 847, 108 S.Ct. 143, 98 L.Ed.2d 99 (1987). Accord, Société Des Produits Nestle, S.A. v. Casa Helvetia, Inc., 982 F.2d 633 (1st Cir.1992).

instructions in Spanish, but were otherwise the same product. The U.S. manufacturer refused to register these dolls, leading to numerous complaints by parents and children. These complaints supported the court's injunction against importation of the dolls from Spain under Section 32. Section 32 provides trademark owners with remedies against persons who, without consent by the owner, use a "reproduction, counterfeit, copy or colorable imitation" of a mark so as to cause confusion, mistake or deception.[6] However, a Ninth Circuit decision relying of Sections 32 and 43(a) (country of origin markings) of the Lanham Act leads to the opposite conclusion, finding no support for the argument that gray market imports can be remedied under those provisions.[7]

Sections 103 and 602 of the Copyright Act provide that importing goods into the U.S. without the consent of copyright owners is an infringement.[8] But Section 109 limits the distribution rights of copyright owners under what is known as the "first sale doctrine."[9] This doctrine limits the owner's control over copies to their first sale or transfer. Two Third Circuit decisions split on the use of copyright law against gray market imports in spite of the first sale doctrine.[10] In *Sebastian,* the Third Circuit held that a U.S. manufacturer who sells goods with copyrighted labels to foreign distributors is barred by the first sale doctrine from obtaining import infringement relief. In *Scorpio,* where the goods were manufactured abroad under license by the U.S. copyright holder, such relief was granted. The Supreme Court subsequently held that the first sale doctrine bars injunctive relief under the Copyright Act[11] against good previously exported from the USA. However, if the goods are foreign made, injunctive relief under the Copyright Act may be had.[12]

§ 24.11   Gray Market Goods in Other Jurisdictions

An excellent review of the treatment of gray market goods in other jurisdictions is presented in an article by Takamatsu.[1] This review is of particular interest to U.S. *exporters* of gray market goods. For the most part, his review indicates that other jurisdic-

6.   15 U.S.C.A. § 1114.

7.   NEC Electronics v. CAL Circuit Abco, Inc., 810 F.2d 1506 (9th Cir.1987), *cert. denied* 484 U.S. 851, 108 S.Ct. 152, 98 L.Ed.2d 108 (1987).

8.   17 U.S.C.A. § 106.

9.   17 U.S.C.A. § 109.

10.   Columbia Broadcasting System v. Scorpio Music Distributors, 569 F.Supp. 47 (E.D.Pa.1983), *affirmed* 738 F.2d 424 (3d Cir.1984) (relief granted); Sebastian Int'l, Inc. v. Consumer Contacts (PTY), Ltd., 847 F.2d 1093 (3d Cir.1988) (relief denied).

11.   Quality King Distributors, Inc. v. L'ANZA Research International, Inc., 523 U.S. 135, 118 S.Ct. 1125, 140 L.Ed.2d 254 (1998).

12.   See Parfums Givenchy, Inc v. Drug Emporium, 38 F.3d 477 (9th Cir. 1994)., *cert. denied* 514 U.S. 1004, 115 S.Ct. 1315, 131 L.Ed.2d 197 (1995).

§ 24.11

1.   Takamatsu, Parallel Importation of Trademarked Goods: A Comparative Analysis, 57 Wash.L.Rev. 433 (1982).

tions permit gray market goods to enter. This is true of the *Parker Pen* cases under Japanese law,[2] the *Maja* case under German law[3] and the *Agfa–Gevaert* case in Austria,[4] all of which are reviewed by Takamatsu. Canadian Superior Court law strongly supports free trade in gray market goods.[5] The legal analysis contained in these opinions has been very influential in European Community licensing law.[6] EC law basically posits that once goods subject to intellectual property rights of common origin have been sold on the market with authorization, the holders can no longer block importation of those goods ("parallel imports") through the use of national property rights. Such use is not thought to have been intended as part of the original grant of rights and is said to have been "exhausted" upon sale. An extensive body of law permits parallel imports (even of qualitatively different goods) as part of the promotion of the Common Market and rejects attempts to divide the market territorially along the lines of national property rights. Product labeling as to source and contents is thought sufficient notice to consumers that qualitatively different goods are involved.

In a major decision, the European Court of Justice has ruled that trademark rights can be used to block gray market imports into the Common Market. These rights are not exhausted once the goods are voluntarily put into the stream of international commerce. An Austrian maker of high-quality sunglasses was therefore entitled to bar imports from Bulgaria.[7] In *Zino Davidoff, SA*, and *Levi Strauss* the European Court of Justice affirmed the right of trademark owners to block gray market sales of their goods sold at prices below those they utilize in the EU. No "implied consent" to gray market imports was found via the sale of goods outside the EU.[8]

§ 24.12   Section 337—Complaint and Response

Section 337 complaints may be filed by domestic producers with the International Trade Commission in Washington, D.C.,

2. NMC Co. v. Schulyro Trading Co., Feb. 20, 1970 (Osaka Dist. Ct., 234 Hanrei Taimuzu 57) reprinted in English at 16 Japanese Annual of Int'l Law 113 (1972) affirmed by Osaka High Court. See Nestle Nihon K.K. v. Sanhi Shoten (unreported Tokyo Dist.Ct. May 29, 1965) summarized in T. Doi, Digest of Japanese Court Decisions in Trademarks and Unfair Competition Cases (1971).

3. Fed.Sup.Ct. (W.Ger.) Jan. 22, 1964, 41 Bundesgerichtshof 84 summarized in 54 Trademark Rep. 452 (1964).

4. Agfa–Gevaert GmbH v. Schark, Sup.Ct. (Aus.), Nov. 30, 1970.

5. Consumers Distributing Co., Ltd. v. Seiko Time Canada Ltd., 1 Sup.Ct. 583 (1984). But see Mattel Canada Inc. v. GTS Acquisitions, 27 C.P.R.(3d) 358 (1989) (preliminary injunction against identical gray market goods).

6. See Chapter 23.

7. Silhouette International v. Hartlauer, 1998 WL 1043033 (July 16, 1998).

8. Cases C–414–99, 415/99 and 416/99, 2001 WL 1347061 (Levi jeans sold by supermarket in Britain) (Nov. 20, 2001).

provided the complainants have not agreed by contract to litigate all disputes elsewhere.[1] The complainant must be a representative of the industry. The complaint itself must contain a statement of the facts alleged to constitute unfair import methods or acts. The complaint must also specify instances when unlawful importations occurred, the names and addresses of respondents, and if they exist, a description of any related court proceeding. The complaint must describe the domestic industry that is affected by the import practices and the petitioner's interest in that industry. If the case involves intellectual property rights, detailed information regarding the patent, copyright, trademark or mask work must be provided. Lastly, the complaint must indicate what relief is sought.[2] Section 337 complainants are subject to the "duty of candor" recognized in *Convertible Rowing Exercisers*.[3] This duty is violated by (1) a failure to disclose material information or a submission of false material information and (2) an intent to mislead.

Once a complaint is filed, or the Commission decides to start a Section 337 proceeding on its own initiative, an investigation is normally commenced. The Commission takes the position that it is not obliged to commence an investigation after the filing of a private complaint. Its Office of Unfair Imports (OUI) takes 30 days to examine the sufficiency of the complaint. This Office is an independent party in Section 337 proceedings charged with representing the public interest. Pre-filing review of draft complaints by the OUI is possible, and counsel for the respondents may also seek to have the OUI recommend against proceeding with a Section 337 complaint. Although it is a rare event, the Commission occasionally has declined to pursue a Section 337 investigation. If this happens, the complaint is dismissed.[4] The Commission has maintained its discretionary authority to review Section 337 complaints despite statutory language which would appear to be mandatory.[5] Thus, it has dismissed complaints where there is insufficient data to support the allegations, or the allegations themselves are insufficient to prove a Section 337 violation.[6] The complainant may of course amend and refile its complaint. Furthermore, a rejection of Section 337 complaints by the Commission can be appealed to the Federal Circuit Court of Appeals.[7]

§ 24.12

1. See Texas Instruments Inc. v. Tessera, Inc., 231 F.3d 1325 (Fed.Cir. 2000) (agreement that all litigation must take place in California precludes Section 337 complaint).

2. C.F.R. § 210.20 (1990).

3. Inv. No. 337–TA–212, U.S.I.T.C. Pub. No. 2111 (1988).

4. See 19 C.F.R. § 210.12.

5. See 19 U.S.C.A. § 1337(b)(1).

6. See Certain Fruit Preserves in Containers Having Lids With Gingham Cloth Design, Docket 1056 (May 21, 1984); Certain Architectural Panels, Docket 1122 (November 30, 1984).

7. See Syntex Agribusiness, Inc. v. U.S. International Trade Commission, 617 F.2d 290 (C.C.P.A.1980) and 659 F.2d 1038 (C.C.P.A.1981).

The respondents in Section 337 proceedings are given an opportunity to submit written briefs regarding the complaint. Such briefs should respond to each allegation in the complaint and set forth any defenses. Section 337 complaint and response requirements are reproduced in Section 20.27 of this chapter. Failure to provide a response to the complaint can result in a determination that the facts alleged in the complaint are deemed admitted.[8] For example, if the complaint is based upon patent infringement, the respondent would typically allege non-infringement by suggesting that the product is not covered by the patent and/or the invalidity of the patent. An unusual aspect of Section 337 proceedings is the appointment of an investigative attorney by the ITC to represent the public interest. This attorney is a party to the investigation and may participate in discovery and hearings to the full extent of the complainant and respondent.[9]

§ 24.13   Section 337—Temporary Relief

If the Commission decides, in the process of its investigation, that there is reason to believe that a violation of Section 337 has occurred, it may order the goods to be excluded from entry into the United States or permit entry only under a bond as a temporary remedy.[1] Such remedies require proof not only of the reasons to believe in the violation, but also of an immediate and substantial injury to the domestic industry in the absence of a temporary remedy.[2] The statute now requires that the Commission consider the public interest in making temporary remedial decisions in connection with Section 337. Thus, the Commission ends up balancing the probability of the complainant's success on the merits, the prospect for immediate and substantial harm to the domestic industry if no relief is granted, the harm to the respondent if such relief is granted, and the effect that temporary remedies would have on the public interest.[3] If the Commission is concerned that the complainant may possibly have filed a frivolous claim or that the harm to the respondent is particularly large, it can require the complainant to post a bond in order to get temporary relief. Decisions about temporary relief are made by the administrative law judge in the case, although they may be modified or vacated by the Commission upon review.[4]

---

8.   19 C.F.R. § 210.21.

9.   19 C.F.R. § 210.4.

§ 24.13

1.   19 U.S.C.A. § 1337(e).

2.   See Certain Apparatus, 12 ITRD 1841, U.S.I.T.C. Pub. No. 1132 (April 1981).

3.   19 U.S.C.A. § 1337(e).

4.   19 C.F.R. § 210.24(17).

§ 24.14   Section 337—Administrative Process

Section 337 investigations normally last one year but may be extended to eighteen months in complicated cases. This relatively short period has been described as "due process with dispatch." Section 337 investigations are the only investigations conducted by the International Trade Commission that are governed by the Administrative Procedure Act. Thus, the investigation will follow the established procedures for discovery under the Federal Rules of Civil Procedure, pre-hearing conferences, an initial determination of the issues by an administrative judge, and final review by the Commission.[1] One problem is the frequent need for extraterritorial discovery in Section 337 cases. Another problem is the absence of effective sanctions for abuse of discovery.[2] Although the Commission is authorized to promulgate rules allowing costs and attorneys' fees as sanctions, it has not yet done so. In contrast, the Commission has aggressively enforced its protective orders against disclosure of confidential and business information of a proprietary character.[3] At any point during its investigation, the Commission may decide to settle the proceedings by consent order or by agreement of the parties. This happens reasonably often, especially when the parties to an intellectual property case agree to a licensing arrangement. In either case, the Commission will review the motion to terminate or a proposed consent order from the standpoint of the public interest in the proceeding. An arbitration agreement between parties who are contesting a Section 337 proceeding is no grounds for terminating the ITC investigation.[4]

When the International Trade Commission reviews the advisory decision of the administrative law judge in Section 337 proceedings, it need not undertake a review of that entire determination. It is sufficient for purposes of appeal that the Commission decides the case on the basis of a single dispositive issue. For example, in patent infringement litigation, if the Commission decides that there was no infringement, it need not render decisions concerning any other issues in the Section 337 proceeding.[5] Thus it was only this issue that could be appealed to the Federal Circuit Court of Appeals. Put another way, the only issues that can be appealed are

§ 24.14

1. See 19 C.F.R. §§ 2210.1–2210.71.

2. See Certain Concealed Cabinet Hinges and Mounting Plates, 12 ITRD 1841 (Jan. 8, 1990).

3. See Certain Electrically Resistive Monocomponent Toner, 10 ITRD 1672 (1988).

4. Farrel Corp. v. U.S. ITC, 949 F.2d 1147 (Fed.Cir.1991), *cert. denied* 504 U.S. 913, 112 S.Ct. 1947, 118 L.Ed.2d 551 (1992).

5. Beloit Corp. v. Valmet Oy, 742 F.2d 1421 (Fed.Cir.1984), *cert. denied* 472 U.S. 1009, 105 S.Ct. 2706, 86 L.Ed.2d 721 (1985).

those upon which the Commission has decided, and this is true even in cases concerning temporary relief under Section 337.[6]

§ 24.15 Section 337—Sanctions

If the Commission ultimately decides that an unfair import method or act has been committed, it is authorized to issue a cease and desist order or an exclusion order barring the goods from entering the United States. Any violation of those orders is punishable by civil penalties up to $100,000 per day or twice the value of the merchandise in question. Final ITC determinations under Section 337 are appealed directly to the Federal Circuit Court of Appeals.

The Federal Circuit Court of Appeals has ruled that the ITC may impose civil penalties for violation of consent orders (as well as cease and desist orders) that terminate patent infringement investigations under Section 337.[1]

§ 24.16 Section 337—Settlements

As the Section 337 investigation proceeds, the complainant may move for a summary determination by the ITC. This is analogous to summary judgment under the Federal Rules of Civil Procedure.[1] If the complaint concerns patent infringement, one solution is for the parties to enter into a licensing agreement. However, the parties must give the Commission a copy of their complete agreement. The Commission's investigative attorney then comments on the settlement and the administrative law judge makes an initial decision as to whether to terminate the investigation on the basis of the settlement. This determination is sent to the Commission for final approval.[2] The purpose of these procedures is to insure that the public interest is preserved as part of the patent infringement dispute settlement.

In non-patent cases, the typical route for settlement is by consent order. To do this, a joint motion is filed by all of the complainants, the Commission's investigative attorney, and one or more of the respondents.[3] This typically occurs before the commencement of the hearing before the administrative law judge. Consent settlements of this type must contain admissions of all jurisdictional facts, waivers of rights to seek judicial review or other

---

6. See Warner Bros., Inc. v. U.S. International Trade Commission, 787 F.2d 562 (Fed.Cir.1986).

§ 24.15

1. San Huan New Materials High Tech, Inc. v. ITC, 161 F.3d 1347 (Fed. Cir.1998).

§ 24.16

1. 19 C.F.R. § 210.50.

2. 19 C.F.R. § 210.51.

3. 19 C.F.R. § 211.20.

means of challenging the consent order, and an agreement that the enforcement, modification and revocation of the order will be undertaken pursuant to ITC rules. The consent order typically is not deemed to constitute an admission of a violation of Section 337 and usually states that it is undertaken solely for settlement purposes.[4] There is a ten-day notice period which allows any interested party to comment on the proposed termination of a Section 337 proceeding on the basis of a consent order.[5]

§ 24.17   Section 337—ITC Public Interest Review

The International Trade Commission is not required to impose a Section 337 remedy if it finds a violation. Its remedial powers are discretionary. In deciding whether to accept proposed consent orders or to impose any remedy, the Commission is required to consider all of the public comments that have been received, the effect upon the public health and welfare of the United States, the effect upon competitive conditions in the U.S. economy, the effect on production of like or directly competitive articles in the United States, and its effect upon U.S. consumers.[1] The Commission has rarely invoked the public interest exception to Section 337 relief. When it has, the domestic industry typically was unable to supply critically needed items[2] or the public's strong interest in the research overrode patent rights.[3]

§ 24.18   Section 337—ITC General Exclusion and Cease and Desist Orders

The International Trade Commission may issue three different kinds of remedies under Section 337. The first is an exclusion order of a limited or general nature, and this type of relief predominates in intellectual property cases. The second is a cease and desist order, and this type of relief is often issued if there are significant inventories of the offending product already imported into the United States. The effect of such a cease and desist order is to prevent further distribution within the country. The Commission is expressly authorized to issue exclusion orders and cease and desist orders together.[1] In either case, the Commission may authorize entry of the goods under bond pending the President's final determination in the proceeding. The amount of the bond varies from

4.   19 C.F.R. § 211.22.
5.   19 C.F.R. § 211.20.

§ 24.17

1.   19 U.S.C.A. § 1337(d), (e), (f).
2.   See Automatic Crankpin Grinders, 2 IRTD 5121, U.S.I.T.C. Pub. No. 1022 (1979) (engine parts needed to meet fuel efficiency standards); Certain

Fluidized Supporting Apparatus reported at 7 I.T.R.D. 1089 (1984).

3.   Certain Inclined–Field Accelerated Tubes, 2 ITRD 5572 (1990).

§ 24.18

1.   19 U.S.C.A. § 1337(f).

case to case, but is generally intended to offset the competitive advantages that are perceived to exist. Such bonds have ranged upwards to 600 percent of the value of the imports.[2] Many Section 337 bonds have been determined by measuring the difference between the complainant's prices in the U.S. and the customs value of the imports. Forfeiture orders are relatively uncommon and typically follow notice by the Secretary of the Treasury that forfeiture would result from further importation of goods that offend Section 337.

Plaintiffs usually wish to obtain general exclusion orders in intellectual property cases. Such orders will keep out all infringing products. The problem with this approach is that it may unfairly bar the importation of goods that resemble but do not infringe the patented product. This is a generally undesirable result that the Commission will try to avoid.[3] Consequently, the Commission requires those seeking general exclusion orders to prove a widespread pattern of unauthorized use of the patented invention and reasonable inferences that foreign manufacturers other than the respondents may attempt to enter the United States market with infringing goods.[4] A widespread pattern of unauthorized use can be demonstrated by the importation of the infringing goods by numerous companies, by pending foreign infringement suits based upon foreign patents which correspond to the United States patent at issue, or by other evidence which demonstrates a history of unauthorized foreign use of the invention.[5] In providing evidence that it is reasonable to infer that other foreign manufacturers may attempt to enter the U.S. market, plaintiffs may offer proof of the established demand for the product, the existence of a distribution system in the United States for its marketing, the cost to foreigners of manufacturing or creating a facility capable of manufacturing the goods, the ease and number of foreign manufacturers who could retool so as to produce the offending article, and the cost of such retooling.[6] As these criteria suggest, obtaining a general exclusion order is not always easy, and certainly not automatic.

Patent-based Section 337 proceedings are multiplying. ITC decisions take about 12 to 15 months, versus three to five years for federal court lawsuits. General exclusion orders are typically sought. Hearings are held before one of four administrative law judges specializing in patent law, with final decisions taken by the ITC. Infringing products are excluded from importation during the appeals process. About one-fourth of all 337 proceedings find in-

2. See Certain Cube Puzzles, supra.

3. See Certain Cloisonne Jewelry, 8 ITRD 2028, U.S.I.T.C. Pub. No. 1822 (March 1986).

4. See Certain Airless Spray Pumps and Components Thereof, 3 ITRD 2041, U.S.I.T.C. Pub. No. 1199 (1981).

5. Id.

6. Id.

fringements. An increasing number of foreign owners of U.S. patents are invoking 337 procedures. About half of all such complaints are settled, often using cross-licensing among the parties.

§ 24.19   Section 337—Presidential Veto

Any order issued by the International Trade Commission under Section 337 goes into effect immediately. However, the President may veto that order for public policy reasons.[1] Vetoes by the President of Commission orders in Section 337 proceedings are rare and not generally reviewable by the courts.[2] The President has sixty days within which to make a decision concerning ITC orders under Section 337. If the President does not take action within this period, then the order becomes final.[3] Final ITC orders under Section 337 remain in effect until the Commission decides that there is no longer reason to continue the order.[4] Any violation of an outstanding ITC order under Section 337 can incur a civil penalty of up to $10,000 per day or twice the domestic value of the goods sold, whichever is greater.[5]

§ 24.20   Section 337—ITC Opinion Letters

The ITC follows the practice of issuing informal or formal opinion letters in connection with Section 337 matters. Requests for informal opinions from the ITC staff should be addressed to the Assistant General Counsel of the Commission. Formal opinions actually issued by the Commission itself may be obtained if the staff opinion letter is adverse or a formal opinion is just simply necessary. Requests for such opinions are filed with the Secretary of the Commission.[1]

§ 24.19

1. 19 U.S.C.A. § 1337(j).

2. Duracell, Inc. v. U.S. International Trade Commission, 778 F.2d 1578 (Fed.Cir.1985).

3. Id.

4. 19 U.S.C.A. § 1337(k).

5. 19 U.S.C.A. § 1337(j).

§ 24.20

1. 19 C.F.R. § 211.54.

*

Chapter 25

INTRODUCTION TO FOREIGN DIRECT INVESTMENT

Table of Sections

§ 25.1 Why Invest Abroad?

Foreign direct investment (FDI) abroad often occurs subsequent to less extensive experience with the foreign country in the form of trading goods, or transferring technology to have goods produced under license in a foreign nation. Persons and multinationals have many reasons to invest abroad. It may be part of an initial overall plan to produce goods or provide services worldwide. It may be the next progression considered after the home market is saturated. But the investment may be less voluntary, undertaken to maintain the enterprise's market share at home as some stages of competitors' production move offshore to seek lower labor costs. It may be to avoid high tariffs for imported finished products in the foreign nation. It may be a consequence of an unhappy relationship with a licensee abroad, and a belief that the company can make a better product or provide a better service on its own. Poor-quality products or services produced by licensees is often the reason for assuming control of production abroad. Whatever the motivation, foreign investment will almost always encounter laws in the host nation that differ from the laws regulating investment in the home nation.[1]

Investment abroad involving the creation of new businesses, and the capital transfers to underwrite them, is often referred to as foreign direct investment (FDI).[2] It means ownership and control of the enterprise abroad, whether branch or subsidiary in form. Enterprises which undertake foreign investment are referred to by several names, multinational corporations (MNCs) or enterprises (MNEs), or transnational corporations (TNCs) or enterprises (TNEs). More important than what they are called are their percentages of ownership and control by the home-nation person or entity. That discloses whether or not the enterprise is a joint venture, and which country is likely to assert authority over the enterprise in the host or foreign nation. Both the governments of the home nation (place of incorporation) and the foreign host nation (place of the productive part of the business) may attempt to assert such authority, leading to intergovernmental conflicts.

Foreign investment is a major part of the business of many companies chartered in developed nations. Especially since the early 1980s, multinational enterprises have moved toward global production and division of labor. As a result, global foreign direct investment rose to over $2 trillion by the opening of this century. Intraregional foreign investment is another aspect of this development. The creation of the European Community (now European Union) in 1958, and the adoption of the North American Free

§ 25.1

1. Host-nation is used to identify the nation in which the investment is made. Home-nation is used to designate the nation from which the investment capital and technology comes, meaning usually the nation in which the multinational parent is located.

2. In contrast to indirect investment such as by purchases of shares of an existing company.

Trade Agreement in 1994, stimulated increased foreign investment within these trading areas.[3] The completion of the Uruguay GATT Round in late 1993 added new WTO investment rules (TRIMs). These new rules have encouraged even more foreign investment.

The composition of the rules which should govern foreign investment has been a subject of frequent debate among developed and developing countries. The North–South dialogue[4] led in the 1970s to both restrictive United Nations General Assembly Resolutions,[5] and restrictive foreign investment laws in many developing nations.[6] But after the debt crisis in the early 1980s, and the subsequent election of governments more determined to join the developed world than to lead the third world, impediments to foreign investment began to be dismantled. Nationalizations in the 1960s and 1970s gave way to privatizations in the 1980s and 1990s. Investment restrictions gave way to investment incentives. Involuntary joint ventures gave way to voluntary joint ventures. But even though this recent liberalization has provided investors with significant opportunities in many foreign nations, obstacles to foreign investment remain, and old ones may be exhumed as governments change. This chapter focuses upon some of the typical regulations that investors may confront in attempting to *establish* or *acquire* enterprises in foreign countries. Later chapters discuss more specif-

---

3. There are many other regional trade groups which have promoted increased investment as well as trade.

4. The North–South dialogue split developed countries in the northern hemisphere and less developed countries generally in the southern hemisphere. The less developed countries argued that they were poor because the developed countries were rich, and that the development gap was increasing. The less developed countries made demands that were largely aspirational, and unrealistic. They wanted transfers of the most advanced technology at little or no cost, increased investment capital in companies with majority local control and ownership, and both forgiveness of old debt and assurances of new borrowing with few restrictions as to use. The dialogue was most active in the late 1960s and through the 1970s. It became unraveled with the debt defaults in the early 1980s, and the election of more market oriented leaders in many developing nations who realized that development lay more in local effort than foreign largesse.

5. The two most significant were the Charter of Economic Rights and Duties

of States, Dec. 12, 1974, U.N.G.A.Res. 3281 (XXIX), 29 U.N. GAOR, Supp. (No. 31) 50, U.N.Doc. A/9631 (1975), reprinted in 14 Int'l Legal Mat. 251 (1975), and the Declaration on the Establishment of a New International Economic Order, May 1, 1974, U.N.G.A.Res. 3201 (SBVI), 6 (Special) U.N. GAOR, Supp. (No. 1) 3, U.N.Doc. A/9559 (1974), reprinted in 13 Int'l Legal Mat. 715 (1974). A proposed U.N. Code of Conduct on Transnational Corporations was never enacted. These "aspirational" declarations of the developing nations and the UN General Assembly were never very effective, and with the focus on incentives for investment since the early 1980s, they are very much on the back burner.

6. See, e.g., Mexican Law to Promote Investment and Regulate Foreign Investment of 1973, translated in 1 Michael Wallace Gordon, Multinational Corporations Law (1982); Indian Foreign Investment Regulation Act of 1973, in 1982 Bus. Int'l 92 (Mar. 19); Nigerian Enterprises Promotion Decree of 1977, in 6 Investment Laws of the World (ICSID1982). Each of these restrictive laws of the 1970s has been repealed, amended or emasculated by regulation or policy.

ically investment issues in developing and in nonmarket or transitional economy nations, and in regional areas in Latin America and Europe. This chapter also examines efforts to reduce or limit foreign investment barriers by means of bilateral or multilateral agreements, especially within the GATT/WTO and the NAFTA.

§ 25.2   The Language of Investment Barriers—TRIMs

Foreign investment barriers that individual nations impose have come to be described in the past few years as "trade related investment measures" or TRIMs, language incorporated in the WTO. Although many countries impose TRIMs, the developed and developing countries have different views regarding their economic effects. Developed nations argue that TRIMs cause investors to base their decisions on considerations other than market forces. The principle of national treatment, that mandates that foreign-controlled enterprises receive no less favorable treatment from governments than their domestic counterparts, embodies this idea. Led by the United States, the developed nations have tried to limit TRIMs through the General Agreement on Tariffs and Trade (GATT)/ World Trade Organization (WTO) process.

Developing nations take a less negative view of TRIMs. They believe TRIMs provide a means of host nation control over various aspects of foreign multinational enterprise activity. Specifically, they believe that TRIMs serve as useful policy tools to promote government objectives in furthering economic development and ensuring balanced trade. Additionally, developing nations have quite vigorously defended the use of TRIMs as an aspect of national sovereignty, historically to maintain control over natural resources, and more recently to preserve domestic culture.

The overall data as to whether TRIMs successfully meet policy objectives or always cause inefficiency appears mixed. Also unclear is exactly which practices the term TRIMs encompasses. The Uruguay Round of GATT, leading to the creation of the WTO, defined fourteen practices as TRIMs. U.N. commentators have broken these into four categories: local content, trade-balancing, export requirements, and the broad area of investment incentives.[1] The first three serve as restrictions or barriers, while the fourth encourages investment. Some viewers divide foreign investment laws into different

§ 25.2

1. Sometimes, however, a foreign investment law that is actually restrictive is introduced by a government as an investment encouraging law, and therefore an "incentive" law. This may be the first law adopted that allows foreign investment after a long period of little or no foreign investment, such as the 1982 Cuban joint venture foreign investment law. The Cuban government viewed it as an incentive law, a view nearly unanimously rejected by potential foreign investors.

groups.[2] Rather than discuss the broad area of incentives, which typically involves tax benefits, this chapter focuses more on barriers to investment.

The term "performance requirements" often refers to barriers that governments use to condition entry, often through a screening mechanism. In order to distinguish between the incentives and barriers, barrier TRIMs are often called trade related performance requirements (TRPRs).[3]

§ 25.3 Governance by Home Nations

Governance of multinational enterprises may be divided into three spheres. They are governance by the home nation, by the host nation or by multi-nation organizations. One might also wish to add a fourth, governance by international law. Although the latter might constitute an ideal method in an ideal world, international legal norms that govern multinational enterprises are few in number and contested in status.

The regulation of U.S. multinationals abroad, or governance by the home nation, is essentially a matter of federal law. These laws tend to fall into one of two classes. First are those laws enacted to deal with domestic issues, and without serious consideration of their impact on foreign activities of U.S. enterprises. Examples are the federal securities and antitrust laws. Both have extraterritorial effect, although the potential impact abroad was not seriously debated when they were enacted. Second are laws that address specific foreign policy issues and are intended to achieve what are largely political goals. Examples are the Foreign Corrupt Practices Act (FCPA) and the antiboycott laws. There are other laws that affect multinationals' actions abroad, such as tax laws that may encourage investment in friendly nations, customs provisions allowing assembly abroad of U.S. made parts with duties applied only to the value added abroad when the products re-enter the United States, and the generalized system of preferences (GSP), that is intended to assist development. But what is missing are laws of home nations enacted to address special interests of the developing nations when they host foreign investment. Foreign nations should nevertheless understand that home nations in which multinationals are registered and usually "seated" tend only to enact laws that are in the best interests of the home nations, usually without serious

---

2. Foreign investment laws are divided into four categories as well: export requirements, local content requirements, investment incentives, and transfer of technology requirements. See also Cynthia Day Wallace, Legal Control of the Multinational Enterprise 37 (1983).

3. The term "trade related investment measure" is sometimes considered synonymous with performance requirements, but it may more accurately encompass all measures, including incentives. The U.S. government does not clearly distinguish these measures.

regard for any special interests of the various possible host nations. Thus it is only the host nations' laws that may effectively regulate multinational activity in the host nation.

One form of governance by home nations, in a kind of collective sense, is the work of the Organisation for Economic Cooperation and Development (OECD). The OECD was for many years composed of developed Western European nations plus such other nations as the United States, Japan, Australia, New Zealand, Canada, Finland and Turkey. But it began to expand in the 1990s with the transition of non-market economies to market economies. The OECD recommends only a modest form of "governance", and its efforts have not been enacted into national laws. What the OECD has accomplished is the creation of Guidelines for the conduct of multinational enterprises. The Guidelines consist of recommendations regarding how multinationals ought to act in foreign nations. In the late 1990s the OECD engaged in extensive discussions to develop a Multilateral Agreement on Investment (MAI). But it stalled over several issues, as discussed below. The discussions are certain to continue, especially in view of the success of the OECD in completing the Convention on Combating Bribery of Foreign Officials in International Business Transactions.

§ 25.4   Governance by Host Nations

The laws enacted in the 1970s by host nations to govern foreign investment tended to be very restrictive. Some of their characteristics are discussed below.[1] Mandatory joint ventures was a key element.[2] But foreign investors in developing nations with restrictive laws often were able to avoid joint ventures. An "operational code" or unwritten law existed that allowed much needed

---

§ 25.4

1. In addition to restrictions based on the desire to have host nation nationals participate in equity and management, restrictions may be imposed when investment is believed to infringe upon national sovereignty, is contrary to a development plan, is unbalanced in favor of the foreign party, creates environmental damage, or violates host nation law.

2. See, e.g., Wolfgang G. Friedmann & J.P. Beguin, Joint International Business Ventures in Developing Countries (1971); Andrzej Burzynski & Julian Jurgensmeyer, Poland's New Foreign Investment Regulations: An Added Dimension to East—West Industrial Cooperation, 14 Vand.J.Transnat'l L. 17 (1981); Thomas M. Franck & K. Scott Gudgeon, Canada's Foreign Investment

Control Experiment: The Law, the Context and the Practice, 50 N.Y.U.L.Rev. 76 (1975); Michael Wallace Gordon, The Joint Venture as an Institution for Mexican Development: A Legislative History, 1978 Ariz.St.Univ.L.J. 173; Martin F. Klingenberg & Joseph E. Pattison, Joint Ventures in the People's Republic of China: The New Legal Environment, 19 Va.J.Int'l L. & Econ. 807 (1979); Covey Oliver, The Andean Foreign Investment Code: A New Phase in the Quest for Normative Order as to Direct Foreign Investment, 66 Am. J.Int'l L. 763 (1972); James F. Pederson, Joint Ventures in the Soviet Union: A Legal and Economic Perspective, 16 Harv.Int'l L.J. 390 (1975); Niki Tobi, Legal Aspects of Foreign Investment in Nigeria, 18 Indian J.Int'l L. (1978).

foreign investment to avoid the harsh rules generally believed to be mandatory rules affecting foreign investment.[3]

Host nation laws of the 1970s that governed foreign investment tended to evolve from two quite different perspectives. One group which enacted restrictive laws mandating joint ventures included nations which already had considerable foreign investment, such as India, Mexico and Nigeria. These nations viewed the new laws as a way to gain greater control over foreign multinationals and to allow their nationals to participate in the equity and management of the means of production in the nation. At the same time nonmarket economy nations were beginning to adopt joint venture laws that were used to admit for the first time in decades some limited foreign equity. The reason was usually that the nation needed technology that would not be transferred unless it accompanied an equity investment. Nations adopting such laws included several Eastern European nations, plus China and Cuba.[4] Nearly all of the world's nations that experimented with a nonmarket economy have more recently adopted investment laws that have eliminated many of the more restrictive features of investment laws of the 1970s.[5] Foreign investors often preferred to establish an investment in these nations rather than in the developing, market economy nations. That decision was perplexing to the latter nations. Those latter nations failed to realize that they were becoming more restrictive than they had been before, while the nonmarket economy nations were becoming less restrictive than before. Overall, whether nonmarket or developing (or both), new investment entered these nations far more cautiously than it has since the late 1980s, when the restrictive laws began to be dismantled, in application if not in existence.

Governance by host nations has been a dynamic process. By the early 1990s the restrictiveness of the earlier laws had largely been replaced by laws encouraging foreign investment. The changes were both internally induced after the financial crises of the early 1980s when foreign debts could not be paid in many nations, and

3. See Michael Wallace Gordon, Of Aspirations and Operations: The Governance of Multinational Enterprises by Third World Nations, 16 Inter–American L.Rev. 301 (1984).

4. The development of investment laws in China and Cuba are discussed in Jian Zhou, National Treatment in Foreign Investment Law: A Comparative Study From a Chinese Perspective, 10 Touro Int'l L. Rev. 39 (2000); Zhang Lixing, The Statutory Framework for Direct Foreign Investment in China, 4 Fla.Int'l L.J. 289 (1989); Lynn McGil-

vray—Saltzman, Joint Venture Associations: Cuba Reopens its Doors to Foreign Investment, 1 Fla.Int'l L.J. 45 (1984).

5. See, e.g., Foreign Investment Law of Mongolia of 1990, translated in 30 Int'l Leg.Mat. 263 (1991); National Investment (Promotion and Protection) Act of 1990 (applicable on the mainland only, the 1986 act remains effective in Zanzibar), 30 Int'l Leg.Mat. 890 (1991); Foreign Investment Law of Vietnam of 1987, amended several times.

externally induced in order to participate in regional pacts and the GATT. The decade of the 1990s was clearly one of marketization and privatization, rather than nationalization.

In addition to legislation governing foreign investment, there may be constitutional provisions that affect investment. These may reserve areas for national ownership,[6] allocate regulation to or among specific government agencies,[7]and generally outline the form of economy the nation has adopted.[8] When China initially welcomed foreign investment with the adoption of a law on joint ventures in 1979, it first amended the Constitution of 1978 to sanction foreign investment. If a foreign investment law is inconsistent with the nation's constitution, but is not questioned by the current government, problems may arise for the foreign investor with a later government not inclined to view the investment law as liberally as the prior government. In many civil law nations the weight given to the constitution is less than in the United States, often because there may be no process of judicial review to test legislation against the constitution.

§ 25.5 Governance by Multi–Nation Organizations and International Law

The principal multi-nation organization that has attempted to regulate multinationals is the United Nations. The United Nations and its subsidiary organizations, however, have had little success in developing an effective, widely accepted regulatory scheme for multinationals. This should not be surprising because the United Nations is a large organization with diverse cultural, economic and political norms. However laudable have been the efforts to develop a code of conduct for multinationals, the record to date has not been impressive. The role of the United Nations, especially the Centre on Transnational Corporations, has become somewhat obscure as developing nations and nonmarket economies increasingly adopt less restrictive investment laws. The aspirations of developing nations of the 1970s, to achieve development through transfers (reparations for alleged abuses of colonialism, transfers of technology based on ideas being the patrimony of mankind rather than subject to private ownership, etc.), have been largely subordinated to a desire to achieve development through self help.

---

6. The Mexican Constitution reserves basic petroleum production to the nation by vesting ownership of the land in the nation. The nation retains all subsurface rights when surface ownership is sold. Mex. Const., art. 27.

7. The Indian Constitution outlines government involvement in investment, including the ability to exclude private participation. Indian Const., arts. 19 and 301.

8. The constitutions of nonmarket economies often reserve the means of production and distribution to the state.

Part of the efforts of the developing nations in the 1970s involved the creation of international norms that would control multinationals, such as the UN initiated code of conduct. Not only did these efforts fail, but the development of international law in general has been disappointing in its failure to establish legal norms for both multinationals and host nations. For example, the most contentious issue, compensation rights subsequent to expropriation, was before the International Court of Justice in the *Barcelona Traction* decision, but the court focused on a narrow issue of ownership and did not address compensation.[1]

The OECD has also participated in developing rules governing foreign investment. It has conducted work on a Multilateral Agreement on Investment (MAI). The United States has urged that this Agreement further liberalize investment, and address such issues as national treatment, standstill, roll-back, non-discriminatory most favored nation treatment, and transparency. The OECD is considering such issues as free movement of executives, foreign investor rights to participate in privatization, monopolies, intellectual property rights, portfolio investment, restrictions on investment in sensitive areas, relations with regional organizations, authority over investment by sub-federal government (i.e., states and provinces), protection of culture by limitations on investment and dispute settlement. Developing nations have expressed concern that the MAI may be an attempt by the OECD to monopolize market share by industrialized nations' corporations in the developing world. There were expectations that the MAI would be completed by April, 1998, for the annual OECD ministerial meeting. But the United States would not agree to EU insistence that an exception would be created for the EU, so that it could deny non-EU investment benefits granted within the market. The United States further rejected the "cultural exception" and the "public order" clause. The cultural exception would allow nations to limit investment when it had an adverse impact on the host nation's culture (promoted by France and Canada). The public order clause would permit withholding national treatment in industries considered essential to national security, law enforcement and public order. The United States tabled many exceptions to the applicability of the Agreements provisions, and insisted that the MAI would not extend to the states. April came and went and the MAI remained in the negotiation stage. France, in frustration, withdrew from the talks in October. The year (1998) ended without completion of the Agreement, and without any expectation that it would soon conclude.

§ 25.5

1. Barcelona   Traction,   [1970] I.C.J.Rep. 3.

The earlier focus on investment rules by the United Nations has been renewed, but this time as a joint effort with the International Chamber of Commerce (ICC) in Paris. Rather than the restrictive approach taken by the United Nations in the 1960s and 1970s, the UN–ICC effort will produce investment guides for the private sector to promote better private sector involvement in the UN's decision-making processes, and more private sector participation in the economic development of the poorest countries.

The World Bank, home of the successful International Centre for the Settlement of Investment Disputes (ICSID), is another organization that has drafted guidelines on foreign investment. They are important to investors seeking World Bank assistance.

A study in Canada (Industry Canada) suggests that the MAI will not eliminate some important barriers because it does not lead to the "deeper integration" that may be the only way to eliminate some barriers.[2] The report illustrates how as some barriers are eliminated, such as mandatory joint ventures or local content requirements, others arise. It notes some of the following barriers:

1. Antitrust policies such as merger laws that prohibit takeovers for economic or social reasons.

2. Administrative procedures such as using required takeover reviews to demand performance requirements.

3. Structuring corporations with voting schemes that permit effective control by a small group representing a small proportion of the shares but with ability to block a takeover.

4. Antitakeover laws that restrict voting rights of individuals or groups, such as in some American states.

5. Restrictions on privatized government companies such as the U.K. and Italian use of "golden shares" to prevent changes of control.

6. Structures such as the Japanese keiretsu that essentially precludes a hostile takeover, or large bank holdings that block takeovers.

7. Limited role of stock markets with few listings, and high local concentrations of ownership that are hard to dislodge.

The report noted how such trade agreements as the NAFTA (Chapter 11) may dismantle some barriers, but also emphasized the limited range of issues that the NAFTA addressed in opening foreign investment. Some of the barriers are deeply rooted and

---

2. "Foreign Investment Research: Messages and Policy Implications," Industry Canada.

long-established practices, that were never adopted as barriers, but have come to function as such.

Despite the efforts of the UN and OECD, the most effective control of the multinational is by the laws of the host nation, as might be expected. It is thus the form of those laws that is of most concern to an investor planning a foreign investment, and is the subject of the some of the comments below. The form of these laws has been more recently regulated by the WTO TRIMs and for the NAFTA nations Chapter 11 on investment rather than by the discussions within the UN or OECD.

§ 25.6   Restrictions Upon Entry

At what point in the investment process the government regulation or law takes effect presents another key distinction. Some nations make *entry* very difficult, by mandatory review of proposed investment, requirements of joint ventures or exemptions gained only after long negotiation and concessions, restrictions on acquisitions, and numerous levels of permission from various ministries and agencies. Mexico, until the late 1980s, possessed in its legal structure an example of each such restriction. But by 1994 it had repealed nearly all of these restrictions.

Restrictions upon entry tend to assume one of two forms. Nations which recognize the corporate form sometimes restrict the maximum equity allowed to foreign ownership. Additional rules may also limit the foreign management or control to a minority interest. The enterprises resulting from these restrictions are referred to as equity joint ventures. But where host nations do not recognize the corporate entity, foreign equity cannot be governed by way of limiting share ownership. These nations are the nonmarket economies, which have not allowed private ownership of the means of production and distribution and thus do not have corporation laws. The manner of control over permitted foreign investment is by means of contract. The foreign investor's rights are detailed in what is referred to as a contractual joint venture.[1] The foreign party receives a percentage of the profits and is granted certain management rights. As nonmarket nations have converted to market economies, they have adopted corporation laws and shifted from the use of contractual to equity joint ventures. Many have also shifted from mandatory to voluntary joint ventures. In some cases the shift has involved a change from contractual joint ventures

§ 25.6

1. See, e.g., Van Uu Nguyen, Foreign Investment in Vietnam Through Business Cooperation Contracts, 28 Int'l Lawyer 133 (1994). Vietnam does allow the creation of a limited liability company, but it is not required for foreign investment.

directly to permitting wholly foreign owned corporate entities, without an intermediate stage of mandating equity joint ventures.

§ 25.7 Restrictions During Operations

Some nations allow entry with comparative ease. Once established, however, the *operation* of the enterprise may be subject to various restrictions that divert time and resources from the main purpose of the investment. Government oversight may be extensive, with frequent visits from different officials to the degree that it becomes more harassment than regulation. Restrictions are often imposed on repatriating capital or sending profits or royalties abroad, or receiving hard currency to pay for needed imports. Currency restrictions have long been associated with foreign investment in developing nations such as Brazil, but less so with Mexico.

Another form of restriction on operations are performance requirements that mandate minimum local content, specify use of local labor and mandate levels of technology used in production. The elimination of performance requirements has been a focus of multinational negotiations, especially in the GATT, where the adoption of the WTO TRIMs Agreement has resulted in a diminished use of such restriction.

§ 25.8 Restrictions Upon Withdrawal

The withdrawal of foreign investment may be subject to restrictions. These restrictions may affect the ability to repatriate capital, the liability of the foreign parent or other subsidiaries in the country for debts of the withdrawing entity, and the removal of physical assets from the country. Potential investors should evaluate the restrictiveness at each level in determining whether or not to invest. Termination of an investment by bankruptcy may introduce the foreign investor to different theories of bankruptcy, including liability of the parent for debts of the foreign subsidiary.

§ 25.9 Prohibitions and Limitations on Ownership

Although restrictions may assume a seemingly infinite number of alternatives, there are several forms that continue to appear in the laws of various nations. They may be laws that generally govern foreign investment, or laws that limit foreign investment under antimonopoly or restrictive trade practice rules.[1] Or they may be a more general law restricting the flow of foreign capital, with a consequent ability of the nation to govern the purpose of capital inflows for investment.

§ 25.9

1. See, e.g., the Indian Monopoly and Restrictive Trade Practices Act of 1969, which applied to investments exceeding a certain size or which were "dominant undertakings."

Total prohibition in certain sectors. Almost every nation prohibits foreign investment in certain sectors. Both developed and developing nations limit investment where national security is threatened. But the developing nations sometimes increase the scope of prohibited investment to a degree that may suggest the nation is really a nonmarket economy—it mandates state ownership of most of the means of production and distribution. Foreign investment is most often prohibited in the exploitation of the nation's most important natural resources.[2] Mexico, for example, has long prohibited foreign investment in the petroleum industry. Canada's early foreign investment regulations discouraged foreign investment in railroads by limiting ownership of Canadian railroads receiving government aid to only British subjects. Canada also restricted natural resources, limiting oil and gas leases, mining, and exploration assistance grants to Canadian companies, or those having at least 50 percent Canadian ownership or listed on the Canadian stock exchange.

Outside this hemisphere, similar restrictions on foreign investment have been imposed by many nations. For example, India reserved some industries to its public sector in its Industrial Policy Resolution of 1948.[3] Additionally, some sectoral barriers through legislation and national monopolies remain impediments to FDI and intraregional direct investment in the European Union.[4] Other areas often restricted in various nations relate to the nation's infrastructure, such as transportation (in addition to railroads), communications, and electricity. The prohibitions may further reach some basic petrochemical production.

Reservation of investment to domestic private investors. A second group of industries may be permitted as private rather than national ownership, but the private owners must be host-nation nationals. These are industries where the nation believes that public national ownership is not necessary, but the nation prefers to reserve the areas for their own nationals. The reasons may be no greater than protectionism and the power of lobbying efforts of domestic indus-

2. Cynthia D. Wallace, Legal Control of Multinational Enterprise 45 (1983) (giving examples of broad bans in Sweden, Norway, Switzerland, and particularly Japan, which had indicated as many as 22 protected industries, some going beyond those that might reasonably be attributed to national sovereignty, such as drugs and data processing). Aeronautics, high-tech, petroleum, and iron and steel industries, also rank high among the key sectors protected by European nations, even those with generally open investment policies, such as Germany.

3. Note, Foreign Investment in India, 26 Colum.J. Transnat'l L. 609, 640 (1988).

4. S. Thomsen & S. Woolcock, Direct Investment and European Integration Competition Among Firms and Governments 89 (1993) (citing transportation, telecommunications, and utilities as typical protected industries; also noting that intra-EU investors have much less trouble than non-EU investors as the EU removes many barriers within the region).

try which does not wish to compete with foreign owned investment. If the nation admits private ownership in a specific industry, it may have difficulty reserving that industry for its own nationals if the nation is a member of the GATT/WTO. The current trend is to require that the nation offer the same investment opportunities to foreigners that it offers to its own nationals, under the concept of national treatment. This could cause nations to move these industries not to ownership by nationals or foreigners, but exclusively to state ownership.

Foreign investment allowed. Industries not included in the protected classes mentioned above may have foreign ownership participation. But that foreign private ownership may be limited to joint ventures, and possibly only minority interests. In some joint venture laws, it appears at first that all areas are open to foreign investment, because the law does not reserve any spheres of activity for the state or its nationals. This was true of the Cuban joint venture law of 1982,[5] but it was clear that foreign investment was to be directed to restoring Cuba's tourist industry, which would help obtain foreign currency. The Tanzanian law specifically prohibited foreign participation only in petroleum and minerals, but the Investment Promotion Centre could refuse investments in other areas, particularly if they were not joint ventures.[6] The Namibian law referred only to "eligible investment", without defining what areas were open or closed to foreign investment.[7]

Outright bans on foreign investment appear less frequent than equity limitations, but such laws present the first question a foreigner looking to invest abroad must consider—is the industry in which I am interested open to me? If the industry is one which is historically sensitive, such as natural resources and transportation, the answer may remain—no, it is not open to foreign investment. Where foreign investment is limited to minority participation in joint ventures in all industries not subject to even greater restrictions, the country is not a very receptive location for foreign investment. It is also unlikely to be a member of the GATT/WTO.

5. Economic Associations Between Cuban and Foreign Entities, No. 50 (Feb. 15, 1982), translated in Possibility of Joint Ventures in Cuba, Cámara de Comercio de la República de Cuba 8 (Feb. 1982). Regulations were issued in September, 1982. See Regulations complimentary to decree Law No. 50 of 15 Feb. 1982, Cámara de Comercio de la República de Cuba (Sept. 1982). Cuba adopted a new investment law in 1995.

6. The law does not address joint ventures, but it appears that the Centre has the authority to demand them for approval.

7. Namibia Foreign Investments Act of 1990, 31 Int'l Leg.Mat. 205 (1992). But the Act allowed the Ministry to issue notices regarding areas reserved for Namibians, which was broadly defined as areas of "services or the production of goods which can be provided or produced adequately by Namibians."

Equity percentage limitations. The equity percentages allowed to be owned by foreign investors have varied with the type of industry and the host nation's goal in applying the restriction. The reason for equity percentage limitations may be to allow the amount to depend on (1) what the investment is perceived to offer the nation, such as needed technology, or (2) an economic/social philosophy based notion that foreign investment is inherently evil and to be prohibited. The former may be overcome by the foreign investor, the latter often may not. For years the nonmarket economy nations adopted the latter view, but moved to the former when it was apparent that those nations' development levels had remained at best static.

When nations adopt mandatory joint venture rules, they often limit foreign ownership to a minority share, usually 49 percent.[8] The reason is stated to be a preference to keep a majority of the ownership and control in the hands of nationals. If the nation decides to allow majority control to be owned by foreign investors, it often takes the additional step and allows the investment to be *wholly* foreign owned. If there is one certain characteristic of equity percentage limitations, it is that they are neither likely to remain static over a number of years, nor likely to be enforced absolutely. An unwritten code usually allows selective, needed investment to enter with total foreign ownership. The host nation often will waive restrictive equity limitations. Several reasons are commonly found in exception provisions in written investment laws, or in the unwritten "operational code", the unwritten policy of the government. They include the following:

> 1. *Technology.* Some companies with high technology, such as IBM, have been able to avoid joint venture mandates and retain total ownership.[9] What form of technology will gain such a waiver is likely to vary from one nation to another. Where there is a transfer of technology law, it is likely to state several reasons for registering a technology agreement that disclose the nation's interests. They include technology that assists import substitution, the most up-to-date technology, technology in high priority areas such as computers, technology intended to enhance job opportunities, and technology viewed as reasonable in cost.

8. The arrangement is called differently in different nations. For example, in India it is "foreign collaboration." See Kurk, Foreign Collaboration Agreements: Policy as Law, 9 J. Indian L. Inst. 66 (1967); Note, Foreign Investment in India, 26 Colum. J. Transnat'l L. 609 (1988).

9. The experience of IBM in Mexico is an example. But IBM withdrew from India in the late 1970s when India demanded that IBM convert its wholly foreign parent owned investment in India to a joint venture. Minority shares would be owned by the parent with the majority owned by Indian nationals. See generally, Gucharan Das, India Unbound (2001).

2. *Plant location.* The willingness to locate a production facility away from already saturated areas, such as the capital city, will increase chances of gaining a waiver. Some countries specify areas that the nation feels are already sufficiently industrialized,[10] other specify areas that they have designated for industrial development, or simply mention "less developed" areas.[11]

3. *Education.* The willingness to establish training centers in the host nation, especially centers that will teach jobs to function with new technology, is a method of gaining a waiver.[12]

4. *Research and development.* A major criticism of many nations is that multinationals only export their technology while undertaking all the research to develop that technology in their home nation. Being willing to undertake some research and development in a host nation may gain a waiver of maximum equity participation requirements.

5. *Balance imports with exports.* Because of chronic shortages of hard currencies, many host nations grant waivers of investment restrictions where the investment will require little demand upon the host nation's scarce hard currency reserves. Thus, exporting part of the production to earn sufficient hard currency to pay for imports and cover profit and royalty payments may be decisive. The host nation's appreciation will increase as the export earnings continue to exceed the import demand. China placed great emphasis on exports, it was the key to obtaining permission to establish a wholly owned foreign investment under the 1986 joint venture law.[13]

6. *Sourcing capital from abroad.* In addition to shortages of foreign currency, some nations have shortages of domestic currency to lend to companies. They often wish to reserve that lending capacity for locally owned business. Thus, commencing an investment with capital from outside the host nation is another possible key to gaining a waiver.

Not only developing nations have experimented with limitations on foreign ownership of domestic business. During the 1970s, Canada enacted a restrictive investment law, although the provisions were never as restrictive as the foreign investment laws of India, Mexico and Nigeria. The Foreign Investment Review Act of

---

10. Mexico has preferred to keep new investment out of Mexico City, Guadalajara and Monterrey.

11. Namibia Foreign Investment Law of 1990, art. 6(3)(b)(iv).

12. The Namibian Investment Law of 1990, for example, gives special re-

gard to the training of Namibians. Art. 6(3)(b)(ii).

13. Law of the People's Republic of China on Wholly Foreign–Owned Enterprises of 1986, art. 3.

1973 placed Canada in a unique position. It rendered Canada a legitimate contender to the title "developing nation." There were complex rules governing foreign investment, especially acquisitions. There was a Foreign Investment Review Agency with powers not greatly different than the powers of the Mexican Foreign Investment Commission. But this restrictive Canadian law was replaced in 1985 with the more investment-encouraging law—the Investment Canada Act. Parts of that Act have remained in place and were integrated into the framework of investment rules both under the Canada–United States Free Trade Agreement and the subsequent North American Free Trade Agreement.

Reasons for accepting equity restrictions. Foreign investors generally prefer to have total ownership of their foreign investments. Why would a foreign investor agree to limit participation to a minority interest?

An investment in place at the time of enactment of a government demand to convert to a joint venture or withdraw from the nation may be less costly to continue as a joint venture with a minority position than to withdraw from the country. A local partner may be an asset if market penetration is difficult or political contacts are critical. But it is unlikely that the parent company will increase its investment or transfer the latest technology to the joint venture enterprise. The foreign entity will thus become quite unlike other wholly owned foreign investments of the multinational. It will remain relatively static while other foreign wholly owned company investments receive any needed additional capital and the latest technology.

If the market in the host nation has good long term prospects, and the restrictive joint venture laws are viewed as being transitory and likely to be modified in the future, it may be appropriate to accept a joint venture and invest. In Mexico in the 1970s, the willingness of Japanese investors to enter joint ventures with minority participation placed pressure on U.S. firms to accept the same limits on ownership, and even to offer better deals because of the growing Mexican desire to lessen reliance on U.S. investment. But new investment was never as extensive as it would have been without the restrictive laws of the 1970s, illustrated by the rapid increase in new foreign investment since those laws were repealed in the 1990s.

If the host nation offers attractive investment incentives, accepting limitations on equity and management participation may be a fair trade, especially if the incentives are available immediately and the joint venture rules are likely to fade in time.

Retroactive effect of equity limitations. To force foreign investment already in existence to convert to joint ventures may give rise to claims of expropriation. Consequently, countries usually applied the laws to new investment, but often added provisions that made it very difficult for current investment to continue without conversion. For example, the Mexican 1973 Investment Law was not retroactive on its face,[14] but regulations denied permission to enter new lines of products or establish new locations without conversion to a joint venture.[15] India's Foreign Exchange Regulation Act of 1975 separately classified existing and new investment, granting the latter favorable treatment because it complied with joint venture mandates.[16] But the Indian government began to place pressure on all foreign investment to convert to joint ventures, leading to conflicts with many companies, and the withdrawal of Coca Cola and IBM. Conversion to a joint venture for Coca Cola would have meant disclosing the "secret formula";[17] conversion for IBM would have been contrary to a long-held policy to not participate in joint ventures.[18]

§ 25.10   Limitations on Acquisitions

A frequently used method to invest abroad is to acquire a locally owned company in the foreign nation. Such foreign acquisition has all the characteristics of an acquisition in the United States. That includes the loss of an opportunity to increase the number of competitors in the business were the investing company to commence a new company ("greenfields investment") rather than acquire an existing company, consequences of vertical integration if the company acquired is the distribution channel while the company acquiring is the producer, or vice versa. But these antitrust issues have not been the reason foreign nations have often prohibited foreign investment by means of acquisition of a host nation company. The reason has been the replacement of a locally owned business by a foreign owned business. The nation may be particularly concerned where the proposed acquisition is of a large domestic industry that is thought to *be* a domestic industry. For example, a proposed foreign acquisition of General Motors would

---

14. One Mexican author, however, considered the law to constitute "creeping" expropriation. See Luis Creel, "Mexicanization": A Case of Creeping Expropriation, 22 Sw.L.J. 281 (1968).

15. See Ignacio Gomez–Palacio, Defining "New Lines of Products" Under Mexico's Foreign Investment Law, 8 Calif.West.Int'l L.J. 74 (1978).

16. See A. Jayagovinda, Regulation of Foreign Enterprises in India: An Enquiry into Foreign Exchange Regulation Act, 1973, 17 Indian J.Int'l L. 325 (1977).

17. See Dennis J. Encarnation & Sushil Vachani, Foreign Ownership When Hosts Change the Rules, 63 Harv. Bus.Rev. 152 (1985).

18. See McLellan, Why IBM Must Withdraw from India in June, 24 Datamation 181 (1978). IBM's experience with Mexico, contrastingly, was successful. It was granted waivers from the mandatory joint ventures. See IBM to Bid Again to Build Computers in Mexico, Miami Herald, Feb. 4, 1985, Bus. Monday, at 23.

create far more objection than proposed foreign acquisitions of 1,000 companies, each one–1,000th the size of GM, but not thought of *as American.* Even more sensitive may be proposed acquisitions of enterprises bearing the name of the nation, such as Mexicana airlines or Canadian Pacific railway. The objection is thus often more cultural and emotional than economic. Foreign acquisition may provide an infusion of needed capital not available at home, and bring new management ideas where old management has been uncreative and stagnant. Restrictions on acquisitions are thus often based more on the feared *loss* of a domestic company, than the feared *addition* of a new foreign company. This means foreign investors and their lawyers have a different obstacle to overcome to obtain approval of an acquisition as opposed to a new investment.

Prohibiting *any* foreign investment in a particular sector is protective of domestic industry. Prohibiting foreign investment by means of *acquisitions* does not assure protection for domestic industry, since it allows competition to exist by the establishment of a new industry that is foreign owned. Thus protectionist arguments urge restrictions on all investment, not only acquisitions. The decision is often given to a foreign investment review agency.

§ 25.11   Limitations on Management

A limitation on the permitted foreign equity may not mean an inability to control the investment. Host nation majority owners may elect foreign management. Some host nation laws, however, stipulate that the percentage of foreign management may be no greater than the permitted equity participation.[1] But even this limitation may be unimportant if the local board is dominated by host nation nationals who are all profit motivated entrepreneurs whose goals are far more aligned with the foreign affiliate than with host nation government officials who believe that local management should be committed to pursuing national social goals.

§ 25.12   Performance Requirements

Restrictive investment laws often include performance requirements. These may mandate that manufactured products contain a certain minimum percentage of local content, thus protecting many smaller local suppliers. Other requirements may address the use of local labor. Labor requirements may cover both the employment of local persons, and establishing facilities for training new employees, including management level positions. The performance require-

---

§ 25.11

1. The 1973 Mexican Investment Law stated, "The participation of foreign investment in the administration of the business enterprise may not exceed its participation in the capital." Law to Promote Mexican Investment and to Regulate Foreign Investment, art. 5 (1973). The provision does not appear in the current Mexican investment law.

ments may also mandate that a certain percentage of the production be exported, often in order to balance import needs against exports to avoid drawing on scarce foreign exchange.[1] Finally, there may be mandates regarding the level of technology used in the production, often requiring that the technology be as current as technology of the company used in the home nation. Transfer of technology requirements may also include mandated licenses to locals, or stipulations as to what technologies the investor may introduce. Performance requirements have been limited by the adoption of the WTO TRIMs Agreement.

§ 25.13   Limitations on Transfer of Capital and Earnings

One aspect of the import/export performance requirement is to alleviate trade imbalances, reflected in part by the flow of capital in or out of a country. Some countries have no systematic restrictions on movements of capital such as foreign exchange controls, limits on borrowing, transfer pricing, as well as repatriation of earnings. Ironically, restricting remittance of earnings does not always solve balance-of-payments problems; it may rather cause companies to maintain a static position with respect to their capital, and freeze the flow of currency, both positive and negative, to the nation.

Repatriation of assets, profits or royalties may have to be reviewed by a national bank. This is often the case even where the general policy is to allow relatively free transfer of currencies. Similar approval may be needed to pay for necessary imports. Some countries have been notorious for demanding that all receipts in foreign currencies be converted to the host nation (usually soft) currency. Any foreign currency thereafter needed to pay for imports or to remit home as profits, must be approved. This restrictive policy often leads to double billing for exports, with part of the price going directly to the home nation. Such transfers are as commonly practiced as they are as commonly deemed unlawful.

Brazil and Argentina are examples of nations that have relied heavily on currency restrictions. The restrictions have been government responses to a frustrating inability to control inflation and indexation. Argentina has more recently reduced previously severe levels of inflation, partly by linking the Argentine currency with the U.S. dollar, which is a form of official dual currency in Argentina. Brazil has reduced restrictions on capital and profit repatriations, but it has a history of currency restrictions and investors are

---

§ 25.12

1. The Mexican 1989 investment regulations required that a company established under the regulations (which exempted the company from joint venture mandates) maintain "during the first three years of its operations, a position of equilibrium in its balance of foreign currency." Regulations of the Law to Promote Mexican Investment and to Regulate Foreign Investment, Diario Oficial, art. 5, IV, 16 May 1989.

always concerned that restrictions will be restored. Mexico, contrastingly, imposed currency restrictions only during a brief four-month period in 1982.[1] As a result of considerable inflation, capital flight from Mexico increased dramatically in the early 1980s. To conserve remaining hard currency, the government nationalized banks and imposed exchange controls in August, 1982. The elected but not yet inducted president terminated the controls a few months later. The banking industry was partially opened to foreign investment several years later. Mexico's entry into NAFTA a decade later accelerated Mexico's return to private ownership of and foreign participation in banking.

India seems to have stood somewhere between Mexico and Brazil. While repatriations were generally freely allowable, they were controlled by the Reserve Bank of India and subject to numerous restrictions. Yet the Indian practice was generally thought to be accommodating to foreign investment.[2] If a repatriation or divestment was particularly large, the Indian government might stagger it over several years to cushion its impact on India's persistent foreign-exchange difficulties.

China, as part of obtaining export-oriented or technologically-advanced status, encourages investors to reinvest profits in China rather than remitting them abroad.[3] Such encouragement is generally present in most nations, both because it reduces demand on foreign-currency reserves and adds to the industrial base of the nation. Reinvestment is often the only real choice for a foreign investment, since idle funds may be taxed or diminished in value if there is indexation in the nation which does not apply to such funds.

§ 25.14 Current Trends in Enacting and Enforcing Restrictions

The enactment of restrictive investment laws was most prominent in the 1970s. Two important occurrences in the 1980s tended to stop the enactment of restrictive investment laws. The first was the debt crisis in the early 1980s, which caused nations to realize that restrictive investment laws did not contribute to economic growth and exports. The second was the dismantling of the USSR and the commencement of the transition of many nonmarket economies toward the direction of market economies. Even nonmarket economies outside the Eastern Europe and USSR group

§ 25.13

1. See Stephen Zamora, Peso–Dollar Economics and the Imposition of Foreign Exchange Controls in Mexico, 32 Am.J.Comp.L. 99 (1984).

2. See Khanna, Licensing Technology and Joint Ventures in India, Indo–Am. Bus. Times, May, 1987, at 24.

3. Zhang Lixing, The Statutory Framework for Direct Foreign Investment in China, 4 Fla.J.Int'l L. 289, 305, 310–11 (1989).

were making such changes. Vietnam, for example, first adopted a foreign investment law in 1987, and has since amended it several times.[1] Tanzania and Mongolia both enacted investment laws in 1990, neither of which has any reference to mandatory joint ventures.[2] The former USSR first adopted joint venture legislation in 1987, with modifications in 1988 and 1989, and a new law in 1990.[3] The law was quite liberal, which is the direction taken by the new nations that were formerly part of the USSR. Poland enacted a series of investment laws, each more liberal than the previous. The 1991 law eliminated the previously required approval process for many investments.[4]

By the late 1980s nearly all developing and nonmarket economies had begun to open their economies to more foreign direct investment, even though their earlier announced reservations about extensive participation in the means of production and distribution by foreign enterprises remained in many existing written laws. There was a reluctance at first to repeal these laws, which were often popular with the liberal media and academics. The nations instead began to relax their enforcement of the restrictive laws. While foreign nations, both developing and nonmarket, previously had brought many, and sometimes all, industries within the ambit of foreign equity limitations or prohibitions, these governments began in the mid–1980s to administer those laws with increasing flexibility. At times, the way the laws read and the way they were applied seemed quite opposite.[5] In the 1990s, the laws began to be modified to reflect the reality of practice, and to reflect obligations under bilateral investment agreements and multilateral agreements such as the GATT/WTO.

§ 25.15 TRIMs

The GATT Uruguay Round produced important new investment rules. Prior to this Round, the GATT had not directly

§ 25.14

1. See Van Uu Nguyen, Foreign Investment in Vietnam Through Business Cooperation Contracts, 28 Int'l Lawyer 133 (1994). The Vietnamese laws become important to United States investors because of the restoration of trading relations in early 1994.

2. Foreign Investment Law of Mongolia of 1990, translated in 30 Int'l Leg. Mat. 263 (1991); National Investment (Promotion and Protection) Act of 1990 (Tanzania), in 30 Int'l Leg.Mat. 890 (1991).

3. A brief description of the USSR laws is included in William G. Frenkel, Introductory Note to the 1990 Decree,

30 Int'l Leg.Mat. 913 (1991). See also 30 Int'l Leg.Mat. 266 (1991).

4. Polish Law on Companies with Foreign Participation, June 14, 1991, translated in 30 Int'l Leg.Mat. 871 (1991), including a useful Introductory Note by Ania M. Frankowska & Radoslon Gronet.

5. There was in effect an operational code, an unwritten law which stated "how things really worked". See Michael Wallace Gordon, Of Aspirations and Operations: The Governance of Multinational Enterprises by Third World Nations, 16 Inter–American L.R. 301 (1984).

governed foreign investment.[1] The new rules are thus quite a significant development. But as must be expected with any large organization with members possessing divergent views, the investment provisions of the GATT are not as comprehensive as those in the much smaller NAFTA.

The GATT/WTO investment rules are included in the "Agreement on Trade–Related Investment Measures." These measures, commonly called TRIMs, first set forth a national treatment principal. TRIMs, which are considered inconsistent with GATT/WTO obligations, are listed in an annex, and include such performance requirements as minimum domestic content, imports limited or linked to exports, restrictions on access to foreign exchange to limit imports for use in the investment, etc. Developing countries are allowed to "deviate temporarily" from the national treatment concept, thus diminishing in value the effectiveness of the GATT/WTO investment provisions, and obviously discouraging investment in nations which have a history of imposing investment restrictions, and making such agreements as the NAFTA all the more useful and likely to spread.

The essence of the GATT/WTO TRIMs is to establish the same principle of national treatment for investments as has been in effect for trade. TRIMs are incorporated in the overall structure of the GATT/WTO, alongside trade measures, rather than being treated as a quite distinct area. Because all the deficiencies of the GATT/WTO with regard to trade measures may apply to TRIMs, it remains to be seen how effective these measure will be in governing foreign investment. Because the measures are much less certain than those included in bilateral investment treaties and small-area free trade agreements, it is likely that much of the regulation of foreign investment will develop in their context rather than within the GATT/WTO.

The WTO has a working party on trade and investment which has been discussing new investment rules. To some degree the collapse of the OECD discussions regarding the proposed Multilateral Agreement on Investment in late 1998 shifted the discussion to the WTO. The EU wants investment policy to be a major issue in a comprehensive millennium round of trade talks it had hoped to commence in 1999. The unsettled nature of the Seattle WTO meeting in early 2000 has delayed further development. By early 2005 there was no immediate prospect of new WTO investment rules.

§ 25.15

1. Foreign investment was originally to have been governed by a proposed World Trade Organization, discussed at the Bretton Woods conference near the end of World War II. The U.S. Senate was hostile to the idea, and the ensuing GATT did not cover foreign investment.

§ 25.16   Foreign Investment Treaties

The decade of the 1990s was an active period for the signing of bilateral investment treaties. The principal focus was the protection and promotion of foreign investment.[1] It is not only the United States which has emphasized these treaties; they are common features of most developed nations in their relations with host nations for foreign investment. For example, China has investment protection agreements with such nations as Australia, Austria, Belgium, Luxembourg, Denmark, France, Germany, Japan, the Netherlands, and the United Kingdom. A benefit of such an agreement is that its provisions prevail over domestic law, although the agreements usually allow for exceptions to investment protection when in the interests of national security.

The investment treaties of interest to U.S. investors are those which have been concluded by the United States with other nations. Because the process of enactment of these agreements is a continuing one, the number in existence is certain to increase in the coming years. The existence of the WTO TRIMs provisions may reduce the number of bilateral treaties, but they will be used because they are able to tailor the provisions to meet the unique needs of the two nations. The parties must be careful, however, that concessions granted may be demanded by other WTO members under MFN concepts.

§ 25.17   United States Investment Treaties

The United States has entered into numerous bilateral investment treaties (BITs) in the past two decades. The reason is twofold. The earlier Friendship, Commerce and Navigation treaties (FCNs) were not effective investment-protection treaties. Furthermore, other multinational forums, especially the United Nations, failed to enact investment protection and promotion rules, leaving the gap to be filled by bilateral agreements, especially between developed and developing nations respectively. The WTO TRIM rules are a step in the right direction, but remain less specific than agreements among smaller groups of nations (such as the NAFTA) or bilateral agreements.

The United States may participate in bilateral arrangements which are not treaties, but rather constitute cooperative statements of policies regarding direct investment. Japan and the United States signed such a statement by means of letter exchanges on a diplomatic level. One of the objectives of the letter exchange was to increase foreign investment in each nation by the other nation's

---

§ 25.16

1. Another form of treaty important to foreign investment has been for the avoidance of double taxation and prevention of tax evasion.

investors.[1] But the exchange seems more a U.S. attempt to further remove obstacles to U.S. investment in Japan than the reverse.

§ 25.18   The Unwritten Law, Operational Codes[1]

Nations currently allowing foreign investment often strive to create regulations that narrowly fall short of the degree of restrictiveness that would cause a large scale withdrawal of foreign direct investment. Multinationals react adversely to any form of regulation and often attempt to convince host nation authorities that the nation either has achieved the nadir of restrictiveness, or, more likely, that the nation is retarding development. They argue that the restrictiveness has increased above the "Edge of Discouragement", that level of restrictiveness beyond which foreign investors will withhold investment. Each host nation has such a level which the combination of its written and unwritten laws must not exceed if the nation truly wants to receive foreign investment.

The Edge of Discouragement slopes upwards in the degree of acceptable restrictiveness over time. Foreign investors learn to function in an atmosphere of increasing restrictiveness, as long as the point of investment impossibility is not reached. It is difficult for host nations to determine the optimum level for the regulation without discouraging foreign direct investment. No two developing or nonmarket nations possess such similar domestic, political, economic, and social characteristics that a uniform code of regulation of foreign direct investment could be produced. The framework of any one nation for the governance of foreign direct investment consequently may consist of a sophisticated and finely tuned set of norms, or it may include elements of regulatory absurdity, based on misconceptions either of the impact of the foreign investment, or the ability of the host nation to regulate without causing the withdrawal of needed foreign investment.

A tier of multinational governance consists of regulations by multi-nation organizations, although the adequacy of this type of regulation is questionable when directed at conduct in developing host nations. The principal multi-nation organization which has attempted to regulate multinationals is the United Nations. The United Nations and its subsidiary associations have had little success, however, in developing an effective, widely accepted regulatory scheme for multinational enterprises. This should not be

§ 25.17

1. Japan–United States: Policies and Measures Regarding Inward Direct Investment and Buyer–Supplier Relationships, reprinted in 34 Int'l Legal Materials 1341 (1995).

§ 25.18

1. This material is extracted from Michael Wallace Gordon, Of Aspirations and Operations: The Governance of Multinational Enterprises by Third World Nations, 16 Inter–American L.Rev. 301 (1984).

surprising because it is a large organization with extreme diversity of cultural, economic and political characteristics and goals. That is as it should be. However ideally conceived to govern multinationals objectively the United Nations may have been, the record to date is not impressive.

Whether several of the United Nations pronouncements affecting multinationals constitute international law is an important issue that has become largely academic. Of greater importance is their disclosure of the aspirations of the large majority of the developing and nonmarket members, and a few developed nations. Because they reflect the aspirations of these nations, they may be called "Aspirational Declarations". They are written, but not law.

Aspirational Declarations assume particular importance not because they may constitute international law but because they disclose current sentiments and possible future law. They create a norm of expected conduct, a moral code promoted by developing and nonmarket nations as proper and reasonable conduct for multinationals. But they are more than a moral code. They may be a precursor of customary international law or they may become part of the written or unwritten laws of specific host nations governing foreign investment. The laws and policies of several host nations share a close identity with Aspirational Declarations of multination organizations.

Apart from being indicators of future action, Aspirational Declarations serve another important function. They offer developing nations strong words to use that may temper adverse public reaction to governments plagued by economic and political troubles. They may serve, in a sense, as doctrines of collective insecurity.

On a graph, the Aspirational Declarations belong above the Edge of Discouragement. If these declarations were the norm of regulation, most foreign direct investment would withdraw. The reluctance of host nations to incorporate these declarations into their domestic law, and the Operational Code's extreme variance with the concepts of the declarations, also reinforces that they are more restrictive than is acceptable.

If one is asked how multinationals are governed, the common response is to concentrate exclusively on those written laws of the host nations that directly or indirectly regulate foreign direct investment. This is the second level of governance, referred to as the "Public Code". This code is written and it is law, in contrast to the Aspirational Declarations, which are written but are not law. A nation's Public Code includes constitutional provisions affecting foreign direct investment (such as labor and social security rules), statutes, published administrative regulations and widely distributed regulations or decisions of foreign investment agencies.

Although a nation's Public Code governing foreign direct investment may be extensive, it serves as the basis—the mental framework—of regulation of foreign direct investment for that developing nation. But even in those nations that have an extensive Public Code, multinational advisors should not rely on that written law as constituting the total framework of investment regulation. Awareness of the Operational Code is necessary, as is awareness of any impact that the nation's participation in the formulation of Aspirational Declarations would have on the functioning of both the Operational and Public Codes.

Properly locating the Public Code on a graph creates some difficulty because the graph generally applies to foreign direct investment in all developing and nonmarket nations. But a graph may be done for individual nations. Conclusions drawn as to the plotting of the restrictiveness over time are limited to an increasing degree of restrictiveness, or an upward sloping line, because Public Codes differ from nation-to-nation. It is preferable to show this line not as a constantly increasing line but one which increases in abrupt increments. Elements of the Public Code are enacted periodically, usually when the Operational Code has become so cumbersome and confusing that it is necessary to transfer some elements to the Public Code. This reduces investor confusion and increases predictability for those investors only familiar with the Public Code.

The Operational Code, the third control level, is the pivotal concept for multinational enterprises to understand. It is important largely because it is not written, or, where written, is not publicly disclosed. Indeed, by definition it may not be publicly disclosed. When elements of the Operational Code become so well-known to the investing community and are no longer considered secret, these elements tend to assume the status of the Public Code, yet remain unwritten. There is consequently a small part of the Public Code which is not formally written. But it is likely to become part of the written Public Code in its next revision. Nevertheless, the government may continue to deny its existence, even in the face of overwhelming public acknowledgment of its existence.

The definition of the Operational Code suggests that it is limited to formal unwritten regulations and decisions, but it may also include formal written regulations and decisions that either are not publicly available or discoverable. Two examples of written elements of the Operational Code illustrate this point. The National Commission on Foreign Investment in Mexico reviewed petitions from foreign investors requesting exceptions from the now-repealed 1973 Mexican Investment Law. A company could request a waiver from the requirement of Mexicanization to allow it to expand its current production at a new location or begin production of new products. Either, in the absence of being granted an exception, required Mexicanization of the entire company.

The Commission's written decisions were not released to the public, but they disclosed a great deal about the Operational Code and the criteria the government applied in reaching decisions on these petitions. Over time, these decisions were obtained by some Mexican lawyers representing multinationals. Their release eventually would become so extensive they would be common knowledge. They were then no longer part of the Operational Code but transformed by the extent of the public knowledge to the Public Code. These decisions were already written and constituted pronouncements of an entity with decision-making authority, therefore, there was no need to pass through the formal legislative process to become part of the Public Code. When the Public Code was next revised, these concepts would very probably integrated into the investment regulation laws. That happened with the enactment of the 1993 Mexican Investment Law.

In contrast to formerly non-disclosed pronouncements, there are regulations issued by various ministries which have not been kept secret. Although technically part of the Public Code, they exist in such large numbers and are so difficult to locate that they must be considered part of the Operational Code. Brazilian lawyers deal with such rules in the form of what are known as "drawer" regulations. These are regulations that have been issued by various ministries that, even though not labeled secret, have not been publicly disseminated. They are kept in a ministry official's drawer, removed on one occasion when considering a proposed foreign investment, and left in the drawer on another. Even when a drawer regulation is noted by the official it may be applied with an inconsistency permitted by the lack of public disclosure. Both the Mexican Commission decisions and these Brazilian regulations may be considered part of the Operational Code, although they are in fact *written* decisions and regulations.

The Operational Code is always somewhat at variance with the Public Code, but it must not deviate from the Public Code so extensively that it generates so much uncertainty that it reduces foreign investor confidence in the regulatory structure. The Operational Code directly conflicts with the Public Code when, although positive law provisions of the Public Code do not contain exceptions, the law is waived according to the Operational Code. Any such waiver would be an Operational Code provision directly contrary to written law which would constitute a serious source of misunderstanding for potential foreign investors. This would be a far more serious problem than where a sizable variance exists between the Codes only in an indirect form. A direct conflict with the Public Code may lead to litigation against a host country over the Operational Code.

An indirect variance exists when positive statements of the Public Code are conditioned by exception provisions, but the government so routinely grants exceptions that the positive law effectively becomes a nullity. It is a potential source of conflict because unknowing foreign investors may believe the Public Code to be routinely applied. If the variance between the Operational Code and Public Code becomes extreme, it is mandatory, and in the best interest of a nation, to enact a new investment law. The new law should add to the Public Code those elements of the Operational Code the government wishes to acknowledge as now being appropriately part of the Public Code, and those which it believes create unacceptable conflicts by remaining within the Operational Code. The government will still not acknowledge Operational Code provisions it does not want admitted to the public. For example, Operational Code requirements mandating payments to government officials to expedite services, to grant exceptions, or even to refuse to enforce the Public Code, are not appropriate subjects to publicly acknowledge, and thus remain perpetually hidden in the Operational Code.

To place the Operational Code in the graph it must be emphasized that Operational Codes by their nature are not well defined. But for a general representation the line should relate to the Public Code and move upwards (or downwards)without the abrupt steps of the Public Code since the Operational Code is constantly undergoing modification.

It is as important for a host nation government to be aware of the divergence of its Operational Code from the Public Code, as it is for multinationals to be aware of that divergence and the progressively changing content of the Operational Code. A company failing to appreciate these movements is not in a secure position to predict future movements if it is ignorant of the existence of the Operational Code and the degree to which it varies from the Public Code. In some cases, particularly in the small dependent nations, the government tries to maintain a narrow gap between the Public Code and the Operational Code. If a dominant multinational enterprise in that nation is able to influence the Operational Code, it may function according to a lenient Operational Code but defend its actions on the basis of the more restrictive Public Code. The graph of such a nation would show a more restrictive Public Code than the Operational Code (at least for the dominant investor). There may be a benefit to the nation because it limits the single, dominant multinational to benefitting from the lenient Operational Code and enforces the more restrictive Public Code for other new investments.

The Operational Code has numerous facets. It has different rules applicable to multinationals with different levels of power to demand a lenient Operational Code. It reflects the nation's need to be flexible so as to obtain investment, particularly in crucial areas. The Operational Code under which IBM functions in many nations, where its computer technology has a monopoly position and where such a monopoly is of critical need to development, is in stark contrast to the Operational Code applicable to a multinational entering an industry saturated by domestic-owned enterprises. The Operational Code applicable to IBM may be less restrictive than the Public Code, while that applicable to the latter multinational may be so severely restrictive that it works to eliminate foreign direct investment that might compete with inefficient local industry.

The Operational Code occupies an important position in a host nation's governance of foreign direct investment because it allows the government to treat different multinational enterprises in specific ways thought to be best for the nation. It may even treat different nations' multinational enterprises differently, hidden from obligations of MFN treatment. An investor with leverage may be able to enter without accepting a joint venture with majority host nation equity, but other enterprises, even those manufacturing similar products, may be required to comply with a Public Code mandating the joint ventures. More important than permitting unequal treatment, however, is that a potentially unpopular, flexible, Operational Code is hidden from public criticism. Nationalistic pressures may have caused the enactment of a restrictive Public Code for foreign investment that is unrealistic and certain to discourage all investment. By use of a liberal Operational Code, however, the government is able to function pragmatically while public opinion remains nationalist.

The most successful multinational enterprises are those that are aware of the various sources of law affecting foreign investment. This awareness, however, should not be misinterpreted as constituting control by the multinational enterprise. A multinational that appears to have a foreign investment with attributes that differ from provisions of the Public Code, may simply understand the Operational Code better than others. The Operational Code cloaks much activity of foreign direct investment. It may lead to increased criticism from the public sector, particularly the press and academia, that may identify practices of multinationals that appear to the public to be at variance with the Public Code. The multinationals, however, have not necessarily violated the law; they have rather followed the Operational Code completely in accordance with the practices of the host nation government.

§ 25.19   Other Forms of Foreign Investment

There are some unique forms of foreign investment that have gathered their own rules as an overlay to the rules discussed above.

Countertrade. Investment may assume the form of a countertrade agreement, where production is established in the host nation and the profit is received exclusively as a share of the production.[1] This is usually called "compensation" or "buy-back". In such case the foreign investor may agree to build a production plant in the foreign nation and take as compensation or profit a part of the production of the plant. It is a form used mainly when the foreign nation is very short of hard currency. Compensation agreements are usually of fairly long duration, since it may take years to pay for the plant by the share of the plants production. The foreign investor must be able to market the production, and often negotiates a low price for the goods (in the form of a higher percentage of the production than might otherwise be called for).

Border industries and economic zones. A unique form of foreign investment has taken place for several decades along the borders of the United States and Mexico, called the border industries or *maquiladoras.* A foreign, primarily United States, company establishes an assembly plant across the border in Mexico to take advantage of low labor costs. Mexico in turn would not apply its former, restrictive foreign investment rules to the maquiladoras. With the adoption of the NAFTA, and Mexico's dismantling of its restrictive rules, the advantages of the maquiladora are considerably reduced.[2] The maquiladora concept is related to the use of free trade or economic zones, common in many countries.

Free trade or economic zones. Free trade or economic zones are geographic areas, often at a port, where foreign investors are allowed to exist with few domestic restrictions.[3] The foreign investor provides raw materials and goods are manufactured or assembled in the economic zone for subsequent export. One common rule is that the products may not be distributed in the domestic market.[4] The benefit of the zone is that the country in which the zone is located does not impose tariffs on either the parts entering the zone or the products leaving the zone, provided that they are exported.

§ 25.19

1. Countertrade is discussed in chapter 5.

2. See, e.g., Panel Discussion, The Mexican Maquiladora: Rumors of its Death Are Premature, 7 U.S.–Mexico L.J. 203 (1999); Cheryl Schechter & David Brill, Jr., Maquiladoras: Will the Program Continue? 23 St. Mary's L.J. 697 (1992); Note, Mexico's Maquiladora Industry & Other Manufacturing Facili-

ties in Mexico, 15 Loyola L.A. Int'l & Comp.L.J. 965 (1993).

3. See, e.g., Samuels, Freeports, Free Trade Zones, 9 Bus.L.Rev. 109 (1988); D.L.U. Jayawardena, Free Trade Zones, 17 J.World Trade L. 427 (1983).

4. There may be exceptions, but in such case import duties will almost certainly be applied.

The benefit of the zone to the host nation is principally the jobs produced in the zone.

Lease financing. Lease financing involves financial (or operational) leasing of equipment to manufacture products. It is often a part of an investment arrangement, and may help reduce demands on foreign exchange (lease versus purchase). It also may allow the nation to obtain high technology equipment under lease.

§ 25.20   Taxation of Foreign Investment

As noted above, many developed nations have concluded tax treaties with nations in which their multinationals invest, essentially to avoid double taxation. Even though a nation may have a liberal foreign investment law, unless there is a reasonably clear expression of the form of taxation facing the investment, investment will be slow to enter. Some nations offer tax incentives to foreign investment, such as tax holidays that defer tax for a certain number of years, or rebates when profits are reinvested rather than repatriated. The tax benefits are often linked to investment in high priority areas, such as those that generate foreign exchange. Tax benefits may extend beyond tax on profits to taxation of royalties, taxes on imports and exports, sales and consumption taxes, and taxes on personal income of expatriates. One problem for foreign investors is the dynamics of taxation in foreign nations. Tax burdens change frequently and incentives received one year may be far less valuable in another.

Tax units, whether nations or states, are always concerned when reporting methods tend to diminish income expectations. Two issues relate to transfer pricing and the unitary tax. If a foreign company reduces its taxable income in a host nation by artificial transfers, such intracompany transfers at prices which do not reflect arms-length transactions, the host nation may respond with methods to restructure the transfers, and possibly with sanctions. Secondly, when the subsidiary reports an income that as a percentage of the world wide corporate entity's income is considerably lower than the percent of assets, employees and sales within the host nation, the host nation may adopt a unitary tax that replaces a tax based on reported income by adjusting that income to parallel the percent of assets, employees and sales in the jurisdiction.

§ 25.21   Currency Issues

Currencies of developing nations are almost uniformly considered to be "soft" currencies, although they are rarely as controlled as the *soft* currencies of nonmarket economies. It may be that merely being a developing nation means that the currency is soft But within the developing nation world there are *soft* currencies and there are softer currencies. The softest of these currencies may be as nearly controlled as the currencies of a nonmarket economy. But few developing nations have the kind of controls used in some nonmarket economies, where entering persons are required to convert so much hard currency for the soft local currency, and where no currency may be taken out of the nation. Every transaction by foreigners must be accounted for upon exiting the country, and what local currency has not been spent must be left within the country, often used to purchase tourist items in a shop at the point of departure. Common as such practices were two decades ago, they are rapidly being dismantled as part of the transitional process to market economies.

The currency controls in developing nations often amount to attempts to fix the rate of exchange rather than allow it to freely float, or to link the currency to a hard currency. When the currency is formally linked to a hard currency, such as to the dollar for many Latin American nations, the currency has two problems. First, the country's monetary policy effectively is transferred to the linked nation.[1] Second, the linking may prove to be artificial and cause a parallel market rate to arise.[2] The country may use the parallel free market rate as a guide against which to devalue the fixed official rate. Mexico has for many years linked the Mexican peso to the dollar, and for the past few years adjusted the peso daily, often with a slight daily slippage or decline in the peso against the dollar.

Many developing nations compound currency problems with high inflation. High inflation tends not to be a characteristic of nonmarket economies, at least until they become nations in transition. A nation with high inflation cannot long keep its currency pegged to that of a low inflation developed-nation. There must be periodic devaluations or the developing nation currency will be highly overvalued. This will cause a parallel market at market rates to develop, will encourage nationals to move currency abroad, and may cause the economy to "dollarize." The latter occurs when there is little faith in the local currency and nationals begin to deal with a hard foreign currency. As inflation reaches four figures or more, business persons are often more concerned with currency issues than with the primary purpose of the business.

Western traders normally require that goods or services be paid for in hard currency, the rate of which generally reflects market conditions and is convertible to other currencies. But a few developing nations' currencies are relatively hard, and generally convert-

---

§ 25.21

1. If the dollar falls against other hard currencies, such as the yen or Euro or Pound Sterling, the developing nation's currency also falls.

2. The parallel market may be allowed to exist, or be suppressed to the extent possible, and become a black market currency.

ible to other hard currencies. Some developing nations have laws that mandate that any international contract performed in the nation, or any debt due, must be paid in the official national currency. Such laws do not succeed where the currency is soft and unacceptable as a commercial form of payment. Thus an international agreement may stipulate that the contract is to be considered performed outside the developing nation and payment is to be made in a hard currency outside the developing nation. It may even be helpful to have the contract executed in the United States (or another hard currency nation), and stipulate that title to exports from the United States passes before shipment, so as to have as many links as possible outside the developing nation, even though that is where the much of the performance actually occurs.

Currency issues tend to complicate trade and investment. Currency issues tend not to halt trade and investment, however, unless they become so extreme that they overwhelm the principal trade or investment project. Since currency problems are usually an incident of being a developing nation, traders and investors have learned how to deal with them.

Currencies in nonmarket economies are also usually "soft" currencies. Nonmarket economy currency "official" exchange rates are established and rigidly protected by the government. These rates do not reflect market factors. Nonmarket economies frequently have multiple exchange rates. There is an "official" rate, and such other rates as a tourist rate, and perhaps a commercial rate. All are artificial and set by the government. There is likely additionally to be a black-market rate that the government may attempt to suppress. Any artificial exchange rate tends to cause the currency to be rejected in international currency markets, although the nonmarket economy may attempt to keep the currency completely out of any international trading. But most transitional nations are attempting to stabilize their currencies. The transitional process has brought some "hardness" to these currencies. One intermediate measure for nations in transition from nonmarket to market economies has been to peg the domestic currency at a floating rate to a Western hard currency, initially the German Deutschmark, and currently the Euro.

Loans to purchase products usually must be repaid in hard currency. Such demands have a restrictive effect on trade. Hard currency reserves must be earned to be spent. Many nonmarket economies are reluctant to spend their hard currency reserves unless the product is of high priority.

Several of the new nations created by the changes in the former Soviet Union have an even more basic currency problem. These newly independent nations have only recently introduced a national currency. They are attempting the very difficult task of simultaneously establishing an independent nation, introducing major structural reforms, and modernizing their infrastructure and industry. Several new nations formerly part of the Soviet Union continued to use the ruble until their own currency was established, or having established their own, used both. The ruble's problems thus extended beyond Russia's borders. The new currencies often had few assets backing them. The nations' leaders have little experience in developing an economy or dealing with financial markets. But these new linked currencies have become independent from the ruble, and many have been gaining reputations as reasonably stable currencies.

§ 25.22   Goals of Privatization

Developing nations. The reasons countries privatize is not always made clear. Many developing nations have struggled with a mix of private and state ownership which they call a "mixed" economy. But the proportion of the mix is never very clear. Furthermore, it is also uncertain how the government will allocate the private sector between host nation nationals and foreign investors. While privatization has important economic consequences for the nation, it is always the result of political decisions.

Developing nations have turned to privatization to reduce the financial burden on the state from operating many businesses at a loss. But privatization is also thought to make profitable state-owned businesses operate even more profitably. A company might operate in the domestic market with a profit, where its products are necessaries and there is no foreign competition. But as the nation reduces tariffs on imports, these businesses must change to survive. Privatization is sometimes the first change.

Privatization was much discussed in developing nations in the mid–1980s, but in practice the idea was mostly mythical. Privatization plans were announced, but the obstacles to a successful privatization were often considerable. Brazil once announced a sale of "one company per month" but added little detail to assure success. It never materialized. To some extent actual and effective privatization in many developing nations did not commence until the nonmarket nations in Eastern Europe began serious privatizations at the beginning of the 1990s. Privatization in developing nations is obviously less extensive than privatization in nonmarket economies. In the latter, often all the means of production and distribution were state owned, even small stores. Furthermore, all housing was often state owned. Developing nations' privatization usually affects medium to large businesses.

There is no common plan of privatization. Nations have developed many different plans, often carefully watching how privatization functions in other nations and making small adjustments. There are common characteristics to privatization plans, such as dealing with retention of employees, granting employees or nationals priority in purchasing businesses, and listing enterprises to be privatized. Because privatization is a relatively new phenomenon, there has been much trial and error in developing a plan appropriate to the particular state and appropriate to the goals of privatization.

The goals of privatization in developing economies are more associated with the need to reduce state expenditures than with a philosophical change of economic theory from socialism to capitalism. Most nonmarket economies have pursued privatization to assist the change to a nonmarket economy. Certainly, some philosophical change has occurred in developing nations. Many of the governments of the 1970s thought greater state ownership of the means of production and distribution was an appropriate social goal. Having established that in a usually quite nominal dimension, changes in attitudes reversed based on more fundamental theories than the need to reduce state subsidization of business. Many transitional and developing nation administrations are theoretically committed to the idea of a market economy. But it is often difficult to gain public acceptance of the idea when populist remnants endure, and even assume control. In nonmarket economies privatization is one element of the commitment to change. In developing nations there is usually no such pronounced change in process.

Once the concept of privatization has been accepted by a nation, rules must be developed to carry out the privatization. If the rules are unrealistic state owned businesses will remain unsold. The concept will remain a myth. The nation will either abandon the process or make adjustments to make the plan successful. Those adjustments must be made in many areas where there are obstacles to privatization.

Nonmarket economy nations. State ownership of the means of production and distribution has not been successful. It has caused inefficiency and the production of poor quality goods that have not found markets abroad. The cost of maintaining so many state enterprises has placed an unbearable economic burden on the state. Nearly all of the nonmarket economies have chosen as a principal method of transition greater private ownership of commercial enterprises. Privatization of state owned firms has been a major method of foreign investment in these nations. The process has gone beyond factories to stores and apartment buildings, and selected services. Not all industries and services are on national schedules for privatization, many associated with national security and some "essential" services remain state owned.

The pace of privatization and the methods used vary country-to-country. Few of these nations have had much experience, even prior to communist rule, with modern Western style capitalism and private ownership of property and business enterprises. Some Eastern European nations have a history of capitalism and industrialization, with small shops and farms. But the history of the region consists primarily of agrarian peasant societies with a landed aristocracy. Entrepreneurs and shopkeepers were not at the center of government or society, and there are few persons left who had actual experience with markets where they existed during the first half of the last century.

Most of the nonmarket economies have learned that privatization increases productivity and removes a very costly burden from government financial support. Success in one privatized industry leads to more privatization. But there seems to be an inconsistency in the motivations behind privatization in different countries.

Some nations are using privatization to achieve what they refer to as a "mixed" economy, allowing private enterprise in certain sectors but retaining substantial state ownership in others. What the proper mix is to be is never very clearly identified, and the concept seems subject to continual alteration as industries retained under state ownership become a financial burden. Some nations have used privatization to lower the foreign debt, using the proceeds to pay down outstanding obligations. Others have used the process to broaden the base of private ownership in the middle class. The plans of some countries often seem based only on political publicity, such as Brazil's idea of "one company per month." There is some dislike of the idea of privatization, not only in the nonmarket economies but developing nations as well. To avoid public anger, Mexico has referred to the process as "disincorporation" rather than privatization. There is yet no clear plan in many countries that informs potential foreign investors of the nation's real commitment to the privatization process.

Once the process is made part of the nation's economic transitional plan, it must be realized that it is a long process to change a nation with no private ownership of the means of production and distribution to one where private ownership is the dominant mode. Full conversion must be measured in several decades rather than several years, even where the goal is made clear and principal obstacles are removed. Those obstacles are many.

§ 25.23 Obstacles to Privatization

Developing nations. The once largely myth of privatization in developing nations has turned to reality. But the process has proven difficult. There are many obstacles which if not corrected or surmounted, tend to return the plan to mythology.

Absence of an adequate legal infrastructure. Developing nations usually have in place a legal infrastructure with market economy characteristics, unlike the situation facing nonmarket economies in transition. But there are often inadequate structures to help raise capital, such as a viable stock market and securities regulation law. Also, few developing nations have effective rules governing monopolies and restrictive trade practices. Mexico, for example, has only a little more than a decade ago created a commission to deal with restrictive trade practices.[1] Nevertheless, most developing nations have effective company laws, commercial codes, laws governing property transfers, and bankruptcy or insolvency laws. Even when the laws and institutions are created there may be an absence of the educated human resources required to function effectively. The result may be no enforcement or a very harsh and arbitrary enforcement.

One concern special about privatization is dealing with claims against the property being privatized by former owners. This is a serious issue in privatization in former nonmarket economy nations. In most developing nations the state owned enterprises were not formerly privately owned entities that were expropriated, and the issue is not often present.

There is another infrastructure that is often lacking in developing nations, and in nonmarket economics. It is the infrastructure of airports, roads, ports, waterways, telecommunications, water treatment, and power plants, all needed to allow business to function and grow. Often these are all state-owned and operated inefficiently and without adequate capital. They are areas where privatization is often most needed to diminish such a serious obstacle to encouraging foreign investment. In recent years there has been a major emphasis in some developing nations, especially in Latin America, in developing this infrastructure with foreign private assistance.

Government approval process. Because the essence of privatization is the sale of state-owned properties, the government is obviously involved. Often, the state creates a privatization commission to carry out the process. But, where a specific case becomes a public issue, there may be pressure on the central administration to influence decisions of the special commission. Privatization can become a very volatile issue, especially when the workers feel

---

§ 25.23

1. The absence of laws often also means an absence of regulatory institutions. In some cases the rules are in place but there are no enforcement institutions, such as in the area of protecting the environment.

threatened by the process and seek public support for stopping the process.

The government must decide what to privatize. In nonmarket economies the question is "is everything to be sold?" But in developing nations the state does not own everything, and the question is more limited to "is everything the state does own on the list?" The state is likely to control the process by controlling what will be sold at a given time. There may be a list of state enterprises to be sold, or the state may be open to offers to purchase almost any state-owned enterprise.[2]

Government approval creates opportunities for requests for bribes. Many developing nations governments have institutionalized corruption. The privatization process creates new opportunities and new forms of corruption. Management (i.e., government employees) of the state-owned enterprises may oppose the privatization unless they are paid-off, or hired-on, by the purchasers. Many government employees see the proceeds of the sale as a one time windfall, which they have an opportunity to share in personally. It is difficult to participate in privatization in many countries without confronting demands for payments that will certainly create issues under the U.S. Foreign Corrupt Practices Act.[3]

Participation of workers in the approval process. Workers often view privatization as a threat to their jobs. They have good reason. Usually the state enterprise has more employees than are needed to perform the business function. Privatization means a reduction of the workforce in most cases. As a consequence of this, workers are sometimes given some voice in the sale of an enterprise. But they are rarely given the final say, since they are likely to vote against the sale to preserve their jobs. What they may receive are rights to participate in the equity of the new privately-owned enterprise. They may be similar to rights sometimes granted generally to nationals.

Rights of nationals to preferences. While employees may participate in the approval process, all nationals may have preference rights to purchase shares in the entity being sold. The reason is to allow nationals to share in the sale of assets. But there is less such motivation in developing nations than in nonmarket economies. In the latter, nationals have not been able to own the means of production and distribution, and privatization is a method of allowing them to begin to become owners. In developing nations, ownership has always been a possibility, if not of the particular industry

---

2. There are likely to be some state enterprises not on the list, such as petroleum and some natural resource related industries.

3. The Foreign Corrupt Practices Act is the subject of chapter 17.

or plant being privatized. Furthermore, nationals of developing nations are more likely to have had the means to become owners, since unlike in the nonmarket economies, there were no limits on their earnings.

When governments set aside so much of the enterprise to be privatized for possible purchase by nationals or employees, they may issue coupons or vouchers to the nationals or employees. The vouchers may be used for any privatization, or for a specific industry being privatized. A danger is to allow too much of the enterprise to be acquired by nationals at a nominal price paid for the coupons or vouchers. The principal purchaser of the majority interest will not be willing to subsidize the acquisition of shares by nationals. If the per share price paid by nationals is far less than that paid by the foreign investor, the latter may reject the acquisition unless the price is low, notwithstanding the sale of some shares to nationals. The value of a privatized enterprise is one of the most difficult calculations for the government to make.

Method of valuation. There is probably no more difficult aspect of privatization than establishing a value for an enterprise to be privatized. The book value of a developing nation state-owned company is not likely to be any more reflective of the value than in the case of a privately-owned business in the United States.

Where it is difficult to determine a fair value, the government may wish to have an auction.[4] Foreign investors may not wish to engage in a bidding process, and the auction process clearly drives away some prospective buyers. Most purchasers wish to be the only negotiating company, so as to avoid losing the expense of competitive bidding.

Valuation difficulty is not limited to developing nation privatizations. It is even more difficult in nonmarket economies. Furthermore, there have been experiences in developed nations that have privatized state owned companies at either too high prices (bringing no interest), or too low prices (bringing many buyers and the creation of a second market after the sale at a considerably higher price).

Treatment of *foreign investment.* The privatization process in developing nations assumes the participation of foreign investment. There is usually thought to be insufficient capital in the private sector to purchase the enterprises. However, some enterprises which are to be privatized may be limited to private ownership by

---

4. They may wish to use an auction method even where there is a reasonably certain calculation of value. The auction may bring a buyer who is willing to pay more than the enterprise would be worth to most buyers. But a purchase at too high a price could lead to disappointment with the business by the purchaser, and an early insolvency.

host nation nationals. Or there may be limitations on the foreign share acquired, bringing into the privatization mandatory joint ventures. Sometimes there are attempts to first sell the business to nationals, with a subsequent opening of the remaining shares to foreign investment. This is not likely to attract many foreign investors when it means acquisition of a minority share. The reality is that the capital needed to privatize is usually mostly located abroad, and sooner or later the nation must adapt the privatization plan to including foreign investors. If there are limits on foreign investment, the largest industries will go unsold.

Miscellaneous. Privatization contains many unknowns for both the government and potential foreign investors. The government views the process as relieving it of a financial burden and acquiring a substantial payoff. The foreign investor often views the process as a means of entering the nation and possibly obtaining a good investment at a favorable price. Neither the nation nor the foreign investor may be fully satisfied, and may discover that the time and expense necessary to complete the privatization is far in excess of what was expected.

Additional problems that face foreign investors acquiring an enterprise through privatization include the possibility that there may be demands that the company continue to produce the same products, or export so much production. The company must know what the demands will be that will interfere with its making choices.

State-owned companies may not have shares. There may have to be a creation of a new enterprise with shares by the government so that there are shares to sell. Alternatively, the state may sell the assets to a party which creates a business to accept such assets. This latter may be more favorable if there are hidden liabilities that must be addressed if shares are bought. Buying specific assets may avoid assuming non-disclosed liabilities. In any event, even when shares are bought, there may be an agreement by the selling government to assume all liabilities not stipulated in the sales agreement.

Privatization has been especially successful in nonmarket economies with small to medium businesses. But in developing nations, there are usually few small to medium sized business that are state owned. Where there are they have sold reasonably well. Selling the largest businesses in any form of economy has greater problems than selling smaller businesses. The workforce is likely to be more vocal and more powerful in the largest businesses. Valuation is usually more difficult, and there are fewer buyers who can afford such businesses. In many cases, the largest business have been acquired by consortia, often comprising investors from several foreign nations.

The complexities of the privatization process, and especially the problems associated with being unable to fire workers, replacing obsolete technology, assuming responsibility for environmental damage claims, valuing the business, understanding and correcting poor (or different) accounting procedures, and having little previous quality control, have led many foreign investors to follow the "greenfields" method of investing. That method suggests forming an entirely new company rather than acquiring an existing state-owned one.

Nonmarket economy nations. Until a very few years ago, privatization was much discussed but little activated. It was one of the myths of foreign investment. As the myth became reality, mainly with the political changes in Eastern Europe and the former USSR, it became apparent that the process of privatization would be difficult, even with a new positive government backing.

Absence of an adequate legal infrastructure. Nonmarket economies long functioned without the legal framework necessary in a market economy. Constitutional amendments have been required to change the fundamental philosophy, and alter fundamental notions of ownership of property. New laws have been acted to address the formation and operation of business enterprises, transfers of property, bankruptcy, banking, and securities regulation.[5] Many new laws have been viewed by foreign investors as being too broad and allowing too much discretion to governmental officials. In addition to the laws, new institutions have to be established, such as a stock market and securities regulation agency.[6] There have been disputes regarding whether federal or local (state or provincial) laws ought to govern, with federal law predominating. As the nations began to acknowledge private ownership, many citizens and emigres presented claims for the return of properties expropriated decades ago. Such claims affect foreign investors, who may be pursuing an acquisition of a small business claimed by a host nation citizen. Of major concern has been the obligation of new owners to clean up past environmental damage. Foreign investors need to learn if there are any claims of environmental damage against the state and whether there are laws allocating the responsibility for their correction. An agreement to acquire a state-owned business ought to have

5. Principal models have been the laws of Germany and the United States.

6. Part of the problem with the earlier structures was that so much was done by a kind of unwritten law or administrative policy that was often elusive in source. See, e.g., Bernard Black, Reinier Kraakman & Anna Tarassova, Russian Privatization and Corporate Governance: What Went Wrong? 52 Stan. L. Rev. 1730 (2000).

an indemnification provision obligating the state to pay any former claims.

As nonmarket economies in transition develop new market oriented laws, the risk of investing will be much reduced. The manner of development of the new legal infrastructure discloses much about the commitment of the host nation to a serious process of allowing foreign investment and achieving a market economy.

Government approval process. Many nonmarket economies have added a special agency to deal with privatization. That is helpful if it does not merely add one additional layer of bureaucracy to the approval process. In some cases the specialized agency shares authority with another. The agency may develop a list of approved companies for privatization. But "spontaneous" privatization, where foreign investors identify a company and propose privatization, has been accepted and successful in some cases.

Government approval creates the possibility of requests for bribes. Unfortunately, the nonmarket economies in transition have been a major source of such requests, matching some of the developing nations in demanding payments for official action.

Participation of workers in the approval process. Workers may have to participate in the approval of the sale of enterprises. Before the disintegration of Yugoslavia, workers owned the plants in which they worked and there was thus a constitutional obstacle to the sale. In other nations, enterprise workers' councils may have the right to approve. Even where there does not seem to be any formal process for workers' approval, the concern for the workers sometimes leads to a kind of informal approval, a sensing of the workers' attitudes before official government approval is granted. The likely concern of the workers is loss of employment. One reason privatization is adopted is to reverse the overemployment consequence of state ownership with no accountability for costs of production. If workers are given approval, privatization may prove impossible, and essentially be a mythical characteristic of the transition.

Rights of nationals to preferences. While workers in the factory may participate in the approval process, both workers and nationals in general may have preference rights to purchase shares. The national motivation is to allow nationals to share in ownership. But since nationals do not have very much savings, they cannot afford to pay the per share price offered by a foreign investor. Governments have thus sometimes set aside so much percentage of a company to be privatized for local ownership. It is often accomplished by a coupon or voucher scheme, where the government issues coupons or vouchers of a set value to all nationals. The state privatization agency first determines the approximate value of an enterprise to be privatized. The agency then issues an appropriate number of stock shares. The coupons or vouchers may be redeemed for shares of an enterprise or traded with others, or sold. Shares may then be redeemed through the state privatization agency or on the stock exchange.

In some countries, employees are granted the first opportunity to purchase shares of the factory or store where they work. The initial issue of coupons or shares are to employees or specific buyers only, and may not be freely transferred. This method is consistent with the nonmarket economy tradition of common or collective ownership, only under this system the workers truly own the factory instead of the state owning it for them. This program has run into resistance particularly in Russia from factory managers who fear losing their jobs to the workers, or worse yet to strangers when the workers later trade or sell their shares. The nationals are allowed to sell the vouchers to other nationals, or use them to acquire shares in companies. Because nothing is paid for such shares, a foreign investor is likely to calculate the per share value considering the dilution effect by the percentage of shares acquired by nationals. While the process is fair to nationals, it overlooks the fact that the nations need capital, and for every percent given to nationals, the foreign investor is going to reduce its offer to offset the "free" shares to nationals.

Treatment of foreign investment. The privatization framework may include limitations on foreign participation. That may be by absolute prohibition in some privatizations, leaving the enterprises for exclusively local private ownership, or by limitations allowing joint ventures. The joint venture law thus becomes interrelated with the privatization process. Sometimes foreign investors are given last priority, to allow as many enterprises as possible to be owned by nationals, with foreign investors allowed to invest in what remains. But while this might suggest that foreign investors are given only the scraps, the fact is that nationals do not have the resources to purchase anything but a small fraction of their nation's industries.

Some of the rules are based on incorrect assumptions regarding what foreign investors want. They are interested in direct investment, not a scattered portfolio investment. And they are interested in control. If the host nations expect to obtain foreign technology, capital and distribution outlets, they have to give up more than many governments have been willing to acknowledge.

Method of valuation. Establishing a value for an enterprise to be privatized is as difficult in a nonmarket economy nation as in a developing nation. Book value possesses all the problems of book value in the United States, plus even greater distortions due to accounting practices that do not adhere to market policies. But book value may be used, especially to set the value (at a low amount) for purchases by workers. The government may use one valuation method for purchases by nationals, another (higher value) for purchases by foreign investors.

One prevalent form of valuation is really not a valuation method at all. It is by auction, perhaps with a minimum base. But many foreign investors prefer to negotiate a price and not be one of several players in bidding for a company. Former losers at auctions may be discouraged from committing the time and expense to be a participant in the future.

Setting the value of a company to be privatized is not only a problem for nonmarket economy nations. The experience of the United Kingdom in privatizing several state-owned companies illustrates setting prices too low or too high. When too low, the market quickly raises the price to a market level and the government is quickly aware of what they have lost by undervaluation. When too high, there may be no buyers and the process has to be repeated. It is a costly procedure.

Miscellaneous. Privatization is a rather traumatic experience for the government, and also for the foreign investor. There are many uncertainties, as noted above. The government sees a benefit in both raising a great deal of hard currency, and ending a constant drain on the economy in subsidizing an unprofitable enterprise.[7] The most difficult obstacle is concern for workers. Mythical privatization procedures stipulated that no workers could be fired. That meant the foreign private investor would be expected to subsidize overemployment in the same way as the state had in the past. That could hardly be called a market economy system.

Some additional problems facing the foreign investor involve demands that the company continue to produce the traditional products, export demands, and limitations on salary disparities of foreign managers and domestic employees. Another problem is whether to sell the assets and then have a new company formed, or form a new state owned company and then sell the company with all its assets. The practice seems to be to create a company that is then sold.

Privatization has thus far been very successful with small to medium sized enterprises. This applies whether the enterprise is sold to domestic or foreign investors. Many foreign investors have preferred to acquire smaller companies in the service sector, thus avoiding some of the many problems associated with large manufacturing state controlled industries. It is more complex to establish valuation for the larger factories, and it is much more difficult to

---

7. Not all enterprises privatized were unprofitable. The government may be privatizing to get out of ownership altogether, or to sell an enterprise that is profitable but could be even more so under private ownership.

locate willing buyers, especially if the operation is inefficient, uses outdated technology, or requires environmental repair.

Ironically, privatization may be more successful where a single agency has the primary responsibility for devising and executing the plan. Where decentralization has occurred, bureaucracy has been replaced by chaos and unpredictability. For example, in Russia, the government issued vouchers for individual stock purchase, but delegated the implementation and schedule of privatization to municipal authorities. Consequently, in several cities, the authorities and factory managers conspired to either block privatization or to appropriate the enterprises for themselves. The legal system has proved inadequate to cope with such corruption and misappropriation.

Rather than proceed with immediate privatization, some nations are taking an intermediate step of reforming the structure of state enterprises. These governments are introducing market factors of production and commercial accountability, while retaining state ownership. This requires a separation of the functions of management of state owned property and the management activity of the enterprise. Companies are restructured as either joint stock or limited liability companies, while remaining under the control of the appropriate ministries.

A variation of the above transforms the state-owned enterprises into single owner corporations, with the state as the initial owner. Management is then contracted out. A majority percentage of the shares is turned over to investment groups, and the companies become joint stock corporations upon termination of the management contract. To encourage local purchase, some will offer a lease-to-own option or credit at preferential loan rates.

The complexities of the privatization process in nonmarket as well as developing nations have led many foreign investors to reject the privatization route and follow the "greenfields" method of investing.

§ 25.24 Human Rights and Environmental Challenges to Foreign Investors

Foreign investors have always faced possible litigation in the host nation. Jurisdiction in the host nation is rarely a problem because the company is clearly there and doing business. But the subsidiary in the host nation often has few assets. While they may be sufficient to satisfy judgments dealing with such common issues as a job related injury to an employee, or a contract breach, they are insufficient when multiple plaintiff actions are brought for alleged large scale injury such as environmental damage or labor abuses. In such actions the defendant is the parent as well as the host nation subsidiary, leading to jurisdictional issues if the suit is brought in the host nation. But such suits are brought in the United States, often in state courts where juries are perceived as hostile to multinational corporations, such as South Texas or Mississippi.[1] Initiated by attorneys' with contingent fee contracts and who demand punitive damages, human rights abuses, environmental damages and even cultural genocide have been the charges in an increasing number of suits against some of the largest corporations in the United States, including Del Monte, Dupont, Exxon Mobil Corp., Ford Motor Company, Freeport–McMoran, Texaco, Union Carbide and United Technologies. The principal basis for these suits has been alleged violations of international law and specifically of the U.S. Alien Tort Claims Act. Much of this litigation has evolved since the 1980 *Filártiga v. Peña-Irala* decision.[2]

The *Filártiga* case did not involve a corporate defendant. It was brought by a Paraguayan citizen, Filártiga, residing in the United States, against one Peña, another Paraguayan citizen in the United States on a tourist visa. Peña had been the Inspector General of the Police in Asunción, Paraguay, and allegedly tortured and killed the son of Filártiga. The case was based principally on violations of the Alien Tort Claims Act, a 1789 enactment of Congress to address quite different concerns, such as acts of piracy. It was rarely used until *Filártiga*. But its brevity and breadth provided the court a foundation to find Peña in violation as the court had little trouble in finding death by torture a violation of international law. When the court gave its opinion in 1980 the floodgates opened for many suits that tried to enlarge the scope of violations of international law. And for another challenge important to international business—could the defendants be foreign corporations?

How expansive an interpretation should be given the ATCA's "violation of the law of nations" language is yet undetermined. Certainly torture and extra-judicial killing are such violations. So perhaps are hostage taking and aircraft sabotage, and acts of terrorism. But the cases have tested the ATCA's language in two ways. One is the scope of acts within a category that appear at first glance to constitute international law violations, but may encompass less clear violations, such as torture (e.g., cutting off hands versus sleep deprivation) and human rights (extra-judicial killing of political dissidents versus relocating indigenous people to build a dam). The second debate is whether to bring within violations of international law areas where there is uncertainty whether acts

---

§ 25.24

1. The U.S. parent will usually argue lack of jurisdiction over the parent because it operates in the foreign host nation solely through a host nation cor-

poration. This usually leads to veil piercing charges.

2. 630 F.2d 876 (2nd Cir. 1980).

violate treaties or customary international law. The most litigated may be violations of environmental laws. While there are many domestic environmental laws, there is considerable debate as to whether there is any international environmental law, especially customary law. A more recent basis for litigation is alleged "cultural genocide,"[3] charging displacement and relocation of indigenous peoples.

While the above issues could be debated and litigated in cases against officials of the foreign nations, subject to jurisdiction in U.S. courts, the far deeper pockets are those of multinational corporations. It was inevitable that suits would be brought against corporate defendants. The first to establish corporate liability was *Doe v. Unocal,* brought by Burmese nationals charging human rights violations by the defendant for complicity with the government in using forced labor in the construction of an oil pipeline.[4] It remains unclear how the 2004 *Sosa v. Alvarez–Machain* decision will affect corporate liability.[5]

Sosa did not involve a corporate defendant, but an individual claiming that his abduction constituted a violation of international law under the ATCA. The case brought the U.S. Supreme Court into the debate over the limits of the ATCA. The Court rejected the defendant's argument that the ATCA does not provide a cause of action, but found that the abduction of Alvarez–Machain in Mexico and transportation to the United States for trial did not violate the law of nations. The Court gave several reasons for judicial caution in applying too broad an interpretation of the ATCA.

Sosa v. Alvarez–Machain may have diminished the availability of reliance upon the ATCA for suits against foreign corporations, not because the defendants are corporations but because the scope of the ATCA seems more limited than prior to the decision. *Sosa* has probably not ended suits against foreign investors, since other grounds remain, such as the Racketeer Influenced and Corrupt Organizations Act, the federal question statute, and such traditional actions as wrongful death, false imprisonment, assault, intentional infliction of emotional distress and negligence.[6]

---

3. Beanal v. Freeport–McMoran, Inc., 197 F.3d 161 (5th Cir. 1999) (brought on grounds of human rights violations, environmental torts and abuses, and genocide and cultural genocide).

4. 110 F.Supp.2d 1294 (C.D.Cal. 2000). The chronology of corporate liability under the ATCA is in Presbyterian Church of Sudan v. Talisman Energy, Inc., 244 F.Supp.2d 289, 308 (S.D.N.Y. 2003). See also Courtney Shaw, Uncer-

tain Justice: Liability of Multinationals Under the Alien Tort Claims Act, 54 Stan.L.Rev. 1359 (2002).

5. ___ U.S. ___, 124 S.Ct. 2739, 159 L.Ed.2d 718 (2004).

6. The ATCA and each of these examples of causes of action were grounds in Doe v. Unocal Corp., 110 F.Supp.2d 1294 (C.D.Cal.2000). The case was appealed, 395 F.3d 932 (9th Cir.2002). After a majority of the 9th Circuit voted to have an en banc rehearing, and a few

§ 25.25 The Applicable Law and Dispute Resolution

Investment disputes often involve claims by the foreign investor that the host nation interfered with the investment to the degree that it constitutes a taking of property. A taking may violate international law, but that area is poorly defined in international law and disputed by different nations.[1] Investors prefer to rely on other means for dispute settlement.

Host-nation law may include how investment disputes are to be resolved. Often the law provides for stages beginning with a form of mediation, then arbitration, and if not satisfied through use of the courts. This may be unsatisfactory to the foreign investor if the membership of the mediation and arbitration panels, and the rules under which they operate, favor the host nation. A more neutral settlement process is usually preferred.

In host nations which are federations of states or provinces, there may be concern regarding the applicability of local law. Where there are differences in national and local laws, the general rule is that the national law will prevail. But where the local law supplements or fills gaps in the national law, foreign investors will have two sets of laws with which to comply. There is an added cost to functioning in such a system. United States investors should have no difficulty in understanding such a system, there is none more complex than the federation of states which is our own.

§ 25.26 Bilateral Investment Treaties (BITs)

International law has been slow to establish standards regarding how nations should treat foreign investment. The United Nations' efforts to draft a code of conduct for multinational enterprises did not include provisions for the conduct of host nations. Such process was thus quite unsatisfactory to foreign investors, who sought assistance from their home nations when their property was taken by the host nation. Bilateral investment treaties have provided some help. To promote national treatment and protect U.S. investors abroad, the United States embarked on the BIT program in the early 1980s.[1] The BIT program followed earlier extensive use of Friendship, Commerce, and Navigation (FCNs) treaties. Unlike the FCNs, the model BIT distinguishes treatment for foreign-owned, domestically incorporated subsidiaries and branches of foreign firms for some provisions, particularly employment. As a result

months after the Sosa decision, a settlement was reached.

§ 25.25

1. The expropriation of property is the subject of chapter 29.

§ 25.26

1. See K. Scott Gudgeon, United States Bilateral Investment Treaties, 4 Int'l Tax & Bus.Law. 105 (1986); Pamela Gann, The United States Bilateral Investment Treaty Program, 21 Stanford J.Int'l L. 373 (1985).

of the *Sumitomo Shoji America v. Avagliano* decision,[2] the FCN treaty afforded no protection to a foreign company using its nationals in hiring. Under the typical BIT, explicit freedom to hire nationals exists in a narrow range of management provisions, helping roll back the traditional TRIM of local management provisions. But investment-screening mechanisms and key sectors often remain exempt from BIT protections, typically listed in an Annex to a BIT. While elimination of FDI screening and imposition of performance requirements has been an object of the BIT program, these provisions of the model BIT have been weakened in the treaties currently in force.[3]

The United States has entered into a number of bilateral investment treaties (BITs), as well as a number of less formal bilateral trade agreements. The trade agreement may refer to investment as an area for further discussion.[4] The bilateral *investment* treaties do address investment issues. They tend to replace earlier Friendship, Commerce & Navigation treaties because they apply to investments. While many of the first BITs were negotiated with small developing countries,[5] more recently the United States has signed BITs with such important trading nations as Argentina.[6] The Argentina–United States BIT follows the U.S. BIT prototype of addressing both *investment protection* and *investor access* to each other's markets.

The BITs do not prohibit nations from enacting investment laws, but provide that any such laws should not interfere with any rights in the treaty. The free access aspect of some BITs may not be perceived as a right. Thus investment laws might be enacted that limit access to certain areas, but would not create a right of the other party to challenge the law under the BIT.

One important provision the United States seeks to include in its BITs is the "prompt, adequate and effective" concept (if not always the language) of compensation subsequent to expropriation. Many of the nations that have recently agreed to this language disputed its appropriateness during the nationalistic North–South dialogue years of the 1960s and 1970s. But as the developing

---

2. 457 U.S. 176, 102 S.Ct. 2374, 72 L.Ed.2d 765 (1982).

3. See Gudgeon, supra note 1, at 126–7 (observing that BITs with Egypt, Haiti, and Zaire have the weakest language ["shall seek to avoid" TRPRs], while BITs with Senegal and Panama include qualifications, such as exemption for Panama's investment incentive program).

4. The Mongolia–United States Agreement on Trade Relations, Jan. 23,

1991, 30 Int'l Leg.Mat. 515 (1991), provides for further cooperation in the form of reaching agreement on investment issues, including the repatriation of profits and transfer of capital. See art. X(1).

5. For example, Haiti, Mongolia, Panama, Senegal, Sri Lanka and Zaire.

6. Argentina–United States Treaty Concerning the Reciprocal Encouragement and Protection of Investment, Nov. 14, 1991.

nations began to promote rather than restrict investment, they began to accept the idea that expropriated investment had to be compensated reasonably soon after the taking ("prompt"), be based on a fair valuation ("adequate"), and be paid in a realistic form ("effective"). The Argentina–United States BIT uses language referring to the "fair market value ... immediately before the expropriatory action".[7]

Most BITs do not include provisions for consultations when differences arise in the interpretation of the treaty. The Argentina–United States and Sri Lanka–United States BITs are exceptions. BITs do often provide for arbitration, sometimes with no necessary recourse to prior exhaustion of local remedies.

The BIT process is quite dynamic. Each successive agreement with a new country may include some new provisions. The United States has a prototype agreement, but it has been modified as host nations have sought new foreign investment and have been willing to sign a BIT to establish the most attractive conditions for that investment. It is certain that the BITs in existence today will not be identical to BITs executed in years ahead. BITs are an important contribution of the developed home nation to their multinationals investing abroad. They establish some ground rules for investment on a bilateral treaty basis that should not be unilaterally altered by the host nation to impose restrictions on the investments that are inconsistent with the BIT. Certainly, revolutionary governments have ignored similar agreements in the past and may in the future. But the BITs do provide some investment security, at least as long as the host governments remain relatively stable, and receptive to foreign investment.

§ 25.27 International Centre for the Settlement of Investment Disputes (ICSID)

More than 100 nations have become parties to the 1966 Convention on the Settlement of Investment Disputes Between States and Nationals of Other States.[1] The Convention provided for the creation of the International Centre for the Settlement of Investment Disputes as part of the World Bank.[2] The Convention and Centre provide for a form of arbitration of investment disputes, offering an institutional framework for the proceedings. Jurisdiction under the Convention extends to "any legal dispute arising

---

7. Argentina–United States BIT, art. IV(1).

§ 25.27

1. TIAS 6090, implemented in the United States in 22 U.S.C.A. §§ 1650 and 1650a.

2. The Centre publishes the useful semiannual journal, the ICSID Review–Foreign Investment Law Journal.

directly out of an investment, between a Contracting State or ... any subdivision ... and a national of another Contracting State." But the parties must consent in writing to the submission of the dispute to the Centre. Once given, the consent may not be withdrawn.

Disputes regarding jurisdiction may be decided by the arbitration panel and appealed to a committee (ad hoc) created from the Panel of Arbitrators by the Administrative Council of the ICSID. The jurisdiction of the tribunal, challenged in a United States court, may well lead to a refusal to uphold the decision.[3] Concern regarding the jurisdictional limitations led to the creation of the Additional Facility, which may conduct conciliations and arbitrations for what are rather special disputes.[4] It was not created to deal with the ordinary investment dispute, but with disputes between parties with long-term special economic relationships involving substantial resource commitments. The Additional Facility may be used only with the blessing of the ICSID Secretary General.

Chapter 11 of the North American Free Trade Agreement governs foreign investment and provides for the resolution of investment disputes between the government of a member state and a private investor of another member state. These disputes may be submitted to arbitration under the ICSID Convention where the government and investors are both from member countries. But Canada and Mexico are not yet ICSID members, leaving the arbitration to be done under either the ICSID Additional Facility Rules or the UNCITRAL Rules.[5] Only UNCITRAL Rules are available for disputes between Mexico and Canada since neither is an ICSID member.

The World Bank has another organization important to foreign investment, the Multilateral Investment Guarantee Agency (MIGA). MIGA provides investment insurance not unlike the United States Overseas Private Investment Corporation's (OPIC) insurance programs.[6]

---

3. The ICSID is discussed in W. Michael Reisman, Systems of Control in International Adjudication & Arbitration (1992).

4. The Additional Facility has its own arbitration rules.

5. The first two NAFTA investment disputes, each involving a U.S. investor and the Mexican government, chose to use the ICSID Additional Facility Rules, the first investment disputes anywhere to do so. See Metalclad Corp. v. United Mexican States (Case ARB(AF)/97/1); Azinian et al and the United Mexican States (Case ARB(AF)/97/2)(reported in 14 ICSID Review—Foreign Investment L.J. 538 (1999).

6. Both MIGA and OPIC are discussed in chapter 28.

Chapter 26

INVESTING IN EUROPE

Table of Sections

This chapter focuses upon investing in Europe. It is written primarily for an audience located outside Europe, and its emphasis is on investing in the European Union. The underlying assumption is that foreign investors are seeking to and will increasingly treat Europe as a regional market, not a series of individual national markets nor as a group of regional markets. Thus, although the relevant laws of the European country where the investment will be made always need to be consulted and can vary greatly, this chapter primarily covers regional investment and trade law in Europe. It is this body of law that governs the operational realities of the market called Europe. And it is this market potential that so attracts foreign investors. **For much more extensive coverage, see Folsom's** *Principles of European Union Law.*

§ 26.1   Introduction

Investors in the European Union have a great interest in how well its common market works. Their basic goal is to sell in a regional (not a national) market. This section highlights the law governing free movement of goods, money and services. It also very selectively focuses upon the development of common policies of particular concern to foreign investors (with emphasis on U.S. interests). Space does not permit treatment of European law governing medical and food products, free movement of people, worker and professional rights, banking, insurance, investment advisors, transportation, value-added and excise taxation, broadcasting and media products, computer software, commercial agents, corporate taxation, subsidies, industrial and intellectual property, procurement, products liability, consumer protection, advertising, companies, the environment, energy, telecommunications, agricultural and fisheries policy, customs, trade,[1] franchising,[2] patent and know-how licensing,[3] distribution and antitrust.[4]

§ 26.2   A Single Market

The campaign for a European Community without internal frontiers was the product of Commission studies in the mid–1980s which concluded that a hardening of the trade arteries of Europe had occurred. The Community was perceived to be stagnating relative to the advancing economies of North America and East Asia. Various projections of the wealth that could be generated from a truly common market for Western Europe suggested the need for revitalization. A "white paper" drafted under the leadership of Lord Cockfield of Britain and issued by the Commission in 1985 became the blueprint for the campaign.

The Commission's white paper identified three types of barriers to a Europe without internal frontiers—physical, technical and fiscal. Physical barriers occur at the borders. For goods, they include national trade quotas, health checks, agricultural monetary compensation amount (MCA) charges, statistical collections and transport controls. For people, physical barriers involve clearing immigrations, security checks and customs. Technical barriers mostly involve national standards and rules for goods, services, capital and labor which operate to inhibit trade among the member states. Boilers, railway, medical and surgical equipment, and pharmaceuticals provide traditional examples of markets restrained by technical trade barriers. Fiscal barriers centered on different value-added and excise taxation levels and the corresponding need for tax

§ 26.1

1. See Chapters 12 and 13.

2. See Chapter 22.

3. See Chapter 23.

4. See Chapter 20.

collections at the border. There were, for example, wide value-added tax (VAT) differences on auto sales within the Common Market.

The Commission (Cecchini Report) estimated that removal of all of these barriers could save the Community upwards of 100 billion ECUs (European Currency Units) in direct costs. In addition, another roughly 100 billion ECUs may be gained as price reductions and increased efficiency and competition take hold. Overall, the Commission projected an increase in the Common Market's gross domestic product (GDP) of between 4.5 to 7 percent, a reduction in consumer prices of between 6 to 4.5 percent, 1.75 to 5 million new jobs, and enhanced public sector and external trade balances. These figures were thus said to represent "the costs of non-Europe."

Single European Act

Major amendments to the Treaty of Rome were undertaken in the Single European Act (SEA) which became effective in 1987. Amendments to the Treaty can occur by Commission or member state proposal to the Council which calls an intergovernmental conference to unanimously determine their content. The amendments are not effective until ratified by all the member states in accordance with their respective constitutional requirements. Proposals originating in the Commission's 1985 white paper on a Europe without internal frontiers were embodied in the Single European Act. The SEA amendments not only expanded the competence of the European institutions, but also sought to accelerate the speed of integration by relying more heavily on qualified majority (not unanimous) voting principles in Council decision-making.

The Single European Act envisioned the adoption of hundreds of new legislative measures designed to fully integrate the Common Market by the end of 1992. Nearly all of these measures and more have been adopted by the Council. Implementation at the national level has proceeded more slowly and is still a concern, especially regarding insurance, investment advisors and procurement.

§ 26.3   Economic and Monetary Union, A Common Currency

The legal basis for the European Monetary System (EMS) and European Currency Unit (ECU) was substantially advanced by the addition to the Treaty of Rome of Article 98 by the Single European Act of 1987. This article committed the member states to further development of the EMS and ECU, recognized the cooperation of the central banks in management of the system, but specifically required further amendment of the Treaty if "institutional changes" were needed. In other words, a common currency managed by an European central bank system was *not* a part of the 1992 campaign. In 1990 however, draft plans for such developments surfaced in the Commission using the U.S. Federal Reserve Board as a model. Britain, always concerned about losses of economic sovereignty (what greater loss is there than the power to print money?), proposed an alternative known as the "hard ECU." This proposal would have retained the national currencies but added the hard ECU as competitor of each, letting the marketplace in most instances decide which currency it prefers.

In December of 1989, the European Council (outvoting Britain) approved a three stage approach to economic and monetary union (EMU). Stage One began July 1, 1990. Its focus was on expanding the power and influence of the Committee of Central Bank Governors over monetary affairs. This Committee was a kind of EuroFed in embryo. It was primarily engaged in "multilateral surveillance." Stage One also sought greater economic policy coordination and convergence among the member states. Stage Two anticipated the creation of a European central banking system, but functioned with the existing national currencies in the context of the EMS and its exchange rate mechanism. Stage Two was a learning and transition period. In October of 1990, it was agreed (save Britain) that Stage Two would commence January 1, 1994. This deadline was actually met, and the European Monetary Institute was installed in Frankfurt. It was the precursor to the European Central Bank.

Stage Three involved the replacement of the national currencies with a single currency, the EURO, managed by a European Central Bank. In December of 1991, agreement was reached at Maastricht to implement Stage Three no later than Jan. 1, 1999 with a minimum of seven states. Britain reserved a right to opt out of Stage Three. All member states had to meet strict economic convergence criteria on inflation rates, government deficits, long-term interest rates and currency fluctuations. To join the third stage of the EMU in 1997, a country was supposed to have an inflation rate not greater than 1.5 percent of the average of the three lowest rates in the Union, long-term interest rates no higher than 2 percent above the average of the three lowest, a budget deficit less than 3 percent of gross domestic product (GDP), a total public indebtedness of less than 60 percent of GDP and no devaluation within the ERM during the prior two years. These criteria will likewise govern admission of the new member states from Central Europe to the EURO zone.

European Central Bank

It was also agreed at Maastricht that, in the third stage, the European Central Bank (ECB) and the European System of Central Banks (ESCB) would start operations. The ECB and ESCB are governed by an executive board of six persons appointed by the member states and the governors of the national central banks. The ECB and the ESCB are independent of other regional institutions and free from member state influence. Their primary responsibility is to maintain price stability, specifically keeping price inflation below two percent per year. In contrast, the U.S. Federal Reserve has three primary responsibilities: maximum employment, stable prices and moderate long-term interest rates. The main functions of the ECB and ESCB are: (1) define and implement the monetary policy; (2) conduct foreign exchange operations; (3) hold and manage the official foreign reserves of the member states; and (4) supervise the payments systems. The ECB has the exclusive right to authorize the issue of EURO bank notes. It sets interest rates to principally achieve price stability. The Court of Justice may review the legality of ECB decisions. The ECB works closely with the Ecofin Council which issues broad guidelines for economic policy. If the Ecofin considers a national government's policy to be inconsistent with that of the region, it can recommend changes including budget cuts. If appropriate national action does not follow such a warning, the Ecofin can require a government to disclose the relevant information with its bond issues, block European Investment Bank credits or levy fines and penalties. By 2004, half the Euro zone states were under threat of sanctions for failure to comply with the 3 percent budget deficit rule, which does not appear to be enforceable before the Court of Justice.[1]

EURO Zone

The economic performance of member states in 1997 became the test for admission to the economic and monetary union. Since both France and Germany had trouble meeting the admissions criteria, this opened a window for much more marginal states such as Belgium, Italy and Spain to join immediately. In May of 1998, at a special European Council summit, it was decided that all but Greece would qualify. As expected, Denmark, Britain and Sweden opted out of initial participation in the common currency. Danish voters voted in 2000 against joining the EURO zone, as did the Swedes in 2003. Greece was deemed to qualify and joined the EURO zone January 1, 2001. The ten nations that joined the EU in 2004 will likewise need to qualify to join the EURO zone.

On January 1, 1999, the participating states fixed the exchange rates between the EURO and their national currencies. National notes and coins will be removed from the market by July 2002 as the EURO is installed. Until then, many companies maintain dual

§ 26.3

1. See Commission v. Council (2004) Eur.Comm.Rep. I–00000 (Case C–27/04).

EURO and national currency accounts and prices. The EURO has been used for most commercial banking, foreign exchange and public debt purposes since 1999. It has also been adopted (voluntarily) by the world's securities markets, and by Monaco, San Marino, the Vatican, Andorra, Montenegro and Kosovo.

The arrival of the EURO has important implications for the United States and the dollar. For decades, the dollar has been the world's leading currency, although its dominance has been declining since the early 1980s. Use of the Deutsche Mark and Yen in commercial and financial transactions, and in savings and reserves, has been steadily rising. The EURO is likely to continue the dollar's decline in all of these markets. It is certainly the hope of many Europeans that they have successfully created a rival to the dollar.

§ 26.4   Free Movement of Goods

North American traders and investors should understand that the free movement of goods within Europe is based upon the creation of a customs union. Under this union, the member states have eliminated customs duties among themselves.[1] They have established a common customs tariff for their trade with the rest of the world. Quantitative restrictions (quotas) on trade between member states are also prohibited, except in emergency and other limited situations.[2] The right of free movement applies to goods that originate in the Common Market *and* to those that have lawfully entered it and are said to be in "free circulation."[3]

Measures of Equivalent Effect

The establishment of the customs union has been a major accomplishment, though not without difficulties. The member states not only committed themselves to the elimination of tariffs and quotas on internal trade, but also to the elimination of "measures of equivalent effect."[4] The elastic legal concept of measures of equivalent effect has been interpreted broadly by the European Court of Justice and the Commission to prohibit a wide range of trade restraints, such as administrative fees charged at borders which are the equivalent of import or export tariffs.[5] Charges of equivalent effect to a tariff must be distinguished from internal taxes that are applicable to imported and domestic goods. The latter must be levied in a nondiscriminatory and nonprotective manner (Article 95), while the former are prohibited entirely (Arti-

---

§ 26.4

1. Article 25, Treaty of Rome.

2. Articles 28–29, Treaty of Rome.

3. Articles 23–24, Treaty of Rome.

4. See especially Articles 25, 28 and 29, Treaty of Rome.

5. Rewe Zentralfinanz v. Landwirtschaftskammer Westfalen–Lippe (1973) Eur.Comm.Rep. 1039; Commission v. Italy (1969) Eur.Comm.Rep. 193. But see Commission v. Germany (1988) Eur. Comm.Rep. 5427.

cles 9, 12). There has been a considerable amount of litigation over this distinction.[6]

The elasticity of the concept of measures of an equivalent effect is even more pronounced in the Court's judgment relating to quotas. This jurisprudence draws upon an early Commission directive (no longer applicable) of extraordinary scope.[7] In this directive, the Commission undertook a lengthy listing of practices that it considered illegal measures of effect equivalent to quotas. It is still occasionally referenced in Commission and Court of Justice decisions. Its focus is on national rules that discriminate against imports or simply restrain internal trade.

Cassis Formula

This "effects test" soon found support from the ECJ. In a famous case, the Court of Justice ruled that Belgium could not block the importation of Scotch whiskey via France because of the absence of a British certificate of origin as required by Belgian customs law.[8] The Court of Justice held that any national rule directly or indirectly, actually or potentially capable of hindering internal trade is generally forbidden as a measure of equivalent effect to a quota. However, *if* European law has not developed appropriate rules in the area concerned (here designations of origin), the member states may enact "reasonable" and "proportional" (no broader than necessary) regulations to ensure that the public is not harmed.[9] This is often referred to as the *"Cassis* formula". Products meeting reasonable national criteria, the *Cassis* opinion continues, may be freely traded. This is the origin of the innovative "mutual reciprocity" principle used in significant parts of the legislative campaign for a Europe without frontiers.

The *Cassis* decision suggests use of a Rule of Reason analysis for national fiscal regulations, public health measures, laws governing the fairness of commercial transactions and consumer protection. Environmental protection and occupational safety laws of the member states have been similarly treated. Under this approach, for example, a Danish "bottle bill" requiring use of approved containers was therefore unreasonable.[10] However, the Danes' argument that a deposit and return system was environmentally neces-

---

6. See e.g. Industria Gomma, Articoli Vari v. Ente Nazionale ENCC (1975) Eur.Comm.Rep. 699.

7. Procureur du Roi v. Dassonville (1974) Eur.Comm.Rep. 837.

8. Commission Directive 70/50 on the Abolition of Measures which have an Effect Equivalent to Quantitative Restrictions, 1970 O.J. L13/29 (Special Edition) (I), p. 17.

9. See the "Cassis de Dijon" case, Rewe Zentral AG v. Bundesmonopolverwaltung für Branntwein (1979) Eur. Comm.Rep. 649 (German *minimum* alcoholic beverage rule not reasonable).

10. Commission v. Denmark (1988) Eur.Comm.Rep. 4607.

sary prevailed. This was a reasonable restraint on internal trade recognized by the Court under the *Cassis* formula for analyzing compelling state interests. Likewise, a Belgian law prohibiting the importation of general wastes from neighboring countries was found reasonable and not in breach of Community free trade principles.[11]

Under *Cassis*, national rules requiring country of origin or "foreign origin" labels have fallen as measures of effect equivalent to quotas.[12] So have various restrictive national procurement laws, including a "voluntary" campaign to "Buy Irish."[13] Minimum and maximum retail pricing controls can also run afoul of the Court's expansive interpretations.[14] Compulsory patent licensing can amount to a measure of equivalent effect nullified by operation of regional law. The U.K. could not compulsorily require manufacturing within its jurisdiction.[15] Member states may not impose linguistic labelling requirements so as to block trade and competition in foodstuffs. In this instance, a Belgian law requiring Dutch labels in Flemish areas was nullified as in conflict with the Treaty of Rome.[16] These cases vividly illustrate the extent to which litigants are invoking the Treaty of Rome and the *Cassis* formula in attempts at overcoming commercially restrictive national laws.

There are cases which suggest that "cultural interests" may justify national restrictions on European trade. For example, British, French and Belgian bans on Sunday retail trading have survived initial scrutiny under the *Cassis* formula.[17] French legislation prohibiting the sale or rental of cassettes within one year of a film's debut also survived such scrutiny.[18] And British prohibitions of sales of sex articles except by licensed sex shops are compatible.[19] National laws prohibiting sales below cost, when applied without discrimination as between imports and domestic products, are not considered to affect trade between the member states. In this

---

11. Commission v. Belgium (1992) Eur.Comm.Rep. I–4431 (Case C–2/90).

12. Commission v. Ireland (1981) Eur.Comm.Rep. 1625; Commission v. United Kingdom (1985) Eur.Comm.Rep. 1202.

13. Commission v. Ireland (1988) Eur.Comm.Rep. 4929 (product standards); Commission v. Ireland (1982) Eur.Comm.Rep. 4005 (Buy Irish). But see Apple and Pear Development Council (1983) Eur.Comm.Rep. 4083 (permissible promotion of local agricultural products).

14. Re Ricardo Tasca (1976) Eur. Comm.Rep. 291; Openbaar Ministerie v. Van Tiggele (1978) Eur.Comm.Rep. 25.

15. Commission v. United Kingdom (1992) Eur.Comm.Rep. I–0829 (Case C–30/90).

16. Piageme ASBL v. Peeters BVBA (1991) Eur.Comm.Rep. I–2971 (Case C–369/89).

17. Torfaen Borough Council v. B+Q PLC Ltd (1989) Eur.Comm.Rep. 3851; UDS v. Sidef Conforma & Ors (1991) Eur.Comm.Rep. 997 (Case C–312/89); Re Marchandise & Ors (1991) Eur.Comm.Rep. 1027 (Case C–332/89).

18. Cinéthéque SA v. Federation Nationales des Cinémas Francaises (1985) Eur.Comm.Rep. 2605.

19. Quietlynn Ltd. v. Southend Borough Council (1990) 1 Eur.Comm.Rep. 3051.

remarkable decision signaling a jurisprudential retreat, the ECJ ruled that such laws may not be challenged under the traditional *Cassis* formula.[20] Deceptive trade practices laws ordinarily do not amount to "selling arrangements,"[21] but national laws regulating sales outlets[22] and advertising[23] may.

In recent years, member state regulations capable of being characterized as governing "marketing modalities" or "selling arrangements" have sought shelter under *Keck*. For example, the French prohibition of televised advertising (intended to favor printed media) of the distribution of goods escaped the rule of reason analysis of *Cassis* in this manner. Some commentators see in *Keck* and its progeny an unarticulated attempt by the Court to take subsidiarity seriously. Others are just baffled by its newly found tolerance for trade distorting national marketing laws. But the Court of Justice has poignantly refused to extend *Keck* to the marketing of services.

The Court has made it clear that all of the Rule of Reason justifications for national regulatory laws are temporary. Adoption of Common Market legislation in any of these areas would eliminate national authority to regulate trading conditions under *Dassonville, Cassis* and (presumably) *Keck*.[24] These judicial mandates, none of which are specified in the Treaty of Rome, vividly illustrate the powers of the Court of Justice to expansively interpret the Treaty and rule on the validity under European law of national legislation affecting internal trade in goods.

§ 26.5 Article 30 and the Problem of Nontariff Trade Barriers

The provisions of the Treaty of Rome dealing with the establishment of the customs union do not adequately address the problem of nontariff trade barriers NTBs. As in the world community, the major trade barrier within Europe has become NTBs. To some extent, in the absence of a harmonizing directive completely occupying the field,[1] this is authorized. Article 30 (formerly 36) of

20. See Re Keck & Mithouard (1993) Eur.Comm.Rep. 6097 (Cases C–267/91, C–268/91).

21. Verband Sozialer Wettbewerb v. Clinique Laboratories (1994) Eur. Comm.Rep. I–317.

22. Commission v. Greece (1995) Eur.Comm.Rep. I–1621.

23. Societe d'Importation Edouard Leclerc–Siplec v. TFI Publicite (1995) Eur.Comm. I–179. *Compare* Konsumer-tombusmannen (KO) v. Gourmet Inter-

national Products ABS, (GIP) (2001) Eur.Comm.Rep. I–6493.

24. Oberkreisdirektor des Kreises Borken v. Moorman B.V. (1988) Eur. Comm.Rep. 4689.

§ 26.5

1. See Firma Eau de Cologne v. Provide (1989) Eur.Comm.Rep. 3891 and Pubblico Ministero v. Ratti (1979) Eur. Comm.Rep. 1629 (Article 30 preempted by directives). But see Article 95 of the Treaty of Rome regarding internal mar-

the Treaty of Rome permits national restraints on imports and exports justified on the grounds of:

(1) public morality, public policy ("ordre public") or public security;

(2) the protection of health and life of humans, animals or plants;

(3) the protection of national treasures possessing artistic, historical or archeological value[2]; and

(4) the protection of industrial or commercial property.

Article 30 amounts, within certain limits, to an authorization of nontariff trade barriers among the member nations. This "public interest" authorization exists in addition to, but somewhat overlaps with, the Rule of Reason exception formulated in *Dassonville* and *Cassis* above. However, in a sentence much construed by the European Court of Justice, Article 30 continues with the following language: "Such prohibitions or restrictions shall not, however, constitute a means of arbitrary discrimination or a disguised restriction on trade between member states."

Case Law

In a wide range of decisions, the Court of Justice has interpreted Article 30 in a manner which generally limits the ability of member states to impose NTB barriers to internal trade. Britain, for example, may use its criminal law under the public morality exception to seize pornographic goods made in Holland that it outlaws,[3] but not inflatable sex dolls from Germany which could be lawfully produced in the United Kingdom.[4] Germany cannot stop the importation of beer (e.g., Heineken's from Holland) which fails to meet its purity standards.[5] This case makes wonderful reading as the Germans, seeking to invoke the public health exception of Article 30, argue all manner of ills that may befall their populace if free trade in beer is allowed. Equally interesting are the unsuccessful Italian health protection arguments against free trade in pasta

ket directives where member states retain certain Article 30 prerogatives and cases allowing member states to "supplement" directives on the basis of genuine need, including Ministére Public v. Grunert (1980) Eur.Comm.Rep. 1827; In re Motte (1985) Eur.Comm.Rep. 3887; Ministére Public v. Muller (1986) Eur. Comm.Rep. 1511; Ministére Public v. Bellon (1990) Eur.Comm.Rep. 4683.

2. See Council Directive 93/7 securing the right of return of national cultural treasures removed unlawfully after Dec. 31, 1992.

3. Regina v. Henn and Darby (1979) Eur.Comm.Rep. 3795.

4. Conegate Ltd. v. H.M. Customs and Excise (1986) Eur.Comm.Rep. 1007.

5. Commission v. Germany (1987) Eur.Comm.Rep. 1227. But see Aragonesa de Publicidad Exteriro SA (APESA) + Anor v. Departemento de Sanidad y Seguridad Social (1991) Eur.Comm.Rep. 4151 (Cases C–1/90 and C–176/90) (advertising ban applied to strong alcoholic beverages can be justified on public health grounds).

made from common (not durum) wheat.[6] But a state may obtain whatever information it requires from importers to evaluate public health risks associated with food products containing additives that are freely traded elsewhere in the Common Market. This does not mean that an importer of muesli bars to which vitamins have been added must prove the product healthful, rather that the member state seeking to bar the imports must have an objective reason for keeping them out of its market.[7] Assuming such a reason exists, the trade restraint may not be disproportionate to the public health goal.[8] A notable 2002 ECJ opinion invalidated a French public health ban on U.K. beef imports maintained after a Commission decision to return to free trade following the "mad cow" outbreak.[9]

Public security measures adopted under Article 30 can include external as well as internal security. An unusual case under the public security exception contained in Article 30 involved Irish petroleum products' restraints.[10] The Irish argued that oil is an exceptional product always triggering national security interests. Less expansively, the Court acknowledged that maintaining minimum oil supplies did fall within the ambit of Article 30. The public policy exception under Article 30 has been construed along French lines (ordre public). Only genuine threats to fundamental societal interests are covered.[11] Consumer protection (though a legitimate rationale for trade restraints under *Dassonville* and *Cassis*), does not fall within the public policy exception.[12] Permitting environmental protesters to block the Brenner Pass for 30 hours is acceptable public policy in support of fundamental assembly and expression rights.[13]

§ 26.6   Intellectual Property Rights as European Trade Barriers

A truly remarkable body of case law has developed around the authority granted national governments in Article 30 to protect industrial or commercial property by restraining imports and exports. These cases run the full gamut from protection of trademarks and copyrights to protection of patents and knowhow. There

6. Re Drei Glocken GmbH and Criminal Proceedings against Zoni (1988) Eur.Comm.Rep. 4233, 4285.

7. Officer van Justitie v. Sandoz BV (1983) Eur.Comm.Rep. 2245.

8. Commission v. United Kingdom (UHT Milk) (1983) Eur.Comm.Rep. 203.

9. National Farmers' Union v. Secrétariat Général (2002) Eur.Comm.Rep. I–9079.

10. Campus Oil Ltd. v. Minister for Industry and Energy (1984) Eur. Comm.Rep. 2727.

11. See Regina v. Thompson (1978) Eur.Comm.Rep. 2247 (coinage).

12. Kohl KG v. Ringelhan and Rennett SA (1984) Eur.Comm.Rep. 3651.

13. Schmidberger v. Austria (2003) Eur.Comm.Rep. I–5659 (Case C–112/00).

is a close link between this body of case law and that developed under Article 81 concerning restraints on competition.[1]

Trade restraints involving intellectual property arise out of the fact that such rights are nationally granted. Although considerable energy has been spent by the Commission on developing Common Market patents that would provide an alternative to national intellectual property rights, these proposals have yet to be fully implemented. Late in 1993, the Council reached agreement on a Common Market trademark regime. And the Council has adopted Directive 89/104, which seeks to harmonize member state laws governing trademarks. In the copyright field, several directives have harmonized European law, perhaps most importantly on copyrights for computer software (No. 91/250).

Exhaustion Doctrine

The European Court of Justice has addressed the problems under Article 30 and generally resolved against the exercise of national intellectual property rights in ways which inhibit free internal trade. In many of these decisions, the Court acknowledges the existence of the right to block trade in infringing goods, but holds that the *exercise* of that right is subordinate to the Treaty of Rome. The Court has also fashioned a doctrine which treats national intellectual property rights as having been *exhausted* once the goods to which they apply are freely sold on the market. One of the few exceptions to this doctrine is broadcast performing rights which the Court treats as incapable of exhaustion.[2] Records and cassettes embodying such rights are, however, subject to the exhaustion doctrine once released into the market.[3] Such goods often end up in the hands of third parties who then ship them into another member state.

The practical effect of many of the rulings of the Court of Justice is to remove the ability of the owners of the relevant intellectual property rights from successfully pursuing infringement actions in national courts. When intellectual property rights share a common origin and have been placed on goods by consent, as when a licensor authorizes their use in other countries, then infringement actions to protect against trade in the goods to which the rights apply are usually denied. It is only when intellectual property rights do not share a common origin or the requisite consent is absent that they stand a chance of being upheld so as to stop trade

§ 26.6

1. See Chapter 20.

2. See Coditel v. Ciné Vog Films SA (1980) Eur.Comm.Rep. 881; (1982) Eur. Comm.Rep. 3381.

3. Musik–Vertrieb membran Gmbh v. GEMA (1981) Eur.Comm.Rep. 147.

in infringing products.[4] Compulsory licensing of patents, for example, does not involve consensual marketing of products. Patent rights may therefore be used to block trade in goods produced under such a license.[5] But careful repackaging and resale of goods subject to a common trademark may occur against the objections of the owner of the mark.[6]

Centrafarm Case

An excellent example of the application of the judicial doctrine developed by the Court of Justice in the intellectual property field under Article 30 can be found in the *Centrafarm* case.[7] The United States pharmaceutical company, Sterling Drug, owned the British and Dutch patents and trademarks relating to "Negram." Subsidiaries of Sterling Drug in Britain and Holland had been respectively assigned the British and Dutch trademark rights to Negram. Owing in part to price controls in the UK, a substantial difference in cost for Negram emerged as between the two countries. Centrafarm was an independent Dutch importer of Negram from the UK and Germany. Sterling Drug and its subsidiaries brought infringement actions in the Dutch courts under their national patent and trademark rights seeking an injunction against Centrafarm's importation of Negram into The Netherlands.

The Court of Justice held that the intellectual property rights of Sterling Drug and its subsidiaries could not be exercised in a way which blocked trade in "parallel goods." In the Court's view, the exception established in Article 30 for the protection of industrial and commercial property covers only those rights that were specifically intended to be conveyed by the grant of national patents and trademarks. Blocking trade in parallel goods after they have been put on the market with the consent of a common owner, thus exhausting the rights in question, was not intended to be part of the package of benefits conveyed. If Sterling Drug succeeded, an arbitrary discrimination or disguised restriction on Union trade would be achieved in breach of the language which qualifies Article 30. Thus the European Court of Justice ruled in favor of the free movement of goods within the Common Market even when that negates clearly existing national legal remedies.

Only in the unusual situation where the intellectual property rights in question have been acquired by independent proprietors

---

4. See CNL–Sucal v. HAG (1990) Eur.Comm.Rep. 3711 (Case C–10/89) (wartime expropriation of trademark removes common origin).

5. Pharmon BV v. Hoechst AG (1985) Eur.Comm.Rep. 2281.

6. Hoffman–LaRoche & Co. AG v. Centrafarm Vertriebsgesellschaft Phar-

mazeutischer Erzeugnisse mgH (1978) Eur.Comm.Rep. 1132; Pfizer, Inc. v. Eurim–Pharm GmbH (1981) Eur. Comm.Rep. 2913.

7. Centrafarm BV and Adriann de Peipjper v. Sterling Drug Inc. (1974) Eur.Comm.Rep. 1147.

under different national laws may such rights inhibit internal trade.[8] While the goal of creation of the Common Market can override national intellectual property rights when internal trade is concerned, these rights apply fully to the importation of goods from outside the European Union.[9] North American exporters of goods allegedly subject to rights owned by Europeans may therefore find entry into the EU challenged by infringement actions in national courts. This is notably true regarding trade in gray market goods.[10] Levi Strauss successfully cited *Silhouette* to keep low-price (made in the USA) Levi's out of the EU.

§ 26.7   NTBs and the Single Market

Nontariff trade barrier problems were the principal focus of the campaign for a fully integrated Common Market. Many legislative acts have been adopted, or are in progress, which target NTB trade problems. There are basically two different methodologies being employed. When possible, a common European standard is adopted. For example, legislation on auto pollution requirements adopts this methodology. Products meeting these standards may be freely traded in the Common Market. Traditionally, this approach (called "harmonization") has required the formation of a consensus as to the appropriate level of protection.

Once adopted, harmonized standards must be followed. This approach can be deceptive, however. Some harmonization directives contain a list of options from which member states may choose when implementing those directives. In practice, this leads to differentiated national laws on the same so-called harmonized subject. Furthermore, in certain areas (notably the environment and occupational health and safety), the Treaty of Rome expressly indicates that member states may adopt laws that are more demanding. The result is, again, less than complete harmonization.

Harmonization Principles

Many efforts at the harmonization of European environmental, health and safety, standards and certification, and related law have been undertaken. Nearly all of these are supposed to be based upon "high levels of protection."[1] Many have criticized what they see as the "least common denominator" results of harmonization of na-

---

8. See Terrapin (Overseas) Ltd. v. Terranova Industrie CA Kapferer & Co. (1976) Eur.Comm.Rep. 1039; CNL–Sucal v. HAG (1990) Eur.Comm.Rep. 3711 (Case C–10/89).

9. See E.M.I. Records Ltd. v. CBS United Kingdom Ltd. (1976) Eur. Comm.Rep. 811 and Silhouette International v. Hartlauer, No. C–355/96 (July 16, 1998) (graymarket goods).

10. Silhouette International v. Hartlauer (1998) Eur.Comm.Rep. I–4799 (Case C–355/96); Zino Davidoff SA v. A + G Imports Ltd. (2001) Eur. Comm.Rep. I–8691 (Cases C–414/99 to 416/99).

§ 26.7

1. Article 95, Treaty of Rome.

tional laws under the campaign for a Europe without internal frontiers. One example involves the safety of toys. Directive 88/378 permits toys to be sold throughout the Common Market if they satisfy "essential requirements." These requirements are broadly worded in terms of flammability, toxicity, etc. There are two ways to meet these requirements: (1) produce a toy in accordance with CEN standards (drawn up by experts); or (2) produce a toy that otherwise meets the essential safety requirements. Local language labeling requirements necessary for purchaser comprehension have generally, though not always, been upheld.[2]

The least common denominator criticism may be even more appropriate to the second legislative methodology utilized in the internal market campaign. The second approach is based on the *Cassis* principle of mutual reciprocity. Under this "new" minimalist approach, European legislation requires member states to recognize the standards laws of other member states and deem them acceptable for purposes of the operation of the Common Market.[3] However, major legislation has been adopted in the area of professional services.[4] By mutual recognition of higher education diplomas based upon at least three years of courses, virtually all professionals have now obtained legal rights to move freely in pursuit of their careers. This is a remarkable achievement.

§ 26.8   Product Standards and Testing

An important part of the single market campaign against nontariff trade barriers (NTBs) of great interest to international business involves product testing and standards. More than half of the legislation involved in the single market campaign concerned such issues. Since 1969, there has been a standstill agreement among the member states to avoid the introduction of new technical barriers to trade. A 1983 directive requires member states to notify the Commission of proposed new technical regulations and product standards. The Commission can enjoin the introduction of such national rules for up to one year if it believes that a regional standard should be developed.[1] The goal was to move from national regulatory approvals to one unified system embodying essential requirements on health, safety, the environment and consumer protection. Goods that meet these essential requirements bear a "CE mark" and can be freely traded. Manufacturers self-certify

2. *See* Piageme & Orrs v. Peeters (1995) Eur.Comm.Rep. I–2955; Colim v. Bigg's Continent Noord (1999) Eur. Comm.Rep. I–3175.

3. See, e.g., Council Resolution on a New Approach to Technical Harmonization and Standards, 1985 O.J. C136/1.

4. See Council Directives, 89/48, 92/51.

§ 26.8

1. Council Directive 83/169.

their compliance with relevant European standards. Design and production process standards generally follow the ISO 9000 series on quality management and assurance. Firms must maintain a technical file documenting compliance and produce the file upon request by national authorities.

Standards Bodies

Private regional standards bodies have been playing a critical role in the development of this system. These include the European Committee for Standardization (CEN), the European Committee for Electrotechnical Standardization (CENELEC), and the European Telecommunications Standards Institute (ETSI). Groups like these have been officially delegated the responsibility for creating thousands of technical product standards. They have been turning out some 150 common standards each year. For example, directives on the safety of toys, construction products and electromagnetic compatibility have been issued.[2] These directives adopt the so-called "new approach" of setting broad standards at the regional level which if met guarantee access to every member state market. Under the "old approach", which still applies to most standards for processed foods, motor vehicles, chemicals and pharmaceuticals, European legislation on standards is binding law. The technical specifications and testing protocols of these directives must be followed and (unlike the new approach) the member states may add requirements to them. Under either approach, goods meeting these standards will bear a CE mark. North American producers have frequently complained that their ability to be heard by European standards' bodies is limited. They have had little influence on product standards to which they must conform in order to sell freely in the Common Market.

Testing and Certification

Testing and certification of products has been another part of the single market campaign. The main concern of North American companies is that recognition be granted of U.S., Canadian and Mexican tests. In the past, many North American exporters have had to have their goods retested for European purposes. The EU is generally committed to a resolution of such issues under what it calls a "global approach" to product standards and testing. This involves creation of a regional system for authorizing certification and testing under common rules and procedures.[3] In negotiations undertaken as part of the Uruguay Round on revising the Standards Code of the GATT, the EU indicated its commitment to giving recognition to "equivalent technical regulations" of other nations, and to avoidance of unnecessary obstacles to trade. The

2. See Council Directives 88/378, 89/106 and 89/336.

3. Council Resolution Dec. 21, 1989, O.J. C10 (Jan. 16, 1990).

Transatlantic Partnership dialogue between Europe and the United States has successfully achieved mutual recognition on a range of product standards and testing.

§ 26.9 Freedom to Provide and Receive Services Across European Borders

The freedom of nonresidents to provide services within other parts of the Common Market is another part of the foundations of the Treaty of Rome.[1] The freedom to provide services (including tourism) implies a right to receive and pay for them by going to the country of their source.[2] Industrial, commercial, craft and professional services are included within this right, which is usually not dependent upon establishment in the country where the service is rendered.[3] In other words, the freedom to provide or receive services across borders entails a limited right of temporary entry into another member state.

The Council has adopted a general program for the abolition of national restrictions on the freedom to provide services across borders. This freedom is subject to the same public policy, public security and public health exceptions applied to workers and the self-employed.[4] The Council's program has slowly been implemented by a series of legislative acts applicable to professional and nonprofessional services. As with the right of self-establishment, discrimination based upon the nationality or nonresidence of the service provider is generally prohibited even if no implementing law has been adopted.[5] However, in parallel with law developed in connection with the free movement of goods, the Court of Justice in *van Binsbergen* indicated that member governments may require providers of services from other states to adhere to professional public interest rules. These rules must be applied equally to all professionals operating in the nation, and only if necessary to ensure that the out-of-state professional does not escape them by reason of establishment elsewhere.

§ 26.9

1. Articles 49 and 50, Treaty of Rome.

2. Luisi and Carbone v. Ministero del Tesoro (1984) Eur.Comm.Rep. 377; Cowan v. Le Tresor Public (1986) Eur. Comm.Rep. 195 (British tourist entitled to French criminal injury compensation).

3. Commission v. Germany (1986) Eur.Comm.Rep. 3755; Ministère Public

v. van Wasemael (1979) Eur.Comm.Rep. 35 (employment agencies).

4. Article 55, Treaty of Rome.

5. Van Binsbergen v. Bestuur van de Bedrijfsvereniging voor de Metaalnijverheid (1974) Eur.Comm.Rep. 1299 (legal representation); Coenen v. Sociaal Economische Raad (1975) Eur.Comm.Rep. 1547 (insurance intermediary).

Financial Services

In other words, if the professional rules (e.g., ethics) of the country in which the service provider is established are equivalent, then application of the rules of the country where the service is provided does not follow. Following *Cassis,* and notably not *Keck,* the Court of Justice has affirmed member state marketing controls over the sale of lottery tickets (social policy and fraud interests) and over "cold calling" solicitations for commodities futures. Telemarketing in most other areas is forbidden, except with prior consumer consent, under a 1977 directive.

Bankers, investment advisors and insurance companies have long awaited the arrival of a truly common market. Their right of establishment in other member states has existed for some time. The right to provide services across borders without establishing local subsidiaries was forcefully reaffirmed by the Court of Justice in 1986.[6] This decision largely rejected a requirement that all insurers servicing the German market be located and established there.

Legislative initiatives undertaken in connection with the single market campaign promise to create genuinely competitive cross-border European markets for banking, investment and insurance services. Licensing of insurance and investment service companies and banks meeting minimum capital, solvency ratio and other requirements as implemented in member state law is done on a "one-stop" home country basis. Banks, for example, cannot maintain individual equity positions in non-financial entities in excess of 15 percent of their capital funds, and the total value of such holdings cannot exceed 50 percent of those funds.[7] They can participate and service securities transactions and issues, financial leasing and trade for their own accounts. The proposed investment services directive requires home country supervision of the "good repute" and "suitability" of managers and controlling shareholders.

Member states must ordinarily recognize home country licenses and the principle of home country control. For example, Council Directive 89/646 ("the Second Banking Directive") employs the home country single license procedure to liberalize banking services throughout the region. However, host states retain the right to regulate a bank's liquidity and supervise it through monetary policy and in the name of the "general good." Similarly, no additional insurance permits or requirements may be imposed by host countries when large industrial risks (sophisticated purchasers) are involved. However, when the public at large is concerned (general risk), host country rules still apply.[8] Major auto and life insurance

---

6. Commission v. Germany (1986) Eur.Comm.Rep. 3755.

7. Council Directive 89/646.

8. Council Directive 88/357 ("the Second Non–Life Insurance Directive").

directives employing one-stop licensing principles were adopted in 1990.[9] The auto insurance directive reproduces the large versus general risk distinctions found in the Second Non–Life Insurance Directive. Host country controls over general risk auto insurance policies were retained until 1995. Host country permits are also required when life insurers from other member states actively solicit business.

Reciprocity and the United States

There was a rush by non-member state bankers, investment advisors and insurers to get established before January 1, 1993 in order to qualify for home country licenses. North Americans and others have been particularly concerned about certain features of the legislation mandating effective access in foreign markets for European companies before outsiders may benefit from the liberalization of services within the Common Market. This problem is generally referred to as the "reciprocity requirement." It is this kind of requirement that gave the campaign for a Europe without internal frontiers the stigma of increasing the degree of external trade barriers. Many outsiders, in rhetoric which sometimes seems excessive, refer to the development of a "Fortress Europe" mentality and threat to world trading relations.

Since state and federal laws governing banking, investment services and insurance are restrictive, and in no sense can it be said that one license permits a company to operate throughout the United States, one result of European integration has arguably been reform of United States regulatory legislation. Since 1994, the U.S. has noticeably relaxed its rules on interstate banking and largely repealed the Depression-era Glass–Steagall Act limitations on universal banking.

§ 26.10 Equal Pay and Equal Treatment (Comparable Worth)

Article 141 (formerly 119) is probably the most prominent element in European social policy. It is derived from International Labor Organization Convention No. 100 which three states, including France, had adopted by 1957. The French were rightfully proud of this tradition of nondiscrimination between the sexes on pay. They also appreciated that gender-based inequality in pay in other member states could harm the ability of their companies to compete. Article 141 thus enshrines the principle that men and women shall receive equal pay for equal work, a rough equivalent to what is termed "comparable worth" in the United States and a brave new world for investors in Europe.

9. Council Directives 90/619 (life insurance) and 90/618 (auto insurance).

Equal Pay, Comparable Worth

Article 141 has been the subject of voluminous legislation and litigation. It applies, quite appropriately, to the European Community as an employer.[1] Early on, the Court of Justice decided that the Article 141 on equal pay for equal work is directly effective law.[2] This decision allows individuals to challenge pay discrimination in public and private sector jobs. The ruling was applied prospectively by the Court of Justice so as to avoid large numbers of lawsuits for back pay.

In *Defrenne,* a flight attendant for Sabena Airlines was able to allege illegal discrimination in pay and pension benefits (as a form of deferred pay) to stewards and stewardesses on the basis of Article 141 law before a Belgian work tribunal. European law in this area enshrines the principle of "comparable worth," a most controversial issue in United States employment law. Furthermore, women who are paid less than men performing work of less worth may claim relief.[3] The hard questions are how to determine what constitutes "equal work" requiring equal pay under Article 141 or what "women's work" is worth more than that being done by men (again requiring pay adjustments). For example, does secretarial work equal custodial work? Is the work of an airline attendant worth more than that of an airline mechanic? What about speech therapists (mostly women) and pharmacists (mostly men).[4]

Council Directive 75/117 complements Article 141. It makes the principle of equal pay apply to work of *equal value* (to the employer). This mandates establishment of nondiscriminatory job classifications to measure the comparable worth of one job with another. The Commission successfully enforced Directive 75/117 in a prosecution before the European Court of Justice against the United Kingdom. The Sex Discrimination Act of 1975, adopted expressly to fulfill Article 141 obligations, did not meet European standards because employers could block the introduction of job classification systems.[5] Danish law's failure to cover nonunionized workers also breached the equal pay directive.[6] But its implementation under German law, notably by constitutional provisions, sufficed to meet regional standards.[7]

§ 26.10

1. Sabbatini, née Bertoni v. European Parliament (1972) Eur.Comm.Rep. 345; Razzouk v. Commission (1984) Eur. Comm.Rep. 1509 (working conditions).

2. Defrenne v. Sabena (1976) Eur. Comm.Rep. 455.

3. Murphy v. An Bord Telecom Eireann (1988) Eur.Comm.Rep. 673.

4. *See* Enderby v. Frenchay Health Authority (1993) Eur.Comm.Rep. I–5535.

5. Commission v. United Kingdom (1982) Eur.Comm.Rep. 2601.

6. Commission v. Denmark (1986) 1 Common Mkt.L.Rep. 44.

7. Commission v. Germany (1986) 2 Common Mkt.L.Rep. 588.

In determining equal or greater values, most states favor a job content approach. Content is determined through job evaluation systems which use factor analysis. For example, in Great Britain a job is broken down into various components such as skill, responsibility, physical requirements, mental requirements, and working conditions. Points or grades are awarded in each of these categories and totaled to determine the value of the job. Different factors may be balanced against each other. In Ireland, the demand of physical work can be balanced against the concentration required in particular skills. This is known as the "total package" approach. The equal job content approach relies on comparisons. This raises the question of which jobs should be deemed to be suitable for comparison. The member states have taken different approaches to this question. In Britain the comparison must be drawn from the same business establishment. In contrast, the Irish Anti–Discrimination Pay Act provides for "comparisons in the same place," and "place" includes a city, town or locality. This approach is designed to ensure that legitimate regional differences in pay are not disturbed.

Defenses

Employer defenses also vary from member state to member state. In Ireland, employers may justify a variation if they can show "grounds other than sex" for a disputed variation in pay. In Britain, employers will succeed if they can prove a "genuine material factor which is not the difference of sex." In Germany, the employer can prove that "material reasons unrelated to a particular sex" justify the differential. A further consideration in the implementation of equal pay laws has been the existence of pre-existing wage schedules set by collective agreement. In Britain and Italy, courts have held that collective agreements relating to pay cannot be changed or altered except where direct discrimination can be shown.

The burden of proving "objectively justified economic grounds" to warrant pay differentials is on the employer.[8] When a woman succeeds a man in a particular position within a company (here a warehouse manager), she is entitled to equal pay absent a satisfactory explanation not based upon gender.[9] The same is true of part-time (female) workers doing the same job as full-time (male) workers.[10] Free travel to railway employees upon retirement cannot go only to men.[11] And "pay" includes retirement benefits paid upon involuntary dismissal, which cannot be discriminatory.[12] But a

---

8. Council Directive 97/80.

9. McCarthays Ltd. v. Smith (1980) Eur.Comm.Rep. 1275.

10. Jenkins v. Kingsgate (Clothing Productions) Ltd. (1981) Eur. Comm.Rep. 911.

11. Garland v. British Rail Engineering, Ltd. (1982) Eur.Comm.Rep. 359.

12. Barber v. The Guardian Royal Exchange Assurance Group (1990) 1 Eur.Comm.Rep. 1889.

protocol adopted at the 1991 Maastricht Summit makes this ruling prospective only. Pay also includes employer-paid pension benefits which cannot be for men only.[13] In this decision the Court refused to remove the retroactive effect of its judgment suggesting that *Defrenne* was adequate notice of the direct effect of Article 141 upon employers. Mobility, special training and seniority may be objectively justifiable grounds for pay discrimination.[14]

Equal Treatment

The principle of equal pay for equal work has been extended by Council Directive to *equal treatment* regarding access to employment, vocational training, promotions, and working conditions (e.g. retirement deadlines).[15] This directive prohibits discrimination based upon sex, family or marital status. The Equal Treatment Directive is limited by three exceptions. Member states may distinguish between men and women if: (1) sex is a determining factor in ability to perform the work; (2) the provision protects women; or (3) the provision promotes equal opportunity for men and women. Equal treatment must be extended to small and household businesses.[16] Dutch Law compulsorily retiring women at age 60 and men at age 65 violated the directive.[17] Women cannot be refused employment because they are pregnant even if the employer will suffer financial losses during maternity leave.[18] Maternity and adoption leave benefits for women, however, need not be extended to men.[19] The dismissal of a woman because of repeated absences owing to sickness is lawful provided the same absences would lead to the dismissal of men.[20] General prohibitions against night work by women but not men violate equal treatment Directive 76/207. The French government failed to justify this criminal law on any special grounds.[21]

Equality also governs social security entitlements[22] such as disability or caring for the disabled pay.[23] Social security benefits

---

13. Worringham and Humphreys v. Lloyds Bank Ltd. (1981) Eur.Comm.Rep. 767.

14. Union of Commercial and Clerical Employees v. Danish Employers Assn *ex parte* Danfoss, 1989 Eur. Comm.Rep. 3199.

15. Council Directive 76/207 (issued under Article 235).

16. Commission v. United Kingdom (1983) Eur.Comm.Rep. 3431.

17. Beets–Proper v. Van Lanschot Bankiers NV (1986) Eur.Comm.Rep. 773. See Council Directive 86/378 (equal treatment regarding pensions).

18. Dekker v. Stichting Vormingscentrum voor Jong Volwassenen Plus

(1990) Eur.Comm.Rep. 3941 (Case C–177–88).

19. Hoffmann v. Barmer Ersatzkasse (1984) Eur.Comm.Rep. 3047; Commission v. Italy (1983) Eur.Comm.Rep. 3273 (adoption leave benefits).

20. Hertz and Aldi Marked (1990) Eur.Comm.Rep. 3979 (Case C–179/88).

21. Ministère Public v. Stoeckel (1991) Eur.Comm.Rep. 4047 (Case C–345–89).

22. Council Directive 79/7. An important exception allows state pension schemes to retain different retirement ages for men and women. See Regina v. Secretary of State for Social Security (1992) Eur.Comm.Rep. 4297 (Case C–

23. See note 23 on page 627.

cannot be based upon marital status.[24] Women police officers cannot be denied arms when men are not, even in the interest of "public safety" and "national security."[25] Equal treatment requires the elimination of preferences based upon gender in laws governing collectively bargained employment agreements.[26] The Council adopted a declaration in December 1991 endorsing the Commission's recommended Code of Practice on sexual harassment. This Code rejects sexual harassment as contrary to equal treatment law, specifically Council Directive 76/207. But the equal pay and equal treatment directives fail to cover significant categories of women workers; part-time, temporary and home workers.[27] Additional legislation in these areas can be expected.

Although Article 141 on equal pay is directly effective law binding upon public and private employers, it is not yet clear to what degree the equal treatment directives discussed above have that effect. Clearly these directives are binding on the member states and public corporations as employers.[28] The private sector must comply after national implementing legislation is adopted, but if that legislation is deficient the only remedy is a prosecution of the member state by the Commission.[29] There is a trend within the jurisprudence of the Court of Justice towards recognition of a broad human right of equality before the law. This is evidenced in a number of Article 141 cases, which suggests that the private sector will eventually be bound by all European legislation on equal pay and equal treatment even in the absence of or in spite of national implementing law.

Affirmative Action

Predictably, questions of "affirmative action" have arisen in the context of Article 141 law. A controversial decision of the Court of Justice invalidated a Bremen regulation giving women of equal

9/91) and Article 7(1)(a) of Directive 79/7. But severe disablement allowances (SDA) and invalid care cannot be provided on the basis of different ages. Secretary of State for Social Security v. Thomas (1993) Eur.Comm.Rep. 4297 (Case C–328/91).

23. Drake v. Chief Adjudication Officer (1986) Eur.Comm.Rep. 1995.

24. Id.

25. Johnston v. Chief Constable (1986) Eur.Comm.Rep. 1651. See generally Articles 223–225, Treaty of Rome.

26. Commission v. France (1988) Eur.Comm.Rep. 6315 (Case 312/86) (preferences for women must be removed).

27. See Jenkins v. Kingsgate Ltd. (1981) Eur.Comm.Rep. 911 (part-time workers paid less, and though largely female, no EC law violation). Compare Bilka–Kaufhaus v. Weber 1986–2 Common Mkt.L.Rep. 701.

28. See especially Marshall v. Southampton and South–West Hampshire Area Health Authority (Teaching) (1986) Eur.Comm.Rep. 723 (discriminatory retirement ages unlawful); Foster v. British Gas (1990) Eur.Comm.Rep. 3313 (Case 188/89).

29. See Duke v. GEC Reliance Ltd. (1988) 1 All Eng.Rep. 626 (discriminatory retirement ages lawful).

qualifications priority over men where women made up less than half the relevant civil service staff. While not strictly a quota, the Court found that Bremen had exceeded the limits of the equal treatment directive in promoting equality of opportunity.[30] Article 141(4) of Treaty of Rome, as amended by the Amsterdam Treaty in 1999, attempts to address such issues. It allows member states to maintain or adopt "measures for specific advantages" in order to make it "easier" for the "under represented sex" to pursue vocational activity or to prevent or compensate for "disadvantages" in professional careers. Specific reservation of University professorships for women in Sweden likewise fell upon ECJ review.[31] Sweden now uses increasing targets for women in full professorships.

Gender and Other Discrimination

Although Article 141 on equal pay is directly effective law binding upon public and private employers throughout the Union (*Defrenne*), it is not yet clear to what degree the equal treatment directives cited above have that effect. Clearly these directives are binding on the member states and public corporations as employers.[32] The private sector must comply after national implementing legislation is adopted, but if that legislation is deficient the only remedy may be prosecution of the member state by the Commission.[33] There is a trend within the jurisprudence of the Court of Justice towards recognition of a broad human right of equality before the law. This is evidenced in a number of Article 141 cases, reliance upon the European Human Rights Convention in developing general principles of EU law,[34] and in revised Articles 2, 3 and 13 of the Treaty of Rome (1999), which suggests that the private sector will eventually be bound by all European Union legislation on equal pay and equal treatment even in the absence of or in spite of national implementing law.[35]

Transsexuals[36] and homosexuals have begun to benefit from this trend. But the Court notably refused to require equal employer travel benefits for same sex partners under Article 141 law,[37] and

---

30. Kalanke v. Freie Hansestadt Bremen (1995) Eur.Comm.Rep. I–3051.

31. Abrahamsson and Anderson v. Fogelgvist (2000) Eur.Comm.Rep. I–5539.

32. *See especially* Marshall v. Southampton and South–West Hampshire Area Health Authority (Teaching) (1986) Eur.Comm.Rep. 723 (discriminatory retirement ages unlawful); Foster v. British Gas (1990) 1 Eur.Comm.Rep. 3313.

33. *See* Duke v. GEC Reliance Ltd. (1988) 1 All Eng.Rep. 626 (discriminatory retirement ages lawful).

34. *See* Section 2.12.

35. *See* Section 3.1 (discussion of duty of national courts to interpret national law in furtherance of EU directives).

36. P. v. S. (1996) Eur.Comm.Rep. I–2143; K.B. v. National Health Services Pensions Agency (2004) Eur.Comm.Rep. I–00000 (Case No. C–117/01).

37. Grant v. South–West Trains Ltd. (1998) Eur.Comm.Rep. I–621.

likewise the Court of First Instance refused to recognize homosexual partnerships as the equivalent of marriage for household allowance purposes.[38] Revisions of the 1976 equal treatment directive emphasizing an approach called "gender mainstreaming" are in progress. Directive 2000/43 broadly provides for equal treatment irrespective of racial or ethnic origin. Directive 2000/78 more narrowly prohibits employment discrimination on grounds of religion or belief, disability, age or sexual orientation.

§ 26.11 Social Policy—Occupational Safety, the Social Fund and Social Charter

Investors in the European Union encounter a host of "social policy" regulations. The Treaty of Rome is dominated by economic affairs. Nevertheless, Europe has always sought to provide for some of the concerns of the human beings who are impacted by the winds of economic change. The Treaty of Rome seeks to improve working conditions and standards of living on a harmonized basis. The right of nationals to move freely to take up employment has been solidified. Europe's social policy builds upon this basic right. Article 144, for example, led to the enactment of social security legislation to insure coverage for those who exercise their right to move freely to work.

A major impetus came in 1987 with the addition of Article 138 (formerly 118a) by the Single European Act. This article focuses on health and safety in the working environment. Acting by a qualified majority vote, the Council in cooperation with the Parliament is empowered to issue directives establishing minimum requirements in this field. It has done so, for example, on visual display units, heavy load handling and exposure to biological agents and carcinogens. More generally, Council directives now establish minimum safety and health requirements for most workplaces, equipment used by workers, and protective devices. Article 138 specifically requires such directives to avoid imposing administrative, financial and legal constraints that would hold back the creation and development of small and medium-sized enterprises. Like the 1987 Treaty amendments creating the Environmental Policy, Article 138 allows member states to maintain or introduce more stringent legal rules on working conditions, provided these are compatible with the Treaty of Rome.

The European Social Fund comes out of the regional budget. It is used to pay up to 50 percent of the costs of the member states under their vocational retraining and worker resettlement pro-

---

38. *See* D. and Sweden v. Council (2001) Eur.Comm.Rep. I–04319 (May 31, 2001).

grams. European rules have substantially harmonized these programs. Unemployment compensation is also funded when plants are converted to other production for workers who are temporarily suspended or suffer a reduction in working hours. They retain the same wage levels pending full re-employment. Commission Decision 83/516 extended the operation of the European Social Fund to promoting employment among those under age 25, women who wish to return to work, the handicapped, migrants and their families, and the long-term unemployed.

Social Charter

The single market campaign has a social dimension. Labor unions have been especially concerned about the prospect of "social dumping," the relocation of companies to states with weaker unions and lower wages. There is no regional legislation on minimum wages and none is expected in the near future. One response to these concerns led to the Charter of Fundamental Social Rights For Workers, adopted in 1989 by 11 member states less Britain through the European Council. The Charter proclaims the following fundamental social rights for workers:

(1) freedom of movement and choice of occupations;

(2) fair remuneration (sufficient to have a decent standard of living);

(3) improved living and working conditions (e.g., paid leave);

(4) adequate social security benefits;

(5) free association in unions, including the right *not* to join, and the right to strike;

(6) nondiscriminatory access to vocational training;

(7) equal treatment for women and men;

(8) development of rights to access to information, and rights of consultation and participation;

(9) satisfactory health and safety conditions at work;

(10) for the young, a minimum employment age of 15, substantial limitations on night work for those under 18, and start-up vocational training rights;

(11) for retirees, the right to assistance "as needed" and a decent standard of living; and

(12) for the disabled, assistance to integrate socially and professionally.

The Charter was to be implemented immediately by the member states in "accordance with national practices." In addition, for each item listed above, regional legislation was anticipated.

Adoption of this legislation was slow chiefly because Britain held a veto power in the Council over employment matters under the Single European Act. The Commission, however, drafted a number of Social Action Program legislative measures. One such measure guaranteeing minimum maternity leave benefits of 14 weeks at statutory sick pay rates was adopted by the Council in 1992. A woman's employment cannot be terminated because she is pregnant. In addition, pregnant women are entitled to switch from night work, exempted from work detrimental to their health, and entitled to take paid leave for pre-natal check-ups. This directive required substantial improvements to existing legislation in Ireland, Portugal and the United Kingdom.

Social Protocol and Policy

In December 1991 at the Maastricht Summit agreement was reached, save Britain, on a "social policy protocol" facilitating adoption by the other eleven member states of laws by qualified majority vote governing many areas which bridge workers' interests and company operations. Some suggested that the "social protocol" would have been more accurately labeled a "workers' rights protocol". It focused on working environment issues including conditions of labor, health and safety, disclosure of information, sex discrimination, and worker consultation. The "social protocol" thus overlapped considerably with the Social Charter.

Despite its repeated opposition to development of a "social dimension," the United Kingdom under Conservative rule adopted or implemented over half of the measures noted in the Social Charter. What the Conservatives consistently objected to were rules relating directly to the employee-employer relationship, not worker benefits such as pregnancy leave or health or safety measures. Nevertheless, the Court of Justice repeatedly ruled against Britain in litigation challenging the adequacy of its implementation of worker-related directives (e.g., on collective redundancies and transfers of enterprises). And, in a major decision, the Court ruled over vehement objection that the "working time" directive (No. 93/104) was properly adopted by qualified majority vote on the basis of Article 138's authorization of worker health and safety law.[1] This ruling had the practical effect of avoiding Britains's Social Protocol opt out rights. The directive creates, inter alia, a minimum right to four weeks of paid vacation. The United Kingdom under the Labour Party administration of Prime Minister Blair has since opted into the EU's Social Policy.

§ 26.11

1. United Kingdom v. Council (1996) Eur.Comm.Rep. I–5755.

As amended, Articles 136–145 of the Treaty of Rome (the "social chapter") embrace social goals reflecting the Social Charter. There is express authority for EU legislation on worker health and safety, work conditions, information and consultation of workers, and gender equality, mostly using qualified majority voting and co-decision Parliamentary powers. However, there is no authorization for EU action on matters of pay, and rights of association, strike and lock-out. EU legislation can occur by unanimous vote on social security, co-determination, worker protection upon termination, and employment of third country nationals.

§ 26.12   Company Law, European Companies

Article 293 of the Treaty of Rome obliges member states to enter into negotiations with each other about equal protection of citizens, abolition of double taxation, mutual recognition of firms and companies, the possibility of international mergers, and simplification of enforcement of judgments. Article 293 was the backdrop against which member states signed in 1968 a Convention on Mutual Recognition of Companies and Other Bodies Corporate. This Convention sought to ensure that Treaty benefits extend to such legal personae. Unfortunately, it never achieved full ratification by the member states. Article 43 on the right of establishment entitles companies based in one member state to set up agencies, branches or subsidiaries in other member states, even when this avoids paid-in capital requirements.[1] In the absence of an EU convention on legal personalities, nothing in the right of establishment permits a company to freely transfer its place of incorporation (seat) and administrative center to another member state without home state permission where that is required. In this case, the British Daily Mail newspaper sought to change to Dutch citizenship to take advantage of lower taxes.[2]

However, two decisions of the European Court of Justice, *Überseering*[3] and *Inspire Art*,[4] hold that a company formed under the laws of one member state of the European Union may move or establish its entire operations to or in any other member state. The other member state may not impose any restrictions on or deny the legal capacity of such a company even if there is no connection to the member state in which it was formed other than statutory registration. The Court explicitly clarified that it does not constitute an abuse of the principle of freedom of establishment if the

§ 26.12

1. Centros v. Erhvervs–OG Selskabsstyrelsen (1999) Eur.Comm.Rep. II–1459.

2. Re Daily Mail (1988) Eur. Comm.Rep. 5483.

3. Uberseering BV v. NCC Nordie Construction Co. (2002) Eur.Comm.Rep. I–9919.

4. (2003) Eur.Comm.Rep. 0000 (Sept. 30, 2003) (Case 167/01).

purpose is to circumvent the application of the stricter company laws of the member state in which the company is operating through its branch by forming the company in another member state with more liberal laws. It further stated that all questions relating to the company's status (liability of limited partners and managing directors, capital requirements, etc.) must be governed by the law of incorporation of the company. It is widely thought that these decisions will avoid restrictive Germany company law rules by, for example as in *Uberseering*, incorporation in the Netherlands.

Company Law Directives

The Council has adopted a number of non-controversial coordination directives under Article 44 advancing Union company law. These in theory seek to avoid the race to the bottom problems associated with Delaware corporate law in the United States. The first directive sets out requirements for disclosure, validity and nullity of share capital companies. The ECJ has ruled that the listing of grounds for nullifying the formation of a company found in the First Company Law Directive 68/151 exhausts all such possibilities. Grounds for nullification based upon the Spanish Civil Code requirement of "causa" could not be utilized since that Code must be construed in conformity with Directive 68/151.[5] The second deals with the classification, subscription and maintenance of capital of public and large companies.[6] Increases in share capital must be approved by company shareholders with preemptive rights preserved. This obligation is derived from Article 25 of the Second Company Law Directive, which has direct effect in Union law.[7] Companies are generally forbidden from acquiring their own shares. Governmental acts authorizing increases in company capital to ensure survival which prejudice the preemptive rights of shareholders are impermissible under Directive 77/91.[8] The Second Company Law Directive was amended in late 1992 to close a loophole by prohibiting parent companies from buying through subsidiaries more than 10 percent of their own shares when faced with hostile takeovers.[9]

---

5. Marleasing SA v. La Comercial Internacional de Alimentación SA. (1990) 1 Eur.Comm.Rep. 4135. Regarding the first directive, *see also* Daihatsu Handler v. Daihatsu Deutschland (1997) Eur. Comm.Rep. II–6843; Commission v. Germany (1998) Eur.Comm.Rep. II–5449.

6. Karella & Anor v. Greek Minister for Industry, Energy and Technology (1991) Eur.Comm.Rep. I–2691 (Cases C–19 and C–20/90).

7. *Id.* Regarding the second directive, *see also* Siemens v. Nold (1996) Eur.Comm.Rep. I–6017; Pafitis v. Trapeza Kentrikis Ellados (1996) Eur. Comm.Rep. I–1347.

8. Kerafina–Keramische und Finanz Holding AG & Anor v. Hellenic Republic (1992) Eur.Comm.Rep.I–5699 (Cases C–234/91, C–135/91).

9. *See* Council Directive 92/101.

The Third Company Law Directive concerns the internal merger of public companies. Modern procedures for mergers with related and unrelated companies are established. Asset and liability acquisitions and new company formations are allowed. Shareholder rights are specified. The sixth directive governs sales of assets of public companies, including certain shareholder, creditor and workers' rights. The fourth standardizes the treatment of annual accounts (*e.g.*, in their presentation, content, valuation and publication). It requires public presentation of a "true and fair view" of company assets, liabilities, finances, profits and losses. Small and medium-sized firms can publish abridged accounts. All companies must present comparable figures for the preceding year. Valuation of assets and liabilities must be prudent, consistent and reflect the company as a going concern. The fourth directive even details the notes that must accompany annual accounts. In addition, shareholders must be given a report by management annually on the development of the business, future plans, research activities and company purchases of its own shares. There is a permissive provision relating to inflation or current cost accounting. There is some doubt about the degree of relation to similar requirements of the United Kingdom accounting bodies or "generally accepted accounting practices" in the United States. Directive 2001/65 spells out "fair value" accounting rules, notably for derivatives. Regulation 1606/2002 mandated use of International Accounting Standards by publicly traded companies.

The Sixth Company Law Directive adopted in 1982 complements the third directive and addresses the division or "scission" of public limited companies, where they wind up without liquidation. The seventh concerns requirements for consolidated accounts of groups of companies. Consolidated accounts must follow the rules of the fourth directive as supplemented by the seventh. Consolidated accounts are required if an EU firm has legal or *de facto* control over other companies through majority shareholdings, appointment or removal power over management in a subsidiary, the right to exercise dominant influence, or the possibility of shareholder agreements conveying majority voting rights. Consolidated accounts must treat the group as a single enterprise regarding transactions among the companies. The Eighth Company Law Directive provides certain minimum standards and qualifications for auditors of company accounts.

Works Councils

Several controversial proposals for company law directives are in varying stages of evolution. These include a fifth directive on company structure and administration which has been long delayed due to differing views about the functions of single and two-tier boards of directors and officers, and worker representation at these levels. Another controversial topic (the "Vredeling proposal") would have required substantial information sharing between companies and their employees. The 1994 "works council" Directive 94/45 requires councils in companies with more than 1000 employees operating with 150 employees in at least two member states. Workers must be given information on and an opportunity to respond to a broad range of topics including the firm's economic and financial situation, employment, work methods and mergers and layoffs. But the information can be withheld when disclosure might "seriously harm" the functioning of the company or be "prejudicial" to it. Thousands of works councils now operate with little controversy. The European Court of Justice has held Directive 94/45 applies to parent companies located outside the EU.[10]

Other less controversial directives are also planned. The ninth directive concerns liability on the part of parent companies for the debts of subsidiaries they effectively control. The tenth directive deals with cross-border company mergers. The eleventh (adopted in 1989) involves disclosure by branches operating in other EU states, and the twelfth (also adopted in 1989) affects single member private limited liability companies. Hostile takeovers, a sensitive area, are the subject of the thirteenth proposed company law directive. This directive would require equal treatment of shareholders and specify permissible defensive measures, and was denied in 2001 by a tie vote in Parliament.

European Companies

An amended proposal for a European Company was submitted by the Commission to the Council in August 1989. Nineteen years had passed since the submission of the first proposal in 1970, and 14 years since the last amended proposal in 1975. In that period, considerable harmonization had been accomplished by way of directives. Finally, late in 2001, a European Company Statute was finalized, taking effect in 2004. Forming a European Company ("Societas Europeae" or SE) is optional. An SE operates on a European-wide basis governed by EU law. A regulation establishes its company law rules, while a directive covers worker involvement in SE. Under the Statute, an SE registered in one member state can freely move its registered office to another. SEs may be privately or publicly traded companies. SE, at least in theory, will remove the need for costly networks of subsidiaries throughout the European Union. Large legal and administrative cost savings are expected to be realized. SE must be registered in the member state where it has its administrative head office, and the Statute does not significantly alter applicable taxation.

---

10. Gesamtbetriebsrat der Kühne + Nagel AG + Co. KG v. Kühne + Nagel AG + Co. KG (2004) Eur.Comm.Rep. I–00000 (Case 440/00).

Regarding worker participation, the issue that held up the SE proposal for over 30 years, the first duty is to try negotiate agreement on employee involvement. Failing that, Standard Principles attached to the directive require regular reports, consultation and information exchange between management and worker representatives. Such reports must detail business plans, production and sales, management changes, mergers, divestments, potential closures and layoffs, and the implications of all this to workers. In the case of a European Company created by merger, the Standard Principles apply when at least 25 percent of the employees had the right to participate before the merger. However, member states need *not* implement the directive on participation for SEs created by mergers, but if so the SE can be registered only if an agreement with the employees is reached, or when no employees were covered by participation rules before the SE was created.

§ 26.13 Early Law on Mergers and Acquisitions

One alternative to direct investment in Europe is to purchase an existing business. Traditionally, the law governing such acquisitions was almost exclusively national. Since 1990, the EU actively regulates sizeable mergers and acquisitions as part of its competition policy. European law in this area is summarized below. Special attention should also be paid to the United States–European Community Antitrust Cooperation Agreement (1991) under which coordinated exchanges of information and review of transnational mergers occur. This Agreement is reviewed in Chapter 20.

In 1965 the Commission announced in a memorandum to the member states that concentration ought to be encouraged to achieve efficiency and economies of scale, and to combat competition from large United States and Japanese multinational firms. These rationales have supported a long line of merger approvals by the Commission under its coal and steel concentration controls. It was not until a European merger boom was in progress and extensive studies revealed increasing trends toward industrial concentration that the Commission took action against a merger in *Continental Can*.[1]

The Commission decided Continental Can abused its dominant positions in the manufacture of meat and fish tins and metal caps in Germany in only one fashion, by announcing an 80 percent control bid for the only Dutch meat and fish tin company. The Commission reasoned that Continental Can would strengthen its dominant German market position through this Dutch acquisition, to the detriment of consumers, and that this amounted to an abuse. The Commission emphasized that potential competition between

§ 26.13

1. (1972) Common Mkt.L.Rep. D11.

companies located within Europe was to be eliminated. Acting quickly before the merger was a *fait accompli,* the Commission underscored its inability to block proposed mergers. Continental Can was given six months to submit proposals for remedying its infringement.

On appeal to the Court of Justice, Continental Can argued that the Commission was acting beyond its powers in attempting to control mergers under Article 82 (formerly 86).[2] The Advocate General to the Court concurred. Nevertheless, the Court chose to go beyond the limits of the language of Articles 81 and 82 and interpret them in light of Articles 82 and 83 of the Treaty of Rome. These Articles set out basic tasks and activities. Article 3 calls for the erection of a system of nondistorted competition in the Common Market.

The Court reasoned teleologically that both Articles 81 and 82 were intended to assist in the maintenance of nondistorted competition. If businesses could freely merge and eliminate competition (whereas Article 81 agreements, decisions or concerted practices merely restrict competition), a "breach in the whole system of competition law that could jeopardize the proper functioning of the common market" would be opened.

> There may therefore be abusive behavior if an enterprise in a dominant position strengthens that position so that the degree of control achieved substantially obstructs competition, i.e. so that the only enterprises left in the market are those which are dependent on the dominant enterprise with regard to their market behavior.[3]

One problem with relying on Article 82 for control of mergers and acquisitions was the absence of any pre-merger notification system. Once a merger is completed, it is always difficult to persuade a court or tribunal that dissolution is desirable or even possible. The key to effective mergers regulation, as the United States has learned under its Hart–Scott–Rodino pre-merger notification rules,[4] is advance warning and sufficient time to block anticompetitive mergers before they are implemented.

The possibility of using Article 81 against selected mergers was surprisingly dismissed by the Commission in an early 1966 competition policy report.[5] Article 81(3) notifications seeking individual exemptions[6] could conceivably have been used for pre-merger regulatory purposes. One explanation for the Commission's early dis-

---

2.　(1973) Eur.Comm.Rep. 215.

3.　Id.

4.　15 U.S.C.A. § 18A.

5.　Commission Competition Series No. 3, The Problem of Industrial Con-

centration in the Common Market (1966).

6.　See Chapter 20.

missal of this possibility is the contrast between the Treaty of Rome's complete absence of specific coverage of mergers and the Treaty of Paris' detailed grant of authority to the Commission of control over coal and steel concentrations.[7] By the 1980s, with industrial concentration continuing to increase in Europe, the Commission reversed its position on the applicability of Article 81 to mergers and acquisitions. It challenged a tobacco industry acquisition as an unlawful restraint under Article 81(1). The Court of Justice held that Article 81 could be applied to the acquisition by one firm of shares in a competitor if that acquisition could influence the behavior in the marketplace of the companies involved.[8] Likewise, Article 82 could apply if the acquisition resulted in effective control of the target company.[9]

After the ruling of the Court of Justice in *Continental Can,* the Commission submitted a comprehensive mergers' control regulation to the Council for its approval. Nearly twenty years later, a regulation on mergers was finally implemented.

§ 26.14 Commission Regulation of Mergers and Acquisitions

In December of 1989, the Council of Ministers unanimously adopted Regulation 4064/89 on the Control of Concentrations Between Undertakings ("Mergers Regulation"). This regulation became effective Sept. 21, 1990 and was expanded in scope by amendment in 1997 (Regulation 1310/97) and significantly revised in 2004. It vests in the Commission the *exclusive* power to oppose large-scale mergers and acquisitions of competitive consequence to the Common Market and the European Economic Area. For these purposes, a "concentration" includes almost any means by which control over another firm is acquired. This could be by a merger agreement, stock or asset purchases, contractual relationships or other actions. Most full function joint ventures creating autonomous economic entities are caught by this test. Thus "control" triggering review can be achieved by minority shareholders, such as when they exercise decisive influence over strategic planning and investment decisions.[1] "Cooperative joint ventures" between independent competitors may also be subject to from the Mergers Regulation.[2]

7. See Article 66 of Treaty of Paris.

8. British American Tobacco Co. Ltd. and R.J. Reynolds Industries, Inc. v. Commission (1987) Eur.Comm.Rep. 4487.

9. Id.

§ 26.14

1. See Conagra/IDEA, 1991 O.J. C175/18; EIF/BC/CEPSA, 1991 O.J. C172/8; Usinor/ASD 1991 O.J. C193/34.

2. See Article 4(2).

The control process established by the Mergers Regulation commences when a concentration must be notified to the Commission on Form CO in one of the official languages. This language becomes the language of the proceeding. Form CO is somewhat similar to second request Hart–Scott–Rodino pre-merger notification filings under U.S. antitrust law. However, the extensive need for detailed product and geographic market descriptions, competitive analyses, and information about the parties in Form CO suggests a more demanding submission. Form CO defines a product market as follows:

> A relevant product market comprises all those products and/or services which are regarded as interchangeable or substitutable by the consumer, by reason of the products' characteristics, their prices and their intended use.

Meeting in advance of notification with members of the Commission on an informal basis in order to ascertain whether the "concentration" has a regional dimension and is compatible with the Common Market has become widely accepted. Such meetings provide an opportunity to seek waivers from the various requests for information contained in Form CO. Since the Commission is bound by rules of professional secrecy, the substance of the discussions is confidential.

The duty to notify applies within one week of the signing of a merger agreement, the acquisition of a controlling interest or the announcement of a takeover bid.[3] The Commission can fine any company failing to notify it as required.[4] The duty to notify is triggered only when the concentration involves enterprises with a combined worldwide sales turnover of at least 5 billion ECUs (approximately $6 billion)[5] *and* two of them have an aggregate regional turnover of 250 million ECUs (approximately $300 million).[6] Additionally, since 1997, mergers with a combined aggregate worldwide turnover of more than 2500 million ECUs and significant member state and regional turnovers must be notified.[7]

As a general rule, concentrations meeting these criteria cannot be put into effect and fall exclusively within the Commission's domain. The effort here is to create a "one-stop" regulatory system. However, certain exceptions apply so as to allow national authorities to challenge some mergers. For example, this may occur under national law when two-thirds of the activities of each of the companies involved take place in the *same* member state.[8] The

---

3. Article 4(1).

4. Article 14(1).

5. For banks and insurance companies, an amount equal to one-tenth of

assets will be used as a proxy for sales turnover.

6. Article 1(2).

7. Article 1(3).

8. Article 1(2).

member states can also oppose mergers by appealing Commission decisions when their public security is at stake, to preserve plurality in media ownership, when financial institutions are involved or other legitimate interests are at risk.[9] If the threshold criteria of the Mergers Regulation are not met, member states can ask the Commission to investigate mergers that create or strengthen a dominant position in that state.[10] States that lack national mergers' controls seem likely to do this. Similarly, if the merger only affects a particular market sector or region in one member state, that state may request referral of the merger to it. This is known as the "German clause" reflecting Germany's insistence upon it. It has been sparingly used by the Commission.

Once a concentration is notified to the Commission, it has one month to decide to investigate the merger. If a formal investigation is commenced, the Commission ordinarily then has four months to challenge or approve the merger.[11] During these months, in most cases, the concentration cannot be put into effect. It is on hold.

The Commission evaluates mergers in terms of their "compatibility" with the Common market. The 1990 Mergers Regulation stated that if the concentration created or strengthened a dominant position such that competition was "significantly impeded," it was incompatible. Effective May 1, 2004, this test was replaced by a prohibition against merges that "significantly impede effective competition" by creating or strengthening dominant positions. Thus the new test focuses on effects not dominance. A set of Guidelines on Horizontal Mergers issued by the Commission in 2004 elaborate upon this approach. It is thought that this change will bring EU and U.S. mergers law closer together (the U.S. test is "substantial lessening of competition").

During a mergers investigation, the Commission can obtain information and records from the parties, and request member states to help with the investigation. Fines and penalties back up the Commission's powers to obtain records and information from the parties.[12] If the concentration has already taken effect, the Commission can issue a "hold-separate" order.[13] This requires the corporations or assets acquired to be separated and not, operationally speaking, merged. Approval of the merger may involve modifications of its terms or promises by the parties aimed at diminishing its anticompetitive potential. Negotiations with the Commission to obtain such approvals follow the pattern of negotiations associated with negative clearances and individual exemptions under Article 81. If the Commission ultimately decides to oppose the merger in a

---

9. Article 21(3).

10. Article 22(3).

11. Article 10.

12. Articles 11–15.

13. Articles 7 and 10.

timely manner, it can order its termination by whatever means are appropriate to restore conditions of effective competition (including divestiture, fines or penalties). Such decisions can be appealed to the Court of First Instance. The Court has confirmed that mergers resulting in collective (oliogopolistic) dominance of a market fall within European mergers regulation.[14]

Case Examples

The first merger actually blocked by the Commission on competition law grounds was the attempted acquisition of a Canadian aircraft manufacturer (DeHaviland-owned by Boeing) by two European companies (Aerospatiale SNI of France and Alenia e Selenia Spa of Italy).[15] Prior to this rejection in late 1991, the Commission had approved over 50 mergers, obtaining modifications in a few instances. The Commission, in the DeHaviland case, took the position that the merger would have created an unassailable dominant position in the world and the European market for turbo prop or commuter aircraft. If completed, the merged entity would have had 50 percent of the world and 67 percent of the European market for such aircraft. In contrast, the Commission approved (subject to certain sell-off requirements) the acquisition of Perrier by Nestlé.[16] Prior to the merger, Nestlé, Perrier and BSN controlled about 82 percent of the French bottled water market. Afterwards, Nestlé and BSN each had about 41 percent of the market. The sell-off requirements were thought sufficient by the Commission to maintain effective competition. The case also presents interesting arguments that the Commission, in granting approval, disregarded fundamental workers' social rights. This issue was unsuccessfully taken up on appeal by Perrier's trade union representative.

In 1997, the Commission dramatically demonstrated its extraterritorial jurisdiction over the Boeing–McDonnell Douglas merger. This merger had already been cleared by the U.S. Federal Trade commission. The European Commission, however, demanded and (at the risk of a trade war) got important concessions from Boeing. These included abandonment of exclusive supply contracts with three U.S. airlines and licensing of technology derived from McDonnell Douglas' military programs at reasonable royalty rates. The Commission's success in this case was widely perceived in the United States as pro-Airbus.

The Commission blocked the MC Worldcom/Spring merger in 2001, as did the U.S. Dept. of Justice. Both authorities were worried about the merger's adverse effects on Internet access. For the Commission, this was the first block of a merger taking place

---

14. Gencor Ltd. v. EC Commission, 1999 CEC 395. *See* France v. EC Commission, 1998 Eur.Comm.Rep. I–1375.

15. 1991 O.J. L334/42.

16. O.J. L356/1 (Dec. 5. 1992).

outside the EU between two firms established outside the EU. Much more controversy arose when in 2001 the Commission blocked the GE/Honeywell merger after it had been approved by U.S. authorities. The Commission was particularly concerned about the potential for bundling engines with avionics and non-avionics to the disadvantage of rivals. Appeal of this decision is pending. The United States and the EU, in the wake of GE/Honeywell, have agreed to follow a set of "Best Practices" on coordinated timing, evidence gathering, communication and consistency of remedies.

The Court of First Instance overturned a 1999 decision of the European Commission blocking the $1.2 billion merger of Airtours and First Choice Holidays. The June, 2002 CFI decision was the first reversal of a merger prohibition since the 1990 inception of the review process. The CFI judgment confirmed that transactions can be blocked on collective dominance grounds, but found that the Commission had failed to meet the three conditions for proving collective dominance: (1) each member of the dominant group is able to determine readily how the others are behaving, (2) there is an effective mechanism to prevent group members from departing from the agreed-upon policy, and (3) smaller competitors are unable to undercut that policy.

In June of 2002 the European Court of Justice issued three decisions on the use by member states of so-called "golden shares." Such shares allow governments to retain veto rights with respect to acquisitions of or other significant accumulations in privatized businesses. The court outlawed a golden share decree allowing France to block a foreign takeover of a privatized oil company. The golden share decree created a barrier to the free movement of capital. The court also outlawed a law giving Portugal the ability to block the acquisition of controlling stakes in privatized state companies, but determined as a matter of public interest that Belgium could retain its golden share in recently privatized canal and gas distribution companies.

In October of 2002, acting under its new fast track review procedures, the Court of First Instance overturned two additional mergers decisions of the Commission. In both the Court found serious errors, omissions and inconsistencies. Credible evidence, not assumptions or "abstract and detached analysis," must be tendered to prove both the strengthening or creation of a dominant position, and the likelihood that the merger will significantly impede competition.

Chapter 27

INVESTING IN NAFTA

Table of Sections

§ 27.1 Investment Laws of Canada

Although U.S. persons often view Canada in a mirror and see themselves, thus assuming that Canadians and the Canadian government will be very receptive to foreign investment, the policies of Canada over the years reflect an ambivalence toward investment. Canada has long regulated foreign investment by both federal and provincial laws. Soon after its creation as a federation in 1867, Canada established high tariffs to protect infant industries from imports from the United States. This caused U.S. manufacturers to invest in Canada to surmount the tariff wall. Soon the United States was the principal source of foreign investment, and for many U.S. companies Canada was a natural location for their first foreign investments.

Most Canadian investment laws have focused on specific sectors, such as financial institutions, transportation, natural resources[1] and, quite importantly, publishing.[2] Canada was always a

---

§ 27.1

1. Oil and gas acquisitions were pro-

hibited until the *Masse Policy*, adopted in 1992, was rescinded, leaving such reg-

natural target for investment from the United States, especially since so much of the industrial development of the United States occurred relatively near the Canadian border. Canada's attitude toward foreign investment remained quite receptive until nationalistic forces in the 1960s began to challenge an open investment policy. The first measure of significance was the creation of the Foreign Investment Review Agency (FIRA) in 1974, which allowed the federal government to review proposed foreign investment, especially acquisitions of Canadian companies, and in some cases deny their development. The National Energy Program in 1980 was intended to *reduce* foreign ownership in the oil and gas industry. Most of that foreign ownership was by U.S. companies. A Conservative government elected in 1984 replaced the FIRA with the Investment Canada Act (ICA) (1985),[3] that continues to govern foreign investment in Canada—especially acquisitions. When the CFTA was adopted, it incorporated part of the ICA, providing that a review of an acquisition under the ICA would not be subject to the CFTA dispute settlement provisions.[4] The ICA was to be amended to comply with the CFTA, but considerable definitional language in the ICA was retained by reference. When NAFTA was adopted, excluded from its dispute settlement provisions were decisions by Canada following a review under the ICA. This, plus Canada's exclusion of "cultural industries" by incorporation of the CFTA provisions, indicates that Canada has insisted in retaining some domestic control over foreign investment, especially the acquisition of Canadian owned industries, and most especially "cultural" industries.

§ 27.2   Investment Laws of Mexico

The United States has never viewed Mexico with the same mirror as it does Canada, seeing itself in the reflection. Despite all the differences between Canada and the United States, Canada usually has been viewed an equal by the United States. Not so with Mexico. The United States has viewed Mexico as something less than a partner. The United States views Mexico as needing the United States, but the United States has not viewed itself as needing Mexico. Mexico has responded accordingly, with suspicion

ulation to the Investment Canada Act, which allowed such investment but required approval of some acquisitions. However, the threshold before approval was required was quite high, making the law less restrictive than it otherwise appeared.

2.   Canada considers publishing to be a cultural industry. Until restrictions in

the Canadian *Baie Comeau Policy* on ownership of publishing were relaxed, foreign investment in publishing was very difficult.

3.   R.S. 1985, ch. 28 (1st Suppl.), *as amended* by 1988 ch. 65 and Investment Canada Regulations SOR/85–611, *as amended* by SOR/89–69.

4.   CFTA Art. 1608(1).

and deliberation. Canada never really flirted with socialism, as Mexico did in the 1970s by substantially increasing national ownership of the means of production and distribution. The Mexican investment law, the transfer of technology law, and the trade names and inventions law, all enacted in the 1970s, were models of restrictive laws of developing nations adopted during the tense and often bitter North–South dialogue, when developing nations argued that they were poor because the developed nations were rich, and that there had to be a transfer of wealth from the latter to the former.

Several Mexican government actions reducing foreign ownership of specific foreign investment brought considerable industrial production and distribution into government ownership long before the 1973 law. Mexico opened to foreign investment with few restrictions during the *Porfiriato*, the 1876–1911 reign of Porfirio Díaz. But the state assumed a more restrictive role with the new 1917 Constitution, which followed the revolutionary turmoil begun in 1910. It soon became apparent that the state would begin to intervene in many areas of established foreign investment. After an unsuccessful attempt by Mexico to participate in the foreign owned petroleum industry in 1925, a labor dispute led to the total nationalization of the industry in 1938, reducing in the minds of many Mexicans the apparent conflict with Article 27 of the Mexican Constitution, that decreed that all natural resources were owned by the nation. Two years later, the government severely limited foreign participation in the communications sector. A 1944 Emergency Decree was the first broad attempt to regulate foreign investment, and limited certain investments to joint ventures. The joint venture concept was extended by a Mixed Ministerial Commission established in 1947, although it was of limited effectiveness. The 1950s saw the introduction of further limited control of specific industries, and electric power was nationalized in 1960. Mining became subject to a 1961 Act, but the next dozen years were relatively free of significant changes.

A strict 1972 Law for the Registration of the Transfer of Technology and the Use and Exploitation of Patents and Marks,[1] forewarned the coming restrictiveness towards foreign investment. The 1973 Law to Promote Mexican Investment and Regulate Foreign Investment,[2] to some degree pulled together the policies of encouraging but limiting foreign investment, that had been introduced during the past several decades, and were clearly part of the Echeverrían administration policy, that began in 1970. The 1973 law classified investments, limiting some to state ownership, some

---

§ 27.2   **2.**   Diario Oficial, Mar. 9, 1973.

1. See Diario Oficial, Dec. 30, 1972.

to private ownership exclusively by Mexican nations, and some where minority foreign participation would be allowed. The law did not apply retroactively, but if a company expanded into new lines of products or new locations, it was expected to Mexicanize, meaning to sell majority ownership to Mexicans. But escape provisions and the operational code in Mexico (the way things really work), resulted in few existing companies converting to Mexican majority ownership. What the laws did accomplish was to significantly curtail new foreign investment. A new institution, the National Commission on Foreign Investment, assumed substantial discretionary power to carry out the new rules.

What President Echeverría started, his successor, José López Portillo, continued when he entered office in 1976. His final year in office, 1982, saw first the amendment of the 1972 Transfer of Technology Law, retaining its restrictiveness and extending its scope, and second, the nationalization of the banking industry. His successor, Miguel de la Madrid, assumed control of a nation with a defaulted national debt, a plunging currency, and diminished interest of foreign investors. Realizing that Mexico must change its policies, de la Madrid issued investment regulations in 1984 that partly relaxed the restrictiveness of the 1970s. Further regulations were issued in the following years, and in 1989, the first year of Carlos Salinas de Gortari's presidency, new regulations were issued that were so inconsistent with the clear philosophy of the restrictive 1973 law that their constitutionality was questioned. The direction was turned: Mexico's ascension into the stratosphere of developing-nation restrictiveness toward foreign investment had reached its apogee in 1982, and was coming back to earth. Foreign investment was returning. It was further encouraged by Mexico's admission into the GATT in 1984, after years of internal debate. The 1993 replacement of the 1973 Investment Law, twenty years after its introduction, ended an unsettling era of Mexican foreign-investment policy.

This 1993 Investment Act[3] was a highlight of the Salinas administration, an encouragement to the many investors who had made commitments to Mexico during his administration, and a stepping stone to participation in the NAFTA the following year. The 1993 law improved access to investment in Mexico, containing investment-attracting provisions absent from the earlier law. Formally abandoned was the mandatory joint-venture focus, although it was never successful. But some significant restrictions remained, including control over natural resources, reservation of some areas of investment for Mexican nationals, and retention of remnants of the Calvo doctrine that attempted to limit a foreign investor's use

3. See Diario Oficial, Dec. 27, 1993.

of its own nation as diplomatic efforts in the event of an investment conflict with Mexico. But the law nevertheless was a huge reversal of the policies of the 1970s, and it both established a more efficient National Registry of Foreign Investment and allowed proposals to be assumed to have been approved if they were not acted upon within the established time-frame. Regulations adopted in 1999 are consistent with both the 1993 law and its investment-encouraging philosophy. As the new century began, Mexico was not yet as open to foreign investment as were Canada and the United States, but it had established a sufficiently respectful base from which to participate in the NAFTA foreign-investment framework. It was quite a remarkable transformation and a credit to several of Mexico's leaders.[4]

§ 27.3   Mexican and Canadian Foreign Investment Review Procedures

If foreign investment is allowed under certain conditions, there must be some entity assigned the decisional role in accepting or rejecting proposals. Quite obviously where foreign investment is totally prohibited, no such review entity is necessary. Consequently, as nations which prohibited investment begin to open to limited foreign investment, an entity was created to review proposed foreign investment. Investment-screening agencies were granted, or over time assumed, very substantial power in molding the nation's foreign investment sector. This was especially true where the agency had discretion to admit otherwise prohibited foreign investment under exception clauses, whether those exceptions were contained in written law or unwritten administrative policy. Sometimes review power was given to a ministry, other times to a specialized agency.

A screening process allows a government to control foreign entry on a case-by-case basis. The written law may be quite restrictive, but the screening process may allow the entry of foreign investment deemed necessary for development. That may mean admission of investment which brings to the country advanced technology. Proposals granted permission and proposals denied permission often illustrated what the nation was willing to grant exceptions for, which could help a prospective foreign investor. But decisions of foreign investment review agencies which might disclose the reasoning process were usually not available to the public. Some of the reasons a nation might give approval to a proposed

---

4. See generally Jorge A. Vargas, Mexico's Foreign Investment Act of 1993, Mexican Law (J. Vargas ed. 1998); Ewell E. Murphy Jr., Access and Protection for Foreign Investment in Mexico under Mexico's New Foreign Investment Law and the North American Free Trade Agreement, 10 ICSID Rev. Foreign Investment L.J. 54 (1998).

investment are discussed above as reasons a nation might grant a waiver from restrictive maximum equity percentages.

The individual analysis of proposed foreign investment by a review agency makes evaluation of potential foreign investments very flexible. This in turn makes government action more difficult to predict, but allows governments the ability to place conditions on foreign investment without a total ban.

Screening agencies are often thought to be the exclusive patrimony of developing and nonmarket economy nations. That is not the case. Essentially all nations limit foreign investment, including the most developed nations. The reasons may appear to be different, but may mask the most common reason—the protection of domestic industries. The United States has a process to review foreign investment. The European Union also has restrictions on foreign investment.

The examples of Canada and Mexico. The investment screening processes introduced by Canada and Mexico in the early 1970s departed from their earlier unrestrictive foreign investment policies. Their 1970s screening mechanisms have survived, notwithstanding the dismantling of most investment restrictions in the 1980s and the creation of the North American Free Trade Agreement.

The Foreign Investment Review Agency (FIRA), the first Canadian foreign investment screening process, arose in part from political pressures, with the ruling Liberal party looking to maintain its legislative coalition.[1] The FIRA provided the cornerstone of an expanded effort to control foreign investment in Canada, while maintaining some of the traditional open investment attitude of previous years. A grandfather clause exempted from review existing investments as well as profits reinvested in similar businesses. The FIRA appeared to target the expansion of foreign control of Canada's economy, rather than foreign investment as a whole.[2] The overall goal remained simple: to ensure that new foreign investment would benefit Canada.

The Investment Canada Act of 1985 replaced the Foreign Investment Review Agency with Investment Canada, a new agency "to advise and assist" the Minister in reviewing investment and

---

§ 27.3

1. Thomas M. Franck & K. Scott Gudgeon, Canada's Foreign Investment Control Experiment: the Law, the Context and the Practice, 50 N.Y.U.L.Rev. 76, 111 (1975).

2. FIRA § 2(1) (describing the purpose of the Act, to ensure that acquisi-

tion of Canadian enterprises by those not already carrying on business in Canada, or those whose new businesses in Canada would be unrelated to the businesses they already have, would continue only if the investment would be likely to significantly benefit Canada).

more generally in administering the Act. What was to be reviewed was considerable less encompassing than under the earlier FIRA.

The Canada–United States Free Trade Agreement of 1989 included a full chapter on investment,[3] which further opened Canada for U.S. investment under the principal of national treatment. The Agreement allowed Canada to continue to review the acquisition of control of Canadian businesses, but included within the scope of such review far fewer businesses. Canada's participation in the NAFTA brings additional investment rules into force. It is incorporates the national treatment principal. The review process established under the Investment Canada Act remains in place, with specific reference in the NAFTA that decisions of Canada in reviewing acquisitions are not subject to Chapter 11 or Chapter 20 dispute resolution panels or procedures.[4] The Canadian policy thus has been to retain a modest measure of reviewing authority of only the largest acquisitions.

The since-repealed Mexican 1973 Investment Law also created a screening agency, the National Commission on Foreign Investment.[5] The Commission was granted considerable review power over approving new foreign investment, including exemptions from joint venture mandates, acquisitions, and expansion of existing investment. The Investment Law allowed quite flexible administration, but it was unclear at the outset whether that flexibility would serve the government's or foreign investor's goals. The law imposed fines and prison terms for using Mexican nominees to subvert the requirements. The Mexican law included an investment limitation not present in the Canadian regime—existing enterprises could not expand in similar businesses without agency review, because *foreign controlled* Mexican firms were considered foreign investors. The result of both the Canadian FIRA and Mexican FIL acts was similar: the imposition of entry conditions upon foreign investors.

The 1989 Regulations to the 1973 Mexican Investment Law changed the screening process in some key respects, but not the screening entity. The Regulations, designed to increase foreign investment, waived Commission approval for investments that met certain conditions. While the screening process did become more streamlined, performance requirements did not vanish. The 1993 Investment Law, that replaced both the 1973 law and the 1989 regulations, retained the Commission as a review agency, but with review authority closer to review procedures in the Regulations than to procedures in the earlier restrictive law.

3. CFTA, chapter 15.

4. NAFTA chapter 11, Annex 1138.2.

5. Mexican 1973 Investment Law, chapter III, art. 11.

Mexico's participation in the NAFTA means the applicability of the same Chapter 11 investment rules as for Canada. The difference is that while Canada has retained the review process developed under the Investment Canada Act, Mexico specifically is allowed to retain review by the Mexican National Commission on Foreign Investment, with such review of acquisitions not subject to the Chapter 11 or Chapter 20 dispute resolution panels and procedures.[6] For comparison, the United States reserved no process of review of acquisitions in the NAFTA, but it is certain that review under the U.S. Exon–Florio law will continue.

The trend to reduce the restrictiveness of foreign investment laws has led to a reduction of the role of a review agency or commission, if not an abolition of the agency itself. That is true not only of Canada and Mexico. India, for example, also streamlined its foreign investment approval scheme during the mid–1980s.[7] But even the much more liberal written laws of India in the 1990s continue to retain the use of review agencies, even though they may not have as much authority to restrict foreign investment as in previous decades.[8]

The process of review by foreign investment review agencies usually includes the application of specific guidelines, but nevertheless allowing considerable discretion in the evaluation of the investment. Since foreign investment has to benefit the host nation for approval, the review process necessarily requires an evaluation of what constitutes a benefit. The process usually requires an application filed with the review agency with approval in the form of permission or a kind of license. While the agency granting permission or issuing licenses may have considerable discretion, some nations have formal development plans (usually a five-or ten-year plan) with which the reviewing agency must comply in granting permission.[9] The review process usually includes scrutiny regarding the proposed investment's benefits to the nation. It is likely to consider some of the following:

1. Effect on the economic development of the nation;

2. Degree of participation of host-nation citizens in the business;

---

6. NAFTA chapter 11, Annex 1138.2.

7. Note, Foreign Investment in India, 26 Colum.J.Transnat'l L. 609, 630 (1988).

8. See Indian Foreign Exchange Regulation Act of 1973. See 1982 Bus. Int'l 92 (Mar. 92). Another example in Africa is the 1990 Namibia Foreign Investment Act, which establishes an Investment Centre in the Ministry of Trade and Industry to administer the Act. 31 Int'l Leg.Mat. 205 (1992).

9. While nonmarket economies are often most associated with such plans, such market economy nations as Mexico and India have used plans. Knowledge of these plans is important; they may disclose sectors in which a nation is especially interested in developing, and which may be the beneficiary of incentives.

3. Location of the new business;

4. Effect on competition in the industry;

5. Effect on productivity, efficiency, technological development and product innovation;

6. Effect on balance of payments, which may mean amount of exports generated by the new business;

7. Ability of the nation to increase its role in the world market;

8. Creation of new training and job opportunities;

9. Establishment of research and development facilities;

10. Impact on culture; and

11. Use of external capital sources for borrowing.

Many of these points may have to be addressed in seeking approval of a new investment or acquisition. It means a lengthy process in many cases, and an expensive one. It is never clear how much weight will be given any one of the different factors. The weight may change according to circumstances within the nation. For example, if the nation has a favorable trade balance and substantial hard currency, little weight is likely to be given to whether exports exceed imports and raise hard currency. How the process proceeds in two nations, Canada and Mexico, is discussed immediately below as an example.

The decision of the review agency may be final, or it may be appealable to another agency within the government or to the courts. But the process of review is largely a factual determination, and the foreign investor is advised to place great emphasis on establishing the benefit of the proposed investment to the host nation.

Canadian review process. The factors that the Canadian Foreign Investment Review Agency uses in evaluating whether new investment will "significantly benefit" Canada are included in the Investment Canada Act and reflect the TRIMs described above, and some of the various separate criteria noted immediately above. These factors include the effects on economic activity, participation by Canadians, productivity, efficiency, innovation, technological development, competition, culture and role in world markets.[10]

Most new foreign investment in Canada is not reviewed,[11] review being limited to *acquisitions*.[12] The Investment Canada Act

---

10. Investment Canada Act of 1985, art. 20.

11. Canada has reserved the right to review investment in certain stipulated cultural industries. See ICA arts.

14.1(9), 15. This right is retained in the NAFTA.

12. The earlier Canadian Foreign Investment Review Act did provide for a review of new investment, with complex provisions regarding investor eligibility

raised the minimum threshold level of dollars for a reviewable acquisition, shortened the time for government review, and streamlined the process and standards for review. The ICA also included a series of stages where acquisitions by Americans (principally U.S. nationals) would not require review if they exceeded certain levels.[13]

Mexican review process. The factors that the Mexican National Commission of Foreign Investment (Commission) will consider in allowing exceptions to the 49 percent maximum for foreign equity, reflect, as in Canada, the four trade related investment measures (TRIMs) and trade related performance requirements (TRPRs). The Commission also issues general resolutions of interpretation and application. The procedure requires the Commission to act within 45 business days, or the application is automatically approved.

§ 27.4   U.S. Regulation of Foreign Investment

The Exon–Florio amendment to the Defense Production Act of 1950, passed as part of the Omnibus Trade and Competitiveness Act of 1988,[1] grants the President the authority to investigate and suspend or prohibit transactions leading to the control of American firms by foreign persons, based on national-security concerns.[2] Exon–Florio is the only U.S. law that broadly regulates foreign investment. Furthermore, its application may arise throughout the investment process.

Although a trade regulation provision based upon national security such as Exon–Florio may pose a potential for mischief against foreign investors by the government, foreign acquisitions of U.S. companies were thought at the inception of Exon–Florio not likely to be obstructed. History has verified this prediction, with perhaps one or two notable exceptions.

There are two basic problems that Exon–Florio presents to foreign investors. The first is that Exon–Florio issues may arise throughout the investment process. Foreign acquisitions that could affect national security must be reported to CFIUS at the outset to allow the government to make a determination; otherwise, the

---

and control. Under the Investment Canada Act, new investment is subject only to notification procedures. Part III, Arts. 11–13.

13. The stages progressed from review for any acquisition above $25 million at the time of enactment, to only those above $150 million after 1992. Art. 14.1.

§ 27.4

1. 50 U.S.C.A.App. § 2170; See also 31 C.F.R. § 800.101.

2. See generally Jose Alvarez, Political Protectionism and United States International Investment Obligations in Conflict: The Hazards of Exon–Florio, 30 Va.J.Int'l. 1 (1989).

The main point of contact in the United States for inquires about the Exon–Florio law is the Committee on Foreign Investment in the United States (CFIUS), in the Office of International Investment, Department of the Treasury. See generally <www.treas.gov/.

government may be prompted to investigate on its own and possibly order divestment. The result could be that foreign investors have acquired property without very clear title.[3]

The second problem is the uncertainty about the definition of national security under Exon–Florio. The Exon–Florio Regulations offer few bright-line tests. That confirms CFIUS, the President's designated center of investigation, as the omnipotent reviewer of foreign acquisitions. Exon–Florio initially earned the nickname "Lawyers Full Employment Act" because of the potentially broad scope of national security.[4] CFIUS has interpreted national security on a case-by-case basis, leaving other companies, even in similar industries, somewhat baffled about the criteria used to evaluate the transaction. But Exon–Florio does include a list of factors to be considered in the evaluation of a transaction's national-security implications.[5] There nevertheless remains concern about the potential abuse of the broad language and consequent wide scope of Exon–Florio's national-security language.

§ 27.5 History of CFIUS and Evolution of Exon–Florio

Before the enactment of Exon–Florio, when the concern for widespread Arab buyouts of American businesses in the 1970s was perceived as a threat to national security, the U.S. executive, seeking a compromise with the Congress, agreed to create the Committee on Foreign Investment in the United States (CFIUS) as an interagency, interdepartmental group to investigate inward foreign direct investment and recommend policy. CFIUS, which would have no real screening or review power, would serve at the President's discretion; for example, President Carter's administration investigated only one transaction.

During President Reagan's second term, the concern turned more toward the increasing trade deficit and the "Japanese threat." There were large inflows of foreign investment in the 1980s, although they were not limited to Japanese investors. The administration began to intervene in these inflows more frequently, especially when they constituted planned acquisitions of U.S. companies. The policy of open versus controlled investment seemed most confused when the Japanese electronics conglomerate Fujitsu

3. See Group Sees Problems with Treasury's Draft Foreign Acquisition Regulations, 57 Antitrust & Trade Reg. Rep. (BNA) No. 1425, at 95 (July 20, 1989).

4. Soon after the law was passed, CFIUS reportedly received notice of a

planned acquisition of swimming pool companies. See Martin Tolchin & Susan J. Tolchin, Selling Our Security: The Erosion of America's Assets 51 (1992).

5. See 50 U.S.C.A.App. § 2170(f)(4).

sought to acquire an 80 percent share in Fairchild Semiconductor.[1] Fairchild had openly solicited the bid. Even though the French concern Schlumberger already owned Fairchild, the Commerce, Defense and Justice departments all joined to oppose the proposed acquisition. The Department of Justice was concerned with antitrust implications,[2] while the departments of Commerce and Defense appeared to object primarily in order to force Japanese markets to open more. Because of the extensive concern, Fujitsu withdrew its proposed acquisition even though CFIUS at the time lacked the power to block the sale.

By 1988, Congress seemed intent on creating some mechanism to review proposed foreign investment in the United States. The determination was increased when the proposed foreign purchase of Phoenix Steel was announced. Phoenix Steel was a producer of many items procured by the Department of Defense. The purchaser, represented by a Hong Kong agent, was to obtain financing for the acquisition from the People's Republic of China.[3] CFIUS had no authority to block the sale, but it nevertheless began an investigation because many of Phoenix's products were subject to export controls. Representative Florio of New Jersey proposed foreign-investment control legislation that would allow the President to block the sale of a U.S.-owned company to any entity with financing by a potential enemy, to ensure that the U.S. firm's controlled technology would not be acquired by the foreign nation. The administration accepted the Exon–Florio proposal as a compromise because competing bills would have imposed even greater reporting and disclosure requirements on foreign investors, which the administration opposed. One competing proposal required any foreign investor acquiring a five percent or greater interest to report to the Department of Commerce certain information which would become available to the public.

After the enactment of Exon–Florio in 1988, several amendments were proposed that would have increased the regulation of foreign investment. These proposals were partly due to the belief that Treasury was attempting to weaken the law through the adoption of lenient regulations.[4] Consequently, some of the pro-

§ 27.5

1. The policy issues of foreign investment, such as whether it benefits or harms the United States, should controls be extended beyond national security, etc., have never been addressed thoroughly. Exon–Florio's vague language does not help resolve these questions.

2. See Division is Probing Effects of Merger of California, Japanese Comput-

er Firms, 51 Antitrust & Trade Reg.Rep. (BNA) No. 1282, 803 (Nov. 27, 1986).

3. See Bid for U.S. Steel Mill by Company Backed by P.R.C. Raises Export Control Questions, 5 Int'l Trade Rep. (BNA) 239 (Feb. 24, 1988).

4. See Treasury Official Concedes Aim to Weaken Rules for Exon–Florio Takeover Amendment, 55 Antitrust & Trade Reg. Rep. (BNA) No. 1395, at 1013 (Dec. 15, 1988).

posed amendments would have replaced Treasury as the chair of CFIUS with either the department of Commerce or Defense.[5] Nevertheless, the amendments that were passed in 1992 did not alter CFIUS's structure but did modify when and how CFIUS must investigate.[6]

§ 27.6   When and How CFIUS Reviews Proposed Foreign Investment Under Exon–Florio

Exon–Florio authorizes the President or President's designee to investigate the national-security impact of "mergers, acquisitions, and takeovers" by or with foreign persons that could result in control by foreign persons.[1] Most investigations are at the discretion of CFIUS after receipt of written notification as prescribed by the regulations.[2] CFIUS has 30 days after notification to decide whether or not to investigate,[3] and 45 days after that to investigate and make a recommendation to the President. The President next has 15 days to either (1) suspend or prohibit the acquisition, merger, or takeover, or (2) seek divestiture for an already completed transaction.[4] He may direct the Attorney Gener-

---

5. See Bill Offered to Strengthen Law Governing Foreign Acquisitions, 8 Int'l Trade Rep. (BNA) 947 (June 19, 1991).

6. The 1992 Byrd Amendment included a non-binding resolution that to CFIUS membership should be added the Director of the Office of Science and Technology Policy and the Assistant to the President for National Security. Congress wanted more representation which would be likely to be concerned with foreign acquisitions and take a harder line than would other departmental heads on CFIUS. In response to this resolution, Executive Order 12860 was issued expanding CFIUS' membership to add the two aforementioned persons and also the Assistant to the President for Economic Policy, bringing the membership to eleven.

§ 27.6

1. See 50 U.S.C.A. App. § 2170(a); 53 Fed.Reg. 43,999 (1988) (President naming Secretary of Treasury as lead investigator and head of CFIUS); 31 C.F.R. § 800.203 (1992) (defining "Committee" and "Chairman of the Committee" as CFIUS and the Secretary of the Treasury); Executive Order No. 11858, 40 Fed.Reg. 20,263, 3 C.F.R. 1971–1975 Comp., 990 as amended, reprinted in 15 U.S.C.A. § 78b note (establishing CFIUS, which includes Treasury, State, De-

fense, Commerce and Justice Departments, the U.S. Trade Representative, and other executive chairs); 31 C.F.R. §§ 800.202—800.221 (definitions unique to Exon–Florio).

2. See 31 C.F.R. § 800.401 (establishing procedures for notice to CFIUS; providing for notification by individual members of the Committee, where the member has reason to believe national security to be adversely affected; and setting a three-year time limit for such self-starting notice); 31 C.F.R. § 800.402 (describing the information that CFIUS requires for voluntary notices). But see 50 U.S.C.A. App. § 2170(b) (requiring mandatory investigations when an entity seeking control in a merger, takeover or acquisition is itself controlled or acting on behalf of a foreign government).

3. The investigation is mandatory where a foreign government controlled entity or agent is involved. This was part of the 1992 Byrd Amendment resulting from the Thomson/LTV case discussed below.

4. Notice may be submitted and CFIUS review commenced at any time while the transaction is pending or after it is completed. But there is a three-year limitation after the transaction is completed, unless the CFIUS chairman, consulting with other members, requests an

al to seek appropriate relief in U.S. district courts to enforce his decision.

The President must make two findings in order to exercise his authority. First, he must believe that there is "credible evidence" that the foreign interest would exercise "control" which might threaten "national security." Second, he must believe that other provisions of law, aside from the International Emergency Economic Powers Act, provide inadequate authority to safeguard national security. Although these two findings remain prerequisites to presidential action, they are not subject to judicial review under the statute.

Although considerable debate occurred, "national security" remains undefined in either the law or regulations. But the Exon–Florio provisions suggest that the President consider several factors in evaluating national security concerns. These are mainly directed to the capacity of domestic industry to meet national-defense requirements in view of the proposed takeover. Amendments to Exon–Florio have added as factors for presidential consideration both the potential for proliferation of missiles and nuclear and biological weapons, as well as the potential effect of the transaction on U.S. leadership in technology that affects national security.

Any information filed with CFIUS is largely confidential, although some releases of information may be made to authorized members of Congress. Critics have charged that CFIUS has abused the confidentiality provisions in some cases, and also has left important players out of the investigation process until after CFIUS has made its decisions.[5] The confidentiality provision has made official reports of cases impossible but has protected both the interests of foreign investors and national security. The manner in which CFIUS and the President have applied the law, and the criticism generated from such application, have focused on the proper meaning of three terms—"mergers, acquisitions, and takeovers," "control", and "national security." The statute and regulations confine the application of Exon–Florio to "mergers, acquisitions, and takeovers" of U.S. businesses leading to foreign control. Any such transaction concluded on or after the effective date of Exon–Florio, August 23, 1988, is subject to review.

The regulations take into account devices created to avoid Exon–Florio review, such as foreign-controlled corporations seeking

investigation. To avoid the possibility of having a completed transaction questioned, companies sometimes submit a voluntary notice to commence review before completing the transaction. Any transaction which has been the subject of CFIUS review or investigation is not subject to later Presidential action.

Thus, even when there seems to be little apparent impact on national security, a review request might be useful.

5. See Martin Tolchin & Susan J. Tolchin, Selling Our Security: The Erosion of America's Assets 61 (1992).

to purchase U.S. businesses using American agents supposedly acting independently. As Treasury drafted the regulations, Rep. Florio and other commentators wondered about the applicability of the law toward other types of transactions, such as proxy solicitations which might lead to foreign control, foreign bank financing which might lead to control by default, joint ventures, and "greenfield" investments.[6] The regulations address most of those issues, although they include few "bright-line" tests.

Exon–Florio does not apply to portfolio investments, such as investments where the foreigner obtains ten percent or less of voting securities solely for investment purposes; investments where the foreign buyer has the same parent as the target; or other investments where the foreign investor does not acquire managerial control of a U.S. business. Joint ventures, originally thought to be exempt from Exon–Florio review, are included. Foreign persons soliciting proxies in order to obtain control are also covered. The regulations do not subject lending transactions by foreign persons to Exon–Florio review, unless the lender assumes some degree of control, at either the time that the loan is made or when default appears imminent.

As the above comments suggest, what *control* would be exercised by the foreign person is the key to determining whether a transaction is within the scope of Exon–Florio. The regulations define "control" without limitation on voting percentages or majority ownership, but as "the power, direct or indirect, whether or not exercised ... to determine, direct, take, reach or cause decisions" in a series of key areas. These areas include the transfer (sale, lease, mortgage or pledge) of assets, the dissolution of the business, the closing or relocation of research and development facilities, terminating or not fulfilling the business contracts, and amending the Articles of Incorporation of the business with regard to any of the aforementioned matters.[7] In addition, when examining control, if more than one foreign person is involved, CFIUS may consider the possibility of their acting in concert. However, an *unrelated* group of foreign investors holding a majority of shares in a U.S. company will not be assumed to control that company.

In contrast with the attempt to define "control," Exon–Florio and its associated regulations do not define "national security." Many of the public comments during Treasury's drafting of the regulations urged a specific definition, but the statute and regula-

6. See Treasury Proposes Rules on Foreign Mergers, Acquisitions, and Takeovers, 57 Antitrust & Trade Reg. Rep. (BNA) No. 1424, at 46 (July 13, 1989).

7. The Industrial Security Regulations, allowing the DOD to block an acquisition where there will be access to classified information, include a much more extensive definition of "foreign ownership, control or influence."

tions consciously leave the determination of a national-security concern to the President's discretion.[8] Few involved in regulating foreign investment outside the administration were satisfied with that result. Some in Congress thought that the White House interpreted "national security" under Exon–Florio too narrowly, equating it only with military security.[9] The General Accounting Office (GAO) criticized CFIUS for not determining if anti-competitive behavior by foreign firms might jeopardize national security. A former Attorney General and Secretary of Defense, speaking for a segment of the foreign-investment regulatory community, criticized the rules lack of national-security criteria because more mergers and acquisitions may fall under review than Congress intended.[10] Nevertheless, administration officials stressed the need for "national security" to have a broad scope and not be confined to particular industries, and be particularly applicable should the target company provide products or technologies essential to the U.S. defense industrial base.[11]

§ 27.7   Application of Exon–Florio: Cases

The application of Exon–Florio in real situations resolves some of the apparent ambiguity with regard to the meaning of "national security" and the other important statutory and regulatory terms. By 1992, CFIUS had reviewed 650 proposed acquisitions. Twelve detailed investigations led to two withdrawals, but only one presidential order of divestment. Because of CFIUS' confidentiality requirements, no official reports or summaries of its investigations under Exon–Florio exist for lawyers or investors to consult. Instead, secondary sources must be used to draw meanings given to the statute and regulations. The cases when the President chose not to act when the parties themselves withdrew and the one case when the President actually ordered divestment present some general patterns of what foreign investors may expect from a CFIUS investigation under Exon–Florio.

Huels AG of Germany/Monsanto. The Department of Defense prompted one of the first investigations under Exon—Florio, be-

---

8. See H.R. Conf. Rep. No. 576, 100th Cong. (1988). See also Set of Principles on S & T Cooperation Would Be Valuable. NEC Official Says, 10 Int'l Trade Rep. (BNA) 663 (Apr. 21, 1993) (a White House official hinting that a definition of "national security" may be forthcoming).

9. See Narrow Interpretation of Statute Hobbles Exon–Florio Reviews, Lawyers Told, 9 Int'l Trade Rep. (BNA) 325 (Feb. 19, 1992).

10. See Seminar Probes Impact of Investment by Japanese Firms in the U.S. Economy (Elliot Richardson quoted), 57 Antitrust & Trade Reg. Rep. (BNA) No. 1426, at 137 (July 27, 1989).

11. See Foreign Acquisitions and National Security: Hearing Before House Subcom. on Commerce, Consumer Protection, and Competitiveness of the Comm. on Energy and Commerce, 101st Cong. (1990) (statements of assistant secretaries in Treasury and Commerce).

cause the U.S. semiconductor research consortium that the DOD sponsors, SEMATECH, wanted guaranteed access to silicon wafers manufactured by Monsanto Electronic Materials Co., which was about to be sold to Huels AG, a German company. Although CFIUS recommended that the President allow the transaction to go forward, notwithstanding the objections of 29 congressmen, CFIUS obtained as part of its approval written assurances that SEMATECH would retain access and no technology would transfer for five years.[1] There appeared to be a quid pro quo that CFIUS would not disapprove the takeover in return for Huels' assurances, creating a performance requirement for foreign investment. CFIUS apparently imposed a similar requirement on Matra SA of France when it sought to purchase Fairchild industries, requiring a restructured export-control system as a condition for CFIUS approval. Foreign investors therefore may have to agree to government-imposed conditions on their transactions, with CFIUS approval received only after an Exon–Florio investigation is conducted as a bargaining tool.

British Tire & Rubber (UK)/Norton. The administration is not alone in using Exon–Florio as a bargaining tool. U.S. companies which are targets of hostile takeovers by foreign investors have used Exon–Florio as one method to oppose proposed takeovers.[2] Within two months of passage of the law, companies began to invoke Exon–Florio to delay or discourage takeovers.[3] This led many to conclude that the Exon–Florio process was easily abused. Critics argued that existing DOD regulations could handle true national-security concerns, and that Exon–Florio only added a political element to the ability of foreign investors to acquire U.S. companies.

A good example of an American firm using political pressure on a foreign buyer through Exon–Florio and other mechanisms is the attempted purchase of the Norton Company of Worcester, Mass., by British Tire and Rubber, PLC (BTR). Norton manufactured ceramic ball bearings used in the space shuttle. More than 200 congressmen urged an investigation, including Senator Kerry of Massachusetts, who noted Norton's role in the Massachusetts economy as justification for an investigation in addition to national-security reasons. The Massachusetts state legislature soon enacted a law

---

§ 27.7

1. See Bush Clears Sale of U.S. Manufacturer of Silicon Wafers to German Corporation, 56 Antitrust & Trade Reg. Rep. (BNA) No. 1402 at 232 (Feb. 9, 1989) (Rep. Florio observing that Huel's parent's owners could not be identified).

2. See Jonathan A. Knee, Limiting Abuse of Exon–Florio by Takeover Targets, 23 Geo.Wash.J.Int'l L. & Econ. 475 (1989).

3. See New Omnibus Trade Law May Provide Weapon Against Foreign Takeover Bids, 55 Antitrust & Trade Reg.Rep. (BNA) No. 1390, at 853 (Nov. 10, 1988).

depriving BTR of control should the purchase succeed, leading BTR to pull out, and a French buyer to make a friendly offer at a much higher price. No security concerns were raised when the friendly French buyer appeared offering a better price, even though Norton had earlier argued that BTR planned to dismember Norton and reduce its research and development budgets to the detriment of national security.[4] This led many to conclude that the Exon–Florio process was easily abused. Critics argued that existing DOD regulations could handle true national-security concerns, and that Exon–Florio only added a political element to the ability of foreign investors to acquire U.S. companies.

China Nat'l Aero Tech./NAMCO. While some firms use a CFIUS investigation to scare away hostile foreign investors, the one transaction that the President decided to reject had already been finalized at the time of the order.[5] The order forced the foreign entity to divest. The target was MAMCO Manufacturing, Inc., a U.S. company in Seattle that manufactured metal parts for commercial aircraft made by Boeing. MAMCO mainly supplied Boeing, and although some of its products were subject to export controls, MAMCO had no contracts involving classified information. The buyer was China National Aero–Technology Import and Export Corp. (CATIC), owned by the People's Republic of China. During the investigation, it appeared that CATIC had previously violated export-control laws concerning aircraft engines purchased from General Electric. But concerns about CATIC went beyond export-control problems with China. Administration sources revealed that CATIC had been trying to obtain technology to build jet fighters capable of refueling during flight. In addition, there were concerns by the administration and Congress that the Chinese government used CATIC as a base for covert operations in the United States.

The Executive Order directing CATIC to divest itself of MAMCO contained none of the above concerns or information, but simply stated that the two requirements of Exon–Florio had been satisfied: There existed credible evidence of a threat to national security, and no other provision of law could protect the national-security interest. Considering the relatively low level of technology involved, however, the President's action on CFIUS' unanimous recommendation to terminate the investment surprised many observers, leading some to believe that the national-security concern was a pretext for other political motives. Foreign-investor lobbying

---

4. See John Burgess, Norton's Defense: The British Are Bad

5. See President Invokes Exon–Florio, Blocks Acquisition of Aircraft Components Maker, 58 Antitrust & Trade Reg.Rep. (BNA) No. 1452, at 225 (Feb.

8, 1990); Bush Cancels China Purchase of U.S. Firm, San Francisco Chronicle, Feb. 3, 1990, at A1; Stuart Auerbach, President Tells China to Sell Seattle Firm, Wash. Post, Feb. 3, 1990, at A1.

organizations agreed with this perception, fearing that Exon–Florio would become a foreign-policy tool. But the administration stressed that the order did not constitute a change in America's general policy of openness toward investment from foreigners or reflect upon the PRC in particular. But the order seemed to be some indication that investment owned or supported by foreign governments would receive particular scrutiny under Exon–Florio.

Nakamichi/Applied Magnetics. MOST, a U.S. incorporated subsidiary of Nakamichi Corp. of Japan, agreed to purchase the Optical Products Division of U.S. Applied Magnetics Corporation. Although about 98 percent of OPD's sales were optical heads for computers, the products have application in some weapons systems. CFIUS reviewed the application and approved the sale one day before the inauguration of President Clinton. Congress was unaware of the ongoing review until the announced approval. But some members quickly intervened and produced evidence allegedly showing that the CFIUS review was based on misleading and incomplete information. That would allow reopening of the review process. Although much publicity followed there was no further review, but a clear warning sounded that a clearance by CFIUS may lead to public outcry if the process had remained silent until the CFIUS decision.

Thomson/LTV. By 1992, Congressional dissatisfaction with how the President and CFIUS had interpreted Exon–Florio led to proposals for new and stricter controls. The circumstances that led to the first substantive amendments to the Exon–Florio law involved foreign-government participation in a proposed acquisition, the attempted purchase of the missile division of LTV Corp. by Thomson–CSF, a conglomerate partially owned (58 percent) and financed by the French government.[6]

LTV, a defense contractor, had been operating under bankruptcy protection since 1986. Thomson made a bid for $450 million in association with an American investment bank and Northrop, the U.S. aircraft company, to buy LTV's aircraft and missile business.[7] Thomson outbid the U.S. defense contractor Martin Marietta by nearly $100 million. Martin Marietta was the buyer LTV favored because of the prospective problems Thomson would have with CFIUS.[8] To diminish concerns regarding national security, Thomson initially proposed to the DOD to structure its purchase of LTV through an agreement that would allow some control over LTV. As pressure increased, Thomson withdrew that proposal and stated

---

6. See Foreign Investment: Thomson—CSF Bid for LTV "Watershed Event," Leading to New Controls, ABA Seminar Told, 9 Int'l Trade Rep. (BNA) 1781 (Oct. 14, 1992).

7. The bankruptcy court approved the sale.

8. Thomson filed the notice for review under Exon–Florio.

that a proxy agreement would suffice, with the proxies being U.S. citizens who had no prior connection to the parties. But Thomson was unable to satisfy DOD demands to protect classified information.[9]

There was immediate adverse Congressional reaction, acknowledging that the United States and France were allies, but noting that French interests have not always been the same as America's.[10] Administration officials were reluctant to discuss even the general policy of allowing a foreign government-owned or-controlled company to purchase a U.S. defense contractor while the investigation was in process. Because the DOD apparently did not at first intend to object to the sale, it was criticized for failing to consider the questionable record of Thomson and the French government in exporting weapons to countries with which the United States did not have good relations, such as Iran, Libya and Iraq, and also for ignoring a Defense Intelligence Agency warning of extensive technology leakage. The lesson is that even "friendly" nations may have skeletons in the closet which the DOD and other critics of a proposed investment will quickly make public. France's military policy, which is made independently of NATO's, did not help.

Other commentators remained equally critical of Thomson's proposal suggesting that although an open-door policy makes sense for *private* foreign investors, that policy should be reexamined where foreign *governments* are involved, especially in this case, where LTV's products could not be replaced by another domestic firm. Exon–Florio (as it then existed) did not seem an appropriate vehicle to carry out a policy intended to prevent foreign-government ownership of defense contractors.

It became apparent during the controversy over LTV that the CFIUS was almost certain to recommend that the President block the transaction. Consequently, Thomson first withdraw its bid to restructure the deal and ultimately withdrew completely, leading to a suit by LTV for breach of contract.[11] Martin Marietta soon submitted a higher bid, justified because it would not have to compete with the inexhaustible resources of a government-assisted competitor.

---

9. The DOD has separate authority under the Industrial Security Regulations to protect classified information, including the ability to block an acquisition.

10. See French Government Ownership of Thomson Should Bar LTV Acquisition, Panel Told, 9 Int'l Trade Rep. (BNA) 1017 (June 10, 1992). The Senate even passed a non-binding resolution (vote of 93–4) finding the proposed acquisition to be harmful to national security.

11. See LTV Sues Thomson—CSF for Failure To Pay $20 million After Bid Withdrawal, 9 Int'l Trade Rep. (BNA) 1395 (Aug. 12, 1992).

During and following the Thomson–LTV attempted merger, Congress, not the President and CFIUS, assumed the lead role. Congress led the effort to gain more information on Thomson, and as a result of its hearings to reconsider the policy of open direct investment involving foreign governments, Thomson's bid was withdrawn. Because of the perception that the administration took up the case only with prompting by Congress, amendments to Exon–Florio soon appeared on Capitol Hill.

The committee working on what would become the Byrd Amendment to Exon–Florio identified three factors of greatest concern in the attempted merger. First, LTV was a substantial contractor with the DOD and NASA, and was the largest contractor ever for sale to a foreign firm. Second, as much as 75 percent of the work LTV did for the DOD required access to highly classified information that is generally prohibited for foreign nationals or representatives of foreign interests. Third, the French government owned 58 percent of Thomson's stock.[12] Of considerable concern to the committee was that government ownership would introduce into the company's decision-making process the foreign government's political and diplomatic interests, which may contrast with those of the United States.

Two major amendments to Exon–Florio are directly attributable to the experience of the failed Thomson purchase of LTV. When Congress assumed the lead in that investigation, the President appeared to be slow to react to the attempted takeover involving a foreign government. The first change sought by Congress was to remove any presidential and CFIUS reticence in carrying out their responsibilities under Exon–Florio. The Byrd Amendment *requires* the President or his designee to investigate if the purchasing foreigner is "controlled by or acting on behalf of a foreign government." The "acting on behalf" language is not without some ambiguity. It remains unclear whether this would include a lesser form of control as defined in the regulations (issued before the Byrd Amendment), consequently increasing Exon–Florio's coverage when a foreign government is involved. But the Byrd Amendment does add a new concept of "effective control" by a foreign government, which may increase the ambiguity of the meaning of "control by a foreign government."

The second important amendment forbids the sale of some U.S. companies to certain foreign investors, principally those involved with foreign governments. In a separate section of Exon–Florio, entities controlled by a foreign government are prohibited from

12. See S.Rep. No. 352, 102d Cong. (1992); see also H.R. Conf. Rep. No. 966, 102d Cong. (1992).

acquiring certain department of Energy or Defense contractors. Such contractors may not be acquired by entities controlled by or acting on behalf of foreign governments if they work under a national-security program that cannot be done without access to a "proscribed category of information." Furthermore, any firm awarded at least $500 million in prime DOD contracts or at least $500 million in prime Department of Energy contracts under national-security programs may not be acquired. There may be an escape clause, however. Section 2170a(b) suggests that if foreign investors are patient and go through an investigation that ends without suspension or prohibition, the acquisition restraints may not apply.[13]

There is an additional amendment which requires the President to report to Congress his Exon–Florio decision, including a detailed explanation of how the decision was reached. These reports are not disclosed to the public under an exemption to the Freedom of Information Act.

The Thomson–CSF experience nearly established a process that Congress decided that it did not want followed. The earlier-described proposed acquisition by CATIC, owned by the Chinese government, also resulted in a failed acquisition attempt, although due to action rather than a somewhat coerced withdrawal. Although the cases involve different national-security concerns, the pattern exists that if a foreign government plays a role in a foreign investment, CFIUS, or perhaps its apparent watchdog, the Congress, will examine the proposal very carefully. Exon–Florio has proven to be a law the operation of which Congress views very carefully, ready to enter into the review of a proposed acquisition with the threat of amendments that would undo any CFIUS or presidential approval.

§ 27.8   Defenses to Exon–Florio

If a foreign investor's proposed transaction is blocked, or if a completed transaction is ordered divested, the foreign investor may have some recourse, despite a finding that the investment adversely affects national security. As noted above, the Exon–Florio law states that the President's findings with regard to national security are not subject to judicial review. But courts may find that statutes designed to protect nationals security do not preclude all judicial

---

13. This section may mean either that such acquisitions are permitted only if an Exon–Florio review has been completed. And a decision made not to block, or that such acquisitions are permitted unless they are actually blocked by an Exon–Florio proceeding. As a practical matter, an Exon–Florio notice filing is most likely in such a case, and, consequently, there will be an examination by CFIUS.

review on the merits.[1] The requirement in § 2170(g) that the President report his findings in detail to Congress indicates that Congress intended to oversee the President's discretion. Additionally, the Fifth Amendment, as interpreted in *Goldberg v. Kelly*,[2] recognizes due-process rights in an administrative proceeding based upon a balancing test of the party's and the government's interests. If the President orders divestment, the foreign investor might claim that the consequence of such summary action is a "grievous loss" because of the President's action, not justified by an inadequate government interest cloaked in a nebulous concept of national security. Depending on the sensitivity of the nation-security interest, a divestment order, because of the substantial property loss, may justify more formal procedural protections than CFIUS standard procedures of investigation. There is nevertheless a mystique about national security that may lead courts to avoid opening the door to a proceeding in which the injured investor attempts to mandate that the government prove what the government will insist cannot be made the subject of inquiry for national-security reasons.

Additionally, foreign investors could challenge a divestment order issued pursuant to Exon–Florio as a taking for public use requiring just compensation, provided investors could prove a property loss. But such an argument must overcome the government's substantial public purpose in protecting national security.

Application of Exon–Florio might also produce conflicts with bilateral investment treaties (BITs) and friendship, commerce, and navigation treaties (FCNs) that the United States has concluded with other nations to promote open investment and guarantee national treatment in the United States and abroad. Foreign-investment proponents have argued that the government should interpret national security under Exon–Florio as defined in these treaties, rather than a broader version including economic issues.[3] Under FCN treaties, however, national security usually constitutes an exception to the principal of national treatment. Foreign investors may attempt to have presidential orders under Exon–Florio reviewed by means of an interpretation of the exception that requires resolution by the International Court of Justice (ICJ). The principal obstacle, however, is that standing before the ICJ is provided only to governments, thus requiring the foreign investor's home nation to commence the proceeding.[4] By contrast, bilateral

---

§ 27.8

1. See Note, Proposals for Limiting Foreign Investment Risk Under the Exon–Florio Amendment, 42 Hastings L.J. 1175, 1229 (1991).

2. 397 U.S. 254, 90 S.Ct. 1011, 25 L.Ed.2d 287 (1970).

3. See Martin Tolchin & Susan J. Tolchin, Selling Our Security: The Erosion of America's Assets 67 (1992).

4. It is further likely that under present attitudes toward the ICJ in the United States, jurisdiction of the ICJ

investment treaties provide procedures for resolving investment disputes through binding arbitration. But it is unclear whether their security exceptions are wholly discretionary or subject to judicial review.[5]

One further option, considering the political sensitivity of foreign investment in the United States, is to advance policy arguments to Congressional members interested in the investment. More than 100 members of Congress prompted the investigation into the proposed purchase of the Massachusetts-based Norton Company by British Tire and Rubber. The case demonstrated the politicization of the review process. In addition to the usual justifications for following a generally open investment policy, as described above, foreign investors might argue that a broad interpretation of Exon–Florio would cause defense-production companies needing capital to survive would be forced to dissolve in the absence of a foreign infusion through an acquisition, thus causing a loss of production.[6] But in most cases the foreign interest in the U.S. target company is matched by domestic interest, although by means of an offer for less than that offered by the foreign investor.

§ 27.9   Exon–Florio Viewed From Abroad

Foreign nations have not viewed the Exon–Florio law very favorably. The C.D. Howe Institute of Canada has noted that Canadian investors are concerned with the vague definition of "national security" and likely variations in interpretations by successive administrations.[1] The 1992 amendments were viewed in Canada as a further barrier to investment because they failed to define "defense critical technology."[2] The European Union also objects to Exon–Florio's vagueness in the definition of national security.[3]

If national security is to mean something more than national security, the law ought to be modified to express an intention to use foreign investment review as a review based on economic and/or

---

would not be recognized by the United States.

5. See Jose Alvarez, Political Protectionism and United States International Investment Obligations in Conflict: the Hazards of Exon–Florio, 30 Va.J.Int'l L. 1, 37 (1989). Bilateral investment treaties are discussed in chapter 25 on investment control laws.

6. See Tolchin & Tolchin, supra note 6, at 67.

§ 27.9

1. See NAFTA's Investment Provisions Improve Over FTA's, But Prob-

lems Remain Report Says, 10 Int'l Trade Rep. (BNA) 498 (Mar. 24, 1993).

2. See Canadian List of U.S. Trade Barriers Wide–Ranging but Small, Wilson Says, 10 Int'l Trade Rep. (BNA) 582 (Apr. 7, 1993), (discussing Canada's 1993 register of U.S. barriers to trade).

3. See EC Report on U.S. Barriers Issued on Eve of Talks Between Officials, 10 Int'l Trade Rep. (BNA) 659 (Apr. 21, 1993); EC's Van Agt Expresses Concern with U.S. Protectionist Tendencies, 10 Int'l Trade Rep. (BNA) 994 (June 16, 1993).

political concerns. Most of the trading partners of the United States view Exon–Florio in its current clothes as a law used differently by successive administrations to achieve political goals in permitting foreign investment, with little real analysis of the national security implications that are purportedly the foundation of the review process.

It is fair to comment that Exon–Florio is not well regarded abroad. It has allegedly led to diminished foreign investment in U.S. defense contractors.[4] But that is of course intended if such investment would threaten national security. Exon–Florio seems unlikely to go away. Exon–Florio is part of the government's "discretionary" power to deal with foreign trade and investment. Once given, it is hard to retrieve. But, in focus, some 98 percent of proposed acquisitions since 1988 that have been notified under the law have been approved without a full investigation.

§ 27.10   The Development of NAFTA Investment Rules

Unsuccessful attempts to develop an International Trade Organization under the failed Havana Charter after (WWII) (when the successes included the creation of the IMF, World Bank and GATT), left an investment rule abyss until bilateral investment treaties began to be used by European nations in the late 1950s.[1] While rules for investment were not successfully developed on a multilateral basis by the UN's Code of Conduct attempts during the 1970s, the issue of the settlement of investment disputes took a major step with the 1965 conclusion of the Convention on the Settlement of Investment Disputes Between States and Nationals of Other States.[2] The Convention established within the World Bank an affiliated institution called the International Center for the Settlement of Investment Disputes.

The GATT was never intended to include investment rules, they were to be in the failed ITO agreement. Although one of the later GATT rounds might have addressed the issue, there were many obstacles, not the least being the problem of potential U.S. Congressional opposition to such a major change or addition to the GATT, that had not been approved by the Congress in the first place. When the Uruguay Round of negotiations to develop the

4. See Changes Since Thomson/LTV Controversy Have Shrunk Defense Investment, Bar Told, 10 Int'l Trade Rep. (BNA) 1859 (Nov. 3, 1993).

§ 27.10

1. See A.J. Pappas, References on Bilateral Investment Treaties, 4 ICSID Rev. 189 (1989). The United States

joined in their use in the 1970's. See K. Scott Gudgeon, United States Bilateral Investment Treaties: Comments of Their Origin, Purposes, and General Treatment Standards, 4 Int'l Tax & Bus. L. 105 (1986).

2. Mar. 18 1965, 17 U.S.T. 1270, T.I.A.S. 6090, 575 U.N.T.S. 159.

World Trade Organization began, intending to lead to an expansion of the GATT, it was clear that it would have to face a vote in Congress. Investment rules were a major focus of the negotiations. By the time the WTO was adopted, with its Trade Related Investment Measures (TRIMs), the NAFTA, with its Chapter 11 on investment, was already in place. The Canada–U.S. Free Trade Agreement had covered investment in a modest manner, but with little attention to investment-dispute settlement.

The NAFTA a provisions carry further the investment provisions of the CFTA. Adding Mexico to form the NAFTA meant addressing several investment law problems that had not been at issue in relations between Canada and the United States. One was Mexico's adherence to the Calvo doctrine.[3] Furthermore, Mexico was reluctant to accept international law as the law applicable determining compensation subsequent to an expropriation. Mexico has long rejected the U.S. view that international law requires prompt, adequate and effective compensation. Mexico believed the applicable law was domestic law, and the standard to be closer to "appropriate" or "just" than to the U.S. view.[4]

§ 27.11   The Scope of Coverage of the NAFTA

The NAFTA investment provisions in Chapter 11 are divided into two major sections. Section A covers investment rules, and Section B the settlement of investment disputes. Chapter 11 applies to all investments, as defined in Article 1139; exempted are financial services contained in Annex III, and where special social services (police, public health, etc.) are performed. But if a provision of Chapter 11 conflicts with a provision in another chapter, the latter prevails.

The investment provisions of Chapter 11 are a major step in the multilateral agreement process. They are far more developed than those contained in the earlier CFTA, and even than those in the more recent WTO. They are a model for the development of a Free Trade Agreement of the Americas (FTAA). But however rational the progress in the development of the NAFTA investment rules may appear, these rules are not without their critics. The absence of serious attention to the environment and labor issues led to the adoption of NAFTA-saving environmental and labor side

3. See generally Donald R. Shea, The Calvo Clause: A Problem of Inter–American and International Law and Diplomacy (1955).

4. See generally Gloria L. Sandrino, The NAFTA Investment Chapter and Foreign Direct Investment in Mexico: A Third World Perspective, 27 Vand. J. Transnat'l L. 259 (1994); Stephen Zamo-

ra, NAFTA and the Harmonization of Domestic Legal Systems: The Side Effects of Free Trade, 12 Ariz. J. Int'l & Comp. L. 401 (1995); Note, NAFTA's Provision for Compensation in the Event of Expropriation: A Reassessment of the "Prompt, Adequate and Effective" Standard, 31 Stan. J. Int'l L. 423 (1995).

agreements. The negotiations for the FTAA must address both of these issues. But that is not enough to satisfy some critics. The rhetoric of the North–South dialogue of the 1960s and 1970s has never really gone away. It appears in the legal academy within the larger framework of "critical legal studies." Turning their attention to the NAFTA, some scholars suggest that the NAFTA is little more than a way for the United States to further dominate investment in Mexico, by establishing rules which for the most part govern the conduct of Mexico in admitting investment, but omitting any consideration of the responsibilities of the foreign investor. Often spoken in the broad language of the UN of the 1970s, if they are to be understood their criticisms need to be expressed in more specific and less rhetorical language that may allow fair consideration during the process of negotiation of future multinational trade agreements. The process of the development of the FTAA will tell us whether critical legal studies has any role to play.

While we have often stereotyped Mexico as a difficult nation in which to invest, and Canada as welcoming, we are to learn that stereotypes are often mythical. The NAFTA does not require each Party to repeal all laws governing foreign investment. What it does require is that each Party treat investors of other Parties in certain ways. But there are also exceptions that allow the perpetuation of some vestiges of earlier restrictionist policies. Whether or not justified, they are part of the NAFTA, and they are effective. Our interest is principally in the way in which the NAFTA affects our investment, rather than in whether or not national or local laws of the Parties are violated by the acts of the Canadian and Mexican governments. But we have learned that national laws remain applicable; what NAFTA tries to accomplish is to control those laws.

§ 27.12 NAFTA Chapter 11—General Rules

Section A of NAFTA Chapter 11 includes several general rules which require each Party to offer specific treatment to investors of each other Party. The most important is *national treatment*, requiring treatment to investors of another Party "no less favorable than that it accords" to the Party's own investors. This is similar to the provision that follows, *most-favored nation treatment*, that a Party accord investors of another Party treatment no less favorable than that it accords to any other Party or non-Party. There is also a requirement that the treatment of investors of another Party meet a minimum standard, incorporating a rule of "international law, including fair and equitable treatment and full protection and security." These provisions are a kind of boiler-plate framework, and they have roots in the GATT treatment obligations applicable to international trade in goods. The concept in the NAFTA applies equally to goods, services, technology and investment. But foreign investment has some special requirements, and several NAFTA provisions attempt to deal with them.

One ongoing concern of foreign investors has been *performance requirements,* local mandates that a certain percentage of the goods or services be exported, or be of domestic content, or meet a balance between import needs and exports, or link local sales to the volume of exports, or contain certain technology transferred from abroad, or mandate meeting certain exclusive sales targets. Each of these is addressed in the NAFTA, with certain exceptions. Perhaps the second-most disliked domestic restriction on foreign investment are mandated levels of local equity, the *involuntary joint venture.* A prohibition against a minimum level of domestic equity is included in the national treatment provision. There is also a prohibition against a minimum number of local persons being appointed to senior management. But there may be a local requirement that a majority of the board of directors (or a board committee) be nationals or residents, as long as the investor is not therefore impaired in controlling the investment. A fourth investor concern is free transferability of profits, royalty payments, etc., both during the operation and upon liquidation of the investment. The agreement attempts to assure this right, with some exceptions dealing with such issues as bankruptcy, securities trading, and criminal offenses (money laundering).

The above areas of concern deal mostly with the ability to commence and operate an investment free from certain restrictions. There is another time in the life of a business that has long been perhaps the most significant risk for foreign investors: when the business is nationalized or expropriated. The NAFTA includes an eight-part article outlining rules for both the taking and the compensation. Nowhere do the words "prompt, adequate and effective" appear, although that has long been the standard the U.S. government has argued to be the mandate of international law. It is a standard specifically rejected by Mexico subsequent to the nationalization of petroleum in 1938. The language of the NAFTA addresses each of these areas, however. Compensation shall be "equivalent to the fair market value of the expropriated investment immediately before the expropriation took place ... ", which certainly meets a prompt standard. But there may be disputes over whether an expropriation has occurred. In such instance prior compensation will not have been made. The adequacy issue is covered by the NAFTA requirement of "fair market value," and the effectiveness by the requirement of payment in a "G7 currency," or by implication one convertible to such currency. The expropriation article is likely to be the subject of considerable debate. Indeed, it has already been used to challenge actions that are not traditional nationalizations, but are more common regulatory standards that act as impediments to the effective operation of an investment.[1]

§ 27.13   NAFTA   Chapter   11—Investment   Dispute Resolution

Section B of NAFTA Chapter 11 governs the settlement of investment disputes between a Party and an investor of another Party.[1] This part of Chapter 11 establishes a procedure for claims against states. It proceeds first by consultation or negotiation, and then moves directly to arbitration under the ICSID Convention, the latter's Additional Facility Rules, or UNCITRAL Arbitration Rules. Arbitration is to be under the ICSID Convention where both the disputing Party *and* the Party of the investor are parties to the Convention (only the United States is an ICSID party), or under the ICSID Additional Facility Rules if either the disputing Party or the Party of the investor is not a party to the Convention(applicable for disputes between United States and Mexico, or United States and Canada), or under the UNCITRAL arbitration rules (applicable for disputes between Canada and Mexico). But the matter is not fully shifted to these forms of arbitration: such issues as the selection of arbitrators, the place of arbitration, and enforcement are covered in the NAFTA. There have been numerous investor–state claims' proceedings under Section B.[2]

§ 27.12

1. See, e.g., Anthony DePalma, Mexico is Ordered to Pay a U.S. Company $16.7 Million, N.Y.Times, Aug. 31, 2000, at C4 (state government's enforcement of environmental laws amounted to an expropriation); Timothy Pritchard, Law Suits are Prompting Calls for Changes to Clause in NAFTA, N.Y.Times, June 19, 1999, at C2 (Canadian claiming California environmental law violated Ch. 11); William Glaberson, NAFTA Invoked to Challenge Court Award, N.Y. Times, Jan. 28, 1999, at C6 (Canadian company claiming Mississippi jury award violated Ch. 11).

§ 27.13

1. See, e.g., Donald S. Macdonald, Chapter 11 of NAFTA: What Are the Implications for Sovereignty?, 24 Can.-U.S. L.J. 281 (1998).

2. See R. Folsom, *NAFTA and Free Trade in the Americas* Nutshell (2004), Chapter 6.

*

Chapter 28

OPIC AND MIGA INVESTMENT INSURANCE

Table of Sections

§ 28.1 OPIC Role and Structure

OPIC's mandate is to "mobilize and facilitate the participation of U.S. private capital and skills in the economic and social development of less developed friendly countries and areas, thereby complementing the development assistance objectives of the United States."[1] Guided by the expected economic and social development impact of a project, and its compatibility with other U.S. projects,[2] preferential consideration is given to investment projects in countries having low per-capita income. OPIC must further restrict its activities in countries with low per-capita incomes. But the President may designate other countries as beneficiaries under separate authority.[3] Countries may be denied OPIC insurance if they do not extend internationally recognized workers' rights to workers in that country, but the President may waive this prohibition on national economic interest grounds.[4]

§ 28.1

1. 22 U.S.C.A. § 2191.
2. 22 U.S.C.A. § 2191(1).
3. 19 U.S.C.A. § 2702.

4. 22 U.S.C.A. § 2191a. A subsection makes China ineligible for insurance unless the President grants authorization.

OPIC has broad power to engage in such insurance activities as to insure, reinsure,[5] cooperate in insuring,[6] enter into pooling or risk-sharing agreements, and hold ownership in investment insurance entities.[7] But its role is not limited to insurance. In addition to insuring investment risks, OPIC has some financing authority.[8] It provides loans which are sponsored by or significantly involve U.S. small businesses. OPIC may also guarantee loans, regardless of the size of the company.[9] Although OPIC provides financing worldwide, much of its initial focus was for investments in Latin America. It does not offer financing in nations which do not have bilateral agreements with OPIC. There has been a dramatic increase in financing in Eastern Europe. More recently, OPIC created new private equity investment funds—the Modern Africa Growth and Investment Company Fund, and the New Africa Opportunity Fund. These two funds address nations long thought overlooked.

OPIC operates with a 15–member board of directors, that includes eight appointed by the President from outside the government.[10] At least two of the eight must be experienced in small business, one each in organized labor and cooperatives. Other board of director members include the Director of the U.S. International Development Cooperation Agency and the U.S. Trade Representative, and an official from the Department of Labor. The OPIC President and CEO is appointed by the President, taking into account private business experience.[11] It is this composition that causes it to be referred to as a "quasi private/quasi public" organization.

§ 28.2   OPIC—Investor Eligibility

OPIC is a U.S. program for U.S. business. Eligibility is limited to U.S. citizens, U.S. corporations, partnerships, or other associations "substantially beneficially owned" by U.S. citizens. "Substantial beneficial ownership" ordinarily means that more than 50 percent of each class of issued and outstanding stock must be directly or beneficially owned by U.S. citizens. Foreign corporations, partnerships and other associations are also eligible if they are 95 percent owned by U.S. citizens.[1] If it appears from all the circumstances that foreign creditors can exercise effective control over an otherwise eligible corporation, no insurance will be written.

---

5.   22 U.S.C.A. § 2194(f).

6.   22 U.S.C.A. § 2194(a)(2).

7.   22 U.S.C.A. § 2194(f).

8.   22 U.S.C.A. § 2194(c).

9.   22 U.S.C.A. § 2194(b).

10.   22 U.S.C.A. § 2193(b).

11.   22 U.S.C.A. § 2193(c).

§ 28.2

1.   22 U.S.C.A. § 2198(c).

§ 28.3   OPIC—Insurance Programs

Three principal investment risks were the initial reason for the existence of OPIC. They are risk of loss of an investment due to (1) inconvertibility of currency, (2) expropriation or confiscation of property, and (3) property loss caused by war, revolution, insurrection or civil strife. A fourth class has been added called "business interruption" due to any of the principal three risks.

Inconvertibility. Before insurance against inconvertibility of currency is approved, the investor must obtain assurance from the host country that investor earnings will be convertible into dollars and that repatriation of capital is permitted. If the currency thereafter becomes inconvertible by act of the government, OPIC will accept the foreign currency, or a draft for the amount, and will provide the investor with U.S. dollars.

Expropriation. Expropriation "includes, but is not limited to, any abrogation, repudiation, or impairment by a foreign government of its own contract with an investor with respect to a project, where such abrogation, repudiation, or impairment is not caused by the investor's own fault or misconduct, and materially adversely affects the continued operation of the project."[1] OPIC contracts have followed a more specific and enumerative approach, because the law does not define specifically what actions constitute expropriation. OPIC's standard insurance contract contains a lengthy description of what is considered to be expropriatory action sufficient to require OPIC payment. That definition may help an investor in drafting a contract with the foreign host government, because that government will have to deal with OPIC once OPIC has paid the investor's claim.

The OPIC insured U.S. investor must exhaust local remedies before OPIC is obligated to pay any claim. All reasonable action must be taken by the investor, including pursuing administrative and judicial claims, to prevent or contest the challenged action by the host government. Upon payment of the claim, OPIC is subrogated to all rights to the investor's claim against the host government. Because the United States (OPIC) must deal with the foreign government, OPIC will not write any insurance in a foreign country until that country agrees to accept OPIC insurance and thus to negotiate with OPIC after claims have been paid.[2]

War, Revolution, Insurrection or Civil Strife. The third form of coverage, "war, revolution, insurrection, or civil strife," (political violence) is not defined by the statute. The usual OPIC contract provides protection against:

§ 28.3

1. 22 U.S.C.A. § 2198(b).

2. 22 U.S.C.A. § 2197(a).

injury to the physical condition, destruction, disappearance or seizure and retention of Covered Property directly caused by war (whether or not under formal declaration) or by revolution or insurrection and includes injury to the physical condition, destruction, disappearance or seizure and retention of Covered Property as a direct result of actions taken in hindering, combating or defending against a pending or expected hostile act whether in war, revolution, or insurrection.[3]

Civil strife is politically motivated violence (e.g., civil disturbances, riots, acts of sabotage, terrorism). Added to the OPIC statute in 1985 was a provision providing that:

Before issuing insurance for the first time for loss due to business interruption, and in each subsequent instance in which a significant expansion is proposed in the type of risk to be insured under the definition of "civil strife" or "business interruption", the Corporation shall ... submit to [Senate and House Committees] ... a report with respect to such insurance, including a thorough analysis of the risks to be covered, anticipated losses, and proposed rates and reserves and, in the case of insurance for loss due to business interruption, an explanation of the underwriting basis upon which the insurance is to be offered.[4]

§ 28.4 OPIC—Investment Insurance Terms

OPIC is authorized to issue up to $7.5 billion in investment insurance. While OPIC may not apply more than 10 percent of the maximum to any one investor,[1] it would seem unjustified according to risk management principles to allocate anywhere near that to a single investor, especially if most of the investment was located in a single foreign nation. OPIC in 1990 insured General Electric Company's Hungarian investment for $141 million, which might be questioned were risk management principles to govern investment decisions.[2] Foreign policy often appears to influence the decision.

§ 28.5 OPIC—Eligible Investments

The creating legislation authorizes OPIC to carry out its functions "utilizing broad criteria".[1] OPIC must consider investment eligibility in accordance with extensive guidelines that provide that OPIC conduct operations on a self-sustaining basis. It must consid-

---

3. OPIC Contract Art. 1.07.

4. 22 U.S.C.A. § 2194(a)(4).

§ 28.4

1. 22 U.S.C.A. § 2194(a)(3).

2. The World Bank's MIGA reinsured $50 million of this project, thus lessening the full exposure of OPIC.

§ 28.5

1. 22 U.S.C.A. § 2191.

er the economic and financial soundness of the project; use private credit and investment institutions along with OPIC's guarantee authority; broaden private participation and revolve its funds through selling its direct investments to private investors; apply principles of risk management; give preferential consideration to projects involving small business (at least 30 percent of all projects); consider less developed nation receptiveness to private enterprise; foster private initiative and competition and discourage monopolistic practices; further balance of payment objectives of the United States; support projects with positive trade benefits to the United States; advise and assist agencies of the United States and other public and private organizations interested in projects in less developed nations; avoid projects which diminish employment in the United States; refuse projects which do not have positive trade benefits to the United States, and refuse projects which pose an unreasonable or major environmental, health, or safety hazard, or result in significant degradation of national parks and similar protected areas. OPIC must also operate consistently with the goals of U.S. law relating to protection of environment and endangered species in less developed nations. Additionally it must limit operations to nations which provide or are in the process of providing internationally recognized rights for workers. Finally, OPIC must consider the host nation's observance of and respect for human rights. The political and economic changes in Eastern European countries have resulted in considerable OPIC activity in that area.

OPIC participates only in *new* investments (loans or insurance) because its role is to encourage new investment, not facilitate existing investment. Each proposed investment is evaluated by OPIC to consider, in addition to the above eligibility requirements, the extent to which the U.S. participant has long-term management arrangements with the new enterprise, the extent of private participation and whether the project is likely to assist further development of the host-nation's private sector. Loans or the contribution of goods or services to foreign governments will not be insured unless they are part of a construction contract. Nor will OPIC insure the credit or solvency of the foreign government. OPIC insures or provides a guarantee only for projects in countries that have signed an agreement with the United States for OPIC programs.

§ 28.6   OPIC—Claims and Dispute Settlement

Claims presented by insured investors are "settled, and disputes arising as a result thereof may be arbitrated with the consent of the parties, on such terms and conditions as OPIC may determine.''[1] OPIC insurance contracts have stated that "any controversy arising out of or relating to this Contract or the breach thereof shall be settled by arbitration in accordance with the then prevailing Commercial Arbitration Rules of the American Arbitration Association." The arbitration process is important; OPIC has challenged a number of claims presented to it by U.S. companies claiming to have lost property through expropriations.

Under AID, prior to 1969, six investor expropriation claims and one inconvertibility claim were denied. Between 1969 and 1978, under OPIC, about eight percent of claims were denied for a variety of reasons, such as investor failure to fulfill contractual obligations to the OPIC, or insurance not in effect at the time of the expropriation. As of 1997 OPIC had denied 23 claims and eight had been submitted to arbitration by the investors. Since 1978, OPIC has had the authority to deny loss claims if the investor, a controlling shareholder, or any agent of the investor has engaged in any act which resulted in a conviction under the 1977 Foreign Corrupt Practices Act, and such act has been the "preponderant" cause of the loss.[2] There have been few convictions under the FCPA, however, since most charges lead at most to a consent decree.

§ 28.7 OPIC—Private Insurers

OPIC continues to investigate methods of transferring its insurance coverage to private insurers. Even though some members of Congress view insurance of private investment abroad as best allocated to the private sector, it seems likely that OPIC will survive because its programs provide insurance for risks not broadly acceptable to the private insurance industry, and there are foreign policy considerations which may conflict with traditional risk management principles in establishing insurance premium rates.

§ 28.8 Investment Insurance on an International Level

The concept of offering insurance for various investment risks which led to the creation of OPIC in the United States, and to similar programs in several other nations, has been built upon on an international level by the World Bank's 1988 creation of the Multilateral Investment Guarantee Agency (MIGA). This organization, the newest part of the World Bank group, is intended to encourage increased investment to the developing nations by offering investment insurance and advisory services.[1] Voting power is

---

§ 28.6

1. 22 U.S.C.A. § 2197(i).

2. 22 U.S.C.A. § 2197(*l*).

§ 28.8

1. MIGA publishes a newsletter "MIGA NEWS", available at MIGA, World Bank, 1818 H Street, N.W., Wash-

equally divided between the industrial and developing nation groups. Shares are proportional to member nations' shares of World Bank capital.

Creating MIGA within the World Bank structure offers benefits a separate international organization lacks. MIGA has access to World Bank data on nations' economic and social status. This gives considerable credibility to MIGA, and encourages broad participation. It is not certain how MIGA has affected national programs, such as OPIC.[2] A U.S. based company, for example, may prefer dealing with OPIC because of greater confidence of claims being paid (until MIGA has developed a record of claims payments), of maintaining information confidentiality, and benefiting from legal processes established in bilateral investment treaties. But U.S. companies may find MIGA insurance available where OPIC is not. Rather than being an alternative to OPIC, MIGA should be viewed as compatible with OPIC. For example, International Paper Investments of the United States obtained MIGA insurance for risks of currency transfer, expropriation and war and civil disturbance, plus additional political risk insurance from OPIC.

Banks have found MIGA attractive because bank regulators in some countries have exempted commercial banks from special requirements for provisioning against loss where loans or investments are insured by MIGA. Furthermore, investors in nations without adequate national insurance programs have very much welcomed MIGA's creation. But even some of the newly industrializing nations, such as India and Korea, have adopted national programs. MIGA is not intended to replace national programs, but to extend the availability of investment insurance to many areas where it was not previously available, which in turn is expected to assist economic development in those areas. MIGA's success will likely be where it fills gaps rather than where it competes with established and successful national insurance programs. Those gaps are substantial and MIGA has a very major role to play in the world.

Unlike national programs, such as OPIC, MIGA has the force of a large group of nations behind it when it presses a claim. Only experience will disclose the extent to which politics (and particularly the North–South dialogue) will enter MIGA's claims procedures. The clear intention of MIGA is to avoid political interference and

---

ington, D.C. 20433. The advisory service is provided by MIGA's Foreign Investment Advisory Service, a joint venture with the IFC and World Bank. MIGA has a homepage at www.miga.org, and it's Investment Promotion Agency Electronic Network is at www.ipanet.net.

2. Several U.S. foreign investment projects have turned to MIGA for insurance, including McDonald's in Chile, Citibank in Argentina, Turkey and Pakistan, Bank of America in Pakistan, Bank of Boston in Argentina, Mobil Corporation in Saudi Arabia, and Coca–Cola in Poland.

consider the process solely as creating legal issues. The 1980s and 1990s thus far have been quiet times for foreign investment with regard to the risks insured against by OPIC and MIGA. But the risks are perceived as sufficiently likely that OPIC and MIGA have been quite busy writing new insurance.

§ 28.9 MIGA—Insurance Programs

Risks covered by MIGA are noncommercial and include risks of currency transfer, expropriation, war and civil disturbance, and breach of contract by the host government. Only developing nations are eligible locations for insured investments.

Currency Transfer. This insurance is similar to that offered by OPIC. It covers losses incurred when an investor is unable to convert host-nation currency into foreign exchange and transfer that exchange abroad. Host-nation currency may be that obtained from profits, principal, interest, royalties, capital, etc. The insurance covers refusals and excessive delays where the host government has failed to act, where there have been adverse changes in exchange control laws or regulations, or where conditions in the host-nation that govern currency transfer have deteriorated. Currency devaluations are *not* covered. Such devaluations are often the cause of substantial losses, but these are commercial losses attributed to changes that are to some extent predictable, and are not carried out by host nations to harm investment. Indeed, currency devaluations are usually extreme measures to address changing demand for the nation's currency.

Expropriation. This is insurance for partial or total loss from acts that reduce ownership of, control over, or rights to the insured investment. Included is "creeping" expropriation, where a series of acts has the same effect as an outright taking. Not covered are nondiscriminatory actions of the host government in exercising its regulatory authority.

Valuation for compensation is net book value; that may mean inadequate compensation where book value reflects historic costs. Loans and loan guarantees are compensated to the extent of the outstanding principal and interest. Compensation is paid at the same time as the insured assigns its rights in the investment to MIGA, which then may take action against the expropriating government.

War and Civil Disturbance. Losses for damage, disappearance, or destruction to tangible assets by politically motivated acts of war or civil disturbance, such as revolution, insurrection, *coups d'etat*, sabotage and terrorism. Compensation is for the book value or replacement cost of assets lost, and for the repair of damaged assets. This insurance also covers losses attributable to an interruption in a project for a period of one year. This is business interruption coverage, and becomes effective when the investment is considered a total loss. Book value is the measure of compensation.

Breach of Contract. This special insurance covers losses caused by the host government's breach or repudiation of a contract. When there is an alleged breach or repudiation, the foreign investor must be able to invoke an arbitration clause in the contract and obtain an award for damages. If that award is not paid by the host government, MIGA provides compensation.

§ 28.10   MIGA—Eligible Investments

MIGA insurance may cover, to a maximum of U.S. $50 million, new equity investments, or loans made or guaranteed by holders of equity. Also covered are service and management contracts, and licensing, franchising and production sharing agreements, if they are at least of three years duration and the investor's remuneration is related to the operating results of the project. MIGA will insure acquisitions under a state privatization program, an important program in view of the rapid pace of privatization in developing nations, Eastern European nations and parts of the former Soviet Union.

Two member countries are involved. First, investors must be from a member country, and only foreign investors qualify. With Agency approval, however, domestic investors may receive coverage for projects where they bring assets back to their nation. This special allowance is intended to promote the return of capital transferred to safe havens during times of political or economic uncertainty. Second, the location of approved investments must be in developing member nations which approve the insurance. There was considerable discussion regarding insuring only in developing nations which adopted standards for protecting foreign investment, but the final Convention did not include any such standards. Member nation standards for protecting foreign investment may nevertheless be a factor in writing insurance, if any measure of risk management principles is to be followed. Since the viability of MIGA is dependent both on its care in selecting risks to insure, and its ability to negotiate settlements after paying claims, the right of subrogation is extremely important.

§ 28.11   MIGA—Eligible Investors

An investor seeking MIGA insurance must be a national or member country *other than* the country in which the investment is to be made. The test of nationality for corporations is incorporation and having its principal place of business in the member nation, *or* being majority owned by nationals of the member nation. Commercially operated state owned corporations are eligible.

§ 28.12 MIGA—Scope of Coverage

MIGA covers investments under a standard term of 15 years, which may be increased to 20 years if MIGA determines that the longer term is justified by the nature of the project. If the insurance is for a loan, the term follows the duration of the loan agreement. Once written, MIGA is not able to terminate the coverage except for default by the investor. The insured investor, however, is entitled to cancel the insurance on any anniversary date after the third.

Premiums are based on risk assessment which include consideration of the political and economic conditions in the host nation. Rates vary depending on the industry and type of coverage. MIGA can insure equity investments to 90 percent of the initial contribution, plus 180 percent to cover earnings. Contracts such as for technical assistance are covered to 90 percent of the value of the payments due under the agreement. Loans and loan guarantees are also insured to 90 percent of the principal and interest that will accrue over the term of the loan. These figures are maximum available guarantees. The *current* amount is that in force for the given year. The difference between the maximum and current amount is referred to as the *standby* amount of guarantee, and constitutes a reserve coverage that the investor may place in effect each year to cover changes in the value or amount of investment at risk.

Chapter 29

EXPROPRIATION OF AN INVESTMENT

Table of Sections

§ 29.1   Avoiding the Risk of Expropriation

The risk of expropriation and cannot be fully avoided, and insurance should be considered, especially that provided either by the U.S. Overseas Private Investment Corporation (OPIC) or the World Bank's Multilateral Investment Guarantee Agency (MIGA). Taking measures to avoid the risk of expropriation cannot assure a foreign investor that expropriation will not occur. Many of the expropriations of the last century resulted from revolutions (USSR, Cuba, Mexico, Nicaragua) or very significant alterations in the government through elections (Chile), or in post-independence nationalism (Indonesia).

§ 29.2   Legal Choices Following Expropriation

If a taking occurs, there are several issues that will face the expropriated foreign investor. What law will apply, the law of the place of the taking, international law, or the law of the forum? Was the taking for a public purpose, or was it retaliatory or discriminatory? Was proper compensation forthcoming? Must remedies be exhausted in the taking nation? If the investor whose property has been taken attempts to sue the taking government in courts in the United States, or in third nations, what are the likely defenses?

§ 29.3   What Law Applies and What Is That Law?

There has been continuing debate about both the choice of law issue with respect to expropriation law and, assuming international law applies or is to be considered, what does that law state? The Mexican expropriation of foreign petroleum interests in 1938 commenced a dialogue between Mexico and the United States regarding the applicable law.[1] Mexico insisted that Mexican domestic law applied, which required compensation. The United States insisted that international law applied, which also required compensation. The United States argued that compensation had to be made in accordance with an alleged "prompt, adequate and effective" international law standard. The U.S. government position has continued to be that the standard is "prompt, adequate and effective," even though this view receives inconsistent support abroad and even within the United States by most jurists. The U.S. business community, nevertheless, tends to support the U.S. government position.

§ 29.3

1. The views expressed in letters exchanged by the governments are includ- ed in 3 Green H. Hackworth, Digest of International Law 655–65 (1942).

§ 29.4   Applying Domestic Law of the Taking Nation

While there does seem to be agreement that international law is applicable to takings of foreign property, that has been challenged in two ways. First, the U.N. Charter of Economic Rights and Duties of States affirms the right of nations to expropriate property, and states that compensation issues are to be settled by "domestic law of the nationalization State," unless otherwise agreed.[1] Second, when a nation expropriates foreign property, it tends to find greater comfort in arguing the applicability of its own law, which invariably is less demanding than whatever standard the international community has approved.

§ 29.5   Applying International Law

Even if the parties agree that international law is applicable, it may be difficult to determine what international law requires. It may be "prompt, adequate and effective" compensation, as the United States argues, or "just" compensation, as the Restatement of Foreign Relations suggests, or "appropriate" compensation, as U.N. Resolution 1803 dictated in 1962 proposes, and which seems to have been adopted by tribunals and courts more than any other standard.

§ 29.6   Investment Treaties

The possibility of having to address these issues suggests that investment agreements should include a provision providing for compensation under a standard of prompt, adequate and effective. The United States continues to try to include in bilateral investment treaties (BITs) a provision for compensation based on such standard. That is helpful to U.S. investors abroad. But governments change, and the most contentious compensation issues have arisen when there is an expropriation following a revolution or radical realignment of a government, such as in Cuba. In such case, even contractual provisions for payment according to prompt, adequate and effective criteria may be ignored by the new government in the taking nation.

§ 29.7   Public Purpose Under International Law

A sovereign nation has full and permanent sovereignty over its natural resources and economic activities.[1] That sovereignty gives

§ 29.4

1. Dec. 12, 1974, U.N.G.A. Res. 3281 (XXIX), 29 U.N. GAOR, Supp. (No. 31) 50, U.N. Doc. A/9631 (1975), reprinted in 14 Int'l Legal Mat. 251 (1975). This Charter, which does not constitute international law, was passed over the objection to this provision by 16 nations, mostly the largest industrialized nations, including the United States. The Charter illustrates the diversity of opinion regarding expropriation arising with the achievement of independence by many former colonies of the industrialized nations.

§ 29.7

1. That is clearly stated in the U.N. Resolution on Permanent Sovereignty

the nation the right to take privately-owned property, whether that property is owned by the country's nationals or foreigners. These are long-held concepts that exist on both an international and domestic level. Most national constitutions express this right. But the theory of taking does not allow the taking for any reason or any whim of the prevailing government. There must be a public purpose. There are two problems with the public purpose. First is its definition, and second is determining who is to measure public purpose in an international expropriation.

§ 29.8   Defining Public Purpose

There has never been a very clear definition of public purpose. It is often expressed in such broad words as "improvement of the social welfare or economic betterment of the nation." Does this mean such specific goals as improved infrastructure, better medical care, lower rates for basic services such as electricity, more adequate housing, or a lower infant-mortality rate? Or does it mean something more general, such as a shift to a different fundamental economic theory, by increasing or making exclusive the state ownership of the means of production and distribution.[1] The proper definition may be what the taking nation says it is, but at least there seems to be agreement that some legitimate public purpose is a necessary component of a lawful expropriation, and the taking nation must offer some rational purpose for the taking.

§ 29.9   Who Measures Public Purpose?

Defining public purpose does not end the problem. When one state has taken the property of nationals of another, what courts should sit in judgment of the public purpose issue, both to define it and to determine whether it is likely to be or already has been met? A court in the taking nation is not likely to overrule the taking for lack of public purpose justifications. The ideal setting for establishing these rules is the International Court of Justice. But that court has not yet proven to be an effective body to develop an international law of expropriation. Such development is thus left to national courts and various tribunals. These have tended to shy away from addressing the public purpose issue.[1] That has been because of

Over Natural Resources, Dec. 14, 1962, U.N.G.A.Res. 1803 (XVII), 17 U.N. GAOR, Supp. (No. 17) 15, U.N.Doc. A/5217 (1963), reprinted in 2 Int'l Legal Mat. 223 (1963).

§ 29.8

1. Public purpose, with respect to the Cuban expropriations, is explored in

Michael Wallace Gordon, The Cuban Nationalizations: The Demise of Foreign Private Property (1976).

§ 29.9

1. See Martin Domke, Foreign Nationalizations, 55 Am.J.Int'l L. 585 (1961).

both the conceptual difficulty with the issue, and the fact that foreign investors whose properties have been expropriated usually are not interested in restitution of their property as long as the taking government is in office. The foreign investors are interested in receiving compensation. Consequently, while the public purpose element of expropriation is present and should be considered, there are other elements of expropriation more likely to be the subject of investor concern.

§ 29.10   Retaliation and Discrimination Defined

In addition to lacking a public purpose, an expropriation may be unlawful if it were in retaliation for acts of the government of the person who owned the property,[1] or if it discriminated against a particular person or government.[2] The Cuban expropriations were examples of both. The first expropriations were exclusively of U.S. property (i.e., discrimination), and were in response to the United States eliminating the Cuban sugar quota (i.e., retaliation). Both were reasons for U.S. courts holding the expropriations to have been unlawful.[3]

The taking of some property of only one nation's nationals is not necessarily discriminatory. A country may decide to nationalize one sector, such as mining. That sector might be owned exclusively by nationals of one foreign nation. It could be difficult in such case to conclude whether the taking was based on the desire to have the state own all mining interests because it was believed more sound economically or preferable for national security reasons, or was based on an intention to discriminate against one nation and take its property, whether it consisted of mining properties or hotels or anything else.

§ 29.11   Retaliation and Discrimination Subordinated to Compensation

However important it may be to understand the issues of public purpose, retaliation and discrimination, the real issue is likely to be the payment of compensation. If a foreign investor is compensated satisfactorily, there is likely to be little concern with the technicalities of lawfulness or unlawfulness of the taking under

---

§ 29.10

1. Proof of a retaliatory purpose may actually constitute proof of the *absence* of a public purpose. If the reason for an expropriation is retaliation, it can hardly be considered a public purpose.

2. If an expropriation is undertaken solely to discriminate against a foreign nation, it may constitute proof of both a lack of a public purpose and retaliation.

The three elements, public purpose, retaliation and discrimination, are thus often quite interrelated.

3. See Banco Nacional de Cuba v. Sabbatino, 376 U.S. 398, 84 S.Ct. 923, 11 L.Ed.2d 804 (1964), and especially the decisions of the district court, 193 F.Supp. 375 (S.D.N.Y.1961), and court of appeals, 307 F.2d 845 (2d Cir.1962).

international law because of the public purpose, retaliation or discrimination characteristics of the taking. The investor may be concerned with the loss of future business, however, and may wish to consider the prospects of a return of the property after the new, hostile government is either replaced or adopts a different attitude toward foreign investment or the foreign investor.

§ 29.12   The Uncertainty of International Law

As noted above, if the expropriated foreign property owner is satisfactorily compensated, that is likely to end the matter. A ruling by any dispute settling entity, court or tribunal, domestic or international, that the expropriation was unlawful, is a purely pyrrhic victory if there is no satisfactory compensation. What, therefore, is the proper measure of compensation?

The U.S. government's repeatedly stated position regarding compensation is that it is (1) required under international law, and it (2) must be prompt, adequate and effective.[1] The first view, that international law requires compensation, is generally shared by jurists within the United States and abroad. But the second view, the prompt, adequate and effective standard, is the subject of vigorous debate and generally is rejected by many U.S. and foreign jurists. The two parts are often discussed as one issue.

The first international court case usually referred to that discusses expropriation is the 1928 *Chorzów Factory* decision of the Permanent Court of International Justice (PCIJ).[2] That case refers only to a duty of the "payment of fair compensation." That seems less stringent than the "prompt, adequate and effective" standard alleged to be the prevailing international law by U.S. Secretary of State Hull in 1938 in his notes to the Mexican government.[3] There has been little further guidance from the PCIJ, replaced by the International Court of Justice. The narrow focus in the *Barcelona Traction* decision[4] added very little, if anything, to the international law of expropriation compensation. A subsequent dispute involving an intervention which allegedly caused the company to file for bankruptcy was decided by a Chamber of the International Court of

---

§ 29.12

1. See Oscar Schachter, Editorial Comment, Compensation for Expropriation, 78 Am.J.Int'l L. 121 (1984).

2. P.C.I.J., Ser.A, No. 17 (1928). The earlier 1922 Norwegian Shipowners' Claims arbitration referred to "just compensation" as determined by the "fair actual value at the time and place". Norwegian Shipowners' Claims (Norway v. U.S.), 1922 1 U.N.Rep.Int'l Arb.Awards 307.

3. 3 Green H. Hackworth, Digest of International Law 655 (1942).

4. Barcelona Traction, Light & Power Co. (Second phase) (Belg. v. Spain), 1970 ICJ Rep. 3. The case is discussed in Herbert W. Briggs, Barcelona Traction: The *Jus Standi* of Belgium, 65 Am. J.Int'l L. 327 (1971); F.A. Mann, The Protection of Shareholders' Interests in the Light of the *Barcelona Traction* Case, 67 Am.J.Int'l L. 259 (1973).

Justice.[5] It involved the interpretation of the Treaty of Friendship, Commerce and Navigation between the United States and Italy, most specifically issues regarding interference with the U.S. company's right to "control and manage" its operation in Italy. The measure of damages became an issue, and was not dealt with very clearly, partly because of the uncertainty of the company's ability to function during the period of intervention and the appropriateness of damages after filing bankruptcy. But the ruling was that Italy had not violated international law in its requisition or intervention. Furthermore, since the damages were conditioned upon liability, there was no final decision as to their measure.

Debate over the proper level of compensation continues without anything resembling a consensus. But some standards have developed that might be applied by a court or tribunal. The alternatives seem to use elastic words or terms, but when further defined, there may be less difference than is at first thought to exist.

§ 29.13 Prompt, Adequate and Effective Compensation

The "prompt, adequate and effective" standard is likely to be applied by (1) U.S. courts or tribunals applying a U.S norm of compensation theory, or searching for an international standard, or (2) U.S. courts or tribunals applying an agreement between the parties or nations that calls for the application of the prompt, adequate and effective standard, such as a bilateral investment treaty. There is no assurance, however, that a U.S. court or tribunal searching for "the" international law will arrive at a prompt, adequate and effective rule. The 1981 *Banco Nacional v. Chase Manhattan Bank* decision suggested that the consensus of nations was to apply an "appropriate" standard, and quoted one highly regarded American author who rejected the prompt, adequate and effective standard as a norm of international law.[1]

Because of the very limited number of judicial decisions discussing the compensation issue, decisions of arbitration panels are often useful to compare with cases. In the *LIAMCO* arbitration, the arbitrator suggested that the prompt, adequate and effective standard was not the only standard, and interpreted the contract to conclude that under general principles of law only "equitable"

---

5. Elettronica Sicula S.p.A. (ELSI), Judgment (U.S. v. Italy), 1989 ICJ Rep. 15. The case is discussed in Ignaz Seidl–Hohenveldren, ELSI and Badger: The Two Raytheon Cases, 26 Rivista de Diritto Internazionale Privato e Processuale 261 (1990); F.A. Mann, Foreign Investment in the International Court of Justice: The *ELSI* Case, 86 Am.J.Int'l L. 92 (1992).

§ 29.13

1. Banco Nacional de Cuba v. Chase Manhattan Bank, 658 F.2d 875 (2d Cir. 1981). The court quoted Professor Wolfgang G. Friedmann.

compensation was required.[2] But the arbitrator included in the award a substantial amount for lost profits, a conclusion suggesting the adoption of a *full* compensation standard.

§ 29.14 Appropriate Compensation

The "appropriate" compensation norm is the standard in U.N. Resolution 1803 of 1962, which in the view of many jurists,[1] remains the most likely norm to be applied. It has been suggested as the standard in the *Banco Nacional* decision noted above, and in at least two important international arbitrations, the *TOPCO/CALASIATIC* and *AMINOIL* cases.[2]

§ 29.15 Fair Compensation

The "fair" compensation standard was used in the much-discussed but little-followed *Chorzów Factory* PCIJ decision, noted above. However, fair compensation has not generally been accepted as the proper standard, and has not become an accepted norm of international law. That is at least partly due to the broad sense of what fair might include. A legal norm deserves greater definition.

§ 29.16 Just Compensation

The Restatement (Third) of the Foreign Relations Law of the United States adopted "just" in place of "appropriate", largely to avoid a possible inclusion of host nation demanded deductions under an "appropriate" standard. Several expropriating nations had calculated compensation by taking the company's value of the property and deducting what were called "excess profits" or "improper pricing" of resources to arrive at a conclusion that either no compensation was due, or that the company actually owed the expropriating nation. But it is hard to envision a taking nation agreeing that while such deductions could be allowed under an "appropriate" standard, they could not under a "just" standard.

§ 29.17 Restitution as a Substitute for Compensation

The expropriated foreign investor may prefer to have the property returned rather than receive compensation. This is not

---

2. Libyan American Oil Co. v. Libyan Arab Republic, 20 Int'l Legal Mat. 1 (1981).

§ 29.14

1. See, e.g., Richard B. Lillich, The Valuation of Nationalized Property in International Law: Toward a Consensus or More "Rich Chaos"?, in Richard B. Lillich (ed. & contrib.), 3 The Valuation

of Nationalized Property in International Law 183 (1975).

2. Texas Overseas Petroleum Co/California Asiatic Oil Co. v. Government of the Libyan Arab Republic, 17 Int'l Legal Mat. 3, 29 (1978), 53 ILR 389 (1979) (English trans.); Arbitration between Kuwait and the American Independent Oil Co. (AMINOIL), 21 Int'l Legal Mat. 976 (1982).

likely to be the case where there has been a revolution with an investment-hostile government, such as Cuba, but may be appropriate where a counter-revolution has soon restored an investment-welcoming government. There is some precedent for restitution. In the *TOPCO/CALASIATIC* arbitration, following expropriations of Texas Overseas Petroleum Corporation and California Asiatic Oil Company by Libya, the sole arbitrator, Professor Dupuy (Secretary General of the Hague Academy of International Law), noted that the *Chorzów Factory* decision suggested that *restitutio in integrum* remains international law, and ordered Libya to resume performance of the agreement.[1] But in the *BP Arbitration* the arbitrator, Swedish Judge Lagergren, stated that the *Chorzów Factory* rule of *restitutio in integrum* was meant only to be used to calculate compensation, suggesting adherence to a full compensation theory.[2]

§ 29.18 Mandatory Questions Under Any Standard

Whatever standard is chosen, three questions must be asked. First, *how much* is to be paid? Second, in *what form* is it to be paid? And third, *when* must it be paid? If the answers to these questions are the full value of the property, in convertible currency, and immediately or very soon, then the standard that is being applied seems to be the "prompt, adequate and effective" standard argued by the United States to constitute international law. The Iran–United States Claims Tribunal, meeting in the Hague for over two decades, never formally applied a "prompt, adequate and effective" standard.[1] But claims approved by the tribunal have been paid *promptly* from the funds established for the purpose, they have been paid in dollars (that surely constitutes *effective* payment), and the methods of valuation used seem to satisfy any reasonable *adequacy* standard.[2]

If the consensus is an "appropriate" standard, tribunals that have gained the respect of the majority of the international community, including the main industrialized nations, seem to be applying a standard that is "fair, just and appropriate" as well as "prompt,

§ 29.17

1. 17 Int'l Legal Mat. 1, 32 (1978).

2. British Petroleum Exploration Co. v. Libyan Arab Republic, 53 ILR 297 (1973).

§ 29.18

1. The Tribunal has used a "just" standard, which is stated in the U.S.-Iran Treaty of Amity, Economic Relations and Consular Rights. Aug. 15, 1955, 8 UST 899, ITAS No. 3853, 284 UNTS 93. The standard is stated as "prompt payment of just compensation." But it goes on to state that it must be paid in "an effectively realizable form" and must be for the "full equivalent of the property taken", thus becoming nearly a prompt, adequate and effective standard. See David Caron, The Nature of the Iran–United States Claims Tribunal and the Evolving Structure of International Dispute Resolution, 84 Am.J. Int'l L. 104 (1990).

2. The Iran–United States Tribunal is quite unique, however, because of the initial agreement to deposit considerable funds to meet claims.

adequate and effective". For now, and perhaps until or unless the investment restrictiveness of the 1970s returns, the demand for a norm allowing only partial compensation has little backing.[3]

§ 29.19   Exhaustion of Local Remedies

Seeking compensation from the expropriating government is not only appropriate, but may be a precondition for initiating an insurance claim.[1] It is reasonable to first seek compensation from the one who has committed the wrong.[2] That idea makes sense when the expropriation is not part of a total change in economic theory following a revolution that includes the expropriation of all private property. The taking nation may be prepared to compensate properties taken in a selective nationalization, such as a taking of all telecommunications or air transportation enterprises. But when a nationalization occurs of the dimensions of those in the former Soviet Union, China, Eastern Europe and Cuba, there is little reason either for the expropriated property owner to attempt to exhaust local remedies, or for that party to be forced to do so before insurance claims are presented. Nevertheless, it is probably appropriate for the expropriated party to make some attempt against the taking government, if nothing more than a formal written protest of the taking and a demand for compensation. The problem arises when the nation expresses a willingness to hear such claims, but the circumstances, and unfolding facts, seem clearly to suggest that the willingness to discuss compensation is illusory.[3] The expropriated property owner may have to be prepared to establish that local remedies are inadequate before seeking remedies at home or in third-party nations. Adequate proof justifying the futility of pursuing local remedies may take time to accumulate. The proof should illustrate deficiencies with the court or tribunal system of the taking nation, the method of valuation, the ability of the country to pay settled claims, and the appropriateness of the form of any payment the taking nation can afford. The experience with taking nations where the taking is part of a major economic, political and social revolution clearly suggests that local remedies are likely to very unsatisfactory to the expropriated property owners, and that they will have to seek assistance outside the taking nation.

3. See Patrick M. Norton, A Law of the Future or a Law of the Past? Modern Tribunals and the International Law of Expropriation, 85 Am.J. Int'l L. 474 (1991).

§ 29.19

1. See G. Law, The Local Remedies Rule in International Law (1961).

2. See Mummery, Increasing the Use of Local Remedies, 58 Proceed.Am. Soc'y Int'l L. 107 (1964), tracing the idea to the Bible.

3. Cuba offered compensation in the form of bonds that deserved the term "junk bonds" long before Wall Street popularized them decades later.

§ 29.20 Assistance of the Government—The "Calvo Clause"

Expropriated U.S. investors usually report the expropriation to the U.S. Department of State. Diplomatic pressure may be essential to success in dealing with the taking nation. The U.S. executive has frequently intervened subsequent to foreign nationalizations of U.S. property. While diplomatic intervention may be helpful and may lead to government sanctions against the taking nation, there is one concern that frequently faces the U.S. investor abroad—the application by the taking nation of the "Calvo Clause".[1]

The Calvo Clause espouses a theory, sometimes expressed in an agreement signed by the foreign investor, that a foreign investor is entitled to treatment no different than that given domestic investors,[2] and recourse to one's diplomatic channels may result in a *forfeiture* of the property. The Calvo Clause was included in Article 3 of the restrictive 1973 Mexican Investment Law, but there is no instance of any property forfeiture in Mexico, or in other nations which have either adopted the Calvo Clause concept formally in investment legislation, or made it a part of investment rhetoric.[3] The idea of the Calvo Clause improperly frustrates the right of a nation to diplomatic intervention to protect property of its citizens. If a government does intervene, it may not be clear whether it does so at the request of the expropriated foreign investor, or on its own initiative. If the latter, it is unfair to conclude that the property is therefore forfeited because of any act of the investor. While the idea that foreign investors ought to be entitled to no better treatment than nations may seem sensible, the real world does give foreign investors alternatives not available to nationals. One is diplomatic negotiations. When the Calvo Clause goes beyond being a statement of exhaustion of local remedies to being an exclusionary rule precluding any other subsequent remedies, it loses much of its respect and viability.

§ 29.21 Lump–Sum Agreements and Claims Commissions

Where there has been an extensive nationalization of foreign property, such as by the Soviet Union, China, Eastern European

---

§ 29.20

1. Donald R. Shea, The Calvo Clause (1955).

2. This part of the concept means that the foreign investor is entitled to no better treatment than a national, and thus is left exclusively to local remedies. It is consequently interrelated with the exhaustion of local remedies concept.

3. The concept was not included in the 1993 Mexican Investment Law, which is more investor friendly than the 1973 law. The NAFTA foreign investment provisions eliminate the Calvo Clause as a threat to a Canadian or U.S. investor, a major concession by Mexico.

nations, and Cuba, the most likely conclusion is by a lump-sum settlement by a later binational agreement. Lump-sum settlements are common, but they remain questionable as a part of the jurisprudence of the international law of compensation.[1] Any agreed-upon lump sum is subsequently divided among claimants who have quite likely filed claims years earlier, soon after the expropriations occurred.[2] For example, the Cuban nationalizations occurred between 1959 and the early 1960s. The Cuban Claims Act was passed in 1964, providing for claims to be filed between 1965 and 1967, extended later to 1972. At the end claims allowed amounted to U.S. $1.76 billion.[3] The valuation method ranged from strict reliance on book value to a usually much higher going concern value.[4] The Iran–United States Claims Tribunal has tended to interpret its obligation to provide full compensation to mean something closer to going concern value than book value.[5] Arguing for acceptance of a claim under a going concern value does not assure that one will receive that higher amount, but it may mean a claim accepted for an amount higher relative than other U.S. claimants, and thus ultimate receipt of a higher amount in the pro rata apportioning of any agreed settlement.

Cuba will not be able to pay the full amount of the claims. A Cuban government willing to negotiate the claims will not likely agree that the amount as determined by the United States is correct, partly because there was never any Cuban representation at the claims hearings. Cuba will not be able to afford to pay some $2 billion in claims, and the experience of U.S. claims commissions is the ultimate payment of a substantially lower negotiated amount than the full value of previously documented claims.

§ 29.21

1. Dictum in Barcelona Traction suggests that lump-sum settlements are not sources of law for compensation. Barcelona Traction, Light & Power Co., Ltd. (Belgium v. Spain), 1970 I.C.J. 3, 40. See also Brice Clagett, Just Compensation in International Law: The Issues Before the Iran–United States Claims Tribunal, in Richard B. Lillich (ed. & contrib.) 4 The Valuation of Nationalized Property in International Law 31 (1987). Other scholars dispute this narrow view of international law sources.

2. See generally Richard B. Lillich, International Claims: Their Adjudication by National Commissions (1962).

3. See Michael Wallace Gordon, The Cuban Claims Act: Progress in the Development of a Viable Valuation Process in the FCSC, 13 Santa Clara Law. 625 (1973).

4. The statute authorizes the use of several methods of valuation. See 22 U.S.C.A. § 1623(a). The valuation is to use "applicable principles of international law, justice, and equity." Id. See 22 U.S.C.A. § 1623(k).

5. The experience with Iran differs markedly from the case of Cuba. Iran agreed to the payment of claims only because it had very substantial sums on deposit in the West, which were blocked. It agreed to the claims process as a means to gain access to those funds. But Cuba had no such large sums in foreign banks. Sums that remain frozen in U.S. banks will probably be part of a future settlement agreement, with additional sums to be paid from renewed trade with the United States, possibly with restoration of some sugar quota.

The Cuban Claims Act process is part of the larger U.S. Foreign Claims Settlement Commission. A *mixed* commission to settle claims was created following the U.S. revolutionary war.[6] But it was not effective and was followed by a *national* commission to determine claims after a lump-sum settlement agreement was concluded in 1803. Over the next century the United States established national commissions to distribute funds received in settlements with Great Britain, Brazil, China, Denmark, France, Mexico, Peru, the Two Sicilies and Spain. Between World Wars I and II both national and mixed claims commissions were used, but the national commission prevailed. Foreign countries often prefer the use of a national claims commission to distribute an agreed upon total sum as the country prefers. The Iran–United States Claims Tribunal is quite unique in this respect, it varies from the norm at least partly because the U.S. hostages were involved, and there was no time to conduct a lengthy process to determine how much money to demand from Iran. But the use of a national commission, in the manner of the Cuban Claims Commission, is likely to be the way future claims are settled that lack the unique characteristics of the Iranian case.

The Foreign Claims Settlement Commission was established in 1954 as a separate entity, when the earlier International Claims Commission was abolished. Its function is essentially judicial, and the benefit of its existence (as opposed to using the district courts, for example) is its ability to acquire expertise in the narrow area of adjudication of foreign claims. Evidence of valuation of property lost abroad is difficult to obtain, and that form of evidence demanded in the courts is rarely available. In 1980, after a number of years of relative inactivity, the FCSC was transformed into a separate and independent agency within the Department of Justice. Any sums obtained by the United States are distributed according to the statute.

Special funds have been created in the Treasury for specific claims, relating to claims and agreements with Yugoslavia and the People's Republic of China. Each real or expected settlement with an expropriating nation must necessarily be kept separate from another, thus the statutes have titles covering special procedures for various specific takings. These include claims against Bulgaria, Hungary, Romania, Italy and the Soviet Union; Czechoslovakia; Cuba and China; German Democratic Republic; and Vietnam. Each is related to takings following significant disturbances, principally war and revolution. The statute illustrates a pattern of procedural provisions which will likely be adopted for any future losses by U.S.

6. The Jay Treaty of 1794 established the first claims commission for the new United States.

citizens abroad where the takings are of all the property of U.S. citizens.

Some claimants might prefer bringing their own suits against the foreign government, where they are able to locate property owned by that foreign government situated in the United States. That has not proven very successful in most cases, however. When a nation undertakes a massive expropriation of the property of a foreign nation, it usually removes as much property as possible from that nation. The inability of Iran to do so required Iran to agree to the Iran–United States Claims Tribunal. Cuba successfully transferred large sums out of the United States before remaining assets were frozen by the Congress. Thus there may be little sense in seeking a judgment in a U.S. court, if there is no property to attach and it is evident that the hostile taking nation will reject any attempt to enforce the judgment in the taking nation. Furthermore, the United States may make filing claims before a national commission the only available procedure. Many investors who were in the process of suing Iran at the time of the resolution of the hostage dispute and establishment of the claims tribunal were angered that the agreement included removal of their claims from courts to the tribunal. Requiring all U.S. claimants to use this same process may benefit relations between the nations, but may not satisfy some claimants who were able to attach certain property of the foreign government and believe they might receive a greater share of their claim by separate litigation.

Separate litigation will often be attempted by frustrated expropriated investors, perhaps more successfully when the expropriations have not been massive takings as discussed above, but more selective takings of only certain property. Thus, some thought should be given to these individual suits against foreign governments for expropriations.

§ 29.22 Suing in United States Courts

When a U.S. investor sues a foreign government for taking property, two special defenses are likely to be made by the foreign government. The first is that the defendant is a sovereign which is immune from suit. The second is that the act of taking was a sovereign act occurring within the territory of the nation and is thus an "act of state" that should not be adjudicated in the courts of a foreign nation. There is much written on these two subjects. There are some principal features of these two theories, particularly as they apply to expropriation.

§ 29.23 Foreign Sovereign Immunity

When the circumstances for state immunity are present, the court relinquishes jurisdiction to adjudicate or enforce over the foreign state. Because state immunity is influenced by the state's concepts of separation of powers and notions of comity, state immunity theory assumes different forms in different nations. Somewhat paradoxically, state immunity is contained in statutes in several common law tradition nations, but is found only in the case law of many civil law tradition nations. State immunity theory in the United States developed in case law exclusively until the enactment of the Foreign Sovereign Immunities Act (FSIA) of 1976.[1] The experience in the United Kingdom is similar, case law prevailed until the enactment of the State Immunity Act 1978.[2] On the continent, the theory long remained in case law, but is now under the European Convention on State Immunity and Additional Protocol 1972.

§ 29.24   History and Rationale

The roots of U.S. state immunity precedent go back to *The Schooner Exchange v. McFaddon.*[1] Chief Justice Marshall stated in this Supreme Court decision that the courts of the United States lacked jurisdiction over an armed ship of a foreign state (France) located in a U.S. port. When engaged in official acts (*jure imperii*) the sovereign (whether ancient prince or modern state):

> [b]eing in no respect amenable to another; and being bound by obligations of the highest character not to degrade the dignity of his nation, by placing himself or its sovereign rights within the jurisdiction of another, can be supposed to enter a foreign territory only under an express license, or in the confidence that the [absolute] immunities belonging to his independent sovereign station, though not expressly stipulated, are reserved by implication, and will be extended to him.[2]

But Chief Justice Marshall was also aware of the logic of limits on immunity, acknowledging a distinction between the private property of a person who happens to be a prince, and the military force of a sovereign power. Had he been confronted with a case of commercial activity by a sovereign, the long struggle with state immunity theory in the United States might have been prevented.

Immunity of a sovereign was nevertheless consistently found to be absolute, regardless of the nature of the activity. Although it may have appeared from *The Schooner Exchange* that state immunity is domestic law, it is as well an accepted principle of customary

§ 29.23

1. 28 U.S.C.A. §§ 1330, 1602–1611.

2. See Michael Wallace Gordon, Foreign State Immunity in Commercial Transactions § 17 (Butterworths 1991).

§ 29.24

1. 11 U.S. (7 Cranch) 116, 3 L.Ed. 287 (1812).

2. 11 U.S. (7 Cranch) at 137.

international law.[3] Customary international law offered some support in the mid-part of the 20th century to nations (i.e., United Kingdom) confronting the absolute/restrictive debate, but the evolution from absolute to restrictive theory was less influenced by international law than developing state concepts of the role of the state in modern society.

The doctrine of state immunity would have caused little difficulty had sovereigns engaged only in "sovereign" acts. But modern states engage in many private transactions (*jure gestionis*). The doctrine of absolute and unqualified immunity gave way to a restrictive theory which denied immunity when the sovereign descended into the market placer.

Many states became private traders, engaging in the operation of transportation, telegraph and telephone services, radio and television communications and the production of goods (extraction of natural resources, tobacco and matches, etc.). Commercial transactions gave rise to disputes and brought into the courts of one nation the trading sovereigns of another. National courts were slow to alter the absolute immunity doctrine. Rather surprisingly, in civil law tradition nations on the Continent case law was where the evolution from absolute theory to restrictive theory occurred, while in common law tradition nations' courts struggled with such evolution and the restrictive theory only took root clearly with the enactment of legislation. As early as 1857 in Belgium, in *Etat du Perou v. Krelinger*,[4] restrictive theory began to be accepted on the Continent. An Italian decision in 1882, *Morellet C. Goveruo Danese*,[5] continued the movement, as have Austrian and German courts in this century.

The Department of State regularly requested immunity when friendly nations were sued in U.S. courts. But in 1952, the Department of State sent what became known as the "Tate Letter" to the Department of Justice, announcing that Department of State policy was "to follow the restrictive theory of sovereign immunity in the consideration of requests of foreign governments for a grant of sovereign immunity."[6] The letter stated:

It is realized that a shift in policy by the executive cannot control the courts but it is felt that the courts are less likely to allow a plea of sovereign immunity where the executive has declined to do so. There have been indications that at least some Justices of the Supreme Court feel that in this matter courts should

---

3. See Berizzi Brothers Co. v. The Pesaro, 271 U.S. 562, 46 S.Ct. 611, 70 L.Ed. 1088 (1926).

4. P.B. 1857–II–348.

5. (1882) Guir. It. 1883–I–25.

6. 24 Dept. State Bull. 984 (1952).

follow the branch of the Government charged with responsibility for the conduct of foreign relations.

Although the Tate Letter announced an acceptance of the restrictive theory of sovereign immunity, it offered no guidelines or criteria to distinguish a state's public acts from its private acts. Until the passage of the Foreign Sovereign Immunities Act twenty-four years later, the application of the restrictive theory proved troublesome. The courts generally complied with "suggestions" of immunity from the Department of State, and foreign sovereigns were often successful in urging the Department to support immunity for the kind of private acts the restrictive theory was intended to address. But even when state immunity was codified in the 1976 FSIA, it was uncertain to what degree separation of powers principles would induce a judicial caution about embarrassing the executive branch in its role as the primary organ of international policy. Moreover, and "(p)erhaps more importantly, in the chess game that is diplomacy only the executive has a view of the entire board and an understanding of the relationship between isolated moves."

§ 29.25   The Foreign Sovereign Immunities Act of 1976

The enactment of the Foreign Sovereign Immunities Act was intended to relieve the government of diplomatic pressures, "thereby eliminating the role of the State Department in such questions and bringing the United States into conformity with the immunity practice of virtually every other country."[1] The FSIA additionally illustrated to litigants that sovereign immunity decisions would be made on legal rather than political grounds. The old suggestion of immunity made by the executive was abrogated by the FSIA.[2] In adopting the restrictive theory, the FSIA established legal standards applicable to claims of immunity made by foreign sovereigns, whether the litigation were in a state or federal court in the United States. But the FSIA also guarantees foreign states the right to remove civil actions from a state court to a federal court, thus allying fears of "local" treatment and contemplating the development of a fairly uniform body of law in the federal courts. That body has proven to be less than uniform; one court has described it as a "statutory labyrinth that, owing to the numerous interpretive questions engendered by its bizarre structure ... has ... been a

§ 29.25

1. Martropico Compania Naviera S.A. v. Perusahaan Pertambangan Minyak Dan Gas Bumi Negara (Pertamina), 428 F.Supp. 1035, 1037 (S.D.N.Y.1977).

2. Republic of Philippines v. Marcos, 665 F.Supp. 793 (N.D.Cal.1987).

financial boon for the private bar but a constant bane of the federal judiciary".[3]

A further goal of the FSIA was to provide a procedure for service of process and obtaining in personam jurisdiction, thus avoiding the past practices of plaintiffs seizing property of foreign states to force an appearance. And finally, the FSIA allows execution upon commercial assets, although the requirements for execution are stricter than those for jurisdiction to adjudicate.

§ 29.26 Who Is a Sovereign?

State immunity is a defense that is the patrimony of foreign states. A "foreign state" includes "a political subdivision of a foreign state or an agency or instrumentality of a foreign state."[1] An "agency or instrumentality of a foreign state" is any entity:

(1) which is a separate legal person, corporate or otherwise, and

(2) which is an organ of a foreign state or political subdivision thereof, or a majority of whose shares or other ownership interest is owned by a foreign state or political subdivision thereof, and

(3) which is neither a citizen of a State of the United States [as defined in the Act], ... nor created under the laws of any third country.[2]

The distinction between a foreign state and agency or instrumentality is important: a foreign state is not liable for the acts of its agencies or instrumentalities in the absence of piercing the corporate veil. There is a presumption that the foreign state is separate from its instrumentalities that may only be overcome by showing (1) that the corporate entity was so controlled that there was a principal/agent relationship, or (2) that allowing the distinction would work fraud or injustice.[3] The Vatican has been held to be a foreign state.[4] The PLO has been denied such status.[5] Foreign trade organizations of nonmarket nations have usually been held to be instrumentalities, as have state owned corporations engaged in a wide variety of activities, such as airlines, mining, shipping, banking and production such as steel.

3. Gibbons v. Udaras na Gaeltachta, 549 F.Supp. 1094, 1105 (S.D.N.Y.1982).

§ 29.26

1. 28 U.S.C.A. § 1603(a).

2. 28 U.S.C.A. § 1603(b).

3. First Nat'l City Bank v. Banco Para El Comercio Exterior De Cuba

(Bancec), 462 U.S. 611, 103 S.Ct. 2591, 77 L.Ed.2d 46 (1983).

4. English v. Thorne, 676 F.Supp. 761 (S.D.Miss.1987).

5. National Petrochemical Co. of Iran v. M/T Stolt Sheaf, 860 F.2d 551 (2d Cir.1988).

The FSIA does not address the status of international organizations as foreign states. Courts have denied such status to OPEC,[6] granted it to the British West Indies Central Labour Organization,[7] and in other cases suggested that it did not have to reach a decision because immunity would exist (or not exist) whether absolute or restrictive theory applied.

§ 29.27   Jurisdictional Issues

The FSIA is federal law. The law is based on the theory that a foreign state is "presumptively immune" from the jurisdiction of a U.S. court. The court lacks subject matter jurisdiction unless a specific exception applies.[1] Subject matter jurisdiction is conferred by § 1330(a) to permit a nonjury civil action against a foreign state not entitled to immunity. If the court has subject matter jurisdiction under § 1330(a), and if service of process is made in accordance with § 1608, and if constitutional due process requirements are met, then the court has personal jurisdiction over the foreign state under § 1330(b). But, as noted, this jurisdiction is effective only when the foreign state is not entitled to immunity. The principal function of the FSIA is to confer immunity upon a defendant foreign state. A court clearly lacks jurisdiction unless one of the exceptions applies. It should thus be apparent that "(u)nder the analytic structure of the Act, the existence of subject matter and personal jurisdiction, the requisites for service of process, and the availability of sovereign immunity as a defense are intricately coordinated inquiries."[2] Understanding the Congressional pattern of subject matter and personal jurisdiction under the FSIA requires one additional essential comment, that the "Act cannot create personal jurisdiction where the Constitution forbids it. Accordingly, each finding of personal jurisdiction under the FSIA requires, in addition, a due process scrutiny of the court's power to exercise its authority over a particular defendant."[3] The FSIA "is designed to embody the 'requirements of minimum jurisdictional contacts and adequate notice.' "[4]

6. International Ass'n of Machinists and Aerospace Workers v. OPEC, 477 F.Supp. 553, 560 (C.D.Cal.1979), aff'd, 649 F.2d 1354 (9th Cir.1981), cert. denied, 454 U.S. 1163, 102 S.Ct. 1036, 71 L.Ed.2d 319 (1982).

7. Rios v. Marshall, 530 F.Supp. 351 (S.D.N.Y.1981).

§ 29.27

1. See Saudi Arabia v. Nelson, 507 U.S. 349, 113 S.Ct. 1471, 123 L.Ed.2d 47 (1993); Argentine Republic v. Amerada Hess Shipping Corp., 488 U.S. 428, 109 S.Ct. 683, 102 L.Ed.2d 818 (1989); Verlinden B.V. v. Central Bank of Nigeria, 461 U.S. 480, 103 S.Ct. 1962, 76 L.Ed.2d 81 (1983).

2. Velidor v. L/P/G Benghazi, 653 F.2d 812, 817 (3d Cir.1981).

3. Texas Trading & Milling Corp. v. Federal Republic of Nigeria, 647 F.2d 300, 308 (2d Cir.1981), cert. denied 454 U.S. 1148, 102 S.Ct. 1012, 71 L.Ed.2d 301 (1982).

4. East Europe Domestic Int'l Sales Corp. v. Terra, 467 F.Supp. 383, 387 (S.D.N.Y.1979).

§ 29.28   Exceptions to Sovereign Immunity—Waiver

A foreign state is not immune in any case "in which [it] has waived its immunity either explicitly or by implication, notwithstanding any withdrawal of the waiver ... except in accordance with the terms of waiver."[1]

Implied waivers are not easily established. A foreign state does not waive its state immunity by entering into a contract with another nation. That contract may give rise to a commercial exception issue, but a waiver must be intentional and knowing.[2] How a foreign state responds to a complaint is important to determining the existence of an implicit waiver. Entering a general appearance may constitute a waiver, as might failure to appear altogether.[3] But failing to timely answer or file motions, such as a motion to dismiss, will not automatically waive immunity.

Explicit waivers are more readily identifiable, such as those found in treaties. For example, the United States has waived immunity with respect to commercial and other activities in some of its treaties of Friendship, Commerce and Navigation (FCN). The language used in the waiver is important—a commonly used provision in FCN treaties that immunity shall not be claimed from "suit, execution or judgment or other liability" is not an explicit waiver from prejudgment attachment.[4]

A second source of explicit waivers is in private agreements. For example, a loan document providing that "The Borrower can sue and be sued in its own name and does not have any right of immunity from suit with respect to the Borrower's obligations under this Letter or the Notes," has been held to be an explicit waiver of a right to raise the defense of state immunity for a prejudgment attachment.

§ 29.29   Exceptions to Sovereign Immunity—Commercial Activity

The commercial activity exception is the reason the FSIA was enacted. Law prior to the passage of the Act was unclear about whether a restrictive theory of sovereign immunity excluded acts which were commercial in *nature* or commercial in *purpose*. The FSIA chooses those commercial in *nature*, by defining "commercial activity" as:

---

§ 29.28

1. 28 U.S.C.A. § 1605(a)(1).

2. Transamerican Steamship Corp. v. Somali Democratic Republic, 767 F.2d 998 (D.C.Cir.1985).

3. Von Dardel v. USSR, 623 F.Supp. 246 (D.D.C.1985, vacated 736 F.Supp. 1

(D.D.C. 1990)). See also Frolova v. USSR, 761 F.2d 370 (7th Cir.1985).

4. Libra Bank Ltd. v. Banco Nacional De Costa Rica, S.A., 676 F.2d 47 (2d Cir.1982).

either a regular course of commercial conduct or a particular commercial transaction or act. The commercial character of an activity shall be determined by reference to the nature of the course of conduct or particular transaction or act, rather than by reference to its purpose.[1]

Determining what activity of the foreign state is alleged to be commercial is obviously a precondition to determine whether that activity is commercial and whether it fits into one of the three classes of commercial activity which deny immunity to the foreign state. The FSIA defines those three classes as:

A foreign state shall not be immune from the jurisdiction of courts of the United States or of the States in any case . . . in which the action is based upon a commercial activity carried on in the United States by the foreign state; or upon an act performed in the United States in connection with a commercial activity of the foreign state elsewhere; or upon an act outside the territory of the United States in connection with a commercial activity of the foreign state elsewhere and that act causes a direct effect in the United States.[2]

The legislative history of the FSIA suggests that a commercial activity is one which an individual might customarily carry on for profit. If the activity is one which normally could be engaged in by a private party, it is commercial and a foreign state is not immune, but if the activity is one in which only a state can engage, it is noncommercial under the FSIA. The focus is not on whether the defendant generally engages in commercial activities, but on the particular conduct giving rise to the action.[3]

The proper focus is on the *nature* of the activity rather than its *purpose*. Cases have found commercial activity to include purchasing grain from a U.S. company under a U.S. government program, a Republic of Ireland joint venture with two U.S. citizens to manufacture plastic cosmetic containers, a Turkish government owned gun manufacturer selling in the United States, artistic contracts for tours of USSR artists to the United States and Great Britain, and a Polish government owned company selling golf carts in the United States. Noncommercial activities have included nationalizing plaintiff's corporation, establishing terms and conditions for removal of natural resources from its territory, and granting and revoking a license to export a natural resource.

In 1992 the U.S. Supreme Court addressed the definition of commercial activity and came down strongly against any interpreta-

§ 29.29

1. 28 U.S.C.A. § 1603(d).

2. 28 U.S.C.A. § 1605(a)(2).

3. Brazosport Towing Co., Inc. v. 3,838 Tons of Sorghum Laden on Board, 607 F.Supp. 11 (S.D.Tex.1984).

tion based on the purpose of the activity.[4] The court said the issue is whether the actions that the foreign state "performs (whatever the motive behind them) are the type of actions by which a private party engages in 'trade and traffic or commerce' ".

The FSIA and pleas of sovereign immunity after expropriations are important. Since considerable U.S. litigation against foreign sovereigns follows noncompensated nationalizations, the view that a "nationalization is the quintessentially sovereign act, never viewed as having a commercial character," obviously is a disappointment to many subjects of nationalization.[5] The exception contained in § 1605(a)(3), discussed in the next section below, rights taken in violation of international law, may apply to some nationalizations, depending on the relation of the property located in the United States to the property nationalized.

The three part commercial activity test of § 1605(a)(2) requires the commercial activity to bear some relationship to the United States. The first part is "action based upon a commercial activity carried on in the United States by the foreign state." This is the easiest part of the test and essentially involves how much commercial activity was done in the United States, and what is the link between the cause of action and the commercial activity. "Substantial contact" with the United States is sufficient. The second part of the test deals with an "act performed in the United States in connection with a commercial activity of the foreign state performed elsewhere." It is the least used of the three parts since many of the acts complained of occur outside the United States; when they do occur in the United States the matter is often considered under or in combination with part one of the test. It is the third part of the test, an "act outside . . . the United States in connection with a commercial activity of the foreign state and that act causes a direct effect in the United States," that has been the most difficult to define. Since many acts do occur abroad, the "direct effect" language is often the focus of attention. The federal circuit courts have been split on what constitutes a direct effect. Some followed the view that it must be "substantial and foreseeable", drawing upon the Restatement of Foreign Relations section on jurisdiction to prescribe.[6] Others have rejected this and believe direct effect to be satisfied where there is some financial loss.[7] This division was answered by the Supreme Court in 1992, when the Court rejected the House Report and Restatement views that direct

4. Republic of Argentina v. Weltover, Inc., 504 U.S. 607, 112 S.Ct. 2160, 119 L.Ed.2d 394 (1992).

5. Alberti v. Empresa Nicaraguense De La Carne, 705 F.2d 250 (7th Cir. 1983).

6. Maritime Int'l Nominees Establishment v. Republic of Guinea, 693 F.2d 1094 (D.C.Cir.1982).

7. Texas Trading & Milling Corp. v. Federal Republic of Nigeria, 647 F.2d 300 (2d Cir.1981).

effect meant both "substantial" and "foreseeable" and ruled that an effect is direct if it "follows 'as an immediate consequence of the defendant's ... activity,' "[8] accepting the *Texas Trading* position.

§ 29.30 Exceptions to Sovereign Immunity— Violations of International Law

Rights in property taken in violation of international law may preclude the defense of sovereign immunity if:

> that property or any property exchanged for such property is present in the United States in connection with a commercial activity carried on in the United States by the foreign state; or that property or any property exchanged for such property is owned or operated by an agency or instrumentality of the foreign state and that agency or instrumentality is engaged in a commercial activity in the United States.[1]

This section may be used to respond to noncompensated expropriations of property, but the decisions have interpreted the provisions more restrictively than what many scholars thought the FSIA intended to reach. The "property tracing" feature of the FSIA severely limits the use of this alternative violation of international law provision of the FSIA. The FSIA is not a helpful statute to persons whose property has been expropriated by a foreign state.

§ 29.31 Act of State Doctrine

The defense of sovereignty immunity often is accompanied by the separate defense of "act of state". Acceptance of either defense generates judicial abstention. The sovereign immunity doctrine mandates that a foreign sovereign may not be sued in the courts of other nations, thus focusing on who should or should not be sued. It is concerned with the *status* of the defendant. Contrastingly, the act of state doctrine suggests that courts of one nation will not sit in judgment of the acts of a foreign sovereign that occurred in the foreign state, thus focusing on what is or is not a proper subject matter. It is concerned with the *acts* of the defendant. The act of state "operates as an issue preclusion device."[1] Sovereign immunity is jurisdictional in nature. If immunity exists, the court lacks jurisdiction. But the act of state doctrine does not deprive a court of jurisdiction. Where the act of state doctrine is at issue, the court

---

8. Republic of Argentina v. Weltover, Inc., 504 U.S. 607, 112 S.Ct. 2160, 2168, 119 L.Ed.2d 394 (1992), citing Texas Trading & Milling Corp. v. Federal Republic of Nigeria, 647 F.2d 300, 311 (2d Cir.1981), *cert. denied* 454 U.S. 1148, 102 S.Ct. 1012, 71 L.Ed.2d 301 (1982).

§ 29.30

1. 28 U.S.C.A. § 1605(a)(3).

§ 29.31

1. National American Corp. v. Federal Republic of Nigeria, 448 F.Supp. 622, 640 (S.D.N.Y.1978), *aff'd*, 597 F.2d 314 (2d Cir.1979).

has jurisdiction but decides, for act of state reasons, not to decide the issue.

Sovereign immunity in the United States is governed by the FSIA, which has exemption provisions for certain commercial activity, and for certain violations of international law. Those two issues have not escaped the act of state doctrine, which has not been the subject of legislation parallel to the FSIA. The act of state doctrine in the United States is not governed by statute but rather by case law. That case law includes debate regarding its application to violations of international law. Congressional anger over *Banco Nacional de Cuba v. Sabbatino*,[2] led to legislation mandating that courts not accept the defense in some instances where there are alleged violations of international law, whether the doctrine applies to bar a counterclaim, whether it applies to an act in violation of a treaty, uncertainty over the situs of an act of state, and most recently, whether it applies to motives rather than acts of foreign state officials. But of most concern to those engaged in international business transactions is the debate regarding the existence of a commercial exception to the doctrine.

§ 29.32   History of Act of State Doctrine

The doctrine can be traced to the 1674 English case of *Blad v. Bamfield*.[1] It also exists in the jurisprudence of France, Germany, Greece, Italy, The Netherlands, Switzerland and other countries. The initial important U.S. decision is *Underhill v. Hernandez*.[2] There the Supreme Court stated that:

> Every sovereign state is bound to respect the independence of every other state, and the courts of one country will not sit in judgment on the acts of the government of another, done within its own territory. Redress of grievances by reason of such acts must be obtained through the means open to be availed of by sovereign powers as between themselves.[3]

The *Underhill* litigation arose from claimed damages suffered by the plaintiff (Underhill) at the hands of a Venezuelan revolutionary army commander (Hernandez) during an alleged false arrest in Venezuela. The United States had subsequently recognized the revolutionary government. The doctrine as expressed in *Underhill* was reaffirmed in the modern classic, *Sabbatino*.

2.   376 U.S. 398, 84 S.Ct. 923, 11 L.Ed.2d 804 (1964).

§ 29.32

1.   36 All E.Eng.Rep. 992, applied in 1981 in Buttes Gas and Oil Co. v. Hammer (No. 3), [1981] 3 All E.R. 616.

2.   168 U.S. 250, 18 S.Ct. 83, 42 L.Ed. 456 (1897).

3.   Id. at 252, 18 S.Ct. at 84.

§ 29.33   Act of State and the Expropriation of Property

Banco Nacional de Cuba v. Sabbatino began the contemporary history of the act of state doctrine and its applicability to expropriations.[1] The case involved rights to property affected by the Cuban nationalization of property in 1960. Justice Harlan stated:

> [T]he Judicial Branch will not examine the validity of a taking of property within its own territory by a foreign sovereign, extant and recognized by this country at the time of suit, in the absence of a treaty or other unambiguous agreement regarding controlling legal principles, even if the complaint alleges that the taking violates customary international law.[2]

Justice White dissented, stating:

> I do not believe that the act of state doctrine, as judicially fashioned in the Court, and the reasons underlying it, require American courts to decide cases in disregard of international law and of the rights of litigants to a full determination on the merits.[3]

The Supreme Court decision was not well received by many members of Congress. The Sabbatino Amendment to the Foreign Assistance Act was quickly passed, and stated:

> Notwithstanding any other provisions of law, no court in the United States shall decline on the ground of the federal act of state doctrine to make a determination on the merits giving effect to the principles of international law in a case in which a claim of title or other right [to property] is asserted by any party including a foreign state ... based upon ... a confiscation or other taking ... by an act of that state in violation of the principles of international law, including the principles of compensation and the other standards set out in this subsection: *Provided*, That this subparagraph shall not be applicable ... (2) in any case with respect to which the President determines that application of the act of state doctrine is required in that particular case by the foreign policy interests of the United States and a suggestion to this effect is filed on his behalf in that case with the court.[4]

This Sabbatino Amendment (also called the Second Hickenlooper Amendment) led to a reversal of the *Sabbatino* decision on

---

§ 29.33

1. 376 U.S. 398, 84 S.Ct. 923, 11 L.Ed.2d 804 (1964).

2. Id. at 428, 84 S.Ct. at 940.

3. Id. at 441, 84 S.Ct. at 946.

4. 22 U.S.C.A. § 2370(e)(2). The bracketed words were added in 1965 to clarify that the doctrine continued to apply to acts not involving the taking of property.

remand.[5] But in the years that followed, the courts have not applied very enthusiastically this hurriedly adopted reversal of a doctrine adopted and long approved by the judicial branch.

§ 29.34   Act of State Encounters Some Limits

The act of state doctrine, subsequent to the formation of much of its characteristics in expropriation cases, was for several years expanded in scope, but in 1990 encountered a Supreme Court contraction in W.S. *Kirkpatrick & Co. v. Environmental Tectonics Corp., Int'l.*[1] In the *Kirkpatrick* case Environmental Tectonics learned that the reason it had lost a contract with Nigeria was that Kirkpatrick had bribed Nigerian government officials. Environmental Tectonics sought damages against Kirkpatrick, which raised the act of state doctrine in that proof of the bribe might require the court to consider an act of the foreign state. The Circuit Court declined to apply the act of state doctrine because the Department of State said that such inquiry would not cause embarrassment to U.S. foreign relations. But the Supreme Court rejected that reasoning, refusing to apply the doctrine because it did not involve an inquiry into the lawfulness of an act of the foreign government, but merely the consideration of the motivations of foreign officials. This test will need some refining. One can think of situations where judicial consideration of an act of a foreign state would cause little embarrassment, but inquiry into the motives of another act would cause great embarrassment to U.S. foreign relations. *Kirkpatrick* is an important decision, suggesting to lower courts a method by which the act of state may be considerably diminished in application in future cases.

§ 29.35   Act of State and the Separation of Powers

The act of state doctrine is punctuated by unclear contours, debatable exceptions and an unsympathetic Congressional response. The cases illustrate that the doctrine is deliberate but flexible. There is general agreement that the doctrine is grounded in self-imposed judicial restraint. The doctrine rests upon considerations of international comity and separation of powers between the executive and judicial branches of the government. It is intended to avoid embarrassment in the conduct of the nation's foreign relations. One has only to envision a justice of peace court in the United States, proclaiming the illegality of actions taken in a

5. Banco Nacional de Cuba v. Farr, 243 F.Supp. 957 (S.D.N.Y.1965), *aff'd*, 383 F.2d 166 (2d Cir.1967), *cert. denied*, 390 U.S. 956, 88 S.Ct. 1038, 19 L.Ed.2d 1151 (1968).

§ 29.34

1. 493 U.S. 400, 110 S.Ct. 701, 107 L.Ed.2d 816 (1990).

foreign country by the highest officers of that government, to sense the international prudence of such a doctrine.[1]

The act of state doctrine's interface with the separation of powers, between the executive and judicial branches of the U.S. government, has been discussed by courts for over twenty years in large part because of *Bernstein v. N.V. Nederlandsche–Amerikaansche Stoomvaart–Maatschappij.*[2] In *Bernstein* the court was inclined to apply the act of state doctrine, but the Department of State urged the court to refrain and to proceed with an examination of the legal issues. The court concluded:

> [I]n the prior appeal in this case ... because of the lack of a definitive expression of Executive Policy, we felt constrained to follow ... [the act of state doctrine] ... Following our decision, however, the State Department issued ... [a policy statement intended] ... to relieve American courts from any [such] restraint upon the exercise of their jurisdiction.... In view of this supervening expression of Executive Policy, we amend our mandate ... [that the act of state doctrine precludes judicial inquiry].[3]

The validity of this *"Bernstein* exception" to the act of state doctrine was before the Supreme Court in *First National City Bank v. Banco Nacional de Cuba.*[4] Reversing the lower court, three justices, as a plurality, wrote:

> [W]here the Executive Branch, charged as it is with primary responsibility for the conduct of foreign affairs, expressly represents to the Court that application of the act of state doctrine would not advance the interests of American foreign policy, that doctrine should not be applied by the courts. In so doing, we of course adopt and approve the so-called *Bernstein* exception to the act of state doctrine. We believe this to be no more than an application of the classical common-law maxim that "[t]he reason of the law ceasing, the law itself also ceases".... Our holding is in no sense an abdication of the judicial function to the Executive Branch.[5]

Two concurring Justices and four dissenting Justices disagreed, however, the latter writing:

> As six members of this Court recognize today, ... [it] is clear that the representations of the Department of State are entitled to weight for the light they shed on the permutation

§ 29.35

1. See DeRoburt v. Gannett Co., Inc., 548 F.Supp. 1370, 1380 (D.Haw.1982).

2. 210 F.2d 375 (2d Cir.1954).

3. Id. at 375–376.

4. 406 U.S. 759, 92 S.Ct. 1808, 32 L.Ed.2d 466 (1972), *reh'g denied,* 409 U.S. 897, 93 S.Ct. 92, 34 L.Ed.2d 155 (1972).

5. Id. at 768, 92 S.Ct. at 1813.

and combination of factors underlying the act of state doctrine. But they cannot be determinative. . . .

The task of defining the contours of a political question such as the act of state doctrine is exclusively the function of this Court. . . . The *"Bernstein"* exception relinquishes the function to the Executive by requiring blind adherence to its requests that foreign acts of state be reviewed. Conversely, it politicizes the judiciary.[6]

Four years later, in *Alfred Dunhill of London, Inc. v. Republic of Cuba*,[7] four dissenting justices wrote:

[S]ix members of the Court in *First National* . . . disapproved finally the so-called *Bernstein* exception to the act of state doctrine, thus minimizing the significance of any letter from the Department of State . . . the task of defining the role of the judiciary is for this court, not the Executive Branch.

Constitutional effect aside, a *Bernstein* letter from the Department of State to a court may be quite persuasive in providing the court a reason to avoid application of the doctrine. Lack of such a letter may not result in a reverse conclusion; in 1982, the Department of State advised the Solicitor General that "courts should not infer from the silence of the Department of State that adjudication in . . . (a pending) case would be harmful to the foreign policy of the United States."[8]

The *Kirkpatrick* decision supports the view of *Dunhill* that it is the function of the judiciary rather than the executive to define the role of the judiciary in addressing acts of foreign states. The Supreme Court in *Kirkpatrick* did not reject any role for the executive, but clearly rejected the Circuit Court's giving "full, faith and credit" to the letter from the Department of State.

§ 29.36   Act of State and Some Exceptions

As in the case of the application of sovereign immunity, there are exceptions to the act of state doctrine. One exception, where the act violates international law, has been discussed above. Two other actions that are debated as constituting exceptions are waiver and commercial activity.

Waiver. A sovereign sometimes appears to expressly waive its right to raise the act of state defense. But it is not clear whether the sovereign might retract the waiver. If revocable, it would seem that the doctrine actually cannot be waived. A further question is whether the imposition of a counterclaim by a defendant sovereign

---

6.   Id. at 790, 92 S.Ct. at 1824.

7.   425 U.S. 682, 725, 96 S.Ct. 1854, 48 L.Ed.2d 301 (1976).

8.   See 22 Int'l Legal Mat. 207 (1983).

constitutes a waiver. A majority of the Court in the *First National* decision suggested no, but it was not part of the opinion. If the sovereign brings an action in a U.S. court, it is not stripped of its right to invoke the act of state as a defense to a counterclaim just because it thereby waives its right to avoid a counterclaim on grounds of sovereign immunity. A clear and unambiguous statement by a foreign state that it does not object to judicial scrutiny of a state act may influence a court, but other factors may also be considered.[1]

Commercial activity. Uncertainty also clouds the issue of the existence of a commercial activity exception to the act of state doctrine. The Supreme Court in the *Dunhill* case has stated that:

> [T]he concept of an act of state should not be extended to include the repudiation of a purely commercial obligation owed by a foreign sovereign or by one of its commercial instrumentalities.... In their commercial capacities, foreign governments do not exercise powers peculiar to sovereigns.... Subjecting them in connection with such acts to the same rules of law that apply to private citizens is unlikely to touch very sharply on "national nerves."[2]

The *Dunhill* case has become known as the "commercial exception" to the act of state doctrine notwithstanding that only four justices joined in that part of the opinion, and that four other justices wrote:

> [I]t does not follow that there should be a commercial act exception to the act of state doctrine....

> The carving out of broad exceptions to the doctrine is fundamentally at odds with the careful case-by-case approach adopted in *Sabbatino*.[3]

The ambiguity of the court has led to different views expressed in lower federal courts. One court stated:

> consideration of the commercial nature of a given act is compelled if the doctrine is to be applied correctly. In this connection, attention is owed not to the purpose of the act but to its nature. The goal of the inquiry is to determine if denial of the act of state defense in the case under consideration will thwart the policy concerns in which the doctrine is rooted.[4]

§ 29.36

1. Compania de Gas de Nuevo Laredo, S.A. v. Entex, Inc., 686 F.2d 322 (5th Cir.1982).

2. Alfred Dunhill of London, Inc. v. Republic of Cuba, 425 U.S. 682, 695, 704, 96 S.Ct. 1854, 48 L.Ed.2d 301 (1976).

3. Id. at 725, 96 S.Ct. at 1876.

4. Sage Int'l, Ltd. v. Cadillac Gage Co., 534 F.Supp. 896, 905 (E.D.Mich. 1981).

But another court observed:

> While purely commercial activity may not rise to the level
> of an act of state, certain seemingly commercial activities will
> trigger act of state considerations.... When the state *qua* state
> acts in the public interest, its sovereignty is asserted. The
> Courts must proceed cautiously to avoid an affront to that
> sovereignty.... [W]e find that the act of state doctrine remains
> available when such caution is appropriate regardless of any
> commercial component of the activity involved.[5]

If a commercial exception is not to be granted, determining that the
situs of the activity (commercial or not) is not in the foreign state
may cause judicial rejection of the doctrine. This has proven important to the international debt issue. If nonpayment is held to have
occurred at the office of the lending bank in the United States, the
doctrine may be rejected as a defense.[6]

---

5. IAM v. OPEC, 649 F.2d 1354, 1360 (9th Cir.1981).

6. Allied Bank Int'l v. Banco Credito Agricola de Cartago, 757 F.2d 516 (2d Cir.1985), *cert. denied*, 473 U.S. 934, 106 S.Ct. 30, 87 L.Ed.2d 706 (1985).

Chapter 30

INTERNATIONAL BUSINESS LITIGATION

Table of Sections

---

§ 30.1 Introduction

An inevitable consequence of increased trade and investment is increased conflict requiring some method of dispute resolution. There are numerous methods to resolve cross-border business disputes. Arbitration is commonly used for commercial contracts. Trade agreements have developed unique processes for dispute resolution especially the dispute panel process, often combining elements of litigation and arbitration. But many international business disputes are handled by traditional litigation.

§ 30.2 Personal Jurisdiction

Development in the United States. Few areas of U.S. law are as difficult to explain to foreign jurists as personal jurisdiction. The history of personal jurisdiction in the United States involves difficult and complex notions of minimum contacts and Constitutional due process.[1] Where a suit is initiated in the United States and the

§ 30.2

1. It is the Constitutional requirements that bifurcate the jurisdictional

question into personal and subject matter jurisdiction.

defendant believes a *forum non conveniens* motion will prevail, possible defects in jurisdiction are overlooked, or deferred pending the resolution of the *forum non conveniens* motion. The reason may be that predicting answers to questions of jurisdiction is less certain than predicting answers to *forum non conveniens*.[2]

Both state and federal courts are limited by federal Constitutional limitations. State courts may be further limited by state Constitutional limitations, but many states have long-arm statutes which extend to, if not beyond, the federal limits.[3] A return to *International Shoe* may cause nightmares to the reader but there is no other way to present personal jurisdiction in international litigation then to start with the classic test of minimum contacts in that venerable decision.[4] Minimum contacts were held necessary to meet constitutional due process requirements under the Fourteenth Amendment. Perhaps in no other area of constitutional law has the court been able to adopt various and varying approaches to the meaning of due process than in the progeny of *International Shoe*.

Although *International Shoe* did not involve a foreign defendant, that extension would later occur.[5] But before the venture into personal jurisdiction over foreign defendants, the Supreme Court issued *Worldwide Volkswagen*.[6] The Court held that a defendant must have "purposefully directed" its activities towards the forum state. The defendant would have to have anticipated being subjected to the forum state's courts, and there should be some link between the injuries and the defendant's activities in the state. The Court listed several factors, emphasizing the number, nature and quality of contacts, and the source and connection of the action with the above three contacts. The often mentioned "stream of commerce" test uses the quantity and quality contacts.

The first significant case with foreign defendants was the *Asahi* decision.[7] A motorcycle tire failed and the driver and passen-

2. A parallel situation arises when a foreign state is sued in a U.S. court. The court may first turn to the Foreign Sovereign Immunities Act and address the questions (1) whether the party is a state, and (2) whether there is a commercial activity, or waiver or other immunity exception. If the defendant is not a state, or an exception is not present, there is no need to address the jurisdiction issue.

3. If they extend beyond they are in violation of the federal Constitution. But not all assertions of jurisdiction are tested in the courts at all, and not all decisions which may be in violation are appealed.

4. International Shoe Co. v. Washington, 326 U.S. 310, 66 S.Ct. 154, 90 L.Ed. 95 (1945).

5. Foreign defendants benefit under the Fifth Amendment due process requirements. See, e.g., Mathews v. Diaz, 426 U.S. 67, 96 S.Ct. 1883, 48 L.Ed.2d 478 (1976), Wong Wing v. United States, 163 U.S. 228, 16 S.Ct. 977, 41 L.Ed. 140 (1896).

6. World–Wide Volkswagen Corp. v. Woodson., 444 U.S. 286, 100 S.Ct. 559, 62 L.Ed.2d 490 (1980).

7. Asahi Metal Indus. Co., Ltd. v. Superior Court, 480 U.S. 102, 107 S.Ct. 1026, 94 L.Ed.2d 92 (1987). Perhaps the Helicopteros Nacionales de Colombia v.

ger were injured and killed, respectively. The valve stem was allegedly the defective part of the tire, and had been made by Asahi, a company in Japan. It was purchased by the Taiwan tire manufacturer. The tire manufacturer was sued in California state court, and cross-complained against Asahi.[8] The California Supreme Court upheld jurisdiction over Asahi, but the U.S. Supreme Court reversed. The Court was unanimous in its ruling that jurisdiction was improper. But the reasoning was not unanimous. There was general agreement that the *International Shoe* decision applied, and that there must be both minimum contacts and constitutional due process. But there was disagreement regarding the standard to determine minimum contacts. Four justices found the "stream of commerce" theory insufficient, rejecting meeting this step by finding the product was brought into the forum by the consumer. Some action by the defendant was needed to satisfy a substantial connection theory. The defendant would have to take some action *"purposefully directed toward the state."*[9] Four other justices preferred the stream of commerce theory without additional conduct. The split of opinion regarding minimum contacts has not helped subsequent cases; federal circuits and state courts have also split on which side they favored.[10]

If the minimum contacts test is satisfied, the court next considers reasonableness—whether exercising jurisdiction meets the *International Shoe* "notions of fair play and substantial justice." It is not easy to show unreasonableness. The finding of minimum contacts seems to imply that reasonableness exists. *Asahi* suggests consideration of the burden on the defendant of litigating in the forum state, the interests of the foreign state, the interests of the plaintiff in obtaining relief, the interests of the interstate judicial system in efficient resolution of cases, and the shared interests of the states in furthering substantive social policies.[11] The Court in *Asahi* was concerned with the burden placed on the Asahi company

Hall, 466 U.S. 408, 104 S.Ct. 1868, 80 L.Ed.2d 404 (1984), decision should be acknowledged as the first, but the Asahi case is the first where the court seems truly aware that the defendants are foreign and that might mean some different analysis.

8. The result might have been different had the action been initiated directly by the California parties against the valve manufacturer. See Restatement (Third) of Foreign Relations Law, § 421, reporters' note 2, at 310.

9. 480 U.S. at 112 (emphasis in original).

10. See, e.g., Gould v. P.T. Krakatau Steel, 957 F.2d 573 (8th Cir.1992), *cert. denied*, 506 U.S. 908, 113 S.Ct. 304, 121

L.Ed.2d 227 (1992) (Sale of Indonesian company's product to N.Y. corporation with subsequent sending of product to Arkansas does not meet test), Mason v. F. LLI Luigi & Franco Dal Maschio, 832 F.2d 383 (7th Cir.1987) (Sale of Italian goods to Maryland with subsequent sending of product to Illinois does meet test), Microsoft Corp. v. Very Competitive Computer Prod. Corp., 671 F.Supp. 1250 (N.D.Cal.1987) (Sale of Taiwanese product to California through another Taiwanese company does meet test).

11. See also Burger King Corp. v. Rudzewicz, 471 U.S. 462, 105 S.Ct. 2174, 85 L.Ed.2d 528 (1985).

in defending the action in a foreign (i.e., U.S.) forum. It additionally noted that "great care and reserve should be exercised when extending our notions of personal jurisdiction in the international field."[12] With these principal cases providing guidelines, however conflicting, the state and federal courts are now left to work out the details when the defendant is foreign. There are certain to be new cases that ultimately reach the Supreme Court.

General and Specific Jurisdiction. An additional jurisdictional issue that had developed in domestic cases and now is confronted in international cases is general versus specific jurisdiction. Specific jurisdiction is generally thought to be where the court may only adjudicate claims related to the defendant's contacts with the forum, while general jurisdiction envisions adjudication of any claims against the defendant because of the aggregate of contacts with the forum.[13] The U.S. Supreme Court views general jurisdiction when the defendant's activities constitute "continuous and systematic general business contacts."[14] Debate reigns whether the standard should be the same for foreign defendants, partly based on concern for reciprocal treatment of U.S. companies abroad.[15]

Veil Piercing to Obtain Jurisdiction. When the defendant is the parent of a subsidiary corporation located in the United States and subject to jurisdiction, a court may extend jurisdiction to the parent in what is often a poorly analyzed piercing of the corporate veil. Veil piercing usually involves linking the two enterprises, but in jurisdiction cases, the analysis often appears less demanding, using agency concepts more freely and replacing "formal relationships" with "economic realities."[16] A conclusion that pierces the veil of the U.S. entity means that jurisdictional factors of minimum contacts and due process are less complex. Additionally, service of process on the U.S. entity will constitute service on the whole entity, including the foreign parent.

International Law and Jurisdiction. International law limitations on extraterritorial extensions of jurisdiction may conflict with U.S. personal jurisdiction rules. U.S. courts considering personal jurisdiction in international cases generally have been disappointing in failing to consider international law rules, instead focusing on the traditional minimum contacts and due process issues.[17] U.S. admin-

---

12.   480 U.S. at 114.

13.   Restatement (Third) of Foreign Relations § 421, reporters' note 3.

14.   Helicopteros Nacionales de Colombia, S.A. v. Hall, 466 U.S. 408, 416, 104 S.Ct. 1868, 80 L.Ed.2d 404 (1984).

15.   See, e.g., Note, Jurisdiction: Personal Jurisdiction Over an Alien Corpo-

ration, 26 Harv. Int'l L.J. 630, 634 (1985).

16.   Andrulonis v. United States, 526 F.Supp. 183, 188 (N.D.N.Y.1981). See also Meyers v. ASICS Corp., 711 F.Supp. 1001, 1004 (C.D.Cal.1989).

17.   See, e.g., Dieter Lange & Gary B. Born, The Extraterritorial Application of National Laws (1989); Harold G. Maier,

istrative agencies have similarly attempted to assert jurisdiction abroad beyond what appear to be acceptable international limits. When *foreign* courts or tribunals have considered the U.S. extraterritorial asserts of jurisdiction, the U.S. rules have not been well received.[18] The Restatement of Foreign relations in its *jurisdiction to adjudicate* provisions suggests "reasonableness" as the standard in assert jurisdiction,[19] but this Restatement provision has received limited acceptance by U.S. courts.[20]

§ 30.3   Subject Matter Jurisdiction

Statutes often express an intention to apply only to domestic actions, or to additionally apply to foreign actions. Subject matter jurisdiction extending beyond the borders becomes limited only by other obstacles such as personal jurisdiction, ability to serve process, and sometimes notions of comity which cause a court to avoid going forward. A court may also avoid the issue by refusing to hear the matter for *forum non conveniens* reasons.

The general rule is that a federal statute is to be applied only within the territory unless there is clear Congressional intent to apply the statute to conduct abroad.[1] But there are statutes with very little expression of such legislative intent with a substantial history of extraterritorial application. The best example is the Sherman Act which refers only to trade "involving" foreign commerce.[2] There was little foreign commerce when the act was passed in 1898 and foreign commerce was not an issue in its debate. Another example is the Securities Exchange Act of 1934, which was directed to securities schemes in the United States, but also has slim reference to foreign commerce.[3] Although the language of the laws may permit extraterritorial application, some courts have

Resolving Extraterritorial Conflicts, or "There and Back Again," 25 Va. J. Int'l L. 7 (1984); Harold G. Maier, Extraterritorial Jurisdiction at a Crossroads: An Intersection Between Public and Private International Law, 76 A. J. Int'l L. 280 (1982).

18. See Compagnie Européenne des Pétroles, S.A. v. Sensor Nederland, B.V., Case 82/716 Rechtspraak van de Week 167 (Dist. Ct., Neth.), reprinted in 22 I.L.M. 66 (1983), Fruehauf Corp. v. Massardy, Court of Appeals of Paris, 14th Chamber. Decision of May 22, 1965, La Gazette du Palais, Paris, 1965, reprinted in 5 I.L.M. 476 (1966).

19. Restatement (Third) Foreign Relations Law § 421.

20. The Restatement on Foreign Relations Law is often more aspirational

than a reflection of the current status of the law. It is as essential to know its limitations as it is important to be familiar with its substance. It reflects a great deal of effort by some exceptionally capable scholars and practitioners.

§ 30.3

1. See EEOC v. Arabian Am. Oil Co., 499 U.S. 244, 111 S.Ct. 1227, 113 L.Ed.2d 274 (1991).

2. 15 U.S.C.A. § 1.

3. 7 U.S.C.A. § 13a–1, 15 U.S.C.A. § 77q, 78aa (fraudulent activities). The extraterritorial application of the securities laws is discussed in Michael Wallace Gordon, United States Extraterritorial Subject Matter Jurisdiction in Securities Fraud Litigation, 10 Fla. J. Int'l L. 487 (1996).

adopted an interest balancing analysis to determine whether the court will go ahead notwithstanding statutory intent. In the extensively debated *Timberlane* decision,[4] the often ambitious federal Ninth Circuit introduced a balancing of interests test. Followed by some courts,[5] and consistent with the Restatement,[6] the test was challenged in the Supreme Court *Hartford Fire Insurance* decision.[7] These decisions at least send a signal to Congress that if it intends to have a law applied extraterritorially, it should make that clear in the legislation. If the intent is clear, the application is more certain and the use of a balancing test in most cases is diminished, if not precluded.

Foreign nations have reacted strongly to the extraterritorial application of U.S. laws, especially the antitrust laws. The reaction has come in two forms. Most reaction has focused on "blocking" laws, which prohibit courts from providing any assistance in these suits, such as allowing the taking of any evidence in the nation.[8] A few countries have gone further and adopted "clawback" provisions, allowing a defendant who has been subjected to a judgment to take at least part of the damages back from any assets the plaintiff has in the country.[9]

§ 30.4   Service of Process

Service of Process abroad is effectively regulated by two conventions. The larger in scope is the Hague Service Convention.[1] The second is the Inter–American Convention.[2] Rule 4(f) of the Federal Rules of Civil Procedure provides for the service of process abroad,

4. Timberlane Lumber v. Bank of America, 549 F.2d 597 (9th Cir.1976).

5. See, e.g., Mannington Mills, Inc. v. Congoleum Corp., 595 F.2d 1287 (3d Cir. 1979).

6. Restatement (Third) of Foreign Relations Law of the United States § 415 (1987).

7. Hartford Fire Ins. Co. v. California, 509 U.S. 764, 113 S.Ct. 2891, 125 L.Ed.2d 612 (1993). See also Laker Airways v. Sabena Belgian World Airlines, 731 F.2d 909 (D.C.Cir.1984).

8. See, e.g., Art. 1A French Penal Code Law (C.Pen) No. 80–538, Protection of Trading Interests Act of 1980 (U.K.), Ontario Business Protection Act, R.S.O. Chap. 56 (1980). See also, Bate C. Toms, The French Response to Extraterritorial Application of United States Antitrust Laws, 15 Int'l Law. 585 (1981); Brigette Ecolivet Herzog, The 1980 French Law on Documents and Information, 75 Am. J. Int'l L. 382

(1981), Note, The Protection of Trading Interests Act of 1980: Britain's Response to U.S. Extraterritorial Antitrust Enforcement, 2 Nw J. Int'l Law & Bus. 476 (1980).

9. See, e.g., Protection of Trading Interests Act of 1980 (U.K.), Art. 6 (recovery of awards of multiple damages).

§ 30.4

1. Hague Convention on the Service Abroad of Judicial and Extrajudicial Documents in Civil or Commercial Matters, done Nov. 15, 1965, 20 U.S.T. 362.

2. Inter–American Convention on Letters Rogatory, *done* Jan 30, 1975, *entered into force for the U.S.,* Aug. 27, 1988, S. Treaty Doc. 98–27, 98th Cong., 2d Sess. (1984); Additional Protocol to the Inter–American Convention on Letters Rogatory, *done* May 8, 1979, *entered into force for the U.S.,* Aug. 27, 1988, S. Treaty Doc. 98–27, 98th Cong., 2d Sess (1984).

requiring use of the treaties. If service is not available under treaty agreements, the Rule provides for alternative means of service. Use of the treaty process should result in service acceptable to the foreign country, but use of the alternative means may not. When using alternative means consideration must be given to the rules in the country where service is to be made. Ineffective service will make enforcement of a judgment very unlikely in the foreign nation.

Service under the Hague Convention is available in some 40 participating countries, including such major nations as Belgium, Canada, China, France, Germany, Italy, Japan, Netherlands, Poland, Spain, Switzerland, the United Kingdom and the United States. Some participating countries have made special reservations which affect the method of service. The service is exclusive, stating in Art. 1 that the Convention "shall apply in all cases, in civil or commercial matters, where there is occasion to transmit a judicial or extrajudicial document for service abroad."[3] Service is made upon a "central authority" in the foreign nation, which subsequently transmits the documents to the proper location. There is some limited authority to send documents by mail,[4] but whether sending constitutes service is debated.[5]

Although the Convention is generally considered to be exclusive, it is not applicable if service may be made on a U.S. subsidiary of a foreign corporation. In *Volkswagenwerk, A.G. v. Schlunk*,[6] service made on Volkswagen of America (VWOA—a U.S. corporation) was held proper to reach Volkswagenwerk (VWAG—the German parent corporation). The Convention was held not to be applicable in a decision applying veil piercing alter ego theory, but without the usual substantive analysis that accompanies veil piercing cases. Cases subsequent to *Schlunk* have been inconsistent in the applicability of the Convention to state law substituted service provisions. But fears that *Schlunk* would cause retaliation abroad have proven unfounded.

The Inter–American Convention and its Additional Protocol have been ratified by most Latin American nations, and the United

---

3. See Société Nationale Industrielle Aerospatiale v. United States Dist. Court, 482 U.S. 522, 107 S.Ct. 2542, 96 L.Ed.2d 461 (1987)(comparing Hague Service Convention with Hague Evidence Convention).

4. Hague Service Convention, art. 10.

5. See, e.g., Ackermann v. Levine, 788 F.2d 830 (2d Cir.1986); Bankston v. Toyota Motor Corp., 889 F.2d 172 (8th Cir.1989); Honda Motor Co., Ltd. v. Superior Court, 10 Cal.App.4th 1043, 12 Cal.Rptr.2d 861 (1992); Suzuki Motor Co., Ltd. v. Superior Court, 200 Cal. App.3d 1476, 249 Cal.Rptr. 376 (1988); Shoei Kako Co. v. Superior Court, 33 Cal.App.3d 808, 109 Cal.Rptr. 402 (1973). The cases are mentioned in David Epstein et al, International Litigation § 4.03 (1998).

6. 486 U.S. 694, 108 S.Ct. 2104, 100 L.Ed.2d 722 (1988).

States. The Convention is limited to letters rogatory, essentially requests from one country through its courts to another country through its courts to assist the administration of justice. Its purpose is similar but less encompassing than the Hague Service Convention. If both are applicable, the Inter–American Convention applies. But the Inter–American Convention is not exclusive, as is the Hague Service Convention. A party thus might use state methods of service that if transmitted to an Inter–American Convention nation would be effective, but that if transmitted to a Hague Service Convention nation not a party to the Inter-American Convention would fail because the Hague Service Convention would be applicable and exclusive.

Service which does not comply with an applicable convention will almost certainly cause any judgment to be rejected if there is an attempt to enforce it abroad. The German government made it very clear in the *Schlunk* case that unless service was made on VWAG under the Convention that German courts would not enforce a judgment.[7] There is thus a certain coercive effect to these service conventions, whether or not they are viewed as exclusive. If they are not followed, enforcement of a judgment will likely be denied.

§ 30.5   Choice of Forum

Choice of forum is associated with several questions. It principally involves conscious choices made by the parties to an agreement. That may be useful for commercial agreements, but is less useful for torts. However, some torts are covered by choice of law agreements, even when they are contained in an agreement not bargained at arm's length, but rather the consequence of purchasing a ticket for an event. Choice of forum is also associated with subject matter jurisdiction, in the sense that a choice of forum agreement by parties does not establish subject matter jurisdiction. It may however, assist courts where there is subject matter jurisdiction in two or more locations. Finally choice of forum by a plaintiff in initiating litigation has some influence on a defendant's motion to dismiss for *forum non conveniens* reasons.

Most jurisdictions accept the parties forum selection. When parties choose a third nation as the forum, there should be some assurance that the courts of that chosen nation will assume jurisdiction. Within the European Union, under the Brussels Convention, parties from two EU nations may select another nation within the EU.[1] Choosing a nation with a civil law tradition legal system introduces a very different form of litigation, where there will be a

---

7. Brief for Volkswagenwerk, A.G. at 16, Volkswagenwerk, A.G. v. Schlunk, 486 U.S. 694, 108 S.Ct. 2104, 100 L.Ed.2d 722 (1988).

§ 30.5

1. Convention on Jurisdiction and Enforcement of Foreign Judgments in

process of gathering evidence until the case is ready for a decision by the assigned judge. There is no trial as known in common law systems. For parties in civil law nations, the idea of a trial may be as much of a concern as the absence of one to a party from a common law system.

If there is any doubt as to the acceptability of forum selection clauses in the United States, the *Carnival Cruise Lines, Inc. v. Shute* decision is mandatory reading.[2] In *Carnival* a plaintiff from Washington state purchased a cruise ticket for a cruise out of Los Angeles. The ticket contained a forum selection clause designating Florida courts, the home of the cruise line. The plaintiff fell and was injured in international waters. The Supreme Court upheld the forum selection provision, which was never negotiated, unconvinced that it would be an unreasonable burden on the plaintiff to bring suit in Florida. The Court did not believe that Florida was a "remote alien forum", language taken from the earlier *Bremen* decision.[3] The Florida court was not "seriously inconvenient", and it was not unreasonable for Carnival Cruise Lines to want to consolidate cases brought against it in Florida. But if a "remote alien forum" is stipulated rather than bargained, a court may reject the clause.[4]

Forum selection clauses are also used to designate arbitration in lieu of judicial resolution. These provisions may conflict with provisions in the legislation generating the conflict that are alleged to give exclusive jurisdiction to courts in the United States. Two U.S. Supreme Court 5–4 decisions involving arbitration selection clauses in antitrust and securities cases upheld such clauses.[5] The reasons were partly because they were international agreements, and international agreements are commonly resolved by international arbitration. The need for predictability in international commerce may be persuasive in overriding notions that the U.S. Congress meant to restrict application of the law to U.S. courts.

§ 30.6 *Forum Non Conveniens*

The *forum non conveniens* doctrine is a creature of equity. It allows a court to dismiss a case that it believes is better brought in

Civil and Commercial Matters at Brussels, Sept. 27, 1968, Art. 17–1. 8 I.L.M. 229 (1969).

2. 499 U.S. 585, 111 S.Ct. 1522, 113 L.Ed.2d 622 (1991).

3. M/S Bremen v. Zapata Off–Shore Co., 407 U.S. 1, 92 S.Ct. 1907, 32 L.Ed.2d 513 (1972) (provision choosing London courts upheld).

4. See Lauro Lines SRL v. Chasser, 490 U.S. 495, 497, 109 S.Ct. 1976, 104 L.Ed.2d 548 (1989). But see Spradlin v. Lear Siegler Management Services Co., 926 F.2d 865 (9th Cir.1991) (Saudi Arabia standard contract forum selection upheld in contract for services to be performed in Saudi Arabia).

5. Scherk v. Alberto–Culver Co., 417 U.S. 506, 94 S.Ct. 2449, 41 L.Ed.2d 270 (1974) (securities law issues), Mitsubishi Motors Corp. v. Soler Chrysler–Plymouth, 473 U.S. 614, 105 S.Ct. 3346, 87 L.Ed.2d 444 (1985) (antitrust issues).

another forum. Not all nations recognize the doctrine, but some reach a similar conclusion under other titles.[1] The U.S. doctrine has origins in *Gulf Oil Corp. v. Gilbert,*[2] a case involving two U.S. forums. In *Gilbert,* the Supreme Court allowed courts to decline to exercise jurisdiction where public and private factors favored another forum. This theory was adopted in two important international cases. First, in *Piper Aircraft Co. v. Reyno,*[3] a court granted a *forum non conveniens* motion to dismiss a suit in the United States in favor of Scotland, where the plaintiffs represented Scottish decedents for a crash of a U.S. made aircraft flown by a Scottish pilot that crashed in Scotland. Scots law was clearly less favorable, but the Court significantly negated the consideration of relative favorableness of the law. Second, in *In re Union Carbide Corp. Gas Plant Disaster,*[4] the court dismissed a case on behalf of numerous Indian nationals injured in an explosion in the Union Carbide subsidiary plant in Bhopal, India. The court accepted as conditions for the dismissal Union Carbide's agreement to submit to jurisdiction in India, a condition that has become common in *forum non conveniens* dismissals. The test has evolved to include several considerations. There must be an available and adequate alternative forum. The plaintiff's choice is weighed against all private interests. When private interests are generally equal public interests are considered.[5] The defendant should submit to the jurisdiction of the foreign forum.

Forum non conveniens motions are presented by defendants as part of litigation strategy. If they are successful, the case is sometimes moved to a forum far distant where the case dies. The death is because the U.S. attorneys no longer have visions of large punitive damage awards. Indeed, they may have little involvement as attorneys in the foreign forum. The defendants in both the *Piper* and *Bhopal* cases were obviously pleased with the outcome. The *Piper* case has never gone to trial in Scotland. The *Bhopal* case resulted in a settlement far less than what might have been a jury's award in the United States, and there is doubt that the settlement funds have ever reached the injured plaintiffs. Courts have thus increasingly asked about the nature of the proceeding in the foreign forum, especially about the nature of the process. If there is a

§ 30.6

1. There appear to be some Scottish origins. See generally Paxton Blair, The Doctrine of Forum Non Conveniens in Anglo–American Law, 29 Colum. L. Rev. 1 (1929).

2. 330 U.S. 501, 67 S.Ct. 839, 91 L.Ed. 1055 (1947).

3. 454 U.S. 235, 102 S.Ct. 252, 70 L.Ed.2d 419 (1981).

4. 809 F.2d 195 (2d Cir.1987), *cert. denied*, 484 U.S. 871, 108 S.Ct. 199, 98 L.Ed.2d 150 (1987).

5. In Lubbe et al v. Cape Plc [2000] 4 All E.R. 268, 1 W.L.R. 1545 [2000], the House of Lords in England rejected the use of public interest factors in a *forum non conveniens* decision.

viable legal system that provides for the resolution of disputes of the form presented, the *forum non conveniens* motion may be granted. But if the system is inefficient and corrupt, a *forum non conveniens* motion is unlikely to be granted.

One problem for defendants in obtain a successful *forum non conveniens* ruling is that control over the case may be diminished or lost. If the case is moved abroad, the attorneys will not be able to appear before the foreign court, and foreign counsel must be hired. The U.S. defendant will have to learn about the foreign law and legal system. The better choice for a defendant may be to keep the matter in the U.S. court but to seek application of foreign law. Many such cases merit the application of foreign law, and when a court so rules the difficulty of proving foreign law may be an impossible burden for the plaintiff. It is a difficult choice for lawyers because the law of *forum non conveniens* seems sufficiently elastic that it is hard to predict the outcome, and additionally hard to predict possible conditions that the court may impose upon the defendant in return for granting the *forum non conveniens* motion. The law is a product of equity, and like equity it is somewhat amorphous and difficult to foresee.

§ 30.7   Choice of Law

Choice of law has two sides. First is as part of a conflicts of law determination when a court is using conflicts rules to determine what law applies. Second is when parties wish to argue that a foreign law is applicable and are faced with convincing the court of that request and, if accepted, proving the foreign law. For the conflicts determination, parties to commercial contracts are allowed under most jurisdictions to choose the applicable law in the contract. When they do not, the court will turn to its own conflicts rules in seeking to apply what may be the law that has the "most significant relationship to the transaction",[1] or that "bears an appropriate relation",[2] or of the country "with which it is most closely connected."[3] Torts raise different issues. Because they are not expected, they are less often provided for. But there are many attempts to designate the applicable law (and forum) for torts arising from contracts selling vacations, cruises, etc. They are often upheld. When there is no such "choice" of the applicable law, a court will either apply the law of the place of the injury under the *lex loci delicti* rule, or consider a wide variety of facts to determine the appropriate law.

§ 30.7

1. Restatement, Conflicts of Law (Second)(1971) § 188.

2. U.C.C. § 1–105.

3. Convention on the Law Applicable to Contractual Obligations (EEC) (1980) art. 4.

Cross-border litigation inherently provides for the possibility of the law of at least two nations. Because of the cross-border presence, parties often choose the applicable law, often in conjunction with a choice of forum provision. The parties should be fully aware of the substance of each possibly applicable law before stipulating the chosen law. For example a U.S. party selling goods to a German party might discover that the German law favors the seller in such a transaction. The U.S. party in such case would want to specify that German law applies, and might even gain concessions from the German party on other issues if the German party prefers German law not because it has been researched but because it is German and "probably" better than U.S. law.

Just as a choice of forum agreement may not thrust subject matter jurisdiction upon a court, a choice of law provision may not thrust that decision upon the court. With subject matter jurisdiction and choice of forum, it is usually a matter of whether the court has the capacity to hear the case. Contrastingly, with choice of law, it is usually a question of whether the court is willing to hear the case. Courts usually respect a choice of law provision, especially in a commercial contract where the choice is between the law of the parties' nations. At the other end is where the choice has no relevance to the contract, such as where German and U.S. parties choose the law of Outer Mongolia. A court is likely to reject such choice, perhaps both because the chosen law has no linkage to the case, but also because the court may feel uncomfortable in applying the law of a nation without a highly developed contract law that may be difficult to prove.

A court asked to accept the application of a foreign law is likely to inquire about whether that law will cover the dispute. If a foreign law is chosen that provides no cause of action or inadequate remedies, the court may reject the application of such foreign law. There thus may be some process, possibly a hearing, where the court conducts an analysis of the substance of the foreign law and even whether it is likely that translations of the law can be obtained and experts can be found to explain the law to the court. Because the court does not "know" foreign law, it must be proved.[4] That means the judge has little if any knowledge of the substance of the foreign law and is entirely at the mercy of the experts used by the parties.

A party intending to use foreign law must give notice of such intent. Any form is adequate that does not create an "unfair

---

4. Rule 44.1 of the Federal Rules of Civil Procedure states that the court's determination of foreign law is treated the same as a ruling on a question of law.

surprise."[5] What is presented in proving foreign law is limited only in that it must be relevant.

§ 30.8   Antisuit Injunctions

Complex international litigation may create a situation where a suit is initiated in one nation by a foreign plaintiff against several defendants, including one or more from the foreign plaintiff's nation. Such was the case when Laker Airways initiated litigation in the United States against several U.S. and foreign airlines, including two from the United Kingdom. England was the home of Laker Airways.[1] The British defendants asked an English court to enjoin Laker Airways from pursuing the suit in the United States against the two British airlines because such litigation had only one proper forum—England. The injunction is called an "antisuit-injunction." The U.S. court rejected the injunction granted by the English court, and a serious conflict was avoided only after the House of Lords overturned the injunction, although preserving the concept.

Although the U.S. court in *Laker* rejected the English antisuit injunction, the concept had been accepted in some U.S. courts. Some federal circuits have granted antisuit injunctions, generally applying a multi-part test which considers such issues as would the foreign litigation frustrate a policy of the U.S. forum, be vexatious or oppressive, threaten the court's jurisdiction, or prejudice other considerations.[2] *Laker*, however, narrowed the concept, allowing it to protect the jurisdiction of the court or prevent the litigant from evading public policies of the forum.[3]

Antisuit injunctions are unusual because courts often allow parallel proceedings to continue in two jurisdictions. A judgment of a U.S. court will be considered *res judicata*. So may the foreign judgment. Thus, which party receives the first judgment may have

5. See Laminoirs–Trefileries–Cableries de Lens, S.A. v. Southwire Co., 484 F.Supp. 1063, 1067 (N.D.Ga.1980).

§ 30.8

1. See Laker Airways, Ltd. v. Sabena, Belgian World Airlines, 731 F.2d 909 (D.C.Cir.1984).

2. In re Unterweser Reederei, GMBH, 428 F.2d 888 (5th Cir.1970), *affirmed en banc*, 446 F.2d 907 (5th Cir. 1971), *vacated on other grounds sub nom.*, M/S Bremen v. Zapata Off–Shore Co., 407 U.S. 1, 92 S.Ct. 1907, 32 L.Ed.2d 513 (1972). See also Seattle Totems Hockey Club, Inc. v. National Hockey League, 652 F.2d 852 (9th Cir. 1981), *cert. denied*, 457 U.S. 1105, 102 S.Ct. 2902, 73 L.Ed.2d 1313 (1982).

3. For decisions subsequent to *Laker*, see China Trade & Dev. Corp. v. M.V. Choong Yong, 837 F.2d 33 (2d Cir.1987) (reversing an injunction); Gau Shan Co. v. Bankers Trust Co., 956 F.2d 1349 (6th Cir.1992), *appeal after remand*, 966 F.2d 1452 (6th Cir.1992) (reversing an injunction); Allendale Mut. Ins. Co. v. Bull Data Sys., Inc., 10 F.3d 425 (7th Cir.1993); Mutual Serv. Casualty Ins. Co. v. Frit Indus., Inc., 805 F.Supp. 919 (M.D.Ala.1992), *affirmed without opinion*, 3 F.3d 442 (11th Cir.1993).

the advantage, encouraging a race to judgment. But however undesirable it is to encourage such a race, courts have not granted antisuit injunctions just to stop a race. The impact of parallel proceedings will occur when the judgment is enforced. If the winner of the race's victory is accepted abroad and the judgment is enforced, the judgment was given *res judicata* effect. But it is not clear that it will be so recognized. The foreign court may reject the U.S. decision for traditional reasons justifying nonrecognition and enforcement of foreign judgments, which may incorporate some of the justifications for granting antisuit injunctions. A U.S. judgment entered after an antisuit judgment is granted abroad, will not be enforced in the foreign court. But the intention of an antisuit injunction in a case such as *Laker* is not to allow a judgment in the United States which will be enforced from U.S. assets of the foreign defendant.

§ 30.9 Proving Foreign Law

Proving foreign law may include various forms of written and oral testimony. Often affidavits of experts are submitted,[1] with the experts appearing at trial to support and respond to questions about their opinions.[2] A court may conduct its own research, which may be helpful when the experts are divided on the meaning of the foreign law.

Proof of foreign law often requires obtaining translations. Some foreign laws are available in English, especially constitutions and important codes such as civil and commercial codes. If there is a published version of the foreign statutes, it is likely to have been translated objectively and thus will be accepted by the court. Where the parties have to translate the foreign statutes, they may do so with a choice of words favoring their case. The court may have to choose between two versions. Translations of foreign cases are not often undertaken. When they do exist, they may be very helpful because a U.S. judge may not wish to interpret a foreign statute in a manner that is not clear from the language unless the foreign court has already given a similar or consistent interpretation.

§ 30.10 Depositions   and   Document   Discovery Abroad

For a trial in the United States gathering evidence is far easier when both the defendant and the evidence are in the United States. But when the evidence is located abroad, and especially when the

§ 30.9

1. See Bing v. Halstead, 495 F.Supp. 517 (S.D.N.Y.1980)(affidavits resulting in granting summary judgment).

2. See John R. Brown, 44.1 Ways to Prove Foreign Law, 9 Marq. Law. 179 (1984).

defendant is abroad, obtaining evidence may become very difficult.[1] The principal rules for obtaining evidence are the rules of procedure of the forum. But when personal jurisdiction has been obtained by use of disputed extraterritorial application of the U.S. law, gathering evidence because of the court's authority resulting from personal jurisdiction may conflict with foreign laws blocking the production of evidence. Numerous suits are filed by U.S. lawyers who proceed under the forum's rules of evidence only to discover they need a short-course in obtaining evidence abroad to save their suit. Part of that short-course must be learning that some practices of obtaining evidence permitted in the United States constitute *criminal* conduct in foreign nations.[2]

If U.S. notions of proper evidence paralleled those in foreign nations there would be far less trouble. The problem in gathering evidence abroad is not that all foreign nations prevent other nations from obtaining evidence in their nations. The problem is that the U.S. concept of evidence extends beyond nearly all other nations rules regarding what may be obtained. In most civil law tradition nations, judges with substantial discretion closely regulate the gathering of evidence. Attorneys are not largely left on their own to collect what they think would be useful, with occasional forays into court for new orders of production. Civil law nation judges determine who may be witnesses. The judges ask questions they originate or those referred to them by the lawyers which they approve. Requests for documents must be specific, disallowing requests, for example, for any documents that might have affected the design and manufacture of a product involved in an injury. If we sometimes think of our own process as condoning "fishing expeditions" for evidence, other nations are likely to interpret our method of fishing as using drift nets miles long that catch everything that the net surrounds. Other nations have effectively banned our nets.

As a civil process unfolds in the United States, the search for evidence begins at an early stage, well before the trial. Much that the lawyers are seeking will help in the further development of the case. There may have been very little, if any, evidence present when a brief and general complaint was filed. Much of what is obtained will never be used. This pretrial discovery is neither fully understood nor accepted by many civil law tradition nations. The some-

---

§ 30.10

1. If the defendant is a U.S. citizen or resident, however, a U.S. court may subpoena the defendant to appear in the United States, and produce specified documents. 28 U.S.C.A. § 1783(a).

2. Especially in France and Switzerland. See David Epstein et al, International Litigation § 10.03 n. 5.

times think that "pretrial" means before the suit is filed.[3] Obviously, evidence needs to be gathered before the day of the trial, just as it is gathered over a period of time in a civil law nation and not all presented at one time for the judge's consideration. The dislike for pretrial evidence is made apparent in the Hague Evidence Convention,[4] allowing a convention participant to make a declaration that disallows letters of request seeking "pretrial discovery of documents."[5]

Obtaining evidence abroad comes in two general areas, deposing witnesses and obtaining physical evidence, principally written documents. If depositions are permitted by the foreign nation, they are sometimes taken before a person commissioned by the U.S. court.[6] U.S. consular officers are ordinarily used as the designated commissioner to take the testimony, but a foreign official or private person may be appointed. In some countries the testimony may only be taken under the rules of the country, that disallow the use of a commissioner appointed by the U.S. court. The foreign rules may even prohibit taking any testimony by deposition. In such case the U.S. court may be able to issue a letter of request to a court in the foreign nation asking that it issue an order to take the testimony.[7] The letter may be accepted under notions of comity.

When the court in the United States approves discovery of documents abroad, the laws of the foreign nation may admit or block such discovery. The process of discovery may be similar to taking depositions when letters of request are used as opposed to appointment of a commissioner.

The above discussion involves use of procedural rules of the separate nations, and the application of comity. But another route is present. Many countries, including the United States, are parties to the Hague Evidence Convention. This Convention provides for three methods of obtaining evidence abroad. First is use of a letter of request to the "Central Authority" in the foreign nation. That authority sends the request to the appropriate court. Second is by means of a request to take evidence before a diplomatic or consular officer in the foreign country. Third, a request may be made to have a commissioner appointed to take evidence. These three parallel the methods outlined above under the Federal Rules of Civil Procedure, but there are variations. One most important question for nations

---

3. Their misunderstanding is perhaps because they view the stage like a grand jury proceeding, where evidence is gathered and presented before an indictment.

4. Hague Convention on the Taking of Evidence Abroad in Civil or Commercial Matters, Mar. 18, 1970, 8 I.L.M. 37 (1965).

5. Id., Art 23. Most signatories have issued such a declaration.

6. Fed. R. Civ. P. 28(b)(4).

7. Some nations require the letters of request to be submitted through diplomatic channels rather than court-to-court.

adhering to the Convention is whether it is the exclusive method of taking evidence abroad. For the United States, the Supreme Court answered that it is not the exclusive method in *Societe Nationale Industrielle Aerospatiale v. United States.*[8] The Court did not even impose a rule that the Convention must be used first, with subsequent resort to the rules of the forum. Use of the Convention would seem to mean use of a form approved by the foreign nation, and more likely to be respected. The majority of decisions since *Aerospatiale,* however, have not required use of the Convention as a necessary first option. But the fact remains that the view of the United States is the view of only one side, the requirements of the foreign nation in which discovery is sought have to be considered.

§ 30.11   Recognition and Enforcement of Foreign Judgments

Judgments in the United States are recognized in other states under the "full faith and credit" clause of the U.S. Constitution. But there is no application of this doctrine to foreign judgments. Foreign judgments are recognized and enforced in many nations, but only under often strict rules that allow careful scrutiny of many aspects of the original judgment. No rule exists in the United States prohibiting enforcement. Enforcement is currently a matter for separate state decision. Negotiations at the Hague for an international convention on jurisdiction and the enforcement of foreign judgments have been underway for several years. They are yet to conclude with a final document. When that is accomplished, there is no certainty that it will soon be adopted in the United States.[1]

The rule adopted from English law is that a foreign money judgment is only *prima facie* evidence of the matter decided. The U.S. Supreme Court rejected this position in *Hilton v. Guyot,*[2] and adopted a rule based on comity. This federal law decision presented an analysis of certain elements of the foreign decision, such as whether there was an opportunity for a fair trial before a court of competent jurisdiction, and whether the system of justice was impartial. Additionally discussed was whether the foreign nation would enforce a U.S. judgment, meaning the consideration of reciprocity. But this was not a judgment which established a rule effective in the states, although the evolving state law has drawn heavily from the *Hilton* decision.

---

8.   482 U.S. 522, 107 S.Ct. 2542, 96 L.Ed.2d 461 (1987).

§ 30.11

1. See generally Russell Weintraub, How Substantial is Our Need for a Judgments–Recognition Convention and What Should We Bargain Away to Get It?, 24 Brook. L. Rev. 167 (1998); Cromie, A Choice Between Evils, New Law Journal, at 1244 (Aug. 16, 1996).

2.   159 U.S. 113, 16 S.Ct. 139, 40 L.Ed. 95 (1895).

States courts have differed on the issue of reciprocity. Similarly state legislatures adopting judgment statutes have differed on including reciprocity as a requirement for enforcement. Although the law developed in the courts of the states after *Hilton*, in the last half of the last century states began to adopt the Uniform Foreign Money–Judgments Recognition Act.[3] Those states that have not adopted the UFMJRA either reject judgments and require a de novo trial, or they recognize and enforce judgments after applying tests not usually at great variance from the *Hilton* decision theory.[4] Conditions imposed may include reciprocity, acceptable personal and subject matter jurisdiction by the foreign court, adequate notice to the defendant, absence of fraud, absence of any conflict with public policy of the United States.[5] Those states that have adopted the UFMJRA follow a procedure that includes considerations of some of these very same factors,[6] but the Act does not include reciprocity.[7]

A related issue to the enforcement of the judgment is what the enforcing state should do when the original judgment is in a foreign currency. Judgments are usually given in the currency of the forum, and in some cases this is a mandatory rule.[8] The principal issue for courts has been establishing the time of conversion of the currency of the judgment to the currency of the enforcing forum.[9] Some jurisdictions use the time of the act establishing the cause of action, others use the date of the judgment and others use the date of payment. The Uniform Foreign Money Claims Act has adopted the date of payment.[10] The Restatement of Foreign Relations suggests use of the date which would best "serve the ends of justice in the circumstances."[11]

3. About 30 states have adopted a form of this uniform law.

4. See, e.g., Koster v. Automark Ind., Inc., 640 F.2d 77 (7th Cir.1981)

5. See. E.g., Hunt v. BP Exploration Co. (Libya) Ltd., 492 F.Supp. 885 (N.D.Tex.1980).

6. See, e.g., Bank of Nova Scotia v. Tschabold Equipment Ltd., 51 Wash. App. 749, 754 P.2d 1290 (1988).

7. Reciprocity has nevertheless been added by several states when adopting the UFMJRA.

8. Judgments in U.S. courts may be in foreign currencies. See, e.g., In re Oil Spill by the Amoco Cadiz Off the Coast of France on March 16, 1978, 954 F.2d 1279, 1328 (7th Cir.1992).

9. See Freeman, Judgments in Foreign Currency—A Little Known Change in New York Law, 23 Int'l Law. 73 (1989)(adopting the date of the judgment).

10. About twenty states have adopted this uniform law. See Prefatory Note to Uniform Foreign–Money Claims Act, 13 Uniform Laws Annotated 23 (1990 Supp.).

11. Restatement (Third) of the Foreign Relations Law of the United States § 823.

Chapter 31

INTERNATIONAL COMMERCIAL ARBITRATION

Table of Sections

Dispute resolution in international business transactions runs the gamut from friendly consultations to litigation everywhere. In between nonbinding conciliation and mediation do their best at facilitating a compromise, an approach common to Asia. In between also lies international commercial arbitration (ICA), a binding alternative to days in court. The volume of ICA has grown enormously in recent decades, particularly in the Americas, Europe and the Middle East. ICA is the focus of this chapter.

The ultimate forum selection clause is one that chooses no court at all, but selects an alternate dispute resolution mechanism, such as an arbitration tribunal. For a long period of time, the courts resisted validating such clauses, holding that they deprived the parties of due process of law (a reaction one might expect toward a competitor). However, legislatures were far more sympathetic to arbitration, and around the turn of the century began to enact statutes validating arbitration clauses. The issue now is firmly settled. In addition to arbitration, there are many other even less formal alternative dispute resolution mechanisms. The minitrial, for example, comes in a variety of packages, each with a different impact on resolution of the dispute. It can be nonbinding if used with a "neutral advisor"; it can be semi-binding if its results are admissible in later judicial proceedings; or it can be binding before a court appointed master.[1]

§ 31.1   Why Arbitrate?

The growth of international commercial arbitration (ICA) is in part a retreat from the vicissitudes and uncertainties of international business litigation.[1] More positively, ICA offers predictability and neutrality as a forum (who knows which court you may end up in) and the potential for specialized expertise (most judges know little of international law). ICA also allows the parties to select and shape the procedures and costs of dispute resolution. That said, ICA procedures are often informal and not laden with legal rights. To quote Judge Learned Hand:

> Arbitration may or may not be a desirable substitute for trials in courts; as to that the parties must decide in each instance. But when they have adopted it, they must be content with its informalities; they may not hedge it about with those procedural limitations which it is precisely its purpose to avoid. They must content themselves with looser approximations to the enforcement of their rights than those that the law accords them, when they resort to its machinery.[2]

One of the most attractive attributes of ICA is the enforceability in national courts of arbitral awards under the New York Convention.[3] Roughly 120 nations participate in the New York Convention. There is no comparable convention for the enforcement of court judgments around the world, although a Hague Convention on Jurisdiction and Enforcement of Judgments is being negotiated. The Panama Convention[4] renders arbitral awards enforceable in Latin America.

Another major advantage of ICA is the support of legal regimes that give arbitration agreements dispositive effects. In the United States, for example, the Federal Arbitration Act provides a level of legal security unknown to international business litigation. Many countries have similar statutes, thus avoiding issues of subject matter and personal jurisdiction, *forum non conveniens* and the like.[5] Professor Park has noted that, excepting New York, there are

---

1. For a review of the variety of such alternative dispute resolution mechanisms, see Nelson, "Alternatives to Litigation of International Disputes," 23 *Int'l Lawyer* 187 (1989).

§ 31.1

1. See Chapter 30.

2. American Almond Products Co. v. Consolidated Pecan Sales Co., Inc., 144 F.2d 448, 451 (2d Cir.1944).

3. U.N. Convention on Recognition and Enforcement of Arbitral Awards (1958), 21 U.S.T. 2517, 330 U.N.T.S. 38.

4. Inter–American Arbitration Convention of 1975, 14 I.L.M. 336 (1975).

5. See Park, "When and Why Arbitration Matters" in Hartwell (ed.), The Commercial Way of Justice (1997); Richards v. Lloyd's of London, 107 F.3d 1422

no statutory frameworks supporting court selection clauses at the state or federal level.[6] In worst case scenarios, parties selecting a court to resolve their disputes may end up with a court that refuses to hear the case.

One of the least attractive attributes of ICA is the minimal availability of pre-trial provisional remedies.[7] In addition, many arbitrators focus on splitting the differences between the parties, not the vindication of legal rights which in courts might result in "winner takes all." But such extreme results could permanently disrupt otherwise longstanding and mutually beneficial business relationships. Perhaps, therefore, "splitting the baby" through arbitration really is the optimal outcome.

Clearly international commercial arbitration has its pros and cons. Regardless of which way you tip the balance, the use of arbitral dispute resolution methods is certainly increasing. One distinguished set of authors believes that this trend is hardly surprising. Here is their analysis of why:

> Trade and investment across state lines is on the rise, and parties from different jurisdictions who engage in such activity frequently seek the comparative neutrality of a non-state tribunal to resolve their differences. Parties to a transaction from different states may be reluctant to submit to the jurisdiction of the courts of the other. This reluctance may arise from lack of enthusiasm about operating in another language, or according to the procedures and, insofar as it infiltrates procedure, the substantive law of another state. In some circumstances, one party may fear that the courts of the other may have a preference for their own nationals, may share a dislike of a particular foreign nationality or may, in cases involving very large amounts of money, lean toward finding in favor of their national because of the consequences for their national economy and political system. Where one of the parties is a state or state agency, a non-state party may prefer arbitration to submitting a dispute to the courts of the other contracting party. Arbitration may thus serve to "equalize" the non-state entity by transferring the dispute to a setting which may be designed to minimize or ignore the sovereign character of one of the parties rather more than would a national court.

> Arbitration may also be utilized because the various national laws which might be relevant have not developed enough to

(9th Cir.1997) *reversed* 135 F.3d 1289 (9th Cir.1998).

6. Park, "Bridging the Gap in Forum Selection: Harmonizing Arbitration and Court Selection," 8 Transnat'l Law & Contemp. Probs. 19 (Spring 1998).

7. See Borden, Inc. v. Meiji Milk Products Co., 919 F.2d 822 (2d Cir. 1990), *cert. denied*, 500 U.S. 953, 111 S.Ct. 2259, 114 L.Ed.2d 712 (1991).

treat problems raised in a pioneer industry. Thus issues regarding intellectual property rights in computer software of companies from different states may be submitted to arbitration as a way of resolving a dispute by shaping new law on the matter. In some circumstances potential litigants may also seek out arbitration because it is touted as more rapid, private and cheaper than domestic adjudication, though many of these characteristics of international commercial arbitration may be relative and sometimes overstated.

International commercial arbitration is also on the increase because many national court systems not only help international arbitration but appear anxious to externalize a larger amount of the disputes that are formally within their jurisdiction. The willingness of national courts to compel parties who have made prior commitments to engage in private arbitration and then to enforce the awards that ensue, subject only to limited judicial review, increases the likelihood that parties will resort to that mode of dispute resolution.[8]

§ 31.2 Types of International Commercial Arbitrations

There are two distinct types of international commercial arbitrations: ad hoc and institutional. Ad hoc arbitrations involve selection by the parties of the arbitrators and rules governing the arbitration. The classic formula involves each side choosing one arbitrator who in turn chooses a third arbitrator. The ad hoc arbitration panel selects its procedural rules (such as the UNCITRAL Arbitration Rules). Ad hoc arbitration can be agreed upon in advance or, quite literally, selected ad hoc as disputes arise.

Institutional arbitration involves selection of a specific arbitration center or "court," often accompanied by its own rules of arbitration. Institutional arbitration is in a sense pre-packaged, and the parties need only "plug in" to the arbitration system of their choice. There are numerous competing centers of arbitration, each busy marketing its desirability to the world business community. Some centers are longstanding and busy, such as the International Chamber of Commerce "Court of Arbitration" in Paris which has its own Rules of Arbitration. Other centers are more recent in time and still struggling for clientele, such as the Commercial Arbitration and Mediation Center for the Americas (CAMCA).

Ad hoc arbitration presupposes a certain amount of goodwill and flexibility between the parties. It can be speedy and less costly than institutional arbitration. The latter, on the other hand, offers

8. W. Michael Reisman, W. Laurence Craig, William W. Park & Jan Paulsson, International Commercial Arbitration (Foundation Press 1997).

ease of incorporation in an international business agreement, supervisory services, a stable of experienced arbitrators and a fixed fee schedule. The institutional environment is professional, a quality that sometimes can get lost in ad hoc arbitrations. Awards from well established arbitration centers (including default awards) are more likely to be favorably recognized in the courts if enforcement is needed. Many institutional arbitration centers now also offer "fast track" or "mini" services to the international business community.

Uncertainty about identity of the country and the court in which a dispute may be heard, about procedural and substantive rules to be applied, about the degree of publicity to be given the proceedings and the judgment, about the time needed to settle a dispute, and about the efficacy which may be given to a resulting judgment all have combined to make arbitration the preferred mechanism for solving international commercial disputes. Some Western European countries long have been accustomed to arbitration (e.g., see English Arbitration Act of 1889 and English Arbitration Act of 1950, as amended by Arbitration Act of 1979); the London Court of Arbitration, a private arbitration institution, has existed since 1892. The United States has had a Federal Arbitration Act since 1947.[1] Arbitration in international commercial contracts is favored by the Peoples Republic of China, if mediation and conciliation fails, either through the Chinese International Economic and Trade Arbitration Commission (CIETAC) or the Chinese Maritime Arbitration Commission (MAC). Most of the nations of the former Soviet Union also favor arbitration, and have organizations similar to the Chinese CIETAC and MAC. In terms of volume, CIETAC is now the world's largest arbitration center.

The Japan Commercial Arbitration Association has been active since 1953. Virtually all countries in Africa have arbitration statutes. Latin America, historically disadvantaged in many arbitral awards, increasingly is accepting arbitration. For example, the 1975 Inter–American Convention on International Commercial Arbitration[2] provides, in part, that "The Governments of the Member States of the Organization of American States . . . have agreed that . . . an agreement in which parties undertake to submit to arbitral decision any differences . . . with respect to a commercial transaction is valid." The 1979 Inter–American Convention on Extraterritorial Validity of Foreign Judgments and Arbitral Awards expands upon the scope of the 1975 Convention.

§ 31.2   2. See 14 Int'l Legal Mat. 336.

1. 9 U.S.C.A. § 1 et seq.

§ 31.3 Mandatory Law

Almost all jurisdictions have enacted law they consider "mandatory," i.e. public law that private parties cannot avoid by contract. Exactly where the line is drawn between mandatory and non-mandatory law is crucial to ICA.

Many lower U.S. federal courts had held that "mandatory laws" could not be the subject matter of arbitration because of the public interest indicated by the legislative intent underlying the enactment of mandatory law and the public policy favoring judicial enforcement of such law. However, the Supreme Court has now rejected that doctrine. In *Scherk v. Alberto–Culver Co.*[1], the Court held that Securities and Exchange Commission law issues arising out of an international contract are subject to arbitration under the Federal Arbitration Act *(9 U.S.C.A. § 1 et seq.)*, despite the public interest in protecting the United States investment climate. In *Mitsubishi Motors Corp. v. Soler Chrysler–Plymouth, Inc.*[2], the Court held that antitrust claims arising out of an international transaction were arbitrable, despite the public interest in a competitive national economy, and the legislative pronouncements favoring enforcement by private parties. In *Vimar Seguros y Reaseguros, S.A. v. M/V Sky Reefer*,[3] claims that the foreign arbitrators would not apply the United States mandatory COGSA bill of lading law were rejected on the ground that the U.S. could "review" the arbitral award at the award-enforcement stage. That power may, however, be very narrow under the 1958 United Nation's Convention on the Recognition and Enforcement of Foreign Arbitral Awards (the New York Convention), discussed below.

In both *Mitsubishi Motors* and *M/V Sky Reefer*, the Court determined that issues arising out of international transactions involving U.S. mandatory law were arbitrable. However, in *dictum* at the end of the *Mitsubishi* opinion, the Court stated that U.S. courts would have a second chance at the enforcement stage to examine whether the arbitral tribunal "took cognizance of the antitrust claims and actually decided them." Similar language can be found in *M/V Sky Reefer* regarding COGSA claims. It would seem to be difficult to fit any such examination by the U.S. courts properly into the structure of the New York Convention (above). It is not clear whether *Mitsubishi* invites the U.S. courts merely to examine whether the arbitrators state that they considered the

§ 31.3

1. 417 U.S. 506, 94 S.Ct. 2449, 41 L.Ed.2d 270 (1974).

2. 473 U.S. 614, 105 S.Ct. 3346, 87 L.Ed.2d 444 (1985). The Ninth, Eleventh and First Circuits have held on the basis of *Mitsubishi* that private antitrust claims are arbitrable. See Seacoast Motors of Salisbury, Inc. v. DaimlerChrysler Motors Corp., 271 F.3d 6 (1st Cir. 2001), *cert. denied* 535 U.S. 1054, 122 S.Ct. 1911, 152 L.Ed.2d 821 (2002).

3. 515 U.S. 528, 115 S.Ct. 2322, 132 L.Ed.2d 462 (1995).

antitrust issues, or also invites them to examine whether the arbitrators considered these issues *correctly* (review on the merits). The former can be evaded by a mechanical phrase; the latter can harm the arbitral process, especially if the parties have chosen non–U.S. law to govern their agreement.

In either case, arbitrators' enforcement of U.S. antitrust laws may not be to the standards of U.S. courts, and the status of recognition and enforcement of arbitral awards involving antitrust issues is not yet clear. Under the New York Convention, a mere "misunderstanding," or error in interpretation, of a mandatory law by an arbitral tribunal has generally not been held to "contravene public policy." The cases are split as to whether even a "manifest disregard" of United States law constitutes such a violation of public policy. Awards have been upheld which violate the U.S. Vessel Owner's Limitation of Liability Act, previously considered mandatory law. Thus, it is not certain, under the New York Convention, that United States courts retain the review powers assumed by the *Mitsubishi* and *M/V Sky Reefer* Courts to be available at the "award-enforcement stage" of the proceedings.

§ 31.4 International Arbitral Rules: UNICITRAL

The factors considered above are incorporated in Model International Commercial Arbitration Rules[1] issued in 1976 by the United Nations Commission on International Trade Law (UNCITRAL) following ten years of study. The UNCITRAL Rules are intended to be acceptable in all legal systems and in all parts of the world. Rapidly developing countries favor the Rules because of the care with which they have been drafted, and because UNCITRAL was one forum for developing arbitration rules in which their concerns would be heard. The Arbitral Institute of the Stockholm Chamber of Commerce has been willing to work with the UNCITRAL Rules, as has the London Court of Arbitration. The Iran–United States Claims Tribunal has used the UNCITRAL Rules in dealing with claims arising out of the confrontation between the two countries in 1980. Unlike the Stockholm Chamber of Commerce Rules, the UNCITRAL Rules are not identified with any national or international arbitration organization.

Among other things, UNCITRAL rules provide that an "appointing authority" shall be chosen by the parties or, if they fail to agree upon that point, shall be chosen by the Secretary–General of the Permanent Court of Arbitration at the Hague (comprised of a body of persons prepared to act as arbitrators if requested). The UNCITRAL rules also cover notice requirements, representation of the parties, challenges of arbitrators, evidence, hearings, the place

§ 31.4

1. See 15 Int'l Legal Mat. 701 (1978).

of arbitration, language, statements of claims and defenses, pleas to the arbitrator's jurisdiction, provisional remedies, experts, default, rule waivers, the form and effect of the award, applicable law, settlement, interpretation of the award and costs.

In addition to its 1976 Model Arbitration Rules, UNCITRAL has also promulgated a 1985 Model Law on International Commercial Arbitration.[2] The Model Law has been enacted in Australia, Bulgaria, Canada, Cypress, Hong Kong, Nigeria and Scotland. It has also been enacted as state law by several states of the U.S., including California, Florida, North Carolina, Connecticut, Georgia, Ohio, Oregon and Texas. There seems to be no competing federal law which would pre-empt the application of these enactments.

Under the UNCITRAL Model Law, submission to arbitration may be *ad hoc* for a particular dispute, but is accomplished most often in advance of the dispute by a general submission clause within a contract. Under Article 8 of the Model Law, an agreement to arbitrate is specifically enforceable. Although no specific language will guarantee the success of an arbitral submission, UNCITRAL recommends the following model submission clause:

> Any dispute, controversy or claim arising out of or relating to this contract, or the breach, termination or invalidity thereof, shall be settled by arbitration in accordance with the UNCITRAL Arbitration Rules as at present in force.

§ 31.5 International Arbitration Rules: ICSID

These considerations are also incorporated in the text of the Arbitration Rules adopted under the 1966 Convention on the Settlement of Investment Disputes Between States and Nationals of Other States (TIAS 6090), to which over eighty countries are parties. The Convention is implemented in the United States by 22 U.S.C. § 1650 and § 1650a. An arbitral money award, rendered pursuant to the Convention, is entitled to the same full faith and credit in the United States as is a final judgment of a court of general jurisdiction in a State of the United States.[1]

The 1966 Convention provides for the establishment of an International Center for the Settlement of Investment Disputes (ICSID), as a non-financial organ of the World Bank (the International Bank for Reconstruction and Development). ICSID is designed to serve as a forum for conciliation and for arbitration of disputes between private investors and host governments. It provides an institutional framework within which arbitrators, selected

---

2. 2 B.D.I.E.L. 993 (1985). See Lowry, Critical Documents Sourcebook Ann. 345 (1991).

§ 31.5

1. 22 U.S.C.A. § 1650a.

by the disputing parties from an ICSID Panel of Arbitrators or from elsewhere, conduct an arbitration in accordance with ICSID Rules of Procedure for Arbitration Proceedings. Arbitrations are held in Washington D.C. unless agreed otherwise.

Under the 1966 Convention (Article 25), ICSID's jurisdiction extends only "to any legal dispute arising directly out of an investment, between a Contracting State or . . . any subdivision . . . and a national of another Contracting State, which the parties to the dispute consent in writing to submit to the Centre. Where the parties have given their consent, no party may withdraw its consent unilaterally." Thus, ICSID is an attempt to institutionalize dispute resolution between States and non-State investors. It therefore always presents a "mixed" arbitration.

If one party questions such jurisdiction (predicated upon disputes arising "directly out of" an investment, between a Contracting Party and the national of another, and written consent to submission), the issue may be decided by the arbitration tribunal (Rule 41). A party may seek annulment of any award by an appeal to an ad hoc committee of persons drawn by the Administrative Council of ICSID from the Panel of Arbitrators under the Convention (Article 52). Annulment is available only if the Tribunal was not properly constituted, exceeded its powers, seriously departed from a fundamental procedural rule, failed to state the reasons for its award, or included a member who practiced corruption.

The Convention's 1966 jurisdictional limitations have prompted the ICSID Administrative Counsel to establish an Additional Facility for conducting conciliations and arbitrations for disputes which do not arise directly out of an investment and for investment disputes in which one party is not a Contracting State to the Convention or the national of a Contracting State. The Additional Facility is intended for use by parties having long-term relationships of special economic importance to the State party to the dispute and which involve the commitment of substantial resources on the part of either party. The Facility is not designed to service disputes which fall within the 1966 Convention or which are "ordinary commercial transaction" disputes. ICSID's Secretary General must give advance approval of an agreement contemplating use of the Additional Facility. Because the Additional Facility operates outside the scope of the 1966 Convention, the Facility has its own arbitration Rules. It is the basis for most NAFTA Chapter 11 investor-state arbitrations.[2]

§ 31.6 ICC and LCIA Arbitral Rules and Clauses

Many parties use the Rules of the Court of Arbitration of the International Chamber of Commerce (ICC) at Paris or of one of its

---

2. See § 27.13.

national committees, such as the international commercial panel of the American Arbitration Association. The ICC rules are modern and often used in international arbitration. Some 11,000 arbitrations have been administered by the ICC.[1]

The Court of Arbitration of the ICC in Paris recommends use of the following model clause to engage its rules:

> All disputes arising in connection with the present contract shall be finally settled under the Rules of Conciliation and Arbitration of the International Chamber of Commerce by one or more arbitrators appointed in accordance with the said Rules....

Parties who wish to refer any dispute to the equally active London Court of Arbitration may use the following model clause:

> The validity, construction and performance of this contract (agreement) shall be governed by the laws of England and any dispute that may arise out of or in connection with this contract (agreement), including its validity, construction and performance, shall be determined by arbitration under the Rules of the London Court of Arbitration at the date hereof, which Rules with respect to matters not regulated by them, incorporate the UNCITRAL Arbitration Rules. The parties agree that service of any notices in reference to such arbitration at their addresses as given in this contract (agreement)(or as subsequently varied in writing by them) shall be valid and sufficient.

§ 31.7 Enforcement of Arbitral Awards: The New York Convention

In over 120 countries, the enforcement of arbitral awards is facilitated by the 1958 United Nations Convention on the Recognition and Enforcement of Foreign Arbitral Awards (the "New York Convention").[1] "[T]he principal purpose underlying American ... implementation ... was to encourage the recognition and enforcement of commercial arbitration agreements in international contracts and to unify the standards by which agreements to arbitrate are observed and arbitral awards are enforced in the signatory countries."[2] In an abbreviated procedure, under 9 U.S.C.A. §§ 203,

---

§ 31.6

1. See W. Laurence Craig, William W. Park and Jan Paulsson, International Chamber of Commerce Arbitration (3rd Edition, 2000).

§ 31.7

1. 21 U.S.T. 2518, T.I.A.S. No. 6997, 330 U.N.T.S. 38, implemented in the United States by 9 U.S.C.A. §§ 201–208.

2. Scherk v. Alberto–Culver Co., 417 U.S. 506, 520 n. 15, 94 S.Ct. 2449, 41 L.Ed.2d 270 (1974).

208, federal district courts entertain motions to confirm or to challenge a foreign award.

The New York Convention commits the courts in each Contracting State to recognize and enforce arbitration clauses and written arbitration agreements for the resolution of international commercial disputes. Where the court finds an arbitral clause or agreement, it "*shall* ... refer the parties to arbitration, unless it finds that the said agreement is null and void, inoperative, or incapable of being performed" (emphasis added).[3] The New York Convention also commits the courts in each Contracting State to recognize and enforce (under local procedural rules) the awards of arbitral tribunals under such clauses or agreements, and also sets forth the limited grounds under which recognition and enforcement may be refused. Under the New York Convention, grounds for refusal to enforce include:

(1) incapacity or invalidity of the agreement containing the arbitration clause "under the law applicable to" a party to the agreement,

(2) lack of proper notice of the arbitration proceedings, the appointment of the arbitrator or other reasons denying an adequate opportunity to present a defense,

(3) failure of the arbitral award to restrict itself to the terms of the submission to arbitration, or decision of matters not within the scope of that submission,

(4) composition of the arbitral tribunal not according to the arbitration agreement or applicable law, and

(5) non-finality of the arbitral award under applicable law.[4]

In addition to these grounds for refusal, recognition or enforcement may also be refused if it would be contrary to the public policy of the country in which enforcement is sought; or if the subject matter of the dispute cannot be settled by arbitration under the law of that country.[5] Courts in the United States have taken the position that the "public policy limitation on the New York Convention is to be construed narrowly [and] to be applied only where enforcement would violate the forum state's most basic notions of morality and justice."[6] Recourse to other limitations of the Convention, in order to defeat its applicability, has been greeted with judicial caution in the absence of violation of basic U.S. notions of morality and justice.[7] However, the Second Circuit has

3. Article II(3).

4. Article V.

5. *Id.*

6. Fotochrome, Inc. v. Copal Co., Ltd., 517 F.2d 512 (2d Cir.1975).

7. Parsons & Whittemore Overseas Co., Inc. v. Societe Generale De L'Industrie Du Papier (RAKTA), 508 F.2d 969 (2d Cir.1974).

held that the doctrine of forum non conveniens applies in arbitral award confirmation proceedings under the New York Convention.[8]

Whether the N.Y. Convention applies generally turns upon where the award was or will be made, not the citizenship of the parties.[9] A growing number of courts in developing nations are issuing injunctions against arbitral proceedings before they commence. Many of these injunctions seem deliberately intended to protect local companies. Parties who proceed to arbitrate after such an injunction has been issued do so at their peril. Subsequent enforcement of the award under the New York Convention in the enjoining nation will almost certainly be voided on grounds of public policy. Hence enforcement can only proceed in non-enjoining jurisdictions, assuming that their public policy permits this.

§ 31.8 Arbitration Agreements, Arbitrators and Awards Under U.S. Law

Arbitration agreements, traditionally called compromis, come in a variety of forms. Many arbitration centers sponsor model clauses that can be incorporated into business agreements. The New York Convention obliges courts of participating nations to refer upon request disputes to arbitration unless the agreement is "null and void, inoperative or incapable of being performed."[1] The existence and validity of an arbitration agreement must be proved, and can be litigated before the arbitration takes place.

Article II(2) of the New York Convention requires states to recognize written arbitration agreements *signed* by the parties "or contained in an exchange of letters or telegrams." In most jurisdictions exchanges of fax, email and the like embracing arbitration will also be recognized. However, arbitration clauses in unsigned purchase orders do not amount to a written agreement to arbitrate.[2] Pre-arbitration litigation often revolves around motions to compel arbitration.[3] If no such motion is made, and a court judgment is rendered (even by default), the right to arbitrate may be waived.[4] Delays in triggering arbitration or invocation of litigation rights may constitute a waiver of arbitration rights.[5]

8. In re Monegasque de Reassurances S.A.M. v. Nak Naftogaz of Ukraine, 311 F.3d 488 (2d Cir.2002).

9. See Ministry of Defense of the Islamic Republic of Iran v. Gould Inc., 887 F.2d 1357 (9th Cir.1989), *cert. denied,* 494 U.S. 1016, 110 S.Ct. 1319, 108 L.Ed.2d 494 (1990).

§ 31.8

1. Article II(3).

2. Kahn Lucas Lancaster, Inc. v. Lark Int'l Ltd., 186 F.3d 210 (2d Cir. 1999).

3. See, e.g., Tennessee Imports, Inc. v. P.P. Filippi & Prix Italia, S.R.L., 745 F.Supp. 1314 (M.D.Tenn.1990).

4. See Menorah Insurance Co. v. INX Reinsurance Corp., 72 F.3d 218 (1st Cir.1995).

5. See O.J. Distributing, Inc. v. Hornell Brewing Co., 340 F.3d 345 (6th Cir.

Whether a valid agreement to arbitrate exists depends on the specifics of the arbitration clause, not the entire business agreement. The arbitration clause is severable, and issues of validity (such as fraud in the inducement of the arbitration clause and unconscionability) directed to it.[6] Many courts will stretch the limits of the New York Convention in order to uphold an arbitration clause.[7] When there is a battle of forms, the same judicial bias towards arbitration is often found.[8] But, in most cases, the disputes must "arise under" the business transaction to be arbitrable.[9] and legal claims falling outside the transaction remain in court.[10]

The closure or misdescription of an arbitration center designated in the agreement (e.g., the New York Chamber of Commerce) is no barrier to arbitration. A substitute arbitrator will be appointed by the court if the parties cannot agree.[11] The U.S. Supreme Court has held that arbitrators are subject to "requirements of impartiality" and must "disclose to the parties any dealings that might create an impression of possible bias."[12] That said, most U.S. courts are loathe to intrude or vacate an arbitration award on disclosure grounds.[13]

There is a split of opinion as to whether the implied ground of "manifest disregard of the law" bars enforcement of an arbitral award in U.S. courts under the New York Convention. The Second Circuit believes so[14] while the Eleventh Circuit says not.[15] Article V of the New York Convention does not recognize manifest disregard

2003); Colón v. R. K. Grace & Co., 358 F.3d 1 (1st Cir.2003).

6. Prima Paint Corp. v. Flood & Conklin Mfg. Co., 388 U.S. 395, 87 S.Ct. 1801, 18 L.Ed.2d 1270 (1967). See Republic of Nicaragua v. Standard Fruit Co., 937 F.2d 469 (9th Cir.1991). See also Hunt v. Up North Plastics, Inc., 980 F.Supp. 1046 (D.Minn.1997), *cert. denied*, 503 U.S. 919, 112 S.Ct. 1294, 117 L.Ed.2d 516 (1992).

7. See Sphere Drake Insurance PLC v. Marine Towing, Inc., 16 F.3d 666 (5th Cir.1994), *cert. denied* 513 U.S. 871, 115 S.Ct. 195, 130 L.Ed.2d 127 (1994) (absence of signature to standard insurance policy contract no barrier to arbitration).

8. See I.T.A.D. Associates, Inc. v. Podar Bros., 636 F.2d 75 (4th Cir.1981).

9. See Mediterranean Enterprises, Inc. v. Ssangyong Corp., 708 F.2d 1458 (9th Cir.1983).

10. Id. See Coors Brewing Co. v. Molson Breweries, 51 F.3d 1511 (10th Cir.1995).

11. See Astra Footwear Industry v. Harwyn International, Inc., 442 F.Supp. 907 (S.D.N.Y.1978).

12. Commonwealth Coatings Corp. v. Continental Casualty Co., 393 U.S. 145, 89 S.Ct. 337, 21 L.Ed.2d 301 (1968).

13. See Andros Compania Maritima v. Marc Rich & Co., 579 F.2d 691 (2d Cir. 1978).

14. Yusuf Ahmed Alghanim & Sons v. Toys 'R' Us, Inc., 126 F.3d 15 (2d Cir.1997), *cert. denied* 522 U.S. 1111, 118 S.Ct. 1042, 140 L.Ed.2d 107 (1998); Westerbeke Corp. v. Daihatsu Motor Co., Ltd., 304 F.3d 200 (2d Cir.2000); Duferco International Steel Trading v. T. Klaveness Shipping, 333 F.3d 383 (2d Cir.2003); Hardy v. Walsh Manning Securities, LLC, 341 F.3d 126 (2d Cir. 2003).

15. Industrial Risk Insurers v. M.A.N. Gutehoffnungshutte GmbH, 141 F.3d 1434 (11th Cir.1998), cert.*denied* 525 U.S. 1068, 119 S.Ct. 797, 142 L.Ed.2d 659 (1999).

of the law as a basis for denial of enforcement. Another issue concerning the New York Convention is whether to adjourn U.S. enforcement proceedings if parallel proceedings to vacate the award have been commenced in the country of arbitration. Despite the risks of forum shopping and delay, the Second Circuit indicated that adjournment can be appropriate, depending upon the circumstances.[16] The Second Circuit has also denied use of 28 U.S.C. § 1782 to obtain compulsory non-party discovery in private commercial arbitrations. The issue was whether the I.C.C. in Paris constituted a "tribunal" within the scope of that statute.[17]

Cases in the United States have pointed out that parties cannot refer a dispute to a court while an arbitration is in progress[18] or block enforcement of an award in the United States in reliance upon the fact that the award, although binding in the country where rendered, is under appeal there.[19] Interim orders of arbitrators, such as records disclosures, may be enforceable "awards" under the N.Y. Convention.[20] After the arbitration is concluded, a party may not be able to block enforcement of the award in reliance upon the United States Foreign Sovereign Immunities Act[21], but a court may decline to enforce in reliance upon the Act of State Doctrine.[22] One court has granted enforcement, under the Convention, of a New York award rendered in favor of a non-citizen claimant against a non-citizen defendant.[23] Awards entirely between U.S. citizens are not subject to the New York Convention unless they concern property located abroad, envisage performance or enforcement abroad, or have some other reasonable relation with foreign state(s).[24]

When arbitral awards are annulled at their situs, courts in enforcing jurisdictions have taken different positions on the enforceability of the award. French courts enforced an improperly vacated award to the detriment of the claimant who had prevailed in a second arbitration.[25] A U.S. federal district court refused to

16. Europcar Italia, S.p.A. v. Maiellano Tours, Inc., 156 F.3d 310 (2d Cir. 1998).

17. National Broadcasting Co. v. Bear Stearns & Co., 165 F.3d 184 (2d Cir.1999).

18. Siderius, Inc. v. Compania de Acero del Pacifico, S.A., 453 F.Supp. 22 (S.D.N.Y.1978).

19. Fertilizer Corp. of India v. IDI Management, Inc., 517 F.Supp. 948 (S.D.Ohio 1981).

20. See Publicis Communication v. True North Communications, Inc. 206 F.3d 725 (7th Cir.2000).

21. See Ipitrade International, S.A. v. Federal Republic of Nigeria, 465 F.Supp. 824 (D.D.C.1978) and Creighton Ltd. v. Government of Qatar, 181 F.3d 118 (D.C.Cir.1999).

22. Libyan American Oil Co. v. Socialist People's, etc., 482 F.Supp. 1175 (D.D.C.1980).

23. Bergesen v. Joseph Muller Corp., 548 F.Supp. 650 (S.D.N.Y.1982).

24. 9 U.S.C. § 202 (1994).

25. Hilmarton v. OTV, 1997 Rev. Arb. 376, note Ph. Fouchard discussed in Park, "Duty and Discretion in International Arbitration," 93 Am. J. Int'l Law 805 (1999).

honor the clearly legitimate annulment of an arbitral award by an Egyptian court because the parties had agreed not to appeal the award.[26] The Second Circuit, on the other hand, recognized the annulment of two arbitral awards vacated by a Nigerian court and refused enforcement.[27] The New York convention does not address the treatment of annulled arbitral awards.

The U.S. Supreme Court has repeatedly affirmed that arbitrators have jurisdiction to decide their own jurisdiction (compétence-compétence).[28] The United States Supreme Court has indicated that questions of the arbitrability of disputes may be arbitrated, but only if the parties have manifested a *clear* willingness to be bound by arbitration on such issues.[29] Silence or ambiguity should favor judicial review of arbitrability issues.[30] Arbitration clauses that adopt the UNITRAL Rules meet the requirement of clarity to arbitrate arbitrability because Article 21 conveys jurisdictional issues to the tribunal.[31]

U.S. courts are split on whether contract parties may alter the scope of judicial review of arbitration awards. Three Circuits reject expansion of statutory or common law review standards.[32] The Ninth and Tenth Circuits permit contractual expansion of judicial review standards.[33] Attempts at *narrowing* statutory standards are likely to be rejected.[34]

26. Chromalloy Aeroservices v. Egypt, 939 F.Supp. 907 (D.D.C.1996). See Park, *supra*.

27. Baker Marine (Nig.) Ltd. v. Chevron (Nig.) Ltd., 191 F.3d 194 (2d Cir.1999).

28. See, e.g., Howsam v. Dean Witter Reynolds, Inc., 537 U.S. 79, 123 S.Ct. 588, 154 L.Ed.2d 491 (2002); Pacificare Health Systems, Inc. v. Book, 538 U.S. 401, 123 S.Ct. 1531, 155 L.Ed.2d 578 (2003).

29. First Options of Chicago, Inc. v. Kaplan, 514 U.S. 938, 115 S.Ct. 1920, 131 L.Ed.2d 985 (1995).

30. *Id.*

31. Wal–Mart Stores, Inc. v. PT Multipolar Corp., 202 F.3d 280 (9th Cir. 1999) (unpublished).

32. See Roadway Package System, Inc. v. Kayser, 257 F.3d 287 (3d Cir. 2001); Syncor Int'l Corp. v. McLeland, 120 F.3d 262 (4th Cir.1997), *cert. denied*, 522 U.S. 1110, 118 S.Ct. 1039, 140 L.Ed.2d 105 (1998); Gateway Techn., Inc. v. MCI Telecomm. Corp., 64 F.3d 993 (5th Cir.1995).

33. See Kyocera Corp. v. Prudential–Bache Trade Services, Inc., 341 F.3d 987 (9th Cir.2003), *cert. dismissed*, 540 U.S. 1098, 124 S.Ct. 980, 157 L.Ed.2d 810 (2004); Bowen v. Amoco Pipeline Co., 254 F.3d 925 (10th Cir.2001).

34. See Hoeft v. MVL Group, Inc., 343 F.3d 57 (2d Cir.2003).

*

Table of Cases

J

K

*

Index

References are to Sections

---

†